WORLD
CIVILIZATIONS

W·W·NORTON & COMPANY · NEW YORK · LONDON

EDWARD MCNALL BURNS

PHILIP LEE RALPH

ROBERT E. LERNER

STANDISH MEACHAM

WORLD

CIVILIZATIONS

Their History and Their Culture

VOLUME II   SIXTH EDITION

W. W. Norton & Company, Inc. 500 Fifth Avenue, New York, N.Y.
10110
W. W. Norton & Company Ltd. 37 Great Russell Street, London
WC1B 3NU

ISBN 0 393 95095 6

1 2 3 4 5 6 7 8 9 0

To our Students

CONTENTS

Part Six THE WEST AT THE WORLD'S CENTER

MAPS

MAPS IN COLOR

(Maps appear facing or following the pages indicated)

MAPS IN BLACK AND WHITE

XIV

PREFACE

Edward McNall Burns observed in an earlier preface:

"The time has long since passed when modern man could think of the world as consisting of Europe and the United States. Western culture is, of course, primarily a product of European origins. But it has never been that exclusively. Its original foundations were in Southwestern Asia and North Africa. These were supplemented by influences seeping in from India and eventually from China. From India and the Far East the West derived its knowledge of the zero, the compass, gunpowder, silk, cotton, and probably a large number of religious and philosophical concepts. Especially in recent times the East has increased in importance. The exhaustion of Europe by two World Wars, the revolt of the colored races against Caucasian domination, and the struggle for the world between the Communist powers and the United States have made every part of the earth of vital importance to every other. If peace is indivisible, so are prosperity, justice, and freedom; so, in fact, is civilization itself.

"The purpose of this work is to present a compact survey of man's struggle for civilization from early times to the present. No major area or country of the globe has been omitted. Europe, the Commonwealth of Nations, the Middle East, Southeast Asia, Africa, India, China, Japan, and North, Central, and South America have all received appropriate emphasis. Obviously, the history of none of them could be covered in full detail. The authors believe, however, that a broad view of the world as a whole is necessary to understand the basic problems of any of its parts. This thesis acquires additional validity as the nations increase in interdependence. Perspective in history becomes more and more urgent as the momentous problems of our own generation press for solution. If there is any basic philosophical interpretation underlying the narrative, it is the conviction that most of human progress thus far has resulted from the growth of intelligence and respect for the rights of man, and that therein lies the chief hope for a better world in the future."

As its title indicates, this work is not exclusively or even primarily a political history. Political events are recognized as important, but they are not the whole substance of history. In the main, the facts of political history are subordinated to the development of institutions and ideas or are presented as the groundwork of cultural, social, and economic movements. The authors consider the effects of the Industrial Revolutions to be no less important than the Napoleonic Wars. They believe it is of greater value to understand the significance of Buddha, Confucius, Newton, Darwin, and Einstein than it is to be able to name the kings of France. In accordance with this broader conception of history, more space has been given to the teachings of John Locke, Karl Marx, and John Stuart Mill, of Mahatma Gandhi, Mao Tse-tung, and Julius Nyerere than to the military exploits of Gustavus Adolphus or the Duke of Wellington.

The first edition of *World Civilizations* was published in 1955, the second in 1958, the third in 1964, the fourth in 1969, and the fifth in 1974. Each edition has included the whole of Edward McNall Burns' *Western Civilizations,* except for sections on the non-Western world, which are more fully covered in this work. The sixth edition of *World Civilizations* incorporates Burns' *Western Civilizations* as revised for its ninth edition by Robert E. Lerner of Northwestern University and Standish Meacham of the University of Texas at Austin. The qualities that have made the Burns text a leader during the past thirty years have been preserved, while at the same time Professors Lerner and Meacham, utilizing the results of recent scholarship, have sharpened the focus on areas of greatest concern for today's students. The authors' considerable reorganization of the chapters dealing with the Western world has enabled them to give fuller treatment to the Middle Ages and to the nineteenth century, to living conditions during the successive stages of Western development, and to the status of women and minority groups.

In addition to the extensive changes in the chapters on Western history, those devoted to the non-Western and third world have been thoroughly revised. They contain much new material, designed not merely to supply up-to-date information on the course of events but also to take account of new interpretations and to provide a clearer perspective on the character, competing forces, and problems of the troubled era into which contemporary societies have been propelled. In accord with this objective, more space has been allotted to Latin America and to the Middle East than in the previous edition. This edition, like its immediate predecessor, benefits substantially from the contribution of Professor Richard Hull of New York University, who has revised, updated, and expanded the sections on Africa in Chapters 12, 17, 23, 32, and 38. His narrative provides a compact and enlightening account of the peoples and the major civilizations of the African continent and of their present state. For all chapters, the accompanying reading lists have been revised.

The sixth edition of *World Civilizations* has been redesigned for easier reading and to accommodate literally hundreds of new illustrations from Western and non-Western archives. Virtually 50 percent of the 950 illustrations are new to this edition. The text was the first to include color illustrations and continues to include far more color plates than any other book in the field. Most of the 65 maps are either new or thoroughly amended. The new edition is published in both a one-volume and a two-volume format. Available for use with either is a new Teacher's Manual and a thoroughly revised Study Guide, which, as its most distinctive feature, includes numerous extracts from original sources.

In preparing this revision the authors have profited from the assistance and counsel of many individuals whose services no words of appreciation can adequately measure. The list would include not only various specialists but also teachers and students who have used the text in their courses. The authors owe a debt of gratitude to demanding but kindly editors who have worked with them over the years. For this edition, as for the preceding one, Robert E. Kehoe of W. W. Norton & Company has been an indispensable adviser and co-worker. The authors are continually indebted to their wives for often unacknowledged assistance and, even more, for their forbearance, patience, and understanding.

Philip Lee Ralph

WORLD
CIVILIZATIONS

Chapter 21

THE AGE OF ABSOLUTISM
(c. 1500–1789)

There are four essential characteristics or qualities of royal authority.
First, royal authority is sacred.
Second, it is paternal.
Third, it is absolute.
Fourth, it is subject to reason.

> —Jacques Bossuet, *Politics Drawn from the Very Words of Holy Scripture*

It now becomes necessary to go back and attempt to analyze the major political developments which accompanied the birth of modern civilization. During the fourteenth and fifteenth centuries the power of the medieval national monarchies had been gradually tested by the upheavals of the later Middle Ages. But, as we saw in Chapter 13, monarchical power was ultimately not found wanting. In the last quarter of the fifteenth century strong monarchs in the leading states of western Europe—England, France, and Spain—overcame threats of fragmentation and started to make royal power stronger than ever. Thereafter most of Europe experienced the fullest flowering of royal "absolutism," or untrammeled monarchy. The age of absolutism lasted in England until the middle of the seventeenth century, in France until 1789, and elsewhere on the European continent into the nineteenth century. There were several reasons why absolutism predominated in the period after 1500. One was that new wealth helped monarchs to pay for expanding bureaucracies and new departments of government, above all departments that directed military organization and the conduct of foreign policy. Another was that international warfare lasted throughout most of the period, and warfare tended to strengthen the power of the state because it allowed monarchs to maintain standing armies that could enforce peace at home as well as abroad. Finally, the Protestant Revolution contributed consid-

The age of absolutism

Character of absolute monarchy

erably to the growth of royal omnipotence. It broke the unity of the Christian Church, abolished papal overlordship over secular rulers, fostered nationalism, revived the doctrine of the Apostle Paul that "the powers that be are ordained of God," and encouraged the rulers of northern Europe to extend their authority over religious as well as over civil affairs.

Although government was certainly becoming stronger than ever, it is well not to confuse early modern western European absolutism with either despotism or totalitarianism. Western European kings were not really despots because no matter how strong they were they seldom ruled arbitrarily like Oriental pharaohs or caliphs. Owing to the strength of their aristocracies and merchant classes they could not whimsically issue decrees to be carried out by a few henchmen; instead they usually had to justify their policies to hundreds or even thousands before they could be implemented. Moreover, absolute monarchs usually respected due process of law and broke with traditions only in exceptional circumstances. Even less were the absolute monarchs similar to modern dictators. Quite obviously, before the nineteenth and twentieth centuries the state could not interfere very efficiently in the lives of its citizens; it lacked mechanized transportation and communications systems, as well as radio, film, and television for propaganda, and sophisticated instruments of terror. Throughout the period of royal absolutism there were hardly even any policemen. Today most of us fear that the state will become too strong—if it has not already—but between 1500 and 1789 in western Europe it was still only distantly shaping the lives of its subjects.

1. THE GROWTH AND DEFEAT OF ABSOLUTE MONARCHY IN ENGLAND

Reasons for defeat in England

England was the only European country in which absolutism was defeated before 1789. The reasons for this were political, economic, and religious. As we have seen, the principle of consent to royal decision-making was stronger in medieval England than elsewhere. Only in England did a body like Parliament emerge from the Middle Ages to stand as a potential barrier to absolutism. Throughout the sixteenth century, the English Crown knew how to use Parliament to serve its own interests, but in the seventeenth century royal personalities and policies began to provoke parliamentary resistance. When that happened, the economic strength of many members of the parliamentary opposition, which had been brought about by England's major participation in the Commercial Revolution, greatly aided them in fighting and finally defeating the monarchy. The major immediate cause of the revolt against royal absolutism was religious. Radical Protestants strongly objected to royal religious policy and ultimately made their objections a cause for civil war.

Before that happened, it might have seemed that England was moving toward absolutism in the same fashion as the states of the Continent. The Tudor dynasty, initiated by Henry VII in 1485, had gained remarkable success in regulating the consciences of its subjects and in binding the nation to its will. It should be added that the most celebrated Tudors, Henry VIII (1509–1547) and Elizabeth I (1558–1603), gained some of their power through shrewdly maintaining a semblance of popular government. When they desired to enact measures of doubtful popularity, they regularly went through the formality of obtaining parliamentary approval. Or when they wanted more money, they manipulated procedure in such a way as to make the appropriations appear to be voluntary grants by the representatives of the people. But the legislative branch of the government under these sovereigns was little more than a rubber stamp. They limited parliamentary sessions to only three or four months of the year; they interfered with elections and packed the two houses with their own favorites; and they cajoled, flattered, or bullied the members as the case might require in order to obtain their support.

The Tudors

In 1603 Elizabeth I, the last of the Tudors, died, leaving no direct descendants. Her nearest relative was her cousin, James VI of Scotland, who now became the sovereign of both England and Scotland under the name of James I. His accession marked the beginning of the troubled history of the Stuarts, the second and last of the absolute dynasties in England. A curious mixture of stubbornness, vanity, and

The establishment of divine-right monarchy by James I

Queen Elizabeth I. Elizabeth, known to her admiring subjects as "Gloriana," is here depicted standing on a map of Britain.

James I. "The wisest fool in Christendom."

The high-handed policies of James I

Religious dissension during the reign of James I

erudition, James was appropriately called by Henry IV of France "the wisest fool in Christendom." Though he loved to have his courtiers flatter him as the English Solomon, he did not even have sense enough to emulate his Tudor predecessors in being satisfied with the substance of absolute power; he insisted upon the theory as well. From France he appropriated the doctrine of the divine right of kings, contending that "as it is atheism and blasphemy to dispute what God can do, so it is presumption and high contempt in a subject to dispute what a king can do." Although he himself was most undignified in appearance and behavior, in his speech to Parliament in 1609 he declared that "kings are justly called gods, for they exercise a manner of resemblance of divine power upon earth."

That such ridiculous pretensions to divine authority would arouse opposition among the English people was a result which even James himself should have been able to foresee, for England still had traditions of liberty which could not be ignored. The ideal of limited government expressed in Magna Carta had never been entirely destroyed. Moreover, the policies of the new king were of such a character as to antagonize even some of his most conservative subjects. He insisted upon supplementing his income by modes of taxation which had never been sanctioned by Parliament; and when the leaders of that body remonstrated, he angrily tore up their protests and dissolved the two houses. He interfered with the freedom of business by granting monopolies and extravagant privileges to favored companies. He conducted foreign relations in disregard for the economic interests of some of the most powerful citizens. Ever since the days of the Elizabethan sea captains Sir John Hawkins and Sir Francis Drake, English merchants had been ambitious to destroy the commercial empire of Spain. They openly desired a renewal of the war, begun during Elizabeth's reign, for that purpose. But James made peace with Spain and entered into negotiations for marriage alliances favorable to Catholic sovereigns.

It was not marriage alliances alone that involved James in religious troubles. The Elizabethan Compromise, which brought the Reformation in England to a close, had not been satisfactory to the more radical Protestants. They believed that it did not depart widely enough from the forms and doctrines of the Roman Church. During the reign of Queen Mary many of them had been in exile in France and had come under the influence of Calvinism. When Elizabeth's compromise policy took shape, they denounced it as representing too great a concession to Catholicism. Gradually they came to be called Puritans from their desire to "purify" the Anglican Church of all traces of "popish" ritual and observances. In addition, they preached an ascetic morality and condemned the episcopal system of church government. However, they did not form a united group. One faction believed that it could transform the Anglican Church by working within that organization. The other preferred to withdraw from the Anglican fold and

Treaty sites, 1697-1721
Boundary of the
German Empire
Hapsburg dominions

NORWAY
SWEDEN
FINLAND
Nystad 1721
St. Petersburg
INGRIA
ESTONIA
(to Russia, 1721)
LIVONIA
Moscow
Stockholm
NORTH SEA
BALTIC SEA
RUSSIA
Smolensk
SCOTLAND
Edinburgh
DENMARK
Copenhagen
PRUSSIA
Danzig
KINGDOM OF GREAT BRITAIN
Dublin
IRELAND
ENGLAND
WALES
London
POLAND
Warsaw
Kiev
UNITED PROVINCES
Amsterdam
Ryswick 1697
Utrecht 1713
BRANDENBURG
Berlin
(to Turkey, 1718)
Azov
AZOV PROV.
AUSTRIAN NETHERLANDS
Leipzig
SAXONY
Dresden
SILESIA
Prague
BOHEMIA
Cracow
ATLANTIC OCEAN
Versailles
Paris
LORRAINE
Rastatt 1714
ALSACE
BAVARIA
Munich
AUSTRIA
Vienna
HUNGARY
BLACK SEA
FRANCE
FRANCHE-COMTÉ
SWITZERLAND
TIROL
Venice
REPUBLIC OF VENICE
Karlowitz 1699
(to Hapsburgs, 1718)
Passarowitz 1718
0   300 miles
SAVOY
MILAN
(to Hapsburgs, 1714)
PAPAL STATES
Rome
CORSICA
Naples
NAPLES
OTTOMAN EMPIRE
Istanbul
PORTUGAL
Madrid
SPAIN
MINORCA
(to England, 1713)
SARDINIA
(to Hapsburgs, 1714)
MOREA
Lisbon
MEDITERRANEAN SEA
SICILY
(to Turkey, 1711)
Gibraltar
(to England, 1713)
(to Savoy, 1714)

AGE OF ABSOLUTISM

establish separate congregations where they could worship as they pleased. The members of this latter group came to be designated Separatists. They achieved fame in American history as the so-called Pilgrims, who founded Plymouth Colony.

Any brand or faction of Puritans was anathema to King James because he distrusted any religion that did not fit in with his own ideas of relations between church and state. In his estimation the Puritans, by repudiating the episcopal system of church government, were threatening to pull down one of the chief pillars of monarchy itself. Refusal to submit to the authority of bishops appointed by the king was identical in his mind with disloyalty to the sovereign. For this reason he regarded the Puritans as the equivalent of traitors and threatened to "harry them out of the land." He showed little more wisdom in his dealings with the Catholics. For the most part, he favored them, though he could not resist the temptation to levy fines upon them from time to time for violating the severe code which came down from the Reformation. In 1605 a group of fanatical adherents of the Roman faith organized the Gunpowder Plot. They planned to blow

Relations with Puritans and Catholics

up the Parliament building while the king and the legislators were assembled in it, and, in the resulting confusion, seize control of the government. The plot was discovered, and Parliament enacted even more stringent laws against the Catholics. James, however, allowed the measures to go unenforced. Needless to say, his persistent leniency antagonized his Protestant subjects and made him more unpopular than ever.

From 1611 to 1621 James ruled virtually without Parliament. But this did not mean that his troubles were over. In 1613 the rights of the people found a new champion when Sir Edward Coke (pronounced Cook) was appointed chief justice. Coke was no democrat, but he did have a profound reverence for the common law and for the basic liberties inferred from Magna Carta. Moreover, he was a staunch defender of the privileged position of lawyers and judges. When the king insisted that he also had the faculty of reason and could interpret the law as well as the judges, Coke reminded him that he was not learned in the law, and that causes which concerned the lives and fortunes of his subjects were not to be decided by natural reason but only on the basis of long study and experience. Furthermore, the chief justice developed a rudimentary concept of judicial review. In the celebrated Dr. Bonham's case, he held that "when an act of Parliament is against common right and reason, or repugnant, or impossible to be performed, the common law will control it, and adjudge such act to be void." There is evidence that this opinion was highly regarded in colonial America, and that it was one of the factors which later gave rise to the idea that the Supreme Court of the United States has the authority to nullify laws of Congress which conflict with the Constitution.

Sir Edward Coke

The first of the Stuart kings died in 1625 and was succeeded by his son, Charles I (1625–1649). The new monarch was more regal in appearance than his father, but he held the same inflated notions of royal power. As a consequence, he was soon at odds with the Puritans and the leaders of the parliamentary opposition. As in the case of his father, religious tensions were exacerbated by questions of taxation. Soon after his accession to the throne Charles became involved in a war with France. His need for revenue was desperate. When Parliament refused to make more than the customary grants, he resorted to forced loans from his subjects, punishing those who failed to comply by quartering soldiers in their homes or throwing them into prison without a trial. The upshot of this tyranny was the Petition of Right, forced upon Charles by the leaders of Parliament in 1628. This document declared all taxes not voted by Parliament illegal. It condemned also the quartering of soldiers in private houses and prohibited arbitrary imprisonment and the establishment of martial law in time of peace.

But acceptance of the Petition of Right did not end the conflict. Charles soon resumed his old practices of raising money by various ir-

Charles I. This portrait by Van Dyck vividly captures the ill-fated monarch's arrogance.

regular means. He revived obsolete feudal laws and collected fines from all who violated them. He compelled rich burghers to apply for knighthood and then charged them high fees for their titles. He sold monopolies at exorbitant rates and admonished his judges to increase the fines in criminal cases. But the most unpopular of all his expedients for raising revenue was his collection of ship money. Under an ancient custom the English seaboard towns had been required to contribute ships for the royal navy. Since the needs of the fleet were now provided for in other ways, Charles maintained that the towns should contribute money; and he proceeded to apply the new tax not merely to the coastal cities but to the inland counties as well. The levies of ship money were particularly irritating to the merchant class and served to crystallize the opposition of that group to monarchical tyranny. Many refused to pay, and the king's attorney general finally decided to prosecute. A wealthy squire by the name of John Hampden was haled into court in a test case. When convicted by a vote of seven to five, he acquired a sort of martyrdom. For years he was venerated by many as a symbol of resistance to royal autocracy.

The continued tyranny of Charles I

Like his blundering father before him, Charles also aroused the antagonism of the Calvinists. He appointed as archbishop of Canterbury a clergyman by the name of William Laud, whose sympathies were decidedly High Anglican. He outraged the Sabbatarianism of the Puritans by authorizing public games on Sunday. Worse still, he attempted to impose the episcopal system of church government upon the Scottish Presbyterians, who were radical Calvinists. The result was an armed rebellion by his northern subjects and the first step toward full-scale civil war.

Conflict with the Calvinists

In order to get money to punish the Scots for their resistance, Charles was finally compelled in 1640 to summon Parliament, after more than eleven years of autocratic rule. Knowing full well that the king was helpless without money, the leaders of the House of Commons determined to take the government of the country into their own hands. They abolished ship money and the special tribunals which had been used as agencies of tyranny. They impeached and sent to imprisonment in the Tower of London the king's chief subordinates, Archbishop Laud and the earl of Strafford. They enacted a law forbidding the monarch to dissolve Parliament and requiring sessions at least every three years. Charles replied to these acts by a show of force. He marched with his guard into the House of Commons and attempted to arrest five of its leaders. All of them escaped, but the issue was now sharply drawn between king and Parliament, and an open conflict could no longer be avoided. Both sides collected troops and prepared for an appeal to the sword.

The outbreak of civil war

These events ushered in a period of civil strife, which lasted from 1642 to 1649. It was a struggle at once political, economic, and religious. Arrayed on the side of the king were most of the chief nobles

Oliver Cromwell

and landowners, the Catholics, and the staunch Anglicans. The followers of Parliament included, in general, the small landholders, tradesmen, and manufacturers. The majority were Puritans and Presbyterians. The members of the king's party were commonly known by the aristocratic name of Cavaliers. Their opponents, who cut their hair short in contempt for the fashionable custom of wearing curls, were called in derision Roundheads. At first the party of the royalists, having obvious advantages of military experience, won most of the victories. In 1644, however, the parliamentary army was reorganized, and soon afterward the fortune of battle shifted. The Cavalier forces were badly beaten, and in 1646 the king was compelled to surrender. The struggle would now have ended had not a quarrel developed within the parliamentary party. The majority of its members, who were now Presbyterians, were ready to restore Charles to the throne as a limited monarch under an arrangement whereby the Presbyterian faith would be imposed upon England as the state religion. But a radical minority of Puritans, made up principally of Separatists but now more commonly known as Independents, distrusted Charles and insisted upon religious toleration for themselves and all other Protestants. Their leader was Oliver Cromwell (1599–1658), who had risen to command of the Roundhead army. Taking advantage of the dissension within the ranks of his opponents, Charles renewed the war in 1648, but after a brief campaign was forced to concede that his cause was hopeless.

The defeat and execution of the king

The second defeat of the king gave an indisputable mastery of the situation to the Independents. Cromwell and his friends now resolved to put an end to "that man of blood," the Stuart monarch, and remodel the political system in accordance with their own desires. They conducted a purge of the legislative body by military force, ejecting 143 Presbyterians from the House of Commons; and then with the "Rump Parliament" that remained—numbering about 60 members—they proceeded to eliminate the monarchy. An act was passed redefining treason so as to apply to the offenses of the king. Next, a special High Court of Justice was established, and Charles was brought to trial before it. His conviction was a mere matter of form. On January 30, 1649, he was beheaded in front of his palace of Whitehall. A short time later the House of Lords was abolished, and England became an oligarchic republic. The first stage in the so-called Puritan Revolution was now completed.

The Commonwealth and Protectorate

The work of organizing the new state, which was given the name of the Commonwealth, was entirely in the hands of the Independents. Since the Rump Parliament continued as the legislative body, the really fundamental change was in the nature of the executive. In place of the king there was set up a Council of State composed of forty-one members. Cromwell, with the army at his back, soon came to dominate both of these bodies. However, as time went on he became exas-

Cromwell Felling the Royal Oak of England. A Royalist print of 1656 which portrays Oliver Cromwell as a destructive villain.

perated by the attempts of the legislators to perpetuate themselves in power and to profit from confiscation of the wealth of their opponents. Accordingly, in 1653, he marched a detachment of troops into the Rump and ordered the members to disperse. This action was followed by the establishment of a virtual dictatorship under a constitution drafted by officers of the army. Called the Instrument of Government, it was the nearest approach to a written constitution Britain has ever had. Extensive powers were given to Cromwell as Lord Protector for life, and his office was made hereditary. At first a Parliament exercised limited authority in making laws and levying taxes, but in 1655 its members were abruptly dismissed by the Lord Protector. Thereafter the government was but a thinly disguised autocracy. Cromwell now wielded a sovereignty even more absolute than any the Stuart monarchs would have dared to claim. In declaring his authority to be from God he even revived what practically amounted to the divine right of kings.

That Cromwell's regime would have its difficulties was certainly to be expected, since it rested upon the support of only a few people. He was opposed not only by royalists and Anglicans but by various dissenters, including some more radical than he. Like all upheavals of a similar character, the Puritan Revolution tended to move farther and farther in an extremist direction. Some of the Puritans became Levelers, who derived their name from their advocacy of equal political rights and privileges for all classes. Expressly disclaiming any intention of equalizing property, they confined their radicalism to the political sphere. They insisted that sovereignty inheres in the people and that government should rest upon the consent of the governed. Long in advance of any other party, they demanded a written constitution,

Levelers and Diggers

Charles II

The Restoration

Causes of the Glorious Revolution of 1688–1689

universal manhood suffrage, and the supremacy of Parliament. The Levelers were especially powerful in the army and through it exerted some influence upon the government. Still farther to the left were the Diggers, so called from their attempt to seize and cultivate unenclosed common land and distribute the produce to the poor. Though in common with the Levelers the Diggers appealed to the law of nature as a source of rights, they were more interested in economic than in political equality. They espoused a kind of primitive communism based upon the idea that the land is the "common treasury" of all. Every ablebodied man would be required to work at productive labor, and all persons would be permitted to draw from the common fund of wealth produced in proportion to their needs. The Church would be transformed into an educational institution and the clergy would become schoolmasters, giving instruction every seventh day in public affairs, history, and the arts and sciences.

In September 1658, the stout-hearted Lord Protector died. He was succeeded by his well-meaning but irresolute son Richard, who managed to hold office only until May of the following year. Perhaps even a man of much sterner fiber would also have failed eventually, for the country had grown tired of the austerities of Calvinist rule. Neither the Commonwealth nor the Protectorate had ever had the support of a majority of the English nation. Royalists regarded the Independents as usurpers. Republicans hated the disguised monarchy which Oliver Cromwell had set up. Catholics and Anglicans resented the branding of their acts of worship as criminal offenses. Even some members of the merchant class gradually came to suspect that Cromwell's war with Spain had done more harm than good by endangering English commerce with the West Indies. For these and similar reasons there was general rejoicing when in 1660 a newly elected Parliament proclaimed Charles I's exiled son king and invited him to return to England and occupy the throne of his father. The new king, Charles II, had gained a reputation for joyous living and easy morality, and his accession was hailed as a welcome relief from the somber rule of soldiers and zealots. Besides, he pledged himself not to reign as a despot, but to respect Parliament and to observe Magna Carta and the Petition of Right, for he admitted that he was not anxious to "resume his travels." England now entered upon a period known as the Restoration, covered by the reigns of Charles II (1660–1685) and his brother James II (1685–1688). Despite its auspicious beginning, many of the old problems had not really been solved but were simply concealed by the fond belief that the nation had regained its former stability.

Toward the end of the seventeenth century England went through a second political upheaval, the so-called Glorious Revolution of 1688–1689. Several of the causes were grounded in the policies of Charles II. That amiable sovereign was extravagant and carefree but determined on occasion to let the country know whose word was law.

His pro-Catholic attitude aroused the fears of patriotic Englishmen that their nation might once again be brought into subservience to Rome. Worse still, he showed a disposition, in spite of earlier pledges, to defy the authority of Parliament. In 1672 he suspended the laws against Catholics and Protestant Dissenters (i.e., all but Anglicans) and nine years later resolved to dispense with the legislative branch entirely. The policies of Charles II were continued in more extreme form by his brother, who succeeded him in 1685. James II was an avowed Catholic and seemed bent upon making that faith the established religion of England. He openly violated an act of Parliament requiring that all holders of public office should adhere to the Anglican church, and proceeded to fill important positions in the army and the civil service with his Romanist followers. He continued his brother's practice of exempting Catholics from the disabilities imposed upon them by Parliament, even going so far as to demand that the Anglican bishops should read his decrees for this purpose in their churches. As long as his opponents could expect that James II would be succeeded by one of his two Protestant daughters, they were inclined to tolerate his arbitrary rule, lest the country be plunged again into civil war. But when the king acquired a son by his second wife, who was a Catholic, the die of revolution was cast. It was feared that the young prince would be infected with his father's doctrines, and that, as a consequence, England would be fettered with the shackles of despotic and "papist"

Left: *The Trial of Charles I (1649).* Right: *The Arrival of the First Course at James II's Coronation Dinner (1685).* Both of these events took place at Westminster Hall: the first shows English royal power at its low point and the second at its apparent zenith. But James II was to be overthrown even more quickly than Charles I.

Results of the Glorious Revolution

Significance of the Glorious Revolution

rule for an indefinite time to come. To forestall such a result it seemed necessary to depose the king.

The "Glorious Revolution" of 1688–1689 was an entirely bloodless affair. A group of politicians from the upper classes secretly invited Prince William of Orange and his wife Mary, the elder daughter of James II, to become joint rulers of England. William crossed over from Holland with an army and occupied London without firing a shot. Deserted even by those whom he had counted as loyal supporters, King James took refuge in France. The English throne was now declared vacant by Parliament and the crown presented to the new sovereigns. But their enthronement did not complete the revolution. Throughout the year 1689 Parliament passed numerous laws designed to safeguard the rights of Englishmen and to protect its own power from monarchical invasion. First came an act requiring that appropriations should be made for one year only. Next the Toleration Act was passed, granting religious liberty to all Christians except Catholics and Unitarians. Finally, on the sixteenth of December the famous Bill of Rights was enacted into law. It provided for trial by jury and affirmed the right of Englishmen to petition the government for a redress of grievances. It condemned excessive bail, cruel punishments, and exorbitant fines. And it forbade the king to suspend laws or to levy taxes without the consent of Parliament. More sweeping in its provisions than the Petition of Right of 1628, it was backed by a Parliament that now had the power to see that it was obeyed.

The significance of the revolution of 1688–1689 was very great. Since it marked the final triumph of Parliament over the king, it therefore spelled the doom of absolute monarchy in England. Never again was any crowned head in Britain able to defy the legislative branch of the government as the Stuart monarchs had done. The revolution also dealt a death blow to the theory of the divine right of kings. It would have been impossible for William and Mary to have denied the fact that they received their crowns from Parliament. And the authority of Parliament to determine who should be king was made more emphatic by the passage of the Act of Settlement in 1701. This law provided that upon the death of the heiress-presumptive Anne, younger sister of Mary, the crown should go to the Electress Sophia of Hanover or to the eldest of her heirs who might be Protestant. There were some forty men or women with better claim to the throne than Sophia, but all were eliminated by Parliament on the ground of their being Catholics. Finally, the Glorious Revolution contributed much to the American and French Revolutions at the end of the eighteenth century. The example of the English in overthrowing absolute rule was a powerful inspiration to the opponents of absolutism elsewhere. It was the British ideal of limited government which furnished the substance of the political theory of Voltaire, Jefferson, and Paine. And a considerable portion of the English Bill of Rights was incorporated in the French Declaration of the Rights of Man in 1789 and in the first ten amendments to the American Constitution.

In the eighteenth century English political life became far more stable. In 1714 the Electress Sophia's son succeeded Queen Anne as George I (1714–1727) and initiated the reign of the House of Hanover, which continued in England until 1901. Because George, who came to the throne at the age of fifty four, could speak no English and continued to spend much time in his German possession of Hanover, he was content to leave the real government of England to the leader of Parliament, Sir Robert Walpole (1676–1745). The latter deserves to be called the first English prime minister. During his supremacy Parliament became the real executive as well as legislative organ of England, and Walpole as parliamentary leader was the chief executive. Walpole ruled through a new system he devised, forever after called the cabinet system (originally because "cabinet" members met in a small room known as a cabinet). This meant that the leader of the parliamentary party in power (Walpole was a Whig, his opponents Tories) would work together with a group of like-minded parliamentary colleagues to push through legislation in Parliament and for practical purposes run the country. When the dominant party lost control, the opposition party would bring in a new prime minister and a new cabinet. The cabinet system continues in England until the present day.

Walpole remained prime minister until 1742 by following a policy of cautious conservatism. Acting on his motto of *quieta non movere* ("let sleeping dogs lie") he kept England out of war for most of his supremacy and supported the financial interests of the upper classes.

Walpole, first prime minister

George III

Sir Robert Walpole with Members of His Cabinet

New prime ministers continued to rule England more or less along the lines set down by Walpole throughout the rest of the reign of George II (1727–1760). They faced no interference from that monarch because, like his father, George II was really more German than English. But difficulties ensued at the beginning of the reign of George III (1760–1820). The latter was born in England and legend has it that his mother encouraged him to take an active role in English government by constantly saying "George, be king." Desiring to rule as well as reign, George III succeeded for a time in ensuring that only his favorites became prime ministers. But misrule followed. After England lost its American colonies and the king began to suffer from fits of insanity, Parliament regained the unimpeded initiative in governing the country which it has never lost since then.

2. ABSOLUTE MONARCHY IN FRANCE AND SPAIN

Contrasting conditions in England and France

The development of absolutism in France followed a course similar in some respects to early absolutism in England. Although France remained Catholic, its rulers had to contend with a Calvinist (Huguenot) opposition as formidable as that of the Puritans in England. Both nations had their staunch defenders of absolutism among lawyers and political philosophers. But there was one notable difference. England enjoyed an advantage of geographic isolation that sheltered it from foreign danger. It had not been invaded since the Norman Conquest in 1066. As a consequence, the English felt secure, and their rulers found it difficult to justify a huge professional army. They did, of course, maintain large fleets of war vessels, but a navy could not be used in the same manner as an army stationed in inland garrisons to overawe subjects or to stifle incipient revolutions. France, on the other hand, like most continental nations, faced almost constant threats of invasion. France's northeastern and eastern frontiers were poorly protected by geographic barriers and had been penetrated several times. As a result, it was easy for French kings to argue the need for massive armies of professional soldiers. And such troops could readily be utilized to nip domestic disturbances in the bud. It would doubtless be a mistake to give all of the credit to this difference in geographic position for the longer persistence of absolute government in France, but it was certainly a major factor.

The origins of absolutism in France

The growth of royal absolutism in France was the product of a gradual evolution. The most important antecedents were medieval. By 1300 the French kings were perfecting an efficient bureaucratic system of government. By 1450, largely owing to the results of the Hundred Years' War, they had introduced a standing army and had gained the right to collect national taxes. And by 1500 they had reduced regional separatism and the opposition of the provincial nobility. As royal power grew, the nobles were gradually reduced to the level of courtiers, dependent mainly upon the monarch for their titles and prestige. In the reign of Francis I (1515–1547) the crown became even stronger because it gained new control over ecclesiastics. By the Concordat of Bologna, an agreement struck with the papacy in 1516, the king gained the right to choose all French bishops and abbots. Although the pope was granted the first year's income from each new appointment, the agreement greatly favored the monarchy because it virtually conceded to it full political authority over the French Church.

The trend toward absolutism was interrupted during the sixteenth century when France was involved in a war with Spain and torn by a bloody struggle between Catholics and Huguenots at home. Ambitious nobles took advantage of the confusion to assert their power and contested the succession to the throne. Peace was restored to the exhausted kingdom in 1593 by Henry of Navarre (1589–1610), who four years before had proclaimed himself king as Henry IV. He was the founder of the Bourbon dynasty. Though at one time a leader of the Huguenot faction, Henry perceived that the nation would never accept him unless he renounced the Calvinist religion. Flippantly remarking that Paris was worth a Mass, he formally adopted the Catholic faith. In 1598 he issued the Edict of Nantes, guaranteeing freedom of conscience and political rights to all Protestants. With the grounds for religious controversy thus removed, Henry could turn his attention to rebuilding his kingdom. In this work, he had the able assistance of his chief minister, the duke of Sully. Grim, energetic, and penurious, Sully was a worthy forerunner of Colbert in the seventeenth century. For years the king and his faithful servant labored to repair the shattered fortunes of France. Sully devoted his efforts primarily to fiscal reform, so as to eliminate corruption and waste and bring more revenue into the royal treasury. He endeavored also to promote the prosperity of agriculture by draining swamps, improving devastated lands, subsidizing stock-raising, and opening up foreign markets for the products of the soil. The king gave most of his attention to fostering industry and commerce. He introduced the manufacture of silk into France, encouraged other industries by subsidies and monopolies, and made favorable commercial treaties with England and Spain. But Henry did not stop with economic reforms. He was deeply concerned with crushing the reborn power of the nobility, and so successful were his efforts in this direction that he restored the monarchy to the dominant position it had held under Francis I. He was active also in sponsoring the development of a colonial empire in America. During his reign the French acquired a foothold in Canada and began their exploration in the region of the Great Lakes and the Mississippi Valley. In short, his rule was intelligent and benevolent.

The reign of Henry IV was brought to an end by the dagger of a fa-

Francis I of France

Henry IV and the duke of Sully

The Assassination of Henry IV. This contemporary engraving shows Ravaillac climbing on the wheel of Henry's carriage in order to stab the French ruler.

Cardinal Richelieu

natic in 1610. Since the new king, Louis XIII, was only nine years old, the country was ruled by his mother, Marie de'Medici, as regent. In 1624 Louis XIII, no longer under the regency, entrusted the management of his kingdom to a brilliant but domineering cleric, Cardinal Richelieu, whom he made his chief minister. Richelieu dedicated himself to two objectives: (1) to destroy all limitations upon the authority of the king; and (2) to make France the chief power in Europe. In the pursuit of these aims he allowed nothing to stand in his way. He ruthlessly suppressed the nobility, destroying its most dangerous members and rendering the others harmless by attaching them as pensioners to the royal court. Though he fostered education and patronized literature, he neglected the interests of commerce and allowed graft and extravagance to flourish in the government. His main constructive achievements were the creation of a postal service and the establishment of a system under which *intendants,* or agents of the king, took charge of local government. Both were conceived as devices for consolidating the nation under the control of the crown, thereby eradicating surviving traces of independent local authority.

Richelieu's foreign policy

Richelieu's ambitions were not limited to domestic affairs. To make France the most powerful nation in Europe it was necessary to pursue an aggressive diplomacy and eventually to enter into war. France was still surrounded by what Henry IV had referred to as a "Hapsburg ring." On its southern border was Spain, ruled since 1516 by a branch of the Hapsburg family. To the north, less than a hundred miles from Paris, were the Spanish Netherlands. Other centers of Hapsburg power included Luxemburg, the Franche-Comté, and Milan, and still farther to the east the great Austrian Empire itself (see map, p. 665 above). Cardinal Richelieu eagerly awaited an opportunity to break this ring. As we shall see, he finally found it in the Thirty Years' War. Though engaged in suppressing Protestants at home, he did not hesitate to ally himself with Gustavus Adolphus, king of Sweden and leader of a coalition of Protestant states. Long before his death in 1642 the great cardinal-statesman had forged to the front as the most powerful individual in Europe.

Cardinal Richelieu

Absolute monarchy in France attained its zenith during the reigns of the last three Bourbon kings before the French Revolution. The first of the rulers of this series was Louis XIV (1643–1715), known as the "Grand Monarch," who epitomized the ideal of absolutism more completely than any other sovereign of his age. Proud, extravagant, and domineering, Louis entertained the most exalted notions of his position as king. Not only did he believe that he was commissioned by God to reign, but he also regarded the welfare of the state as intimately bound up with his own personality. The famous phrase imputed to him, *l'état c'est moi* (I am the state), may not represent his exact words, but it expresses very clearly the conception he held of his own authority. He chose the sun as his official emblem to indicate his belief that the nation derived its glory and sustenance from him as the planets do theirs from the actual sun. He gave personal supervision to every department and regarded his ministers as mere clerks with no duty but to obey his orders. In general, he followed the policies of Henry IV and Richelieu in consolidating national power at the expense of local officials and in trying to reduce the nobles to mere parasites of the court. But any possible good he may have done was completely overshadowed by his extravagant wars and his reactionary policy in religion. In 1685 he revoked the Edict of Nantes, which had granted freedom of conscience to the Huguenots. As a result, numbers of his most inventive and prosperous subjects fled the country.

Louis XIV, the supreme incarnation of absolute rule

Until the beginning of the revolution in 1789 the form of the French government remained essentially as Louis XIV had left it. His successors, Louis XV (1715–1774) and Louis XVI (1774–1792), also claimed to rule by divine right. But neither of these kings had the desire to emulate the Grand Monarch in his enthusiasm for work and his meticulous attention to the business of state. Louis XV was lazy and incompetent and allowed himself to be dominated by a succession of mistresses. Problems of government bored him, and when obliged to preside at the council table he "opened his mouth, said little, and thought not at all." His grandson, the ill-fated Louis XVI, was weak in character and mentally dull. Indifferent to politics, he amused himself by shooting deer from the palace window and playing at his hobbies of lock-making and masonry. On July 14, 1789 when mobs stormed the Bastille, he wrote in his diary "Nothing." Yet both of these monarchs maintained a government which was more arbitrary

Louis XIV by Rigaud

Philip II of Spain. This painting by Coello shows the famous protruding chin and lower lip which were characteristic features of the Hapsburg family.

Absolutism in Spain

Philip II

than had ever been the case before. They permitted their ministers to imprison without a trial persons suspected of disloyalty; they suppressed the courts for refusing to approve their decrees; and they brought the country to the verge of bankruptcy by their costly wars and by their reckless extravagance for the benefit of their mistresses and favorites. If they had deliberately planned to provoke revolution, they could scarcely have succeeded better.

The growth of absolute monarchy in Spain was less interrupted than was true in France. As we have seen in Chapter 13, by 1500 Ferdinand and Isabella had united Spain and made it a very powerful kingdom. In 1516 the realm was inherited by their grandson Charles I, whose father had been a Hapsburg. Three years later Charles was elected Holy Roman Emperor as Charles V, thereby uniting Spain with central Europe and southern Italy. Charles was interested not merely in the destinies of Spain but in the welfare of the Church and in the politics of Europe as a whole. He dreamed that he might be the instrument of restoring the religious unity of Christendom, broken by the Protestant Revolution, and of making the empire over which he presided a worthy successor of imperial Rome. Though successful in holding his disjointed domain together and in fighting off attempts of the French to conquer his Italian possessions and of the Turks to overrun Europe, he failed in the achievement of his larger objectives. At the age of fifty-six, overcome with a sense of discouragement and futility, he abdicated and retired to a monastery. The German princes chose his brother, Ferdinand I, to succeed him as Holy Roman Emperor. His Spanish and Italian possessions, including the colonies overseas, passed to his son, who became king as Philip II (1556–1598).

Philip II came to the throne of Spain at the height of its glory. But he also witnessed, and to a considerable extent was responsible for, the beginning of its decline. His policies were mainly an intensification of those of his predecessors. He was narrow, despotic, and cruel. Determined to enforce a strict conformity in matters of religion upon all of his subjects, he is reputed to have boasted that he would gather faggots to burn his own son if the latter were guilty of heresy. Therefore, he encouraged the ruthlessness of the Spanish Inquisition and launched the war for suppression of the religious revolt in the Netherlands. Philip was equally shortsighted in his colonial policy. Indigenous peoples were butchered and their territories greedily despoiled of their gold and silver, which were dragged off to Spain in the mistaken belief that this was the surest means of increasing the nation's wealth. No thought was given to the development of new industries in either the colonies or the mother country. Instead, the gold and silver were largely squandered in furthering Philip's military and political ambitions. It can be said, however, in the king's defense that he was following the accepted theories of the time. Doubtless most other monarchs with a like opportunity would have imitated his example.

The Escorial. Built in the sixteenth century by Philip II of Spain, this palace originally served as his retreat.

Philip II's crowning mistake was his war against England. Angered by the attacks of English ships upon Spanish commerce and frustrated in his schemes to bring England back into the Catholic faith, he sent a great fleet in 1588, the "Invincible Armada," to destroy Queen Elizabeth's navy. But Philip had little knowledge of either the new techniques of naval warfare or of the robust patriotism of the English. A combination of fighting seamanship and disastrous storms (the "Protestant Wind") sent many of his 130 ships to the bottom of the Channel and the rest back home in disarray. Spain never recovered from the blow. Though a brilliant cultural afterglow, exemplified the work of great writers and artists like Cervantes and Velasquez, continued for some years, the greatness of Spain as a nation was approaching its end.

The Armada

3. ABSOLUTISM IN CENTRAL EUROPE

The chief countries in central Europe where absolutism flourished most were Prussia and Austria. The founder of absolute rule in Prussia (a state made up primarily of Brandenburg, in north-central Germany, and Prussia, far to the east, near Russia) was the Great Elector, Frederick William, who ruled from 1640 to 1688. He was the first member of the Hohenzollern family to acquire full sovereignty over Prussia and to introduce a standing army. In addition, he began to bring all his dominions under centralized rule. The work of the Great Elector was continued and extended by his grandson, known as Frederick William I (1713–1740), since he now had the title of *king* of Prussia. Frederick William's major concerns were to build up the Prussian bureaucracy and the Prussian army. His bureaucratic officials ran Prussia extremely efficiently and at such small expense that Prussia

Frederick William I of Prussia

Frederick William I

Frederick the Great

Absolutism in Austria: Maria Theresa and Joseph II

was the only continental state in the middle of the eighteenth century with a budgetary surplus, even though the country had very limited natural resources. But Frederick William's really consuming passion was his army. This he more than doubled in size and drilled to a machinelike efficiency. Since he could hardly count on volunteers, he introduced conscription and supplemented that by sending gangs of kidnappers to drag back forced recruits from neighboring German lands. Frederick William had a strange love for particularly tall soldiers: his own private regiment of "Potsdam Giants" was comprised exclusively of soldiers over six feet in height. The king traded musicians and prize stallions for such choice specimens and then spent the bulk of his time marching his "giants" around his palace grounds.

The style but not the substance of Frederick William's militarism was altered by his noted successor, Frederick II (1740–1786), commonly known as Frederick the Great. An earnest disciple of the reformist doctrines of the new rationalist philosophy, Frederick was the leading figure among the "enlightened despots" of the eighteenth century. Declaring himself not the master but merely the "first servant of the state," he wrote essays to prove that Machiavelli was wrong and rose at five in the morning to begin a Spartan routine of personal management of public affairs. He made Prussia in many ways the best-governed state in Europe, abolishing torture of accused criminals and bribery of judges, establishing elementary schools, and promoting the prosperity of industry and agriculture. He fostered scientific forestry and the cultivation of new crops such as the potato. He opened up new lands in Silesia and brought in thousands of immigrants to cultivate them. When wars ruined their farms, he supplied the peasants with new livestock and tools. As an admirer of the French philosopher Voltaire, whom he entertained for some time at his court, he tolerated all sorts of religious beliefs. He declared that he would build a mosque in Berlin if enough Muslims wished to locate there. Yet he was strongly anti-Semitic. He levied special taxes on the Jews and made efforts to close the professions and the civil service to them. Moreover, Frederick continued to invest heavily in his army, and such benevolence as he showed in internal affairs was not carried over into foreign relations. Frederick robbed Austria of Silesia, conspired with Catherine of Russia to dismember Poland, and contributed at least his full share to the bloody wars of the eighteenth century.

The full bloom of absolutism in Austria came during the reigns of Maria Theresa (1740–1780) and Joseph II (1780–1790). Maria Theresa was one of the most capable of all eighteenth-century monarchs. She played the role of a flighty woman when it suited her advantage, but actually ruled with great common sense and determination. During her reign a national army was established, the powers of the Church were curtailed in the interest of consolidated government, and elementary and higher education was greatly expanded. Unlike the rulers of most other countries, Maria Theresa was sincerely devoted to Christian morality. Though she participated in the dismemberment of Poland to make up for the loss of Silesia, she did so with grave misgivings—an attitude which prompted the scornful remark of Frederick the Great: "She weeps, but she takes her share." The reforms of Maria Theresa were extended, at least on paper, by her son Joseph II. Inspired by the teachings of French philosophers, Joseph determined to remake his empire in accordance with the highest ideals of justice and reason. Not only did he plan to reduce the powers of the Church by confiscating its lands and abolishing monasteries, but he aspired to humble the nobles and improve the condition of the masses. He decreed that serfs should become free and promised to relieve them of the obligations owed to their masters. He aimed to make education universal and to force the nobles to pay their proper share of taxes. But most of his magnificent plans ended in failure. He antagonized not merely the nobles and clergy but also the Hungarians, who were deprived of all rights of self-government. He alienated the sympathies of the peasants by making them liable to compulsory military service. He was scarcely any more willing than Louis XIV or Frederick the Great to sacrifice personal power and national glory even for the sake of his lofty ideals.

Maria Theresa of Austria

4. ABSOLUTISM IN RUSSIA

Russia at the beginning of the early modern age was a composite of European and Oriental characteristics. Much of its territory had been colonized by the Norsemen in the early Middle Ages. The Russian religion, calendar, and system of writing had been derived from Byzantium. Even the governing regime, with its boyars, or magnates, and serfs, was not greatly dissimilar to that of western Europe. On the other hand, much of Russia's culture, and many of its customs, were distinctly not European. Russian arts were limited almost entirely to icon painting and religious architecture, characterized by the onion dome. There was practically no literature in the Russian language, arithmetic was barely known, Arabic numerals were not used, and merchants made their calculations with the abacus. Nor were manners and customs comparable to those of the West. Women of the upper classes were veiled and secluded. Flowing beards and skirted garments were universal for men. Table manners were considered superfluous. Seasons of wild revelry alternated with periods of repentance and morbid atonement. It would be a mistake, however, to suppose that Russia was totally cut off from Europe. As early as the fourteenth century, German merchants of the Hanseatic League conducted some trade in Russian furs and amber. In the 1550s English merchants discovered the White Sea and made Archangel a port of entry through

Russia at the beginning of the modern age

which military supplies could be exchanged for a few Russian goods and even products from Persia and China. But with Archangel frozen most of the year, the volume of this trade was undoubtedly small.

Foreign invaders; the Mongols

As late as the thirteenth century Russia was a collection of small principalities. They were attacked from the west by Lithuanians, Poles, and the Teutonic Knights. The last were members of one of several religious and military organizations that sprang from the Crusades. Established originally for charitable purposes, their order developed into a military one which adopted as its mission the conversion and conquest of lands on Germany's eastern frontier. The operations of the Teutonic Knights were part of the famous *Drang nach Osten* (Drive to the East) which occupied such a prominent place in German history. From the east Russia was threatened by the Mongols (Tartars), who had established a great empire in central Asia, eventually including both northern India and China. In 1237 the Mongols began an invasion which led to their conquest of nearly all of Russia. Mongol rule was in several ways a disaster. It marked the development of a stronger Asiatic orientation. Henceforth Russia turned more and more away from Europe and looked beyond the Urals as the arena of its future development. Its inhabitants intermarried with Mongols and adopted some elements of their way of life.

The rise of Moscow; Ivan the Great

Eventually, Mongol power declined. In 1380 a Russian army defeated the Mongols and thus initiated a movement to drive them back into Asia. The state which assumed the leadership of this movement was the Grand Duchy of Moscow. Under strong rulers it had been increasing its power for some time. Located near the sources of the great rivers flowing both north and south, it had geographic advantages surpassing those of the other states. Moreover, it had recently been made the headquarters of the Russian Church. The first of the princes of Moscow to put himself forward as tsar (caesar) of Russia was Ivan the Great (1462–1505). Taking as his bride the niece of the last of the Byzantine emperors, who had perished in the capture of Constantinople in 1453, he proclaimed himself his successor by the grace of God. He adopted as his insignia the Byzantine double-headed eagle and imported Italian architects to work on an enormous building complex, the Kremlin, in demonstration of Russia's new independence and greatness. Avowing his intention to recover the ancient lands that had been lost to foreign invaders, Ivan forced the prince of Lithuania to acknowledge him as sovereign of "all the Russias" and pushed the Tartars out of northern Russia and beyond the Urals.

The first of the tsars to attempt the Europeanization of Russia was Peter the Great (1682–1725). He stands out as the most powerful and probably the most intelligent autocrat yet to occupy the Russian throne. With a reckless disregard for ancient customs, Peter endeavored to force his subjects to change their ways of living. He forbade the Oriental seclusion of women and commanded both sexes to adopt European styles of dress. He made the use of tobacco compul-

Peter the Great. An eighteenth-century mosaic.

sory among the members of his court. He summoned the great nobles before him and clipped their flowing beards with his own hand. In order to make sure of his own absolute power, he abolished all traces of local self-government and established a system of national police. For the same reason, he annihilated the authority of the patriarch of the Orthodox church and placed all religious affairs under a Holy Synod subject to his own control. Deeply interested in Western technology, he made journeys to Holland and England to learn about shipbuilding and industry. He imitated the mercantilist policies of Western nations by improving agriculture and fostering manufactures and commerce. In order to get "windows to the west" he conquered territory along the Baltic shore and transferred his capital from Moscow to St. Petersburg, his new city at the mouth of the Neva river. But the good that he did was greatly outweighed by his extravagant wars and his fiendish cruelty. He put thousands to death for alleged conspiracies against him. He murdered his own son and heir because the latter boasted that when *he* became tsar he would return Russia to the ways of its fathers. To raise money for his expensive wars he debased the currency, sold valuable concessions to foreigners, established government monopolies on the production of salt, oil, caviar, and coffins, and imposed taxes on almost everything, from baths to beehives.

Peter the Great

The significance of Peter the Great is not easy to evaluate. He did not singlehandedly transform Russia into a Western nation. Western influences had been seeping into the country as a consequence of trade contacts for many years. But Peter accelerated the process and gave it a more radical direction. Evidence abounds that he really did aim to

Results of Peter's reign

Peter the Great's Execution of Conspirators. This contemporary print shows scores of corpses gibbeted outside the walls of the Kremlin. Peter kept the rotting bodies on display for months to discourage his subjects from opposing his efforts to westernize Russian society.

The Winter Palace. This contemporary engraving shows the palace built by Peter the Great in the town that bore his name, St. Petersburg.

remake the nation and to give it at least a veneer of cultivation. He sent many of his countrymen abroad to study. He simplified the ancient alphabet and established the first newspaper to be published in Russia. He ordered the publication of a book on polite behavior, teaching his subjects not to spit on the floor or to scratch themselves or gnaw bones at dinner. He encouraged exports, built a fleet on the Baltic, and fostered new industries such as textiles and mining. Though a reaction set in after Peter's death against many of his innovations, some of them survived for at least two centuries. The Church, for example, continued as essentially an arm of the stage, governed by a procurator of the Holy Synod appointed by the tsar himself. Serfdom continued in the extended forms required or authorized by Peter. No longer were serfs bound to the soil; they could be bought and sold at any time, even for work in factories and mines. Finally, the absolutism developed by Peter showed few signs of abating until the early twentieth century. It was an absolutism based upon force, with a secret police, an extensive bureaucracy, and a subordinated Church as instruments for imposing the autocrat's will.

The other most noted of the Russian monarchs in the age of absolutism was Catherine the Great (1762–1796), who before her marriage

Catherine the Great

was a German princess. Frequently classified as one of the "enlightened despots," Catherine corresponded with French philosophers, founded hospitals and orphanages, and expressed the hope that someday the serfs might be liberated. Ambitious to gain for herself a place in intellectual history, she rose at five in the morning to engage in scholarship. She wrote plays, published a digest of Blackstone's *Commentaries on the Laws of England,* and even began a history of Russia. Her accomplishments as a reformer, however, had only a limited scope. She took steps toward a codification of the Russian laws, restricted the use of torture, and remodeled and consolidated local government. Any plans she may have had, however, for improving the lot of the peasants were abruptly canceled after a violent serf rebellion in 1773–1774. Landlords and priests were murdered and the ruling classes terrified as the revolt swept through the Urals and the valley of the Volga. Catherine responded with stern repression. The captured leader of the peasants was drawn and quartered, and, as a guaranty against future outbreaks, the nobles were given increased powers over their serfs. They were permitted to deal with them virtually as if they were chattel slaves. Catherine's chief significance lies in the fact that she continued the work of Peter the Great in introducing Russia to Western ideas and in making the country a formidable power in European affairs. She managed to extend the boundaries of her country to include not only eastern Poland but lands on the Black Sea.

Catherine the Great

5. THE WARS OF THE EARLY MODERN PERIOD

Between 1500 and 1789 the years of peace in Europe were outnumbered by the years of war. The earlier conflicts were largely religious in character and have already been dealt with in Chapter 15. The majority of the wars after 1600 partook of the nature of struggles for supremacy among the powerful autocrats of the principal countries. But religion was also a factor in some of them, and so was the greed of the commercial classes. In general, nationalistic motives were much less important than in the wars of the nineteenth and twentieth centuries. Peoples and territories were so many pawns to be moved back and forth in the game of dynastic aggrandizement.

Character of the wars in the age of absolutism for the despots

The major warfare of the seventeenth century revolved around a titanic duel between Hapsburgs and Bourbons. Originally the rulers of Austria, the Hapsburgs had gradually extended their power over Hungary and Bohemia as well. In addition, the head of the family enjoyed what was left of the distinction of being Holy Roman Emperor. Since the time of Charles V (1519–1556) branches of the Hapsburgs had ruled over Spain, the Netherlands, the Franche-Comté, Milan, and the Kingdom of the Two Sicilies. For many years this expansion of Hapsburg power had been a source of profound disturbance to the rulers of France. They regarded their country as encircled, and longed to break through the enclosing ring. But tensions were building up in other parts of Europe also. The princes of Germany looked with alarm upon the growing power of the Holy Roman Emperor and sought opportunities to restrict him in ways that would increase their own stature. The kings of Denmark and Sweden were also developing expansionist ambitions, which could hardly be realized except at the expense of the Hapsburg Empire. Finally, the seeds of religious conflict, sown by the Reformation, were about ready to germinate in a new crop of hostilities. In 1608–1609 two opposing alliances had been formed, based upon principles of religious antagonism. The existence of these mutually hostile leagues added to the tension in central Europe and

Underlying causes of conflict

contributed toward making an eventual explosion almost a certainty. The conflict that followed, known as the Thirty Years' War (1618–1648), was one of the most tragic in history.

The immediate cause of the Thirty Years' War was an attempt of the Holy Roman Emperor, Matthias, to consolidate his power in Bohemia. Though the Hapsburgs had been overlords of Bohemia for a century, the Czech inhabitants of the country had retained their own king. When the Bohemian throne became vacant in 1618, Matthias conspired to obtain the position for one of his relatives, Duke Ferdinand of Styria. By exerting pressure he induced the Bohemian Diet to elect Ferdinand king. The Czech leaders resented this, since both nationalist and Protestant traditions were strong in the country. The upshot was the invasion of the emperor's headquarters in Prague by Czech noblemen and the proclamation of Bohemia as an independent state with Frederick, the Calvinist Elector Palatine, as king. The war now began in earnest. The success of the Hapsburgs in suppressing the Bohemian revolt and in punishing Frederick by seizing his lands in the valley of the Rhine galvanized the Protestant rulers of northern Europe into action. Not only the German princes but King Christian IV of Denmark and Gustavus Adolphus of Sweden joined the war against Austrian aggression—with the additional purpose, of course, of expanding their own dominions. In 1630 the French intervened with donations of arms and money to the Protestant allies, and after 1632, when Gustavus Adolphus was killed in battle, France bore the brunt of the struggle. The war was no longer a religious conflict, but essentially a contest between the Bourbon and Hapsburg houses for domination of the continent of Europe. The immediate objectives of Cardinal Richelieu, who was directing affairs for Louis XIII, were to wrest parts of Germany from the Holy Roman Empire and to weaken

Two Artistic Broadsides from the Thirty Years' War. On the left the German peasantry is ridden by the soldiery; on the right is an allegorical representation of "the monstrous beast of war."

A Swearing of Oaths at the Peace of Westphalia, 1648

the hold of the Spanish Hapsburgs on the Netherlands. For a time the French armies suffered reverses, but the organizing genius of Richelieu and of Cardinal Mazarin, who succeeded him in 1648, ultimately brought victory to France and its allies. Peace was restored to a distracted Europe by the Treaty of Westphalia in 1648.

Most of the results of the Thirty Years' War were unmitigated evils. By the Treaty of Westphalia France was confirmed in the possession of formerly German territories in Lorraine and Alsace. Sweden also received territory in Germany; the independence of Holland and Switzerland was formally acknowledged, and the Holy Roman Empire was reduced to a complete fiction, since each of the German princes was now recognized as a sovereign ruler with power to make war and peace and to govern his state as he chose. But most of these changes merely laid the foundations for bitter international squabbles in the future. In addition, the war wrought terrible havoc in central Europe. Probably few military conflicts since the dawn of history had caused so much misery to the civilian population. It is estimated that fully one-third of the people in Germany and Bohemia lost their lives as a consequence of famine and disease and the marauding attacks of brutal soldiers. The armies of both sides pillaged, tortured, burned, and killed in such manner as to convert whole regions into veritable desert. In Saxony one-third of the land went out of cultivation, and packs of wolves roamed through areas where thriving villages once had stood. In the midst of such misery, intellectual achievement of every description was bound to decline, with the result that civilization in Germany was retarded by at least a century. Nonetheless, the settlement of 1648 put an end to religious warfare in Europe for all time and initiated a half-century of comparative peace.

In 1700 the French king saw what appeared to be a new opportunity for expanding Bourbon power. In that year Charles II, king of Spain,

Results of the Thirty Years' War

died with neither children nor brothers to succeed him, and willed his dominion to the grandson of Louis XIV. The Austrians denounced this settlement, and formed a new alliance with England, Holland, and Brandenburg. The War of the Spanish Succession, which broke out in 1702 when Louis attempted to enforce the claim of his grandson, was the last important stage in the struggle between Bourbons and Hapsburgs.[1] By the Peace of Utrecht (1713–1714) the grandson of Louis XIV was permitted to occupy the Spanish throne, on condition that France and Spain should never be united. Nova Scotia and Newfoundland were transferred to England from France, and Gibraltar from Spain. The Belgian Netherlands, the Kingdom of the Two Sicilies, and Milan were given to the Austrian Hapsburgs.

It would be difficult to exaggerate the significance of the War of the Spanish Succession. Since it involved most of the nations of Europe and also lands overseas, it was the first of what can be called "world wars." It was fought, however, not by mass armies but chiefly by professional soldiers. It was the prototype, therefore, of most of the wars of the eighteenth century. These were wars between kings, in which the masses of the people were involved only indirectly. Among large-scale conflicts the War of the Spanish Succession was the first in which religion played almost no part. Secular rivalries over commerce and sea power were the major bones of contention. The war put an end to the claims of the smaller states to rank equally with their larger neighbors. Brandenburg and Savoy were the only important exceptions. The first came to be called Prussia and the second, Sardinia. Aside from Sardinia, the rest of the Italian states dwindled into insignificance, and Prussia started to play an important role on the German scene. Holland suffered such a strain from the war that it ceased to be a prime factor in the competition for world power. With a Bourbon king on the throne, Spain was reduced to subservience to France. The Spanish Bourbon dynasty continued to rule, with brief interruptions, until the overthrow of Alphonso XIII in 1931, and the dynasty has returned to Spain since 1975. The War of the Spanish Succession left France and Great Britain as the two major powers in Europe. Of these, the latter was the principal victor. Not only did it acquire valuable possessions, but the British muscled their way into the Spanish commercial empire. By an agreement known as the Asiento, Britain gained the privilege of providing Spanish America with African slaves. This privilege opened the way to the smuggling of all kinds of goods into the Spanish colonies, and contributed toward making Great Britain the richest nation on earth.

The most important of the wars between the War of the Spanish

---

[1] The War of the Austrian Succession (1740–1748), in which France fought on the side of Prussia against Great Britain and Austria, also involved a struggle between Bourbons and Hapsburgs. But the results for France were indecisive: the war was mainly a duel between Prussia and Austria.

Succession and the French Revolution was the Seven Years' War (1756–1763), known in American history as the French and Indian War. The causes of this struggle were closely related to some of the earlier conflicts already discussed. A chief factor in several of these wars had been commercial rivalry between England and France. Each had been striving for supremacy in the development of overseas trade and colonial empires. The Seven Years' War was simply the climax of a struggle which had been going on for nearly a century. Hostilities began, appropriately enough, in America as the result of a dispute over possession of the Ohio valley. Soon the whole question of British or French domination of the North American continent was involved. Eventually, nearly every major country of Europe was drawn in on one side or the other. Louis XV of France enlisted the aid of his relative, the Bourbon king of Spain. A struggle begun in 1740 between Frederick the Great of Prussia and Maria Theresa of Austria over possession of Silesia was quickly merged with the larger contest. The Seven Years' War thus reached the proportions of what virtually amounted to another world conflict, with France, Spain, Austria, and Russia arrayed against Great Britain and Prussia in Europe, and with English and French colonial forces striving for mastery not only in America but also in India.

The outcome of the Seven Years' War was exceedingly significant for the later history of Europe. Frederick the Great won a decisive victory over the Austrians and forced Maria Theresa to surrender all claims to Silesia. The acquisition of this territory increased the area of Prussia by more than a third, thereby raising the Hohenzollern kingdom to the status of a first-rank power. In the struggle for colonial supremacy, the British emerged with a sensational triumph. Of their once magnificent empire in America, the French lost all but two tiny islands off the coast of Newfoundland, Guadeloupe and a few other possessions in the West Indies, and a portion of Guiana in South America. All of the territory given up by the French was acquired by Great Britain, with the exception of Louisiana, which France turned over to Spain as a reward for its part in the war. France was allowed to retain its trading privileges in India, but was forbidden to build any forts or maintain any troops in that country. France's treasury was now depleted, its trade almost ruined, and its chances of dominance on the Continent badly shattered. These disasters, brought on by the stupid policies of the French kings, had much to do with preparing the ground for the revolution of 1789. By contrast, Britain was now riding the crest of the wave—in a literal as well as figurative sense, for its triumph in the Seven Years' War was a milestone in its struggle for supremacy on the seas. The wealth from its expanded trade enriched British merchants, thereby enhancing their prestige in political and social affairs. But perhaps most important of all, its victory in the struggle for colonies gave England an abundance of raw materials which enabled it to take the lead in the Industrial Revolution.

6. THE POLITICAL THEORY OF ABSOLUTISM

The influence of political philosophers in buttressing absolute rule

The autocratic behavior of the rulers of the sixteenth, seventeenth, and eighteenth centuries was sanctioned by the influence of political theory. Several of the Stuart and Bourbon kings, for example, derived justification for their policies from philosophers who expressed the prevailing ideas of their time in systematic and forceful writings.

Jean Bodin

One of the first of the philosophers to lend encouragement to the absolutist ambitions of monarchs was the Frenchman Jean Bodin (1530–1596). He agreed with the medieval philosophers that rulers were bound by the law of God, and he acknowledged that the prince had a moral duty to respect the treaties he had signed. But Bodin had no use for parliaments of any description. He emphatically denied the right of a legislative body to impose any limits upon royal power. And while he admitted that princes who violated the divine law or the law of nature were tyrants, he refused to concede that their subjects had any right of rebellion against them. The authority of the prince is from God, and the supreme obligation of the people is passive obedience. Revolution must be avoided at all costs, for it destroys that stability which is a necessary condition for progress. The main contribution of Bodin, if such it can be called, was his doctrine of sovereignty, which he defined as "supreme power over citizens and subjects, unrestrained by the laws." By this he meant that the prince, who is the only sovereign, is not bound by manmade laws. There is no *legal* restriction upon his authority whatever—nothing except obedience to the natural or moral law ordained by God.

The most noted of all the apostles of absolute government was Thomas Hobbes (1588–1679). Writing during and after the English Civil War and in close association with the royalists, Hobbes was disgusted with the turn which events had taken in England and longed for a revival of the monarchy. However, his materialism and his doctrine of the secular origin of the kingship made him none too popular with the Stuarts. For the title of his chief work Hobbes chose the name *Leviathan,* to indicate his conception of the state as an all-powerful monster. (In the Book of Job, Leviathan is the monster that ruled over the primeval chaos.) All associations within the state, he declared, are mere "worms in the entrails of Leviathan." The essence of Hobbes's political philosophy is directly related to his theory of the origin of government. He taught that in the beginning all human beings lived in a state of nature, subject to no law but brutal self-interest. Far from being a paradise of innocence and bliss, the state of nature was a condition of universal misery. As Hobbes said, "man is a wolf toward man." Life for the individual was "solitary, poor, nasty, brutish, and short." In order to escape from this war of each against all, people eventually united with one another to form a civil society. They drew

The Title Page of Hobbes's *Leviathan*

up a contract surrendering all of their rights to a sovereign, who would be strong enough to protect his subjects from violence. Thus the sovereign, while not a party to the contract, was made the recipient of absolute authority. The people gave up *everything* for the one great blessing of security. In contrast with Bodin, Hobbes did not recognize any law of nature or of God as a limitation upon the authority of the prince. Absolute government, he maintained, had been established by the people themselves, and therefore they would have no ground for complaint if their ruler became a tyrant. On the basis of pure deduction, without any appeal to religion or history, Hobbes arrived at the conclusion that the king is entitled to rule despotically—not because he has been appointed by God, but because the people have *given* him absolute power.

Thomas Hobbes

In a sense, the great Dutchman Hugo Grotius (1583–1645) may also be considered an exponent of absolutism; though with him the question of power within the state was more or less incidental to the larger question of relations among states. Living during the period of the revolt of the Netherlands and the Thirty Years' War, Grotius was impressed by the need for a body of rules that would reduce the dealings of governments with one another to a pattern of reason and order. He wrote his famous *Law of War and Peace* to prove that the principles of elemental justice and morality ought to prevail among nations. Some of these principles he derived from the Roman "law of peoples" and some from the medieval law of nature. So well did he present his case that he has been regarded ever since as one of the chief founders of international law. Grotius's revulsion against turbulence also inspired him to advocate absolutist government. He did not see how order could be preserved within the state unless the ruler possessed unlimited authority. He maintained that in the beginning the people had either surrendered to a ruler voluntarily or had been compelled to submit to superior force; but in either case, having once established a government, they were bound to obey it unquestioningly forever.

Hugo Grotius

The theories just discussed were not simply those of a few isolated philosophers, but rather the widely accepted ideas of an age when order and security were considered more important than liberty. They reflected the desire of the commercial classes, especially, for the utmost degree of stability and protection in the interest of business. Mercantilism and the policies of rulers went hand in hand with the new theories of absolutism. The dictum, "I am the state," attributed to Louis XIV, was not just the brazen boast of a tyrant, but came close to expressing the prevailing conception of government in continental Europe. Those who had a stake in society really believed that the monarch *was* the state. They could hardly conceive of a government able to protect and assist their economic activities except in terms of centralized and unbridled authority. Their attitude was not so far dif-

The significance of philosophers' attempts to justify absolutism ferent from that of some people today who believe that a dictatorship of one form or another is the only means for security and plenty.

7. SIGNIFICANCE OF THE AGE OF ABSOLUTISM

Beginnings of the modern state system

The age of absolutism was important not merely for the establishment of absolute monarchies. It bears even greater significance for its effects upon international relations. It was during this period that the modern state system came into existence. During the era of approximately a thousand years after the fall of Rome, states, in the sense in which we now understand the term, scarcely existed in Europe west of the Byzantine Empire. True, there were kings in England and France, but until almost the end of the Middle Ages, their relations with their subjects were essentially those of lords with their vassals. They had *dominium* but not sovereignty. In other words, they had the highest proprietary rights over the lands which constituted their fiefs; they did not necessarily possess supreme political authority over all the persons who lived on their lands. Only through extension of the taxing power, the judicial power, and the establishment of professional armies, did medieval rulers take steps toward becoming sovereigns in the modern sense.

Causes of the rise of the state system

Some historians consider the beginnings of the modern state system to date from the invasion of Italy in 1494 by King Charles VIII of France. Involved in this war for conquest of foreign territory were considerations of dynastic prestige, the balance of power, elaborate diplomacy, and alliances and counteralliances. It was in no sense a religious or ideological war but a struggle for power and territorial aggrandizement. Other historians conceive of the Reformation as the primary cause of the modern state system. The Protestant Revolution broke the unity of Western Christendom. It facilitated the determination of kings and princes to make their own power complete by repudiating the authority of a universal Church. As early as 1555 the Peace of Augsburg gave to each German prince the right to decide whether Lutheranism or Catholicism should be the faith of his people. It was probably the Treaty of Westphalia, however, that played the dominant role in making the modern state system a political reality. This treaty, which ended the Thirty Years' War in 1648, transferred territories from one rule to another with no regard for the nationality of their inhabitants. It recognized the independence of Holland and Switzerland and reduced the Holy Roman Empire to a fiction. Each of the German princes was acknowledged as a sovereign ruler with power to make war and peace and to govern his domain as he chose. Finally, the treaty introduced the principle that *all* states, regardless of their size or power, were equal under international law and endowed with full and complete control over their territories and inhabitants.

Whatever its origins, the modern state system may be considered to embody the following elements: (1) the legal equality and independence of all states; (2) the right of each state to pursue a foreign policy of its own making, to form alliances and counteralliances, and to wage war for its own advantage; (3) the use of diplomacy as a substitute for war, often involving intrigue and espionage to the extent necessary for political advantage; (4) the balance of power as a device for preventing war or for assuring the support of allies if war becomes necessary. Most of these elements of the state system have continued to the present day. Even the establishment of the League of Nations and the United Nations brought no substantial change, for both were founded upon the principle of the sovereign equality of independent states. Some observers believe that there will be no genuine prospect of world peace until the system of sovereign independent states is recognized as obsolete and is replaced by a world community of nations organized on a federal basis.

Elements of the modern state system

SELECTED READINGS

• *Items so designated are available in paperback editions.*

Ashton, Robert, *The English Civil War: Conservatism and Revolution, 1603–1649,* New York, 1978.

• Birn, Raymond, *Crisis, Absolutism, Revolution: Europe, 1648–1789/91,* Hinsdale, Ill., 1977. A good college-level survey for the second half of the period covered in this chapter.

Carsten, F. L., *The Origins of Prussia,* London, 1954. Standard work, through the reign of the Great Elector.

Cherniavsky, M., *Tsar and People: Studies in Russian Myths,* 2nd ed., New York, 1969. Imaginative study of the symbolism of rulership.

Church, William F., *Louis XIV in Historical Thought,* New York, 1976.

Dorn, W., *The Competition for Empire, 1740–63,* New York, 1940. Excellent old-fashioned study of Europe in the mid–eighteenth century. Particularly strong on military affairs.

• Dunn, Richard S., *The Age of Religious Wars, 1559–1715,* 2nd ed., New York, 1979. The best college level text on this period. Extremely well written.

• Elliott, J. H., *Imperial Spain, 1469–1716,* London, 1963. A masterpiece of sophisticated synthesis.

Elton, G. R., *England under the Tudors,* 2nd ed., London, 1977. Engagingly written and authoritative.

Florinsky, M. T., *Russia: A History and an Interpretation,* Vol. I, New York, 1955. The best textbook on Russian history. Reviews divergent interpretations and emphasizes politics.

• Fraser, Lady Antonia, *Oliver Cromwell,* London, 1973. A popular biography.

Friedrich, Carl J., *The Age of the Baroque, 1610–1660,* New York, 1952.

• Goubert, P., *Louis XIV and Twenty Million Frenchmen,* New York, 1970.

Events of the reign seen against the background of economic and social conditions.

Hatton, Ragnhild, *Europe in the Age of Louis XIV*, London, 1969.

Holborn, H., *A History of Modern Germany: 1648–1840*, New York, 1964.

• Jones, J. R., *Britain and Europe in the Seventeenth Century*, New York, 1966.

———, *Country and Court: England, 1658–1714*, London, 1978. Now the best survey of the period surrounding the Glorious Revolution.

• ———, *The Revolution of 1688 in England*, New York, 1972.

• Mattingly, Garrett, *The Armada*, Boston, 1959. Fascinating narrative; thoroughly reliable but reads like a novel.

Nussbaum, F. L., *The Triumph of Science and Reason, 1660–1685*, New York, 1953.

• Pennington, D. H., *Seventeenth-Century Europe*, London, 1970.

• Rabb, T. K., *The Struggle for Stability in Early Modern Europe*, New York, 1975. A stimulating essay arguing for a shift from crisis to stability around 1650.

Roberts, Penfield, *The Quest for Security, 1715–1740*, New York, 1947.

• Roots, Ivan, ed., *Cromwell, A Profile*, New York, 1973. A collection of readings on problems in interpretation; complements Fraser.

• Rosenberg, Hans, *Bureaucracy, Aristocracy, and Autocracy: The Prussian Experience, 1660–1815*, Cambridge, Mass., 1958. Difficult but rewarding.

• Russell, Conrad, *The Crisis of Parliaments: English History, 1509–1660*, New York, 1971. The best survey covering this broad range of time.

Sabine, George H., *A History of Political Theory*, 3rd ed., New York, 1951. An older work, particularly good on thought of this age.

Smith, Lacey B., *Henry VIII: The Mask of Royalty*, Boston, 1971. A breathtaking interpretation of the last years of Henry VIII and the age in which he lived.

Speck, W. A., *Stability and Strife: England, 1714–1760*, Cambridge, Mass., 1977.

• Steinberg, S. H., *The Thirty Years' War and the Conflict for European Hegemony, 1600–1660*, New York, 1966. The best account.

• Stone, Lawrence, *The Causes of the English Revolution, 1529–1642*, New York, 1972.

• Sumner, B. H., *Peter the Great and the Emergence of Russia*, London, 1950. A good short introduction.

Wedgwood, C. V., *The Thirty Years' War*, London, 1938. More attention to narrative than Steinberg.

Wolf, John B., *The Emergence of the Great Powers, 1685–1715*, New York, 1951.

• ———, *Louis XIV*, New York, 1968. The standard biography in English.

SOURCE MATERIALS

Bodin, Jean, *Six Books Concerning the State*, Cambridge, 1962.

Grotius, Hugo, *The Law of War and Peace*, New York, 1963.

• Hobbes, Thomas, *Leviathan*. (Many editions.)

Chapter 22

THE INTELLECTUAL REVOLU-TION OF THE SEVENTEENTH AND EIGHTEENTH CENTURIES

We are to admit no more causes of natural things than such as are both true and sufficient to explain their appearances. To this purpose the philosophers say that nature does nothing in vain, and more is in vain when less will serve; for nature is pleased with simplicity, and affects not the pomp of superfluous cause.

—Isaac Newton, *The Mathematical Principles of Natural Philosophy*

The years which witnessed the rise of absolutism in Europe were witness, as well, to what can fairly be described as an intellectual revolution. Traditional ideas concerning God, human existence, and the universe were challenged and, to a large extent, either drastically modified or totally cast aside. In their place, philosophers and scientists constructed a new worldview, rational, mechanistic, and largely impersonal, yet at the same time humane, tolerant, and therefore understanding of both the foibles and aspirations of humanity. This intellectual revolution was rooted in the history of the Renaissance and the beginnings of the Commercial Revolution; it derived from the widened intellectual horizons and increased general prosperity that those movements had produced.

The nature of the revolution

The extraordinary galaxy of men and ideas that constitute the revolution make it worth examining in its own right. It must also be studied, however, in order to understand the origins of ideas, institutions, and movements still current today. The self-confidence that compelled men and women to examine their world critically, and the belief in progress that encouraged them to change that world—both characteristic attitudes of this revolution—in turn helped foster the French and Industrial Revolutions, and thus the modern world.

Reasons for examining the intellectual revolution

Engraved Title Page from Bacon's *Novum Organum*

René Descartes

1. THE PHILOSOPHICAL FOUNDATIONS OF THE INTELLECTUAL REVOLUTION

The progenitors of the intellectual revolution were four men: Francis Bacon, René Descartes, John Locke, and Isaac Newton. All four were willing to attack fundamental assumptions about the universe and the human mind; all four were able not only to demolish the old, but to construct new ideas and theories to replace those they had discarded. The son of an Elizabethan government official, Francis Bacon (1561–1626) was both a philosopher and an ambitious courtier, who, as lord chancellor, was sentenced to imprisonment on charges of bribery. Attention to his political career prevented his fully developing those ideas which were to be his intellectual legacy. Yet even granting their limitations, Bacon's conclusions were of immense influence in the history of modern thought. In his two most important works, *Novum Organum* (a treatise on the method of acquiring knowledge, published in 1620) and *The Advancement of Learning* (1623) he insisted upon the importance of doubting all received knowledge.

Bacon's most important contribution to philosophy was the glorification of the inductive method as the basis of accurate knowledge. He believed that all seekers of truth in the past were slaves of preconceived ideas or prisoners of Scholastic logic. He argued that the philosopher should turn to the direct observation of nature, to the accumulation of facts about things and the discovery of the laws that govern them. Induction alone, he believed, was the magic key that would unlock the secrets of knowledge. Authority, tradition, and syllogistic logic should be as sedulously avoided as the plague. Bacon also argued that the worth of any idea depended on its usefulness. The ideas generated and debated by medieval scholastics were, in his opinion, worthless, because they could be put to no real use. Scientific discoveries were a part of "true" knowledge only when they could be applied practically.

René Descartes (1596–1650), like Bacon, constructed a philosophy on the basis of a systematic questioning of received truths. Unlike Bacon, however, his system of belief was built by means of the mathematical instrument of pure deduction. In his famous *Discourse on Method* (1637), and in other scientific writings, he began with simple, self-evident truths or axioms, like those found in geometry, and reasoned from these to particular conclusions. Descartes believed that he had found such an axiom in his famous principle: "I think, therefore I am." From this he maintained that it is possible to deduce a sound body of universal knowledge—to prove, for example, that God exists, and that men and women are thinking animals. These "truths," he declared, are just as infallible as the truths of geometry, for they are products of the same unerring method.

But Descartes is important not only as the founder of the new rationalism. He was also partly responsible for introducing the conception of a mechanistic universe. He taught that the whole world of matter, organic and inorganic alike, could be defined in terms of extension and motion. "Give me extension and motion," he once declared, "and I will construct the universe." Every individual thing—a solar system, a star, the earth itself—is a self-operating machine propelled by a force arising from the original motion given to the universe by God. Descartes did not even exclude the bodies of animals and humans from this general mechanistic pattern. He declared that the whole world of physical nature is one, and that the behavior of animals and humans flow automatically from internal or external stimuli. Yet Descartes was unwilling to include the human mind as part of his mechanistic system. Mind was not a form of matter, but an entirely separate substance implanted in the body by God. The world was therefore *dualistic:* i.e., composed of mind and matter. As a corollary to this assumption, Descartes believed in the existence of innate ideas. He taught that self-evident truths having no relation to sensory experience must be inherent in the mind itself. They are not learned through the use of the senses, but are part of the human mind from birth.

The implications of the thought of Bacon and Descartes were of enormous significance. Those now living, they argued, not only possessed the right but were charged with a duty to reassess the past and, when warranted, to reject its assumptions. They must have the courage to experiment, in order to reveal and understand the mechanical nature of the universe. Such reasoning would have a practical end, since it would result in humanity's mastery of the world. "Understanding the forces and actions of fire, water, air, the stars and heavens," Descartes wrote in the *Discourse,* "we can use these forces . . . for all purposes for which they are appropriate, and so make ourselves masters and possessors of nature."

The principles of rationalism and mechanism were adopted in some form or other by the majority of the philosophers of the seventeenth century. The most noted of Descartes's intellectual successors were the Dutch Jew Benedict Spinoza and the Englishman Thomas Hobbes, whom we have already encountered as a political theorist. Benedict (or Baruch) Spinoza was born in Amsterdam in 1632 and died an outcast from his native community forty-five years later. His parents were members of a group of Jewish immigrants who had fled from persecution in Portugal and Spain and had taken refuge in the Netherlands. At an early age Spinoza came under the influence of a disciple of Descartes and as a result grew critical of some of the dogmas of the Hebrew faith. For this he was expelled from the synagogue and banished from the community of his people. From 1656 till his death he lived in various cities of Holland, eking out a meager existence by grinding lenses. During these years he developed a philoso-

A Diagram Illustrating Cartesian Dualism. The eyes perceive the arrow; the soul, in the pineal gland, transmits an impulse to the muscles, causing the finger to point to the arrow. From the 1677 edition of Descartes's *De Homine.*

phy which incorporated the rationalism and mechanism but not the dualism of Descartes. Spinoza maintained that there is only one essential substance in the universe, of which mind and matter are but different aspects. This single substance is God, who is identical with nature itself. Such a conception of the universe was pure pantheism; but it was grounded upon reason rather than upon faith, and it was intended to express the scientific notions of the unity of nature and the continuity of cause and effect.

Spinoza's ethics

Much more than Descartes, Spinoza was interested in ethical questions. Having come to the conclusion early in life that the things people prize most highly—wealth, pleasure, power, and fame—are empty and vain, he set out to inquire whether there was any perfect good which would give lasting and unmitigated happiness to all who attained it. By a process of geometric reasoning he attempted to prove that this perfect good consists in "love of God"—that is, in worship of the order and harmony of nature. If people would but realize that the universe is a beautiful machine, whose operation cannot be interrupted for the benefit of particular persons, they would gain that serenity of mind for which philosophers have yearned through the ages. We can only be delivered from impossible hopes and cringing fears by acknowledging to ourselves that the order of nature is unalterably fixed, and that human beings cannot change their fate. In other words, we gain true freedom by realizing that we are not free. But with all his determinism, Spinoza was an earnest apostle of tolerance, justice, and rational living. He wrote in defense of religious liberty and, in the face of cruel mistreatment, set a noble example in his personal life of kindliness, humanity, and freedom from vengeful passions.

Hobbes

Another of the great rationalists of the seventeenth century was Thomas Hobbes. Born before either Descartes or Spinoza, he outlived both. Hobbes agreed with his two contemporaries in the belief that geometry furnished the only proper method of discovering philosophic truth. But he denied the Cartesian doctrine of innate ideas, maintaining that the origin of all knowledge is in sense perception. He refused to accept either the dualism of Descartes or the pantheism of Spinoza. According to Hobbes, nothing exists except matter. Mind is simply motion in the brain or perhaps a subtle form of matter, but in no sense a distinct substance. God, also, if we can believe that He exists, must be assumed to have a physical body. There is nothing spiritual anywhere in the universe of which the mind can conceive. This was the most thoroughgoing materialism to make its appearance since the days of the Roman Lucretius. It was combined with mechanism, as materialism usually is. Hobbes contended that not only the universe but humanity as well can be explained mechanically. All that human beings do is determined by appetites or aversions, and these in turn are either inherited or acquired through experience. In similar fashion, Hobbes maintained that there are no absolute standards of good and evil. Good is merely that which gives pleasure; evil, that which brings pain.

John Locke

Spinoza and Hobbes, though important as recruits in the army of intellectual revolutionaries, were not, like Bacon and Descartes, primary instigators of that revolution. John Locke (1632–1704), the English philosopher, was. Locke, in his *Treatise of Civil Government,* posited a political philosophy based upon natural law which was used to justify the Glorious Revolution of 1688, and, later, the American and French Revolutions of the eighteenth century. He was, as well, the author of an extremely influential new theory of knowledge. Rejecting Descartes's doctrine of innate ideas, Locke maintained that all knowledge originates from sense perception. This theory had already been asserted by Hobbes; but Locke systematized and enlarged it. In his *Essay Concerning Human Understanding* (1690), he insisted that the human mind at birth is a blank tablet, a *tabula rasa,* upon which absolutely nothing is inscribed. It does not contain the idea of God or any notions of right and wrong. Not until the newborn child begins to have experiences, to perceive the external world with its senses, is anything registered in its mind. But the simple ideas which result directly from sense perception are merely the foundations of knowledge; no human being could live intelligently on the basis of them alone. These simple ideas must be integrated and fused into complex ideas. This is the function of reason or understanding, which has the power to combine, coordinate, and organize the impressions received from the senses and thus to build a usable body of general truth. Sensation and reason are both indispensable—the one for furnishing the mind with the raw materials of knowledge, the other for working them into meaningful form.

Locke

Locke's theory of knowledge was as effective as were the ideas of Bacon and Descartes in freeing men and women from the restraints of received beliefs. If there was evil in the world, Locke's argument implied, it was not the result of some divine plan but rather of an environment and educational system that men and women had made and that men and women could change. Improve society, Locke was saying, and you will improve human behavior, since the latter takes its shape from the former. The optimism implicit in Locke grew explicit in the writings of other theorists as the eighteenth century progressed.

Locke's optimism

The fourth "founding father" of the intellectual revolution was the English scientist Isaac Newton (1642–1727). With the publication in 1687 of his *Mathematical Principles of Natural Philosophy,* Newton offered the world for the first time a single, coherent mechanical theory for the understanding of the universe. All measurable motion could be described by the same formulas. "Every particle of matter in the universe attracts every other particle with a force varying inversely as the square of the distance between them and directly proportional to the product of their masses." This force was gravity, which Newton dis-

Newton

Sir Isaac Newton

*Implications of Newton's
work*

*The strength of
superstition*

covered, and the proposition defining that force he held to be valid not only on the earth but throughout the endless expanse of the solar system. Newton's discoveries were "true" knowledge, in the Baconian sense, since they had been arrived at through observation, and since they were useful in assisting men and women in mastering the world in which they lived. The measurement of tides; the locating of ships on the ocean; the predictability of a cannon ball's trajectory—all this and much more was the practical result of Newton's scientific achievement.

The implications of Newton's work were those of the entire philosophical and scientific revolution to which he himself contributed so signally: first, that it is the task of philosophers and scientists—and of all thoughtful people—to challenge the received opinions of the past, to think matters out for themselves anew; second, that nature is governed neither by mysterious divine intervention nor by caprice, but by rational, universal laws, which can be formulated as precisely as mathematical principles. From this latter conclusion it was but one further step to the assumption that there exists a set of natural laws governing the politics of the nations of the earth. Those laws were presumed to be reasonable in the freedoms they afforded legitimately constituted authority, yet stern in their prohibitions against arbitrary power that operated against their fixed principles. Third, men and women, though subject to all the laws governing the universe, could, by discovering the way those laws worked, put them to use to ensure the progress of the human race.

2. THE PERSISTENCE OF SUPERSTITION

Despite remarkable achievements in thought, the period of the intellectual revolution was by no means free from superstitions. Numerous quaint and pernicious delusions continued to be accepted as valid truths. The illiterate masses clung to their beliefs in goblins, satyrs, and wizards and to their fear of the devil, whose malevolence was assumed to be the cause of diseases, famine, storms, and insanity. But superstition was not harbored in the minds of the masses alone. The astronomer Kepler believed in astrology and depended upon the writing of almanacs, with predictions of the future according to signs and wonders in the heavens, as his chief source of income. Not only did Francis Bacon accept the current superstition of astrology, he also contributed his endorsement of the witchcraft delusion. Newton also lent his voice to superstition; for example, he searched the Bible for hidden references predicting the reign of Anti-Christ.

The worst of all the superstitions that flourished in this period was unquestionably the witchcraft delusion, under which women were tortured and burned as the assistants of Satan. Belief in witchcraft was by no means unknown in the Middle Ages or the Renaissance, but it never reached the proportions of a dangerous hysteria until after the beginning of the Protestant Revolution. The persecutions attained their most virulent form in the very countries where religious conflict raged the fiercest, that is, in Germany and France. The witchcraft superstition was a direct outgrowth of the belief in Satan which obsessed the minds of so many of the Reformers. In general, the tendency of each camp of theologians was to ascribe all the victories of their opponents to the uncanny powers of the Prince of Darkness. With such superstitions prevailing among religious leaders, it is not strange that the mass of their followers should have harbored bizarre and hideous notions. The belief grew that the devil was really more powerful than God, and that no one was safe from destruction. It was assumed that Satan not only tempted mortals to sin, but actually forced them to sin. This was the height of his malevolence, for it jeopardized chances of salvation.

According to the definition of the theologians, witchcraft consisted in selling one's soul to the devil in return for supernatural powers. It was believed that a woman who had concluded such a bargain was thereby enabled to work all manner of spiteful magic against her neighbors—to cause their cattle to sicken and die, their crops to fail, or their children to fall into the fire. But the most valuable gifts bestowed by Satan were the power to blind husbands to their wives' misconduct or to cause women to give birth to idiots or deformed infants. It is commonly assumed that the so-called witches were toothless old hags whose cranky habits and venomous tongues had made them objects of suspicion and dread to all who knew them. However, the writers on the Continent and in England generally imagined the witch to be a "fair and wicked young woman," and a large percentage of those put to death in Germany and France were adolescent girls and women not yet thirty.

The earliest persecutions for witchcraft were those initiated by Pope Innocent VIII in 1484, who instructed his inquisitors to use torture in procuring convictions. But it was not until after the beginning of the Protestant Revolution that witchcraft persecution became a mass hysteria. Luther himself provided some of the impetus by recommending that witches should be put to death with fewer considerations of mercy than were shown to ordinary criminals. Other Reformers quickly followed Luther's example. Under Calvin's administration in Geneva, twenty-one women first had their right hands cut off and were then burned for the alleged crime in 1545. From this time on the persecutions spread like a pestilence. Women, young girls, and even mere children were tortured by driving needles under their nails, roasting their feet in the fire, or crushing their legs under heavy weights until the marrow spurted from their bones, in order to force them to confess filthy orgies with demons. To what extent the persecutions were due to sheer sadism or to the greed of magistrates, who were sometimes permitted to confiscate the property of those con-

Burning of Witches at Dernberg in 1555. From a sixteenth-century German pamphlet denouncing witchcraft.

victed, is impossible to say. There were few people who did not believe that the burning of witches was justifiable. One of the most zealous defenders of the trials was the French political philosopher, Jean Bodin. The final number of victims will never be known. In the 1620s there was an average of 1,000 burnings a year in the German cities of Würzburg and Bamberg, and around the same time it was said the town square of Wolfenbüttel "looked like a little forest, so crowded were the stakes."

Decline of witchcraft

After about 1650 the mania gradually began to subside. The reasons for the decline are difficult to discern. Most likely the principal causes were the revival of reason and the influence of scientists and skeptical philosophers. At the very zenith of the witch-burning frenzy certain lawyers began to have doubts as to the value of the evidence admitted at the trials. In 1584 an English jurist by the name of Reginald Scot published a book condemning the belief in witchcraft as irrational and asserting that most of the lurid crimes confessed by accused women were mere figments of disordered minds. Such eminent scientists as Pierre Gassendi (1592–1655) and William Harvey also denounced the persecutions. The physician Harvey coolly dissected a toad that was alleged to be a witch's accomplice in order to show that it was just like any other and that there was no devil in it. Such appeals to scientific demonstration finally put the witch-hunting mania to an end.

3. THE ENLIGHTENMENT

Enlightenment concepts

The eighteenth-century cultural climate known as the Enlightenment was grounded on the rational, optimistic foundations laid by the seventeenth-century thinkers of the intellectual revolution. Enlightenment philosophy, as expressed in the writings of its leading exponents and popularizers, embodied among its principal tenets the following ideas and assertions:

The place of men and women within the universe: Men and women were no longer perceived as the explanation for the existence of the universe, as they had been in the theologically conceived worldview of the medieval period. Instead, they were considered only one link in a rationally ordered chain of being that included all living things. Yet their subjection to universal ordering by no means rendered them powerless or without purpose. Men and women, recognizing the extent to which their senses could ensnare them in acts of individual folly, were urged to exercise their reason as responsible beings in campaigns to eradicate folly from human society as a whole.

Attitudes toward God and organized religion: A rationally ordered universe, subject to invariable laws, precluded the existence of a capricious God, who could intervene through the agency of miracles to contradict those laws. If God did exist, as most Enlightenment philosophers believed, it was simply as a prime mover, as the force which had devised the laws, set them in motion, and ensured their continued functioning. Men and women who held to this view called themselves Deists. They attacked the biblical foundations of Christianity by subjecting the Bible to scholarly criticism and then arguing that it was no more than mythology. They joined a larger body of critics in denouncing institutionalized religions as instruments of exploitation, devised by rogues and scoundrels to enable them to prey upon the ignorant masses. They rejected the prayers and sacraments of organized Christianity as useless; God, they argued, cannot be persuaded to disregard natural law for the benefit of particular persons. They condemned the doctrine of original sin as pernicious. Men and women have the freedom and the rational ability to choose between good and evil; the notion that some are predestined for salvation and others for damnation denies humanity the dignity with which its reason has endowed it.

Classical civilization as exemplar: Enlightenment philosophers, having for the most part rejected the moral pronouncements of organized Christianity as an inspiration for right living, sought guidance instead in the history of the classical civilizations of Greece and Rome. By making the Greeks and Romans the arbiters of civilized behavior, Enlightenment thinkers were helping to deny to Christianity its claim as the central fact of human history. They rifled the vast store of ancient wisdom for precepts from writers as diverse as Socrates and Marcus Aurelius. They delighted in those passages where the Greeks and Romans attacked superstition and praised toleration; but they exercised extreme selectivity, ignoring the fact that classical civilization, taken as a whole, was more prey to irrationality and intolerance than was that of eighteenth-century Europe.

Emphasis upon the affairs and concerns of this world: The substitution of earthly for divine models of behavior was part of a broader movement, characteristic of the Enlightenment, which stressed the importance of thoroughly understanding the workings of this world, while dismissing as either unknowable or inconceivable the existence of some heavenly world-to-come. Travel to distant parts of the globe, which increased considerably during the eighteenth century, encouraged men and women to study other contemporary civilizations. As they observed the Chinese, the Persians, or the Tahitians, they began to argue the relative virtue of various ways of life, very often praising the attitudes of the supposedly inferior "natives"—toward sex and religion, for example—as superior to those characteristic of "civilized" western Europe. Concentration on the life of this world was a reflection of the attitudes expressed by Bacon when he defined "true" knowledge, and by Locke when he expounded his theory of knowledge. Truth was derived from the here-and-now, the practical concrete business of daily life. Knowledge came with the daily experiences imprinted upon the "blank tablet" of one's mind.

Humanitarianism: True understanding of the present world could lead, Enlightenment thinkers insisted, to an improved world in the future. A more perfect society could be realized once men and women applied reason to the task of banishing superstition and inhumanity. Happiness was perceived as a goal attainable on earth. As we shall see, this belief translated itself into practical programs of reform which went some way toward eliminating social evils and improving the general lot of humanity.

Although the Enlightenment derived much of its inspiration from the work of Englishmen, and although it was a general European phenomenon, it blossomed to its fullest glory in France, where its ideas were expressed in the writings of a group calling themselves *philosophes.* Without question, its leading exponent and propagandist in France was François Marie Arouet, a writer who signed himself Voltaire. Voltaire epitomized the Enlightenment as Luther did the Reformation or Michelangelo the Italian Renaissance. Voltaire was born in 1694 and, despite his delicate physique, lived until 1778, within eleven years of the outbreak of the French Revolution. He developed a taste for satiric writing early in his life and got himself into numerous scrapes by his ridicule of noblemen and pompous officials. As a consequence of one of his lampoons he was sent to prison and afterwards exiled to England. Here he remained for three years, acquiring a deep admiration for British institutions, and composing his first philosophic work, which he entitled *Letters on the English.* In this work he popularized the ideas of Newton and Locke, whom he had come to regard as two of the greatest geniuses who ever lived. Most of his later writings—the *Philosophical Dictionary, Candide,* his histories, and many of his poems and essays—were also concerned with exposition of the doctrine that the world is governed by natural laws, and that reason and concrete experience are the only dependable guides for men and women to follow. Voltaire had contempt for the smug optimism of some Enlightenment thinkers, who taught that the ills of

Voltaire by Houdon

0   500 miles

SCOTLAND   • ADAM SMITH, 1723
△ • Edinburgh
HUME,
BURNS,   1711
1759

GOLDSMITH,   *SEA*
1728   ENGLAND   PRIESTLEY, 1733
• Dublin
IRELAND   SWIFT,   Liverpool •   NEWTON, 1642
1667
BOYLE,   RICHARDSON,   PAINE,
1627   1689   DRYDEN, • 1737
     S. JOHNSON,   1631   VERMEER,
     1709   GAINSBOROUGH, 1632   SPINOZA, 1632
LOCKE, 1632   WREN,   1727   Delft • Leiden
FIELDING,   1632 △   JENNER, 1749 REMBRANDT,
1707   HOBBES,   London   1606
      1588   HOOKE,   HARVEY,   VAN DYCK,
        1635   1578   1599
BACON, 1561   CORNEILLE,
DEFOE, 1659   1606   WATTEAU,
GIBBON, 1737   1684   CONDORCET,
MILTON, 1608   1743
POPE, 1688   VOLTAIRE, 1694   RACINE,
LAVOISIER, 1743   Paris 1639
         MOLIERE,
DESCARTES,   1622
1596   DIDEROT,
         1713 △ Dijon
FRANCE   SWITZ.
     ROUSSEAU, Geneva
PASCAL,   1712
1623
MONTESQUIEU,
Bordeaux •   1689
      Turin •
• Toulouse   • Genoa
     Marseilles •   GALILEO,
          1564

DENMARK   △ • Copenhagen

• Hamburg

LEEUWENHOUK,   Elbe R.
1632   NETHERLANDS   HANDEL,   • Berlin
           1685
    Göttingen △   Oder R.
RUBENS,   BACH, △ Erfurt
1577   1685
HOLY   ROMAN
       GOETHE, 1749
       Frankfurt • △ Nuremberg
       • Mannheim   Danube R.
EMPIRE   GLUCK, Vienna
      KEPLER,   1714 △
      1571   • Munich   HAYDN,
     Salzburg •   1732
       MOZART,   AUSTRIA
       1756

LINNAEUS,
1707

KANT, 1724
Königsberg •

POLAND

Vistula R.

BALTIC
SEA

HUNGARY

Verona •
   • MONTEVERDE,
      156?
   • Bologna
MALPIGHI,   OTTOMAN
1628 • • Florence   EMPIRE
     I T A L Y
       ADRIATIC
         SEA

CORSICA   Rome • △
          BERNINI,
          1598
          • Naples

ATLANTIC

OCEAN

Seine R.   Rhine R.   Loire R.   Rhone R.   Garonne R.

Barcelona •

PORTUGAL   Tagus R.   • Madrid
• Lisbon   SPAIN

VELAZQUEZ,
1599
  • Seville

BALEARIC
ISLANDS

SARDINIA

SICILY

MEDITERRANEAN   *SEA*

THE INTELLECTUAL REVOLUTION
OF THE SEVENTEENTH AND EIGHTEENTH CENTURIES

   ●   Birthplaces of scientists, artists, and writers

   △   Scientific academies

  —·—·   Boundaries ca. 1740

England and Scotland Crowning Charles I, Rubens. This scene was part of a series painted in Whitehall Palace, London, to glorify the Stuart family. (Minneapolis Institute of Art)

The Last Judgment, Peter Paul Rubens (1577–1640). Vivid colors, voluptuous figures, and classical themes are typical of Rubens' work. (Alte Pinakothek, Munich)

Pope Innocent X, Velásquez. (Doria-Pamphili Collection)

The Marchessa Durazzo, Anthony Van Dyck (1599–1641). This portrait of a Genoese noble-woman suggests the Italian Renaissance sophistication admired by the Flemish burghers. (MMA)

The Night Watch, Rembrandt. (The Rijksmuseum)

The Anatomy Lesson, Rembrandt van Rijn (1606–1669). Rembrandt scorned the classical themes of his contemporaries and turned to character analysis and the portrayal of life. (Mauritshuis, The Hague)

The Stonemason's Yard, Canaletto (1697–1768). A quiet scene of everyday life, in strong contrast to the portrait below. (National Gallery, London)

Marriage à la Mode, William Hogarth (1697–1764). A satirical look at the arranged marriage: the financial needs of the nobleman and the social aspirations of his middle class counterpart dominate the negotiations. (National Gallery, London)

Le Mezzetin, Antoine Watteau (1684–1721). Mezzetin was a popular character in Italian comedy who was much liked in France. Watteau enjoyed portraying the make-believe world of the court with its festivals and formalized elegance. (MMA)

The Blue Boy, Thomas Gainsborough (1727–1788). Though the costume suggests the romantic ideal of Prince Charming, the face is a penetrating study of the moodiness and uncertainty of adolescence. (Huntington Library)

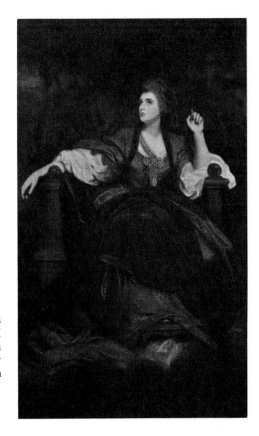

Sarah Siddons as the Tragic Muse, Sir Joshua Reynolds (1723–1792). Mrs. Siddons, a famous actress of the XVIII cent., is here portrayed as the Queen of Tragedy, in accordance with Reynolds' habit of depicting wealthy patrons in impressive classical poses. (Huntington Library)

Madame de Pompadour, François
Boucher (1703–1770). This portrait
idealizes the favorite mistress of
Louis XV. (The Wallace Collection,
London)

Madame Recamier, Jacques Louis David (1748–1825). David was the exponent of
a new classicism during and after the French Revolution. The couch, the lamp,
and the costume are copied from Rome and Pompeii. (Louvre)

Execution of the Rioters, Francisco Goya (1746–1828). Unlike most artists of his time, Goya dealt unflinchingly with suffering, violence, fear, and death. Depicted here is the execution of Spanish rebels by Napoleon's soldiers in 1808. This harshness caused the rebellion to spread over the whole peninsula. (Prado)

The Raft of the Medusa, Théodore Géricault. Agony and suffering is vividly portrayed in Géricault's realistic figures. (Louvre)

THE EMPIRE OF NAPOLEON
AT ITS GREATEST EXTENT · 1812

French territory

Allied with
Napoleon

French
dependencies

Independent
states

RUSSIA

Moscow
Borodino

NAPOLEON 1812

Tilsit
Friedland
Warsaw

DUCHY
OF
WARSAW

PRUSSIA

AUSTRIAN
EMPIRE

BALTIC SEA

SWEDEN

NORWAY

DENMARK
Copenhagen

Berlin

Leipzig
Elbe R.

CONFEDERATION
OF THE
RHINE

Austerlitz

Vienna

Ulm

HELVETIC
REPUBLIC

KINGDOM OF ITALY

ILLYRIAN PROVINCES

Po R.

ADRIATIC SEA

BLACK SEA

OTTOMAN EMPIRE

AEGEAN SEA

KINGDOM
OF
NAPLES

Naples

KDM. OF
SICILY

PAPAL
STATES

Rome

CORSICA

KDM.
OF
SARDINIA

MEDITERRANEAN SEA

HOLLAND
Amsterdam

Rhine R.

Waterloo
Brussels

★ Paris

FRENCH
EMPIRE

Bordeaux

Marseilles

NORTH
SEA

ENGLAND

London

IRELAND

English Channel

ATLANTIC
OCEAN

SPAIN

Madrid

KDM. OF
PORTUGAL

Lisbon

500 miles

0

each make up the good of all, and that everything is for the best in the best of all possible worlds. He saw, on the contrary, universal misery, hatred, strife, and oppression. Only in his utopia of El Dorado, which he described in his novel *Candide* and placed somewhere in South America, were freedom and peace conceivable. Here there were no priests, no lawsuits, and no prisons. The inhabitants dwelt together without malice or greed, worshiping God in accordance with the dictates of reason, and solving their problems by logic and science. But this idyllic life was made possible only by the fact that the land was cut off by impassable mountains from the "regimented assassins of Europe."

Voltaire is best known as a champion of individual freedom. He regarded all restrictions upon liberty of speech and opinion as barbarous. In a letter to one of his opponents he wrote what has often been quoted as the highest criterion of intellectual tolerance: "I do not agree with a word that you say, but I will defend to the death your right to say it." But if there was any one form of repression that Voltaire abhorred more than others, it was the tyranny of organized religion. He blasted the cruelty of the Church in torturing and burning those who dared to question its dogmas. With reference to the whole system of persecuting and privileged orthodoxy, he adopted as his slogan, "Crush the infamous thing." He was almost as unsparing in his attacks upon political tyranny, especially when it resulted in the slaughter of thousands to satisfy the ambitions of despots. "It is forbidden to kill," he sarcastically asserted, "therefore all murderers are punished unless they kill in large numbers and to the sound of trumpets."

Religious toleration

Among the other philosophers of the Enlightenment in France were Denis Diderot (1713–1784), Jean d'Alembert (1717–1783), and the marquis de Condorcet (1743–1794). Diderot and d'Alembert were the chief members of a group known as the Encyclopedists, so-called from their contributions to the *Encyclopedia,* which was intended to be a complete summation of the philosophic and scientific knowledge of the age. In general, both of them agreed with the rationalism and liberalism of Voltaire. Diderot, for example, maintained that "men will never be free till the last king is strangled with the entrails of the last priest." D'Alembert, while accepting the rationalist and individualist tendencies of the Enlightenment, differed from most of his associates in advocating a diffusion of the new doctrines among all the people. The general attitude of his contemporaries, notably Voltaire, was to despise the common people, to regard them as fools beyond redemption from ignorance and grossness. But for d'Alembert the only assurance of progress lay in universal enlightenment. Accordingly, he maintained that the truths of reason and science should be taught to the masses in the hope that eventually the whole world might be freed from darkness and tyranny. Condorcet, who committed suicide during the course of the French Revolution, was, like

Diderot, d'Alembert, and Condorcet

See color map facing page 704

The *Philosophes* at Supper. An imaginary convocation of some of the greatest of the French Enlightenment thinkers. The seated figures are Voltaire, with his left hand raised, and, moving to his left, Diderot, Père Adam, Condorcet, d'Alembert, Abbé Maury, and La Harpe.

d'Alembert, a devout believer in the theory of human progress. His book, *The Outline of the Progress of the Human Mind,* written while he was in hiding from revolutionary extremists, argued the possibility of general social improvement as a result of the application of reason to the problems of the world.[1]

Lessing

Although the Enlightenment had much less influence in Germany than in France or England, it did give birth there to significant and progressive ideas. The most widely recognized of its German leaders was Gotthold Lessing (1729–1781), primarily a dramatist and critic but also a philosopher of humane and far-sighted views. The essence of his philosophy was tolerance, founded upon a sincere conviction that no one religion has a monopoly of truth. In his play, *Nathan the Wise,* he expounded the idea that nobility of character has no particular relation to theological creeds. Largely for this reason he condemned adherence to any one system of dogma and taught that the development of each of the world's great religions (Christianity included) was simply a step in the spiritual evolution of humanity.

Hume

Two other philosophers commonly given a place in the Enlightenment—the Scotsman David Hume (1711–1776) and the Frenchman Jean-Jacques Rousseau (1712–1778)—were neither of them in full agreement with the majority of their contemporaries. Hume is noted above all for his skepticism. Like Hobbes, he taught that the mind is a bundle of impressions, derived exclusively from the senses and tied together by habits of association. That is, we learn from experience to associate warmth with fire and nourishment with bread. If we had

[1] The political and economic doctrines of the Enlightenment will be treated more fully in the following chapter on the French Revolution.

never actually experienced the sensation of warmth, no reasoning faculty in our minds would enable us to draw the conclusion that fire produces heat. But constant repetition of the fact that when we see a flame we generally experience warmth leads to the habit of associating the two in our minds. Impressions and associations are all that there is to knowing. Since every idea in the mind is nothing but a copy of a sense impression, it follows that we can know nothing of final causes, the nature of substance, or the origin of the universe. We cannot be sure of any of the conclusions of reason except those which, like the principles of mathematics, can be verified by actual experience. All others are likely to be the products of feelings and desires, of animal urges and fears. In his challenge to preconceived ideas, Hume was following Enlightenment practice. Yet in denying the competence of reason, Hume placed himself almost entirely outside the mainstream of contemporary thoughts.

In similar measure, Rousseau repudiated many of the basic assumptions which originated with Newton and Locke. An unhappy man, Rousseau failed in nearly every occupation he undertook. He preached lofty ideals of educational reform, but abandoned his own children to a foundling asylum. He quarreled with everybody and reveled in morbid self-disclosures. Undoubtedly it was these qualities of temperament which were largely responsible for his revolt against the coldly intellectual doctrines of his contemporaries. He maintained that to worship reason as the infallible guide to conduct and truth is to lean upon a broken reed. In the really vital problems of life it is much safer to rely upon feelings, to follow our instincts and emotions. These are the ways of nature and are therefore more conducive to happiness than the artificial lucubrations of the intellect. The "thinking man is a depraved animal." Yet notwithstanding his contempt for reason, Rousseau was in other ways thoroughly in agreement with the viewpoint of the Enlightenment. He extolled the life of primitive civilizations more fervently than did any of his associates. He shared the impatience of the Enlightenment with every sort of restriction upon individual freedom, though he was much more concerned about the liberty and equality of the masses than were the other reformers of his time. Rousseau's dogmas of equality and popular sovereignty, though frequently misinterpreted, became the rallying cries of late–eighteenth-century revolutionaries and of thousands of more moderate opponents of the existing regime. And, as the chapter on the French Revolution will show, it was Rousseau's political philosophy that provided the inspiration for the modern ideal of majority rule.

Jean-Jacques Rousseau

A movement as profoundly disturbing to Western society as the Enlightenment was bound to have its effects upon social customs and individual habits. Not all of the social progress of this time can be traced to intellectual influences; much of it derived from the prosperity induced by the expansion of trade in the Commercial Revolution.

Broader effects of the Enlightenment

Nevertheless, the progress of philosophy and science had more than incidental effects in clearing away ancient prejudice and in building a more humane society.

Humanitarianism

Mention has already been made of the influence of the Enlightenment in promoting the cause of social reform. A characteristic expression of this influence was agitation for revision of drastic criminal codes and for more liberal treatment of prisoners. With regard to both, the need for reform was urgent. Penalties even for minor offenses were exceedingly severe in practically all countries, death being the punishment for stealing a horse or a sheep or for the theft of as little as five shillings in money. During the first half of the eighteenth century no fewer than sixty crimes were added to the capital list in England. The treatment accorded to bankrupts and debtors was also extremely harsh. Beaten and starved by their jailers, they died by the thousands in filthy prisons. Conditions such as these eventually challenged the sympathies of several reformers. Foremost among them was Cesare Beccaria (1738–1794), a jurist of Milan, who had been deeply influenced by the writings of French rationalist philosophers. In 1764 he published his famed treatise *Crimes and Punishments,* in which he condemned the common theory that penalties should be made as severe as possible in order to deter potential offenders. Insisting that the purpose of criminal codes should be the prevention of crime and the reform of the wayward, rather than vengeance, he urged the abolition of torture as unworthy of civilized nations. He likewise condemned capital punishment as contrary to the natural rights of humans, since it cannot be revoked in case of error. Beccaria's book created a sensation. It was translated into a dozen languages, and stimulated efforts to improve conditions in many countries. By the end of the eighteenth century some progress had been made in reducing the severity of penalties, in relieving debtors from punishment, and in providing work and better food for prisoners.

Antislavery

The humanitarian spirit of the Enlightenment found an outlet also in other directions. Several of the scientists and philosophers denounced the evils of slavery. Many more condemned the slave trade. The efforts of intellectuals in this regard were warmly seconded by the leaders of certain religious groups, especially by prominent Quakers in America. Pacifism was another ideal of many of the Enlightenment thinkers. Voltaire's strictures on war were by no means the only example of such sentiments. Rousseau attacked as illogical attempts to draw a distinction between just and unjust wars. From the pens of other *philosophes* emanated various ingenious plans for insuring perpetual peace, including a scheme drafted by a Frenchman, the Abbé de Saint-Pierre (1658–1743), for a league of nations to take concerted action against aggressors.

Influential though the ideas of the Enlightenment were, they were not all-pervading, nor did everyone who encountered them find them

persuasive. The intellectual revolution we have been describing occurred within a society the majority of whose members was illiterate
and, as we have seen, deeply superstitious. When Halley's comet,
named for the English astronomer Edmund Halley, made its appearance in 1682, popular imagination took it as an omen of impending
cataclysm, much as it interpreted the devastating Lisbon earthquake of
1755 as a sign of divine displeasure. Men and women, literate or not,
found it exceedingly difficult to surrender the reassuring idea that
humankind and its activities were the center upon which the world was
fixed. They continued to believe, despite what philosophers might tell
them, that God was interested in their individual plight, and that their
supplications would bring them the relief and support they sought.
The ignorant still resorted to the full demonology and mythology of
medieval folklore. The more thoughtful, dissatisfied with the theological and spiritual thinness of Deism or, indeed, of conventionally practiced orthodoxies, had recourse to an evangelicalism whose beliefs
were the antithesis of Enlightenment rationalism. Quietists, whose
greatest strength was in France, argued that God spoke directly to
them of salvation. They denied the need for institutionalized religion,
but for reasons far different from those of the Deists. The Jansenists,
another French sect, revived a belief in predestination. And in England, John Wesley (1703–1791), the founder of Methodism, stirred
mass meetings of thousands from mid-century on by preaching salvation through faith in God's love for sinful men and women.

Yet the impact of the Enlightenment, qualified though it must be,
was nevertheless profound, both upon individuals and upon society as
a whole. Those who read and accepted its doctrines and discoveries
found their perceptions of themselves and their universe vastly altered. Its rationalism undoubtedly helped in some measure to improve
the human condition. And its insistence upon a social order controlled
by natural law and governed according to the practical experiences of
this world was eventually instrumental in bringing an end to the remaining vestiges of feudalism and the monopolies of unearned privilege.

*The Enlightenment's
impact*

4. SCIENCE AND THE INTELLECTUAL REVOLUTION

The intellectual revolution celebrated the triumph not only of reason
but of science as well. Prior to the seventeenth century, scientists had
worked in isolation from one another and in opposition to a worldview which was inclined to regard their work as suspect, if not as outright blasphemy. From the mid–seventeenth century on, however,
science became an international enterprise, encouraged by that willingness we have already noted to challenge accepted ideas, and supported by governments, as anxious as scientists themselves to put new

The prestige of science

An Illustration of a Laboratory from an Eighteenth-Century Edition of Diderot's *Encyclopedia*. The Enlightenment stressed the importance of scientific experiment.

discoveries to practical use. The Royal Society of London, founded in 1662 with King Charles II as its patron, and the French Academy of Sciences, founded four years later, stimulated the publication of scientific treatises and the exchange of scientific knowledge. Science was no longer seen as an esoteric field of inquiry, existing apart from the everyday business of the world. Instead it was welcomed for the very reason that its discoveries were proving to be of great value to humanity. Scientists themselves worked to apply their researach to the needs of society. Newton, for example, devised a series of navigational tables, by which the changing positions of the moon among the stars could be accurately predicted. And he invented the sextant for measuring these positions and thereby determining latitude and longitude.

Electricity   Some preliminary progress was made during this period in the understanding of electrical phenomena. At the beginning of the seventeenth century the Englishman William Gilbert (1540–1603), discovered the properties of lodestones and introduced the word "electricity" into the language.[2] Other scientists quickly became interested, and sensational results were anticipated from experiments with the marvelous "fluid." A learned Jesuit even suggested that two persons might communicate at a distance by means of magnetized needles which would point simultaneously to identical letters of the alphabet. Late in the eighteenth century Alessandro Volta (1745–1827) constructed the first battery. Still another important achievement in elec-

[2] "Electric" comes from the Greek word for amber. Gilbert and others had observed that amber rubbed on fur will attract paper, hair, straw, and various other things.

trical physics was the invention in 1746 of the Leyden jar for the storage of electric energy. It was mainly as a result of this invention that the American Benjamin Franklin (1706–1790) was able to show that lightning and electricity are identical. In his celebrated kite experiment in 1752 he succeeded in charging a Leyden jar from a thunderstorm.

Almost as spectacular as the progress in physics was the development of chemistry. If any one scientist can be called the founder of modern chemistry, it is Robert Boyle (1627–1691). The son of an Irish nobleman, Boyle achieved distinction in 1661 with the publication of his *Sceptical Chymist, or Chymico-Physical Doubts and Paradoxes*. In this work he rejected the theories of the alchemists and thereby contributed toward the establishment of chemistry as a pure science. In addition, he distinguished between a mixture and a compound, learned a great deal about the nature of phosphorus, produced alcohol from wood, suggested the idea of chemical elements, and reviewed the atomic theory. No scientist before his time had foreshadowed so much of the knowledge of modern chemistry.

Chemistry: Boyle

Despite the work of Boyle, little further development of chemistry occurred for almost a hundred years. The reason lay partly in the wide acceptance of errors concerning such matters as heat, flame, air, and the phenomenon of combustion. The most common of these errors was the so-called phlogiston theory. The theory was based on the idea that phlogiston was the substance of fire—i.e., when an object burned, phlogiston was supposed to be given off. The remaining ash was said to be the "true" material. In the second half of the eighteenth century important discoveries were made which ultimately overthrew this theory and cleared the way for a real understanding of some of the most familiar chemical reactions. In 1766 the Englishman Henry Cavendish reported the discovery of a new kind of gas obtained by treating iron, zinc, and other metals with sulphuric acid. He showed that this gas, now known as hydrogen, would not of itself support combustion, and yet would be rapidly consumed by a fire with access to the air. In 1774 oxygen was discovered by another Englishman, the Unitarian minister Joseph Priestley. He found that a candle would burn with extraordinary vigor when placed in the new gas—a fact which indicated clearly that combustion was not caused by any mysterious principle or substance in the flame itself. A few years after this discovery, Cavendish demonstrated that air and water, long supposed to be elements, are actually a mixture and a compound, respectively, the first being composed principally of oxygen and nitrogen and the second of oxygen and hydrogen.

Cavendish and Priestley

Lavoisier's Apparatus for the Decomposition of Air

The final blow to the phlogiston theory was administered by the Frenchman Antoine Lavoisier (1743–1794), one of the greatest of all scientists of the intellectual revolution, who later lost his life in the French Revolution. Lavoisier proved that both combustion and respiration involve oxidation, the one being rapid and the other slow. He

Lavoisier

provided the names for oxygen and hydrogen, demonstrated that the diamond is a form of carbon, and argued that life itself is essentially a chemical process. But undoubtedly his greatest accomplishment was his discovery of the law of the conservation of mass. He found evidence that "although matter may alter its state in a series of chemical actions, it does not change in amount; the quantity of matter is the same at the end as at the beginning of every operation, and can be traced by its weight." This "law" has, of course, been modified by later discoveries regarding the structure of the atom and the conversion of some forms of matter into energy. It is hardly too much to say, however, that as a result of Lavoisier's genius chemistry became a true science.

Biology

Although the physical sciences received the major attention in the intellectual revolution, the biological sciences were by no means neglected. One of the greatest of the early biologists was the Englishman Robert Hooke (1635–1703), the first to see and describe the cellular structure of plants. This achievement was soon followed by the work of Marcello Malpighi (1628–1694) in demonstrating the sexuality of plants and in comparing the breathing function of vegetable leaves with that of the lungs of animals. About the same time a Dutch businessman and amateur scientist, Anthony van Leeuwenhoek (1632–1723), discovered protozoa and bacteria and wrote the first description of human sperm. The seventeenth century also witnessed some progress in embryology. About 1670 the Dutch physician, Jan Swammerdam (1637–1680), carefully described the life history of certain insects from the caterpillar stage to maturity and compared the change of tadpole into frog with the development of the human embryo.

Linnaean classification

In many ways the end of the seventeenth century appeared to mark a decline of originality in the sciences that deal with living things. During the next hundred years biologists were inclined more and more to center their efforts upon description and classification of knowledge already in existence. The most brilliant classifier of biological knowledge was the Swedish scientist, Carl von Linné (1707–1778), more commonly known by his Latinized name of Linnaeus. In his *System of Nature* and in his *Botanical Philosophy* Linnaeus divided all natural objects into three kingdoms: stone, animal, and vegetable. Each of these kingdoms he subdivided into classes, genera, and species. He invented the system of biological nomenclature still in use, by which every plant and animal is designated by two scientific names, the first denoting the genus and the second the species. Thus he called humans *Homo sapiens*. Linnaeus's system of classification was widely adopted even in his own time.

Buffon

The second great genius of descriptive biology in the eighteenth century was the Frenchman Georges Buffon (1707–1788). His *Natural History* in forty-four volumes, though intended as a general summation of science, dealt mainly with humans and other vertebrates. While much of the material in this work was taken from the writings of other scientists and from the accounts of travelers, the author was able to reduce a vast body of knowledge to orderly arrangement and enliven it with his own interpretations. Buffon recognized the close relationship between humans and the higher animals. Though he could never quite bring himself to accept the full implications of a theory that linked human evolution directly to that of other animals, he was nonetheless strongly impressed by the striking resemblances among all of the higher species. He admitted the possibility that the entire range of organic forms had descended from a single species.

Despite the notable scientific advances of the seventeenth and eighteenth centuries, the development of physiology and medicine progressed rather slowly during the same period, and for several reasons. *Medicine* One was the inadequate preparation of physicians, many of whom had begun their professional careers with little more training than a kind of apprenticeship under an older practitioner. Another was the common disrepute in which surgery was held as a mere trade, like that of a barber or blacksmith. Perhaps the most serious of all was the prejudice against dissection of human bodies for use in anatomical study. As late as 1750 medical schools which engaged in this practice were in danger of destruction by irate mobs. Despite these obstacles some progress was still possible. About 1670 Malpighi and Leeuwenhoek confirmed the famous discovery of the Englishman William Harvey by observing the actual flow of blood through the network of capillaries connecting the arteries and veins. At approximately the same time an eminent physician of London, Thomas Sydenham, proposed a new theory of fever as a natural process by which diseased material is expelled from the system.

Medical progress during the eighteenth century was somewhat more rapid. Among the noteworthy achievements were the discovery of blood pressure, the founding of histology or microscopic anatomy, *Inoculation* the development of the autopsy as an aid to the study of disease, and the recognition of scarlet fever as a malady distinct from smallpox and measles. But the chief milestones of medical advancement in this period were the adoption of inoculation and the development of vaccination for smallpox. Knowledge of inoculation came originally from the Near East, where it had long been employed by the Muslims. Information concerning its use was relayed to England in 1717 through the letters of Lady Montagu, wife of the British ambassador to Turkey. The first systematic application of the practice in the Western world, however, was due to the efforts of the American Puritan leaders, Cotton and Increase Mather, who implored the physicians of Boston to inoculate their patients in the hope of curbing an epidemic of smallpox which had broken out in 1721. By the middle of the century inoculation was quite generally employed by physicians in Europe and in

America. In 1796 a milder method of vaccination was discovered by the Englishman Edward Jenner. It was now revealed that direct inoculation of human beings with the deadly virus of smallpox was unnecessary: a vaccine manufactured in the body of an animal would be just as effective and much less likely to have disastrous results. The vast possibilities thus opened up for the elimination of contagious diseases appeared to confirm the Enlightenment belief in the ability of men and women to make nature's laws work for the betterment of the human condition.

5. CLASSICISM IN ART AND LITERATURE

Classical models

The history of European art and literature during the seventeenth and eighteenth centuries reflects the respect for the classical world which we have noted as a particular characteristic of Enlightenment thought. Artists and writers strove to imitate classical models. They chose classical titles and themes for many of their works and embellished them wherever possible with allusions to antique mythology. Deploring the destruction of ancient civilization by "Christian barbarians," they were unable to see much value in the cultural achievements of later centuries. In particular, they despised what they termed the "Middle Ages" as a long night of barbaric darkness stretching between the classical period and their own. Most would have agreed with the dictum of Rousseau that the Gothic cathedrals were "a disgrace to those who had the patience to build them."

Left: *St. Peter's Cathedral, Rome.* The sweeping colonnades, designed by Bernini and begun in 1656, express the dramatic splendor that was characteristic of baroque architecture. Right: *St. Paul's Cathedral, London.* Designed by Christopher Wren, the boldness of the structure reflected the emergence of England as a world power.

The Chateau of Versailles. Dramatically expanded by Louis XIV in the 1660s from a hunting lodge to the principal royal residence and the seat of government, the chateau became the standard of secular baroque architecture and a monument to the international power and prestige of the Grand Monarch.

These attitudes were an inheritance from the Renaissance humanists. Yet the classicism of the seventeenth and eighteenth centuries was no mere copy of that espoused by earlier artists and writers. As adopted by architects, painters, and sculptors, classicism emerged in new forms as the baroque style. This style was initially developed as part of the Catholic Reformation of the late sixteenth century. Churches were built in a manner designed to inspire renewed reverence and respect for the Church of Rome. Classical elements such as columns, domes, and architectural sculpture were combined in such a way as to express both aggressive restlessness and extraordinary power. The results are clearly visible in a structure such as Giovanni Lorenzo Bernini's (1598–1680) colonnades at St. Peter's in Rome. The Englishman Christopher Wren (1632–1723), with Bernini among the most gifted of baroque architects, employed the same style in his design for St. Paul's Cathedral in Protestant London, an architectural statement whose grandeur challenged the authority claimed by Roman Catholicism.

The baroque style

The baroque style was soon adopted by the absolutist monarchs of seventeenth-century Europe to symbolize their power and magnificence. The palace of Louis XIV at Versailles is undoubtedly the supreme example of secular baroque architecture. Buildings and grounds together are a remarkable expression of the formality and hierarchy of the autocratic state, and of the power invested in the person of the monarch. Other European rulers commissioned royal residences in the style of Versailles: Peter the Great, for example, built the Peterhof at his capital of St. Petersburg; King William of England employed Wren to embellish the already standing palace of Hampton Court. None of these structures, however, could rival Versailles, ei-

Royal Baroque

Left: *The Petit Trianon, Versailles.* Added as a royal retreat in the gardens of Versailles by Louis XV, this structure expresses the refined elegance that characterized rococo architecture. Right: *The Interior of the Pilgrimage Church, Bavaria.* An example of the flamboyance of the late baroque architectural style.

ther in its grandeur or its total devotion to the harmony and proportion which characterized the baroque.

During the eighteenth century the baroque style gradually gave way to further adaptations of the classical. On the Continent, the baroque

Rococo

was succeeded by the rococo, a term perhaps derived from the French words for rock and shell (*rocaille* and *coquille*), two natural forms often employed in both exterior and interior rococo ornamentation. The rococo differed from the baroque in several ways: it was lighter, less majestic; it created an impression of grace and refinement. In place of a struggle for dynastic power and colonial empire, much of European society by now focused its attention on the dilletantism and elegance of the court of Louis XV, which set the standard for continental behavior among the ruling classes. The rococo both represented and reflected this change in focus. Well-known examples of the rococo are the Petit Trianon, a small palace built on the grounds of Versailles, which was designed as a royal retreat, and the palace of Sans Souci (literally, "Without Care") at Potsdam, built by Frederick the Great.

In England reaction to the baroque took the form of a return to the severer classicism of Renaissance architecture, adapted from the de-

Palladianism

signs of the Italian architect, Andrea Palladio (1508–1580) and from those of the seventeenth-century Englishman, Inigo Jones. Most of the imposing country houses built by the landed gentry in this period displayed a fidelity to the precise mathematical equations of neo-Palladianism. As such they reflected the general Enlightenment worship of reason and order.

To a certain extent the evolution of painting during the seventeenth and eighteenth centuries paralleled that of architecture. The greatest painters in the baroque tradition were the Flemish artists, Peter Paul Rubens (1577–1640) and Anthony Van Dyck (1599–1641), and the Spaniard, Diego Velásquez (1599–1660). Rubens was the outstanding genius among these three. In such works as *The Fates Spinning* and *Venus and Adonis,* he combined classical themes with sumptuous baroque color and richness pleasing to the affluent merchants and nobles of his day. The pink and rounded flesh of his full-blown nudes is thoroughly in keeping with the robust vitality of the age. Both Rubens and his gifted pupil, Anthony Van Dyck, are noted for their portraits of rulers and nobles, with full attention paid to the gorgeous details of elegant apparel and opulent furnishings in the background. Van Dyck's best-known portraits are those of the English kings, James I and Charles I, and their families. Velásquez, the third great artist of the baroque tradition, was the court painter to Philip IV of Spain. Much of his work consisted of royal portraits, suffused in soft and silvery light but fundamentally empty of meaning or emotional expression, a testimony, perhaps, to the waning power of the Spanish Empire.

Rubens's Portrait of His Son Nicolaus

See color plates following page 704

Venus and Adonis by Peter Paul Rubens. Rubens often painted classical themes, which he conceived on a grand scale and executed with sweeping vigor.

Self-Portrait by Rembrandt

All of the painters mentioned thus far were exponents in some degree of the classical influence. But there were others in both the seventeenth and eighteenth centuries who refused to be bound by the prevailing artistic conventions. Foremost among them was Rembrandt van Rijn (1606–1669), now universally considered one of the greatest painters of all time. The son of a well-to-do miller of Leyden, Rembrandt was allowed to begin his artistic education at an early age. Under a series of native masters he learned the technique of subtle coloring and a skillful depiction of natural phenomena. Famous by the time he was twenty-five, he fell upon evil days later in his life, mainly as a consequence of bad investments and the failure of critics to appreciate his more recondite works. In 1656 he was stripped by his creditors of all he possessed and driven from his house. Apparently these reverses served mainly to broaden and deepen his philosophy, for in this very same year he produced some of his greatest achievements. As a painter Rembrandt surpassed all the other members of the Dutch school and deserves to be ranked with the painters of the High Renaissance in Italy like Titian and Leonardo. No artist had a keener understanding of the problems and trials of human nature or a stronger perception of the mysteries of life. His portraits, including those of himself, are imbued with an introspective quality and with a suggestion that the half is not being told. Rembrandt departed from the subjects of classical mythology, preferring to portray solemn rabbis, tattered beggars, and scenes from the Old and New Testaments, rich in drama and in human interest. Some of his best-known works include *The Good Samaritan, The Woman Taken in Adultery, The Marriage of Samson,* and *The Night Watch.*

The history of literature in the seventeenth and eighteenth centuries exhibited tendencies quite similar to those of art. The most popular literary ideal was classicism, which generally meant not only a studied imitation of classical forms but also an earnest devotion to reason as a way of life. Although literary classicism was not confined to any one country, its principal center was France. The most noted member of the French group of poets and dramatists was Jean-Baptiste Poquelin (1622–1673), who is much better known by his adopted name of Molière. Less respectful of ancient formalism than any of his associates, Molière was the most original of French comedians. Few keener critics of human nature have ever lived. "The business of comedy," he once declared, "is to represent in general all the defects of men and especially of the men of our time." The mortal weakness he delighted most to ridicule was pretentiousness, as he did so brilliantly in plays such as *Tartuffe.* But with all of this penchant for satire, Molière had a measure of pity for the evil fortunes of humankind. In a number of his plays sympathy and even melancholy go hand in hand with clever wit and pungent scorn. His genius was probably broader in scope than that of any other dramatist since Shakespeare. Two French play-

Aristotle Contemplating the Bust of Homer by Rembrandt. A fine example of Rembrandt's obsession with the effects of light and shade as means of expression.

wrights whose work more directly mirrored the classical tradition were Pierre Corneille (1606–1684) and Jean Racine (1639–1699). Both took as their subjects the heroes and heroines of ancient literature and history—Medea, Pompey, and Phaedra, for example; and both chose as their literary models the poets and dramatists of classical Greece and Rome.

Seventeenth-century England also produced writers in the classical style. The greatest was the renowned Puritan poet, John Milton (1608–1674). The leading philosopher of Cromwell's Commonwealth, Milton wrote the official defense of the beheading of Charles I. Nearly all of his writings were phrased in the reasoned and formal expression of the classical tradition, while many of the lesser ones took their themes from Greek mythology. But Milton was as much a Puritan as he was a classicist. He could never escape from the idea that the essence of beauty is morality. Moreover, he was deeply interested in theological problems. His greatest work, *Paradise Lost,* is a synthesis of the religious beliefs of his age, a majestic epic of the Protestant faith. In spite of the fact that Milton was a Puritan, his views reflected ideas characteristic of the intellectual revolution. The principal themes of *Paradise Lost* are the moral responsibility of the individual and the importance of knowledge as an instrument of virtue. Paradise is lost repeatedly in human life to the extent that men and women allow passion to triumph over reason in determining the course of their actions.

Classicism in English literature reached its zenith in the eighteenth century with the poetry of Alexander Pope (1688–1744). Pope was a great exponent in verse of the mechanistic and Deist doctrines of the Enlightenment. In such poetic works as his *Essay on Man* and his *Essay on Criticism* he set forth the view that nature is governed by inflexible laws, and that men and women must study and follow nature if they

Milton

John Milton. From the First Edition of his poems, 1645.

Gin Lane by William Hogarth. Hogarth, like his friend Henry Fielding, believed in portraying human nature as he found it. In this famous engraving, he is preaching a sermon against the gin trade, one of the besetting evils of eighteenth-century London.

Literature in eighteenth-century England

would bring any semblance of order into human affairs. Other English writers, however, turned from classical models to describe, castigate, and celebrate present-day eighteenth-century society. Jonathan Swift (1667–1745), Daniel Defoe (1660–1737), and Henry Fielding (1707–1754) all took as their subjects human nature as it manifested itself in the lives of their contemporaries. Swift, in *Gulliver's Travels,* ridiculed current human pretensions and political realities by contrasting them with the perceptions of a series of mythical races. Defoe, in *Robinson Crusoe,* the tale of one man's survival on a desert island, extolled practical ingenuity and defended the subjugation of indigenous peoples by Europeans. Fielding, in *Tom Jones,* the first modern novel, and one of the greatest, declared that men and women, if they are to be portrayed as they should be, must be depicted not as impossibly virtuous heroes and heroines, but simply as real people, responsible for their actions.

6. MUSIC IN THE SEVENTEENTH AND EIGHTEENTH CENTURIES

Italian opera

The seventeenth century witnessed a dramatic change in the form of musical structure and composition, one which reflected shifts occurring elsewhere in the intellectual world. As we have previously observed, the end of the sixteenth century had marked the culmination of a long era of choral, polyphonic music. Almost immediately, however, a reaction set in, so powerful that the polyphonic style became obsolete within twenty-five years of the death of its most gifted and advanced practitioner, Palestrina, in 1594. A new ideal, that of primary voice accompanied by one of several musical instruments, swept Italy in a remarkably short time, and became known as monody. One of the major reasons for this change was a growing and characteristically baroque insistence upon the dramatic, and a realization on the part of Italian composers that the intense feelings of an individual cannot be adequately expressed by a many-voiced chorus. The same impulses that produced the architecture of Bernini and the paintings of Rubens led to the creation of opera, which reached its first powerful manifestation in *Orfeo* (1607) by the Italian Claudio Monteverdi (1567–1643), the dominating musical personality in the first half of the new century. Within a generation operas were performed in most important cities in Italy; by 1736 Venice boasted an opera house for every parish. Opera, staged within magnificent settings, and calling upon the talents of singers, musicians, artists, dramatists, and as master of the grand design—the conductor—expressed as clearly as any art form the dedication of the baroque to grandeur, complexity, and display.

During this same period, the instrumental tradition of the Renaissance began to produce works for organ, harpsichord, and the various string and wind instruments. In the last third of the century instrumental music created the concerto, along with opera one of the greatest original stylistic accomplishments of the Italian baroque. Both opera and concerto soon spread beyond the Alps. Though the seventeenth century was preoccupied with musical experiments, it created an impressive synthesis upon which the first half of the eighteenth century could build the final great achievements of late baroque music.

The concerto

The late baroque culminated in two towering composers: Johann Sebastian Bach (1685–1750) and George Frederick Handel (1685–1759). Though both were born in Saxony, Bach became the epitome of German musical genius, while Handel, who lived for almost half a century in London and became a British subject, embodied an English national style. Bach combined an unbounded imagination and a capacious intellect with heroic powers of discipline and an unquenchable zeal for work. By lifelong study he made himself the master of most existing types and styles of music, from little dance pieces for the clavichord to gigantic choral works. As a church musician, Bach's duty was to provide new music for elaborate Sunday and holy day services. Therefore the bulk of his work is made up of cantatas (over 200 preserved), oratorios, Passions, and Masses. His settings of the Gospels according to St. John and St. Matthew represent the unsurpassable peak of this genre. Fundamentally, though, Bach was an instrumental composer, the creator of tremendous works for organ and harpsichord, and of spacious concertos and sonatas for various combinations of instruments, and suites for orchestra. Bach was steeped in German Protestantism in a way that makes him, in one sense, uncharacteristic of the generally antireligious Enlightenment.

Johann Sebastian Bach

"The Charming Brute." A contemporary caricature of Handel, engraved by Joseph Groupy, 1754.

Classical music

Mozart

Yet no one who has heard Bach's music or studied his scores can deny the extent to which they reflect the attention to rational order and mathematical harmony that lay at the heart of the intellectual revolution.

Handel was the absolute antithesis of his great fellow-Saxon. After four years spent in Italy he completely absorbed Italian techniques and modes of composition, subsequently settling in England, where for years he ran an opera company that produced nothing but Italian operas, mostly his own. Italian opera did not suit the English middle class public, however, and after decades spent in composing and producing dozens of operas, Handel realized that he must turn to something more acceptable to the English taste. This he found in the "oratorio," a musical drama intended for performance in concert form. With the exception of *Messiah,* the most famous of his oratios, these works were not religious music, although their themes came from the Old Testament. Undoubtedly one reason for Handel's success in his adopted country was the fact that his virile and heroic oratorios could be said to symbolize the English people, their pride in their institutions and their attainment of national greatness.

After the mid–eighteenth century, the center of the musical world shifted to Vienna, where a group of highly gifted composers achieved a remarkable stylistic synthesis by reconciling baroque weightiness, rococo charm, and preromantic excitement into the form that has been labeled classical. Christoph Willibald von Gluck (1714–1787) reformed the declining "serious" opera into a noble drama that recalls the tone of classical antiquity. The appeal of the mischievous, Italian comic opera, the *opera buffa,* forced a fusion with serious opera which reached its greatest height in the operas of Wolfgang Amadeus Mozart (1756–1791), while chamber and orchestral music achieved a new formal and expressive level under the leadership of Joseph Haydn (1732–1809).

The eighteenth century was full of music, but its social organization severely hampered the creative artist. Handel, who ran his own business and left behind a respectable estate, was an exception to the general rule. In most instances, if a composer or musician was not employed by a court, noble house, church, or municipality, or if he was not an internationally acclaimed virtuoso or a renowned teacher, he ran the risk of being ground down in an effort to make a living. Mozart was among the first to shed the security of a position as "musical lackey" and to try the free artistic economy of the metropolis. While a child prodigy he was adored and admired, but when he left the employ of the archbishop of Salzburg to take up the career of a freelance artist in Vienna, he could support himself only with the greatest difficulty. Although the remaining ten years of his life were spent in bountiful productivity, he had to live from hand to mouth.

Mozart, at the Age of Six, Plays Before Empress Maria Theresa. This contemporary illustration suggests the importance of royal patronage and the often demeaning relationship between artists and patrons in this era.

Financial troubles pursued him until his death at the age of thirty-five.

When appraising the music of the classical era we must realize that in spite of its magnificent sonatas and symphonies, the stylistic core of the era was still in the dramatic music of the opera. Mozart used the operatic form to shape the characters, fates, and conflicts of human beings in a way that other forms too became permanent. Each great Mozart opera—*The Marriage of Figaro, Don Giovanni, The Magic Flute*—provides a center from which the form of piano sonatas, quartets, quintets, concertos, and symphonies were subsequently derived by his successors.

Mozart's operas

Haydn was carved from sterner timber than Mozart; his peasant background made him tenacious and stubborn. If Mozart embodied the aristocratic spirit, Haydn did that of the liberated plebeian. It was because of their diametrically opposed personalities that the two musicians got along so well; they complemented each other, learned from each other, and, in fact, were friends. Haydn had a sharp intellect and acquired his extensive knowledge of music through incessant study and experimentation. His art conveys the impressions of the village and the countryside, but also the elegance of the princely Austrian household that patronized him for many years. Haydn's compositions are so numerous that a complete edition of them has never been made. They include many operas and Masses, oratorios, concertos, over eighty string quartets, and more than 100 symphonies. It was Haydn who firmly established the technical and stylistic principles of symphonic construction, creating, with Mozart, the pattern of the symphony orchestra which remained the basis for all future musical developments.

The careers of Mozart and Haydn suggest both the achievements

Joseph Haydn

The era of revolution

and limitations of the revolution we have traced. Their compositional innovations were a part of that broad series of intellectual changes that assisted in carrying Europe forward into the modern world. Yet Haydn's dependence upon aristocratic patronage, and Mozart's inability to live apart from it, make clear the extent to which the world of the Enlightenment remained a world bound together by rank and privilege. Only at the very end of the eighteenth century, with the coming of the French and Industrial Revolutions, did the ideas of the intellectual revolution begin to play an active role in altering, in any major way, the structure of the social and political institutions of the West.

SELECTED READINGS

• *Items so designated are available in paperback editions.*
• Carl Becker, *The Heavenly City of the Eighteenth-Century Philosophers,* New Haven, Conn., 1932. Relates the Enlightenment to its medieval origins.
• Burford, W. H., *Germany in the Eighteenth Century: The Social Background of the Literary Revival,* London, 1935. A combination of social and intellectual history, this work remains the best introduction in English to the German Enlightenment.
  Cassirer, Ernst, *The Philosophy of the Enlightenment,* Princeton, N.Y., 1951. Emphasizes the role of critical thinking on the part of the *philosophes* and the nature of reason in the Enlightenment.
  Cobban, Alfred, *In Search of Humanity: The Role of the Enlightenment in Modern History,* London, 1960.
• Gay, Peter, *The Enlightenment: An Interpretation;* Vol. I, *The Rise of Modern Paganism;* Vol. II, *The Science of Freedom,* New York, 1966–69. A brilliant work by the leading authority on the eighteenth-century intellectual world. Argues that the Enlightenment represented a complete break with the medieval past and the first stage of the modern world. Contains superb bibliographies.
  Gillespie, C. C., *The Edge of Objectivity: An Essay in the History of Scientific Ideas,* Princeton, N.J., 1960.
• Grimsley, Ronald, *Jean-Jacques Rousseau: A Study in Self-Awareness,* Cardiff, 1961. An excellent biography concerned with Rousseau's psychological development.
  Haldane, E. S., *Descartes, His Life and Times,* London, 1905. An old but thorough biography.
• Hall, A. R., *The Scientific Revolution, 1500–1800: The Formation of the Modern Scientific Attitude,* rev. ed., New York, 1966.
• Hampshire, Stuart, *Spinoza,* London, 1952.
  Havens, George R., *The Age of Ideas: From Reaction to Revolution in Eighteenth-Century France,* New York, 1955. Short biographies of the major French *philosophes.*

Humphreys, A. R., *The Augustan World: Society, Thought, and Letters in Eighteenth-Century England,* London, 1954.

Manuel, Frank E., *A Portrait of Isaac Newton,* Cambridge, Mass., 1968. A psychoanalytic interpretation.

Mellone, S. H., *The Dawn of Modern Thought: Descartes, Spinoza, Leibniz,* London, 1930. Explains the Cartesian system and its influence.

Monter, E. W., ed., *European Witchcraft,* New York, 1969. Selected readings with fine introductions by one of the world's leading experts.

More, L. T., *Isaac Newton: A Biography,* New York, 1934. The standard biography.

Ornstein, Martha, *The Role of Scientific Societies in the Seventeenth Century,* rev. ed., Hamden, Conn., 1963.

Palmer, R. R., *Catholics and Unbelievers in Eighteenth-Century France,* New York, 1939. Argues that Catholic thinkers were as enlightened as the *philosophes,* and that, ironically, their very tolerance contributed to the anticlericalism of the age.

• Phillipson, Coleman, *Three Criminal Law Reformers: Beccaria, Bentham, Romilly,* rev. ed., London, 1970.

Shackleton, Robert, *Montesquieu: A Critical Biography* London, 1961. The man and his thought.

Shryock, Richard H., *The Development of Modern Medicine: An Interpretation of the Social and Scientific Factors Involved,* London, 1948.

• Thomas, Keith, *Religion and the Decline of Magic,* London, 1971. A marvelously insightful study of popular belief in England.

SOURCE MATERIALS

Beccaria, Cesare, *An Essay on Crimes and Punishments, with a Commentary by M. de Voltaire,* Stanford, 1953. A reprint of the 1767 edition. Beccaria advocates a rational approach to punishment, with the good of the state outweighing motives for revenge. Voltaire's Commentary contains some interesting remarks on witchcraft.

• Boswell, James, *Life of Johnson,* London, 1970. The classic biography of the English man of letters, Samuel Johnson, written by his protégé; contains a superb portrait of eighteenth-century London.

Gibbon, Edward, *Autobiography,* London, 1961.

• ———, *The Decline and Fall of the Roman Empire,* 3 vols., New York, 1960. Published in 1776, this classic work exemplifies the skeptical, anticlerical nature of much of Enlightenment thought of the eighteenth century, especially Chapters 15 and 16 of Volume I.

• Kors, Alan C., and E. Peters, eds., *Witchcraft in Europe, 1100–1700: A Documentary History,* Philadelphia, 1972.

• Kramer, Heinrich, and James Sprenger, *The Malleus Maleficarum,* New York, 1971. An extraordinary work, the *Malleus* ("The Hammer of Witches") was the handbook of the witchcraft prosecutors of the Inquisition.

• Locke, John, *Two Treatises of Government,* ed. by Peter Laslett, London,

1960. Locke's celebrated tracts invoking the concept of the contractual nature of government and the sanctity of private property. An excellent introductory essay by Laslett.

• Voltaire, *Candide,* New York, 1956. Voltaire's satirical critique of the contemporary philosophy that "this is the best of all possible worlds," traced through a series of disasters experienced by his protagonist. First published in 1759.

Chapter 23

INDIA, THE FAR EAST, AND AFRICA DURING THE EARLY MODERN ERA (c. 1500-1800)

Fuji-ichi was a clever man, and his substantial fortune was amassed in his own lifetime. . . . He noted down the market ratio of copper and gold; he inquired about the current quotations of the rice brokers; he sought information from druggists' and haberdashers' assistants on the state of the market at Nagasaki; for the latest news on the prices of ginned cotton, salt, and saké, he noted the various days on which the Kyoto dealers received dispatches from the Edo branch shops. Every day a thousand things were entered in his book, and people came to Fuji-ichi if they were ever in doubt. He became a valuable asset to the citizens of Kyoto.

—I. Saikaku, *The Tycoon of All Tenants* (1688)

Between the sixteenth and the nineteenth centuries a reinvigorated Indian empire headed by a new dynasty attained the rank of a major power; China, under the last of a long series of imperial dynasties, waxed even stronger, becoming the largest and most populous country in the world; and Japan adapted her feudal institutions to the requirements of a despotic government. In both India and China, and to a lesser degree in Japan, splendor and magnificence reflected the tastes of wealthy societies and mighty rulers, as was also true in much of Europe during this same period. In the long run, however, the great Asian states found themselves at a disadvantage because they played a passive rather than an active role in the Commercial Revolution. As western European nations turned to empire building and expanded their naval forces, they established direct contacts with the coastal regions of Asia, took over the bulk of the trade between East and West, and frequently threatened the independence of non-European peoples. For several centuries the principal Eastern states were strong enough to protect themselves against the threat of aggression from the West. Faced with rigid trade restrictions in China and almost totally excluded from Japan, the seafaring Europeans

Impact of the West upon the East

turned to other quarters. In the 1570s the Spanish occupied the Philippines, subduing the native tribes and the communities of Chinese colonists in the Islands. A few years later the Dutch, through their East India Company, laid the foundations of a rich empire in Indonesia, dislodging the Portuguese who had preceded them by almost a century. The British and French somewhat belatedly turned their attention to the mainland of India, where they secured valuable trading posts in the course of the seventeenth century. During this same period the Portuguese, the British, and the Dutch established commercial enclaves on the coast of Africa.

I. INDIA UNDER THE MOGUL DYNASTY

Babur "the Tiger"

In the sixteenth century a new invasion of India by Muslim forces from the north produced very different results from those that had accompanied the Turkish inroads and the institution of the Delhi Sultanate. It led to the establishment of the dynasty known as the Mogul—a Persian variant of the word "Mongol"—which created an efficient and, on the whole, successful pattern of government and, most significant, demonstrated the possibility of an integration of the Indian people regardless of religious profession. Actually, the ruling family and the administrative officers were far from pure-blooded Mongols. Babur ("the Tiger"), the founder of the dynasty, was descended on his father's side from Timur (of Turkish stock) and on his mother's side from the Mongol conqueror Genghis Khan. His own descendants were of mixed parentage, including Turkish, Persian, and Indian strains. Babur, like many another conqueror, began his career as the head of a small state in Turkestan. By advancing into Afghanistan he secured control of the frontier mountain passes commanding the route to the Punjab. Within the space of five years (ended by his death in 1530) he conquered the greater part of Hindustan, while retaining his territories in Afghanistan and southern Turkestan. His conquest was facilitated by the fact that he possessed artillery and match-fired muskets of European manufacture, although these guns were very primitive. The empire which Babur had begun to mark out was fully established and also given its most distinctive character by his grandson, Akbar.

Akbar, the Great Mogul

Akbar, deservedly termed "the Great Mogul," was truly remarkable both as a personality and as a sovereign. He is generally considered India's greatest ruler, although he evidently fell short of the noble idealism exemplified by Asoka some 1,800 years earlier. Perhaps the scarcity of records for Asoka's reign makes a comparison unfair. At any rate, enough data are available for Akbar's period to show that he was unquestionably one of the world's outstanding political figures in the sixteenth century. His reign was a long one—from 1556 to 1605 (the dates almost coincide with the reign of Elizabeth I of England). Much of it was devoted to schemes of conquest, unsuccessfully in the Deccan but resulting in the extension of Mogul authority over all northern India and the neighboring portion of Afghanistan. Far more important was Akbar's determination to conciliate and secure the support of the Hindu population, a decision to which he adhered inflexibly throughout his reign. For his large harem (said to number over 5,000) he chose wives of several different nationalities, partly with an eye toward political expediency. By contracting marriage alliances with the proud Rajput clans, whose spirit had never been broken by the Turks, he hoped to win their allegiance. (Akbar's favorite wife and the mother of his successor to the throne was a Rajput princess.) Early in his reign he took the important step of abolishing the special taxes on non-Muslims, and he appointed Hindus—especially Rajputs—to civil and military office. A Hindu raja served in the highly responsible post of minister of finance. Akbar abandoned entirely all attempts to win converts to Islam by coercion and introduced a policy of religious toleration, although he tried to discourage those Hindu practices which he considered reprehensible, such as animal sacrifice, child marriage, and suttee.

Akbar's administration was bureaucratic and relatively efficient. At the head of each of the provinces and districts into which he divided

The Court of the Emperor Babur "the Tiger," Founder of the Mogul Dynasty

THE MOGUL EMPIRE IN INDIA

Akbar's administrative methods

the state he placed a military governor who was paid a generous salary but was required to maintain a prescribed number of troops and was held to a strict accountability for his actions. Thus the government was not feudal in basis, although there was a nobility of various grades (including some Hindus and Indian Muslims as well as Moguls). While Akbar was unable to keep an adequate check on every part of his large dominions, he made a sincere effort to enforce justice among his mixed population, and he severely punished officials whose corruption was detected. The criminal code was a savage one, but not more barbarous than in most European countries of that day. Civil law was based largely upon Islamic tradition and the Koran. Akbar's chief source of revenue was a land tax, assessed upon the fields actually under cultivation and amounting to one-third of the annual value of the crop, based on the average yield over a ten-year period. This assessment, though heavy enough to provide a huge income to the state, was actually less than that exacted by other rulers both before and after Akbar; also it was applied uniformly and with safeguards against the cupidity of local officials.

The latter part of Akbar's long reign was generally peaceful, and, in spite of the invasions and the murderous strife of preceding centuries, a high level of prosperity seems to have been reached in India. Akbar maintained a sound currency, typified by gold coins of extraordinary fineness. Commerce throve, cities expanded, and a substantial middle class of traders and skilled artisans flourished. Common laborers, however, were far from prosperous, and many were slaves. The country villagers also, who made up the majority of the population, apparently subsisted on a very low standard of living. Great wealth and lavish display were confined to large landowners and officials and were most conspicuous in the court of the emperor. It is estimated that Akbar's total revenue from all sources was equal to more than $200,000,000 a year. Of a total population approximating 100 million, country villagers made up the majority, as they have down to the present day. Although their standard of living was pitifully low, it was probably higher than in modern times.

Prosperity for the rich, hardships for the poor

Akbar's unusual personality and rare combination of interests left their mark upon all aspects of his reign. Endowed with a superb physique, he loved feats of strength and dangerous exploits, sometimes risking his life in the most reckless fashion by attacking a lion single-handed or by riding wild elephants. In a fit of temper he could be pitilessly cruel, but he was generally fair in judgment and frequently generous to a defeated opponent. This high-strung emperor was endowed with lively intellectual curiosity and a capacious mind. He is credited with several inventions, chiefly in connection with the improvement of artillery. Although he stubbornly refused to learn to read or write, he was fond of literature and metaphysical speculation and collected a huge library. A gifted musician, he not only acquired skill as a performer (especially on a type of kettle drum) but also became versed in the highly intricate theory of Hindu vocalization. The promotion of art and architecture was another of his ardent pursuits.

Abkar's personality and his cultural interests

The Mogul rulers did not lack heirs, but each reign usually ended with princes revolting against their father and joining in fratricidal strife with one another. Nevertheless, the administrative system and policies of Akbar were retained substantially for half a century after his death. The most renowned of his successors was Shah Jahan, whose reign extended from 1627 to 1658. Shah Jahan devoted much of his resources to the erection of costly buildings to gratify a sumptuous but exquisite taste. He established his chief royal residence at

Shah Jahan

Top: *Mumtaz Mahal ("Ornament of the Palace")*. The favorite wife of Shah Jahan, who died in childbirth in 1631 at the age of 39. Bottom: *Shah Jahan (1627–1658)*. The Mogul emperor was famous for his luxurious court and his magnificent buildings.

The Sikhs

Delhi, where he laid out a new city and named it after himself. Both Delhi and Agra in the seventeenth century were among the world's greatest cities in respect to number of inhabitants and impressive public buildings. Agra, with a population of 600,000, was divided into separate sections for the different types of merchants and artisans and contained 70 great mosques and 800 public baths. The new Delhi was protected by walls rising 60 feet above the river. Here was constructed a huge royal palace that beggars description. It housed the famous Peacock Throne, inlaid with precious metals and jewels, the value of which has been estimated as in excess of $5,000,000. His extravagant tastes and luxurious court, coupled with fruitless military expeditions against Persia and into Central Asia, so depleted the royal treasury that the emperor raised the land tax to one-half of the annual crop value, putting a crushing burden upon the poorer peasants. Shah Jahan's most celebrated monument is the Taj Mahal, located at Agra and designed as a mausoleum and memorial to his favorite wife (who died while bearing her fourteenth child to the emperor). The Taj engaged the labor of 20,000 workmen and was some twenty years in construction. The building is a unique blend of Persian and Indian architectural elements, executed with meticulous craftsmanship. Its charm is enhanced by its setting, amid shaded walks, lakes, and gardens.

Before the Moguls had completed their cycle of power, they were confronted with a hostile Hindu confederacy known as the Marathas, located in the hilly region of the western Deccan. The Maratha tribesmen, reputedly of the lowest (*sudra*) caste, were a sturdy people who, under the leadership of their wily and resourceful king Sivaji, became a scourge to the Moguls' supremacy. Masters of guerrilla tactics, the Marathas could not be crushed, even though their strongholds were taken and the "Mountain Rat" was himself held captive for a time. The confederacy became a state within the state, collecting taxes and governing a large section of the Deccan, apparently with greater satisfaction to the inhabitants than under the Mogul administration.

Another native faction which acquired an undying hatred for the Moguls was the Sikhs of the Punjab. In origin the Sikhs were a religious group with progressive and idealist convictions. The sect had been founded in the fifteenth century by Nanak, a philanthropic and spiritually minded preacher whose teachings and influence have been the subject of conflicting interpretation. Recent scholars question the claim of some admirers that Nanak sought to establish a common bond between Hindus and Muslims by combining the best elements of each of the two faiths. Undoubtedly he drew much of his inspiration from contemporary Hindu beliefs and traditions, but he was a genuinely original thinker. The essence of his teaching was the brotherhood of man, the oneness of God, and the duty of acts of charity:

The Taj Mahal at Agra. Built by Shah Jahan in memory of Mumtaz Mahal, it is considered one of the finest examples of Indian Muslim architecture.

Make love thy mosque; sincerity thy prayer-carpet; justice thy Koran;
Modesty thy circumcision; courtesy thy Kaaba; truth thy Guru; charity thy
  creed and prayer;
The will of God thy rosary, and God will preserve thine honor, O Nanak.[1]

Nanak rejected formal scriptures and mechanical rites, and because he repudiated caste he gained many adherents from among the depressed classes of Hindus. Although his religion contained doctrines common to Islam and Hinduism (and Christianity), the Sikhs ("disciples") became a distinctive community rather than a branch of Hinduism. Akbar had treated the Sikhs kindly and made a grant of land to their Guru (spiritual teacher), but the hostility of later Moguls goaded them to fury. The sect which had begun as a peaceful reformist movement was gradually transformed into a military order. Its members were initiated by a rite called "Baptism of the Sword," and many of them adopted the surname Singh, meaning "Lion." While they retained an antipathy toward caste and subscribed to a strict code of personal discipline, they lost much of the generous idealism of their early leaders. Appearing sometimes as no better than brigands, they showed particular relish for slaughtering Muslims. Thus at the opening of the eighteenth century the Mogul power was menaced not only by the usual court intrigues but also by the spirited defiance of powerful Indian groups—Rajputs, Marathas, and Sikhs.

The evolution of the sect

The long and calamitous reign of Shah Jahan's son Aurangzeb (1658–1707) pushed the empire to its farthest territorial limits but drained it of much of its strength. A man of tremendous energy, sobriety, and fanatical piety, Aurangzeb sacrificed almost every prin-

Aurangzeb

[1] Quoted in H. G. Rawlinson, *India, a Short Cultural History,* p. 378.

ciple of prudent statesmanship in a futile attempt to establish religious conformity and orthodoxy. He demolished Hindu temples and revived the hated poll tax on non-Muslims which Akbar had wisely rescinded. He waged wars not only against Hindu princes but also against heretical Muslim states in the Deccan. Although he devoted some 25 years to military campaigns and won many victories, he created enemies faster than he could subdue them and he left the Marathas—whom he had tried to destroy—more firmly united than ever.

The Persian invasion

One further catastrophe robbed the Mogul Dynasty of most of its remaining vitality, although the Moguls were accorded the formal dignity of ruling sovereigns until long after the British had entrenched themselves in India. In 1739 a usurper to the throne of Persia, Nadir Shah, invaded India and sacked Delhi with terrific carnage. He carried off an enormous quantity of booty, including the Peacock Throne, and left much of the city in ruins.

Mogul architecture

The Mogul period in India was one of considerable activity in intellectual and artistic fields. The emperors were generally cosmopolitan in outlook and welcomed both commercial and cultural intercourse with foreign states. A fusion of Indian, Turkish, Arabic, and Persian elements took place as manifested in literature, the arts, and the general tone of society. As might be expected, architecture illustrates most perfectly the interaction of Hindu and Islamic motifs. Muslim builders introduced the minaret or spire, the pointed arch, and the bulbous dome; Hindu and Jain traditions emphasized horizontal lines and elaborate ornamentation. Because Indian stonemasons and architects were frequently employed even on Muslim religious edifices, there was bound to be a fruitful interchange of ideas, and this culminated in the sixteenth and seventeenth centuries in the production of a distinctive Indo-Muslim architectural style. Some of Akbar's constructions at Agra, of durable red sandstone, are still standing; and so is most of an entire city which he conceived and had completed at a

The Great Mosque in Lahore, Pakistan. Built under the Mogul emperor Aurangzeb, this mosque of red sandstone with marble-covered domes shows Persian influence.

Akbar Inspecting the Progress of the Building of Fatehpur Sikri in 1584. This new city, only 26 miles from Agra, was built in honor of a Sufi saint whose promise of a male heir for Akbar had come to fruition. Described by a contemporary English traveler as larger than London, Fatehpur Sikri was abandoned five years after its completion, possibly due to the failure of its water supply.

site a few miles west of Agra and then abandoned only five years later. But Akbar's forts and government halls lacked the choice materials, the refinement, and the sensuous beauty of the buildings executed for Shah Jahan a half-century later. In place of sandstone, these employed the finest marbles, agate, turquoise, and other semiprecious stones, and were frequently decorated with inlays of gold and silver. Shah Jahan's dazzling structures, contrasting markedly with the robustness of Akbar's work, betray an excessive elegance bordering on decadence.

The Islamic taboos against pictorial representation were almost totally disregarded by the Mogul rulers, who were enthusiastic collectors and connoisseurs of painting. Reflecting the influence of contemporary Persian art, the most typical examples of painting were miniatures, including landscapes and especially portraits, executed with realism and meticulous detail. Calligraphy also enjoyed the status of a fine art, and many manuscripts were illuminated with pictures as in medieval Europe. Texts from the Koran were employed as decorative devices on screens and the façades of buildings, in keeping with a general practice in Muslim countries.

Painting and calligraphy

Probably the most significant expression of Indian creative talent during the Mogul period was literature, which was stimulated by royal patronage and also by the fact that several languages could be drawn upon. Both Turkish and Persian were spoken in court circles; familiarity with Arabic, the language of the Koran, was a necessity for educated Muslims, and a knowledge of the native dialects of northern India was essential for administrators. A permanent result of the intermingling between Turko-Persian and Indian cultures was the rise of

Languages and the foundations of literature

a variety of speech known as Urdu ("the camp language"). While Urdu in its vocabulary includes many Persian and Arabic words and is written in Arabic script, its grammatical structure is basically the same as that of Hindi, the most prevalent Aryan vernacular of northern India. Both Urdu and Hindi came to be standard mediums of communication throughout northern India. (Urdu is now confined chiefly to Pakistan.)

Hindu literature

While the Mogul rulers fostered a cosmopolitan atmosphere at court, attracting thither many Persian scholars and poets, the literary works of most enduring value were produced by Hindus, especially during the tolerant regime of Akbar. This emperor showed great interest in India's literary treasures as well as in her art and music, and he had Persian translations made from the *Vedas* and the Epics. Tulsi Das, one of India's greatest poets, lived during Akbar's reign. His principal work was an idealized and highly spiritual version of the ancient epic, the *Ramayana*. This poem, which combines fine craftsmanship with a warm and fervent moral earnestness, was written in the vernacular tongue rather than in Sanskrit, although its author was a Brahman.

Cultural decline

The reigns of Akbar's later successors, so disastrous to the political fortunes of the Mogul state, were also marked by social unrest and cultural decline. The fanatical Aurangzeb frowned upon art as idolatrous and discouraged literature on the ground that it exalted human vanity. He banished music from his court and, in his extreme mania for orthodoxy, even replaced the Persian solar calendar with the clumsier lunar calendar because the latter had been used by Muhammad. Mogul culture at its best, however, had always been largely a phenomenon of the court and nobility, with few roots among the mass of the populace. Consequently its decline, which was rapid in the eighteenth century, had little effect upon the great body of Hindu society. In many parts of India skillful craftsmanship and exacting artistic standards were carried on much as they had been before the Muslim invasions. Particularly notable was the so-called Rajput school of painting, which was fostered at the courts of native princes in Rajputana and which was more vigorous and less sensuous than the Mogul school.

The coming of Europeans

One aspect of the Mogul period which was bound to have tremendous consequences for the future was the coming of Europeans to India. Although the trading settlements which they established at various points on the coast were small and seemingly insignificant, they denoted the awakening of Europeans to the commercial possibilities of the Far East. The maritime enterprise so highly developed by the Indian states in earlier times had fallen into decay; and even the Mogul empire, for all its splendor, did not long maintain an effective navy. The rise of powerful western European states ended the control of Eastern waters by Arab navigators and brought direct pressure to bear on Indian territory.

Portuguese Goa. A map from Pedro Barreto de Resende's revised edition of Antinio Bocarto's *Curo do Estado da India Oriental,* 1646. Wrested from the Deccan state of Bijapur in 1510, Goa remained under Portuguese control for 451 years.

In the early sixteenth century the Portuguese acquired and fortified several ports on the Indian coast and in Ceylon. Although they lost most of these to more powerful European rivals, they managed to retain Goa, Damão, and Diu until forcibly dispossessed by the government of independent India in December 1961. More significant for the future was the activity of the British East India Company, which was chartered in 1600 and a few years later acquired a port at Surat, north of Bombay on the western coast. This was the fruit of patient negotiation carried on with officials of the Mogul emperor, for whose power the British agents necessarily felt a healthy respect. The Moguls were reluctant to offend the Portuguese as long as the latter commanded the sea routes which Muslim pilgrims used in traveling to Mecca; consequently, only minor concessions were granted to the English in the beginning. William Hawkins, a swashbuckling adventurer, and the more sedate Sir Thomas Roe served successively as English representatives at the court of the Mogul Jahangir, and each wrote a lively account of this eccentric and self-indulgent emperor, who showered hospitality upon his foreign visitors but shrewdly avoided committing himself to a formal treaty. Sir Thomas Roe, while resolutely upholding the dignity of his station before the Mogul courtiers, at the same time warned his own countrymen not to repeat the Portuguese policy of seizing territory and attempting to found

The Portuguese and British footholds

colonies in India. The English, he urged, should seek profit "at sea and in quiet trade," remembering that "war and traffic are incompatible." This advice was little heeded in the subsequent history of the East India Company. Before the close of the seventeenth century the company had secured three locations, of strategic as well as commercial importance, in widely separated regions of India: the island of Bombay off the western coast (given by Portugal in 1661 when the English king, Charles II, married a Portuguese princess), Madras on the soueastern coast, and Fort William (Calcutta) at the mouth of the Ganges.

2. CHINA UNDER THE MANCHU (CH'ING) DYNASTY

*Establishment of Manchu
rule*

With the disintegration of the Ming Dynasty it was China's fate to succumb, for the second time in her history, to conquest by a foreign invader. By the early seventeenth century a strong military organization had been formed in the Amur River region by the Manchus, kinsmen of the Juchên who had divided China with the Sung emperors 500 years before. Taking advantage of China's weakness and factional strife, the Manchu forces pushed southward through Manchuria and occupied Peking in 1644. A few years previously their chieftain had exchanged his tribal title of khan for that of emperor and assumed a Chinese dynastic name—Ch'ing, meaning "Clear" or "Pure." While the Manchu (or Ch'ing) Dynasty, which lasted until the revolution of 1911, is dated from 1644, it was not firmly established until considerably later. Northern China was occupied with little opposition, but many campaigns were required to subdue the stubbornly resisting southern Chinese. Near the end of the seventeenth century a rebellion led by Chinese generals was so nearly successful that it threatened to detach southern China from Manchu rule entirely, but it was finally crushed in 1681 by the young Manchu emperor. Not until 1683 was the last anti-Manchu regime overthrown in Formosa (Taiwan), which was then incorporated into the Chinese empire. The Manchu rulers took steps to make revolt more difficult in the future. They strengthened the control of the central government at Peking over the provinces and distributed the authority in each province among several officials so that each could exercise a check upon the others. Also they won the support of the influential gentry of the Yangtze valley by promising them security in their land holdings. Instead of uprooting Chinese political institutions, the Manchu conquerors adapted them to the requirements of a uniform and centralized administrative system and laid the foundations for a long period of internal peace.

*The dimensions of the
Manchu empire*

From the material standpoint the Manchu Dynasty, which proved to be the last of China's imperial ruling houses, was one of the most successful of all. The state was larger than at any other time in its history except for the brief period in the thirteenth century when

China was part of the pan-Asian Mongol empire. It included Manchuria, Mongolia, Sinkiang, and Formosa, while Tibet was a protectorate, and Korea, Burma, Nepal, and parts of Indochina were tributary dependencies. The government was also remarkably efficient during the first century and a half of the dynasty's history, partly because most of this period was covered by the reigns of two very able and long-lived emperors. One, who while still a youth had broken the rebellion in south China and whose role period is called K'ang Hsi, reigned for sixty-one years (1661–1722). He was therefore a contemporary of King Louis XIV of France, but he was far more of a statesman than the celebrated "Sun King." Under his grandson, who ruled for another sixty years (1736–1796, known as Ch'ien Lung), the dynasty reached the climax of its prestige and effectiveness. Thus, while Europe was in a condition of turbulence and shaken by the wars of rival despots, China enjoyed the advantages of unity and peace under a government which was stable if not entirely benevolent. That Chinese society was generally prosperous is indicated by a phenomenally rapid growth in population under the Manchus. But while China in the eighteenth century was one of the best-governed and most civilized states in the world, its society was highly inequitable and, under a double standard of morals, women were more oppressed than ever before. While prostitution and concubinage flourished, widows were expected to remain in permanent mourning or even prove their fidelity to a departed husband by committing suicide. The cruel and crippling custom of female foot-binding, which was supposed to make a woman more attractive to a man and effectively ensure her remaining dependent upon him, grew in popularity in spite of the efforts of several emperors to stamp it out. Not until the twentieth century was the practice of foot-binding completely abandoned.

Ch'ien Lung (1736–1796). The great Manchu emperor under whom the Ch'ing Dynasty reached its climax. (Painting on silk by a nineteenth-century artist.)

Manchu administrative policies

Obviously, the Manchu Dynasty was by no means a repetition of the Mongol, even though it was founded by northern invaders of nomadic origin. From the outset the Manchu emperors attempted to identify themselves with the culture and institutions of their Chinese subjects and to rule in accordance with accepted traditions. As a safeguard against rebellion they stationed garrisons in various parts of the country, composed of Chinese and Mongol troops as well as Manchu. They required Chinese men to braid their hair in a queue after the Manchu fashion and to adopt the Manchu style of dress as a token of submission. At the same time they preserved the ancient administrative framework, continued the civil-service examinations, and exalted the state cult of Confucius by requiring temples to be maintained in every district and by elevating the spirit of the ancient sage to the highest rank of official deities. In appointments to office the Manchus showed partiality to their own national group, but nothing like the extreme discrimination which had characterized the Mongol rule. More than 80 percent of the lower governmental offices were filled by Chinese. The top administrative posts were divided about equally between Manchus and Chinese, with half of the Chinese quota going to northerners and half to southerners. Unfortunately, this seemingly equitable arrangement was somewhat unfair to southern China because this region was the more heavily populated.

Problems of population growth

The substantial material progress that took place during the Manchu period was not an unmixed benefit to the entire nation. Nothing equivalent to an industrial revolution occurred, but there were sufficient social and economic changes to create serious problems for the future. While Chinese society remained basically unaltered in organization and structure between the tenth and the nineteenth centuries, it experienced a great increase in numbers. From time to time the imperial government had taken a census of the population, and the returns—though probably incomplete and inaccurate—indicate an upward trend, especially during the period of Manchu rule. By the early twelfth century, under the Sung, the number of Chinese people had grown to about 100 million. Following the Mongol conquest there was an appreciable decline, but this was only temporary. During the first two centuries of the Manchu Dynasty the population seems to have increased nearly fourfold. It is estimated that by the middle of the nineteenth century the empire included approximately 400 million inhabitants. The causes of this rapid growth are not entirely clear, but it is certain that before the end of the Manchu Dynasty, China was feeling acute distress from the pressure of population upon food supply. The lack of sufficient arable land to support such large numbers led to the clearing and cropping of areas in the upper river valleys which had hitherto been left to nature. Soil erosion subsequently increased the danger of floods and droughts, thus aggravating China's agrarian problem in the modern era.

Sectional differences

Although the Chinese were basically one people in their fundamental institutions and cultural heritage, significant sectional differences, which augured trouble for the Manchu regime, had developed between the northern and the southern portions of the country. The sectional contrasts were largely the result of geographic and climatic differences between north and south, but they were intensified by historic factors. The Yangtze valley and the southeastern coastal region were by far the most productive agricultural areas and also contained the largest cities which had long been centers of international commerce. The inhabitants of these areas were characterized by a breadth and diversity of interests and frequently by an independence of spirit which stemmed not so much from an extreme individualism as from a strong sense of family solidarity. Southern Chinese resented the fact that they paid the greater share of taxation, and yet the government seemed to spend most of its money for the benefit of the Peking region. They also felt that they were discriminated against in the competitive examinations, so that the leadership they might have supplied was denied adequate recognition. In spite of their efforts toward conciliation, the Manchu emperors were never able to repose complete confidence in the loyalty of the southern Chinese, and the revolution which finally overthrew the dynasty had its origin in the south.

Not the least among the problems with which the Manchu regime ultimately had to contend was that caused by the penetration of Europeans into the Far East, although as long as the dynasty remained vigorous it experienced little difficulty in holding the foreigners within bounds. The overseas expansion of the Western nations during the Commercial Revolution affected China as well as India and other Eastern lands. By the early sixteenth century the Portuguese had occupied Malacca, and one of their trading vessels reached Canton in 1516. The Chinese authorities, long accustomed to peaceful commercial intercourse with Arabs and other foreigners, at first had been disposed to grant the normal privileges to the newcomers. Portuguese adventurers, however, pillaged Chinese ships engaged in trade with the Indies and raided coastal cities, looting and massacring the inhabitants. Such actions convinced the Chinese that Europeans were no better than pirates; nor was their opinion favorably revised with the arrival, a little later, of the Dutch and the English. The wanton depredations perpetrated by these early Western seafarers were responsible for the unflattering name which the Chinese came to apply to Europeans—"Ocean Devils." The government finally determined to exclude Europeans from the coastal cities but allowed the Portuguese to maintain a trading center and settlement at Macao in the far south. Established in 1557, this post has been retained by the Portuguese to the present day. As a security measure, the local officials constructed a wall blocking off the Portuguese settlement on the island of Macao and imposed rigid restrictions upon the activities of the foreigners. The trade was too profitable for the Chinese to want to abolish it altogether, and the Portuguese were soon extended the privilege of docking at Canton at prescribed times and under strict supervision.

Father Adam Schall with His Astronomical Instruments. Director of the Imperial Board of Astronomy, he wears the "mandarin square" of a Manchu civilian official.

Thus, before the Manchu conquest of China, precedents had already been set for dealing with Western traders. When the Manchus attacked the Ming empire, the Portuguese assisted the Ming court, supplying artillery and some military personnel. This intervention was a portent of things to come, suggesting the ominous possibilities of European interference in Chinese affairs; but its immediate effect was to implant in the Manchu rulers a prejudice against the meddling "Ocean Devils" at the very time when the new regime was being inaugurated. Nevertheless, as the Manchu emperors succeeded in strengthening their position, they were willing to allow European trade to continue, though restricting it chiefly to Canton. Meanwhile, the suspicion attaching to Europeans had been partially dispelled through contacts with Christian missionaries, especially the Jesuits, who had been active in the Far East since the sixteenth century. Many of these Catholic missionaries impressed the Chinese with their breadth of scholarship, their respect for Chinese culture, and their sincere interest in the people among whom they had come to work.

Father Matteo Ricci of Macerata, the First Jesuit Missionary to Work in China, and His Chief Convert, Hsü Kuang-ch'i Pao-lu of Shanghai

*Encroachments of the
Russians*

Cultural conservatism

Vitality in philosophy

Consequently they were permitted to win converts to Christianity and were welcomed into intellectual circles. The early Manchu emperors were generally cordial to Christian missionaries, particularly the French Jesuits, whom they employed at court in such various capacities as instructors in science, mathematics, and cartography.

While the maritime expansion of Western nations was bringing Portuguese, Spanish, French, and others into the Far East, China came into more direct contact with another European power as Russia extended the frontier of her empire overland toward the Pacific. By the latter seventeenth century the Russians were encroaching on the Manchurian border. The success of the Manchus in meeting this threat from the north illustrates the strength of the state at this time, in decided contrast to the weakness which it exhibited before the great Western powers a century and a half later. In 1689 a treaty negotiated with Russian officials defined the boundary between the two countries, provided for a limited commercial intercourse, and arranged for the reciprocal extradition of criminals. This treaty (and subsequent ones negotiated during the eighteenth century) in no way impaired the sovereignty or prestige of China. Her day of humiliation under the impact of Western imperialism was yet to come.

In cultural fields the Manchu period was one of abundant productivity but little originality. It is probably correct to say that the overall trend was toward sterility or even decadence. Chinese culture was still of high level and even brilliant, but it was largely an echo of the genius of earlier centuries. This does not mean that the Chinese had deteriorated in vitality or innate capacity. The decline was partly due to the rigidity of their social institutions and to the fact that they had developed an extreme veneration for ancient authorities, which fostered an attitude of stiff conservatism. More directly it was the result of the government's policy of encouraging docility among the people and frowning upon all innovation. Under the Manchu emperors more than under any native Chinese dynasty the accumulated dogmas of orthodox Confucianism (the Neo-Confucianism of Chu Hsi) were upheld inflexibly and perpetuated in the civil-service examinations through which officials were recruited. Inevitably, as the bureaucracy grew ever more conventional and inelastic in its thinking, it was ill prepared to cope with new problems as they arose. The exalting of orthodoxy above every other virtue led slowly but surely to a state of intellectual stagnation.

Examples can be found, however, of vigorous and independent thinkers among the Chinese of this period, even in the field of philosophy. Valuable contributions were made by a school of critical scholars who pioneered in the objective and scientific study of ancient classics. The prime objective of this school was to purge Chinese philosophy of the Buddhist and Taoist influences which had encrusted it during the Sung period. Hence, in spite of their perceptiveness and their defiance of conventions, the "Han Learning" scholars were attempting to rehabilitate the distant past rather than to deal directly with the needs of the present. While they were unable to dislodge the narrow conservatism that prevailed in high quarters, the movement was not devoid of results. That such was the case is indicated by the decline of Buddhism as an intellectual force in China even though it remained a popular religion.

If freshness and originality were lacking in most fields of expression, a notable exception was provided by the novel, which continued to be a successful literary medium and reached an even higher state of excellence than it had under the Ming. The best Chinese novels of this period readily bear comparison with significant prose works of other nations, Eastern or Western. As under the Ming, the novel was sometimes a vehicle for satire or trenchant criticism of governmental policies. One early nineteenth-century novel embodied an attack upon the subjection of women and advocated sweeping social and educational reforms.

During the early Manchu period Chinese culture—retrogressive as it may have been—created a more distinct impression upon the civilized nations of the West than had ever been true before. In the eighteenth century especially, Chinese-style gardens, pagodas, and pavilions became fashionable among the wealthy classes of western Europe. Other items borrowed from China included sedan chairs, lacquer, and incense, while the craze for Chinese porcelain reached such proportions that it had the unfortunate effect of lowering the quality of the product. In addition, largely through translations and commentaries prepared by the Jesuits, European intellectuals were introduced to Chinese thought and literature. European acquaintance with these subjects was, of course, limited and superficial, but it was sufficient to arouse curiosity and admiration. Spokesmen of the Enlightenment upheld the somewhat mythical "Chinese sage" as an example of how man could be guided by reason, and fragments of Confucian texts were cited in support of deism.

The Manchu rulers had demonstrated their ability to adapt themselves to the institutions and traditions of their subjects. At the same time, they proved their inability to escape the enfeebling influences that tended to undermine every successful Chinese dynasty. By the nineteenth century their leadership had degenerated seriously, control was slipping into the hands of palace eunuchs, and the court was becoming the scene of soft living and intrigue. As the rulers grew less effectual, they were inclined to compensate for their own deficiencies by appearing more stern and arrogant than their predecessors. Occasionally they instigated persecution of the Christians, and they displayed a haughty and overbearing attitude toward the few European delegations which sought an audience with the emperor. Meanwhile, domestic discontent was manifest in rebellions—both incipient and overt—in various parts of China. Secret societies, hostile to the Manchu government, were organized. The dynasty was probably doomed

Originality in the novel

Chinese Porcelain. Decorated with "famille verte," a vivid green enamel typical of the K'ang Hsi period (1661–1722).

The seeds of decline

even before friction with the Western powers later in the nineteenth century created new and distressing problems.

3. JAPAN UNDER THE TOKUGAWA SHOGUNATE

The end of feudalism

The most turbulent period of Japanese feudalism was ended rather abruptly at the close of the sixteenth century when a series of military campaigns forced the daimyo (great lords) to acknowledge the authority of a single ruler. The rise of the daimyo[2] had led to the establishment of fairly effective government within their individual domains, some of which were large enough to include several of the ancient provinces. Hence, when the great lords were brought under a common central authority, the way was open for a genuine unification of the country, and Japan entered upon an era of comparative peace and stability extending to the threshold of modern times.

Nobunaga

The establishment of a stable central government after the ravages of 100 years of feudal warfare was achieved in the space of one generation by three military heroes whose careers were marked with bloodshed, treachery, and pitiless cruelty, but whose work endured. Nobunaga, a small provincial lord who dared to challenge the great daimyo fought his way to control of the imperial city of Kyoto, where he rebuilt palaces and took the Shogun under his protection. When this official proved troublesome, Nobunaga expelled him, thus ending the Ashikaga Shogunate (1573). He moved swiftly to break the power of the great Buddhist monasteries, storming their strongholds and massacring thousands of monks, women, and children. Before his death in battle (1582) he had conquered about half of Japan's provinces.

Hideyoshi

The work of consolidation was carried forward by Nobunaga's ablest general, Hideyoshi, who is commonly regarded as the greatest man in Japanese history. Hideyoshi was a brilliant commander, highly intelligent, and usually sound in judgment, but his fame rests equally on the fact that he is the only figure in Japan's history to rise from the lowest rank (he was a peasant's son) to ruler of the nation. By 1590 he had broken all resistance in Japan and nourished still larger ambitions. He sent an army into Korea, insulted envoys from the Ming imperial court, and launched a second ill-fated expedition with the avowed intention of conquering China.

Tokugawa Ieyasu

The third member of the triumvirate of heroes was Tokugawa Ieyasu. Once a vassal of Nobunaga, he had become the most powerful of the daimyo by the time of Hideyoshi's death in 1598. Following a decisive military victory over rebellious rivals, Ieyasu had himself appointed Shogun in 1603 (the title had been in abeyance for thirty years) and took steps to ensure that this office would remain hence-

[2]See above, p. 541.

forth in his family, the Tokugawa. Reaping the fruits of the labors of his two predecessors, Tokugawa Ieyasu made the Shogunate a much more efficient instrument of government than it had ever been before.

Under the Tokugawa Shogunate (1603–1867), Japan's feudal institutions remained intact, but they were systematized and made to serve the interests of a strong central government. Ieyasu founded his capital at Edo (now Tokyo), where he built a great castle surrounded with moats and an elaborate series of outer defenses. The great domains of central and eastern Japan were held by members of the Tokugawa or by men who had helped Ieyasu in his campaigns. These trusted supporters of the regime were known as "hereditary daimyo," while the lords who had acknowledged Ieyasu's supremacy only when forced to do so were called "outer daimyo." The members of both groups were hereditary vassals of the Shogun and were kept under careful surveillance lest they should try to assert their independence. The Shogun employed a corps of secret police to report any signs of disaffection throughout the country. As a special precaution he required all daimyo to maintain residences in Edo and reside there every other year, and also to leave their wives and children as hostages when they returned to their own estates. The system Ieyasu devised was so well organized and thorough that it did not depend on the personal ability of the Shogun for its operation. For the first time Japan had a durable political framework, which remained undisturbed in the hands of the

Centralization of authority

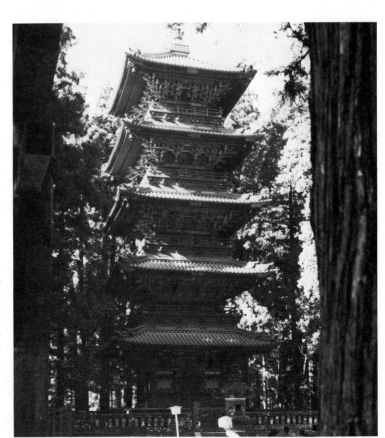

Five-storied Pagoda at Nikko, in Central Japan. It was built in 1636 and dedicated to Tokugawa Ieyasu, founder of the Tokugawa Shogunate. The structure (about 100 feet high) is ornately carved, painted, and lacquered, but is given a magnificent natural setting by the surrounding forest.

Tokugawa for two and a half centuries. While the Shogunate was essentially a feudal power structure, it developed for administrative purposes a large bureaucracy of carefully recruited and competent officials.

*Persistence of dual
government*

It should be noted that the Japanese government was still dual in form. The imperial family and a decorative court nobility continued to reside at Kyoto, while the real power was lodged in the Bakufu, the military hierarchy headed by the Shogun at Edo. The Tokugawa Shoguns cultivated the fiction that they were carrying out the will of a divine emperor. By emphasizing the emperor's sanctity they added an aura of invulnerability to their own position, and by keeping him in seclusion they rendered him harmless. The shadow government at Kyoto was now entirely dependent upon the Shogun even for its financial support, but it was carefully and respectfully preserved as a link with Japan's hallowed past.

Relations with Europeans

The most serious problem of the early Tokugawa period concerned relations with Europeans. Before the close of the sixteenth century both the Portuguese and the Spanish were carrying on considerable trade in Japan, and the Dutch and the British secured trading posts early in the following century. Europeans had been accorded a favorable reception by the Japanese, who seemed eager to learn from them. Firearms, acquired from the Portuguese, came into use for the first time in Japan and played a part in the feudal battles of the late sixteenth century. The introduction of gunpowder had the effect temporarily of stimulating the construction of heavy stone castles by the daimyo, a practice which was carefully regulated by the Tokugawa after they had seized the Shogunate.

*The growth and
suppression of Christianity*

Along with the Western traders came missionaries, who at first encountered little hostility. Vigorous proselyting by Portuguese Jesuits and Spanish Franciscans met with remarkable success in winning converts to the Catholic faith among all classes of the population, including some of the feudal nobles. By the early seventeenth century there were close to 300,000 Christian converts in Japan, chiefly in the south and west where the European trading centers were located. Eventually, however, the Shoguns decided that Christianity should be proscribed, not because they objected to the religion as such but because they were afraid it would divide the country and weaken their authority. They were annoyed by the bickering between rival European groups and also feared that their subjects were being enticed into allegiance to a foreign potentate, the pope. The first persecutions were mild and were directed against Japanese Christians rather than against the Europeans; but when the missionaries refused to halt their work they were severely dealt with, and many were executed. Finally, in 1637, when a peasant revolt against oppressive taxation developed into a Christian rebellion, the Shogun's forces conducted a real war against the Christian strongholds in southwestern Japan and, in spite of the most heroic resistance, wiped out the Christian communities and exterminated the religion almost completely.

Following this bloody purge, the Shoguns adopted a policy of excluding all Europeans from Japanese settlement. That they were able to enforce it shows how strong their government had become. Reluctant to cut off Western trade entirely, they made a slight exception in the case of the Dutch, who seemed to be the least dangerous politically. The Dutch were permitted to unload one ship each year at the port of Nagasaki in the extreme western corner of Japan, but only under the strictest supervision. Going even further along the line of reaction, the Shogun next forbade his Japanese subjects to visit foreign lands on pain for forfeiting all their rights and commanded that no ship should be built large enough to travel beyond the coastal waters of the island empire. Although traffic with China was continued, the Shoguns forced upon their country a policy of almost complete isolationism, thus reversing the course which had been followed advantageously during many centuries preceding.

The expulsion of Europeans and the adoption of isolationism

The Tokugawa era gave Japan a long period of peace and orderly government and promoted the ideal of a perpetually hierarchical society. Theoretically, the social structure was arranged in accordance with the classes of China, which ranked, in order of importance: (1) scholar-officials, (2) farmers, (3) artisans, (4) merchants, and (5) soldiers, bandits, and beggars. In Japan, however, the realities of a feudalized society produced a peculiar distortion of the ideal arrangement, which was somewhat fanciful even in China. The warrior (*samurai*), who had enjoyed a position of leadership for centuries, was elevated from the lowest category to the highest. In return for the place of honor assigned to him he was expected to exhibit the qualities of the scholar also, and to a considerable extent he did. The daimyo and the samurai were no longer the uncouth, lawless ruffians of early feudal days but refined aristocrats, who cultivated literature and the arts and took pride in the rigorous discipline to which they were bred. Still, their pre-eminence had been won in the first instance by force, and their position was regarded as a hereditary right, not to be challenged by men of superior ability who had been born to a lower class.

A hierarchical society; exaltation of the warrior

The artificiality and formal rigidity of the Tokugawa regime did not stifle economic progress. By the early eighteenth century Japan's population had reached a total of 30 million; thenceforth it increased but slightly for a century and a half. This slow rate of population growth apparently was more the result of voluntary family planning than of a scarcity of resources, although occasional famines did occur. The country as a whole was prosperous; industry and internal trade continually expanded even though foreign commerce had been curtailed. Communication was relatively easy through all parts of Japan, both by waterways and by improved highways. A brisk exchange of agricultural and manufactured goods promoted the growth of a capitalist economy. Rice merchants occupied a strategic position in the world of finance and their establishments, offering commercial credit and daily price quotations, bore some resemblance to a modern stock exchange. Cities grew in size, especially in the central area of the

Prosperity and stability

*Japanese Bronze, Eighteenth
Century.* The figure depicted is
Kuan Ti, Chinese "God of
War"—actually a deified military hero of the early third century A.D. Regarded as the patron of military officials, he was
particularly revered in China
during the late Ch'ing (Manchu) period.

*Expansion of agricultural
productivity*

country. By the late eighteenth century Edo had attained a population
of one million and was probably the largest city in the world at that
time.

Economic progress, coupled with a rigid and inherently authoritarian political regime, produced severe strains within society. The position of the samurai became more and more anomalous. While they
possessed a monopoly of the profession of arms, they found little
opportunity to practice it because the Shogun discouraged feudal
quarrels, and there were no foreign wars. Thus the samurai became,
by and large, a group of respectable parasites, although many of them
displayed both talent and energy. They were often employed in
administrative functions by the daimyo, and sometimes took over the
management of a great domain so completely that the daimyo was
reduced to little more than a figurehead. On the other hand the merchants, who were ranked at the bottom of the social pyramid, steadily
accumulated wealth, formed their own trade associations to replace
the older and more restrictive guilds, and exerted a potent influence
over the whole national economy. Inevitably they imparted a bourgeois tone to society in the bustling cities.

Until recently historians commonly assumed that the peasants' lot
under the Tokugawa was a miserable one, but research in Japanese
sources has discredited this assumption. It is true that peasant labor
supported the upper classes of daimyo and samurai as well as the Shogun and his bureaucracy. It is also true that peasants endured privation
and sometimes cruel treatment at the hands of their social superiors,
who dismissed them contemptuously as seeds to be pressed or cattle
to be driven. The outbreak of riots and actual local rebellions—in a
society as disciplined as the Tokugawa—indicates the reality and the
depth of popular discontent. But the evidence is undeniable that Japanese farmers and tenants not only contributed to but also shared in
the country's rising prosperity. Forbidden to bear arms, they were
relieved from the burden of military service, and they benefited from
the two and a half centuries of almost uninterrupted peace that followed the accession of Tokugawa Ieyasu.

Japanese agriculture was vastly more progressive than in earlier
times. The amount of land under cultivation doubled, new crops were
introduced, intensive fertilization and better tools, including a
mechanical thresher, came into use, and irrigation was extended
through the cooperative efforts of farm villages. A steady expansion
in productivity, together with regional specialization keyed to market
demands, enabled the majority of peasants to sustain a rising standard
of living in spite of tax increases during the eighteenth century. But
while agriculture enjoyed a flourishing condition, its rewards were
not evenly distributed. A trend away from large family combinations
to smaller units that could be run more efficiently widened the spread
between prosperous and indigent peasants, and there was an increase
in tenantry as opposed to individual farm ownership. At the same

Woman Weaving Cloth

time the emergence of a mobile class of wage earners stimulated growth of village industries—processing silk, cotton, salt, tobacco, saké, and sugar cane—and provided a reserve labor force which eventually contributed to the rapid industrialization of Japan in the post-Tokugawa period.

During the Tokugawa era Japanese culture, being largely cut off from outside contacts, acquired a distinctive national character. This is not negated by the fact that intellectual circles manifested a heightened interest in Chinese philosophy. A number of Chinese scholars had fled to Japan when the Ming Dynasty was overthrown by the Manchus and, more importantly, the Shoguns encouraged study of the Confucian classics, particularly among the aristocracy, because they thought it would help to inculcate habits of discipline in their subjects. These writings, of course, had long been honored in Japan, but now they were diligently examined for the purpose of developing a native school of philosophers who, through their example and through their position as administrators, could inculcate the principles of virtue—especially obedience—among all classes of the population.

The growing interest in Chinese philosophy

The most significant social and cultural changes were those related to the growth of large cities, such as Edo, Osaka, and Kyoto, where men of wealth were creating an atmosphere of comfort and gaiety in contrast to the restrained decorum of the feudal nobility. In these populous commercial and industrial centers the trend in art and literature and especially in the field of entertainment was toward a distinctly middle-class culture, which was sometimes gaudy but appealing in its exuberance and spontaneity. In the pleasure quarters of the cities an important figure was the geisha girl, who combined the qualities of a

Life and customs in the large cities

The Art of Tile Making. A wood block by Hokusai (1760–1849), an artist famous for landscapes.

Woman Playing the Flute. The flutist is by Harunobu (1724–1770), earliest master of the multicolored-print technique.

modern beauty queen with the talents of a nightclub entertainer. Trained in the art of conversation as well as in song and dance, she provided the sparkling companionship which men too often missed in their own homes because of the habits of docility and self-effacement that they instilled into their wives and daughters. Prostitution, also, was prevalent on a large scale in the towns, in spite of attempts by the authorities to curtail the evil. Inherently sordid as was the practice, it took on a specious refinement under the patronage of the well-do-do, and some courtesans acquired an enviable standing in the loose but highly sophisticated society which flouted established conventions. Not only merchants and businessmen but even samurai and daimyo were attracted by the gay diversions of city life, and surreptitiously exchanged the boredom of their routine existence for the delights of a "floating world" of pleasure and uninhibited self-expression.

The dissolute society of the Tokugawa cities was by no means utterly degenerate. Some of the best creative talents in Japan catered to bourgeois appetites, just as they did in Italy during the Renaissance. Racy novels, satirizing contemporary figures and piquant with gossip, innuendo, and scandal, came into vogue. Previously art had been chiefly aristocratic and religious except for the exquisitely designed articles of ordinary household use produced by the various handicrafts. Now a type of folk art was appearing that mirrored society realistically and also was enlivened with humor and caricature. Its chief medium was the wood-block color print, which could be produced cheaply enough to reach a wide public and which has ever since been a popular art form. Another proof of the influence that urban tastes were exerting in the aesthetic sphere is seen in the evolution of the Kabuki drama. In contrast to the No, the highly stylized and austere dance-drama that had been perfected a few centuries earlier under the patronage of the aristocracy, the Kabuki offered entertainment appealing to the middle and lower classes of the towns. Although it owed something to traditional dance forms, the Kabuki drama was derived more immediately from the puppet theater and, unlike the No, it was almost entirely secular in spirit. As developed in the seventeenth and eighteenth centuries, the Kabuki drama attained a high degree of realism, with exciting plots, lively action, and effective stage devices. In the opinion of some theatrical experts, it deserves to rank as the greatest drama any civilization has ever produced.

Various forces at work in Japan tended to undermine the foundations of Tokugawa institutions in spite of their apparent durability. The partial transformation of Japan's economy from an agrarian to a mercantile basis enhanced the importance of men engaged in manufacture, trade, and transport. As a result feudalism was rendered obsolete, and the feudal classes began to feel the pinch of adversity. Although money had been in circulation for many centuries, the incomes of daimyo and of their samurai retainers were still computed in measures of rice, the chief agricultural staple. The merchants who provisioned such great cities as Edo and Osaka controlled the market-

Economic changes

Kabuki Theater. Left: Kabuki actor (Matsumoto Koshiro) portrayed here as a fishmonger by Sharaku, a wood-block artist noted for his caricatures of actors (1794 or 1795). Right: Famous actor Mitsugoro Bando portraying the aged warrior Ikyu in the play *Sukeroku.*

ing of a large proportion of the rice crop; hence they were able to foresee fluctuations in price and sometimes even to induce fluctuations for their own benefit. Naturally, the daimyo and samurai were at a disadvantage in a period of unstable prices, because their incomes were from land rents, and because their necessities were increasingly supplied by articles that had to be purchased in the cities. Often the price of rice was considerably below the general price level; and even when it was high, the middleman appropriated most of the profit. The landed aristocrats found their real incomes diminishing while low-born traders and brokers grew richer and richer.

The disruption of classes

Inevitably, class lines began to break down, just as they did in western Europe under similar conditions during the period of the Commercial Revolution. Wealthy Japanese merchants purchased samurai rank and title, while nobles adopted children of bourgeois families or contracted marriage alliances with this class in an effort to recoup their fortunes. Feeling honor-bound to maintain their accustomed style of living—at least in appearances—the aristocrats borrowed recklessly. As early as 1700 the indebtedness of the daimyo class was reputed to have reached a figure one hundred times greater than the total amount of money in Japan. Impoverished samurai pawned their ceremonial robes and even the swords which were their badge of rank. While townspeople in large numbers were entering the lower grades of samurai, samurai and farmers were flocking to the towns, where the more successful ones merged into the bourgeois class.

Cultural trends generate unrest

The unrest generated by economic dislocation was further augmented by cultural trends in the later Tokugawa period. As a national spirit developed, it was accompanied by a renewal of interest in Japan's past. Shintoism, the ancient cult over which the imperial family presided, had been largely eclipsed by Buddhism. Gradually its popularity revived, and several new Shinto sects obtained an enthusiastic following. The study of ancient records (historical and mythological) stimulated reflection on the unique character of Japan— "founded by a heavenly ancestry, country of the gods"—and on the alleged origins of the imperial office. It directed attention to the fact that the Shogunate was a comparatively recent innovation or actually a usurpation, not an authentic part of the ancient political structure. At the same time, familiarity with China's political heritage—fostered by the vogue of Confucian scholarship which the Shoguns themselves had promoted—raised doubts among Japanese intellectuals as to the merits of a dual administrative system and of feudal institutions. Moreover, Western books and ideas were seeping into Japan through the port of Nagasaki where the Dutch were permitted a very limited trade. Even before Japan was "opened" in the nineteenth century, considerable interest had been aroused in Western guns, ships, watches, glassware, and scientific instruments. Thus Japan's insulation from the outside world was beginning to develop cracks at the same time that internal discontent had reached a dangerous point. By the opening of the nineteenth century the Shogun's position was precarious, unlikely to withstand the shock of a severe crisis, especially since other powerful families were eagerly watching for any sign of weakness on the part of the Tokugawa.

The sweeping and revolutionary changes in Japan since the abolition of the Shogunate in 1867 have made it difficult to view the Tokugawa period with an undistorted perspective. Inward-looking, conservative, and devoted to hierarchy as it was, the Tokugawa regime went far toward unifying the nation, instilled habits of discipline, and provided a long period of security. Class structure was not so rigid as to prevent the realization of a fairly homogeneous society, especially as urban centers grew and communication improved. Education advanced significantly; by the end of the Tokugawa period about 45 percent of the male population was literate (only 15 percent of the female), a record unmatched in the rest of Asia and better than that of many countries today. Although Japan was still a predominantly agrarian society, capital techniques had been developed and applied to agriculture as well as to commerce and manufacture. Seemingly, although certainly unintentionally, the Tokugawa Shoguns had laid the foundation for Japan's transformation into a modern state.

*Contributions of the
Tokugawa period*

Recently a group of Japanese historians—disillusioned with the effects of modernization and proponents of what they call "people's history"—have depicted the Tokugawa period as a kind of golden age. They claim that it contained the seeds of a freer society and even of democracy, evidenced by the growth of village cooperatives which stimulated social initiative and active participation among the peasants. They indict the imperial restoration as a "failed vision," a regretable step toward state worship, and they argue that the Tokugawa era could have provided the base for a structure different from and better than a duplication of Western industrialized society.[3]

*An unconventional
interpretation*

4. AFRICA UNDER DIVINE RULERS AND RITUAL CHIEFS

The period 1500 to 1800 marked the beginning of Africa's incorporation into the capitalist world economy. From about 1500, western Europe transformed Africa into a satellite of its own burgeoning capitalistic system. The network of international trade established by the Arabs by the thirteenth century was seized and extended by the Europeans from the opening of the sixteenth century. This maritime contact ended Africa's long isolation from the West and brought all coasts of the continent into the European commercial orbit.

*Africa as Europe's
Economic Satellite*

[3]Carol Gluck, "The People in History: Recent Trends in Japanese Historiography," *Journal of Asian Studies,* November 1978, pp. 25–50.

*European presence on the
coast forces a reorientation
of trade*

This period also witnessed the arrival of European traders and adventurers on Africa's sub-Saharan shores. A revolution in maritime and military technology enabled Europeans to navigate beyond sight of land and to conduct an efficient ocean-borne trade with swift, well-armed ships. For West Africans this necessitated a reorientation of trade from their ancient North African markets across the Sahara to western Europe and the Americas via the Atlantic. A voluminous and highly profitable Atlantic traffic ensued with explosive force and required a concentration of territorial power in the hands of a few rulers. Instability generated by the introduction of arms trafficking and slave raiding forced weaker communities either to coalesce in self-defense or to seek the protection of larger, better organized societies in neighboring areas. First coastal kingdoms, then empires, emerged in the tall forests after the 1650s in response to increasing opportunities for trade in guns, gunpowder, and exotic luxury items.

Long-distance trading networks from coast to interior and coastwise by canoe from the Niger Delta to the Ivory Coast antedated European contact. Indeed, small, independent fishing communities had dotted the palm-studded coast at least since 1300. Fisherfolk exchanged ocean salt and dried fish with forest farmers for yams, goats, and cattle. Later, such local industries as fishing, weaving, and brewing were weakened when communities turned to the less expensive though often inferior European substitutes. Ultimately, European traders fostered economic rivalries and precipitated civil wars between African communities to prevent indigenous traders and chiefs from uniting. Such unity could inflate prices and weaken the European trade advantage. Nevertheless, on an individual basis, African traders sometimes proved superior to Europeans in the art of bargaining.

Between about 1730 and 1800 the less accessible interior states sought to extend their authority to the sea in order to trade directly with the Europeans. Seldom, however, were foreign traders permitted to operate beyond the coast. In Benin, Dahomey, and Oyo they were restricted to designated seaports and could only lease the land upon which they constructed their warehouses, fortresses, and slave markets.

Some states, like Oyo, Benin, and Asante, prospered and became territorial empires. Others, particularly Kongo, Ngola, and Mwenemutapa, failed to keep the Europeans at arm's length or to comprehend fully their true motives. Their history was punctured by foreign intrigue, political instability, and eventual collapse. Numerous African governments became so dependent on European trade that a shift in pattern spelled economic doom.

During this era, kings, claiming divine attributes, aggrandized their authority through military force. Often, neighbors were reduced to tributary status. Royal subordinates, dispatched to the conquered areas, guarded against conspiracies and assimilated the vanquished.

Folkways and authority patterns, if strong, were usually left intact, while prisoners of war and dissidents were sold into slavery in order to replenish supplies of gunpowder. Africa's human losses were America's gains in this vicious circle initiated by amoral white traffickers and facilitated by selfish black collaborators.

Like the divine emperors of Japan, the Obas of Benin, Asantehenes of Asante, Manikongos of Kongo, Alafins of Oyo, and other African monarchs shrouded themselves in mystery and appeared only on ceremonial occasions. Much of their time was devoted to state rituals and sacrifices to ancestral heroes. They evolved rigid codes of court etiquette and communicated with commoners only through intermediaries. Some wore finely crafted, oversized sandals to shield their feet from direct contact with the sacred earth. All of them fostered a hieratic art, aimed as exalting the sanctity of the state. To achieve this, guild artists were supported by the monarchy and forced to remain within the palace confines so that their talents would not pass to others.

Royal Dignitary. Bronze plaque fragment. Bini tribe, Benin.

These kings, their paramount chiefs, and lesser titled hereditary officials devised ingenious systems of checks and balances to prevent a concentration of power in any single office. In the Oyo empire (in western Nigeria) the Alafin served as hereditary secular leader. Yet his power had to be shared with a royally appointed nobility, which organized itself into a kind of electoral college and administrative watchdog called the Oyo *Mesi*. Its leading member, the *Bashorun,* acted as prime minister and as spokesman for most of the powerful national cults or religious orders. As a counterforce to the Oyo *Mesi,* the Alafin appointed trusted slaves, called *Ilari*. They were responsible for collecting tribute and overseeing local government. At the same time, every important town was headed by a hereditary mayor or *Oba*. Though the *Oba*'s authority derived from ancestral mandate and tradition, his powers were limited by the Ogboni Society. This organization of influential and prosperous townsfolk linked the masses of peasants, traders, and artisans to royal authority. Everyone in the Oyo empire, from the Alafin down to the poorest peasant, swore allegiance to the Oni of Ifé. Ifé was the founding city-state of the Oyo empire, the fount of Yoruba civilization; and the ancient office of Oni served as the supreme authority over spiritual matters. Power was therefore diffused throughout society. From at least the fifteenth to the late eighteenth century the Yoruba peoples of Oyo were well served by this unwritten constitution.

Political organization

In the 1790s, the authority and prestige of the Alafin's office, so vital to national solidarity, was severely diminished when its holder challenged the spiritual supremacy of the Oni of Ifé. The time-honored rules of the game eroded further when the *Bashorun,* or prime minister, tested his own strength against the Alafin's. Preoccupation with such power struggles weakened central authority and enabled the tributary states to secede. Civil war erupted, and in the mid-nine-

Weakening of the central authority

Yoruba civilization

Belt Mask. Ivory. Bini Tribe,
Benin.

*Afro-European relations
poisoned by the demands
of the slave trade*

teenth century the crumbling empire fell prey to European intrigue from the south and Muslim Fulani challenges from the north.

Even though the Oyo empire disintegrated, its artistic and musical traditions continued to thrive. In both Oyo and neighboring Benin, guilds of Yoruba craftsmen turned out a rich variety of sculpture in brass, bronze, ivory, and wood. Metal commemorative busts and plaques, some antedating European contact by centuries, were delicate, strikingly naturalistic, and secular in intent. Companies of professional acrobats, dancers, and musicians traveled about the countryside giving performances which were sometimes critical of government practices, royal behavior, and social convention. In many ways, their programs were like an editorial column of a modern newspaper.

Many forest states could boast of magnificent capital cities, holding sprawling palaces and temples with sunken atriums surrounded by columns. Benin city was one of the world's few urban centers to be laid out on a gridiron pattern, with broad tree-lined avenues intersecting streets at near right angles. Kumasi, the capital of Asante, was described by foreigners as Africa's garden city because of its lush flowering undergrowth set against tidy compounds with multicolored stylized facades.

It is significant that most West African forest civilizations had emerged, and in some cases reached their zenith, before European involvement. The Obaship in Benin was well established before Portuguese explorers arrived at Benin's major seaport of Gwato in 1472. Likewise, the Manikongo of Kongo ruled over an expansive domain with almost unchallenged authority before Portuguese contact a decade later. And Ifé was already recognized by the Yoruba as their major religious and cultural center.

Many African leaders received the Portuguese initially with great enthusiasm, hoping to taste the fruits of new techniques in agriculture, industry, and warfare. Before 1505 Benin and Kongo dispatched ambassadors and young intellectuals to Lisbon and the Vatican. But when America's vast resources were discovered by European explorers, it became obvious that the wealth could best be exploited by cheap labor in massive quantities. Only nearby Africa seemed to possess that necessary commodity. Thus, after about 1505, traders, missionaries, and other European visitors to Africa had different intentions from their predecessors. They came not as skilled technicians but as "advisers" who would gradually infiltrate African governments in order to better organize them for the slave trade. Thus, even though the political unification of Portugal and Spain in 1580 sacrificed African involvement to other interests, it in no way spelled an end to the Atlantic trade in humans.

Portuguese initiative in nautical science had already passed to the English, Dutch, and French—all of whom had begun to establish their own colonies of exploitation and settlement in the New World.

View of Benin City before the British Conquest. Note the gridiron street pattern.

Between 1637 and 1642 the Portuguese lost almost all their enclaves in West Africa to the Dutch. The Hollanders, unable to buy enough slaves on the West African coast, soon looked to the Ngola kingdom farther south. Only there did the Portuguese mount a successful resistance.

European rivalries for the African trade

In the course of the seventeenth century, royally chartered companies from many European states formed monopoly enterprises and constructed warehouses and strings of stone fortresses along the West African coast. In 1672 the Royal African Company received a charter from the English crown and soon became the most active buyer of West African gold and slaves. Still, fierce competition with the Dutch in arms and munitions sales to Africans quickly led to a proliferation of deadly weapons among certain forest societies. To many African chiefs, slave raiding and trading became a painful necessity. If they refused to engage in it, the Europeans would supply arms to rivals who might in turn use them to sell their people into captivity. Dahomey and the Kongo, initially opposed to the slave trade, soon found it necessary either to play the European game or face possible economic and political ruin. Benin was one of the few African states that successfully controlled slave trading. It remained an independent political entity until the British invasion of 1897.

Demoralizing effects of the slave and arms trade

A number of small states were born in the seventeenth century in

Dutch Ambassador Welcomed by King Alvaro II of the Kongo. Early in the seventeenth century the Dutch began to rival the Portuguese for control of the kingdoms near the mouth of the Congo River.

the Akan forest behind the Gold Coast. They were known to have supplied by that time more than 20 percent of Europe's gold reserves.

Asante civilization

Under the stimulus of the Royal African Company, this trade increased and led in the late seventeenth century to the rise of the Asante empire. The Akan peoples of Asante grew extremely powerful and wealthy by taxing trade passing through their territory en route to the coast. Between 1721 and 1750 Asante civilization reached its zenith. Asante artisans crafted earrings, anklets, pendants, and armbands from gold and bronze. On horizontal stip looms they wove polychromed togas of varied designs. Each pattern had a name and conveyed a symbolic meaning.

Dahomey: example of extreme centralization

The Atlantic slave trade received a great boost after 1713 when England secured the Spanish *Asiento,* or license, to supply slaves to Spanish New World possessions. In response, the Yoruba state of Oyo expanded into a territorial empire, serving as middleman in the slave trade between the Hausaland interior and the coast. Other states exhibited a similar pattern. Immediately west of Oyo appeared the highly centralized kingdom of Dahomey. Between 1724 and 1729 Dahomey swept into the coastal Aja states and assimilated them.

Unable to foster other sorts of trade with the Europeans, the Dahomeans became both suppliers and brokers in the slave trade. Oyo, fearful of this competition, diverted traffic to its own ports in 1750. To survive the consequent economic dislocation, the Dahomean government developed a state-controlled totalitarian economic and political system unparalleled in the eighteenth century. All state officials were appointed by the king, who ruled as a dictator, and a secret police was established to enforce his will. No system of checks and balances existed; only precedent and ancestral sanction guided his rule. Acting as high priest, the king dominated the major cults. He also controlled the craft guilds which produced pictorial tapestries and graceful statues to glorify royal power. A national military draft of men and women was instituted as well as a census bureau to administer it. Slave-worked plantations were established and placed under the close supervision of a minister of agriculture. Dahomey's economy was tightly regulated with central control over taxation and currency. Prices and wages, on the other hand, were set by producers' organizations. Culturally, westernization was actively discouraged by recourse to an aggressive policy of conquest and enforced assimilation into the traditional Fon way of life. Dahomey outlived the destructive effects of the slave trade and was able to safeguard its dynamic cultural institutions until French guns disrupted them in 1894.

Kongo and Ngola, in the savanna zone of West Central Africa, did not fare as well. After 1482 the Kongolese monarch, anxious to learn the secrets of European technology, assumed a Christian name and converted to Catholicism. But within two decades, Catholic missionaries had driven a wedge between the king and the nobility, who wished to follow the time-honored indigenous traditions. In 1556 rivalries among Portuguese advisers in the Kongo and Ngola dragged these two kingdoms into a destructive war against each other. Ngola won, but the real beneficiaries were European and mulatto slavers who reaped huge profits selling the war prisoners and refugees. Escalating demands for miners in Portuguese Brazil finally led to the total destruction of Kongo and Ngola (called Angola by the Portuguese) in 1665 and 1671 respectively. Their governments collapsed, although the Kongolese tradition of fine raffia cloth weaving remained vigorous. Slave trading persisted and resulted in a further moral and ethical deterioration among certain segments of the population. Successor African Lunda and Luba kingdoms arose deep in the interior, safely beyond direct Portuguese interference. Some of these highly centralized kingdoms survived into the twentieth century, but only to lose their independence to a new wave of Europeans, in search not of slaves but of copper

Portuguese involvement on the East African coast was equally destructive, even though it had little to do with the slave trade. In 1498 Vasco Da Gama rounded the Cape and sailed northward along

*Kongo and Ngola become
major sources for slaves
and fail to survive
European intrusions*

The Portuguese reaction to Swahili civilization

the Swahili coast in search of the East Indies. He was astounded to discover a series of prosperous and highly civilized city-states with strong commercial and cultural links to Arabia, the Persian Gulf, and India. But it was distressing to him that their Sultans were fervent practitioners of Islam. It is no wonder that Da Gama had battles in three of the four city-states he visited. At Milandi his reception was cordial, only because Da Gama had sacked Malindi's commercial rival, Mombasa.

Swahili city-states as Portuguese tributaries

The Portuguese were impressed by the gold and copper flowing out of Central Africa and by the extensive Indian Ocean trading network which carried the ore to distant ports. They hoped to use the Swahili city-states as a springboard to the Indies and as a source of gold for financing commercial operations in India and the Spice Islands. By 1505, after several Portuguese voyages of plunder and bombardment, the city-states were reduced to tributary status.

Fragility of Portuguese rule

The Portuguese did not intend to govern the Swahili city-states. Rather, they attempted, with only limited success, to monopolize the Indian Ocean trade through their Viceroy at Goa on the western coast of India. After troubles with Turkish pirates and pillaging Zimba tribesmen, the Portuguese in 1593 constructed a massive stone citadel, called Fort Jesus, at Mombasa, and the malleable Sultan of Malindi was appointed to govern on their behalf. In 1622 the Portuguese were driven out of Ormuz, their strategic stronghold in the Persian Gulf, by a powerful Persian fleet. The fragility of Porguguese rule soon

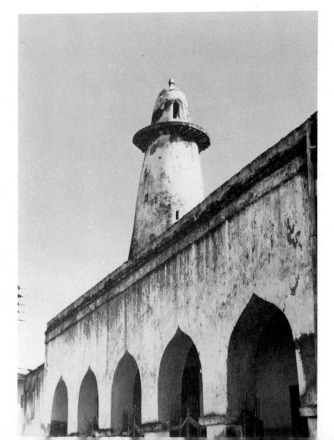

Islam in East Africa. Mombassa Mosque with minaret. Sixteenth century.

Portuguese in East Africa. Fort Jesus was built in 1593 at Mombassa by the Portuguese. It served as their major foothold in East Africa until 1728, when they were driven out under a combined Afro-Arab siege.

became evident to others. From the 1630s they had to suppress costly revolts in numerous Swahili towns. After Muscat, the gateway to the Persian Gulf, fell in 1650, the Omani Arabs emerged as a formidable naval power. In 1698 they drove the Portuguese out of Mombasa, their major port of call en route to India, and Portuguese supremacy north of Mozambique crumbled like a house of cards. In its wake lay the ruins of a once magnificent Swahili civilization. The Omani came to East Africa as liberators, but stayed on as conquerors, practicing a kind of benign neglect which led to further cultural and economic deterioration.

The Portuguese also failed in their attempts to control the gold and copper mines of the Rhodesian and Katangan plateaus. After one hundred eighty years of interference in the political and religious institutions of the Mwenemutapa empire, they were forced to retreat to the Mozambique coast. Their traders and soldiers were simply no match against the more determined and better organized Shona armies. African resistance was clearly stronger than the Portuguese will to conquer. In 1798 the Portuguese attempted to link their colony in Angola with Mozambique in the hope of forging a transcontinental African empire. But malaria and the unwillingness of the crown to administer such a vast area were responsible for its failure.

Portuguese repelled

Africans gained little from the Europeans in their first three centuries of contact. The exchange of guns, powder, alcoholic beverages, and cheap manufactured textiles for humans, gold, ivory, pepper, and palm oil stimulated the centralization of African authority in some areas and contributed to the growth of empires. But it added little to the advance of African civilizations. The south Atlantic trade system also led to the introduction into tropical Africa of new food crops from the Americas, particularly manioc, maize, bananas, cassava, and peanuts. These crops enabled certain regions of the continent to sustain much higher population densities which in turn contributed to

Europeans contribute little to the advance of African civilization

the tendency to state formation. However, disease remained an important determinant in African history. The growth of long-distance trade increased intercommunication among regions in Africa and thus facilitated the transmission of disease among population groups. On the other hand, yellow fever and malaria, so fatal to Europeans, kept white mortality rates high and discouraged extensive direct commercial penetration and colonization in all but the temperate coasts of North and South Africa. Christianity, introduced by force and often for ulterior motives, did not take firm hold. On the other hand, Islam, having suffered a severe setback in the western Sudan after the Moroccan invasion of Songhay in 1591, flourished in the Hausa city-states in northern Nigeria. After 1725 Islamic Sufi orders had begun to declare *jihads,* or holy wars, in the Senegal region and to establish theocratic states based on strict adherence to Islamic practices. Yet Islam remained an unknown factor until the nineteenth century for the vast majority of sub-Saharan Africans.

*The nature of trade with
Europe*

Unlike Japan, Africa's real economic growth was slowed by the exploitative, nonproductive nature of the European trade. Europeans exported items which could not be used in the production of other goods. In West Africa, guns and gunpowder by the eighteenth century had become the most important foreign trade commodity. Between 1796 and 1805 more than 1.6 million guns were sent to West Africa from England alone. A strong connection developed between firearms and the acquisition of slaves. The weapons were used mainly for interethnic raids and wars connected with the gathering of people for the slave markets. Wars which created many slaves for the Atlantic markets were particularly stimulated by competition among Africans for control of trade routes to the coast. Some African ethnic groups sold slaves to obtain guns to ensure their own political survival against

Reconstruction of a Kabaka's Reed in Kampala, Uganda. These structures, once common to Buganda royalty, have disappeared.

African Craftsmen. Dye pits in Kano (northern Nigeria) were and still are owned by traditional craft guilds.

internal rivals. In other words, slave exports were sometimes the result of politically motivated warfare rather than of pure economic incentive.

African contact with the Euro–American capitalist system contributed to the evolution of state formation. However, in the long run it generated political instability, bred by struggles for power and status between the old elites and the emerging military and commercial entrepreneurs. The existing bases of political and social differentiation were challenged. Greater popular involvement in warfare and in the trade in gold, slaves, and forest agricultural products enabled clever and ambitious commoners to generate independent wealth. In Asante, Oyo, Dahomey, and elsewhere the traditional royal lineages were forced to alter the hereditary political structures by incorporating ability and meritocracy into them. The rulers who failed to accommodate themselves to the changing order were faced with destructive civil wars and chronic political instability which ultimately rendered them more susceptible to European imperialist conquest in the late nineteenth century.

Political and social change

Yet, in spite of these disruptive influences, these three centuries witnessed steady artistic advancement. Royal families in the centralized states became wealthy and commissioned artisans to fashion rings, pendants, bracelets, and hairpins from gold, copper, ivory, and exotic woods. Impressive mud or reed palaces were constructed with galleries and courtyards adorned with polychromed woven, batik, or tied-and-dyed tapestries. Basic ideals of beauty were expressed through distinct symbols stamped onto cloth, molded in high relief on the façades of buildings, or shaped into fine wood or metal sculpture. Forms such as the circle, rectangle, oval, and square were brilliantly

Artistic advances

Stool with Caryatid. Wood. Luba, Congo.

translated into artistic symbols and given deep philosophical and religious meaning. And complex notions of God and the universe were expressed in the verbal symbolism of proverbs and epic poems or in the intricate designs of royal thrones, scepters, swords, and craftsmen's tools. Over the course of these three centuries, the forest civilizations, with their unlimited supplies of timber, used a wide variety of wood as the primary art medium for sculpturing. They achieved a brilliant artistic synthesis of surrealist and expressionist, abstract and naturalistic elements. The cubist tradition itself was born not in western Europe in the early twentieth century but among artistic circles in the West African forest societies centuries before. Although Europeans robbed Africans of much of their physical and human resources, they did not succeed in weakening their artistic vitality. Indeed, the trauma of European contact seemed to propel Africans toward even greater cultural achievements.

SELECTED READINGS

- *Items so designated are available in paperback editions.*
- Binyon, Laurence, *The Spirit of Man in Asian Art,* New York, 1935.
- Nakamura, Hajime, *Ways of Thinking of Eastern Peoples: India, China, Tibet, Japan,* Honolulu, 1964.

INDIA

Archer, J. C., *The Sikhs,* Princeton, 1946.
- Cole, W. O., and P. S. Sambhi, *The Sihks: Their Religious Beliefs and Practices,* Boston, 1978. Based on recent scholarship.

Garratt, G. T., ed., *The Legacy of India,* Oxford, 1937.

Ikram, Mohamad, *Muslim Civilization in India,* ed. A. T. Embree, New York, 1964.

Kabir, Humayun, *The Indian Heritage,* New York, 1955.

Moreland, W. H., and A. C. Chatterjee, *A Short History of India,* 4th ed., London, 1957.

Prawdin, Michael, *The Builders of the Mogul Empire,* New York, 1965.

Rawlinson, H. G., *A Concise History of the Indian People,* 2d ed., New York, 1950.
- ———, *India, a Short Cultural History,* New York, 1952. An excellent interpretive study.

Smith, V. A., *Akbar the Great Mogul,* Oxford, 1917.

Spear, Percival, *India: A Modern History,* 2d ed., Ann Arbor, 1972. An excellent survey.
- ———, *The Oxford History of Indian, 1740–1975,* 2d ed., New York, 1979.
- Wolpert, Stanley, *A New History of India,* New York, 1977. An admirable survey, informative and well written.

- Eberhard, Wolfram, *A History of China,* 4th ed., Berkeley, 1977.
- Elvin, Mark, *The Pattern of the Chinese Past,* Stanford, 1975.
  Fairbank, J. K., E. O. Reischauer, and A. M. Craig, *East Asia: Tradition and Transformation,* rev. ed., Boston, 1978. A shortened edition of a major text.
- Fitzgerald, C. P., *China, a Short Cultural History,* 3d ed., New York, 1961. Unconventional in viewpoint.
  Honour, Hugh, *Chinoiserie: The Vision of Cathay,* New York, 1962. An account of the rise of European interest in the arts and crafts of the Orient.
  Hucker, C. O., *China's Imperial Past: An Introduction to Chinese History and Culture,* Stanford, 1975. Remarkably clear, comprehensive, and readable.
- Hudson, G. F., *Europe and China: A Survey of Their Relations from the Earliest Times to 1800,* London, 1930.
  Michael, Franz, *The Origin of Manchu Rule in China,* Baltimore, 1942.
- Moore, C. A., ed., *The Chinese Mind: Essentials of Chinese Philosophy and Culture,* Honolulu, 1967.
  Ronan, C. A., ed., *The Shorter Science and Civilization in China,* New York, 1978. Abridgement of the first two volumes of a monumental study by Joseph Needham.
  Rowbotham, A. H., *Missionary and Mandarin: The Jesuits at the Court of China,* Berkeley, 1942.
  Scott, A. C., *The Classical Theater of China,* New York, 1957.
  Shryock, J. K., *The Origin and Development of the State Cult of Confucius,* New York, 1932.
  Sickman, L., and A. Soper, *The Art and Architecture of China,* Baltimore, 1956. Reliable, richly illustrated.
- Sullivan, Michael, *A Short History of Chinese Art,* rev. ed., Berkeley, 1970.
  Tuan Yi-fu, *China,* Chicago, 1970. An excellent cultural geography.

JAPAN

  Boxer, C. R., *The Christian Century in Japan, 1549–1650,* Berkeley, 1951.
- Brandon, J. R., W. P. Malm, and D. H. Shively, *Studies in Kabuki: Its Acting, Music, and Historical Context,* Honolulu, 1978.
  Cole, Wendell, *Kyoto in the Momoyama Period,* Norman, Okla., 1967.
  Dore, R. P., *Education in Tokugawa, Japan,* Berkeley, 1965.
- Duus, Peter, *Feudalism in Japan,* 2d ed. New York, 1975. A concise account of political developments through the nineteenth century.
  Eliot, Charles, *Japanese Buddhism,* New York, 1959. A standard text.
  Embree, J. F., *The Japanese Nation,* New York, 1945. A brilliant and well-balanced study by an anthropologist.
- Hall, J. W., *Japan: From Prehistory to Modern Times,* New York, 1971.
- Keene, Donald, *Japanese Literature: An Introduction for Western Readers,* New York, 1955.
  Langer, P. F., *Japan, Yesterday and Today,* New York, 1966. An excellent summary.

- Moore, C. A., ed., *The Japanese Mind: Essentials of Japanese Philosophy and Culture,* Honolulu, 1967.
- Munsterberg, Hugo, *The Arts of Japan: An Illustrated History,* Rutland, Vt., 1957.
- Reischauer, E. O., *Japan: The Story of a Nation,* 5th ed., New York, 1974. Lucid and well organized.

  Sadler, A. L., *The Maker of Modern Japan: The Life of Tokugawa Ieyasu,* London, 1937.

  Sansom, G. B., *Japan, a Short Cultural History,* rev. ed., New York, 1952. A substantial but highly readable work by an eminent British scholar.

  ————, *The Western World and Japan,* New York, 1950.
- Smith, T. C., *The Agrarian Origins of Modern Japan,* Stanford, 1959.
- Warner, Langdon, *The Enduring Art of Japan,* Cambridge, Mass., 1952.

  Yukio, Y., *Two Thousand Years of Japanese Art,* New York, 1958.

AFRICA

  Curtin, Philip D., ed., *Horizon History of Africa,* New York, 1972.
- Davidson, Basil, *The African Genius,* Boston, 1969.

  Egharevba, Jacob, *A Short History of Benin,* Ibadan, 1960.

  Gailey, H. A., *History of Africa: From Earliest Times to 1800,* New York, 1970.

  Gray, Richard, ed., *The Cambridge History of Africa,* Vol. 4: *c. 1600 to c. 1790,* Cambridge, 1975.

  Hallett, Robin, *Africa to 1875,* Ann Arbor, 1970.

  Hull, Richard W., *Munyakare: African Civilization before the Batuuree,* New York, 1972.

  Roberts, A., ed., *Tanzania before 1900,* Nairobi, 1968.

  Smith, Robert S., *Kingdoms of the Yoruba,* London, 1969.

SOURCE MATERIALS

  Davenport, T. R. H., and K. S. Hunt, eds., *The Right to the Land: Documents on Southern African History,* Capetown, 1974.
- de Bary, W. T., ed., *Sources of Chinese Tradition,* Chaps. XXII, XXIII, New York, 1960.
- ————, ed., *Sources of Indian Tradition,* "Islam in Medieval India"; "Sikhism," New York, 1958.
- ————, ed., *Sources of Japanese Tradition,* "The Tokugawa Period," New York, 1958.

  Gallagher, L. J. tr., *China in the Sixteenth Century. The Journals of Matthew Ricci: 1583–1610,* Milwaukee, 1942.
- Hibbett, Howard, *The Floating World in Japanese Fiction,* New York, 1959.
- Keene, Donald ed., *Anthology of Japanese Literature,* New York, 1960

  Lu, David, ed., *Sources of Japanese History,* Vol. 1, New York, 1973.

  Markham, C. R., ed., *The Hawkins' Voyages,* London, 1878.

  Morse, H. B., ed., *The Chronicles of the East India Company Trading to China,* 5 vols., Cambridge, Mass., 1926–1929.

Oliver, Roland, ed., *The Middle Age of African History,* New York, 1967.

Smith, V. A., ed., *F. Bernier: Travels in the Mogul Empire* A.D. *1656–1668,* London, 1914.

Vansina, Jan, *Kingdoms of the Savanna,* Madison, Wis., 1966.

Wang, C. C., tr., *Dream of the Red Chamber,* New York, 1929.

Whiteley, W. H., compiler, *A Selection of African Prose: Traditional Oral Texts,* Oxford, 1964.

Part Five

THE FRENCH AND INDUSTRIAL REVOLUTIONS AND THEIR CONSEQUENCES

No two events more profoundly altered the shape of Western civilization than the French and Industrial Revolutions. "Modern" history begins with their occurrence. The major happenings of the nineteenth and early twentieth centuries—the spread of middle-class liberalism and economic success; the decline of the old, landed aristocracies; the growth of class consciousness among urban workers—all had their roots in these two revolutions.

The French and Industrial Revolutions took place at about the same time and affected many of the same people—though in different ways and to varying degrees. Together they resulted in the overthrow of absolutism, mercantilism, and the last vestiges of manorialism. Together they produced the theory and practice of economic individualism and political liberalism. And together they ensured the growth of class consciousness, and the culmination of those tensions between the middle and working classes that imparted new vitality to European history after 1800.

Each revolution, of course, produced results peculiarly its own. The French Revolution encouraged the growth of nationalism and its unattractive step-child, authoritarianism. The Industrial Revolution compelled the design of a new, urban social order. Yet despite their unique contributions, the two revolutions must be studied together and understood as the joint progenitors of Western history in the nineteenth and early twentieth centuries.

The French and Industrial Revolutions and Their Consequences

POLITICS	SCIENCE & INDUSTRY

1770

James Watt's steam engine, 1763
Spinning jenny patented, 1770

American War of Independence, 1775–1783

Beginning of factory system, 1780s

French Revolution begins, 1789

Lavoisier discovers the indestructibility of matter, 1789

France declared a republic, 1792
Declaration of Pillnitz, 1792
Reign of Terror, 1793–1794

Cotton gin invented, 1793
Edward Jenner develops smallpox vaccine, 1796

Treaty of Campo Formio, 1797

1800

Napoleon, first consul of France, 1799
Treaty of Lunéville, 1801
Napoleon declared first consul for life, 1802
Napoleon crowns himself emperor of the French, 1804
Continental System established, 1806

Reforms of Hardenberg and Stein, Prussia, 1808

Napoleon's invasion of Russia, 1812
Congress of Vienna, 1814–1815

Battle of Waterloo, 1815

"Peterloo Massacre," England, 1819
Congress of Verona, 1822
Monroe Doctrine, 1823

Louis Pasteur, 1822–1895

1825

"Decembrist" Revolt, Russia, 1825
Greek Independence, 1829
Revolution in France, 1830
"Young Italy," 1831
Reform Bill of 1832, England
Slavery abolished, British colonies, 1833
Poor Law reform, England, 1834
Chartist movement, England, 1838–1848

First railway, England, 1825

Corn Laws repealed, England, 1846
Revolutions in Europe, 1848
Karl Marx, *Communist Manifesto,* 1848
Second Republic, France, 1848
Frankfurt Assembly, Germany, 1848–1849
Reign of Louis Napoleon, 1851–1870

Great Exhibition, London, 1851
Invention of the sewing machine, 1850s

ECONOMICS & SOCIETY	ARTS & LETTERS	
Jean-Jacques Rousseau, *The Social Contract,* 1762		**1770**
	Ludwig van Beethoven, 1770–1827	
Adam Smith, *Wealth of Nations,* 1776		
	Immanuel Kant, *Critique of Pure Reason,* 1781	
Jeremy Bentham, *The Principles of Morals and Legislation,* 1789		
Utilitarianism, 1790–1870	Johann von Goethe, *Faust,* 1790–1808	
	Romantic movement, 1790–1850	
Tom Paine, *The Rights of Man,* 1791–1792		
Thomas Malthus, *An Essay on the Principle of Population,* 1798	William Wordsworth, *Lyrical Ballads,* 1798	
		1800
	G. W. Hegel, *Phenomenology of the Spirit,* 1807	
	I. G. Fichte, *Addresses to the German Nation,* 1808	
Louis Blanc, 1811–1882		
	Francisco Goya, *The Executions of the Third of May,* 1814	
Founding of Prussian Zollverein, 1818		
		1825
	Honoré de Balzac, *The Human Comedy,* 1829–1841	
	Eugène Delacroix, *Liberty Leading the People,* 1830	
	Realism in literature and art, 1840–1870	
Friedrich Engels, *The Condition of the Working Class,* 1844		
John Stuart Mill, *Principles of Political Economy,* 1848	Pre-Raphaelite Brotherhood formed, 1848	

POLITICS	SCIENCE & INDUSTRY

1850

Crimean War, 1854–1856

Invention of the Bessemer process, 1856

Unification of Italy, 1858–1866

Charles Darwin, *Origin of Species,* 1859

Civil War, United States, 1861–1865
Otto von Bismarck's accession to power, 1862
First International, 1864

Parliamentary Reform Bill, England, 1867

Suez Canal opened, 1869
Union Pacific railroad, United States, 1869

Franco-Prussian War, 1870

ECONOMICS & SOCIETY	ARTS & LETTERS

Giuseppe Verdi, *Il Trovatore*, 1853
Richard Wagner, *The Ring of the Nibelung*,
1854–1874
Charles Dickens, *Hard Times*, 1854

Gustave Flaubert, *Madame Bovary*, 1857

Emancipation of the serfs, Russia, 1861

Leo Tolstoy, *War and Peace*, 1866–1869

Karl Marx, *Capital*, 1867

Pope Pius IX, *Syllabus of Errors*, 1869

Chapter 24

THE FRENCH REVOLUTION

Men are born, and always continue, free and equal in respect of their rights. Civil distinctions, therefore, can be founded only on public utility.

The nation is essentially the source of all sovereignty; nor can any individual, or any body of men, be entitled to any authority which is not expressly derived from it.

—*The Declaration of the Rights of Man and of the Citizen,* 1789

I n 1789, one European out of every five lived in France. And most Europeans, French or not, who thought beyond the boundaries of their own immediate concerns, perceived of France as the center of European civilization. It followed, therefore, that a revolution in France would immediately command the attention of Europe, and would from the first assume far more than mere national significance. Yet the French Revolution attracted and disturbed men and women for reasons other than the fact that it was French. Both its philosophical ideals and its political realities mirrored attitudes, concerns, and conflicts that had occupied the minds of Europeans for several decades. When the revolutionaries pronounced in favor of liberty, they spoke not only with the voice of the eighteenth-century *philosophes,* but with those of the English aristocracy in 1688 and the American revolutionaries of 1776. Absolutism was the bane of continental noblemen, jealous to preserve their ancient freedoms from monarchical inroads; it was also the bane of continental merchants, chafing under the constraints of mercantilist authority. Across Europe, monarch, nobility, and middle class confronted each other in uneasy hostilities that varied in intensity, but reflected common mistrust and uncertainty.

The era of revolution

Louis XVI

Governmental structure

Financial problems

I. THE BACKGROUND OF THE FRENCH REVOLUTION

To understand why revolution came to France, we must first understand the major components of French society in the late eighteenth century and the manner in which they stood in opposition to each other. At the head of society stood the king, Louis XVI. Neither the most talented nor the most incompetent of the Bourbons, Louis XVI was attempting to rule France as he believed he should rule: absolutely in theory, yet in practice in consort with the most capable advisors willing to serve under him. He was hampered in his attempts to rule effectively by two major factors.

First, the governmental structure of France was both illogical and unsystematic. Confusion reigned in nearly every department, the product of a long and somewhat irregular growth extending back into the Middle Ages. New agencies had been established from time to time to meet some particular condition, often with a total disregard for those already in existence. As a result there was much overlapping of functions, and numerous useless officials drew salaries from the public purse. Conflicts of jurisdiction between rival departments frequently delayed action on vital problems for months at a stretch. In financial matters there was no more regularity than in other branches of public policy. The collection of public revenues was exceedingly haphazard. Instead of appointing official collectors, the king employed the old Roman system of farming out the collection of taxes to private corporations and individuals, permitting them to retain as profit all that they could obtain from the people in excess of a stipulated amount. Similar disorganized conditions prevailed in the realm of law and judicial procedure. Nearly every province of France had its special code based upon local custom. As a consequence, an act punishable as a crime in southern France might be no concern of the law in a central or northern province.

Louis XVI's second major difficulty was financial. England and France had been in conflict for most of the eighteenth century. In all but one of the wars between them, France had emerged the loser and had paid for those losses with surrendered colonies. Ironically, it was the war which the French had helped to win—the American War of Independence—that was now causing them the most immediate problems. The expense of maintaining fleets and armies in the Western Hemisphere had been particularly heavy and had demanded extensive borrowing. The result was a national debt which the inefficient and overly bureaucratic French government found it could not sustain, although it was no greater than that left by Louis XIV in 1714, and no more than half that incurred by the British. Louis pressed his advisors to devise new methods of retrenchment and taxation to keep the government afloat. Yet these men, and Louis with them, recognized that they could make no headway unless by some miracle they could induce the clergy and nobility to surrender the ancient privileges which allowed them to escape payment of an equitable share of the nation's taxes.

The likelihood of this surrender was remote. The system of privilege was one the nobility and the church, the first two of the three "estates" of the realm, were loath to alter. This remained the case despite the clamor of the third estate, the commoners, that they do so. Although many parish priests were as poor as their humble parishoners, the monsignors, bishops, archbishops, and cardinals of the Roman Catholic Church in France enjoyed large incomes, as did the institution of the Church itself. The Church rulers claimed the medieval right to evade taxes on their properties by the payment of a periodic "free gift" to the state, invariably far less than might have been obtained from direct taxation of church property.

*The first and second
estates*

The nobility was also protected by custom from the payment of anything like its proportionate share of taxes. Taxes in France, long before 1789, had come to consist of two main types, direct and indirect. The direct taxes included the *taille,* or tax on real and personal property; the poll tax; and the tax on incomes, originally at the rate of 5 percent, but in the eighteenth century more commonly at 10 or 11 percent. The indirect taxes, or taxes added to the price of commodities and paid by the ultimate consumer, embraced mainly the tariffs on articles imported from foreign countries and the tolls levied on goods shipped from one province of France to another. In addition, the *gabelle,* or tax on salt, was a form of indirect tax. For some time the production of salt had been a state monopoly in France; every individual inhabitant was required to buy at least seven pounds a year from the government works. To the cost of production was added a heavy tax, with the result that the price to the consumer was often as much as fifty or sixty times the actual value of the salt.

Tax structure

While exceedingly burdensome, the indirect taxes were not as a rule unfair distributed. It was difficult for anyone, regardless of social status, to avoid paying them. The case of most of the direct taxes, however, was far otherwise. The clergy escaped payment of both the *taille* and the income tax. The nobles, especially those of higher rank, made use of their influence with the king to obtain exemption from practically all direct levies. As a result, the main task of providing funds for the government fell upon the common people, or members of the third estate. And since few of the artisans and laborers had much that could be taxed, the chief burden had to be borne by the peasants and the middle class.

The tax burden

Not all the nobles opposed the king's plan to abolish their customary exemptions. Many of the most ardent reformers were the *nobles of the robe,* men who had acquired judicial office (hence the "robe") which conferred a title of nobility, as well as an opportunity to ac-

Le Hameau. This rustic villa was constructed in the gardens of Versailles to allow the French court to experiment with the "return to nature" advocated by some of the *philosophes.*

Nobles of robe and nobles of the sword

cumulate a substantial fortune in land and other property. Included in this group were such talented and concerned men as the philosopher the baron de Montesquieu, the lawyer the comte de Mirabeau, and the statesman the marquis de Lafayette, who had come to the aid of the American colonies. Among the nobles of the robe were men who would play prominent roles in the revolution itself. In contrast—and often in opposition—to this group stood the *nobles of the sword,* those whose titles extended back to the feudal lords of the Middle Ages. Many of these aristocrats looked with disdain upon their brethren of the robe. Though in general not nearly so widely representative a group as the nobles of the robe, those of the sword nevertheless held many of the leading positions in the government, delegating their work to subordinates. The nobles of the sword owned large estates, upon which they seldom resided, living instead at the court of Versailles, relying upon bailiffs and stewards to extract all they could from the peasants who lived under their jurisdiction at home. Theirs was an expensive, if not particularly purposeful, existence. Their polished, artificial style of life required increasingly large sums of money. Hence their natural unwillingness to surrender tax exemptions, no matter how hard pressed the government.

Aristocratic demands

To reinforce their political intransigence and economic independence, the nobles had insisted on a greater share in both central and local administration. They asserted their claim by making increased use of three governmental institutions—parliaments, provincial estates, and intendencies. The thirteen French parliaments were regional courts of appeal, but the nobility used them to play an increasingly political role. The provincial estates, also under the control of the nobility, claimed not only judicial but legislative power. Both parliaments and estates insisted, specifically, upon the right to consent to taxation. Both argued that they were exercising this right to protect the population from the never-ceasing demands of a greedy state treasury. In fact, the nobility used these bodies with increasing frequency to do no more than protect its own privileges. Finally, the nobility had entrenched itself in many of the intendencies, those offices from which the thirty-four generalities, or districts, of the country were administered. During the reign of Louis XIV, intendents had, for the most part, been commoners, whose assignment it was to keep the nobility in line. Now many were nobles themselves, less likely to come to the king's aid than to oppose his will.

Within the third estate the peasants, upon whom the nobility depended for much of their income, had come to resent their increasingly intolerable economic situation. A major source of the peasants' discontent were the customary duties that had survived the end of manorialism. True, a vast majority of peasants were free; a considerable proportion owned the lands they cultivated. Others were tenants or hired laborers; the largest percentage appear to have been sharecroppers, farming the lands of the nobles for a portion of the harvest, generally ranging from a third to a half. Even those peasants who were entirely free, however, were required to perform obligations inherited from the later Middle Ages. One of the most odious of these was the payment of an annual rental to the lord who had formerly controlled the land. Another was the donation to the local noble of a share of the price received whenever a tract of land was sold. In addition, the peasants were still required to contribute *banalités,* or fees for the use of various facilities owned by the noble. During the Middle Ages *banalités* had been paid for the use of the lord's flour mill, his wine press, and his bake oven. In spite of the fact that by the eighteenth century many of the peasants owned such equipment themselves and no longer benefited by the services provided by the noble, the *banalités* were still collected in the original amounts.

The third estate: the peasants

Probably the most exasperating of all the relics of manorialism were the *corvée* and the hunting privileges of the nobility. The *corvée,* formerly a requirement of labor on the lord's demesne and in the building of roads and bridges on the manorial estate, had become an obligation to the government. For several weeks each year the peasant was forced to put his own work aside and devote his labor to maintaining the public highways. No other class of the population was required to perform this service. Even greater inconvenience was suffered as a result of the hunting privileges of the nobles. From time immemorial the right to indulge in the diversions of the chase had been regarded as a distinctive badge of aristocracy. The property rights of the peasants were not allowed to stand in the way of this gentlemanly pastime. In some parts of France the peasants were forbidden to weed or mow in

The relics of manorial custom

Enclosure of common land

breeding time lest they disturb the nests of partidges. Rabbits, crows, and foxes could not be killed regardless of how much damage they did to the crops or to domestic fowl and young animals. Furthermore, the peasant was expected to resign himself to having his fields trampled at any time by the horses of a thoughtless crew of noble hunters.

Not only did the peasants suffer under the vestiges of manorial custom. During the eighteenth century they also came under pressure as a result of the increasingly frequent enclosure of what had been common land. Fields allowed to lie fallow, together with those tilled only infrequently, were considered "common," land on which all persons might graze their livestock. These common lands, particularly extensive in the west of France, were an important resource for the peasants. In addition to the above-mentioned right to pasturage, they enjoyed that of gathering wood and of gleaning cultivated fields following a harvest. Now the king's economic advisors—Charles Calonne, Étienne Loménie de Brienne, the Swiss banker Jacques Necker—declared these collective rights to be obstacles in the path of agricultural improvement. Anxious to increase their income by increasing the efficiency of their estates, the landlords agreed. The result was authorization, by the crown, of the breakup of common lands and their enclosure as private property.

Here, then, were peasants pressed on the one side to acknowledge the duties of an outmoded manorial system and on the other to acquiesce in the exactions of modern agricultural capitalism, all the while paying taxes from which their aristocratic neighbors were exempt.

The frustrations of the peasants mirrored those of the most dynamic element within French eighteenth-century society, the middle class. This group was by no means homogeneous; there were within it

A Gentleman of the Third Estate with His Family. A contemporary engraving which illustrates the respectability the Third Estate wished to see translated into political power.

many ranks, graded according to both occupation and income. At the top stood financiers and wholesale traders. Many of these men were also shareholders in various enterprises and in the government bonds which had been issued throughout the eighteenth century. (Noblemen invested in business as well; the economic line between the second and third estate was not as heavily drawn as was the social.) Professionals ranged throughout the ranks of the middle class: doctors and lawyers, many of the latter to play roles central to the revolution. Industry remained subordinate to trade: although a few factories existed in France prior to 1789, most manufacturing took place in homes, and most consumers were supplied by local craftsmen. For every capitalist entrepreneur, there were scores of small-scale masters, lodged somewhere in the lower reaches of the middle class, at home in the workshop yet removed by virtue of their ownership of that shop from the ranks of the laboring classes below them.

The third estate: the middle class

While these men acknowledged the gradations that separated them from each other, they resented the privileges that excluded them from any consequential participation in the affairs of state. No matter how much money a merchant, manufacturer, banker, or lawyer might acquire, he was still excluded from political privileges. He had almost no influence at the court; he could not share in the highest honors; and, except in the choice of a few petty local officers, he could not even vote. He was looked down upon as an inferior by the nobility. As the middle class rose in affluence and in consciousness of its own importance, its members were bound to resent such social discrimination. Above all, it was the demand of the commercial, financial, and industrial leaders for political power commensurate with their economic position that turned members of the middle class into revolutionaries.

Lack of political power

A demand for political power was not the only consequence of the growing prosperity of the middle class; there was also an increasing clamor for the abandonment of mercantilist policies. In earlier times mercantilism had been welcomed by merchants and manufacturers because of its effects in procuring new markets and fostering trade. But those times occurred at the beginning of the Commercial Revolution, when business was still nascent. As commerce and industry flourished through succeeding centuries, the middle class became increasingly confident of its ability to stand on its own feet. The result was a growing tendency to look upon the regulations of mercantilism as oppressive restrictions. Merchants disliked the special monopolies granted to favored companies and the interference with their freedom to buy in foreign markets. Manufacturers chafed under the laws controlling wages, fixing prices, and restricting the purchase of raw materials outside of France and its colonies. These were only a few of the more annoying regulations enforced by a government operating under the twin objectives of paternalism and economic self-sufficiency.

Antimercantilism

Like the peasantry, the middle class saw itself bearing a major por-

Peasants vs. middle class

tion of the state's financial burdens. Unlike the peasants, however, the middle class—at any rate its upper echelons—represented an economic force that was compelling change in a new and untried direction. The peasants, opposing enclosure, wanted to return to what had been. The prosperous financiers, the frustrated lawyers, the emerging entrepreneurs wanted to play leading roles in encouraging an expansion of international trade and in moving France ahead in its commercial competition with Britain.

France divided

France on the eve of revolution was thus a country divided against itself. Monarchy struggled to exact money from an aristocracy increasingly determined not to pay and increasingly anxious in turn to exact what it could from a sullen peasantry. The middle classes resented a government that appeared at best an anachronism and at worst a tyranny, frustrated and furious that a country as prosperous as France should find it impossible to pay its debts. France did not fall to revolution because it was poor. It succumbed because those who knew best how rich it was were dissatisfied with the slow rate of its commercial progress.

Intellectual background

No event as all-encompassing as the French Revolution occurs in a cultural vacuum. Although ideas may not have "caused" the revolution, they played a most important role in giving shape and substance to the discontent experienced by so many, particularly among the middle class. These ideas derived from the thought of the Enlightenment. Two theories, in particular, expressed the concerns and aspirations of the revolutionaries. The first was the *liberal* theory of such writers as Locke, Voltaire, and Montesquieu; and the second was the *democratic* theory of Rousseau. While the two were fundamentally opposed, they nevertheless had elements in common. Both were predicated upon the assumption that the state is a necessary evil and that government rests upon a contractual basis. Each had its doctrine of popular sovereignty, although with contrasting interpretations. Both upheld in some measure the fundamental rights of the individual. And both contained elements appealing to those who, for various reasons, were dissatisfied with things as they were.

The liberal political theory of John Locke

The father of the liberal theory of the seventeenth and eighteenth centuries was John Locke. His philosophy of education, as we have seen, was intrinsic to the development of Enlightenment thinking. His political beliefs are contained chiefly in his *Second Treatise of Civil Government,* published in 1690. In this book he developed a theory of limited government, which was used to justify the new system of parliamentary rule set up in England as a result of the Glorious Revolution. He maintained that originally all humans had lived in a theoretical state of nature in which absolute freedom and equality prevailed, and in which there was no government of any kind. The only law was the law of nature, which each individual enforced for himself in order to protect his natural rights to life, liberty, and property. It was not long, however, until men began to perceive that the inconveniences of the state of nature greatly outweighed its advantages. With individuals attempting to enforce their own rights, confusion and insecurity were the unavoidable results. Accordingly, the people agreed among themselves to establish a civil society, to set up a government, and to surrender certain powers to it. But they did not make that government absolute. The only power they conferred upon it was the executive power of the law of nature. Since the state is nothing but the joint power of all the members of society, its authority "can be no more than those persons had in a state of nature before they entered into society, and gave it up to the community."[1] All powers not expressly surrendered are reserved to the people themselves. If the government exceeds or abuses the authority explicitly granted in the political contract, it becomes tyrannical; and the people then have the right to dissolve it or to rebel against it and overthrow it.

Locke condemned absolutism in every form. He denounced despotic monarchy, but he was no less severe in his strictures against the absolute sovereignty of parliaments. Though he defended the supremacy of the law-making branch, with the executive primarily an agent of the legislature, he nevertheless refused to concede to the representatives of the people an unlimited power. Arguing that government was instituted among people for the preservation of property (which he generally defined in the inclusive sense of life, liberty, and estate), he denied the authority of any political agency to invade the natural rights of a single individual. The law of nature, which embodies these rights, is an automatic limitation upon every branch of the government. Regardless of how large a majority of the people's representatives should demand the restriction of freedom of speech or the confiscation and redistribution of property, no such action could legally be taken. If taken illegally it would justify effective measures of resistance on the part of the majority of citizens. Locke was much more concerned with protecting individual liberty than he was with promoting stability or social progress. If forced to make a choice, he would have preferred the evils of anarchy to those of despotism in any form.

Locke's condemnation of absolutism

The appeal of Locke's ideas to the French middle class can be readily understood. His doctrines of natural rights, limited government, and the right of resistance to tyranny, as well as his stout defense of property, reflected the values of that element in French society. Like their American counterparts, who a decade earlier had incorporated Locke's theories into the Declaration of Independence, these middle-class Frenchmen opened their minds to Lockean suppositions and explanations.

Locke's appeal

In France the foremost exponents of the liberal political theory were Voltaire and Montesquieu (1689–1755). As was indicated earlier, Voltaire considered orthodox Christianity to be the worst of the enemies

[1] *Second Treatise of Civil Government* (Everyman Library ed.), p. 184.

Montesquieu

*The separation of powers;
checks and balances*

of humanity; he reserved contempt for tyrannical government as well. During his exile in England he had studied the writings of Locke and had been deeply impressed by their vigorous assertions of individual freedom. In common with Locke he conceived of government as a necessary evil, with powers which ought to be limited to the enforcement of natural rights. He maintained that all are endowed by nature with equal rights to liberty, property, and the protection of the laws. But Voltaire was no democrat. He was inclined to think of the ideal form of government as either an enlightened monarchy or a republic dominated by the middle class.

A more systematic political thinker than Voltaire was his older contemporary, Montesquieu. Though, like Voltaire, a student of Locke and an ardent admirer of British institutions, Montesquieu was a unique figure among the political philosophers of the eighteenth century. In his celebrated *Spirit of Laws* he brought new methods and new conceptions to the theory of the state. Instead of attempting to found a science of government by pure deduction, he followed the Aristotelian method of studying actual political systems as they were supposed to have operated in the past. He denied that there is any one perfect form of government suitable for all peoples under all conditions. He maintained, on the contrary, that political institutions in order to be successful must harmonize with the physical conditions and the level of social advancement of the nations they are intended to serve. Thus he declared that despotism is best suited to countries of vast domain; limited monarchy to those of moderate size; and republican government to those of small extent. For his own country, France, he was disposed to think that a limited monarchy would be the most appropriate form, since he regarded the nation as too large to be made into a republic unless on some kind of federal plan.

Montesquieu is especially famous for his theory of the separation of powers. He avowed that it is a natural human tendency to abuse any power, and that consequently every government, regardless of its form, is liable to degenerate into despotism. To prevent such a result he argued that the authority of government should be broken up into its three natural divisions of legislative, executive, and judicial. Whenever any two or more of these are allowed to remain united in the same hands, liberty, he declared, is at an end. The only effective way to avoid tyranny is to enable each branch of the government to act as a check upon the other two. For example, the executive should have the power by means of the veto to curb the encroachments of the lawmaking branch. The legislature, in turn, should have the authority of impeachment in order to restrain the executive. And, finally, there should be an independent judiciary vested with power to protect individual rights against arbitrary acts of either the legislature or the executive. This favorite scheme of Montesquieu was not intended, of course, to facilitate democracy. Its purpose was largely the opposite: to prevent the absolute supremacy of the majority, expressed as it normally would be through the people's representatives in a legislature. Montesquieu's ideas thus appealed to both nobility and middle class. The nobility read his writings as a defense of their ancient privileges—elevated by Montesquieu into "liberties." The provincial estates, where noblemen exercised considerable political power, were the constituted bodies which would provide a check to royal power. The middle class welcomed further theoretical support to substantiate its preference for something other than the monarchical absolutism and centralized mercantilism of eighteenth-century France.

Additional arguments in favor of governmental nonintervention was provided by another group of libertarians—theoreticians who were redefining the study of economics.

In the second half of the eighteenth century a number of writers began attacking traditional assumptions with regard to public control over production and trade. Their special target of criticism was mercantilist policy. To a large extent the new economics was founded upon the basic conceptions of the Enlightenment, particularly the idea of a mechanistic universe governed by inflexible laws. The economists argued that the sphere of the production and distribution of wealth was subject to laws just as irresistible as those of physics and astronomy. The new economic theory was a counterpart of political liberalism. The cardinal aims of the two doctrines were quite similar: to reduce the powers of government to the lowest minimum consistent with safety and to preserve for the individual the largest possible measure of freedom in the pursuit of his own devices.

The new economists

The greatest of all the economists of the age of the Enlightenment and one of the most brilliant of all time was Adam Smith (1723–1790). A native of Scotland, Smith began his career as a lecturer on English literature at the University of Edinburgh. From this position he was soon advanced to a professorship of logic at Glasgow College. In 1776 he published his *Inquiry into the Nature and Causes of the Wealth of Nations.* In this work he maintained that labor, rather than agriculture or the bounty of nature, is the real source of wealth. While in general he accepted the principle of laissez faire, avowing that the prosperity of all can best be promoted by allowing all individuals to pursue their own interests, he nevertheless recognized the necessity for certain forms of governmental interference. The state should intervene for the prevention of injustice and oppression, for the advancement of education and the protection of public health, and for the maintenance of necessary enterprises which would never be established by private capital. Notwithstanding these rather broad limitations upon the principle of laissez faire, Smith's *Wealth of Nations* was adopted as holy writ by the economic individualists of the eighteenth and nineteenth centuries. Its influence in causing the French

The economics of Adam Smith

Revolution was indirect but nonetheless profound. It furnished the final answer to mercantilist argument and thereby strengthened the ambition of the middle class to have done with a political system which continued to block the path to economic freedom.

The second of the great political ideals which occupied an important place in the intellectual background of the French Revolution was the ideal of democracy. In contrast with liberalism, democracy, in its original meaning, was much less concerned with the defense of individual rights than with the enforcement of popular rule. What the majority of the citizens wills is the supreme law of the land, for the voice of the people is the voice of God.

The foremost theoretician of democracy in eighteenth-century Europe was Jean-Jacques Rousseau (1712–1778). The most significant of his writings on political theory were his *Social Contract* and his *Discourse on the Origin of Inequality*. In both of these he upheld the popular thesis that humans had originally existed in a state of nature. But in contrast with Locke he regarded this state of nature as a veritable paradise. People suffered no inconvenience from maintaining their own rights against others. Indeed, there were very few chances of conflict of any sort; for private property did not exist for a long time, and every person was the equal of every other. Eventually, however, evils arose, due primarily to the fact that some staked off plots of land and said to themselves, "This is mine." It was in such manner that various degrees of inequality developed; and, as a consequence, "cheating trickery," "insolent pomp," and "insatiable ambition" soon came to dominate the relations among men.[2] The only hope of security was now to establish a civil society and to surrender all rights to the community. This was accomplished by means of a social contract, in which each individual agreed with the whole body of individuals to submit to the will of the majority. Thus the state was brought into existence.

Rousseau developed an altogether different conception of sovereignty from that of the liberals. Whereas Locke and his followers had taught that only a portion of sovereign power is surrendered to the state, the rest being retained by the people themselves, Rousseau contended that sovereignty is indivisible, and that all of it became vested in the community when civil society was formed. He insisted further that each individual in becoming a party to the social contract gave up all rights to the people collectively and agreed to submit absolutely to the general will. It follows that the sovereign power of the state is subject to no limitations whatever. When Rousseau referred to the state he did not mean the government. He regarded the state as the politically organized community, which has the sovereign function of expressing the general will. The authority of the state cannot be repre-

---

[2] *Discourse on the Origin of Inequality* (Everyman Library ed.), p. 207.

sented, but must be expressed directly through the enactment of fundamental laws by the people themselves. The government, on the other hand, is simply the executive agent of the state. Its function is not to formulate the general will but merely to carry it out. Moreover, the community can set the government up or pull it down "whenever it likes."[3]

Rousseau's influence was great. His appeal, however, was not so much to those members of the middle class whose thoughts and actions dominated the first stage of the revolution. Although they might have agreed with Rousseau's opposition to hereditary privilege, they were, as convinced individualists, unmoved by arguments in favor of surrender to a "general will." Rousseau's influence upon the revolution was greatest during its second stage, when a more democratic and radical coterie emerged to lead events, first in the direction of democracy and then along a course toward an absolutism that nevertheless accorded with Rousseau's notions of the sovereign state.

Rousseau's appeal

2. THE DESTRUCTION OF THE ANCIEN RÉGIME

The French Revolution occurred when it did because of the government's inability to resolve its financial crisis. When the king's principal ministers Calonne and Loménie de Brienne attempted in 1787 and 1788 to institute a series of financial reforms in order to stave off bankruptcy, they encountered not just opposition but entrenched aristocratic determination to extract further governmental concessions from the king. To meet the mounting deficit, the ministers proposed new taxes, notably a stamp duty and a direct tax on the annual produce of the soil. The king summoned an assembly of notables from among the aristocracy, in the hope of persuading the nobles to agree to his demands. Far from acquiescing, however, the nobles insisted that to institute a general tax such as the stamp duty the king would first have to call together the Estates General, representative of the three estates of the realm.

The crisis of the monarchy

The summoning of this body, which had not met for over a century and a half. seemed to many the only solution to France's deepening problems. No doubt most of those aristocrats who argued for its calling did so from short-sighted and selfish motives. Yet the politically conscious population as a whole agreed with the idea in an unreasonable and desperate hope that this unusual event might, because of its very strangeness, work a miracle and save the country from ruin. During the period before the rise of monarchical absolutism, when the Estates General was convened more or less regularly, the representatives of each estate had met and voted as a body. Generally this meant that the first and second estates combined against the third.

The Estates General

[3] *The Social Contract* (Everyman Library ed.), p. 88.

FRANCE IN 1789 · THE "GOVERNMENTS"

By the late eighteenth century the third estate had attained such importance that it was not willing to tolerate such an arrangement. Consequently its leaders demanded that the three orders should sit together and vote as individuals. More important, it insisted that the representatives of the third estate should be double the number of the first and second. Leaving this issue unresolved, Louis XVI, in the summer of 1788, yielded to popular clamor and summoned the Estates General to meet in May of the following year.

In the intervening months, the question of "doubling the third" was fiercely debated. When the king pronounced against the idea, he lost support he might otherwise have obtained from the middle class, and virtually preordained the outcome of the convocation. Shortly after

The new political role of the third estate

the opening of the Estates General at Versailles, in May 1789, the representatives of the third estate took the revolutionary step of leaving the body and declaring themselves the National Assembly. "What is the third estate?" asked the Abbé Sieyès, one of the most articulate spokesmen for a new order, in his famous pamphlet of January 1789. The answer he gave then—"everything"—was the answer the third estate itself gave when it constituted itself the National Assembly of France. Sieyès, unlike most other revolutionaries at this point, derived his argument from Rousseau, and claimed that the third estate was the nation and that as the nation it was its own sovereign. Now the middle-class lawyers and businessmen of the third estate acted on that claim. Locked out of their meeting hall on June 20, the commoners and a handful of sympathetic nobles and clergymen moved to a nearby indoor tennis court.

Here, under the leadership of Mirabeau and the Abbé Sieyès, they bound themselves by a solemn oath not to separate until they had drafted a constitution for France. This Oath of the Tennis Court, on June 20, 1789, was the real beginning of the French Revolution. By claiming the authority to remake the government in the name of the people, the Estates General was not merely protesting against the rule of Louis XVI but asserting its right to act as the highest sovereign power in the nation. On June 27 the king virtually conceded this right by ordering the remaining delegates of the privileged classes to meet with the third estate as members of the National Assembly.

The course of the French Revolution was marked by three stages, the first of which extended from June 1789 to August 1792. During most of this period the destinies of France were in the hands of the Na-

Abbé Sieyès

The Tennis Court Oath

The Opening of the Estates General in Versailles, May 5, 1789

The Tennis Court Oath by David. In the hall where royalty played a game known as *jeu de paume* (similar to tennis) leaders of the revolution swore to draft a constitution. In the center of this painting, with his arm extended, is Jean Bailly, president of the National Assembly. Seated at the table below him is Abbé Sieyès. Somewhat to the right of Sieyès, with both hands on his chest, is Robespierre. Mirabeau, with a hat in his left hand and wearing a black coat, stands somewhat farther to the right.

The first stage of the revolution

Fall of the Bastille

tional Assembly. In the main, this stage was moderate, its actions dominated by the leadership of liberal nobles and equally liberal men of the third estate. Yet three events in the summer and fall of 1789 furnished evidence that the revolution was to penetrate to the very heart of French society, ultimately touching both the urban populace and the rural peasants.

News of the events of late spring 1789 had spread quickly across France. From the very onset of debates on the nature of the political crisis, public attention was high. It was roused not merely by abstract interest in matters of political reform, however. Prices had risen to a point where the cost of bread alone consumed more than 50 percent of a poor family's income in August 1788, and 80 percent in February and July 1789. Belief was widespread that the aristocracy and king were together conspiring to punish an upstart third estate by encouraging scarcity and high prices. Rumors circulated in Paris during the latter days of June 1789. At their clubs and in their shops, those men and women who would come to be called the sans-culottes[4]—workshop masters, craftspeople, shopkeepers, petty tradespeople—worried about their fate. Determined to obtain arms to defend themselves from the threat of counterrevolution, they successfully stormed the ancient fortress of the Bastille on July 14, thereby establishing the fact of the king's impotence within his own capital. Built in the Middle Ages as a stronghold, the Bastille was no longer much used; but it symbolized royal authority to the masses. When crowds demanded

[4] So-called because the men did not wear upper-class breeches.

arms from its governor, he refused and opened fire. The crowd took revenge, not only by capturing the fortress but by murdering the governor.

The fall of the Bastille was the first of those events which were to demonstrate the commitment of the common people to revolutionary change. The second occurred in the countryside, where the peasants were suffering the direct effects of economic privation. They, too, feared a monarchical and aristocratic counterrevolution. Eager for news from Versailles, their anticipation turned to fear when they began to understand that a middle-class revolution might not address itself to their problems. Frightened and uncertain, peasants in many areas of France panicked in July and August, setting fire to manor houses and the records they contained, destroying monasteries and the residences of bishops, and murdering some of the nobles who offered resistance.

The "Great Fear"

The third instance of popular uprising, in October 1789, was also brought on by economic crisis. This time women, angered by the price of bread and fired by rumors of the king's continuing unwillingness to cooperate with the assembly, marched to Versailles on October 5 and demanded to be heard. Not satisfied with its reception by the assembly, the crowd broke through the gates to the palace, calling for the king to return to Paris. On the afternoon of the following day the king yielded. The National Guard, sympathetic to the agitators, led the crowd back to Paris, the procession headed by a soldier holding aloft a loaf of bread on his bayonet.

The "October Days"

In each case, these three popular uprisings produced a decided effect on the course of political events as they were unfolding at Versailles. The storming of the Bastille helped persuade the king and nobles to treat the National Assembly as the legislative body of the nation. The "Great Fear" inspired an equally great consternation among the debaters in the assembly. On August 4, with one sweep, the remnants of manorialism were largely obliterated. Ecclesiastical tithes and the *corvée* were formally abolished. Serfdom was eliminated. The hunting privileges of the nobles were declared at an end. Exemption from tax-

Achievements of the first stage: (1) the destruction of feudal privilege

The Departure of the Women of Paris for Versailles, October 1789. Note that the contemporary caption refers to the "heroines of Paris." An early example of revolutionary propaganda.

(2) the Declaration of the Rights of Man

(3) secularization of the Church

An Assignat

(4) constitution of 1791

ation and monopolies of all kinds were sacrificed as contrary to natural equality. While the nobles did not surrender all of their rights, the ultimate effect of these reforms of the "August Days" was to annihilate distinctions of rank and class and to make all French citizens of an equal status in the eyes of the law.

Following the destruction of privilege the assembly turned its attention to preparing a charter of liberties. The result was the Declaration of the Rights of Man and of the Citizen, issued in September 1789. Property was declared to be a natural right as well as liberty, security, and "resistance to oppression." Freedom of speech, religious toleration, and liberty of the press were held to be inviolable. All citizens were declared to be entitled to equality of treatment in the courts. No one was to be imprisoned or otherwise punished except in accordance with due process of law. Sovereignty was affirmed to reside in the people, and officers of the government were made subject to deposition if they abused the powers conferred upon them.

The king's return to Paris during the October Days confirmed the reforms already underway and guaranteed further liberalization along lines decreed by the middle-class majority in the assembly. In November 1789, the National Assembly resolved to confiscate the lands of the Church and to use them as collateral for the issue of *assignats,* or paper money, which, it was hoped, would resolve the country's inflationary economic crisis. In July of the following year the Civil Constitution of the Clergy was enacted, providing that all bishops and priests should be elected by the people and should be subject to the authority of the state. Their salaries were to be paid out of the public treasury, and they were required to swear allegiance to the new legislation. The secularization of the Church also involved a partial separation from Rome. The aim of the assembly was to make the Catholic Church of France a truly national institution with no more than a nominal subjection to the papacy.

Not until 1791 did the National Assembly manage to complete its primary task of drafting a new constitution for the nation. The constitution as it finally emerged gave eloquent testimony to the dominant position now held by the middle class. The government was converted into a limited monarchy, with the supreme power virtually a monopoly of the well-to-do. Although all citizens possessed the same civil rights, the vote was allowed only to those who paid a certain amount in taxes. About half the adult males in France made up this latter category of "active" citizen. Yet even their political power was curtailed, for they were to vote for electors, whose property ownership qualified them for that position. Those electors, in turn, chose department officials and delegates to the National—or, as it was now called, Constituent—Assembly. The king was deprived of the control he had formerly exercised over the army and local governments. His ministers were forbidden to sit in the assembly, and he was shorn of all power over the legislative process except a suspensive veto, which in fact could be overridden by the issuance of proclamations.

The economic and governmental changes the Constituent Assembly adopted were as much a reflection of Enlightenment liberalism as were its constitutional reforms. To raise money, it sold off Church lands, but in such large blocks that peasants seldom benefited by the sales as they had expected to. In opposition to the interests of the peasantry, the assembly proceeded with the enclosure of common lands in order to facilitate the development of capitalist agriculture. To encourage the growth of unfettered economic enterprise, guilds and trade unions were abolished. To rid the country of authoritarian centralization and of aristocratic domination, local governments were completely restructured. France was divided into eighty-three equal departments. All towns henceforth enjoyed the same form of municipal organization. All local officials were locally elected. This reorganization and decentralization expressed a liberal belief in the necessity of individual liberty and freedom from ancient privilege. As such these measures proclaimed, as did all the work of the assembly, that the "winners" of this first stage of the revolution were the men and women of the middle class.

(5) economic and governmental changes

3. A NEW STAGE: RADICAL REVOLUTION

Their triumph did not go unchallenged, however. In the summer of 1792, the revolution entered a second stage, which saw the downfall of moderate middle-class leaders and their replacement by radical republicans claiming to rule on behalf of the common people. Two major reasons accounted for this abrupt and drastic alteration in the course of events. First, the politically literate lower classes grew disillusioned as they perceived that the revolution was not benefiting them. The uncontrolled free-enterprise economy of the government resulted in constantly fluctuating and generally rising prices. These increases particularly exasperated those elements of the Parisian population that had agitated for change in preceding years. Rioting urban mobs demanded bread at prerevolutionary prices, while their spokesmen called for governmental control of the ever-growing inflation. Their leaders articulated as well the frustrations of a mass of men and women who felt cheated by the constitution. Despite their major role in the creation of a new regime, they found themselves deprived of any effective voice in its operation.

The second stage: (1) disappointment of the common people

The second major reason for the dramatic turn of events was the fact that France now found itself at war with much of the rest of Europe. From the outset of the revolution, men and women across Europe had been compelled, by the very intensity of events in France, to take sides in the conflict. What we have called the first revolution

(2) the revolution abroad

A Contemporary Engraving of the September Massacres in Paris, 1792

won the support of a wide range of thoughtful intellectuals, politicians, businessmen, and artisans. Strikes and revolts broke out in Germany and Belgium. In England, philosophical radicals such as Joseph Priestley, the scientist, and Richard Price, a Unitarian minister, joined with businessmen such as James Watt and Matthew Boulton to welcome the overthrow of privilege and absolutism. Others opposed the course of the revolution from the start. Edmund Burke, in his famous pamphlet, *Reflections on the Revolution in France,* denounced the egalitarian actions of the revolutionaries. The monarchs of Europe responded with at least passive sympathy to the distressed clamorings of Louis XVI, Marie Antoinette, his impetuous, ultra-conservative queen, and the émigré nobles who soon fled to the courts of German principalities in pursuit of assistance for their doomed cause.

It is questionable, however, whether that sympathy would have turned to active opposition, had not the French soon appeared as a threat to international stability and the individual ambitions of the great powers. It was that threat which led to war in 1792, and which kept the Continent in arms for a generation.

This state of war had a most important impact on the formation of political and social attitudes during this period in Europe. Once a country declared war with France, its citizens could no longer espouse sympathy with the revolution without paying severe consequences. Those who continued to support the revolution, as did a good many among the artisan and small tradespeople class, were persecuted and punished for their beliefs. To be found in Britain, for example, possessing a copy of Tom Paine's revolutionary tract, *The Rights of Man* (1791–1792), a prorevolutionary response to Burke's *Reflections,* was enough to warrant imprisonment. As the moderate nature of the early revolution turned to violent extension, entrepreneurs and business-

The impact of international war

men eagerly sought to live down their radical sentiments of a few years past. The wars against revolutionary France came to be perceived as a matter of national survival; to ensure internal security, it seemed, particularly to the English, that patriotism demanded not only a condemnation of the French but of French ideas as well.

The first European states to express public concern about events in revolutionary France were Austria and Prussia. They were not anxious to declare war; their interests at the time centered upon the division of Poland between themselves. Nevertheless, they jointly issued the Declaration of Pillnitz in August 1791, in which they avowed that the restoration of order and of the rights of the monarch of France was a matter of "common interest to all sovereigns of Europe." The leaders of the French government at this time were the moderate Girondists, many of whom came from the mercantile Girondist department. The Girondists drew their support largely from regions outside Paris, and were inclined to mistrust urban radicals. Afraid of losing political support in France, they pronounced the Declaration of Pillnitz a threat to national security, hoping that enthusiasm for a war would unite the French and result also in enthusiasm for their continued rule. They were aided in their scheme by the activities of monarchists, both within and outside France, whose plottings and pronouncements could be made to appear an additional threat, though to a greater extent than they actually were. On April 20, 1792, the assembly declared war against Austria and Prussia.

Although the Girondist faction expected that military success would solidify the loyalty of the people to the regime, many anti-Girondist radicals were clamoring for war in the secret hope that the armies of France would suffer defeat, and that the monarchy would thereby be discredited. A republic could then be set up, and the heroic soldiers of the people would turn defeat into victory and carry the blessings of freedom to all the oppressed of Europe. As the radicals had hoped, the forces of the French met serious reverses. By August 1792 the allied armies of Austria and Prussia had crossed the frontier and were threatening the capture of Paris. A fury of rage and despair seized the capital. The belief prevailed that the military disasters had been the result of treasonable dealings with the enemy on the part of the king and his conservative followers. As a consequence, a vigorous demand arose from the radicals for drastic action against all who were suspected of disloyalty to the revolution. It was this situation more than anything else which brought the extremists to the fore and enabled them to gain control of the assembly and to put an end to the monarchy.

From this point, the country's leadership passed into the hands of an equalitarian-minded "middle" middle class. These new leaders called themselves Jacobins, after the Parisian political club to which they belonged. The hallmarks of the Jacobin, or second, stage of the French Revolution were its radical republicanism and its "Reign of Terror."

Edmund Burke

Declaration of Pillnitz

The course of war

Thomas Paine

The government during the second stage: the national convention

One of the Jacobins' first actions was to ask all Frenchmen to vote for delegates to a national convention, to draft a new and more republican constitution. This convention, which assembled in September 1792, became the effective governing body of the country for the next three years. It was composed entirely of republicans; 486 of its 749 members were men who had not sat in the old assembly. On September 21, the convention abolished the monarchy and declared France a republic. In December, the convention placed the former king, Louis XVI, on trial; in January he was, by one vote, condemned to death. He and his queen suffered death on the guillotine, the frightful mechanical headsman that was one of the most famous and feared instruments of revolutionary fervor.

Domestic reforms

Meanwhile, the convention turned its attention to the enactment of further domestic reforms. Among its most significant accomplishments over the next three years were the abolition of slavery in French colonies; the prohibition of imprisonment for debt; the establishment of the metric system of weights and measures; and the repeal of primogeniture, so that property might not be inherited exclusively by the oldest son, but be divided in substantially equal portions among all immediate heirs. The convention also attempted to supplement the decrees of the assembly in abolishing the remnants of manorialism and in providing for greater freedom of economic opportunity for the commoner. The property of enemies of the revolution was confiscated for the benefit of the government and the lower classes. Great estates were broken up and offered for sale to poorer citizens on easy terms. The indemnities hitherto promised to the nobles for the loss of their privileges were abruptly canceled. To curb the rise in the cost of living, maximum prices for grain and other necessities were fixed by

The Execution of Louis XVI. A revolutionary displays the king's head moments after it had been severed by the guillotine in January 1793.

law, and merchants who profiteered at the expense of the poor were threatened with the guillotine. Still other measures of reform were those in the sphere of religion. At one time during the period, an effort was made to abolish Christianity and to substitute the worship of Reason in its place. In accordance with this purpose a new calendar was adopted, dating the year from the birth of the republic (September 22, 1792) and dividing the months in such a way as to eliminate the Christian Sunday. Later, this cult of Reason was replaced by a Deistic religion dedicated to the worship of a Supreme Being and to a belief in the immortality of the soul. Finally, in 1794, the convention decreed simply that religion was a private matter, that Church and State would therefore be separated, and that all beliefs not actually hostile to the government would be tolerated.

While effecting this political revolution in France, the convention's leadership at the same time accomplished an astonishingly successful reorganization of its armies. By February 1793, Britain, Holland, Spain, and Austria were in the field against the French. Britain's entrance into the war was dictated by both strategic and economic reasons. The English feared French penetration into the Low Countries directly across the Channel; they were also concerned that French expansion might pose a serious threat to Britain's own growing mercantile hegemony around the globe. The allied coalition ranged against France, though united only in its desire to somehow contain this puzzling, fearsome revolutionary phenomenon, was nevertheless a formidable force. To counter it, the French organized an army that was able to win engagement after engagement during these years. In August 1793, the revolutionary government imposed a levy on the entire male population capable of bearing arms. Fourteen hastily drafted armies were flung into battle under the leadership of young and inexperienced officers. What they lacked in training and discipline, they made up for in improvised organization, mobility, flexibility, courage, and morale. (In the navy, however, where skill was of paramount importance, the revolutionary French never succeeded in matching the performance of the British.) In 1793–1794, the French armies preserved their homeland. In 1794–1795, they occupied the Low Countries, the Rhineland, parts of Spain, Switzerland, and Savoy. In 1796, they invaded and occupied key parts of Italy and broke the coalition that had arrayed itself against them.

The revolutionary wars

These achievements were not without their price, however. To insure their accomplishment, the rulers of France resorted to a bloody authoritarianism that has come to be known as the Reign of Terror. Although the convention succeeded in 1793 in drafting a new democratic constitution, based upon manhood suffrage, it deferred its introduction because of wartime emergency. Instead, the convention prolonged its own life year by year, and increasingly delegated its responsibilities to a group of twelve leaders known as the Committee of Public Safety. By this time the moderate, upper middle-class Giron-

The dictatorship of the Committee of Public Safety

The Death of Marat. This painting by the French artist David immortalized Marat. The bloody towel, the box, and the tub were venerated as relics of the revolution.

dists had lost all influence within the convention. Complete power had passed to the Jacobins, who, though themselves from the middle class, were ardent disciples of Rousseau and champions of the urban workers.

Marat and Danton

Foremost among the leaders of the extremist faction and members of the Committee of Public Safety, were Marat, Danton, and Robespierre. Jean Paul Marat (1743–1793) was educated as a physician, and, by 1789, had already earned enough distinction in that profession to be awarded an honorary degree by St. Andrews University in Scotland. Almost from the beginning of the revolution he stood as a champion of the common people. He opposed nearly all of the dogmatic assumptions of his middle-class colleagues in the assembly, including the idea that France should pattern its government after that of Great Britain, which he recognized to be oligarchic in form. He was soon made a victim of persecution and was forced to find refuge in sewers and dungeons, but this did not stop him from his efforts to rouse the people to a defense of their rights. In 1793 he was stabbed through the heart by Charlotte Corday, a young woman who was fanatically devoted to the Girondists. In contrast with Marat, Georges Jacques Danton (1759–1794) did not come into prominence until the revolution was three years old; but, like Marat, he directed his activities toward goading the masses into rebellion. Elected a member of the Committee of Public Safety in 1793, he had much to do with organizing the Reign of Terror. As time went on he appears to have wearied of ruthlessness and displayed a tendency to compromise. This gave his opponents in the convention their opportunity, and in April 1794, he was sent to the guillotine. Upon mounting the scaffold he is reported

Danton

to have said: "Show my head to the people; they do not see the like every day."

The most famous and perhaps the greatest of all the extremist leaders was Maximilien Robespierre (1758–1794). Born of a family reputed to be of Irish descent, Robespierre was trained for the law and speedily achieved a modest success as an advocate. In 1782 he was appointed a criminal judge, but soon resigned because he could not bear to impose a sentence of death. Of a nervous and timid disposition, he was never able to display much executive ability, but he made up for this lack of talent by fanatical devotion to principle. He had adopted the belief that the philosophy of Rousseau held the one great hope of salvation for all mankind. To put this philosophy into practice he was ready to employ any means that would bring results, regardless of the cost to himself or to others. This passionate loyalty to a gospel that exalted the masses eventually won him a following. Indeed, he was so lionized by the public that he was allowed to wear the knee breeches, silk stockings, and powdered hair of the old society until the end of his life. In 1791 he was accepted as the oracle of the Jacobin Club, now purged of all but its most radical elements. Later he became president of the National Convention and a member of the Committee of Public Safety. Though he had little or nothing to do with originating the Reign of Terror, he was nevertheless responsible for enlarging its scope. He actually came to justify ruthlessness as a necessary and therefore laudable means to revolutionary progress. In the last six weeks of his virtual dictatorship, no fewer than 1,285 heads rolled from the scaffold in Paris.

Robespierre

The years of the Reign of Terror were years of ruthless dictatorship in France. Pressed by foreign enemies from without, the committee faced sabotage from both the political Right and Left at home. In 1793, a large band of peasants, opposed to military conscription and encouraged by British and royalist agents, revolted in the western area of the Vendée. Girondist fugitives helped fuel rebellions in the great provincial cities of Lyon, Bordeaux, and Marseilles. This harvest of the decentralizing policies of the National Assembly was bitter fruit to the committee. At the same time they met with the scornful criticism of revolutionaries even more radical than themselves. This latter group, known as the *enragés,* was led by the journalist Jacques Hébert, and threatened to topple not only the government but the country itself by its extremist crusades. Determined to stabilize France, whatever the necessary cost, the committee dispatched commissioners into the countryside to suppress the enemies of the state. During the period of the Terror, from September 1793 to July 1794, the most reliable estimates place the number of executions at approximately twenty thousand in France as a whole. A law of September 17, 1793, made every person who had been identified in any way with the Bourbon government or with the Girondists an object of suspicion; and no one who was a suspect or who was suspected of being a suspect was entirely

Jacobins. Contemporary drawings by Heuriot.

A Meeting of the Revolutionary Committee During the Reign of Terror

safe from persecution. When some time later the Abbé Sieyès was asked what he had done to distinguish himself during the Terror, he responded dryly, "I lived."

The achievements of the committee

Three points need to be made with regard to the Committee of Public Safety. First, it dramatically reversed the trend toward decentralization, which had characterized the reforms of the assembly. In addition to dispatching its own commissioners from Paris to quell provincial insurrection, the committee published a *Bulletin des loix,* to inform all citizens what laws were to be enforced and obeyed. And it replaced local officials, some of them still royalist in sympathy, with its own loyal "national agents." Second, by fostering, as it did, the interests of the lower middle class the committee significantly retarded the pace of industrial transformation in France. Through policies which assisted the peasant, the small craftsman, and the shopkeeper to acquire property, the government during this "second" revolution encouraged the entrenchment of a class at once devoted to the principle of republicanism while unalterably opposed to a large-scale capitalist transformation of the economy of France. Third, the ruthless Terror of the committee undoubtedly achieved its end, by saving France from defeat at the hands of the coalition of European states. Whether the human price extracted in return for that salvation was worth the paying is a matter historians—and indeed all thoughtful human beings—may well never finally resolve.

The Thermidorian reaction: stage three

The Committee of Public Safety, though able to save France, could not save itself. It failed to put a stop to inflation, thereby losing the support of those commoners whose dissatisfactions had helped bring the convention to power. The long string of military victories convinced growing numbers that the committee's demands for continuing self-sacrifice, as well as its insistence upon the necessity of the Ter-

ror, were no longer justified. By July 1794, the committee was
virtually without allies. On July 27 (9 Thermidor, according to the
new calendar) the convention "outlawed" Robespierre; on the following day he was executed. The only remaining leaders in the convention were men of moderate sympathies, who, as time went on, inclined toward increasing conservatism. Gradually, the revolution came
once more to reflect the interests of the upper middle class. Much of
the extremist work of the radicals was now undone. The law of maximum prices and the law against "suspects" were both repealed. Political prisoners were freed, the Jacobins driven into hiding, and the
Committee of Public Safety shorn of its absolute powers. The new situation made possible the return of priests, royalists, and other émigrés
from abroad to add the weight of their influence to the conservative
trend.

In 1795 the National Convention adopted a new constitution,
which lent the stamp of official approval to the victory of the prosperous classes. The constitution granted suffrage to all adult male citizens
who could read and write. They were permitted to vote for electors,
who in turn would choose the members of the legislative body. In
order to be an elector, one had to be the proprietor of a farm or other
establishment with an annual income equivalent to at least one
hundred days of labor. The drafters of the constitution thus ensured
that the authority of the government would actually be derived from
citizens of considerable wealth. Since it was not practicable to restore
the monarchy, lest the old aristocracy also come back into power, executive authority was vested in a board of five men known as the Directory, chosen by the legislative body. The new constitution included not only a bill of rights but also a declaration of the *duties* of the
citizen. Conspicuous among the latter was the obligation to bear in

The 1795 constitution

The Death of Robespierre

mind that "it is upon the maintenance of property . . . that the whole social order rests."

The Directory

The reign of the Directory has not enjoyed a good historical press. The collection of *nouveau riche* speculators and profiteers who rose to prominence as they labored to make a good thing for themselves out of the war were not a particularly attractive crew. They were lampooned as ostentatious and vulgar *"merveilleuses"*—outrageously overdressed men and underdressed women. But however anxious they were to live down the self-denying excesses of the past several years by self-indulgent excesses of their own, they were in no mood to see the major accomplishments of the revolution undone. They had no difficulty in disposing of threats from the Left, despite their failure to resolve that bugbear of all revolutionary governments, inflation and rising living costs. When in 1796 the radical "Gracchus" Babeuf[5] launched a campaign to abolish private property and parliamentary government, his followers were arrested, executed, and deported.

Napoleon rescues the Directory

To dispatch threats from the Right was not so easy. Elections in March 1797—the first free elections held in France as a republic—returned a large number of constitutional monarchists to the councils of government. Leading politicians, among them some who had voted for the execution of Louis XVI, took alarm. So too did the Directory's brilliant young general, Napoleon Bonaparte (1769–1821). His plans for permanent French expansion in Belgium and Italy were threatened by a promonarchist "peace" party that was urging an end to war, even if it meant the surrender of recent French conquests. Desperate to save republican France—and themselves—from the monarchists, the directors called for Napoleon's assistance. He sent a general to their aid. With the support of the army thus assured, the Directory in September 1797 annulled most of the election results of the previous

[5] Called "Gracchus" after the Roman tribune Gaius Gracchus, a hero of the people.

The Eighteenth Brumaire. A detail from a painting by Bronchet depicting Napoleon as the man of the hour.

spring. Its bold coup did little, however, to end the nation's political irresolution. Two years later, after a series of further abortive uprisings and purges, and with the country still plagued by severe inflation, Bonaparte seized his opportunity to fill the vacuum of French leadership. Leaving his army as it attempted to free itself from British naval domination in Egypt, Bonaparte appeared in France. Appealing to the desperate Directory, he descended upon them as the answer to their prayers: a strong popular leader who was not a king. Abbé Sieyès, who had once declared for revolution in the name of the third estate, now declared for counterrevolution in the name of virtual dictatorship: "Confidence from below, authority from above." With those words Sieyès foreshadowed the end of the revolutionary period.

4. NAPOLEON AND EUROPE

Few men in Western history have compelled the attention of the world as Napoleon Bonaparte did during the fifteen years of his absolutist rule in France. And few men have succeeded as he has in continuing to live on as myth in the consciousness, not just of his own country, but of all Europe. Without doubt, part of the success of the Napoleonic myth can be credited to the fact that Napoleon never attempted to disguise his less-than-gentlemanly background. Although born in Corsica into a family that held a title of nobility from the Republic of Genoa, he cultivated the rude manners of an *arriviste,* losing his temper, cheating at cards, taking what he could get without regard to the conventions of polite society. As such, he appealed to the new citizens of a triumphantly middle-class Europe. In the minds of his admirers he would remain the "little corporal" who, without the privileges of the aristocrat, had made it to the top on his own.

The character of Napoleon Bonaparte

Yet the myth was also grounded in the important fact of Bonaparte's undoubted abilities. Schooled in France and at the military academy in Paris, he possessed a mind congenial to the ideas of the Enlightenment—creative, imaginative, and ready to perceive things anew. His primary interests were history, law, and mathematics. His particular strengths as a leader lay in his ability to conceive of financial, legal, or military plans and then to master their every detail; his capacity for inspiring others, even those initially oppsed to him; and his belief in himself as the destined savior of the French. That last conviction eventually became the obsession that led to Napoleon's undoing. But supreme self-confidence was just what the French government had lacked since the first days of the revolution. Napoleon believed both in himself and in France. That latter belief was the tonic France now needed, and Napoleon proceeded to administer it in liberally revivifying doses.

His abilities

During the years from 1799 to 1804, Napoleon ruled under the title of first consul, but in reality as a dictator. Once again, France was given a new constitution. Though the document spoke of universal male suffrage, political power was retained, by the now familiar means of indirect election, in the hands of middle-class entrepreneurs and professionals. Recognizing, however, that his regime would derive additional substance if it could be made to appear the government of the people of France, Bonaparte instituted what has since become a common authoritarian device: the plebiscite. The voters were asked to approve the new constitution and did so by the loudly proclaimed vote of 3,011,107 in favor, 1,567 opposed.

Although the constitution provided for a legislative body, that body could neither initiate nor discuss legislation. The first consul made use of a Council of State to draft his laws; but in fact the government depended on the authority of one man. Bonaparte had no desire to undo the major egalitarian reforms of the revolution. He reconfirmed the abolition of estates, privileges, and local liberties, thereby reconfirming as well the notion of a meritocracy, of "careers open to talent," dear to the hearts of the middle class. Through centralization of the administrative departments, he achieved what no recent French regime had yet achieved, an orderly and generally fair system of taxation. His plan, by prohibiting the type of exemptions formerly granted the nobility and clergy, and by centralizing collection, enabled him to budget rationally for expenditures and consequent indebtedness. In this way he reduced the inflationary spiral that had entangled so many past governments.

Napoleon. A famous unfinished portrait by David.

Napoleon's most significant accomplishment was his completion of the educational and legal reforms begun during the revolutionary period. He ordered the establishment of *lycées* (high schools) in every major town and a school in Paris for the training of teachers. To supplement these changes, Napoleon brought the military and technical schools under state control and founded a national university to exercise supervision over the entire system. Like almost all his reforms, this one proved of particular benefit to the middle class; so did the new

legal code promulgated in 1810. The Code Napoleon, as the new body of laws was called, reflected two principles which had threaded their way through all the constitutional changes since 1789: uniformity and individualism. The code made French law uniform, declaring past customs and privileges forever abolished. By underscoring in various ways a private individual's right to property, by authorizing new methods for the drafting of contracts, leases, and stock companies, and by once again prohibiting trade unions, the code worked to the benefit of individually minded entrepreneurs and businessmen.

To accomplish these reforms Napoleon called upon the most talented men available to him, regardless of their past political affiliations. He admitted back into the country émigrés of all political stripes. His two fellow consuls—joint executives, but in name only—were a regicide of the Terror and bureaucrat of the Old Regime. His minister of police had been an extreme radical republi-

Coronation of Napoleon and Josephine by David. Napoleon crowned himself and his wife and assumed the title of Napoleon I, emperor of the French.

can; his minister of foreign affairs was the opportunist aristocrat Talleyrand. The work of political reconciliation was assisted by Napoleon's 1801 concordat with the pope, which reunited Church and State. Though the action disturbed former anti-Church Jacobins, Napoleon, ever the pragmatist, believed the reconciliation of Church and State necessary for reasons both of domestic harmony and of international solidarity. According to the terms of the concordat, the pope received the right to depose French bishops and to discipline the French clergy. At the same time, the Vatican agreed to lay to rest any claims against the expropriation of former Church lands. Hereafter, that property would remain unchallenged in the hands of its new middle-class rural and urban proprietors. In return, the clergy was guaranteed an income from the state. The concordat did nothing to revoke the principle of religious freedom established by the revolution. Although the Roman Catholic clergy received state money, so did Protestant clergy.

Napoleon's agreement won him the support of those conservatives who had feared for France's future as a Godless state. To prove to the old Jacobins, in turn, that he remained a child of their revolution, he invaded the independent state of Baden in 1804 to arrest and then execute the duke of Enghien, a relative of the Bourbons, whom Napoleon falsely accused of a plot against his life. (Three years before he had deported over one hundred Jacobins on a similar charge, but with no permanent political repercussions.) The balancing act only served to increase Napoleon's general popularity. By 1802 the people of France were prepared to accept him as "consul for life." In 1804, they rejoiced when, in the cathedral of Notre Dame, in Paris, he crowned himself Emperor Napoleon I.

Across the boundaries of France, the nations of Europe had watched, some in admiration, others in horror, all in astonishment, at

Napoleon crowned emperor

the phenomenon that was Napoleon. They had fought France since 1792 in hopes of maintaining European stability. Now they faced the greatest threat to that stability yet to arise. The detailed history of the wars fought to contain the French is complex, and of little direct relevance to the patterns of ideas, institutions, and societies we are tracing. Suffice it to say that from 1792 until 1795 France had been at war with a coalition of European powers—principally Austria, Prussia, and Britain. In 1795, Prussia retired from the fray, financially exhausted and at odds with Austria. In 1797, the Austrians, defeated by Bonaparte in northern Italy, withdrew as well, signing the Treaty of Campo Formio, which ceded to France territories in Belgium, recognized the Cisalpine Republic which Bonaparte had established in Italy, and agreed to France's occupation of the left bank of the Rhine.

By the following year, Britain was left to fight the French alone. In 1798 it formed a second coalition against the French, this one with Russia and Austria. The results did not differ significantly from those of the first allied attempt to contain France. Russia and Austria had no success in driving the French from Italy; the French likewise failed to break Britain's advantage at sea. By 1801, the coalition was in tatters, Russia having withdrawn two years previously. The Treaty of Lunéville, signed by France and Austria, confirmed the provisions of Campo Formio; in addition the so-called Batavian, Helvetian, Cisalpine, and Ligurian republics—established by Napoleon from territories in the Low Countries, Switzerland, Italy, and Piedmont—were legitimized. The Austrians also acquiesced to a general redrawing of the map of Germany, which resulted eventually in an amalgamation of semi-independent states under French domination into the Confederation of the Rhine. The following year Britain, no longer able to fight alone, settled with the French as well, returning all the territories it had captured in overseas colonial engagements except Trinidad and Ceylon.

Under Napoleon's reign, the territories of central Europe underwent a revolution. This revolution was a thorough governmental reorganization, one which imposed the major egalitarian reforms of the French Revolution upon lands outside the borders of France, while building a French empire. Most affected were territories in Italy (the "Kingdom of Italy" as it was now called); Germany (the Confederation of the Rhine, including the newly formed Kingdom of Westphalia); Dalmatia (the Illyrian provinces); and Holland. (Belgium had been integrated directly into the empire.) Into all these territories Napoleon introduced a carefully organized, deliberate system of administration, based upon the notion of careers open to talent, equality before the law, and the abolition of ancient customs and privileges. The Napoleonic program of reform in the empire represented an application of the principles that had already transformed postrevolutionary France. Manorial courts were liquidated, and Church courts abolished. Provinces were joined into an enormous bureaucratic network that reached directly back to Paris. Laws were codified, the tax system modernized, and everywhere individuals were freed to work at whatever trade they chose. The one freedom denied throughout this new grand hegemony was that of self-government: i.e., all governmental direction emanated from Paris, and therefore from Napoleon. Despite that fact, middle-class business and professional men, who had chafed against restrictions imposed upon them by petty despotic traditions, welcomed this chance to exercise their talents to a fuller degree than they had ever before enjoyed.

Napoleon's motives in introducing these various radical changes were by no means altruistic. He understood that the defense of his enormous domain depended on efficient administration and the rational collection and expenditure of funds for his armies. His boldest attempt at consolidation, however, a policy forbidding the importation into the Continent of British goods, proved a failure. This "Continental System," established in 1806, was designed as a strategic measure in Napoleon's continuing economic war against Britain. Its purpose was to destroy Britain's commerce and credit—to starve it economically into surrender. The system failed for several reasons. Foremost was the fact that throughout the war Britain retained control of the seas. The British naval blockade of the Continent, implemented in 1807, served, therefore, as an effective counter to Napoleon's system. While the empire labored to transport goods and raw materials overland to avoid the British blockade, the British worked with success to develop a lively trade with South America. Internal tariffs were a second reason for the failure of the system. Napoleon was unable to persuade individual territories to join a tariff-free customs union. As a result Europe remained divided into economic camps, fortified against each other by tariffs, and at odds with each other as they attempted to subsist on nothing more than what the Continent could produce and manufacture. The final reason for the system's collapse was the stark fact that the Continent had more to lose than Britain. Trade stagnated; ports and manufacturing centers grumbled as unemployment rose.

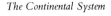

The Continental System

5. THE END OF THE REVOLUTIONARY ERA

The Continental System was Napoleon's first serious mistake. As such it was one of the causes of his ultimate downfall. A second cause of Napoleon's decline was his constantly growing ambition and increasing sense of self-importance. Napoleon's goal was a united Europe modeled after the Roman Empire. The symbols of his empire—reflected in painting, architecture, and the design of furniture and clothing—were deliberately Roman in origin. But Napoleon's Rome was without question imperial, dynastic Rome. The triumphal

The Empress Josephine

Reasons for Napoleon's fall

columns and arches he had erected to commemorate his victories recalled the ostentatious monuments of the Roman emperors. He made his brothers and sisters the monarchs of his newly created kingdoms, which Napoleon controlled from Paris. He divorced his first wife, the Empress Josephine, alleging her childlessness, and insured himself a successor of royal blood by marrying into the house of Hapsburg. Even his admirers began to question if Napoleon's empire was not simply a larger, more efficient, and, therefore, ultimately more dangerous despotism than the monarchies of the eighteenth century. War again broke out in 1805, with the Russians, Prussians, and Austrians joining the British in an attempt to contain France. But to no avail; Napoleon's military superiority led to defeats, in turn, of all three continental allies. Ultimately only the emperor's own unwillingness to recognize that his supply of men, materiel, and good fortune was not limitless brought military defeat upon him.

Invasion of Spain

In 1808, Napoleon invaded Spain on the pretext of guarding its coasts against the British, but with the intention of establishing his brother Joseph as king. Scarcely had the new monarch been crowned than the Spanish people rose in revolt. Though Napoleon sent an army against them, he was never able to crush the rebellion entirely. With encouragement and assistance from the British, the Spaniards kept up a series of guerilla attacks which caused no end of expense and annoyance to the great warlord of France. Further, the courage of Spain in resisting the invader promoted a spirit of defiance elsewhere, with the result that Napoleon could no longer count upon the docility of any of his victims.

See color map facing page 705

A more fateful stage in the downfall of the Corsican adventurer was

The Retreat from Russia. In this painting by Charlet the horrors of the Russian winter can be seen.

the disruption of his alliance with Russia. As a purely agricultural country, Russia had suffered a severe economic crisis when it was no longer able, as a result of the Continental System, to exchange its surplus grain for British manufactures. The consequence was that Tsar Alexander began to wink at trade with Britain and to ignore or evade the protests from Paris. By 1811 Napoleon decided that he could endure this flouting of the Continental System no longer. Accordingly, he collected an army of 600,000 men and set out in the spring of 1812 to punish the tsar. The project ended in disaster. The Russians refused to make a stand, thereby leading the French farther and farther into the heart of their country. They finally permitted Napoleon to occupy their ancient capital of Moscow. But on the very night of his entry, a fire of suspicious origin broke out in the city. When the flames subsided, little but the blackened walls of the Kremlin palaces remained to shelter the invading troops. Hoping that the tsar would eventually surrender, Napoleon lingered amid the ruins for more than a month, finally deciding on October 22 to begin the homeward march. The delay was a fatal blunder. Long before he had reached the border, the terrible Russian winter was upon his troops. Swollen streams, mountainous drifts of snow, and bottomless mud slowed the retreat almost to a halt. To add to the miseries of bitter cold, disease, and starvation, mounted Cossacks rode out of the blizzard to harry the exhausted army. Each morning the miserable remnant that pushed on left behind circles of corpses around the campfires of the night before. On December 13 a few thousand broken soldiers crossed the frontier into Germany—a miserable fraction of what had once been proudly styled the *Grande Armée*. The lives of nearly 300,000 men had been sacrificed in Napoleon's Russian adventure.

The allies now took advantage of Napoleon's depleted forces to engineer victory. By March of 1814 their armies were in Paris and Napoleon prepared for surrender. Exiled to the island of Elba, in the Mediterranean, he plotted return, while his successor Louis XVIII, brother of Louis XVI and the choice of the allies, attempted to fill a space far too great for his mediocre talents. In the spring of 1815, Napoleon returned to France, where he was received enthusiastically. But the rekindled loyalties could not outlast his final defeat at the Battle of Waterloo, in Belgium, on June 18, 1815. This time the allies exiled him to the tiny island of St. Helena, in the south Atlantic, where he died in 1821.

To appreciate the impact of this era of revolution upon Western civilization, one must trace the ideas and institutions it fostered as they work their way into the history of nineteenth- and twentieth-century Europe and America. Liberty—the right to act within the world with responsibility to no one but oneself—was a notion dear to those who made the French Revolution, and one which remained embodied in the reforms it produced. So was equality—the notion of rational laws

EXTRAIT DU MONITEUR.

ACTE
D'ABDICATION
DE
L'EMPEREUR NAPOLÉON.

Napoleon's Abdication Proclamation, 1814

The Russian campaign

The Battle of Waterloo

The era of revolution: liberty, equality, nationality

applied even-handedly to all, regardless of birth or position. National pride, the era's third legacy, was bred in the hearts of the French people as they watched their citizen armies repel attacks against their newly won freedoms. It was instilled, as well, into those whose opposition to the French made them more conscious of their own national identity. The three concepts—liberty, equality, and nationality—were now no longer merely ideas; as laws and as a new way of addressing life, they rested at the center of European reality. They were together one of the two elements upon which a new ruling class—the middle class—now rose to power. The other element—economic success—is the subject of the next chapter.

SELECTED READINGS

• *Items so designated are available in paperback editions.*

• Arendt, Hannah, *On Revolution*, New York, 1963. An analysis of the American and French Revolutions and their meaning for modern man.

Bosher, J. F., *French Finances, 1770–1795: From Business to Bureaucracy*, Cambridge, 1970. An impressive study concerned with the financial apparatus of Old Regime and revolutionary France.

• Breunig, C., *The Age of Revolution and Reaction, 1789–1850*, 2nd ed., New York, 1978.

• Brinton, Crane, *Anatomy of Revolution*, rev. ed., New York, 1961. Attempts to create a general model of revolutions by comparing the English, American, French and Russian Revolutions.

• ———, *A Decade of Revolution, 1789–1799*, New York, 1934. An excellent European survey.

• Bruun, Geoffrey, *Europe and the French Imperium, 1799–1814*, New York, 1938. Describes the impact of Napoleon upon Europe.

Cobban, Alfred, *The Social Interpretation of the French Revolution*, Cambridge, 1964. A penetrating critique of the radical interpretation of the revolution, more important for its questions than its conclusions.

Cone, Carl B., *The English Jacobins: Reformers in Late 18th-Century England*, New York, 1968.

Dansette, Adrien, *A Religious History of Modern France*, Vol. I, New York, 1961. Traces the position of the Catholic Church during the revolutionary and Napoleonic periods.

Ford, Franklin, *Robe and Sword: The Regrouping of the French Aristocracy after Louis XIV*, Cambridge, Mass., 1953. An important social study of the nobility of the robe and its striving for political dominance prior to the revolution.

• Gershoy, Leo, *The French Revolution and Napoleon*, rev. ed., New York, 1964. A good survey with annotated bibliography.

———, *From Despotism to Revolution, 1763–1789*, New York, 1944. Valuable for background on the revolution.

Geyl, Pieter, *Napoleon: For and Against*, rev. ed., New Haven, Conn., 1964. The ways in which Napoleon has been interpreted by French historians and political figures.

Gooch, G. P., *Germany and the French Revolution*, New York, 1920. An old but still valuable account of the German political and intellectual response to the French Revolution.

Goodwin, Albert, *The French Revolution*, rev. ed., London, 1958. A good introduction to the years 1789–1794.

Greer, Donald, *The Incidence of the Terror During the French Revolution: A Statistical Interpretation*, Cambridge, Mass., 1935. An important study which reveals that the lower classes suffered most during the Terror, rather than the nobility or the clergy.

• Hampson, Norman, *A Social History of the French Revolution*, London, 1963.

Herold, J. Christopher, *The Age of Napoleon*, New York, 1963.

• Lefebvre, Georges, *The Coming of the French Revolution*, Princeton, N.J., 1947. An excellent study of the causes and early events of the revolution.

———, *The French Revolution*, 2 vols., New York, 1963–64. An impressive synthesis by the greatest modern scholar of the revolution.

———, *Napoleon*, New York, 1969.

———, *The Thermidorians and the Directory*, New York, 1964.

McManners, John, *The French Revolution and the Church*, New York, 1969. Describes the impact of revolutionary anticlericalism upon the French Church.

Mathiez, Albert, *The French Revolution*, New York, 1928. Sympathetic to Robespierre.

• Palmer, R. R., *The Age of the Democratic Revolution: A Political History of Europe and America, 1760–1800*, 2 vols., Princeton, N.J., 1964. Impressive for its scope; places the French Revolution in the large context of a worldwide revolutionary movement.

———, *Twelve Who Ruled*, Princeton, 1958. Excellent biographical studies of the members of the Committee of Public Safety. Demonstrates that Robespierre's role has been exaggerated.

• Rudé, George, *The Crowd in the French Revolution*, Oxford, 1959. An important monograph which analyzes the composition of the crowds which participated in the great uprisings of the revolution.

Schapiro, J. S., *Condorcet and the Rise of Liberalism in France*, New York, 1934. A splendid study of revolutionary idealism.

Soboul, Albert, *The Sans-Culottes: The Popular Movement and Revolutionary Government, 1793–1794*, Garden City, N.Y., 1972. An outstanding example of "history from below"; analyzes the pressures upon the Convention in the year of the Terror.

Thompson, J. M., *Napoleon Bonaparte: His Rise and Fall*, Oxford, 1958. The standard work.

• ———, *Robespierre and the French Revolution*, London, 1953. An excellent short biography.

• Tilly, Charles, *The Vendée: A Sociological Analysis of the Counter-Revolution of 1793*, Cambridge, Mass., 1964. An important economic and social analysis of the factors that led to reaction in the Vendée.

• Tocqueville, Alexis de, *The Old Regime and French Revolution*. Originally written in 1856, this remains a classic analysis of the causes of the French Revolution.

• Williams, Gwyn A., *Artisans and Sans-Culottes*, New York, 1969.

SOURCE MATERIALS

• Burke, Edmund, *Reflections on the Revolution in France,* London, 1790. The great conservative statement against the revolution and its principles.
• Montesquieu, Baron de, *The Spirit of the Laws,* New York, 1945. See especially Books I, II, III, XI.
• Paine, Thomas, *The Rights of Man,* 1791. (Many editions.) Paine's eloquent response to Burke's *Reflections* resulted in his conviction for treason and banishment from England.
• Rousseau, Jean-Jacques, *Discourse on the Origin of Inequality,* 1754. (Many editions.)
———, *The Social Contract,* 1762, (Many editions.) Rousseau's *Social Contract* provided a philosophical justification for both the American and French Revolutions.
Sieyès, Abbé, *What Is the Third Estate?* 1789. The most important political pamphlet in the decisive year 1789.
Stewart, John Hall, *A Documentary Survey of the French Revolution,* New York, 1951.
Thompson, J. M., *French Revolution Documents, 1789–1794,* Oxford, 1948.
Young, Arthur, *Travels in France during the Years 1787, 1788, 1789,* London, 1912. France on the eve of revolution, as seen by a perceptive English observer.

Chapter 25

THE INDUSTRIAL REVOLUTION

Providence has assigned to man the glorious function of vastly improving the productions of nature by judicious culture, of working them up into objects of comfort and elegance with the least possible expenditure of human labor—an undeniable position which forms the basis of our Factory System.

—Andrew Ure, *The Philosophy of Manufactures*

There have been many revolutions in industry during the history of Western civilization, and there will undoubtedly be many more. Periods of rapid technological change are often called revolutions, and justifiably so, But, historically, there is but one Industrial Revolution. Occurring during the one hundred years after 1780, it witnessed the first breakthrough from a rural, handicraft economy to one dominated by urban, machine-driven manufactuting.

A European revolution: the commercial class

The fact that it was a European revolution was not accidental. Although Europe was, in the mid–eighteenth century, a continent still predominantly agricultural, although the majority of its people remained illiterate and destined to live out impoverished lives within sight of the place they were born—despite these conditions, which in our eyes might make Europe appear "underdeveloped," it was of course no such thing. European merchants and men of commerce were established as the world's foremost manufacturers and traders. Rulers relied upon this class of men to provide them with the wherewithal to maintain the economy of their states, both in terms of flourishing commercial activity and of victorious armies and navies. Those men, in turn, had for the most part extracted from their rulers the understanding that the property they possessed, whether invested in land, or commerce, or both, was theirs outright. That understanding, substantiated by the written contracts that were replacing unwritten, long-acknowledged custom, helped persuade merchants, bankers, traders, and entrepreneurs that they lived in a world that was stable, rational, and predictable. Believing the world was so, they moved out into it with self-confidence and in hopes of prospering. Only in Europe does one find these presuppositions and this class of men in the eighteenth century; only through the activities of such a class could the Industrial Revolution have taken place.

Increasing markets

These capitalists could not have prospered without an expanding market for their goods. The existence of this market explains further why it was in Europe that the Industrial Revolution took place. Ever since the beginning of the seventeenth century, overseas commercial exploration and development had been opening new territories to European trade. India, Africa, North and South America—all had been woven into the pattern of European economic expansion. The colonies and commercial dependencies took economic shape at Europe's behest. Even the new United States had not been able to declare its economic independence. Whatever new design Europe might devise, all would be compelled to accomodate themselves to Europe's demands.

Population growth

A third factor helping to insure that the revolution would occur in Europe was the continuing growth of its population. In England, the population increased from about 4 million in 1600 to about 6 million in 1700, to 9 million in 1800. The population of France grew from 17 million in 1700 to 26 million a century later. Population growth on this scale provided, as did overseas expansion, an ever-increasing market for manufactured goods. It furnished, as well, an adequate pool—eventually a surplus—of laboring men, women, and children to work in the manufacture of those goods either at home or in factories.

Yet these factors—a thriving commercial class, growing markets, and an increasing population—while helping to explain why the Industrial Revolution took place in eighteenth-century Europe, fail to tell us enough about its origins. For that understanding, we must focus our attention from Europe as a whole to its most prosperous state, England.

1. THE INDUSTRIAL REVOLUTION IN ENGLAND

Why in England? (1) an economy of abundance

It was in England that the Industrial Revolution first took hold. England's economy had progressed further than that of any other country in the direction of abundance. In simplest terms: fewer people were engaged in the crude struggle to do no more than remain alive; more people were in a position to sell a surplus of the goods they produced to an increasingly expanding market; and more people had money enough to purchase the goods that market offered. English laborers, though poorly enough paid, enjoyed a higher standard of living than their continental counterparts. They ate white bread, not brown, and meat with some regularity. Because a smaller portion of their income was spent on food, they might occasionally have some to spare for articles which were bought rather than homemade.

Further evidence of this increasing abundance was the number of bills for the enclosure of agricultural land passed by an English Parliament sympathetic to capitalism during the last half of the eighteenth century. The enclosure of fields, pasture, and waste lands into large fenced tracts of land under the private ownership and individual management of capitalist landlords, although it deprived local agricultural laborers of the right to share in the use of common lands as they had in past times, meant an increased food supply to feed an increasing and increasingly urban population. Yet another sign of England's abundance was its growing supply of surplus capital, derived from investment in land or commerce, and available for further employment to finance new economic enterprises. Thus English capitalists had enough money on hand to underwrite and sustain an industrial revolution.

Abundance: food and capital

But the revolution required more than money. It required habits of mind that would encourage investments in enterprises at once risky, but with an enormous potential for gain. In England, far more than on the Continent, the pursuit of wealth was perceived to be a worthy end in life. The aristocracy of Europe had, from the period of the Renaissance, cultivated the notion of "gentlemanly" conduct, in part to hold the line against social encroachments from below. The English aristocrats, whose privileges were meager when compared with those of continental nobles, had never ceased to respect men who made money; nor had they disdained to make whatever they could for themselves. They invested and speculated. Their scramble to enclose their lands reflected this sympathy with aggressive capitalism. Below the aristocracy, there was even less of a barrier separating the world of urban commerce from that of the rural "gentry." Most of the men who pioneered as entrepreneurs in the early years of the Industrial Revolution sprang from the minor gentry or yeoman farmer class. To a degree unknown on the Continent, men from this sort of background felt themselves free to rise as high as their abilities might carry them on the social and economic ladder.

(2) climate of opinion

Eighteenth-century England was not by any means free of social snobbery, however: lords looked down upon bankers, as bankers looked down upon artisans. But a lord's disdain might well be tempered by the fact of his own grandfather's origins in the counting-house. And the banker would gladly lend money to the artisan if convinced that the artisan's invention might make them both a fortune. The English, as a nation, were not afraid of business. They respected the sensible, the practical, and the financially successful. Robinson Crusoe, that desert island entrepreneur, was one of their models. In the novel (1719) by Daniel Defoe, the hero had used his wits to master nature and become lord of a thriving economy. His triumph was not

Respect for financial success

diminished because it was a worldly triumph; far from it. "It is our vanity which urges us on," the economist Adam Smith, defender of laissez faire capitalism, declared. And thank God, Smith implied, for our blessed vanity! An individual's desire to show himself a success worked to produce prosperity for the country as a whole.

(3) increasing markets

England's eighteenth-century prosperity was based upon an expanding market for whatever goods it manufactured. Its small size and the fact that it was an island encouraged the development of a nationwide domestic market. The absence of a system of internal tolls and tariffs, such as existed on the Continent, meant that goods could be moved freely to the place where they could fetch the best price. This freedom of movement was assisted by a constantly improving transportation system. Parliament in the years just before the Industrial Revolution passed acts to finance turnpike building at the rate of forty per year; the same period saw the construction of canals and the further opening up of harbors and navigable streams. Unlike the government of France, whose cumbrous mercantilist adventures as often as not thwarted economic growth, the English Parliament believed that the most effective way in which it could help businessmen was to assist them in helping themselves.

Overseas expansion

Parliament's members had every reason to promote England's economic fortunes. Some were businessmen themselves; others had invested heavily in commerce. Hence their eagerness to encourage by statute the construction of canals, the establishment of banks, and the enclosure of common lands. And hence their insistence, throughout the eighteenth century, that England's foreign policy respond to its commercial needs. At the end of every major eighteenth-century war, England wrested overseas territories from its enemies. At the same time, England was penetrating hitherto unexploited ports and territories, such as India and South America, in search of further potential markets and resources. The English possessed a merchant marine capable of transporting goods across the world, and a navy practiced in the art of protecting its commercial fleets. London, already a leading center for the world's trade, served as a headquarters for the transfer of raw material, capital, and manufactured products. By 1780 England's markets, together with its fleet and its established position at the center of world trade, combined to produce a potential for expansion so great as to compel the Industrial Revolution.

The cotton industry

English entrepreneurs and technicians responded to the compulsion by revolutionizing the production of cotton textile goods. Although far less cotton goods were made in eighteenth-century England than wool, the extent of their manufacture by 1760 was such as to make cotton more than an infant industry. Tariffs prohibiting the importation of East Indian cottons, imposed by Parliament to stimulate the sale of woolen goods, had instead served to spur the manufacture of domestic cotton goods. Thus the revolution, when it did occur, took place in an already well-established industry. Yet without the inven-

The Spinning Jenny. Invented by James Hargreaves in 1767

tion of some sort of machinery which would improve the quality and at the same time dramatically increase the quantity of spun cotton thread, the necessary breakthrough would not have come. The invention of the fly-shuttle, which greatly speeded up the process of weaving, only made the bottleneck in the prior process of spinning the more apparent. The problem was solved by the invention of a series of comparatively simple mechanical devices, the most important of which was the spinning jenny, invented by James Hargreaves, a carpenter and hand-loom weaver, in 1767 (patented 1770). The spinning jenny, named after the inventor's wife, was a compound spinning wheel, capable of producing sixteen threads at once. The threads it spun were not strong enough, however, to be used for the longitudinal fibers, or warp, of cotton cloth. It was not until the invention of the water frame by Richard Arkwright, a barber, in 1769, that quantity production of both warp and woof (latitudinal fibers) became possible. This invention, along with that of the spinning mule, conceived of by Samuel Crompton in 1779, and combining the features of both the jenny and the frame, solved the problems that had heretofore curtailed the output of cotton textiles. They increased the mechanical advantage over the spinning wheel enormously. From six to twenty-four times the amount of yarn could be spun on a jenny as on the wheel; by the end of the century two to three hundred times as much on the mule. Just as important, the quality of the thread improved not only in terms of strength but also of fineness.

Once these machines came into general use, the revolution proceeded apace. Cotton suited the mule and the jenny because it was a tougher thread than wool—fiber which could withstand the rough

Eli Whitney

Growth of factories

The extent of the cotton trade

treatment it received at the mechanical hands of the crude early machines. In addition, the supply of cotton was expandable in a way that the supply of wool was not. The cotton gin, invented by the American Eli Whitney in 1793, separated seeds from fiber, thereby making cotton available at a lower price. The invention kept America's slave plantations profitable, and meant that supply would be available to meet increased demand.

The first machinery was cheap enough to allow spinners to continue to work their own machines at home. But as the machinery increased in size, it was more and more frequently housed not in the cottages of individual spinners, but in workshops or mills located near water which could be used to power the machines. Eventually, with the further development of steam-driven equipment, the mills could be built wherever it might suit the entrepreneur—frequently in towns and cities in the north of England.

The transition from home to factory industry was of course not accomplished overnight. Cotton yarn continued to be spun at home at the same time that it was being produced in mills. Eventually, however, the low cost of building and operating a large plant, plus the efficiency realized by bringing workers together under one roof, meant that larger mills more and more frequently replaced smaller workshops. By 1851, three-fifths of those employed in cotton manufacture worked in medium- to large-sized mills. Weaving remained a home industry until the invention of a cheap, practical power loom convinced entrepreneurs that they could save money by moving the process from home to mill. Hand-loom weavers were probably the most obvious victims of the Industrial Revolution in England. Their unwillingness to surrender their livelihood to machinery meant that they continued to work for less and less—by 1830, no more than a pitiful six shillings a week. In 1815 they numbered about 250,000; by 1850, there remained only 40,000; by 1860, only 3,000.

English cotton textiles flooded the world market from the 1780s. Here was a light material, suitable for the climates of Africa, India, and the more temperate zones of North America. Here was a material cheap enough to make it possible for millions who had never before enjoyed the comfort of washable body clothes to do so. And here was material fine enough to tempt the rich to experiment with muslins and calicos in a way they had not done before. Figures speak eloquently of the revolutionary change wrought by the expanding industry. In 1760, England exported less than £250,000 worth of cotton goods; by 1800 it was exporting over £5 million worth. In 1760, England imported 2.5 million pounds of raw cotton; in 1787, 22 million pounds; in 1837, 366 million pounds. By 1800, cotton accounted for about 5 percent of the national income of the country; by 1812, from 7 to 8 percent. By 1815, the export of cotton textiles amounted to 40 percent of the value of all domestic goods exported from Great Britain. Although the price of manufactured cotton goods fell dramatically, the market expanded so rapidly that profits continued to increase.

Unlike the changes in the textile industry, those occurring in the manufacture of iron were not great enough to warrant their being labeled revolutionary. Yet they were most significant. Britain's abundant supply of coal, combined with its advanced transportation network, allowed the English, from the middle of the eighteenth century, to substitute coal for wood in the heating of molten metal. A series of discoveries made fuel savings possible, along with a higher quality of iron, and the manufacture of a greater variety of iron products. Demand rose sharply during the war years at the end of the century. It remained high as a result of calls for plant machinery, agricultural implements, and hardware; it rose dramatically with the coming of railways in the 1830s and 1840s. Britain was exporting 571,000 tons of iron in 1814; in 1852, it exported 1,036,000 tons out of a total of almost 2,000,000—more iron than was made by all the rest of the world combined.

The need for more coal required the mining of deeper and deeper veins. In 1712, Thomas Newcomen had devised a crude but effective steam engine for pumping water from mines. Though of value to the coal industry, it was of less use in other industries, since it was wasteful of both fuel and power. In 1763, James Watt, a maker of scientific instruments at the University of Glasgow, was asked to repair a model of the Newcomen engine. While engaged in this task he conceived the idea that the machine would be greatly improved if a separate chamber were added to condense the steam, so as to eliminate the necessity of cooling the cylinder. He patented his first engine incorporating this device in 1769. Unfortunately, Watt's genius as an inventor was not matched by his business ability. He admitted that he would "rather face a loaded cannon than settle a disputed account or make a bargain." As a consequence, he fell into debt in attempting to place his

The iron industry

The steam engine

James Watt Working on a Model of Thomas Newcomen's Steam Engine

The Staffordshire Collieries. In the building to the right is a whimsey, or coal-powered steam engine, used to lift loads of coal from the mines.

machines on the market. He was rescued by Matthew Boulton, a wealthy hardware manufacturer of Birmingham. The two men formed a partnership, with Boulton providing the capital. By 1800 the firm had sold 289 engines for use in factories and mines. One must not exaggerate the speed with which the steam engine replaced water as the principle motive force in industry. In 1850 more than a third of the power used in woolen manufacture and an eighth of that used in cotton was still produced by water. Despite those facts, there is no question that without the steam engine there could have been no expansion in those or other industries on the scale that we have described.

Other advances Other industries experienced profound changes during the hundred years of the Industrial Revolution. Many of those changes came in response to the growth of textile manufacture. The chemical industry, for example, developed new methods of dyeing and bleaching, as well as improved methods of production in the fields of soap and glass-making. Production of goods increased across the board, as profits from the boom in manufacturing increased the demand for new and more sophisticated articles. Pottery, metalware—these and other trades expanded to meet demands, in the process adopting methods that in most instances reduced cost and speeded manufacture.

The limits of the Industrial Revolution To understand fully the nature of the Industrial Revolution in England one must not lose sight of two important factors: the first is that dramatic as the revolution was, it happened over a period of two or three generations, at varying paces in different industries. Some men and women continued to work at home, much as their grandfathers and grandmothers had. Old tools and old methods were not immediately replaced by new ones, any more than populations fled the countryside overnight for the city. Second, the revolution was accomplished from a very limited technological and theoretical base. Except in the chemical industry, change was not the result of pure scientific research. It was the product of empirical experimentation—in some cases, of little more than creative tinkering. To say this is not to disparage the work of men such as Arkwright, Hargreaves, Watt, and their like. It is to suggest, however, the reason why England, without a national system of education on any level, was nonetheless able to accomplish the revolution it did. Nor are these remarks designed to belittle the magnitude of the change. What occurred in England was a revolution because of the way in which it reshaped the lives, not just of the English, but of people across the globe. By responding as it did to the demands of its apparently insatiable markets, England made a revolution every bit as profound and long-lasting as that which occurred simultaneously in France.

2. THE INDUSTRIAL REVOLUTION ON THE CONTINENT

The Industrial Revolution came in time to the Continent, but not to any important degree before about 1830. Manufacturing in eighteenth-century France and Germany clustered in regions whose proximity to raw materials, access to markets, and traditional attachment to particular skills had resulted in their development as industrial centers. Flanders and Normandy in France, and Saxony in Germany were centers for the manufacture of woolen cloth; Switzerland, southern Germany, and Normandy, of cottons; Wallonia (the area around Liège in Belgium), the Marne valley, and Silesia in Germany, of iron. Yet for a variety of reasons, these areas failed to experience the late-eighteenth-century breakthrough that occurred in Britain. Nor were they capable at first of imitating Britain's success, once they began to perceive the great economic advantages that its pronounced lead was bringing it. There were a number of reasons for the delay of continental industrialization, most of them opposite to those reasons which had brought the Industrial Revolution first to England. Whereas England's transportation system was highly developed, those of France and Germany were not. France was far bigger than England, its rivers were not as easily navigable, its seaports further apart. Central Europe was so divided into tiny principalities, each with its own set of tolls and tariffs, as to make the transportation of raw materials or manufactured goods over any considerable distance most impractical. Nor was France itself free of the sorts of regulations that thwarted easy shipments. In addition, the Continent was not as blessed with an abundance of raw materials as England. France, the Low Countries, and

*Reasons for delay:
(1) lack of transport and
raw materials*

Germany had to import wool. Europe, though richer than England in timber, lacked an abundant supply of the fuel that was the new source of industrial energy; few major coal deposits had as yet been discovered.

(2) lack of entrepreneurial spirit

Distances and distinctions between social and economic ranks were far greater on the Continent than in England. Money was not the social solvent in France and Germany that it was across the Channel. Before the French Revolution, continental aristocrats were unwilling to invest in commercial enterprises they believed would damage their social standing. More important, after the revolution middle-class Frenchmen, though free in theory to rise as high on the social and economic ladder as they might aspire, appear largely to have remained content to make only enough money to sustain a modest-sized business. Those revolutionary constitutional changes which had favored the lower middle class by encouraging its acquisition of property, prevented the growth of industry by dispersing capital into the hands of innumerable small-scale enterprises. The entrepreneurial spirit that compelled Englishmen to drive competitors to the wall was not as highly developed in France and Germany in the years after 1815. Exhausted by the competitiveness of war, and fearful of the disruptions that war brought in its train, continental businessmen remained far more willing than the English to keep on manufacturing and selling on the same scale they always had.[1]

(3) effect of wars

The Continent did not simply stand idle as England assumed its industrial lead. The pace of mechanization was increasing in the 1780s. But the French Revolution and the wars which followed disrupted the growth which might have otherwise taken place. Battles fought on French, German, and Italian soil destroyed factories and machinery. Although ironmaking increased to meet the demands of the wars, techniques remained what they had been. Commerce was badly hurt both by British destruction of French merchant shipping and by Napoleon's Continental System. Probably the revolutionary change most beneficial to industrial advance in Europe was the removal of previous restraints on the movement of capital and labor; for example, the abolition of trade guilds, and the reduction in the number of tariff barriers across the Continent. On balance, however, the revolutionary and Napoleonic wars clearly thwarted industrial development on the Continent, while at the same time intensifying it in England.

Increases after 1815: (1) population rise

A number of factors combined to produce a climate more generally conducive to industrialization on the Continent after 1815. Population continued to increase, not only throughout Europe, but in those areas now more and more dependent upon the importation of manufactured goods—Latin America, for example. These increases, which doubled the populations of most European countries between 1800 and 1850, meant that the Continent would be supplied with a growing

---

[1] On this point, see David S. Landes, *The Unbound Prometheus*, pp. 132–33.

A Swedish Mining Town, 1790

number of producers and consumers. More people did not necessarily mean further industrialization. In Ireland, for example, where other necessary factors were absent, more people meant less food. But in those countries with an already well-established commercial and industrial base—France and Germany, for example—increased population did encourage the adoption of the technologies and methods of production that had transformed Britain.

Transportation improved in the West both during and following the Napoleonic wars. The Austrian Empire added over 30,000 miles of roads between 1830 and 1847; Belgium almost doubled its road network in the same period; France built, in addition to roads, 2,000 miles of canals. In the United States, where industrialization was occurring at an increasingly rapid rate after 1830, road mileage jumped from 21,000 miles in 1800 to 170,000 in 1856. When these improvements were combined with the introduction of rail transport in the 1840s, the resulting increase in markets available to all Western countries encouraged them to introduce methods of manufacturing that would help meet new demands.

(2) improved transportation

In this endeavor, governments played a more direct role on the Continent than in Britain. Napoleon's rationalization of French and imperial institutions had introduced Europe to the practice of state intervention. His legal code, which guaranteed freedom of contract and facilitated the establishment of joint-stock enterprises, encouraged other rulers to provide a similar framework for commercial expansion. In Prussia, lack of private capital necessitated state operation of a large proportion of that country's mines. In no European country but Britain would railways be built without the financial assistance of the state. In the private sector, as well, more attention was given on the Continent than in England to the need for artificial stimulation to

(3) centralization

produce industrial change. It was in Belgium that the first joint-stock investment bank—the Société Générale—was founded, an institution designed to facilitate the accumulation of ready capital for investment in industry and commerce. Europeans were also willing for the state to establish educational systems whose aim, among others, was to produce a well-trained elite capable of assisting in the development of industrial technology. What Britain had produced almost by chance, the Europeans began to reproduce by design.

(4) the lack of technicians

Until the Continent produced its own technicians it was compelled to rely on British expertise. And another reason why the pace of continental, and also American, industrialization, even after 1815, remained far slower than in Britain was Britain's natural reluctance to see its methods of production pirated by others. Until 1825, British artisans were forbidden to emigrate; until 1842, much innovative machinery could not be exported. Laws did not, however, prevent the movement of creative technician-entrepreneurs and their particular skills; many Englishmen, during the first part of the nineteenth century, made fortunes as they taught others in Europe and America to do what they had taught themselves. But an initial shortage of home-grown experts undoubtedly hampered rapid industrial expansion on the Continent.

Textiles

The growth of the textile industry in Europe was patterned by the circumstances of the Napoleonic wars. The supply of cotton to the Continent had been interrupted, thanks to the British blockade, but the military's greater demand for woolen cloth meant that expansion occurred more rapidly in the latter than in the former industry. By 1820, the spinning of wool by machine was the common practice on the Continent; weaving, however, was still accomplished largely by hand. Centers for the production of wool were located at Rheims and in Alsace, in France; in what is now Belgium; and, in Germany, in

Silk Weavers of Lyon, 1850. The first significant working-class uprisings in nineteenth-century France occurred here in 1831 and 1834. Note the domestic character of the working conditions.

A German Textile Factory, 1848. This is an unusually large manufacturing facility for this period on the Continent.

Saxony and Silesia. Mechanization was retarded by the fact that hand labor was cheap, and by the important fact that since Britain's market was so large, continental profits too often depended upon the manufacture of some particular specialty not made in England, and therefore without broad commercial appeal. Cotton manufacture was curtailed by the same circumstances. In France, as a result, mechanization occurred first in the silk industry and those sections of the cotton industry which produced finer specialty materials—lace, for example. A tradition of prestige associated with the production of luxury goods, dating back to the reign of Louis XIV, encouraged entrepreneurs to invest in this branch of the textile industry. They were willing to forego mass markets in the hope that their products would not meet with British competition. France nevertheless remained the largest continental producer of cotton goods, followed, again, by Belgium, the German territories of the Rhine valley, Saxony, Silesia, and Bavaria.

In the area of heavy industry on the Continent, the picture was much the same as in textiles: i.e., gradual advances in the adoption of technological innovation against a background of more general resistance to change. Here, however, because change came later than in Britain, it coincided with an increased demand for various goods that had come into being as a result of industrialization and urbanization: iron pipe, much in use by 1830 in cities for gas, water, and drainage; metal machinery, now replacing earlier wooden prototypes. Con-

Heavy industry

sequently, the iron industry took the lead over textiles on the Continent, accompanied by an increase, where possible, in the production of coal. Coal was scarce, however; in the Rhineland wood was still used to manufacture iron. The result was an unwillingness on the part of entrepreneurs to make as extensive use of the steam engine as they might have otherwise; it used too much fuel. In France, as late as 1844, hydraulic (i.e., water-driven) engines were employed far more often for the manufacture of iron than were steam engines. One further problem hampered the development of continental heavy industry during the first half of the nineteenth century. British competition forced continental machine construction firms to scramble for whatever orders they could get. This need to respond to a variety of requests meant that it was difficult for firms to specialize in a single product. The result was a lack of standardization, and continued production to order, when rationalization and specialization would have resulted in an increased volume of production.

3. THE COMING OF RAILWAYS

By about 1840, then, European countries, and to some degree, as well, the United States, were moving gradually along the course of industrialization traced by Britain, producing far more than they had, yet nothing like as much as their spectacular pace-setter. Within the next ten years, the coming of the railways was to alter that situation. Though Britain by no means lost its lead, the stimulus provided generally to Western economies by the introduction of railway systems throughout much of the world carried Europe and America far enough and fast enough to allow them to become genuine competitors with the British.

Railways as a stimulus to the European and American economies

Railways came into being in answer to two needs. The first was the obvious desire on the part of entrepreneurs to transport their goods as quickly and cheaply as possible across long distances. Despite already mentioned improvements in transportation during the years before 1830, the movement of heavy materials, particularly coal, remained a problem. It is significant that the first modern railway was built in England in 1825 from the Durham coal field of Stockton to Darlington, near the coast. "Tramways"—parallel tracks along which coal carts were pulled by horses—had long been in use at pitheads to haul coal short distances. The Stockton-to-Darlington railway was a logical extension of this device, designed to answer the transportation needs produced by constantly expanding industrialization. The man primarily responsible for the design of the first steam railway was George Stephenson, a self-made engineer who had not learned to read until he was seventeen. He talked a group of North-of-England investors into the merits of steam traction and was given full liberty to carry out his plans. The locomotives on the Stockton-Darlington line traveled at

Railways as goods carriers

fifteen miles per hour, the fastest rate at which human beings had yet moved overland.

Railways were also built in response to other than purely industrial needs: specifically, the need for capitalists to invest their money. Englishmen such as those who had made sizable fortunes in textiles, once they had paid out workers' wages and plowed back substantial capital in their factories, retained a surplus profit for which they wanted a decent yet reliable return. Railways provided them with the solution to their problem. Though by no means as reliable as had been hoped, railway investment proved capable of more than satisfying the capitalists' demands. No sooner did the first combined passenger and goods service open in 1830, on the Liverpool to Manchester line, than plans were formulated and money pledged to extend rail systems throughout Europe, the Americas, and beyond. In 1830, there were no more than a few dozen miles of railway in the world. By 1840, there were over 4,500 miles; by 1850, over 23,000. The English contractor, Thomas Brassey, the most famous, but by no means the only one of his kind, built railways in Italy, Canada, Argentina, India, and Australia.

Thomas Brassey

The railway boom was a boom to industrialization generally. Not only did it increase enormously the demand for coal and for a variety of heavy manufactured goods—rails, locomotives, carriages, signals, switches; by enabling goods to move faster from factory to salesroom, railways decreased the time it took to sell those goods. Quicker sales meant, in turn, a quicker return on capital investment, money which could then be reinvested in the manufacture of more goods. Finally, by opening up the world market as it had never been before, the railway boom stimulated the production of such a quantity of material goods as to insure the rapid completion of the West's industrialization.

Railways as stimulus to industry

The New Railway Age. Left: Stephenson's "Rocket." A reconstruction of the railway engine built by George Stephenson in 1829. Right: "The Railway Juggernaut of 1845." A cartoon from the English humor magazine *Punch* satirizing speculation—often financially disastrous—in railway stocks.

The building of a railway line was an undertaking on a scale infinitely greater than the building of a factory. Railway construction required capital investment beyond the capacity of any single individual. In Britain, a factory might be worth anything from £20,000 to £200,000. The average cost of twenty-seven of the more important railway lines constructed between 1830 and 1853 was £2 million. The average labor force of a factory ranged from 50 to 300. The average labor force of a railway, after construction, was 2,500. Because a railway crossed the property of a large number of individual landowners, each of whom would naturally demand as much remuneration as he thought he could get, the planning of an efficient and economical route was a tricky and time-consuming business. The entrepreneur and contractor had to concern themselves not only with the purchase of right-of-way. They also contended with problems raised by the destruction of sizable portions of already existing urban areas, to make room for stations and switching yards. And they had to select a route that would be as free as possible of the hills and valleys that would necessitate the construction of expensive tunnels, cuts, and embankments. Railway-builders ran tremendous risks. Portions of most lines were subcontracted at fixed bids to contractors of limited experience. A spate of bad weather might delay construction to the point where builders would be lucky to bring in the finished job within 25 percent of their original bid. Of the thirty major contractors on the London-to-Birmingham line, ten failed completely.

If the business of a contractor was marked by uncertainty, that of the construction worker was characterized by back-breaking labor.

The English "navvies," who built railways not only throughout Britain but around the world, were a remarkable breed. Their name derived from "navigator," a term applied to the construction workers on England's eighteenth-century canals. The work that they accomplished was prodigious. Because there is little friction between a train's wheels and its tracks, it can transport heavy loads easily. But

Construction of the London to Birmingham Railway, London, 1838. This drawing of the building of retaining walls in a new railway cut evokes the chaos created by railway construction within urban areas.

Railway Navvies. Without the aid of machinery, the burden of building Britain's railways fell on the backs of men such as these.

lack of friction ceases to be an advantage when a train has to climb or descend a grade, thereby running the risk of slippage. Hence the need for comparatively level roadbeds; and hence the need for laborers to construct those tunnels, cuts, and embankments that would keep the roadbeds level. In England and in much of the rest of the world, mid-nineteenth-century railways were constructed almost entirely without the aid of machinery. An assistant engineer on the London-to-Birmingham line, in calculating the magnitude of that particular construction, determined that the labor involved was the equivalent of lifting 25 billion cubic feet of earth and stone one foot high. This he compared with the feat of building the Great Pyramid, a task he estimated had involved the hoisting of some 16 billion tons. But whereas the building of the pyramid had required over 200,000 men and had taken twenty years, the construction of the London-to-Birmingham railway was accomplished by 20,000 men in less than five years. Translated into individual terms, a navvy was expected to move an average of twenty tons of earth per day. Railways were laid upon an almost infinite base of human muscle and sweat.

4. INDUSTRIALIZATION AFTER 1850

In the years between 1850 and 1870, Britain remained very much the industrial giant of the West. But France, Germany, Belgium, and the United States assumed the position of challengers. In the iron industry, Britain's rate of growth during these years was not as great as that of either France or Germany (5.2 percent for Britain, as against 6.7 percent for France and 10.2 percent for Germany). But in 1870 Britain

Britain still the leader

The Early Industrial Landscape. Stockport, England, in the 1840s.

was still producing half the world's pig iron; 3.5 times as much as the United States, more than 4 times as much as Germany, and more than 5 times as much as France. Although the number of cotton spindles increased from 5.5 to 11.5 million in the United States between 1852 and 1861, and by significant but not as spectacular percentages in European countries, England in 1861 had 31 million spindles at work in comparison with France's 5.5 million, Germany's 2 million, Switzerland's 1.3 million, and Austria's 1.8 million.

Continuing European advance

Most of the gains experienced in Europe came as a result of continuing changes in those areas we have come to recognize as important for sustained industrial growth. The improved transportation systems that resulted from the spread of railways helped encourage an increase in the free movement of goods. International monetary unions were established, and restrictions removed on international waterways such as the Danube. The Prussian *Zollverein,* or tariff union, an organization designed to facilitate internal free trade, was established in 1818 and was extended over the next twenty years to include most of the German principalities outside Austria. Free trade went hand in hand with further removal of barriers to the freedom to enter trades and to practice business unhampered by restrictive regulation. Control of

See color map facing page 960

guilds and corporations over artisan production was abolished in Austria in 1859 and in most of Germany by the mid-1860s. Laws against usury, most of which had ceased to be enforced, were officially abandoned in Britain, Holland, Belgium, and in many parts of Germany. Governmental regulation of the operation of mines was surrendered by the Prussian state in the 1850s, freeing entrepreneurs to develop resources as they saw fit. The formation of investment banks proceeded apace, encouraged by an important increase in the money supply and therefore an easing of credit, following the opening of the California gold fields in 1849.

A further reason for increased European production was the growing trade in raw materials. Wool and hides imported from Australia helped diminish the consequences of the cotton shortage suffered after the outbreak of the United States Civil War and the Union blockade of the American South. Other importations—guano from the Pacific, vegetable oils from Africa, pyrites (sulphides) from Spain—stimulated the scale of food production and both altered and increased the manufacture of soap, candles, and finished textiles. Finally, discoveries of new sources of coal, particularly in the Pas-de-Calais region of France and in the Ruhr valley in Germany, had dramatic repercussions. Production of coal in France rose from 4.4 million to 13.3 million tons between 1850 and 1869; during the same years, German production increased from 4.2 million to 23.7 million tons.

Increased trade in raw materials

By 1870 Europe had by no means turned its back on agriculture. Fifty percent of France's labor force remained on farms. Agricultural laborers were the single largest occupational category in Britain during the 1860s. Great stretches of the Continent—Spain, southern Italy, eastern Europe—were almost untouched by the Industrial Revolution. And in the industrialized countries, much work was still accomplished in tiny workshops or at home. Yet if Europe was by no means wholly industrial, it was far and away the most industrially advanced portion of the globe—and not by accident. In order to maintain its position of producer to the world, Europe, and Britain particularly, made certain that no other areas stood a chance to compete. Europe used its economic and, when necessary, its military strength to insure that the world remained divided between the producers of manufactured goods—Europe itself—and suppliers of the necessary raw materials—everyone else. Often this arrangement suited those in other parts of the world who made their money by providing the raw materials that fueled the European economy. Cotton-growers in the southern United States, sugar-growers in the Caribbean, wheat-growers in the Ukraine—all remained content with arrangements as dictated by the industrialized West. Those countries which expressed their discontent—Egypt, for example, which in the 1830s attempted to establish its own cotton textile industry—were soon put in their place by a show of force. Western Europeans, believing in their right to industrial leadership in the world, saw nothing wrong with employing soldiers, if they had to, to make others understand their destiny.

Europe's economy within the world

SELECTED READINGS

• *Items so designated are available in paperback editions.*
• Ashton, T. S., *The Industrial Revolution, 1760–1830,* London, 1948. An excellent short introduction.
  Checkland, S. G., *The Rise of Industrial Society in England, 1815–1885,* New York, 1965. Emphasizes the economic organization of England.

• Deane, Phyllis, *The First Industrial Revolution*, Cambridge, 1965.

Henderson, W. O., *The Industrialization of Europe, 1780–1914*, New York, 1969.

———, *The State and the Industrial Revolution in Prussia, 1740–1870*, Liverpool, 1958. A biographical approach. Good on technical education.

• Hobsbawm, Eric, *Industry and Empire: 1750 to the Present Day*, New York, 1968. A general survey of industrialization in Britain.

Hoffman, Walther, *British Industry, 1700–1950*, Oxford 1955. A good source for statistics.

• Landes, David S., *The Unbound Prometheus*, London, 1969. An excellent treatment of the technological innovations and economic results of the Industrial Revolution.

McManners, John, *European History: Men, Machines and Freedom*, New York, 1967.

Mantoux, Paul, *The Industrial Revolution in the Eighteenth Century*, rev. ed., New York, 1961. The beginnings of the modern factory system in England.

• Rostow, Walt W., *The Stages of Economic Growth*, rev. ed., Cambridge, 1971. A synthesis by the exponent of the "take-off" theory of economic development.

• Taylor, George Rogers, *The Transportation Revolution, 1815–1860*, New York, 1968.

Usher, A. P., *A History of Mechanical Invention*, Cambridge, Mass., 1954.

SOURCE MATERIALS

Dodd, George, *Days at the Factories; or the Manufacturing Industry of Great Britain Described, and Illustrated by Numerous Engravings of Machines and Processes*, Totawa, N.J., 1975. A reprint of the 1850 edition.

Mitchell, Brian R., and Phyllis Deane, *Abstract of British Historical Statistics*, Cambridge, 1962. The single best source for statistics on population, trade, manufacturing, etc.

• Smith, Adam, *An Inquiry into the Nature and Causes of the Wealth of Nations*, Chicago, 1977. Written in 1776, this revolutionary work called for the end of mercantilism and the enshrinement of laissez faire.

Ward, J. T., *The Factory System, 1830–1855*, New York, 1970. Excerpts from contemporary documents describing, defending, and criticizing the factory system and industrialization.

Chapter 26

CONSEQUENCES OF INDUSTRIAL-IZATION: URBANIZATION AND CLASS CONSCIOUSNESS (1800–1850)

What Art was to the ancient world, Science is to the modern: The distinctive faculty. In the minds of men the useful has succeeded the beautiful. Yet rightly understood, Manchester is as great a human exploit as Athens.

—Benjamin Disraeli, *Coningsby*

The Industrial Revolution was more than an important event in the economic and technological history of the West. It helped to reshape the patterns of life for men and women, first in Britain, then in Europe and America, and eventually throughout much of the world. By increasing the scale of production, the Industrial Revolution brought about the factory system, which in turn compelled the migration of millions from the countryside and small towns into cities. Once in those cities, men and women had to learn a new way of life, and learn it quickly: how to discipline themselves to the factory whistle and survive in a slum, if they were first-generation urban workers; how to manage a work-force and achieve respectable prominence for themselves in the community, if they were businessmen and their wives. One particular lesson that industrialization and urbanization taught was that of class consciousness. Men and women, to a far greater degree than heretofore, began to perceive themselves as part of a class with interests of its own, and in opposition to the interests of men and women in other classes.

We shall examine this range of social and cultural changes as they occurred during the first fifty years or so of the nineteenth century, after looking briefly first at the condition of the bulk of the popula-

Consequences of the Industrial Revolution

tion, which, despite industrialization, remained on the land. Since the Industrial Revolution came first to Britain, our focus will be on that country. Yet the pattern set by the British was one that was repeated to a great extent in other European countries, as industrialization came to them in time.

1. PEOPLE ON THE LAND

Population increase

The dramatic story of the growth of industrialization and urbanization must not be allowed to obscure the fact that, in 1850, the population of Europe was still overwhelmingly a peasant population. Demographic pressures which helped produce chaos in the cities, likewise caused severe hardship in the countryside. The population increase which took place throughout Europe during this period appears to have been caused by two factors. The first was the occurrence of earlier and more frequent marriages. The second, from which the first followed, was the availability of cheaper food, the result of increased production, improved agricultural technology, and, in many places, the introduction of the potato. Coupled with these factors was a gradually decreasing deathrate. The populations of countries that were predominantly agricultural lept forward with those that were industrializing. The population of Ireland, despite famine, grew from 5.5 to 8 million, Russia's population from 39 to 60 million, in the years from 1800 to 1850.

Wretched rural conditions

Although conditions allowed a population increase, they were not such as to make the life of the poorer inhabitants of Europe anything other than bleak. Overpopulation brought underemployment, and hence poverty, in its train. Conditions in rural areas deteriorated sharply whenever there was a bad harvest, as there was with continuing regularity. Hunger, typhus, and near-starvation were not uncommon. The result was a standard of living—if one can dignify the condition with that name—that for many rural inhabitants of many areas in Europe declined in the first half of the nineteenth century, although not enough to reverse general population growth. Governments in some countries attempted to solve the related problems of population pressure and impoverishment by passing laws raising the age of marriage. In some of the states of southern and western Germany, as well as in Austria, men were forbidden to marry before the age of thirty, and were also required to prove their ability to support a family.

Agricultural capitalism

Even had such laws acted as an effective curb on population growth—which, in the main, they did not—they would nevertheless have failed to prevent the rural stresses that resulted from the continuing spread of agricultural capitalism. The pace of this change varied across Europe; it was furthest advanced in England and Prussia. Wherever landed proprietors determined to meet increased demand

Interior of an English Farm Laborer's Cottage, 1846. Note the wooden crate used as an infant's cradle.

for food by farming large areas as a capital investment, they imposed a series of transformations that were bound to affect the lives of agricultural laborers. First, land must be made a negotiable commodity. It must not, therefore, be tied to ancient customs which clouded its title—as was the case, for example, with common land, to which the poor within a community might have some right of access or cultivation. Second, land must be in the hands of those with capital enough to improve it, in order to make of it a profitable investment. It must be "enclosed"—"regulated" was the term in Prussia—so that it could be properly fertilized and drained, or, if it was grazing land, so that breeds might be scientifically improved without fear of mongrelization. Finally, a mobile force of agricultural laborers must be available to work at the capitalists' behest. They must not be "tied" to a particular piece of land, either through systems of customary rights or bondage. They must be free to go where they were told to go, to work whatever land would bring most profit to its owners.

These requirements, as they were imposed, produced dislocation and hardship. In Scotland, workers were cleared from land which they had farmed as tenants, in order to provide pasturage for the more profitable sheep. In Germany, those serfs emancipated by a reform-minded government in 1807 were compelled to forfeit somewhere between a third to a half of their land in return for their freedom; those who were able to retain small holdings were in most cases pressured to sell out to larger landholders. Not all landlords were ruthless. "Model" improvers among the wealthiest of the English landowners adjusted to capitalist competition without entirely forswearing traditional responsibilities. They built houses for tenants and laborers, and provided them with schools and churches. In eastern Europe there were among the Prussian landlords (Junkers) pietists who acknowledged obligations to their tenants as well as to the market.

Its results

The speed with which agricultural change occurred in various parts of Europe depended upon the nature of particular governments. Those more sympathetic to new capitalist impulses facilitated the transfer and reorganization of land by means of enabling legislation. They encouraged the elimination of small farms and an increase in larger, more efficient units of production. In England, over half the total area of the country, excluding waste land, was composed of estates of a thousand acres or more. In Spain, the fortunes of agricultural capitalism fluctuated with the political tenor of successive regimes: with the coming of a liberal party to power in 1820, came a law encouraging the free transfer of land; with the restoration of absolutism in 1823, came a repeal of the law. Russia was one of the countries least affected by agricultural change in the first half of the nineteenth century. There land was worked in vast blocks; some of the largest landowners possessed over half a million acres. But the institution of manorial serfdom, which bound hundreds of thousands of men, women, and children to particular estates for generations, prohibited the use of land as a negotiable commodity and therefore prevented the development of agricultural entrepreneurship. In France, despite the fact that manorialism had been abolished by the revolution, there was no rapid movement toward large-scale capitalist farming. An army of peasant proprietors, direct beneficiaries of the Jacobins' democratic constitution, continued to work the small farms they owned. The fact that France suffered far less agricultural distress, even in the 1840s, than did other European countries, and the fact that there was less migration in France from the country to the city and overseas than there was in Germany and England, are marks of the general success of this rural lower middle class in sustaining itself on the land. Its members were content to farm in the old way, opposed agricultural innovation, and, indeed, innovation generally. Despite their veneration of the revolution, they were among the most conservative elements in European society.

2. URBANIZATION AND THE STANDARD OF LIVING

If the countryside continued to hold the bulk of Europe's population in the years between 1800 and 1850, the growth of cities nevertheless remains one of the most important facts in the social history of that period. Cities grew in size and number once the steam engine made it practical to bring together large concentrations of men, women, and children to work in factories. Previously, workshops had been located throughout the countryside, close to the water power that provided the primary means of operating machinery. Steam engines freed entrepreneurs from their dependence on water power and allowed them to consolidate production in large cities. In cities, transportation was more accessible than in the countryside. Hence it was less costly to import raw materials and ship out finished goods. Workers were more readily available in cities, as well, attracted as they were in large numbers in the hope—often false—of finding steady work at higher wages than those paid agricultural laborers. Industrialization was not the only reason for the growth of cities in the early nineteenth century, however. General population growth combined with industrialization forced cities to expand at an alarming rate.

Urban population increases

In the ten years between 1831 and 1841 London's population grew by 130,000, Manchester's by 70,000. Paris increased by 120,000 between 1841 and 1846. Vienna grew by 125,000 from 1827 to 1847, into a city of 400,000. Berlin had as large a population by 1848, having increased by 180,000 since 1815. The primary result in these and other fast-growing centers was dreadful overcrowding. Construction lagged far behind population growth. In Vienna, though population rose 42 percent during the twenty years before 1847, the increase in housing was only 11.5 percent. In many of the larger cities, old and new, working men and women lived in lodging houses, apart from families left behind in the country. The poorest workers in almost all European cities dwelt in wretched basement rooms, often without any light or drainage. Governments did their best to encourage emigration to ease the overcrowding, the majority of emigrants relocating in the Americas. Emigration from England rose from 57,000 in 1830, to 90,000 in 1840, to 280,000 in 1850. Ireland, in the early years of the nineteenth century, witnessed the departure of over 1.5 million before the great potato famine of 1846, which increased the flow to a flood. In that year, approximately three out of every four acres of potatoes were blighted. Over 1 million died between 1846 to 1851, either from starvation, or as a result of their weakened physical condition which left them prey to disease.

With cities as overcrowded as they were, it is no wonder that they were a menace to the health of those who lived within them. The middle classes moved as far as possible from disease and factory smoke, leaving the poorest members of the community isolated and a prey to the sickness which ravaged working-class sections. Cholera, typhus, and tuberculosis were natural predators in areas without adequate sewerage facilities and fresh water, and over which smoke from factories, railroads, and domestic chimneys hung heavily. Measures were gradually adopted by successive governments in an attempt to cure the worst of these ills, if only to prevent the spread of catastrophic epidemics. Legislation was designed to rid cities of their worst slums by tearing them down, and to improve sanitary conditions by supplying both water and drainage. Yet by 1850, these projects had only just begun. Paris, perhaps better supplied with water than any European city, had enough for no more than two baths per capita per year; in London, human waste remained uncollected in 250,000 do-

Cities as a health menace

Wentworth Street by Gustav Doré. The artist was much concerned with the over-crowding squalor which resulted from early industrialization in London.

mestic cesspools; in Manchester, no more than a third of the dwellings were equipped with toilets of any sort.

The standard of living debate

Conditions such as these are important evidence in a debate which has occupied historians for the past several decades. The question is: Did the standard of living rise or fall in Europe during the first half-century of the Industrial Revolution? One school, the "optimists," argues that workers shared in the more general increase in living standards which occurred throughout Europe from 1800 onward. It is true, certainly, that some skilled workers within the new factories, along with some artisans in older trades as yet unaffected by industrialization, did benefit by a slight rise in wages and a decline in living costs. But regional variables, along with a constantly fluctuating demand for labor in all countries, have led most commentators to temper their conclusions.

Instability and unemployment

There is no evidence to suggest that the more lowly paid, unskilled worker, whether in England or on the Continent, led anything more than a precarious existence. Textile workers in England, if guaranteed something like full employment, could theoretically earn enough to support a family. Such was not the case in Switzerland, however, where similar work paid only half what was necessary, or in Saxony, where a large portion of the population was apparently dependent upon either poor relief or charity. One of the most depressing features of working-class life in these years was its instability. Economic depressions were common occurrences; when they happened, workers were laid off for weeks at a time, with no system of unemployment insurance to sustain them. Half the working population of England's industrial cities were out of work in the early 1840s. In Paris, 85,000 went on relief in 1840. One particularly hard-pressed district of Silesia reported 30,000 out of 40,000 citizens in need of relief in 1844. Nor must one overlook the plight of those whose skills had been replaced by machinery—the hand-loom weavers being the most notable examples. In the English manufacturing town of Bolton, a hand-loom weaver could earn no more than about three shillings per week in 1842, at a time when experts estimated it took at least twenty shillings a week to keep a family of five above the poverty line. On that kind of pay, workers were fortunate if they did not starve to death. Forced to spend something like 65 percent of their income on food, the per capita meat consumption of the average worker declined to about forty pounds per year in the early nineteenth century.

Such figures make the optimists' generalizations hard to countenance. Figures of whatever sort fail to take into account the stress that urban factory life extracted from the workers. Even workers making thirty shillings a week might well wonder if they were "better off," forced as they were to come to terms with the factory disciplines and living conditions imposed upon them. Though most of those who moved into factory towns migrated but a short distance from their place of birth, the psychological distance they traveled was tremendous. These qualitative factors, admittedly difficult to assess, must be weighed along with more easily quantifiable evidence before reaching any conclusion as to the increased standard of living in early–nineteenth-century cities. Whether or not life in cities was pleasant or ghastly, however, it was, for rapidly increasing numbers, a fact of life. Once we examine that life we will better understand the full impact of industrialization and urbanization upon those who first experienced it.

The quality of life

Soup Kitchen Run by Quakers, Manchester, England, 1862. Enterprises of this sort, which doled out charity "indiscriminately"—that is, without investigating the recipient's character — were condemned by many members of the middle class as encouraging the "worst" elements — idlers and loafers — among the poor.

3. THE LIFE OF THE URBAN MIDDLE CLASS

Isambard Kingdom Brunel. Behind him are lengths of anchor chain from the steamship The Great Western.

Social mobility

The urban middle class which emerged during this period was by no means one homogeneous unit, in terms of occupation or income. In a general category that includes merchant princes and humble shopkeepers, subdivisions are important. The middle class included families of industrialists, such as the Peels (cotton) in England and, at a later period, the Krupps (iron) in Germany. It included financiers like the internationally famed Rothschilds, and, on a descending scale of wealth and power, bankers and capitalists throughout the major money markets of Europe: London, Brussels, Paris, Berlin. It included entrepreneurs like Thomas Brassey, the British railway magnate, and technicians, like the engineer Isambard Kingdom Brunel, designer of the steamship *The Great Western.* It included bureaucrats, in growing demand when governments began to regulate the pace and direction of industrialization, and to ameliorate its harshest social and economic results. It included those in the already established professions—in law particularly, as lawyers put their expertise to the service of industrialists. It included the armies of managers and clerks necessary to the continuing momentum of industrial and financial expansion, and the equally large army of merchants and shopkeepers necessary to supply the wants of an increasingly affluent urban middle-class population. Finally, it included the families of all those who lived their lives in the various subcategories we have listed.

Movement within these ranks was often possible, in the course of one or two generations. Movement from the working class into the middle class, however, was far less common. Most middle-class successes originated within the middle class—the children of farmers, skilled artisans, or professionals. Upward mobility was almost impossible without education; education was an expensive, if not unattainable luxury for the children of a laborer. Careers open to talents, that goal achieved by the French Revolution, frequently meant middle-class jobs for middle-class young men who could pass exams. The examination system was an important path for ascendancy within governmental bureaucracies. If passage from working class to middle class was not common, neither was the equally difficult social journey from middle class to aristocratic, landed society. This was particularly the case on the Continent, where the division between nobility and commoner had traditionally been most pronounced. In Britain, mobility of this sort was easier. Children from wealthy upper middle-class families, if they were sent, as occasionally they were, to elite schools and universities, and if they left the commercial or industrial world for a career in politics, might effect the change. William Gladstone, son of a Liverpool merchant, attended Eton and Oxford, exclusive educational preserves, married a connection of the aristocratic Grenville family, and became prime minister of England. Yet Gladstone was an

Young Gentlemen, 1834. It was to models such as these that the young men of the middle class aspired.

exception to the norm in Britain, and Britain was an exception to the Continent. Movement, when it occurred, did so in less spectacular degrees.

Nevertheless, the European middle class helped sustain itself with the belief that it was possible to get ahead by means of intelligence, pluck, and serious devotion to work. The Englishman Samuel Smiles, in his extraordinarily successful how-to-succeed book *Self Help,* preached a gospel dear to the middle class. Although the gospel declared that anyone willing to exert himself could rise to a position of responsibility and personal profit, however, and although some men actually did so, the notion remained no more than myth for the great majority.

Self-help

Seriousness of purpose was reflected in the middle-class devotion to the ideal of family and home. A practical importance attached to the institution of the family in those areas in England, France, and Germany where sons, sons-in-law, nephews, and cousins were expected to assume responsibility in family firms when it came their turn. Yet the worship of family ignored those practical considerations and assumed the proportions of a sacred belief. Away from the business and confusion of the world, sheltered behind solid masonry and amid the solid comfort of their ornate furnishings, middle-class fathers retired each evening to enjoy the fruits of their daily labors. Inside the home, life was enclosed in a hierarchical and ritualistic system under which the husband and father was absolute master. His wife was called his help-mate but was unquestionably his servant as well. Her task was to keep the household functioning smoothly and harmoniously. She maintained the accounts and directed the activities of the servants—

Family and home

Left: *A Salon in Vienna, 1830s.* A representation of middle-class home life on the Continent. Right: *A Victorian Family at Tea, 1860s*

usually two or three women. Because of the extent of her duties as overseer, she was excused from the everyday drudgeries of washing and cleaning. Called in Victorian England the "Angel in the House," the middle-class woman was responsible for the moral education of her children. Yet she probably spent no more than two or three hours a day at most with her offspring. Until sent to school, they were placed in the custody of a nursemaid or governess. Much of a middle-class woman's day was spent in the company of other women from similar households. An elaborate set of social customs involving "calls" and "at homes" was established in European middle-class society. Women were not expected to improve their minds. They were not expected to be the intellectual companions of their husbands. Rather, they were encouraged to be dabblers, education for them usually consisting of little more beyond reading and writing, a smattering of arithmetic, geography, history, and a foreign language, embellished with lessons in drawing, painting in watercolor, singing, or piano-playing.

Sexuality

Middle-class wives were indoctrinated to believe that they were superior to their husbands in one area only. A wife was "the better half" of a middle-class marriage because she was deemed pure—the untainted Vestal of the hearth, unsullied by cares of the world outside her home, and certainly untouched by those sexual desires which marked her husband, her natural moral inferior. A wife's charge was to encourage her husband's "higher nature." She must never respond to his sexual advances with equal passion; passion was, for her, a presumed impossibility. Instead she must persuade him to seek, through love of home and family, a substitute for the baser instincts with which nature had unhappily endowed the male. Should she fail—and the numberless prostitutes and courtesans in the streets and clandestine boudoirs of nineteenth-century cities suggest that she often did fail—she must accept the fact of her "failure" as she was bound to accept the rest of her life: uncomplainingly. Should she herself succumb to "unwomanly desires" and be discovered to have done so, she could expect nothing less than complete social banishment. The law tolerated a husband's infidelity and at all times respected a husband's rights both to his wife's person and to her property. It made quick work of an "unfaithful" wife, granting to her husband whatever he might desire in terms of divorce, property, and custody, to make him amends for the personal wrongs and embarrassments he had suffered at the hands of his "unnatural" spouse.

Middle-class family rituals helped to sustain this hierarchy. Daily meals, with the father at the head of the table, were cooked and brought to each place by servants, who were a constant reminder of the family's social position. Family vacations were a particularly nineteenth-century middle-class invention. Thanks to the advent of the railways, excursions of one or two weeks to the mountains or to the seashore were available to families of even moderate means. Entrepreneurs built large, ornate hotels, adorned with imposing names—Palace, Beau Rivage, Excelsior—and attracted middle-class customers by offering them on a grander scale exactly the same sort of comfortable and sheltered existence they enjoyed at home.

Domestic rituals

The Middle Class at Leisure. The "morning lounge" at Biarritz, a French resort on the Atlantic coast.

Houses

The houses and furnishings of the middle class were an expression of the material security the middle class valued. Solidly built, heavily decorated, they proclaimed the financial worth and social respectability of those who dwelt within. In provincial cities they were often free-standing "villas." In London, Paris, Berlin, or Vienna, they might be rows of five- or six-story townhouses, or large apartments. Whatever particular shape they took, they were built to last a long time. The rooms were certain to be crowded with furniture, art objects, carpets, and wall hangings. Chairs, tables, cabinets, and sofas might be of any or all periods; no matter, so long as they were adorned with their proper compliment of fringe, gilt, or other ornamentation. The size of the rooms, the elegance of the furniture, the number of servants, all depended, of course, on the extent of one's income. A bank clerk did not live as elegantly as a bank director. Yet in all likelihood both lived in obedience to the same set of standards and aspirations. And that obedience helped bind them, despite the differences in their material way of life, to the same class.

Cities and the middle class

The European middle class had no desire to confront the unpleasant urban by-products of its own success. Members of the middle class saw to it that they lived apart from the unpleasant sights and smells of industrialization. Their residential areas, usually built to the west of the cities, out of the path of the prevailing breeze, and therefore of industrial pollution, were havens from the congestion for which they were primarily responsible. When the members of the middle class rode into the urban centers they took care to do so over avenues lined with respectable shops, or across railway embankments that lifted them above monotonous working-class streets en route to their destination. Yet the middle class, though it turned its face from what it did not want to see, did not turn from the city. Middle-class men and women celebrated the city as their particular creation and the source of their profits. They even praised its smoke—as a sign of prosperity—so

The Paris Opera. An exterior view of the Opera. Designed by Charles Garnier, it was constructed between 1861 and 1875. This grandiose display of wealth and luxury epitomized the taste of the new industrial middle class.

long as they did not have to breathe it night and day. For the most part, it was they who managed their city's affairs. And it was they who provided new industrial cities with their proud architectural landmarks: city halls, stock exchanges, opera houses. These were the new cathedrals of the industrial age, proclamations of a triumphant middle class.

4. THE LIFE OF THE URBAN WORKING CLASS

Like the middle class, the working class was divided into various subgroups and categories, determined in this case by skill, wages, and workplace. The working class included skilled workers in crafts that were centuries old—glassblowing and cabinetmaking, for example. It included as well mechanics equally skilled in new industrial technology. It included the men who built textile machinery and the women and children who tended it. It included the men, women, and children who together worked in mines and quarries. And it included the countless millions who labored at unskilled jobs—railway navvies, coal porters, cleaning women, and the like. The nature of workers' experiences naturally varied, depending upon where they worked, where they lived, and, above all, how much they earned. A skilled textile worker lived a life far different from that of an unskilled dock laborer, the former able to afford the food, shelter, and clothing necessary for a decent existence, the latter so busy trying to keep himself and his family alive that he would have little time to think about anything but the source of their next meal.

Ranks within the working class

Some movement from the ranks of the unskilled to the skilled was possible, if children were provided, or provided themselves, with at least a rudimentary education. Yet education was considered by many parents a luxury, especially since children could be put to work at an early age to supplement a family's meager earnings. There was movement from skilled to unskilled also, as technological change—the introduction of the power loom, for example—drove highly paid workers into the ranks of the unskilled and destitute. Further variations within the working class were the result of the fact that though more men, women, and children were every year working in factories, the majority still labored either in workshops or at home. These variations mean that we cannot speak of a common European working-class experience during the years from 1800–1850. The life we shall be describing was most typical of English workers, during the first half-century of their exposure to industrialization. Only in the years 1850–1900 did continental workers undergo to anything like the same extent, this harsh process of urban acclimatization.

Social mobility

Life in industrial cities was, for almost all workers, uncomfortable at best and unbearably squalid at worst. Workers and their families

Left: *An Urban Courtyard in London.* Right: *A Working-Class Tenement in Glasgow, Scotland.* Courtyards such as these were frequently the only available dumping grounds for household sewage and garbage.

Housing

lived in housing that failed to answer the needs of its inhabitants. In older cities single-family dwellings were broken up into apartments of often no more than one room per family. In new manufacturing centers, rows of tiny houses, located close by smoking factories, were built back-to-back, thereby eliminating any cross-ventilation or space for gardens. Whether housing was old or new, it was generally poorly built. Old buildings were allowed by landlords to fall into disrepair; new houses, constructed of cheap material, decayed quickly. Water often came from an outdoor tap, shared by several houses and adjacent to an outdoor toilet. Crowding was commonplace. Families of as many as eight lived in two or, at the most, three rooms. Housewives could not rely, as in the country, on their own gardens to help supply them with food. Instead, they went to markets that catered to their needs with cheap goods, often stale or nearly rotten, or dangerously adulterated (formaldehyde was added to milk, for example) to prevent further spoilage.

The role of women

The life of working-class wives and mothers was hard. Lack of cheap contraceptive devices and a belief that these devices were immoral helped to keep women pregnant through most of their childbearing years, thus endangering their general health and adding to the burden of their lives. Wives were usually handed a portion of the weekly wage packet by their husbands, and were expected to house, feed, and clothe the family on the very little they were given. Their daily life was a constant round of cooking, cleaning, shopping, and washing—in a tiny space and without enough money. Their problems were compounded, of course, when they themselves had to work, and therefore had far less time to accomplish the household tasks they were still expected to perform.

Since many working-class families had only recently migrated from the country into the city, life there could be a lonely experience for them. If possible, they would live near relatives who had already made the transition and who could assist the newcomers in adjusting to their very different existence. In many cities working-class families lived in districts inhabited primarily by others working at the same trade—weavers in one place, miners in another—and in this way achieved some sense of commonality.

Adjustment to the demands of the factory was every bit as difficult for workers as was acceptance of urban living patterns. Factory hours were long, before 1850 usually twelve to fourteen hours a day. Conditions were dirty and dangerous. Textile mills remained unventilated, so that bits of material lodged in workers' lungs. Machines were unfenced and were a particular danger to child workers, often hired, because of their supposed agility, to clean under and around the moving parts. Manufacturing processes were unhealthy. The use of poison lead in the making of glazed pottery, for example, was a constant hazard to men and women workers in that industry.

As upsetting as the physical working conditions in factories was the psychological readjustment demanded of the first-generation workers in them. Preindustrial laborers had had to work long hours and for very little monetary reward. Yet, at least to some degree, they were free to set their own hours and structure their own activities, to move from their home workshops to their small garden plots and back again as they wished. In a factory, all "hands" learned the discipline of the whistle. To function efficiently, a factory demanded that all employees begin and end work at the same time. Most workers could not tell time; fewer possessed clocks. None were accustomed to the relent-

Loneliness

Factory life

Daily routine

A Laundress and Her Children. Note the cramped and cluttered living quarters.

less pace of the machine. In order to increase production, the factory system encouraged the breaking down of the manufacturing process into specialized steps, each with its own assigned time, an innovation that upset workers accustomed to completing a task at their own pace. The employment of women and children was a further disturbing innovation. In preindustrial communities, women and children had worked, as well as men, but more often than not, all together and at home. In factory towns women and children were frequently hired instead of men: they could be paid less and were declared to be easier to manage. When this happened, the pattern of family life was severely disrupted, and a further break with tradition had to be endured.

Escape

Faced with a drastic reordering of their lives, working-class men and women reacted in various ways. Some sought "the shortest way out of Manchester" by taking to drink (there were 1,200 public houses in that city in 1850). Some women turned to prostitution to supplement their meager wages. Many more men and women struggled to make some sort of community out of the street where they lived or the factory where they worked. It was a long and discouraging process. Yet by mid-century their experiences were beginning to make them conscious of themselves as different from and in opposition to the middle class that was imposing a new way of life on them.

5. THE MIDDLE-CLASS WORLDVIEW

The middle class was not unaware of the many social problems it was generating as it created an industrial society. Despite its general con-

"Capital and Labour." In its earliest years, *Punch,* though primarily a humorous weekly, manifested a strong social conscience. In this 1843 cartoon, the capitalists are seen revelling in the rewards of their investments while the workers—men, women, and children—who toiled in the mines under cruel and dangerous conditions are found crippled and starving.

The Interior of the Crystal Palace. This building of iron and glass was constructed to house exhibits sent to the Exhibition of the Works of Industry of All Nations, held in London in 1851. The exhibition celebrated the triumph of middle-class industrialization.

fidence that the world was progressing—and at its own behest—the middle class was beset by uncertainties. Its belief in its own undoubted abilities was shadowed by concern as to whether its particular talents might ultimately prove irrelevant to the preservation of prosperity. Self-assurance could dissolve in the face of bankruptcy and prosperity vanish in the abyss of economic catastrophe. Those who had risen by their own exertions might fall victim to someone else's ambitions. Nor was it always a simple matter for the middle class to reconcile its own affluence with the poverty of the thousands of workers exploited under its aegis. The middle class was responsible for having wrenched European society out of old patterns of living and thrust it into new ones. To those willing to acknowledge that responsibility, the realization was enough to temper confidence with apprehension. As a result, the middle class worked hard to rationalize its own prosperity, and to make legitimate its ascendancy over both the old society of the land and the urban working poor.

Uncertainty and the need for reassurance

To assist themselves in constructing this congenial worldview, the members of the new industrial middle class made use of the theories of a number of political economists. It is important to recognize that a factory-owner or a banker was not likely to have read the works of these theorists. He might, however, have encountered popular journalistic condensations of their ideas, or have participated in discussions at which the conclusions, if not the reasoned arguments, of the economists were aired. Because those conclusions supported his own inter-

Political economics and the worldview

ests, he grew familiar with them, until, in time, he could talk of the ideas of these men as if they were his own.

We have noted already the manner in which the writings of the economist Adam Smith sustained middle-class respect for individual enterprise. The writings of another group, the classical, or liberal, economists—particularly the Englishmen Thomas Malthus (1766–1834) and David Ricardo (1772–1823)—embodied principles appealing to businessmen who desired a free hand to remake the economies of their countries. The chief elements in the theories as formulated by liberal economists were:

Classical economics

(1) Economic individualism. Individuals are entitled to use for their own best interests the property they have inherited or acquired by any legitimate method. People must be allowed to do what they like so long as they do not trespass upon the equal right of others to do the same.

(2) Laissez faire. The functions of the state should be reduced to the lowest minimum consistent with public safety. The government should shrink itself into the role of a modest policeman, preserving order and protecting property, but never interfering with the operation of economic processes.

(3) Obedience to natural law. There are immutable laws operating in the realm of economics as in every sphere of the universe. Examples are the law of supply and demand, the law of diminishing returns, and so on. These laws must be recognized and respected; failure to do so is disastrous.

(4) Freedom of contract. Individuals should be free to negotiate the best kind of contract they can obtain from any other individual. In particular, the liberty of workers and employers to bargain with each other as to wages and hours should not be hampered by laws or by the collective power of labor unions.

(5) Free competition and free trade. Competition serves to keep prices down, to eliminate inefficient producers, and to ensure the maximum production in accordance with public demand. Therefore, no monopolies should be tolerated, nor any price-fixing laws for the benefit of incompetent enterprisers. Further, in order to force each country to engage in the production of those things it is best fitted to produce, all protective tariffs should be abolished. Free international trade will also help to keep prices down.

Businessmen naturally warmed to theories so congenial to their own desires and intentions. But Malthus and Ricardo made further contributions to the middle-class worldview, based upon their perceptions of conflicting interests within society. Malthus, in his well-known *Essay on Population,* first published in 1798, argued that nature has set stubborn limits to the progress of mankind in happiness and wealth. Because of the voracity of the sexual appetite there is a natural tendency for population to increase more rapidly than the supply of

Thomas Malthus

food. To be sure, there are powerful checks, such as war, famine, disease, and vice; but these, when they operate effectively, further augment the burden of human misery. It follows that poverty and pain are inescapable. Even if laws were passed distributing all wealth equally, the condition of the poor would be only temporarily improved; in a very short time they would begin to raise larger families, with the result that the last state of their class would be as bad as the first. In the second edition of his' work, Malthus advocated postponement of marriage as a means of relief, but he continued to stress the danger that population would outrun any possible increase in the means of subsistence.

Malthus on population

Malthus's arguments allowed the middle class to acquiesce in the destruction of an older society which had made some attempt to care for its poor. In England, for example, officials in rural parishes had instituted a system of doles and subsidized wages to help sustain laborers and their families when unemployed. The attempt failed to prevent distress and was met with increasing resistance by taxpayers. Now Malthus told taxpayers that schemes designed to help the poor damaged both rich and poor alike. Poor relief took money, and therefore food, from the mouths of the more productive members of society and put it into the mouths of the least productive. Malthus helped shift the responsibility for poverty from society to the individual, a shift appealing to the middle class, which wished to be freed from the burden of supporting the urban unemployed.

The application of Malthusian doctrine

Malthusian assumptions played a large role in the development of the theories of the Scottish economist Ricardo. According to Ricardo, wages seek a level which is just sufficient to enable workers "to subsist and perpetuate their race, without either increase or diminution." This Ricardo held to be an iron law, from which there is no escape. If wages should rise temporarily above the subsistence standard, the population would increase, and the ensuing competition for jobs would quickly force the rate of pay down to its former level. Ricardo devised a law of rent as well as a law of wages. He maintained that rent is determined by the cost of production on the poorest land that must be brought under cultivation, and that, consequently, as a country fills up with people an ever-increasing proportion of the social income is taken by the landlords.

Ricardo on wages and rent

Here again, a theorist provided arguments useful to the middle class in its attempt to define and defend itself within a new social order. The law of wages gave employers a useful weapon to protect themselves from their workers' petitions for higher pay. The law of rent justified middle-class opposition to the continuing power of landed interests: a class which derived its income not from hard work but simply from its role as rent-collector was profiting unfairly at the expense of the rest of society and deserved to have its profit-making curtailed.

The uses of Ricardo's laws

As soon as the middle class began to argue in this fashion, however,

Jeremy Bentham

Benthamite utilitarianism

Utilitarianism's appeal to the middle class

it betrayed its devotion to the doctrine of laissez faire. Businessmen and entrepreneurs vehemently opposed to government intervention which might deny them the chance to make as much money as they could, were nevertheless prepared to see the government step in and prevent profiteering landlords from making what *they* could from their property. How could this apparent inconsistency be justified? The answer lay in the theories of the Englishman Jeremy Bentham (1748–1832), without doubt the mainstay of middle-class apologists. Bentham, whose major work, *The Principles of Morals and Legislation,* was published in 1789, argued against the eighteenth-century notion that a satisfactory theory of social order could be grounded in a belief in the natural harmony of human interests. Men and women were basically selfish beings. To suppose that a stable and beneficent society could emerge unassisted from a company of self-interested egos was, Bentham believed, to suppose the impossible. Society, if it was to function properly, needed an organizing principle that would both acknowledge humanity's basic selfishness and at the same time compel people to sacrifice at least a portion of their own interests for the good of the majority. That principle, called utilitarianism, stated that every institution, every law, must be measured according to its social usefulness. And a socially useful law was one which produced the greatest happiness of the greatest number. If a law passed this test, it could remain on the books; if it failed, it should be abandoned forthwith, no matter how venerable. A selfish man would accept this social yardstick, realizing that in the long run he would do himself serious harm by clinging to laws that might benefit him, but produce such general unhappiness as to result in disruptions detrimental to his own interests as well as to those of others.

In what ways did this philosophy particularly appeal to the industrial middle classes? First, it acknowledged the importance of the individual. The interests of the community were nothing more than the sum of the interests of those selfish egos who lived within it. Each individual best understood his or her own interests, and was therefore best left free, whenever possible, to pursue those interests as he or she saw fit. Only when they conflicted with the interests—the happiness—of the greatest number were they to be curtailed. Entrepreneurs could understand this doctrine as a license to proceed with the business of industrialization, since, they argued, industrialization was so clearly producing happiness for the majority of the world's population. At the same time, Bentham's doctrines could be used to justify those changes necessary to bring an industrial world into being. Was the greatest happiness produced, English factory-owners might ask, by an antiquated electoral system which denied representation to growing industrial cities? Obviously not. Let Parliament reform itself so that the weight of the manufacturing interests could be felt in the drafting of legislation.

Utilitarianism was thus a doctrine that could be used to cut two ways—in favor of laissez faire; in favor of governmental intervention. And the middle class proceeded to cut both ways at once. Benthamite utilitarianism provided the theoretical basis for many of the middle-class interventionist reforms, such as a revised poor law in Britain and an expanded educational system in France, achieved between 1815 and 1848.[1] At the same time utilitarianism, combined with the theories of Malthus and Ricardo, fortified the position of those businessmen who believed that unfettered individualism had produced the triumphs of the Industrial Revolution. To restrain that individualism was to jeopardize the further progress of industrialization and hence the greatest happiness of the greatest number.

Individualism and intervention

In arguing as it did, the middle class relied upon the conviction that industrialization and the factory system were together showering benefits on all—not just themselves. As we shall see, there were those who disagreed, who pressed, for example, for regulation of factory wages and hours. But the capitalists claimed intervention would inhibit the distribution of those benefits, and hence the proliferation of general happiness. In their support they could cite the English economist Nassau Senior, who claimed that the net profit of any industrial enterprise was derived solely from its last hour of daily operation. Reduce working hours, said Senior, and you eliminate profits, thereby compelling factories to close and workers to starve. The middle class believed Senior because it was clearly in its interest to do so. The middle class also believed him because the enterprise upon which it was embarked was so new and so uncharted that it was hard to prove him wrong. Their uncertainty led them to believe those theories which provided them with the most reassurance and encouraged them to think that what they were doing was of benefit to their fellow men.

Belief in improvement

Political economists and philosophers in France as well as in England helped provide the new middle class with a congenial worldview. Count Claude de Saint-Simon (1760–1825), while a proponent of utopian schemes for social reorganization, nevertheless preached the gospel of "industrialism" and "industrialists" (two words which he coined). Disciples of Saint-Simon were among the leading proponents in France of industrial entrepreneurship and a standardized and centralized financial system.

Far more generally influential was the Positivist philosophy of Auguste Comte (1798–1857). Comte's philosophy, like utilitarianism, insisted that all truth is derived from experience or observation of the physical world. Comte rejected metaphysics as utterly futile; no one can discover the hidden essences of things—why events happen as they do, or what is the ultimate meaning and goal of existence. All one can really know is how things happen, the laws which control their

Auguste Comte

---

[1] These and other similar reforms will be discussed in the following chapter.

The Positivism of Comte

occurrence, and the relations existing between them. Positivism derived its name from the assertion that the only knowledge of any current value was "positive," or scientific, knowledge. Comte argued that humankind's ability to analyze society scientifically and to predict its future had reached a point which would soon enable Europe to achieve a "positive" society, organized not in terms of belief but in terms of facts. Such an achievement would not be a simple matter, however; "positive" attitudes and institutions could not replace those of the "metaphysical" stage through which Europe had just passed without a struggle. By dividing the history of the world into progressive stages (a "religious" stage had preceded the "metaphysical"), and by declaring that the achievement of the highest stage was not possible without the turmoil of industrialization, Comte assured the middle class of its leading role in the better world that was to be.

6. EARLY CRITICS OF THE MIDDLE-CLASS WORLDVIEW

Honoré de Balzac

Gustave Flaubert

The middle-class worldview did not go unchallenged. Many writers deplored the social disintegration and moral hypocrisy they saw as the legacy of the Industrial Revolution. The Scot Thomas Carlyle (1795–1881), though a defender of the French Revolution and a believer in the need for a new aristocracy of industrialists ("captains of industry"), had nothing but contempt for the theories of the utilitarians. In Carlyle's view, they did no more than excuse the greed and acquisitiveness of the new middle class. Equally scathing in his attacks on the middle class was the English novelist Charles Dickens (1812–1870). In such novels as *Oliver Twist, Hard Times,* and *Dombey and Son,* he wrote with sympathy of the tyrannization of industrial workers by the new rich. In France, the Abbé Félicité Lamennais (1782–1854), though preaching respect for private property, nevertheless attacked self-interest. He argued, in his *Book of the People,* that the "little people" of the world enjoyed far too small a share in the direction of their lives. Honoré de Balzac (1799–1850) wrote *The Human Comedy* to expose the stupidity, greed, and baseness of the middle class. Gustave Flaubert (1821–1880) in his foremost novel *Madame Bovary,* depicted the banal, and literally fatal, nature of bourgeois existence for women.

One of the most trenchant critics of early industrialization was the English philosopher and economist John Stuart Mill (1806–1873). Though Mill as an economist is often considered a member of the classical school, he actually repudiated a number of its most sacred premises. First, he rejected the universality of economic laws. Though he admitted that there are unchangeable laws governing the field of production, he insisted that the distribution of wealth can be regulated by society for the benefit of the majority of its members. Second, he advocated more radical departures from laissez faire than any recommended by his forerunners. He favored legislation, under certain conditions, for shortening the working day, and he believed that the state might properly take preliminary steps toward the redistribution of wealth by taxing inheritances and by appropriating the unearned increment of land. In the fourth book of his *Principles of Political Economy* he urged the abolition of the wage system and looked forward to a society of producers' cooperatives in which the workers would own the factories and elect the managers to run them. On the other hand, Mill was no socialist. He distrusted the state, and his real reason for advocating producers' cooperatives was not to exalt the power of the workers but to give them the fruits of their labor.

Artists, too, attacked the values of industrial society in their painting and sculpture. The art preferred by the European middle class in the nineteenth century was that which in some way either told a story or, better still, preached a message. Beauty was surface decoration, which could be admired for its intrinsic richness and for what it therefore declared about its owner's wealth. Or beauty was a moralism, easily understood and, if possible, reassuring. When the Great Exhibition of the Works of Industry in All Nations was held at the Crystal Palace in London in 1851 to celebrate the triumph of industrialism, one of the most popular exhibits was *The Greek Slave,* a statue by the American sculptor Hiram Powers. Depicting a young Christian stripped bare and standing, according to the catalogue, before the gaze of an Eastern potentate, the work allowed its Victorian male admirers a chance to relish its salaciousness, while at the same time profiting from its depiction of the woman's righteous disdain for her captor.

Some of the artists most critical of the middle class, while repudiating the artificial and decorative, nevertheless reflected the middle-class obsession with art as morality. The self-designated Pre-Raphaelite Brotherhood of English painters was a group of men and women, led by the painter-poet Dante Gabriel Rossetti (1828–1882), determined to express its disdain for contemporary values. They called themselves Pre-Raphaelites as a way of announcing their admiration for the techniques of early Renaissance artists, untainted, supposedly, by corrupted artistic taste. Yet the works of the leading members of the Brotherhood exuded a degree of sentimentality that compromised their rebel nature and rendered them conventionally pietistic and ultimately innocuous as social protest. The same can be said, to a lesser degree, of the work of the Frenchman Jean François Millet (1814–1875). His *Man with the Hoe* is a stark, bitter statement about peasant life; his *The Angelus* softens the statement to sentiment. In both England and France, however, some of the most talented painters seriously questioned many of the values the middle class revered. Gustave Courbet (1819–1877) and Honoré Daumier (1808–1879)

John Stuart Mill

Middle-class art and its critics

The Pre-Raphaelites; Courbet and Daumier

See color plates following page 960

The Angelus by Jean-Fran-
çois Millet. The artist's peasants accept their humble lot
in this sentimental por-
trayal.

both expressed sympathy toward the plight of the French working
class, contrasting scenes of rural and urban misfortune with
unflattering caricatures of the bourgeoisie. Daumier, in particular,
was a powerful satirist of social and political evils, ridiculing the corruption of petty officials and the hypocritical piety of the rich. There
was a harsh bite to most of the work of Daumier and Courbet that
proscribed sentimentalizing.

These writers and artists, while critical of the Industrial Revolution
and middle-class values, proposed nothing very tangible in the way of

Past or present? radical reform. If they opposed the triumph of a materialistic middle
class, they opposed, as well, the idea of complete democracy. Carlyle,
in particular, criticized the present by comparing it with a rosy past
that had never been. In this he was like one of the doughtiest critics
of the new middle-class society, the Englishman William Cobbett
(1763–1835). Cobbett, in his newspaper the *Political Register,* argued
against industrialization itself as well as its effects. His propaganda
mirrored the dilemma most critics had to face: Granted industrialization has brought great social and economic hardship in its train; does
this mean that we should try to return to the life of preindustrial society, also often harsh, and always confining, though probably more
secure?

For some time, a small band of thinkers had been answering that
question with a resounding "no." They argued that there could be no
Utopians return to old times and old ways, but that society could be at the same
time both industrial and humane. These radical thinkers were often
explicitly utopian. Two of the most persuasive were the Englishman

Robert Owen (1771–1858) and the Frenchman Charles Fourier (1772–1837). Though both writers are correctly seen as utopian, with all the practical limitations that label carries with it, in their day many of their followers believed in the possibility of instituting the programs Fourier and Owen propounded. Owen, himself the proprietor of a large cotton factory at New Lanark in Scotland, argued against the middle-class belief that the profit motive should be allowed to shape social and economic organization. Having reorganized his own mills to provide free schooling and a system of social security for his workers, he proceeded to advocate a general reorganization of society on the basis of cooperation, with communities rewarding workers solely on the basis of their actual labor. Fourier urged an even more far-reaching reconstitution, including the abolition of the wage system and the complete equality of the sexes. Followers of Owen and Fourier sought escape from the confusions of the contemporary world in idealist communities founded according to the principles of their leaders. All these attempts failed after a time, victims of faulty leadership and, in the case of Fourierist communities in France, of charges of moral turpitude resulting from Fourier's revolutionary sexual doctrines.

Less utopian radical theories were proposed during the 1840s, years which witnessed recurring economic depressions and their horrifying consequences. The French politician and journalist Louis Blanc (1811–1882), stood, like many contemporary critics, against the competitiveness of the new industrial society and particularly opposed the exploitation of the working class. His solution was to campaign for universal male suffrage, which would give working-class men control of the state. Following their triumph, these workers would make the state the "banker of the poor" and institute "Associations of Production"—actually a system of workshops governed by workers—which would guarantee jobs and security for all. Once these associations became established, private enterprise would wither through competition, and with it the state, for which there would no longer be any need. As we shall see, these workshops were briefly instituted in Paris during the Revolution of 1848. Another Frenchman, Pierre Proudhon (1809–1865), condemned the profits accruing to employers at the expense of their employees. He, too, proposed new institutions, which he argued could be made to produce goods at a price fairer to the worker, a price based solely on the amount of labor devoted to the manufacture of any particular product.

The ideas contained in the works of Blanc and Proudhon and other radical writers received their clearest and most forceful expression by the German theorists Karl Marx (1818–1883) and Friedrich Engels (1820–1895). Both Marx and Engels were sons of wealthy middle class parents. Marx studied philosophy at the University of Berlin. Determined to play an active role in the transformation of a society he was growing to despise, he took a job as editor of the *Rhineland Gazette* in

Louis Blanc

Blanc and Proudhon

Marx and Engels

The Communist
Manifesto

Karl Marx

1842. His radical policies soon put him at odds with his publishers. In 1843, he moved to Paris to devote further thought to the process and possibility of revolutionary change. From there he migrated to Brussels, where he was instrumental in founding the Communist League, a body whose declared aim was the overthrow of the middle class—or to use Marx's terminology, the bourgeoisie. While in Paris, Marx had renewed a former friendship with Engels, who had been living in Manchester where his family owned a cotton mill. While there, Engels wrote a devastating description of the effect of early industrialization upon the workers of England: *The Condition of the Working Class in England in 1844*. Together, Marx and Engels worked to produce a theory that would both explain how society had come to its present state and propose the means whereby it might be altered to benefit all. The theory was published by Marx at the request of the league in 1848, at the height of revolutionary agitation on the Continent, as *The Communist Manifesto*.

In the *Manifesto* Marx outlined a theory of history which owed a good deal to the German philosopher Georg Wilhelm Hegel (see below, p.892). Hegel had argued that ideas, the motive force of history, were in constant conflict with each other, and that this antithetical relationship between ideas in turn would produce an eventual synthesis, representing an advance in the history of the human race. Marx adopted this particular progressive notion of history to his own uses. Whereas Hegel perceived conflict and resolution (a dialectic) in terms of ideas, Marx saw them in terms of economic forces. Society, he argued, was at any time no more than the reflection of a hierarchy dictated by those who own the means of production and control the distribution of its material goods. As history has progressed, so have the means changed. Feudalism and manorialism were vanquished by capitalism. And capitalism, Marx declared, would be vanquished in turn by communism. That process, however, will first involve the concentration of capitalist economic power into fewer and fewer hands, and the consequent opposition of an ever-increasing and ever-debased working class (the proletariat). Once the proletariat overthrows the bourgeoisie by revolution, as it is bound to do eventually, society as a whole will be emancipated. An interim period in which a "dictatorship of the proletariat" rids the world of the last vestiges of bourgeois society will be followed by an end of the dialectical process and the emergence of a truly classless civilization.

Marx insisted that the *Manifesto* was not just another theory. His declaration that the proletariat together could consciously participate in the revolutionary process he described—could actually advance history through its own efforts—helps explain the document's appeal. The writings of Marx and Engels did not bring about an immediate proletarian revolution. Though the *Manifesto*, in its famous declaration, called upon the workers of the world to unite, Marx and Engels realized that this goal would not be achieved quickly. Marx and Engels, however, more than any other political thinkers of the 1830s and 1840s, provided workers with a potential sense of their worth as human beings and of their vital role in the historical process of the world. Engels made workers understand what factory work and urban living was doing to them: turning them from men and women into machines, alienated (a Marxian term) from themselves as human beings because they were alienated from the work over which they had no control. Marx gave workers the sense that those sufferings Engels described had an ultimate purpose, that they represented the workers' own particular contribution to the eventual and inevitable triumph of their class.

The theories of Marx and Engels spread throughout Europe after 1850. Like the theories of those other writers whom we have been considering—both the defenders and the opponents of the middle-class industrial world—they are historically important for two reasons. First, the ideas helped men and women better understand the new social order which had sprung up following the French and Industrial Revolutions, and the part they might play, as members of a class, in that new order. Second, the ideas themselves helped inspire the concrete political, social, and economic changes and events which are the subject of the next two chapters.

Friedrich Engels

SELECTED READINGS

- *Items so designated are available in paperback editions.*
- Berlin, Isaiah, *Karl Marx: His Life and Environment,* New York, 1948. The best short account.

  Briggs, Asa, *The Age of Improvement,* New York, 1959.
- ———, *Victorian People,* London, 1954.
- Burn, W. L., *The Age of Equipoise,* London, 1964. A charming account of the mid-Victorian years.

  Chevalier, Louis, *Laboring Classes and Dangerous Classes,* New York, 1973. An intriguing though controversial study of the quality of life in Paris between 1815 and 1848 which concludes that social mobility was downward and that the fear of crime dominated social consciousness.

  Gide, Charles, and Charles Rist, *A History of Economic Doctrines,* rev. ed., Boston, 1948. A good summary.

  Halevy, Elie, *The Growth of Philosophical Radicalism,* rev. ed., London, 1949. The best introduction to the thought of Malthus, Ricardo, Bentham, and their philosophical heirs.

  ———, *England in 1815,* London, 1949. The classic work by the greatest historian of nineteenth-century England.
- Hammond, J. L., and Barbara Hammond, *The Town Labourer, 1760–1832,* London, 1917. An impassioned account of the economic changes which affected the quality of life of the English worker.

Hobsbawm, Eric, *The Age of Capital, 1848–1875,* London, 1975. A perceptive world survey which traces the global triumph of capitalism and its impact upon the working classes.

• ———, *Labouring Men: Studies in the History of Labour,* London, 1964. A series of essays on workers and the working class in England.

• Langer, William L., *Political and Social Upheaval, 1832–1852,* New York, 1969. Comprehensive survey of European history, with excellent analytical chapters and thorough bibliographies.

Manuel, Frank E., *The Prophets of Paris,* Cambridge, Mass., 1962. An entertaining introduction to the philosophers of progress, from Turgot to Comte.

• Mehring, Franz, *Karl Marx: The Story of His Life,* New York, 1976.

• Rudé, George, *The Crowd in History,* New York, 1964.

• Thompson, E. P., *The Making of the English Working Class,* London, 1963. Argues that the coincidence of the French and Industrial Revolutions fostered the growth of working-class consciousness. A brilliant and important work.

Walker, Mack, *German Home Towns: Community, State, and General Estate, 1648–1871,* Ithaca, N.Y., 1971. Attempts to explain the absence of a strong middle class in Germany.

Zeldin, Theodore, *France, 1848–1951,* 2 vols., Oxford, 1973–77. A highly individualistic synthesis of French history, remarkable for its scope and insight.

SOURCE MATERIALS

• Engels, Friedrich, *The Condition of the Working Class in England,* New York, 1958. A much criticized, but reliable firsthand account by the later collaborator of Marx, written in 1844. Presents a devastating portrait of living and working conditions, especially in Manchester.

• Malthus, Thomas R., *An Essay on Population,* London, 1798 and 1803. Malthus's famous essay relating population growth and food production.

• Marx, Karl, *The Communist Manifesto,* 1848. Written under the spell of European revolutions, this was the young Marx's call for a revolution by the working class.

• Marx, Karl, and Friedrich Engels, *The Marx-Engels Reader,* 2nd ed., ed. by R. C. Tucker, New York, 1978.

• Mayhew, Henry, *London Labor and the London Poor,* New York, 1968. A reprint of the 1851 edition, provides a fascinating view of the population and trades of London. A good factual companion to Dickens.

Owen, Robert, *A New View of Society,* London, 1813. A proposed utopian society based upon cooperative villages by the founder of British socialism.

Chapter 27

THE RISE OF LIBERALISM
(1815–1870)

The general thought, the hope of France, has been order and liberty reuniting under constitutional monarchy.

—François Guizot, "Speech on the State of the Nation," 1831

The history of nineteenth-century Europe was to a great extent shaped by the interplay of the forces of liberalism and nationalism. The middle classes of France and England, where liberalism was strongest, espoused a set of doctrines reflecting their concerns and interests. Liberalism to them meant (1) an efficient government prepared to acknowledge the value of commercial and industrial development; (2) a government in which their interests would be protected by their direct representation in the legislature—in all probability, a constitutional monarchy, and most certainly not a democracy; (3) a foreign policy of peace and free trade; and (4) a belief in individualism and the doctrines of the classical economists.

The components of liberalism

Many middle-class men and women in other European countries shared these beliefs and assumptions, and worked diligently and with some success to carry through specific liberal reforms. But for them, an equally important and often more immediate objective was the achievement of some form of national unity. The middle classes in Germany, Italy, Poland, and the Austrian Empire, however dedicated they were to liberalism, believed that their chances of achieving liberal goals would be greatly enhanced if they could unify the patchwork of principalities that surrounded them into a vigorous, "modern" nation-state. In this chapter, we shall examine the phenomenon of liberalism, primarily as it affected the fortunes of England and France. In the following chapter, we shall describe the way in which liberalism combined with nationalism to reshape the history of central Europe.

The compulsion of nationalism

Congress of Vienna

1. CONSERVATIVE REACTION, 1815–1830

The growth of liberalism occurred, in part, as a reaction to the conservative policies adopted by frightened governments anxious to restore domestic and international order following the Napoleonic wars. For a period of about fifteen years after 1815 the rulers of most European countries did their best to stem the advance of middle-class liberalism. In most instances, however, their repressive policies only made liberals more determined than ever to succeed. The primary concern of governments was to ensure that Europe would never again fall prey to the sort of revolutionary upheavals which it had experienced during the preceding quarter-century. To that end, when representatives of the European powers had met at the Congress of Vienna in 1814 to draw up a permanent peace settlement for Europe, they labored to produce an agreement that would as nearly as possible guarantee international tranquility. At the same time, however, they were by no means unwilling to advance the claims of their own countries to new territories, though such claims threatened conflict, or even war. Although the principle decisions of the congress were made by representatives of the major powers, it was attended by an array of dignitaries from almost all the principalities of Europe. No fewer than six monarchs attended: the tsar of Russia, the emperor of Austria, and the kings of Prussia, Denmark, Bavaria, and Württemberg. Great Britain was represented by Lord Castlereagh and the duke of Wellington. From France came the subtle intriguer Talleyrand, who had served as a bishop under Louis XVI, as foreign minister at the court of Napoleon, and who now stood ready to espouse the cause of reaction.

The dominant roles at the Congress of Vienna were played by Alexander I (1801–1825) and Metternich (1773–1859). The dynamic tsar is one of the most baffling figures in history. Reared at the court of Catherine the Great, he imbibed the doctrines of Rousseau from a French Jacobin tutor. In 1801 he succeeded his murdered father, Paul, as

Alexander I

The Congress of Vienna. The figure to the left of center is Metternich. Seated at the right, with his arms on the table, is Talleyrand.

tsar and for the next two decades disturbed the dreams of his fellow sovereigns by becoming the most liberal monarch in Europe. After the defeat of Napoleon in the Russian campaign, Alexander's mind turned more and more to mystical channels. He conceived of a mission to convert the rulers of all countries to the Christian ideals of justice and peace. But the chief effect of his voluble expressions of devotion to "liberty" and "enlightenment" was to frighten conservatives into suspecting a plot to extend his power over all of Europe. He was accused of intriguing with Jacobins everywhere to substitute an all-powerful Russia for an all-powerful France.

Tsar Alexander I

The most commanding figure at the congress was Klemens von Metternich, born at Coblenz in the Rhine valley, where his father was Austrian ambassador at the courts of three small German states. As a student at the University of Strassburg the young Metternich witnessed some excesses of mob violence connected with the outbreak of the French Revolution, and to these he attributed his life-long hatred of political innovation. After completing his education, he entered the field of diplomacy and served for nearly forty years as minister of foreign affairs. He was active in fomenting discord between Napoleon and Tsar Alexander, after the two became allies in 1807, and he played some part in arranging the marriage of Napoleon to the Austrian archduchess, Marie Louise. In 1813 he was made a hereditary prince of the Austrian Empire. At the Congress of Vienna Metternich distinguished himself for charm of manner and skillful intrigue. His two great obsessions were hatred of political and social change and fear of Russia. Actually the two were related. It was not simply that he feared revolutions as such; he feared, even more, revolutions inspired by the tsar for the sake of establishing Russian supremacy in Europe. For this reason he favored moderate terms for France in its hour of defeat, and was ready at one time to sponsor the restoration of Napoleon as emperor of the French under the protection and overlordship of the Hapsburg monarchy.

Metternich

The basic idea that guided the work of the Congress of Vienna was the principle of *legitimacy*. This principle was invented by Talleyrand as a device for protecting France against drastic punishment by its conquerors, but it was ultimately adopted by Metternich as a convenient expression of the general policy of reaction. Legitimacy meant that the dynasties of Europe that had reigned in prerevolutionary days should be restored to their thrones, and that each country should regain essentially the same territories it had held in 1789. In accordance with this principle Louis XVIII, brother of Louis XVI,[1] was recognized as the "legitimate" sovereign of France, and the restoration of Bourbon rulers in Spain and the Two Sicilies was also confirmed. France was compelled to pay an indemnity of 700 million francs to the victorious

Klemens von Metternich

---

[1] Louis XVII, the young son of the executed king and queen, had died under mysterious circumstances in the hands of revolutionary captors in 1795.

allies, but its boundaries were to remain essentially the same as in 1789.

To ensure that the French would not soon again overrun their boundaries, however, a strong barrier was erected to contain them. The Dutch Republic, conquered by the French in 1795, was restored as the Kingdom of the Netherlands, with the house of Orange as its hereditary monarchy. To its territory was added that of Belgium, formerly the Austrian Netherlands, with the hope that this now substantial power would serve to discourage any future notions of French expansion. For the same reason the German left bank of the Rhine was ceded to Prussia, and Austria was established as a major power in northern Italy.

The principle of legitimacy was not extended to the German principalities, however. There, despite pleas from rulers of the sovereign bits and pieces that had existed before 1789, the great powers agreed to retain the boundaries as redrawn by Napoleon. Fear of an aggressive Russia led the other European nations to support the maintenance—as an anti-Russian bulwark—of the Napoleonic kingdoms of Bavaria, Würtemberg, and Saxony. At the same time, however, Tsar Alexander was demanding that Poland, partitioned into virtual extinction by Russia, Austria, and Prussia in the 1790s, be reconstituted a kingdom with himself as its constitutional monarch. Prussia was prepared to agree with this scheme, provided that it be allowed to swallow Saxony. National avarice for territorial expansion rapidly eclipsed legitimacy as a guiding principle in these negotiations. Metternich, horrified at the double threat thus presented to Austria by Prussia and Russia, allied himself with Talleyrand and Castlereagh, both of whom secretly agreed to go to war against Russia and Prussia, if necessary, in order to prevent them from consumating their Polish-Saxon deal. A compromise was eventually reached, allowing to Russia the major part of Poland and to Prussia a part of Saxony. Britain, no less anxious

"Dividing the Cake." A contemporary cartoonist's impression of the work of the congress diplomats.

KINGDOM OF
NORWAY AND SWEDEN

Stockholm

SCOTLAND

Edinburgh

NORTH

SEA

KINGDOM OF
DENMARK ★ Copenhagen

BALTIC SEA

RUSSIAN

EMPIRE

IRELAND

GREAT BRITAIN

Dublin

Liverpool

Birmingham

ENGLAND

London ★

Amsterdam ★

KINGDOM OF THE
NETHERLANDS

BELGIUM

SCHLESWIG

HOLSTEIN

Hamburg

HANOVER

MECK-
LENBURG

Berlin ★

P R U S S I A

POLAND

Kiev •

ATLANTIC

OCEAN

LUXEMBURG

HESSE

SAXONY

REPUBLIC OF
CRACOW

Paris ★

LORRAINE

ALSACE

BADEN

WÜRTEM-
BERG

BAVARIA

Munich ★

Vienna ★

AUSTRIAN EMPIRE

HUNGARY

• Budapest

MOLDAVIA

KINGDOM OF

FRANCE

Bordeaux •

★ Berne
SWISS CONFED.

LOMBARDY-VENETIA
Milan ★

ADRIATIC SEA

WALLACHIA

O T T O M A N

Marseilles •

KINGDOM OF SARDINIA

PARMA

MODENA

LUCCA

TUSCANY

PAPAL
STATES

MONTENEGRO

E M P I R E

KINGDOM OF
PORTUGAL

KINGDOM OF

Madrid ★

Barcelona •

SPAIN

CORSICA

Rome ★

Naples ★

Constantinople ★

Lisbon ★

BALEARIC ISLANDS
(To Spain)

M E D I T E R R A N E A N

Palermo •

KINGDOM OF

THE TWO

SICILIES

MOROCCO

ALGERIA

TUNISIA

S E A

0   500 miles

EUROPE AFTER THE CONGRESS OF VIENNA · 1815

than the other victorious powers to gain compensation for its long
years at war, received territories principally under French dominion in
South Africa and South America and the island of Ceylon, thus adding
further to its commercial empire.

Following Napoleon's final defeat at Waterloo in 1815, the major
powers reconfirmed the Vienna settlement in the hope that their efforts might result in a permanently stable "Concert of Europe." To
further ensure an end to revolutionary disturbances, they formed the
Quadruple Alliance—Britain, Austria, Prussia, and Russia; when
France was admitted as a fifth member in 1818 it became the Quintuple Alliance. Its members pledged to cooperate in the suppression of
any disturbances which might arise from attempts to overthrow legitimate governments or to alter international boundaries. At the same

The system of alliances

time, Tsar Alexander, his mystic nature now in the ascendant, persuaded the allies to join him in the declaration of another alliance—a "Holy Alliance"—dedicated to the precepts of justice, Christian charity, and peace. The only result of this second league was to confuse Europe's leaders as to Alexander's intentions. Was he a liberal—a Jacobin even, as Metternich feared—or a reliable conservative? The confusion was cleared away, as in one country after another, liberal uprisings were stifled by stern reactionary policies of the allied governments, Alexander's among them.

Suppression of liberal uprisings

Attacks against reactionary governments in Naples and in Spain brought the allies scurrying to a conference at Troppau in Austria in 1820. Secret brotherhoods of young liberals, many of them army officers, had spearheaded these revolts. These organizations, which originated in Italy, called themselves *Carbonari*. They were an active counterreactionary force, whose influence spread throughout Europe in the early 1820s. In both Naples and Spain, they succeeded in forcing the kings to take oaths to establish constitutions modeled on the liberal French constitution of 1789–1791. At Troppau, Austria, Prussia, and Russia reacted to these threats to international order and absolutism by pledging to come to each other's aid to suppress revolution. France and Britain declined to endorse the pledge, not so much because they opposed repression, but because they did not wish to curtail their freedom of action by binding themselves to detailed international treaties. Metternich nevertheless proceeded, with Russian and Prussian concurrence, in a repression of the *Carbonari* rebels through imprisonment or exile.

Defying the congress system

Two years later, in 1822, another congress was convened at Verona, this one to deal with the continuing liberal threat to stability in Spain, with the series of revolutions occurring in Spanish colonies in South America, and with an insurrection in the Near East. To resolve the Spanish problem, the French dispatched an army of 200,000 men to the Iberian peninsula in 1823. Without much difficulty, this force put an end to the Spanish liberals, who opposed King Ferdinand VII's attempt to undermine representative government. The French assisted Ferdinand in restoring his authority to rule as he pleased. Contrary to their experience in Spain, the defenders of the status quo were unable to succeed in stemming the move to independence and liberalism in the colonies. In 1823 President James Monroe of the United States issued the "Monroe Doctrine," which declared that attempts by European powers to intervene in the affairs of the New World would be looked upon as an unfriendly act by his government. Without British maritime support, the doctrine would have remained a dead letter. Britain was ready to recognize the independence of the South American republics, however, since as new countries they were prepared to trade with Britain instead of Spain. The British therefore used their navy to keep Spain from intervening to protect its vanishing empire.

In the Near East, a Greek soldier, Alexander Ypsilanti, was attempting to encourage the formation of a Greek "empire," to be constructed on vaguely liberal principles. In doing so, he had engaged his band of armed followers in battles against the Turks who ruled over Greece. Though Ypsilanti was soon defeated, his movement lived on. Five years later its aims had been narrowed to the more accessible goal of an independent Greece. Supported for reasons of Mediterranean naval strategy by a joint Anglo-French-Russian naval intervention, and by a Russian invasion of the Balkans, the rebels this time succeeded. Their success signaled the extent of changes that had occurred since the Congress of Verona. No longer could Metternich and other reactionaries build alliances on the assumption that, for the powers of Europe, preservation of the status quo was, before everything else, the major goal. Britain, in particular, could not be relied upon. There, by the late 1820s, the liberal movement was gaining momentum fast.

2. LIBERAL GAINS IN WESTERN EUROPE, 1815–1830

Liberal gains in Britain came after an era of reaction that paralleled that which occurred on the Continent. There the conservative Tory party had enjoyed almost unbroken political supremacy since the younger William Pitt had become first minister in 1783. Though Pitt had begun his career as something of a reformer, the French Revolution had turned him, along with his fellow-Tories, into a staunch defender of the status quo. The Tories' political opponents, the Whigs, had throughout the long years of the revolutionary and Napoleonic conflicts, remained to some degree conciliatory to the French. But Whigs were as unsympathetic as Tories to democratic notions and as defensive of their rights to the full fruits of their property.

Hence when rioting broke out in England after 1815 as a result of depression and consequent unemployment, there was general support among the well-to-do for the repressive measures adopted by the British government. Spies were hired to ferret out evidence against popular agitators. In the industrial north, where conditions were particularly severe, radical members of the middle and working classes capitalized on the general unrest to press their demands for increased representation in Parliament. At Manchester a crowd of 80,000, demonstrating for political reform in St. Peter's Fields, was fired upon by soldiers. Eleven persons were killed and over 400 injured, including 113 women. The massacre was thereafter called "Peterloo" by British radicals: i.e., a domestic Waterloo. It was the first of several repressive measures taken by the government to stifle reform. Another was the legislation known as the Six Acts, which was passed by Parliament in 1819, and outlawed "seditious and blasphemous" literature; levied a stamp tax on newspapers; allowed the searching of houses for arms; and restricted the rights of public meeting.

Yet within a surprisingly short time British political leaders re-

The Peterloo Massacre, 1819. A contemporary rendering of the shootings which condemned the "wanton and furious attack by that brutal armed force The Manchester & Cheshire Yeomanry Cavalry."

versed their opposition to everything new. Instead, they displayed an ability to compromise which kept their country free from revolution.

The liberalizing Tories

George Canning, the foreign minister, and Robert Peel, the home secretary, son of a rich cotton manufacturer, were both sensitive to the interests of Britain's liberal-minded capitalist entrepreneurs. Under their direction, the government retreated from its commitment to the intransigent Quintuple Alliance; it was Canning who took the lead in recognizing the new South American republics. At home, these same politicians began to make order of the inefficient tangle of British laws; for example, they abolished capital punishment for about a hundred different offenses. And Canning liberalized, though he did not abolish, the Corn Laws. These laws levied a tariff on the importation of cheap foreign grain. As such, they benefited English landlords, but hurt manufacturers, who had to pay higher factory wages to enable their workers to purchase more expensive bread. These "liberalizers" among the still essentially conservative Tories even succeeded in abolishing the laws which had kept both dissenting Protestants (members of Protestant sects—Baptist, Congregationalist, Methodist—other than Anglican) and Roman Catholics from full participation in public political life.

Parliamentary reform

What the conservatives would not do was reform the system of representation in the House of Commons, heavily weighted on the side of the landed interests. Here the Tories, the majority party in Parliament, drew the line and showed themselves still basically committed to the status quo. Yet members of the liberal middle class argued that such a reform was absolutely necessary before they could themselves play a constant and active role in shaping British policy to comply with their own interests. "Interest" was, indeed, the key word in the debate over parliamentary reform. For centuries Parliament had represented the interests of landowners, the major propertied class in England. About two-thirds of the members of the House of Commons were either directly nominated by or indirectly owed their election to the patronage of the richest landowners in the country. Many of the parliamentary electoral districts, or boroughs, which returned members to the House of Commons, were controlled by landowners who used the pressure of their local economic power—or, in many cases, outright bribery—to return candidates sympathetic to their interests. These were the "rotten" or "pocket" boroughs, so-called because they were said to be in the pockets of those men who controlled them. Those who favored the system as it was argued that it mattered little that electoral politics were corrupt, that electoral districts represented unequal numbers, or that very, very few (about one in a hundred) were enfranchised. What did matter, they claimed, was that the interests of the nation at large, which they perceived to coincide with the interests of landed property, were well looked after by a Parliament elected in this fashion.

Of course the new industrial middle class did not agree with the arguments of the landowners. They insisted, for example, that the Corn Laws did not coincide with the nation's best interest. (If they were followers of the theories of Jeremy Bentham, they might argue that the Corn Laws did not produce "the greatest happiness of the greatest number.") Rather, the Corn Laws worked only for the benefit of landlords, by keeping the price of grain high; and they worked to the disinterest of everyone else. Therefore, said members of the middle class, Parliament must be reformed to represent not only landlords but the interests of industrial England. It is important to note that the liberal middle class was *not* arguing in favor of reform on the basis of a belief in democracy. Some leaders within the emerging working class did make this argument—and, as we shall see, continued to make it after a reform bill was passed in 1832. Most of those who spoke in favor of reform, however, declared that the middle class was capable of representing the interests of the working class, as well as of itself, in Parliament. Reformers took this position either because they believed it; or because they were afraid of working-class representatives; or because they realized that to favor direct representation for the working class would frighten the more timid reformers and hence defeat their whole campaign.

The middle class and reform

Spurred by the example of liberal reformers on the Continent (see below, p. 681) and by the oratory and organizational abilities of middle-class and artisan radicals at home, the movement for reform intensified after 1830. It was strong enough to topple the Tories and to embolden the Whigs, under the leadership of Lord Grey, to bring in a bill to reform the electorate. The government was clearly frightened. Revolution, if it were ever to come in England, would come as a result of the alliance now threatening between middle-class industrialists and the artisan/tradesman leadership of the new working class. In Bir-

A working-class alliance

The Reform Bill of 1832

Liberalism in other parts of the West

mingham, a middle-class banker, Thomas Attwood, organized a "Political Union of the Lower and Middle Classes of the People." By July 1830, there were similar organizations in Glasgow, Manchester, Liverpool, Sheffield, Newcastle, and Coventry. The king, William IV, wrote worriedly to Lord Grey that "miners, manufacturers, colliers, and labourers" appeared ready for some sort of open rebellion.[2] Sensing the grave danger of a possible union of the working and middle classes, the governing class once more accommodated to change, as it had in the 1820s.

The Reform Bill of 1832, however, was not a retreat from the notion of representation by interest. No attempt was made to create equal electoral districts. The franchise, though increased, was defined in terms of the amount of property owned and the length of time one had owned it. In the counties, for example, a man could vote if he paid at least ten pounds annual rental for land held on a long-term sixty-year lease. In other words, the vote was granted to the middle class, but to very few of the working class. Probably more significant than its extension of the franchise, was the bill's scheme for a redistribution of seats. One hundred and forty-three seats were reallocated, most of them from the rural south to the industrial north, thereby increasing representation in and around cities such as Manchester, Leeds, and Birmingham; and thereby increasing, in turn, the political power of the industrial middle classes. Though the bill was the product of change and itself brought change in its wake, it was understood as a conservative measure. It by no means destroyed the political strength of landed aristocratic interests, though it reduced that strength somewhat. And it preserved the notion of representation by interest. The liberal, industrial middle classes had been admitted into junior partnership with the landed oligarchy that had for centuries ruled Britain and was to rule it for at least one more generation.

Efforts to introduce liberal political reforms were not limited to Britain during this period. In the United States, the rule of eastern landed and commercial interests was superseded by the antiprivilege Democratic party, led by the hero of the War of 1812, General Andrew Jackson. Across the world, in Russia, a group of army officers revolted, following the death of Tsar Alexander in 1825, in hopes of persuading his liberally minded brother, Constantine, to assume the throne and guarantee a constitution. In this case, however, the attempt at reform failed. Constantine was unwilling to usurp power from the rightful heir, a third brother, Nicholas. The officers, called Decembrists (because of the month of their rebellion), were harshly punished; Nicholas continued to rule in the severely autocratic ways Alexander had adopted toward the end of his life, creating the Third Section, a political police force, to prevent further domestic disorder.

Meanwhile autocracy also threatened the liberal revolutionary and

[2] Asa Briggs, *The Age of Improvement*, New York, 1959, p. 248.

Napoleonic heritage in France. The upper middle class in France had remained generally content with the domestic settlement agreed upon by the major powers in 1814 and confirmed at the Congress of Vienna the following year. Louis XVIII had issued a "constitutional charter" upon his succession to the French throne. While refusing to deny himself absolute power in theory, in practice Louis XVIII had willingly enough agreed to support those principles most desired by French middle-class liberals: legal equality; careers open to talent; and a two-chamber parliamentary government, with the vote confined to property-holders.

In 1824, Louis died and was succeeded by his reactionary brother Charles X. By his policies Charles immediately declared himself a foe of liberalism, modernization, and the general legacies of the revolutionary and Napoleonic eras. At his direction the French assembly voted indemnities to those aristocratic émigrés whose land had been confiscated by the state. The Church was allowed to reassert its traditionally exclusive right to teach in French classrooms. The upper middle class, strengthened by its role within the country's growing industrial economy, reacted by heading a rebellion against Charles's reactionary policies. In March 1830, members of the Chamber of Deputies, led by bankers, passed a vote of no confidence in the government. Charles dissolved the chamber, as he was constitutionally empowered to do, and called new elections for deputies. When those elections went against his candidates, Charles further retaliated by a series of ordinances, issued on his own authority, which (1) again dissolved the newly elected chamber before it had even met; (2) imposed strict censorship on the press; (3) further restricted suffrage so as to exclude the upper middle class almost completely; and (4) called for new elections.

What Charles got in return for these measures was revolution. Led by republicans—workers, artisans, students, writers, and the like—Parisians took to the streets. For three days, behind hastily constructed barricades, they defied the army and the police, neither of which was anxious to fire into the crowds. Sensing the futility of further resistance, Charles abdicated. Those who had manned the barricades pressed for a genuine republic. But those with the power—bankers, merchants, and industrialists—wanted none of that. Instead they brought the duke of Orleans to the throne as King Louis-Philippe (1830–1848), after extracting a promise from him to abide by the constitution of 1814 which had so suited their particular liberal needs. The franchise was extended, from about 100,000 to 200,000 males. But the right to vote was still based upon property ownership. The major beneficiaries of the change were members of the middle class, those whose interests the Revolution of 1830 primarily served.

Other countries in Europe caught the revolutionary fever in the summer of 1830. As we have already noted, middle- and working-class radicals in England were inspired by the French to press their

The July Revolution of 1830 in Paris. Workers construct street barricades to ward off government troops.

Liberal revolts elsewhere

own case for liberal reform. In Belgium, an insurrection which combined elements of liberal and national sentiment put an end to the union of that country with the Dutch, instituted by the Congress of Vienna. The European powers strengthened Belgium's political structure, and hence its independence, by agreeing to the accession of Leopold of Saxe-Coburg, uncle of the future Queen Victoria of England, as king. Once again, a middle class had succeeded in establishing a constitutional monarchy to its liking, congenial to its liberal and entrepreneurial goals. No such fate awaited the liberal nationalists in Poland, who moved at this time to depose their ruler, the Russian Tsar Nicholas, whose hegemony extended to Poland as a result of the Vienna settlement of 1815. Western Europe did not intervene; Russian troops crushed the Polish liberal rebels, and Poland was merged into the tsarist empire.

Spain

Liberal forces in Spain enjoyed a greater success. There middle-class liberalism was linked to the attempts of Queen Maria Christina, widow of King Ferdinand, to secure the throne for her daughter, Isabella. Though no liberal herself, the queen was prepared to court the favor of urban middle-class elites to win her struggle against her late husband's brother, Don Carlos. During the so-called Carlist Wars, which lasted from 1834 to 1840, liberals extracted from Isabella a constitution which ensured them a strong voice in the legislature, while restricting the franchise in such a way as to keep the more radical lower middle and artisan classes at bay. By mid-century, however, fear of these radicals led the middle class to acquiesce in a government that was nothing more or less than an authoritarian dictatorship, but that did not threaten directly their own economic interests.

3. LIBERALISM IN BRITAIN AND FRANCE, 1830–1848

The Revolution of 1830 in France and the Parliamentary Reform Bill of 1832 in England represented a setback for aristocratic power in both countries. Aristocrats and their supporters did not cease overnight to play an active role in politics, however. Lord Palmerston, for example, was one of England's most influential prime ministers at mid-century and one of Europe's most authoritative arbiters. But no longer would it be possible for the legislatures of France and England to ignore the particular interests of the middle class. Henceforth representatives would include members from that class in sufficient numbers to press successfully for programs which accorded with liberal beliefs.

Decline of aristocratic power

One of the major accomplishments of the first British Parliament elected after 1832 was passage of a new law governing the treatment of paupers. In accordance with the law passed in 1602 under Elizabeth I, each parish in England had been declared responsible for the maintenance of its own poor, either through accommodation in poorhouses, or through a system of doles, coupled with local public employment programs. This system, although it by no means eliminated the debilitating effects of poverty, did provide a kind of guarantee against actual starvation. But by 1830 it had broken down. Population growth and economic depressions had produced a far larger number of underemployed men and women in Britain than had ever before existed, placing tremendous strain upon those funds, levied as taxes, which each parish used to provide relief. Industrialization also demanded that families move in search of employment from one part of the country to another; yet the old poor law provided assistance only to those who applied in the parish of their birth. The old law did not accord with liberal notions of efficiency; the new Parliament set about to amend it. The result, drafted by Jeremy Bentham's former private secretary,

Liberal legislation in Britain: the new poor law

An English Workhouse for the Able-Bodied Poor. This workhouse in the county of Devon was built in the late 1830s.

Edwin Chadwick, and passed almost without dissent, clearly reflected the liberal, middle-class notion of how to achieve "the greatest happiness of the greatest number." Doles were to cease forthwith. Those who could not support themselves were to be confined in workhouses. Here conditions were to be made so severe as to all but compel inmates to depart and accept either whatever work they might find outside, no matter how poorly paid, or whatever charity their friends and relatives might be able to provide them. Parishes were to be grouped together into more efficient unions; the law was to be administered by a central board of commissioners in London. Inspiring this new legislation were the liberal belief that poverty was a person's own fault and the liberal assumption that capitalism, though unregulated, was capable of providing enough jobs for all who genuinely wanted them. Economic depressions in the early 1840s proved that latter assumption false, and wrecked the tidy schemes of the poor-law administrators. Doles were once more instituted, taxes once more increased. Yet the law's failure did not shake the liberal conviction that poverty was, in the end, an individual and not an institutional problem.

Even more symbolic of the political power of Britain's middle class than the new poor law was the repeal of the Corn Laws in 1846. The laws, even after their modification in the 1820s, continued to keep the price of bread artificially high, forcing employers, in turn, to pay wages high enough to allow workers to keep food on their tables. More than that, the Corn Laws symbolized to the middle classes the unwarranted privileges of an ancient and, to their minds, generally useless order: the landed aristocracy. The campaign to accomplish repeal was superbly orchestrated and relentless. The Anti–Corn Law League, an organization of middle-class industrialists and their supporters, held large meetings throughout the north of England, lobbied members of Parliament, and, in the end, managed to persuade Sir Robert Peel, now prime minister, of the inevitability of their goal. They were aided, as well, by the potato famine in Ireland, whose existence argued in favor of ending restrictions against the importation of cheap foodstuffs. That Peel was willing to split the Tory—or as it was now coming to be called, Conservative—party to introduce repeal suggests the power of the middle class and its belief in the gospel of free trade.

Legislation during this period reflected other middle-class concerns, and in some cases, directly conflicted with the liberal doctrine of nonintervention. Many members of the urban middle class professed devotion to the tenets of Christianity, particularly that doctrine which argued that all human beings have within themselves a soul which they must work to preserve from sin for their eternal salvation. This belief in the ability of an individual to achieve salvation, which contradicted the older Calvinist doctrine of a predestined "elect," accorded

Repeal of the Corn Laws

Robert Peel

well with more general middle-class notions about the importance of individualism and the responsibility of the individual for his or her own well-being. It produced legislation such as the abolition of the slave trade in British colonies (1833), and the series of Factory Acts which, in 1847, culminated in the curtailment of the workday in some trades to ten hours. Evangelicals such as William Wilberforce, who was throughout his life an eloquent spokesman for enslaved blacks, and Lord Shaftesbury, who campaigned to end the employment of women and children in mines, maintained that individual souls could not find God when imprisoned in the overworked bodies of plantation slaves or factory operatives. They were joined by others who argued, simply, that to keep people tied to their work for as long as twelve or fourteen hours a day was both inhuman and unnecessary. Middle-class liberals found the arguments confusing. The laws of classical economics pulled them in one direction; the ethics of Christianity in another. Their uncertainty mirrored the extent to which no one could discern a right course in this world of new difficulties and fresh options.

Humanitarian reforms

The years of Louis Philippe's reign in France were not so marked as those in England with significant reforms. In the first place, France was not confronted with anything like the same degree of rapid industrialization that was compelling legislative activity on a number of fronts in England. France had nothing to compare with the problems generated by the growth of urban manufacturing centers in the north of England. Though the Chamber of Deputies contained representatives from the upper middle class, they tended to be bankers and merchants, not industrialists. Some were willing to espouse the notion of free trade, though not with the general enthusiasm of their British counterparts, whose unrivaled position as the world's leading manufacturers gave them a vested interest in that cause. Under the succession of governments dominated by France's leading politician of the period, François Guizot (1787–1874), the French expanded their educational system, thereby further underwriting their belief in the liberal doctrine of a meritocracy, or careers open to talent. A French law of 1833 provided for the establishment of elementary schools in every village. Children of indigent parents were to receive a free education; all others would pay a modest fee. In addition, larger towns were to provide training schools for trade and industry, and departments, schools for teacher training. As a result, the number of pupils in France increased from about 2 million, in 1831, to about 3.25 million in 1846. Little else of lasting importance was accomplished during the liberal regime of Louis Philippe. Guizot became more and more an apologist for the status quo. Everyone was free, he argued, to rise to the upper middle class and thus to a position of political and economic power. His advice to those who criticized his complacency was: "enrich yourselves." Politicians followed his advice, finding in

Louis Philippe

schemes for the modernization of Paris and the expansion of the railway system ample opportunities for graft. Louis Philippe did little to counteract the lifelessness and corruption that characterized his regime. Although he had played a minor part in the first stage of the revolution of 1789, he was no revolutionary. He did not have the dash and glamor of a Napoleon. He was a paunchy, fussy, and undistinguished person, easily caricatured by his enemies and without the talent necessary to rise above his stodgy public image.

Growing dissatisfaction of radicals

Meanwhile radical members of the French and British lower middle and working classes who had assisted—if not propelled—the forces of liberalism to victory in 1830 and 1832 grew increasingly dissatisfied with the results of their efforts. In Britain they soon realized that the Reform Bill had done little to increase their chances for political participation. For a time they devoted their energies to the cause of trade unionism, believing that industrial, rather than political, action might bring them relief from the economic hardships they were suffering.

Trade unionism

Trade union organization had been a goal of militant workers since the beginning of the century. Among the first workers' campaigns in the nineteenth century were those often riotous revolts organized both in England and, later, on the Continent against the introduction of machinery. In some instances, factories were attacked by workers and machines smashed, in the belief that machines, by replacing skilled workers, were producing widespread unemployment. In England, the rioters were called Luddites, after "Ned Ludd," who was the mythical leader of the movement. In other instances, the hostility of trade unionists was not directed so much toward machinery as toward those workers who refused to join in unions against their masters. Yet nowhere in Europe were trade unions able to organize themselves into effective bargaining agents before 1850. They came closest in England. There, artisans and skilled workers had banded together in the mid-1820s to form both Friendly Societies, really mutual aid and insurance organizations, and cooperatives, communal stores which cut prices by eliminating the middleman between producer and consumer. By 1831, there were about 500 cooperative societies in England, with a membership of something like 20,000. These organizations encouraged the parallel growth of trade unions, which, in the early 1830s, reached the peak of their early power and effectiveness. The National Association for the Protection of Labour comprised about 150 separate local unions in the textile and mining industries of the north; the Operative Builder's Union about 30,000 workers throughout the country. In 1834, a new and potentially far more radical organization, the Grand National Consolidated Trades Union of Great Britain and Ireland, was organized by a group of London artisans. Its leadership declared that only by bringing the country to a standstill with a general strike could workers compel the governing class to grant them a decent life. At that point, the governing class realized a serious threat to its existence and decided to put an end to

The Chartist Procession to the Houses of Parliament, April 1848

unions. Six organizers for the Grand National were convicted of administering secret oaths (unions were not themselves illegal) and sentenced to transportation (forced emigration to penal colonies in Australia). Subsequently employers demanded that their workers sign a document pledging their refusal to join a union, thereby stifling opportunities for further organization.

After the defeat of the Grand National, the efforts of radical democratic reformers in England turned back from trade union to political activity, centering on attempts to force further political reform upon the uninterested government through the device of the "People's Charter." This document, circulated across the country by committees of Chartists, as they were known, and signed by millions, contained six demands: universal manhood suffrage; institution of the secret ballot; abolition of property qualifications for membership in the House of Commons; annual parliamentary elections; payment of salaries to members of the House of Commons; and equal electoral districts.

Chartism

The fortunes of the Chartist movement waxed and waned. In some areas its strength depended upon economic conditions: Chartism spread with unemployment and depression. There were arguments among its leaders as to both ends and means: Did Chartism imply a reorganization of industry or, instead, a return to preindustrial society? Were its goals to be accomplished by petition only, or by more violent means if necessary? The Chartist William Lovett, a cabinetmaker, for example, was as fervent a believer in self-improvement as any member of the middle class. He advocated a union of educated workers to acquire their fair share of the nation's increasing industrial bounty. The Chartist Feargus O'Connor, on the other hand, appealed to the more impoverished and desperate class of workers. He urged a rejection of industrialization, and the resettlement of the poor on agri-

Varieties of Chartism

cultural allotments. These polarities and disagreements regarding the aims of the movement suggest the extent of the confusion within the working class, whose consciousness as a separate political force was only just beginning to develop. Events answered most of the Chartists' questions for them. In 1848, revolutionary outbreaks across the Continent inspired Chartist leaders to plan a major demonstration and show of force in London. A procession of 500,000 workers was called, to bear to Parliament a petition containing 6,000,000 signatures demanding the six points. Special constables and contingents of the regular army were marshaled under the now aged duke of Wellington to resist this threat to order. Less than 50,000 made the march to Parliament, however. Rain, poor management, and unwillingness on the part of many to do battle with the well-armed constabulary put an end to the Chartists' campaign, if not their cause.

In France, radical agitation produced very different results. There, as well, those who had manned the barricades in 1830 soon grew disgusted with the liberalism for which they had risked their lives. In their minds they carried memories or myths of the years of the first French Republic—its domestic accomplishments, its foreign victories, if not its Reign of Terror. They were opposed to constitutional monarchy, and only mildly enthusiastic about parliamentary government. They were prepared, if necessary, to use force in order to achieve their ends. Centered in Paris, they were for the most part either writers, students, or working-class leaders. They met in secret, studied the works of the radical theorist, Gracchus Babeuf (see above, p. 802), whose socialist *Conspiracy of Equals,* written during the French Revolution, became their Bible, and succeeded in making constant trouble for the liberal, middle-class governments of Louis Philippe. Their leading spokesman was the socialist Auguste Blanqui (1805–1881). He argued the victimization of the workers by the middle class, and helped organize secret societies which were to become the instruments of eventual insurrection. Radicals waged some of their most successful campaigns in the press. Honoré Daumier's savage caricatures of Louis

A Caricature of Louis Philippe by Daumier. The inscription reads "Louis Philippe, the Last King of France." It reflects a popular sentiment of the time.

Rue Transnomain. A drawing by Daumier to commemorate the victims of government repression in 1834.

The Revolution of 1848 in France.
A contemporary broadside
celebrating the triumph of the
people.

Philippe landed him in prison more than once. But radical campaigning took to the streets as well. In retaliation, the government in 1834
declared radical political organizations illegal. Rioting broke out in
Lyon and Paris in protest, where for two days government troops
massacred hundreds of insurgents, and arrested some 2,000 republican
leaders. In 1835, following an attempt to assassinate Louis Philippe,
the government passed a censorship law, which forbade the publication of articles attempting to inspire contempt for the king and which
prohibited the printing of any drawing or emblem without prior governmental approval.

*French republicans and
socialists*

These repressive measures served only to increase dissatisfaction
with the regime. Guizot was advised by more progressive members of
the legislature to extend the franchise to professionals whose lack of
wealth now denied them the vote, but whose general adherence to the
doctrines of liberalism was unquestioned. Guizot unwisely refused,
thereby driving these moderates into the camp of the more radical
republicans. By 1847, various elements within the opposition were
disaffected enough to instigate a general campaign of agitation
throughout France. At political banquets, republicans such as the poet
Alphonse de Lamartine (1790–1869) and socialist republicans such as
Louis Blanc (see above, p. 857) preached drastic reform, though not
outright revolution. Contrary to the expressed wishes of the king, a
giant protest meeting was announced for February 22, 1848. The day
before, the government forbade the meeting. Rioting and barricading
during the following two days ended in the abdication of Louis Philippe and increased demands for a republic.

*The origins of the
Revolution of 1848 in
France*

4. THE REVOLUTION OF 1848 IN FRANCE

The February revolution in France was a catalyst which, as we shall
see, helped to produce uprisings in the succeeding months throughout
much of Europe. Meanwhile, in Paris, a provisional government was

A National Workshop. When few could read, newspapers were heard rather than scanned. Under government auspices, these workshops achieved a good deal less than Louis Blanc had envisioned.

Republican-socialist split: Blanc's workshops

established consisting of ten men, seven of whom, including Lamartine, were middle-of-the-road republicans; three of whom, including Blanc, were socialists. The tensions between middle-class republicans and radical socialists, which had been masked by a common disgust with the government of Louis Philippe, now emerged to shape the political events of the ensuing months in several specific ways. Blanc insisted upon the establishment of national workshops, institutions he had championed as a writer, which were to be organized by trades as producers' cooperatives, where men and women workers would be trained if necessary, put to work, and paid two francs a day when employed and a smaller stipend when unemployed. Instead, the government established what it called workshops, but what amounted to nothing more than a program of public works in and around Paris, where economic conditions had resulted in widespread unemployment. Initially, plans had called for the employment of no more than ten or twelve thousand in projects throughout the city. But with unemployment running as high as 65 percent in construction trades and 51 percent in textiles and clothing, workers began to flood into the government's so-called workshops, as many as 66,000 by April, and 120,000 by June.

Continuing agitation

Paris meanwhile attracted numbers of radical writers, organizers, and agitators. The provisional government had removed all restrictions upon the formation of political clubs and the dissemination of political literature. As a result, 170 new journals and more than 200 clubs formed within weeks; the club headed by the socialist Auguste Blanqui claimed a membership of some 3,000. Delegations claiming to represent the oppressed of all European countries—Chartists, Hungarians, Poles—moved freely about the city, attracting attention, if not devoted followings, and contributing to tension which was convincing more and more members of the middle class that stern measures were needed to forestall further insurrectionary outbreaks. The middle-class side was strengthened as a result of elections held at the end of April. The provisional government had been pressured by Parisian radicals into decreeing universal manhood suffrage. Yet the election returned only a small proportion of radical socialists. The largest blocs consisted of "true," or moderate republicans and monarchists—this latter group was divided, however, between supporters of the Bourbon dynasty and the Orleanist Louis Philippe. The generally conservative tenor of the newly elected assembly strengthened the hand of those who pressed for the repression of the socialists. It also, naturally, convinced the socialists that once again, as in the 1790s, a potentially radical revolution had been betrayed by the timid, self-serving middle class.

By late spring, a majority of the assembly believed that the workshop system represented both an unbearable financial drain and a serious threat to social order. At the end of May, the workshops were closed to new enrollment as a first step toward barring membership to all who had resided for less than six months in Paris and sending all members between the ages of eighteen and twenty-five to the army. Thousands of workers lost their state-financed jobs, and with them their best chance for survival. Desperate, they and their supporters once more threw up barricades across Paris. From June 23–26, they defended themselves in an ultimately hopeless military battle against armed forces recruited, in part, from willing provincials eager enough to assist in the repression of the urban working class. Whether or not the Parisian insurrectionists were fighting as members of a beleaguered class, or simply as men and women on the brink of starvation, is a matter that historians continue to debate. That they were taken seriously as a revolutionary threat can be seen by the ferocity with which they were hunted out once the street fighting had ceased. About 3,000 were killed and 12,000 more arrested, the majority of whom were deported to Algerian labor camps.

The "June Days"

In the aftermath of the "June Days," the French government moved quickly to bring order to the country. The assembly, faced with the task of drafting a republican constitution, contained a large number of men to whom the idea of a republic was anathema. Assembly members therefore arranged for the immediate election of a president. Their hope was that a strong leader might assist in bringing dissidents to heel. Four candidates stood: Lamartine, the moderate republican; General Eugene Cavaignac, who had commanded the troops in June; Alexander Ledru-Rollin, a socialist; and Louis Napoleon Bonaparte, nephew of the emperor, who polled more than twice as many votes as the other three candidates combined.

The imposition of order

The astonishing upstart Louis Napoleon had spent most of his life in exile. Returning to France after the Revolution of 1830, he was imprisoned a few years later for attempting to provoke a local uprising. But in 1846 he escaped to England, where he was supplied with funds by

*The Rise of Liberalism
(1815–1870)*

*The rise of Louis
Napoleon*

A second emperor

*Napoleon III's Decree Dissolving
the National Assembly*

both British and French reactionaries. By the summer of 1848 the situation in France was such that he knew it was safe to return. In fact, he was welcomed with open arms by members of all classes. Conservatives were looking for a savior to protect their property against the onslaughts of the radicals. Workers were beguiled by his glittering schemes for prosperity in his book, *The Extinction of Pauperism,* and by the fact that he had corresponded with Louis Blanc and with Pierre Proudhon, the anarchist. In between these two classes was a multitude of patriots and hero-worshipers to whom the very name Napoleon was a matchless symbol of glory and greatness. It was chiefly to this multitude that the nephew of the Corsican owed his astounding triumph. As one old peasant expressed it: "How could I help voting for this gentleman—I whose nose was frozen at Moscow?"

With grandiose dreams of emulating his uncle, Louis Napoleon was not long content to be merely president of France. Almost from the first he used his position to pave the way for a higher calling. He enlisted the support of the Catholics by permitting them to regain control over the schools and by sending an expedition to Rome to restore the pope to his temporal power. He courted the workers and the middle class by introducing old-age insurance and laws for the encouragement of business. In 1851, alleging the need for extraordinary measures to protect the rights of the masses, he proclaimed a temporary dictatorship and invited the people to grant him the power to draw up a new constitution. In the plebiscite held on December 21, 1851, he was authorized by an overwhelming majority (7,500,000 to 640,000) to proceed as he liked. The new constitution, which he put into effect in January 1852, made the president an actual dictator. After exactly one year Louis Napoleon Bonaparte ordered another plebiscite and, with the approval of over 95 percent of the voters, assumed the title of Napoleon III, emperor of the French.

What is the significance of the French Revolution of 1848 and its political aftermath in the history of middle-class liberalism, which is our subject? Two points need particular emphasis. First, we must recognize the pivotal role of the liberal middle class. Under Louis Philippe, it increasingly perceived itself and its particular interests as neglected. Denied a direct political voice because of a severely limited franchise, it swung to the left, allying itself with radicals who, by themselves, would probably have stood no chance of permanent success. Yet no sooner had Louis Philippe abdicated than the liberal middle class began to wonder if "success" was not about to bring disaster upon its heels. And so it swung again, this time to the right, where it found itself confronting the mysterious and yet not entirely unattractive prospect of Louis Napoleon. He, in turn, was clever enough to understand this first lesson of 1848, that in France no government could survive that did not cater to the interests of the middle class. By assisting it to achieve its liberal economic goals, the emperor helped it forget just how heavily he was trampling on its political liberties.

Yet 1848 proved that there was now in France another element—class consciousness may, at this point, not yet be the correct term—that governments ignored at their peril. If mid–nineteenth-century Europe saw the middle class closer than ever to the center of power, it saw the workers moving rapidly in from the edge. Their barricades could, if necessary, be destroyed, and their demands ignored, but only at an increasingly grave risk to the fabric of the state. Middle-class liberalism, if it was to thrive, would not only have to pay lip service to working-class demands, but in some measure accommodate to them as well.

Napoleon III

5. LIBERALISM IN FRANCE AND BRITAIN AFTER 1850

Napoleon III recognized the vital role that public opinion had now assumed in the management of affairs of state. He labored hard and successfully to sell his empire to the people of France. He argued that legislative assemblies only served to divide a nation along class lines. With power residing in him, he would unite the country as it had not been for generations. The French, who craved order following their recent political misadventures, bought the program he was selling willingly enough. Napoleon III modeled his constitution upon that of his uncle. An assembly, elected by universal manhood suffrage, in fact possessed almost no power. It could do no more than approve legislation drafted at the emperor's direction by a Council of State. Elections were manipulated by the government to insure the return of politically docile representatives. Control of finance, the army, and foreign affairs rested exclusively with the emperor. France was a democracy only in the sense that its people were periodically afforded a chance, through elections, to express their approval of Napoleon's regime.

Napoleon III's constitution

In return for the gift of almost absolute power, Napoleon III gave the French what they appeared to want. For the middle class, he provided a chance to make a great deal of money. The device of the *Crédit Mobilier,* an investment banking institution, facilitated the expansion of industry by selling its shares to the public and using its income to underwrite various entrepreneurial schemes. In 1863 a limited liability law encouraged further investment by guaranteeing that stockholders could lose no more than the par value of their stock no matter how indebted the company in which they had invested. Railways, owned by the state, spread across the country, and spurred further industrial expansion. So prosperous did the French economy appear that Napoleon was prepared to follow Britain's lead in pressing for tariff-free trade between the two countries. A treaty was signed in 1860; though funds were set aside to compensate French industries for any loss they might suffer, they were never completely expended, suggesting that French manufacturers were now well enough established to meet the threat of British competition. The apparent satisfaction of the middle class with

Napoleon III and the middle class

Paris Under the Second Empire. The Avenue de l'Imperatrice was designed for the enjoyment of the middle class.

Empress Eugénie

Napoleon III and the workers

Napoleon's regime provides a measure with which to assess the state of liberalism in France after 1850. The fact that the country no longer enjoyed a free press, that universities were politically controlled, and that political opposition was repressed seemed to matter very little to most. Liberalism, if it existed at all, existed as the freedom to have one's own economic way.

Napoleon III, though he catered to the middle class, did not fail to court the favor of the workers as well. He encouraged the establishment of hospitals and instituted a program of free medical assistance. More important, he permitted, if he did nothing to encourage, the existence of trade unions and in 1864 introduced legislation to legalize strikes. Ultimately, he appealed to the workers much as he appealed to the middle class, as a glamorous, if not heroic symbol of his country's reemergence as a leading world power. The activities of his court, and of his glamorous empress, Eugenie, were well publicized. The reconstruction of Paris into a city of broad boulevards and grand open spaces was calculated to provide appropriate scenery for the theatre of empire—as well as to lessen the chances for successful proletarian barricade-building across narrow streets.

Grandeur, however, appeared to Napoleon III to demand an aggressive foreign policy. Although early in his regime he declared himself in favor of that central liberal tenet—international peace—he was soon at war: first against Russia in the Crimea; then in Italy; then in Mexico, where he attempted to assist in the establishment of another empire; and finally and disastrously with Prussia. The details of these adventures are part of the subject of the following chapter. It is enough at this point to remark that Napoleon III's foreign policy reflects clearly how far he—and the rest of France with him—had subordinated the liberal heritage of the first French Revolution to that of another of its legacies: national glory.

What, meanwhile, of the liberal tradition in Britain? There the course of liberalism was altered by changes occurring within the working class. Industrialization had, by this time, begun to foster and sustain a growing stratum of labor "aristocrats," men whose particular skills, and the increasing demand for them, allowed them to demand wages high enough to insure them a fairly comfortable standard of living. These workers—concentrated for the most part within the building, engineering, and textile industries—turned from the tradition of militant radicalism that had characterized the so-called hungry forties. Having succeeded within the liberal economic system imposed upon Britain by the middle class, they were now prepared to accept many liberal, middle-class principles as their own. They believed in self-help, achieved by means of cooperative societies or through trade unions, whose major function was the accumulation of funds to be used as insurance against old age and unemployment. They believed in education as a tool for advancement, and patronized the Mechanics Institutes and other similar institutions either founded by them or on their behalf.

Liberalism in Britain: the "labor aristocracy"

Yet the labor aristocracy, as it came to appreciate its ability to achieve a decent life for itself within the capitalist system, grew all the more dissatisfied with a political system which excluded it from any direct participation in the governmental process. Although some pressed for extension of the franchise as democrats, as many argued for it on the same grounds the middle class had used in 1832. They were responsible workers, whose loyalty to the state could not be questioned. As such, they were a bona fide "interest," as worthy of the vote and of direct representation as the middle class. They were joined in their campaign by many middle-class reformers who continued to chafe at the privileged position of national institutions which they associated with the landed society and the old order. Many middle-class men and women, for example, were dissenters from the Church of England; yet they were forced to pay taxes to support a church which was staffed, in the main, by sons of the gentry. Their sons were denied the facilities of the nation's ancient universities, Oxford and Cambridge, unless those sons subscribed to the articles of faith of the Anglican Church.

Middle-class dissatisfaction

Together with working-class leaders, these middle-class dissidents organized a Reform League to campaign across the country for a new reform bill and a House of Commons responsive to their interests. Though by no means revolutionary, the reformers made it clear by their actions that they were determined to press their case to the utmost. Politicians in Britain in the 1860s were confronted by a situation not unlike that which had faced Guizot in France in 1848: middle class, lower middle class, and skilled workers discontented and demanding reform. Unlike Guizot, however, the leaders of both British political parties, Conservative (formerly Tory) and Liberal (formerly Whig), were prepared to concede what they recognized it would be

Reform Bill of 1867

dangerous to withhold. In fact, it was a Conservative government, with the future prime minister Benjamin Disraeli as its leader in the House of Commons, that enacted the second Reform Bill in 1867. The bill doubled the franchise by extending the vote to any males who paid poor rates or rent of ten pounds or more a year in urban areas (this would mean, in general, the skilled workers), and to tenants paying rent of twelve pounds or more in the counties. Seats were again redistributed as in 1832, with large northern cities gaining representation at the expense of the rural south. The "responsible" working class had been deemed worthy to participate in the affairs of state. For the next twenty years it showed its appreciation by accepting its apprentice position without demur, and by following the lead prescribed by the middle class.

The Triumph of British liberalism

The decade or so following the passage of the Reform Bill of 1867 marked the high point of British liberalism. The labor aristocracy was accommodated with the Education Act, virtually guaranteeing a primary education to all, with legalization of trade unions, and with a series of measures designed to improve living conditions in the great cities; yet it was the middle class that set the governmental tone. Under Disraeli and his Liberal counterpart William Gladstone, and with the cooperation of the newly enfranchised skilled workers, Britain celebrated the triumph of the liberal principles of free trade, representative—but not democratic—government, and general prosperity.

SELECTED READINGS

• *Items so designated are available in paperback editions.*

Anderson, R. D., *Education in France, 1848–1870*, New York, 1975. Covers every level of formal education and its practical and theoretical relationship to state and society.

• Artz, Frederick B., *Reaction and Revolution, 1814–1832*, New York, 1934. A European survey, dated but still useful.

• Binkley, Robert C., *Realism and Nationalism, 1852–1871*, New York, 1935.

Blake, Robert, *Disraeli*, London, 1966. A masterful biography.

Duveau, Georges, *1848: The Making of a Revolution*, New York, 1967. Focuses on the working class during the revolution in Paris: their unity at the outset, their division in the "June Days."

Finer, Samuel E., *The Life and Times of Edwin Chadwick*, London, 1952. An excellent biography of the great English Benthamite reformer.

Halèvy, Elie, *A History of the English People*, Vols. II–IV, London, 1949–52. The best survey of nineteenth-century England, comprehensive and analytical.

Harrison, Royden, *Before the Socialists: Studies in Labour and Politics, 1861–1881*, London, 1965. Examines the social and political background of franchise extension in Britain.

• Hobsbawm, E. and Rudé G., *Captain Swing: A Social History of the Great English Agricultural Uprising of 1830*, New York, 1975.
• Houghton, Walter, *The Victorian Frame of Mind, 1830–1870*, New Haven, Conn., 1957. An outstanding attempt to synthesize the Victorian middle-class mentality.
• Kissinger, Henry, *A World Restored: Metternich, Castlereagh, and the Problem of Peace, 1812–1822,* Boston, 1957. By an admirer of Metternich.
• Langer, William L., *Political and Social Upheaval, 1832–1852*, New York, 1969. (Several chapters have been published separately under the title *The Revolutions of 1848.*)
• McCord, Norman, *The Anti–Corn Law League,* London, 1955.
  Magnus, Philip, *Gladstone: A Biography,* London, 1955.
  Merriman, John M., ed., *1830 in France,* New York, 1975. Recent scholarship emphasizing the nature of revolution and examining events outside of Paris.
• Nicolson, Harold, *The Congress of Vienna, a Study in Allied Unity,* New York, 1946.
• Pinkney, David, *Napoleon III and the Rebuilding of Paris,* Princeton, N.J., 1958. An interesting account of the creation of modern Paris during the Second Empire.
  ———, *The French Revolution of 1830,* Princeton, N.J., 1972. A reinterpretation, now the best history of the revolution.
  Roberts, David, *Victorian Origins of the British Welfare State,* New Haven, Conn., 1960. Examines various nineteenth-century reforms in England.
• Robertson, Priscilla, *The Revolutions of 1848: A Social History,* Princeton, N.J., 1952.
  de Sauvigny, G. de Bertier, *The Bourbon Restoration,* New York, 1967. An outstanding work. The best history of a neglected period.
• Stearns, Peter N., *1848: The Revolutionary Tide in Europe,* New York, 1974.
  Thompson, J. M., *Louis Napoleon and the Second Empire,* Oxford, 1954. A good biography. Presents Louis Napoleon as a modern Hamlet.
  Woodward, E. L., *The Age of Reform,* Oxford, 1962. An excellent survey from the Oxford History of England series.
• Zeldin, Theodore, *The Political System of Napoleon III,* New York, 1958. Examines the processes by which Napoleon maintained power as the first modern dictator.
  ———, *France, 1848–1951,* 2 vols., Oxford, 1973–77.

SOURCE MATERIALS

• Flaubert, Gustave, *L'Education Sentimentale,* London, 1961. Contains an unsympathetic but memorable portrait of the Revolution of 1848 and of the bourgeois style of life that contributed to its outbreak.
• Greville, Charles Fulke, *Memoirs,* ed. by Roger Fulford, New York, 1963. Originally published in seven volumes in 1875, these comprise the diaries of the secretary to the Privy Council for the years 1821–1861. An excellent source for the court and politics of the period.

• Mill, John Stuart, *Autobiography,* London, 1873. The life of one of the germinal minds of the century. Serves as an excellent social history of the period.

• ———, *On Liberty,* ed. by P. Appleman, New York, 1975. The classic statement of liberalism first published in 1859.

• Price, Roger, ed., *1848 in France,* Ithaca, N.Y., 1975. An excellent collection of eyewitness accounts, annotated.

Stewart, John Hall, *The Restoration Era in France, 1814–1830,* Princeton, N.J., 1968. A brief narrative and a good collection of documents.

Chapter 28

NATIONALISM AND NATION-BUILDING (1815–1870)

The present problem, the first task . . . is simply to preserve the existence and continuance of what is German.

—Johann Fichte, *Addresses to the German Nation*

The great questions of the day will not be decided by speeches or by majority decisions—that was the mistake of 1848 and 1849—but by blood and iron.

—Otto von Bismarck, speech, 1862

I f the history of nineteenth-century Britain and France can be studied against a general background of middle-class liberalism, that of much of the rest of Europe during the same period must be understood in terms of a more complex combination of the forces of liberalism, nationalism, and nation-building. We shall define nationalism as a sentiment rooted in broad historical, geographical, linguistic, or cultural circumstances. It is characterized by a consciousness of belonging, in a group, to a tradition derived from those circumstances, which differs from the traditions of other groups. Nation-building is the political implementation of nationalism, the translation of sentiment into power.

Nationalism and nation-building defined

Men and women in Britain and France during the nineteenth century entertained national as well as liberal sentiments. When Britain's prime minister, Lord Palmerston, declared in 1850 that any British citizen, in any part of the world, had but to proclaim, like a citizen of the Roman Empire, "civis Romanus sum" ("I am a citizen of Rome") to summon up whatever force might be necessary to protect him from foreign depradations, he was echoing his countrymen's pride in the powers of their nationhood. When the French rejoiced in 1840 at the return of the Emperor Napoleon's remains from St. Helena to an elaborate shrine in Paris, they were reliving triumphs that had become

Nationalism in Britain and France

part of their nation's heritage. Palmerston's boast and Napoleon's bones were both artifacts of national traditions and sentiments bound up in the life of the English and the French.

Nineteenth-century nationalism in other areas of Europe was to be a more assertive phenomenon than it was in Britain and France, which had for centuries existed as particular geographical, cultural, and political entities. Elsewhere, common traditions and assumptions were less clearly articulated, because the political unity that might have helped define them did not exist. East Prussians or Venetians had no difficulty in perceiving of themselves as such; history had provided them with those identities. But history had not provided them, except in the most general way, with identities as Germans or Italians. They had to make a deliberate effort to think of themselves in those terms before the terms could have any political reality.

Neither nationalism nor nation-building stood in necessary opposition to liberalism. Indeed, to the extent that nationalism celebrated the achievements of a particular common people over those of a cosmopolitan aristocratic elite, it reflected liberalism's abhorrence of traditional privilege. Yet to liberalism's readiness to accept the new, nationalism responded with an appreciation, if not veneration, of the past. And to the liberals' insistence upon the value and importance of individualism, nation-builders replied that their vital task might require the sacrifice of some measure of each citizen's freedom. The success of nation-building rested upon the foundation of a general balance of international power, achieved by the European states during the half-century after 1815. The emergence of new nations—a unified Italy and Germany—would require readjustments to that balance. But accommodation remained possible, with only minor skirmishes marring the stability of the settlement achieved at the Congress of Vienna.

1. ROMANTICISM AND NATIONALISM

As we noted in the preceding chapter, nationalism was in part a child of the French Revolution. It was closely related, as well, to the intellectual movement that has been called "romanticism." Romanticism was so broad and so varied that it all but defies definition, if not analysis. Perhaps as much as anything, romanticism represented a reaction against the rationalism of the eighteenth-century Enlightenment. Where the eighteenth century relied on reason, the romantics put their faith in emotion. The eighteenth century understood the mind as a blank tablet, which received knowledge from impressions imprinted upon it through the senses by the external world. Romantics also believed in the importance of sense experience. But they insisted that innate sensibility—that which constituted a person's own particular personality—was inherited, and therefore present in the mind from birth. Knowledge, then, for the romantic, was the product of both innate feelings *and* external perceptions. Romanticism thus stressed individualism, and the individual creativity that resulted from the interaction of unique personality with external experience. At the same time, by stressing the inheritance of attitudes, it also celebrated the past. And that celebration was its link with nationalism.

Romanticism and nationalism were connected by their common belief that the past should be made to function as a means of understanding the present and planning for the future. It was in Germany that this notion received its fullest airing and most enthusiastic reception. One of the earliest and most influential German romantics was Johann von Herder (1744–1803). A Protestant pastor and theologian, his interest in past cultures led him, in the 1780s, to set out his reflections in a lengthy and detailed treatise, *Ideas for a Philosophy of Human History*. Herder traced what he perceived to be the progressive development of European society from the time of the Greeks through the Renaissance. He believed that civilization was not the product of an artificial, international elite—a criticism of Enlightenment thinking—but of the genuine culture of the common people, the *Volk*. No civilization could be considered sound which did not continue to express its own unique historical character, its *Volksgeist*. Herder did not argue that one *Volksgeist* was either better or worse than any other. He insisted only that each nation must be true to its own particular heritage. He broke dramatically with the Enlightenment idea that human beings could be expected to respond to human situations in more or less the same fashion, and with the assumption that the value of history was simply to teach by example.

Johann von Herder

Herder's intellectual heirs, men like the conservative German romantics Friedrich Schlegel (1772–1829) and Friedrich von Savigny (1779–1861) condemned the implantation of democratic and liberal ideas—"foreign" to Germany—in German cultural soil. History, they argued, taught that institutions must evolve organically—a favorite word of the political romantics, and that proper laws were the product of historical growth, not simply deductions from universal first principles. This idea was not peculiar to German romantics. The English romantic poet and philosopher Samuel Taylor Coleridge (1772–1834) argued against the utilitarian state and in favor of giving that ancient institution, the national church, a larger role in the shaping of society. The French conservative Chateaubriand (1768–1848) made much the same case in his treatise, *The Genius of Christianity*, published in 1802. The past is woven into the present, he declared. It cannot be unwoven without destroying the fabric of a nation's society. Religion, both as individual experience and as an expression of national heritage, played a large role in romantic thinking.

The role of history and religion

The theory of the organic evolution of society and the state received its fullest exposition in the writings of the German metaphysician

Georg Wilhelm Hegel

Fichte

Georg Wilhelm Hegel (1770–1831). Professor of philosophy at the University of Berlin, he attracted many adherents. Hegel wrote of history as development: Social and political institutions grew to maturity, achieved their purposes, and then gave way to others. Yet the new never entirely replaced the old, for the pattern of change was "dialectic." When new institutions challenged established ones, there was a clash of "thesis" and "antithesis" producing a "synthesis," a reordering of society that retained elements from the past while adapting to the present. Hegel expected, for example, that the present disunity among the German states (thesis), which generated the idea of unity (antithesis), would inevitably result in the creation of a nation-state (synthesis). Hegel had no use for the theory of a state of nature, so popular with philosophers like Rousseau and Hobbes. Men and women have always lived within some society or other, Hegel argued. The institution of the state was itself a natural historic organism; only within that institution, protected by its laws and customs from personal depradations, could men and women enjoy freedom, which Hegel defined not as the absence of restraint but as the absence of social disorder.

These theories of history and of historical development articulated by the romantics relate directly to the idea of nationalism formulated during the same period. The French Revolution provided an example of what a nation could achieve. Nationhood had encouraged the French to raise themselves to the level of citizenship; it had also allowed them to sustain attacks from the rest of Europe. Applying the historical lessons of the French Revolution and the theories of romantics, Germans, in particular, were roused to a sense of their own historical destiny. The works of the philosopher J. G. Fichte (1762–1814) are an example of this reawakening. As a young professor at the University of Jena, Fichte had at first advanced a belief in the importance of an individual's inner spirit, the creator of its own moral universe. Devoid of national feeling, he welcomed the French Revolution as an emancipator of the human spirit. Yet when France conquered much of Germany, Fichte's attitude changed dramatically. He adopted Herder's notion of a *Volksgeist;* what mattered was no longer the individual spirit, but the spirit of a whole people, expressed in its customs, traditions, and history. In 1808, Fichte delivered a series of *Addresses to the German Nation,* in which he declared the existence of a German spirit, not just one among many such spirits, but superior to the rest. The world had not yet heard from that spirit; he predicted it soon would. Although the French military commander in Berlin, where Fichte spoke, believed the addresses too academic to warrant censorship, they expressed a sentiment that aided the Prussians in their conscious attempt to rally themselves, and, as a political *Volk,* to drive out the French.

Nationalism, derived from romantic notions of historical development and destiny, manifested itself in a variety of ways. The brothers Grimm, editors of *Grimm's Fairy Tales* (1812) traveled across Germany to study native dialects, and collected folktales that were published as part of a national heritage. The poet Friedrich Schiller's (1759–1805) drama of *William Tell,* the Swiss hero (1804), became a rallying cry for German national consciousness. In Britain, Sir Walter Scott (1771–1832) retold in many of his novels the popular history of Scotland, while the poet William Wordsworth (1770–1850) consciously strove to express the simplicity and virtue of the English people in collections such as his *Lyrical Ballads* (1798). Throughout Europe, countries assiduously catalogued the relics of their historical past as in the society for publishing the *Monumenta Germaniae Historica* (Monuments of German History), founded in 1819; the French École des Chartes (1821); and the English Public Records Office (1838). In France, the neoclassical style, typified by the paintings of David, and used by Napoleon to exalt his image, gave way to the turbulent romanticism of painters like Eugène Delacroix, whose painting *Liberty Leading the People* (1830) was a proclamation not only of liberty, but of the courage of the French nation. Music, too, reflected national themes, though not until a generation or so after 1815. Many of Guiseppe Verdi's (1813–1901) operas, for example, *Don Carlo,* contained musical declarations of faith in the possibility of an Italian *risorgimento:* a resurrection of the Italian spirit. The operas of Richard Wagner (1813–1883)—in particular, those based on the German epic, *Song of the Nibelung*—managed to raise veneration for the myths of Nordic gods and goddesses to the level of pious exaltation. Architects, though they found it difficult to escape entirely from the neoclassicism of the eighteenth century, often tried to resurrect a "national" style in their designs. Sir Charles Barry, assigned the task of redesigning the British Houses of Parliament following their destruction by fire in 1836, managed to mask a

Giuseppe Verdi

Romanticism, nationalism, and the arts

See color plates following page 960

Houses of Parliament, London. Redesigned by Sir Charles Barry with a Gothic facade after the earlier structure was destroyed by fire.

*Romanticism and
individuality*

*A William Blake Etching for a
Children's Book Written by Mary
Wollstonecraft*

George Sand

straightforward and symmetrical classical plan behind a Gothic screen, intended to acknowledge the country's debt to its own past. All this creative activity was the spontaneous result of artists' and writers' enthusiastic response to the romantic movement. Yet politicians soon perceived how historical romanticism might serve their nationalist ends. They understood how an individual work of art, whether a painting, a song, a drama, or a building, could translate into a national symbol. And they did not hesitate to assist in that translation when they deemed it useful.

Though romanticism and nationalism shared a common devotion to the past, romantics were not necessarily nationalists. Indeed, romanticism was explicitly international in its celebration of nature, and above all, of individual creativity. The romantics declared that nature was best perceived not by reason, but by the senses. And they respected those elements of nature which appeared the product of chance, not rational order. Whether as a single flower or a mountain range, nature was welcomed as it impressed itself directly on the senses. Men and women were declared free to interpret nature—and life as well—in terms of their individual reactions to it, not simply as it might reflect a set of general rational precepts. The English poet Percy Shelley (1792–1822), the German poet Heinrich Heine (1797–1856), the French novelist Victor Hugo (1802–1885), the Spanish painter Franciso Goya (1746–1828)—all characteristic figures of the romantic movement—expressed in their works romanticism's concern for the experiences of human individuals, a concern that transcended national boundaries. Human experience, romantics believed, was not linked to any one national tradition or *Volksgeist,* but rather to transcendant nature. The paintings of the Englishmen William Blake (1757–1827) and J. M. W. Turner (1775–1851), although they often reflect "Englishness," transcend nationalism by recording a communion with the fundamental elements of nature.

Romantics were internationalists because they enjoyed freedom from the confinement of any boundary—metaphysical or political—which tended to restrict a person's ability to realize his or her potential. In this way romanticism encouraged women to make themselves heard. The Englishwoman Mary Wollstonecraft (1759–1797), author of *A Vindication of the Rights of Woman;* Madame de Staël (1766–1817), an emigré from France to Germany during the revolutionary period, whose essay *De l'Allemagne* (On Germany) was steeped in romanticism; George Sand (1804–1876), whose novels, and whose life, proclaimed allegiance to the standards of radical individualism—these women exemplify romanticism's readiness to break with the past, and its assumptions and stereotypes, if they stood in the path of individual expression.

Romantics, as worshipers of individuality, worshiped "genius." The genius was possessed of a spirit which could not be analyzed and must be allowed to make its own rules. (It was the particular genius of an entire people, of course, that Herder extolled as the *Volksgeist*.) And the human spirit must never allow itself to be fettered by national prescriptions, any more than by social conventions, in such a way as to prevent enjoyment of its most precious possession, its freedom.

Freedom and the problem of self-recognition were major themes in the work of two of the giants of the romantic movement, the composer Ludwig van Beethoven (1770–1827) and the writer Johann Wolfgang von Goethe (1749–1832). The most remarkable quality about Beethoven's compositions is their uniqueness and individuality. In the Fifth Symphony Beethoven reaches the summit of symphonic logic, the Sixth is a glorification of nature, the Seventh a Dionysian revelry, the Eighth a genial conjuring up of the spirit of the eighteenth-century symphony. Then Beethoven, in his later years suffering from deafness, embarks on his last artistic journey: Five piano sonatas, five string quartets, the Ninth Symphony, and the great Mass, *Missa Solemnis,* constitute his final legacy. They fill the listener with awe not so much because of their unusual form or their vast proportions, but because they express boundless individual will and power.

Goethe's dedication to the idea of individual freedom was, in part, the product of his having been born and raised in the free imperial city of Frankfurt. Frankfurt was an international center, a trading place open to intellectual winds from all quarters. Goethe was, in terms of his environment, free from the particularist, nationalist influences which directed the work of other German romantics. Goethe's own "genius" drove him first to the study of law, then medicine, then the fine arts and natural sciences. In 1775 he took up residence at the court

Beethoven

Goethe

Left: *A Page from the Score of Beethoven's Piano Sonata Opus 109 in E Major.* Right: *Ludwig van Beethoven*

An Illustration from Goethe's
Sorrows of Werther

Immanuel Kant

of the young duke of Weimar. Weimar was a tiny German principality with a population of no more than half a million, another cosmopolitan community and in this respect not unlike Frankfurt. Influenced by Herder, Goethe had already published various romantically inclined works, including the immensely popular *Sorrows of Werther,* a novel expressive of Goethe's early restlessness and emotionalism. The almost excessive sensitivity characteristic of Goethe's earlier writings gave way, in his middle years, to the search for a new spirit, equally free and yet more ordered. This mode derived from his experiences in Italy and from his study of the ancient Romans and Greeks. In 1790 Goethe published the first part of his masterpiece, *Faust,* a drama in verse, which he completed a year before his death in 1831. The play, in its retelling of the German legend of the man who sold his soul to the devil in return for universal knowledge, reflects the romantic unwillingness to restrain the spirit; it also expresses Goethe's own recognition of the magnitude of humanity's daring in its desire for unlimited knowledge and its own fulfillment.

The theme of self-realization as humanity's ultimate goal, so characteristic of so much of romantic thinking, contrasted with the notions of those other romantics we have discussed, who, like Herder, insisted upon the subordination of one human spirit to the spirit of a whole people. Immanuel Kant (1724–1804), Goethe's only rival as a thinker during this period, expressed himself as opposed to the idea that unbounded individual freedom was the highest good. Kant, a retiring scholar who lived his life out in the city of Königsberg, where he was born, argued that there were limits to human knowledge, that beyond the world of appearances there lay an unknowable realm of what he called "things in themselves." This thesis, first expounded in his *Critique of Pure Reason* (1781), was further developed in his *Critique of Practical Reason* (1790), in which he attempted to establish proper criteria for personal behavior. If pure reason could neither prove nor disprove the existence of God, Kant argued, practical reason tells us that in the idea of God there exists an idea of moral perfection toward which all people must strive. They must live consistent with what Kant called the "categorical imperative": to act as if one's actions were to become a universal law of nature. Kant argued that only by living according to his categorical imperative could men and women enjoy true freedom. Freedom he defined in terms of self-imposed duty, rather than the absence of restraint or—as in Goethe's case—the compulsion to achieve self-fulfillment.

Whether or not Kant was a romantic is a question that historians have continued to debate. His devotion to reason has often led scholars to consider him a late Enlightenment figure. In one respect, however, Kant certainly thought with the romantics. His insistence that "things in themselves" were ultimately unknowable, reflected the romantics' willingness to surrender to the mysterious. "There is nothing beautiful, pleasing, or grand in life, but that which is more or less mysterious," Chateaubriand wrote, in his defense of Christianity. While Kant was not an explicit defender of Christianity, his philosophy helped perpetuate religious belief, and was thus one in its effect with romanticism. Certainly Kant was not a romantic nationalist, although nationalists used his arguments to support their claim that men and women had a duty to an authority higher than themselves. Kant himself, however, in his treatise *On Perpetual Peace,* published at the height of the revolutionary wars in 1795, argued vehemently against national aggrandizement and in favor of a kind of European federal union.

Kant as a romantic

Romanticism and nationalism bear much the same relationship to each other in the history of nineteenth-century Europe as they do in the thought of the men and women we have just surveyed. At some points, as in England, they appear to run separate courses. At others they join together, as they did in Germany, whose own history lies at the center of the history of both romanticism and nationalism.

*The relationship between
romanticism and
nationalism*

2. NATIONALISM AND NATION-BUILDING: 1800–1848

The humiliating French occupation of Prussia, combined with the growing sense of national destiny exemplified in Fichte's *Addresses,* resulted in a drive on the part of Prussian intellectuals and political reformers to bring their country once more to its former position among European powers. Prussia's crushing defeat by the French in 1806 had been the logical outcome of the inertia that had gripped the country during the half-century or so since the aggressive achievements of Frederick the Great. Unlike the rest of the German states, however, allied directly with France in the Confederation of the Rhine, the separate kingdom of Prussia consciously avoided French "contamination," participating unwillingly in the Continental System, and otherwise holding itself aloof.

*Nationalism and reform in
Prussia, 1806–1815*

Its major task was to rebuild its armies, since only by that means could Prussia reassert itself against Napoleon. To that end, two generals, Gerhard von Scharnhorst and August Gneisenau, instituted changes based on an essential lesson in nation-building they had learned from the French Revolution: that men were far more effective fighters if they believed themselves to have some direct stake in the wars they fought. A reconstituted national army, eventually based upon a system of universal military service, involved the country as a whole in its own defense and grew to become a far more consciously "Prussian" force than it had been heretofore. Officers were recruited and promoted on the basis of merit, not birth, although the large majority continued to come from the Junker (gentry) class. This breach with tradition encouraged the Prussian middle class to take a more ac-

Military reforms

Baron Heinrich vom Stein

*Stein's governmental
reforms*

Economic nationalism

tive and enthusiastic interest in its country's affairs. Old or inefficient officers, despite their social standing, were removed from positions of command; training at the royal cadet school in Berlin was modernized.

These reforms, which illustrate the way in which a liberal desire for modernization might combine with nationalism, paralleled similar changes instituted during the same period under the direction of Prussia's principal minister, Baron Heinrich vom Stein(1757–1831), and his successor, Karl von Hardenberg (1750–1822). Stein was not himself a Prussian; he was initially less interested in achieving a Prussian nation-state than in uniting by some means or other all the various principalities of Germany. Only after the disasters wrought upon the Germans by Napoleon did Stein turn to Prussia as a last resort. He had read Kant and Fichte, and was convinced by them that a state must somehow make its citizens aware of their obligations to the national interest. A sense of duty to the state could hardly be kindled, however, without first convincing men and women that loyalty meant reward as well as obligation. Stein therefore labored to dismantle the caste system which had until that time characterized Prussia, in order to permit individuals to rise within society. Stein's Municipal Ordinance of 1808 was a conscious attempt to increase the middle-class Germans' sense of themselves as citizens—again, a goal shared by both liberals and nationalists. All cities and towns were henceforth required to elect their councilmen, while local justice and security continued to be administered by the central government in Berlin; all other matters, including finance, were left to individual communities. Education played a vital role in nation-building. Schools were ideal agencies for the dissemination of the doctrines of national duty. Recognizing this fact, the Prussian reformers expanded facilities for both primary and secondary education. The University of Berlin, founded in 1808, numbered among its faculty such ardent nationalists as Fichte and Savigny, and was the institutional embodiment of the new spirit that contributed to Prussia's eventual victory over the French.

The history of Prussia between 1815 and 1850 can most easily be understood in terms of its continuing struggle to establish itself as an independent national power within Germany and in opposition to Austria. The most important Prussian victory in this respect was the establishment of the *Zollverein,* or customs union. By the 1840s, the union included almost all of Germany except German Austria. Meanwhile Prussia had produced in the work of the economist Friedrich List (1789–1846), a nationalist response to the internationalism of the liberal free-trade economists. List wrote that while free trade might suit the British, it did not suit Prussia. Economics, he argued, far from being an abstract science equally applicable everywhere, was a discipline which must be grounded in the particular national experience of individual countries. Germany's, and therefore Prussia's, experience demanded not free trade but high tariffs. Only when sheltered behind a protectionist system could Prussia build the factories and manufacture the goods that would guarantee its economic health.

The events which had altered the political shape of Britain and France in the early 1830s—revolution in the latter and liberal reforms in both—did not have lasting counterparts in Germany. A revolutionary movement of sorts, spawned in the universities and youthful secret societies, did result in temporary changes in a few German principalities. But Metternich, still in control of Austrian policy and determined to thwart Prussia's attempts to assert its nationality, used the occasion of those outbreaks to encourage a general antiliberal reaction throughout the German states by playing on the fears of the propertied classes. The diet of the German Confederation, the loose organization of sovereign powers that had replaced the finally defunct "Holy Roman Empire" after 1815, coordinated the repression. Prussia avoided revolution as a result of the reforms instituted a generation before by Stein and Hardenberg. In 1840 Frederick William IV succeeded to the Prussian throne. Apparently devoted to liberal principles, he relaxed censorship laws and encouraged participation in the central government by provincial diets. It soon became apparent, however, that the king was no liberal, but some sort of romantic-nationalist, and an authoritarian as well. He declared himself opposed to constitutionalism, that central doctrine in the liberal canon of beliefs. When middle-class Prussian liberals pressed, in 1847, for control over legislative and budgetary matters in the recently convened assembly of diets (the *Landtag*), the king saw to it that their request was denied. Frederick William then turned his attention to a scheme whereby Prussia might play a far larger role in the confederation. But before his plan could receive a hearing, it was overtaken by the revolutionary movement of 1848, which, as we shall see, engulfed central Europe as it had western Europe, though with different results.

National sentiment, the spirit which served to unite the Prussians, was at the same time operating to divide the heterogeneous elements within the Austrian Empire. Its people, who lived within three major geographical areas—Austria, Bohemia, and Hungary—were composed of a considerable number of different ethnic and language groups: Germans, Czechs, Magyars, Poles, Slovaks, Serbs, and Italians, to name the most prominent. In some parts of the empire, these people lived in isolation; elsewhere they dwelt in direct proximity, if not much harmony, with others. The Austrian Empire attempted to unite these groups by means of a reigning house, the Hapsburgs, and a supposedly benevolent bureaucracy. These devices failed increasingly to satisfy the various groups, in whom a spirit of cultural, if not political, nationalism grew persistently stronger in the years after 1815. In the Polish territories of the empire, where the gentry had for generations been conscious of themselves as Poles, the imperial government succeeded in stifling the sentiment by playing off the serfs against their masters, encouraging a class war as a means of preventing an ethnic one. Elsewhere within the empire they were less adroit. In Hungary, nationalism expressed itself in both cultural and political forms. In 1827, a Hungarian national theatre was established at Budapest. The year before, Magyar was substituted for Latin as the official language of government. A political movement, whose most formidable leader was the radical nationalist Louis Kossuth (1802–1894), was at the same time seeking independence and a parliamentary government for Hungary.

Pan-Slavism

The most widespread of the eastern European cultural nationalist movements was Pan-Slavism, at this period just beginning. Slavs included Russians, Poles, Czechs, Slovaks, Slovenes, Croats, Serbs, and Bulgars. Before 1848 Pan-Slavism was an almost exclusively cultural movement, united by a generalized anti-Western sentiment, yet divided by a tendency to quarrel as to the primacy of this or that particular language or tradition. These divisions did not substantially lessen the effect of Pan-Slavism as a further problem of the Austrian Empire. The literature of the movement—for example, the historian Francis Palacky's (1836–1867) *History of the Bohemian People* and the poetry of the revolutionary Pole Adam Mickiewiez (1798–1855), fed the desires of those who wished to rid themselves of what they considered a foreign yoke. In Russia, slavophilism had been held in check by the Western-looking Alexander I. After his death, however, the notion that the Russian people possessed its particular *Volksgeist* increased in general popularity.

Nationalism in Italy

Two other national movements were growing beyond infancy during the years before 1848: one in Italy, the other in Ireland. Among the organizations formed in the confused period at the end of the Napoleonic wars, none was louder in its nationalist proclamations than the Italian *Carbonari*. One member of that group, Joseph Mazzini (1805–1872) founded a society of his own in 1831, Young Italy, which was dedicated to the cause of uniting the peninsula. In 1834, from Switzerland, Mazzini launched a totally unsuccessful verbal assault against the Kingdom of Sardinia, in the hope that the rest of Italy would join with him. Mazzini subsequently contented himself with propagandizing for the cause of Italian nationalism and republicanism, attracting a devoted following, particularly among British liberals. Liberals in Italy, however, mistrusted him. Although they too wished to see Italy one nation, they were dismayed, as "good" liberals, and members of the middle class, by Mazzini's insistence upon a republic, hoping instead to merge existing principalities together into some sort of constitutional monarchy.

Nationalism in Ireland

If Italian nationalism was primarily a middle-class liberal phenomenon at this time, the same was not true of the Irish movement to repeal the union with England. Headed by Daniel O'Connell (1775–1847), it derived its strength from the support of Irish peasants. O'Connell's remarkably successful appeal was based on the hatred all Irish felt for the English, because of the centuries of oppression Irish Catholics had suffered under English Protestant rule. Both before and after the official union of 1801, the English had imposed on the Irish a foreign rule that had brought with it little but poverty and persecution. O'Connell's campaign for the repeal of the union was grounded in the hope that he would be able to negotiate some sort of moderate agreement with the English ruling class. The desires of his followers exceeded him in being far more radical in nature. Neither the separatist hopes of O'Connell, called by the Irish the "Liberator," nor the more genuinely nationalist hopes of his followers, however, were to achieve realization. Unlike the nationalist movements of central Europe, nationalism in Ireland faced a powerful and determined adversary—England—who would for a century deny it victory.

Joseph Mazzini

3. NATIONALISM, LIBERALISM, AND REVOLUTION, 1848

The history of the revolutions of 1848 in central Europe can most easily be understood in terms of two major themes: the first, the struggle of various nationalities, particularly within the Austrian Empire, to assert their own autonomy; the second, the contention between the forces of liberalism and nationalism in Germany.

News of the February revolution in France traveled quickly eastward. By the end of March the Austrian Empire was split apart. Hungary, with Kossuth in the lead, severed all but the most tenuous of links with the House of Hapsburg and prepared to draft its own constitution. In Vienna, workers and students imitated their counter-

The "March Days" in Austria

The March Days in Vienna, 1848

parts in Paris, erecting barricades and invading the imperial palace. A measure of the political chaos was the fact that Metternich, veteran of a score of threats to the precarious stability he had crafted, found the pressure this time too great, and fled in disguise to Britain. Deserted by that tower of reactionary strength, the Hapsburg emperor, Ferdinand, yielded to nationalist demands from Bohemia and granted that kingdom its own constitution as well. To the south, Italians launched attacks against the Austrian-held territories in Milan, Naples, Venetia, and Lombardy, where the forces of the Sardinian ruler, King Charles Albert, routed the Austrians.

Yet the forces of national sentiment which had brought Austria to its knees then succeeded in allowing the empire to recoup its fortunes. The paradox of nationalism, as it manifested itself in central Europe, was that as soon as a cultural majority had declared itself an independent or semi-independent state, other cultural minorities within that new state complained bitterly about their newly institutionalized inferiority. This is precisely what happened in Bohemia. There the anti-German Czech majority refused to send delegates to an all-German assembly, meeting at Frankfurt to draft a German constitution. Instead, they summoned a confederation of Slavs to Prague. The delegates, most of them from within the boundaries of the old Austrian Empire, immediately recognized that the idea of a united Germany represented a far greater threat to their political and cultural autonomy than the fact of the empire ever had. The German minority in Bohemia, however, was naturally anxious to participate in discussions which might result in closer union with their ethnic counterparts. They resented the Bohemian government's refusal to do so. The resulting animosities made it all the easier for the Austrians to take advantage of a May 1848 insurrection in Prague, subdue the city, send the Slav congress packing, and reassert control in Bohemia. Although the Austrian government was at this time a liberal one, the product of the March revolution in Vienna, it was no less determined than its predecessor had been to prevent the total dismemberment of the empire. For this reason it was quick to restore Lombardy and Venetia to its realm when quarrels among the heretofore united Italian allies had sufficiently weakened their common stand against the Austrians.

Nationalism and counternationalism in Hungary set the stage for the final act of the restoration of Austrian hegemony. Kossuth's radical party was, above all, a Magyar nationalist party. Once in power, in early 1849 it moved the capital from Pressburg, near the Austrian border, to Budapest, and again proclaimed Magyar as the country's official language. These actions offended national minorities within Hungary, particularly the Croats, who prior to the revolution had enjoyed certain liberties under Austrian rule. The Croatians raised an insurgent army and launched a civil war. The Emperor Ferdinand, once more encouraging division along nationalist lines, named the Croatian rebel Josef von Jellachich his military commander against the

Maygars. By this time the Viennese liberals began to recognize—too late—that their turn might come next. They were right. Despite a second uprising in Vienna in October, the revolution was spent. Forces loyal to the emperor descended upon Vienna from Bohemia. On October 31, the liberal government capitulated.

Once the imperial government had reasserted itself, it labored to suppress nationalist impulses as thoroughly as possible. Austria's ministers recognized that, though tactically advantageous at times, nationalist movements operated generally to the detriment of imperial unity. The emperor's chief minister, Prince Felix von Schwarzenberg, and the minister of the interior, Alexander Bach, both nation-builders, together centralized the state within one united political system. Hungary and Bohemia no longer enjoyed separate rights. Peasants of all ethnic groups, liberated from serfdom as part of the general reform movement, were permitted to retain their freedom, on the grounds of their loyalty to the empire. The law was reformed, again to achieve uniformity, and railways and roads were constructed to link the empire. Tariff walls were erected around imperial boundaries to exclude foreign manufactures, while a free trade area within the empire encouraged home industries. Having done all it could to eradicate separatist movements, the Austrian government thus moved to secure its advantage by engaging in a vigorous campaign of nation-building.

Imperial nation-building

In Prussia, revolution ran a similar course. In March, King Frederick William found himself compelled to yield to demands for a popularly elected legislative assembly. When it met, the body proved particularly sympathetic to the plight of the Polish minority within Prussia, and antagonistic toward the Russians, whom radical legislators saw as the major threat to the spread of enlightened political ideas in central Europe. When the assembly's sympathy with Polish nationalism extended to the granting of self-government to Prussian Poland, however, it generated the same feelings among the German minority there that we have seen arousing minorities within the Austrian Empire. In so doing, it precipitated the same eventual results. Germans in Posen, the major city of Prussian Poland, revolted against the newly established Polish government; not surprisingly, Prussian army units on duty sided with the Germans and helped them crush the new government. Power, it now became clear, lay with the army, professionalized since the days of Gneisenau and Scharnhorst, yet still dominated by the Junkers. Against the armed authority of the military, the radical legislators of Berlin were no match; revolution ended in Prussia as quickly as it had begun.

*The failure of revolution
in Prussia*

Meanwhile, at Frankfurt, Germans engaged in the debate that provides the history of central Europe in these revolutionary years with its second theme: liberalism vs. nationalism. Delegates had been chosen from across Germany and Austria to attend the Frankfurt Assembly. They were largely from the professional classes—professors, lawyers, administrators—and generally devoted to the cause of

The Frankfurt Assembly

Procession of the German National Assembly to Its Opening Session at St. Paul's Church, Frankfurt, May 1848

middle-class liberalism. Many had assumed that their task would resemble that of the assembly which had met in 1789 to draft a constitution for the French: i.e., they would draft a constitution for a liberal, unified Germany. That former convocation, however, had been grounded in the simple but all-important fact that a French nation-state already existed. The French assembly had been elected to give the nation a new shape and new direction. But a centralized sovereign power was there to reshape; there was an authority that could be either commandeered or, if necessary, usurped. The Frankfurt Assembly, in contrast, was grounded upon nothing but its own words. It was a collection of thoughtful, well-intentioned middle-class liberals, committed to a belief that a liberal-national German state could somehow be constituted out of abstract principles. These men, from the start of their deliberations, ruled out the use of violence to achieve their ends. At the same time, they failed to ally themselves with the urban workers. If by 1848 the workers were not yet a self-conscious and articulate class, they were nevertheless a force no reformer or revolutionary could reckon without. Yet the Frankfurt debaters by and large ignored them, and thus denied themselves the one source of power they might otherwise have called to their aid.

Almost from the start, the assembly found itself tangled in the problems of nationality. Who, they asked, were the Germans? A majority of the delegates argued that they were all those who, by language, culture, or geography, felt themselves bound to the enterprise now underway at Frankfurt. The German nation that was to be constituted must include as many of those "Germans" as possible. This point of view came to be known as the "Great German" position. Great Germans found themselves stymied, however, by the unwillingness of other nationalities to be included in their fold. The Czechs in Bohemia, as we have seen, wanted no part of Great Germany. In the end the Great Germans settled that the nation for which they were drafting a constitution should include, among other territories, all Austrian lands except Hungary. This decision meant that the crown of their new country might most logically be offered to the Hapsburg emperor. At this point the voice of the "Little Germans" began to be heard. Prussian nationalism took precedence over German nationalism; a minority argued that Austria should be excluded altogether and the crown instead offered to King Frederick William of Prussia.

Great Germans vs. Little Germans

The liberalism of the assembly was put to the test by events in Austria and Poland in the fall of 1848. When the imperial forces crushed the Czech and Hungarian rebellions, when the Prussian Junkers put an end to Polish self-government, liberals found themselves forced to cheer. They were compelled to support the suppression of minority nationalities; otherwise there would be no new Germany. But their cheers were for the forces not only of German nationalism but of antiliberal authoritarianism. The assembly's most embarrassing moment occurred when it found itself compelled to take shelter behind the Prussian army. Riots broke out in Frankfurt protesting the assembly's willingness to withdraw from a confrontation with the Danes over the future of Germans in Schleswig, a Danish province. That particular area, which many considered to be part of Germany, had been annexed by the Danes in March 1848. The Frankfurters had been unable to do more than ask the Prussians to win Schleswig back for them; and the Prussians had refused. Hence the riots; hence a second request, this time heeded, for Prussian assistance.

Liberalism vs. nationalism

Reduced to the status of dependents, the Frankfurt delegates nevertheless, in the spring of 1849, produced a constitution. By this time Austria, fearing its Prussian rival, had decided to have no more to do with Frankfurt. The Little Germans thus won by default and offered their constitutional monarchy to Frederick William of Prussia. Though tempted, he turned them down, arguing that their constitution was too liberal, embodying as it did the revolutionary notion that a crown could be offered to a monarch. Frederick wanted the crown; but on his own terms. The delegates went home, disillusioned by their experience, many of them convinced that their dual goal of liberalism and nationalism was an impossible one. Some, who refused to surrender that goal, emigrated to the United States, where they believed the goal had already been achieved. Many of those who stayed behind convinced themselves that half the goal was better than none, and sacrificed their liberalism to nationalism.

The end of the assembly

Bismarck

Bismarck and the liberals

4. NATION-BUILDING, 1850–1870

The twenty years between 1850 and 1870 were years of intense nation-building in the Western world. Of the master-builders, none was more accomplished than the man who brought Germany under Prussian rule, Otto von Bismarck (1815–1898). He was born into the Junker class. During the revolutionary period of 1848 and 1849, Bismarck had served in the Prussian parliament as a defender of the monarchy. Bismarck was really neither a liberal nor a nationalist; he was a Prussian. When he instituted domestic reforms, he did so not because he favored the "rights" of this or that particular group, but because he thought that his policies would result in a more united, and hence more powerful, Prussia. When he maneuvered to bring other German states under Prussian domination, he did so not in conformity with a grand Germanic design but because he believed that some sort of union was almost inevitable and, if so, that it must come about at Prussia's behest. He prided himself on being a realist; and he became a first-rate practitioner of what has come to be called *Realpolitik*—the politics, not of idealism, but of hard-headed reality.

When Bismarck came to power as minister-president of Prussia in 1862, he was confronted by a liberal parliamentary majority which, since 1859, had opposed a campaign to increase military expenditures despite pressure from the king. This majority had been produced by an electoral system that was part of the constitution granted by Frederick William to Prussia in 1850, following the collapse of the assembly. The parliament was divided into two houses, the lower one elected by universal male suffrage. Votes were apportioned according to one's ability to pay taxes, however; those few who together paid one-third of the country's taxes elected one-third of the legislators. A large landowner or industrialist exercised about a hundred times the voting power of a poor man. Contrary to the king's expectations, however, under this constitution a liberal majority was succeeding in thwarting the plans of the sovereign and his advisors. It was to break this deadlock that King William I, who succeeded his brother Frederick William in 1861, summoned Bismarck. In Bismarck the liberals more than met their match. When they refused to levy taxes, he collected them anyway, claiming that the constitution, whatever its purposes, had not been designed to subvert the state. When liberals argued that Prussia was setting a poor example for the rest of Germany, Bismarck replied that Prussia was admired not for its liberalism but its power.

Whether or not the Germans—or the rest of Europe—admired Prussia's power, they soon found themselves confronted by it. Bismarck proceeded to build a nation that in the short space of eight years came into being as the German Empire. Bismarck was assisted in his task by his readiness to take advantage of international situations as

British Encampment Near Sebastopol, 1854–1855. Photograph taken by Roger Fenton. The Crimean War was the first to be reported to the world by photograph as well as by news dispatch.

they presented themselves, without concerning himself particularly with the ideological or moral implications of his actions. He was aided as well by developments over which he had no initial control but which he was able to turn to his advantage. The first of these, the Crimean War, had occurred in 1854–1856, prior to his taking office. Russia and Turkey, perennial European squabblers, had precipitated the hostilities. Russia invaded the territories of Moldavia and Wallachia (later Rumania) in an attempt to take advantage of the continuing political rot that made the Ottoman Empire an easy prey. In 1854 France and then Britain came to the aid of the Turks by invading Russia's Crimean peninsula. These allies were soon joined by Austria and Sardinia. The quarrel had by this time enlarged to include the question of who was to protect the Christians in Jerusalem from the Turks; it was fueled from the start as well by Britain's continuing determination to prohibit a strong Russian presence in the Near East. The allies' eventual victory was the result primarily of a British blockade of Russia. The peace settlement was a severe setback for Russia, whose influence in the Balkans was drastically curbed. Moldavia and Wallachia were united as Rumania, which, along with Serbia, was granted power as a self-governing principality. Austria, though it had sided with the victor, lost more than it gained from the war. Austrian military resources were severely taxed during the invasion and occupation of Moldavia and Wallachia. It was the subsequent weakness of both Russia and Austria, the result of the Crimean War, that Bismarck used to his advantage in the 1860s.

The Crimean War

In consolidating the German states into a union controlled by Prussia, Bismarck first moved to eliminate Austria from its commanding position in the Germanic Confederation. As a means to this end he inflamed the long-smoldering dispute with Denmark over the possession of Schleswig and Holstein. Inhabited largely by Germans, these two provinces had an anomalous status. Since 1815 Holstein had been

Steps to German unification: (1) weakening of Austria

TOWARD THE UNIFICATION OF GERMANY · 1740-1871

included in the Germanic Confederation, but both were subject to the personal overlordship of the king of Denmark. When, in 1864, the Danish king attempted to annex them, Bismarck invited Austria to participate in a war against Denmark. A brief struggle followed, at the end of which the Danish ruler was compelled to renounce all his claims to Schleswig and Holstein in favor of Austria and Prussia. Then the very sequel occurred for which Bismarck ardently hoped: a quarrel between the victors over division of the spoils. The conflict which followed in 1866, known as the Seven Weeks' War, ended in an easy triumph for Prussia. Austria was forced to give up all claims to Schleswig and Holstein, to surrender Venetia, and to acquiesce in the dissolution of the Germanic Confederation. Immediately following the war Bismarck proceeded to unite all of the German states north of the Main River into the North German Confederation.

To achieve the confederation Bismarck willingly turned himself into a democrat. He saw that if he was to attain his end, which was a strong union with Prussia at its head, he would need to cultivate a constituency hitherto untapped by any German politicians: the masses. He appreciated the manner by which Napoleon III had reinforced his regime through plebiscites. And Bismarck understood that the majority of Germans were not particularly enthusiastic supporters of capitalist liberals, of the bureaucracies of their own small states, or of the Austrian Hapsburgs. The constitution he devised for his confederation provided for two chambers: the upper chamber represented the individual states within the union, though not equally; the lower chamber was elected by universal manhood suffrage. The liberal middle class, to say nothing of the Junkerdom, was astonished and dismayed, as well they might be. Bismarck's intention was to use popular support to strengthen the hand of the central government against the interests of both landlords and capitalists. To this end, he struck a bargain with German socialists, who agreed to exchange support for the confederation for universal suffrage.

(2) courting the masses

Bismarck's final step in the completion of German unity was the Franco-Prussian War of 1870–1871. He hoped that a conflict with France would kindle the spirit of German nationalism in Bavaria, Würtemberg, and other southern states still outside the confederation. Taking advantage of a diplomatic tempest concerning the right of the Hohenzollerns (Prussia's ruling family) to occupy the Spanish throne, Bismarck worked hard to force a Franco-German misunderstanding. King William agreed to meet with the French ambassador at the resort spa of Ems in Prussia to discuss the Spanish succession. When William telegraphed Bismarck that the demands of the French for perpetual exclusion of the Hohenzollern family from the Spanish throne had been refused, Bismarck released portions of the message to the press so as to make it appear that King William had insulted the ambassador—which he had not done. When the garbled report of what happened at Ems was received in France, the nation reacted with a call for war. The call was echoed in Prussia, where Bismarck published evidence which he claimed proved French designs upon the Rhineland. Once war had been declared the south German states rallied to Prussia's side in the belief that it was the victim of aggression. The war was quickly fought. The French were no match for Prussia's professionally trained and superbly equipped forces. Nor did other European powers come to France's assistance. Austria, the most likely candidate, remained weakened by its recent war with Prussia. The Magyars, who at this time had assumed positions of influence within the Austrian government, were quite prepared to welcome a strengthened Prussia; Prussia's growing strength in Germany would further increase Austria's weakness there. And the weaker Austria was as a German power, the stronger would be the claims of the Magyars to predominance. Once more one nationalist consciousness was grinding against another. The war began in July; it ended in September with the defeat of the French and the capture of Napoleon III himself at Sedan in France.

(3) the Franco-Prussian War

The German Empire

Following the collapse of the French imperial government, insurrectionary forces in Paris continued to hold out against the Germans until the winter of 1871. Bismarck meanwhile proceeded to consummate the German union toward which he had worked so assiduously. On January 18, 1871, in the great Hall of Mirrors at Versailles the German Empire was proclaimed. All those states, except Austria, which had not already been absorbed into Prussia declared their allegiance to William I, henceforth emperor or kaiser. Four months later, at Frankfurt, a treaty between the French and Germans ceded the border region of Alsace to the new empire, condemned the French to an indemnity of five billion francs, and thereby broadcast to the world the remarkable success of Bismarck's nation-building.

Italian unification

Events in Italy ran a course almost parallel to that which had led to the unification of Germany. Italy before 1848, it should be remembered, was a patchwork of petty states. The most important of those possessing independence were the Kingdom of Sardinia in the north, the Papal States in the central region, and the Kingdom of the Two Sicilies in the south. The former republics of Lombardy and Venetia were held by Austria, while Hapsburg dependents ruled in Tuscany, Parma, and Modena. As the revolutionary fervor of 1848 swept across the peninsula, one ruler after another granted democratic reforms. Charles Albert of Sardinia outdistanced all the others by providing for civil liberties and a parliamentary form of government. But it soon became evident that the Italians were as interested in nationalism as in liberalism. For some years romantic patriots had been dreaming of the *Risorgimento,* which would restore the nation to the position of glorious leadership it had held in Roman times and during the Renaissance. To achieve this, it was universally agreed that Italy must be welded into a single state. But opinions differed as to the form the new government should take. Young idealists followed the leadership of Mazzini. Religious-minded patriots believed that the most practicable solution would be to federate the state of Italy under the presidency of

Meeting to Arrange Peace Terms at the End of the Franco-Prussian War. On the left is Otto von Bismarck, chancellor of the new German Empire. In the center is Jules Favre and to his right Louis-Adolphe Thiers, both representing the provisional government set up after the overthrow of Napoleon III.

the pope. The majority of the more moderate nationalists advocated a constitutional monarchy built upon the foundations of the Kingdom of Sardinia. The aims of this third group gradually crystallized under the leadership of a shrewd Sardinian nobleman, Count Camillo di Cavour (1810–1861). In 1850 he was appointed minister of commerce and agriculture of his native state and in 1852 prime minister.

The campaign for unification of the Italian peninsula began with efforts to expel the Austrians. In 1848 revolts were organized in the territories under Hapsburg domination, and an army of liberation marched from Sardinia to aid the rebels; but the movement ended in failure. It was then that Cavour, as the new leader of the campaign, turned to less heroic but more practical methods. In 1855, to attract the favorable attention of Great Britain and France, he had entered the Crimean War on their side, despite the fact that he had no quarrel with Russia. In 1858 he held a secret meeting with Napoleon III and prepared the stage for an Italian War of Liberation. Napoleon agreed to cooperate in driving the Austrians from Italy for the price of the cession of Savoy and Nice by Sardinia to France. A war with Austria was duly provoked in 1859, and for a time all went well for the Franco-Italian allies. But after the conquest of Lombardy, Napoleon III suddenly withdrew, fearful of ultimate defeat and afraid of antagonizing the Catholics in his own country by aiding the avowedly anticlerical government of Cavour. Thus deserted by its ally, Sardinia was unable to expel the Austrians from Venetia. Nevertheless, extensive gains were made; Sardinia annexed Lombardy, and acquired by various means the duchies of Tuscany, Parma, and Modena, and the northern portion of the Papal States. Sardinia was now more than twice its original size and by far the most powerful state in Italy.

The second step in consolidating the unity of Italy was the conquest of the Kingdom of the Two Sicilies. This kingdom was ruled by a Bourbon, Francis II, who was thoroughly hated by his Italian subjects. In May 1860 a romantic adventurer, Giuseppe Garibaldi, set out with a regiment of one thousand "red shirts" to rescue his fellow Italians from oppression. Within three months he had conquered the island of Sicily and had then marched to the deliverance of Naples, where the people were already in revolt. By November the whole kingdom of Francis II had fallen to Garibaldi. He at first intended to convert the territory into an independent republic but was finally persuaded to surrender it to the Kingdom of Sardinia. With most of the peninsula now united under a single rule, Victor Emmanuel II, king of Sardinia, assumed the title of king of Italy (March 17, 1861). Venetia was still in the hands of the Austrians, but in 1866, following their defeat in the Seven Weeks' War, they were forced by the Prussians to cede it to Italy. All that remained to complete the unification of Italy was the annexation of Rome. The Eternal City had resisted conquest thus far, largely because of the military protection accorded the pope by Napoleon III. But in 1870 the outbreak of the Franco-Prussian War

Camillo di Cavour

Giuseppe Garibaldi

Garibaldi

Italy and the Papal States

compelled Napoleon to withdraw his troops. In September 1870 Italian soldiers occupied Rome, and in July of the following year it was made the capital of the by now united kingdom.

The occupation of Rome brought the kingdom of Italy into conflict with the papacy. Indeed, the whole movement for unification had been characterized by hostility to the Church. Such was inevitably the case, with the pope ruling in the manner of a secular prince over the Papal States and opposing those who would rob him of his domain for the sake of a united Italy. Following the occupation of Rome in 1870, an attempt was made to solve the problem of relations between the state and the papacy. In 1871 the Italian parliament enacted the Law of

Papal Guaranties, purporting to define the status of the pope as a reigning sovereign. This law the reigning pontiff, Pius IX, promptly denounced on the ground that issues affecting the pope could be settled only by an international treaty to which he himself was a party. Whereupon he shut himself up in the Vatican and refused to have anything to do with a government which had so shamefully treated Christ's vicar on earth. His successors continued this practice of voluntary imprisonment until 1929, when a series of agreements between the Italian government and Pius XI effected settlement of the dispute.

Nation-building was the preoccupation of another major country in the first half of the nineteenth century: the United States. The history of the expansion and consolidation of this newly born country into a nation of remarkable economic potential in little over half a century can best be understood in terms of several major factors. The first is the growth of political democracy.

Nation-building in the U.S.: (1) the growth of democracy

The United States did not begin its history as a democracy. Although a few early leaders professed democratic ideals, these were not the doctrines of the most prominent. The authors of the Constitution were not interested in the rule of the masses. The primary aim of the founders of the United States was to establish a *republic* that would promote stability and protect the rights of private property against the leveling tendencies of majorities. For this reason they adopted checks and balances, devised the Electoral College for choosing the president, created a powerful judiciary, and entrusted the selection of senators to the legislatures of the several states.

Thomas Jefferson by Gilbert Stuart

Following the establishment of a new government under the Constitution of 1789, democratic ideals began to win acceptance in the United States. Until 1801 the Federalist party held the reins of power, representing big landowners, big money, and the conservatives generally. In the latter year the Democratic-Republicans gained control as a result of the election of Thomas Jefferson (1743–1826) to the presidency. This event is often referred to as the Jeffersonian Revolution, on the supposition that Jefferson was the champion of the masses and of the political power of the underprivileged. There is danger in carrying this interpretation too far. In several respects Jefferson's ideas were far removed from democracy in its historic meaning. He strenuously opposed the unlimited sovereignty of the majority. His conception of an ideal political system was an aristocracy of "virtue and talent," in which respect for personal liberty would be the guiding principle.

Yet the Jeffersonian movement had a number of democratic objectives of cardinal importance. Its leaders were vigorous opponents of special privilege, whether of birth or of wealth. They worked for the abolition of established churches. They led the campaign for the addition of a Bill of Rights to the Constitution and were almost exclusively responsible for its success. Although professing devotion to the principle of the separation of powers, they actually believed in the supremacy of the representatives of the people and viewed with abhor-

Jeffersonian principles

Jacksonian democracy

rence the attempts of the executive and judicial branches to increase their power.

By 1820, these notions were being expressed in more direct and forceful terms. Urban populations grew increasingly conscious of their political importance and demanded attention to their interests. The predominance of the agricultural Old South (the South of the original thirteen colonies) had declined. As a result of the Louisiana Purchase (a vast tract bought from the French in 1803) and of increased settlement in the area known as the Northwest Territory (western New York State and Ohio), a new frontier had come into existence. Life there was characterized by a rugged freedom that left little room for class distinctions. In the struggle to survive, hard work and sharp wits counted for more than birth and education. As a consequence a new democratic spirit, which eventually found its leader in Andrew Jackson (1767–1845), took shape around the principle of equality. The Jacksonian Democrats transformed the doctrines of liberalism into a more radical creed. They pronounced all (excluding slaves, American Indians, and women) politically equal, not merely in rights but in privileges. They were devoted adherents to the causes of suffrage for all white males; the election, rather than appointment, of all governmental office-holders; and the frequent rotation of men in positions of political power—a doctrine that served to put more Democratic politicians into federal office. These democratic beliefs helped encourage a spirit of unity within the United States during a period of rapid territorial expansion.

As the United States continued to acquire more territories in the West (the most notable addition resulting from the conquest of lands

"Meal Time." Between the decks on an immigrant ship to the United States in the mid–nineteenth century.

in the southwest from Mexico in 1846), it not only faced the task of binding those areas and their settlers into the nation. There was, as well, the problem of assimilating the thousands of immigrants who came to America from Europe in the first half of the century. Many were Scottish and English; for them the difficulties of adjusting to a new life in a new country were generally not difficult, since they spoke a common language with their fellow-citizens. For others the problems were far greater. For the Irish, who immigrated in great numbers, particularly during the 1840s, there was the fact of their alien religion, Roman Catholicism. For Germans and others from the Continent, there was the language barrier. The United States's policy towards its immigrants was directed against the creation of any foreign nationalist enclaves apart from the main body of its citizenry. Although foreign-language newspapers were tolerated, and immigrants were free to attend churches and social gatherings as they chose, English remained the language of the public schools, the police, the law courts, and the government. To hold a job, a person was almost always forced to learn at least some English. In this way, the United States encouraged immigrants to shed their "foreign" ways and to commit themselves to their adopted nation.

(2) immigration

If there were enclaves in the United States, they existed in the South, where the institution of slavery and the economic dependence of the planters upon England produced two distinct minorities, neither of which was to be assimilated without resort to war. During the nineteenth century, slavery had been abolished throughout much of the Western world, for both economic and humanitarian reasons. Southern planters continued to insist that without the slave system they would go bankrupt. To humanitarians they responded with arguments based upon theories of racial inferiority and upon their self-professed reputation as benevolent masters. The position of these southern spokesmen grew increasingly distasteful and unconvincing to the North. As the country opened to the west, North and South engaged in a protracted tug-of-war as to which new states were to be "free" and which "slave." Northerners were motivated by more than concern for the well-being of southern blacks. The North was industrializing fast. Capitalists there were demanding protective tariffs to assist them in their enterprises. Southerners favored free trade, since they wished to import British goods in return for the cotton they sold to the manufacturers of Lancashire.

(3) slavery and the South

The American Civil War, when it came in 1861, was a war not about the issue of slavery so much as it was about preserving the union of American states and territories. President Abraham Lincoln undertook the war to defend the unity of the United States. European governments, while never recognizing the Confederacy officially, nevertheless remained sympathetic to its cause. They hoped that the fragmentation of the United States would result in the opening up of markets for their manufactured goods, much as the dissolution of the

The Civil War

Nation-building in the West

Spanish Empire had proved a boon to European commercial interests. The victory of the North in 1865, however, insured the continued growth of the United States as a nation. The Fourteenth Amendment to the Constitution stated specifically that all were citizens of the United States, and not of an individual state or territory. In declaring that no citizen was to be deprived of life, liberty, or property without due process of law, it established that "due process" was to be defined by the national, and not the state or territorial governments.

The years following the American Civil War witnessed the binding together of the nation economically under the direction of northern private enterprise. The symbol of the North's triumph as nation-builder came with the driving of the final spike of the transcontinental Union Pacific railroad in 1869. Nation-building in Europe and the United States helped insure the continuing expansion of capitalism. Liberalism had provided a general climate of opinion and a set of attitudes toward government that encouraged industrialization. Nation-building, in its turn, produced the necessary economic units: large enough to generate the wherewithal to sustain economic growth; confident enough to enter into competition with the British Goliath.

SELECTED READINGS

• *Items so designated are available in paperback editions.*

Artz, Frederick B., *France under the Bourbon Restoration, 1814–1830,* New York, 1963. A basic survey with a good treatment of romanticism.

• Binkley, Robert C., *Realism and Nationalism, 1852–1871,* New York, 1935. An excellent synthesis.

Brunschwig, Henri, *Enlightenment and Romanticism in Eighteenth-Century Prussia,* rev. ed., Chicago, 1974.

• Craig, Gordon, *The Politics of the Prussian Army,* Oxford, 1955. Much more than the title implies. An excellent analysis of Prussian social structure and the role of the army in social reform and unification.

Deutsch, Karl W., and W. J. Folz, eds., *Nation-Building,* New York, 1963.

• Eyck, Erich, *Bismarck and the German Empire,* London, 1958. The best one-volume study of Bismarck.

Eyck, Frank, *The Frankfurt Parliament, 1848–49,* New York, 1968. A detailed study of its composition and procedure.

Ford, Guy Stanton, *Stein and the Era of Reform in Prussia, 1807–1815,* New York, 1922. An old but still valuable work on a leading Prussian reformer.

Gewehr, W. M., *The Rise of Nationalism in the Balkans, 1800–1930,* New York, 1931.

• Gleckner, R. F., and G. E. Ersco, eds., *Romanticism,* Englewood Cliffs, N.J., 1962.

Gooch, G. P., *Germany and the French Revolution,* New York, 1920. Examines the origins of reform in Germany in the aftermath of the French Revolution.

Griffith, G. O., *Mazzini: Prophet of Modern Europe*, London, 1931. The standard biography.

• Hamerow, Theodore, *Restoration, Revolution, Reaction*, Princeton, N.J., 1958. An excellent social and economic history of Germany between 1815 and 1871.

• ———, *The Social Foundations of German Unification, 1858–1871*, 2 vols., Princeton, N.J., 1969. Concentrates on economic factors which determined the solution to the unification question. An impressive synthesis.

Hayes, C. J. H., *The Historical Evolution of Modern Nationalism*, rev. ed., New York, 1968.

Holborn, Hajo, *History of Modern Germany*, Vols. II, III, New York, 1964. The best survey of German history in English.

• Kohn, Hans, *The Idea of Nationalism*, New York, 1944. A perceptive analysis.

———, *Panslavism: In History and Ideology*, South Bend, Ind., 1953.

• Langer, William L., *Political and Social Upheaval, 1832–1852*, New York, 1969.

Mack Smith, Dennis, *Garibaldi: A Great Life in Brief*, New York, 1956.

Namier, Lewis B., *1848: The Revolution of the Intellectuals*, London, 1947. A controversial analysis, highly critical of the Frankfurt Assembly.

Noyes, P. H., *Organization and Revolution: Working-Class Associations in the German Revolutions of 1848–49*, Princeton, N.J., 1966. An important monograph.

• Pflanze, Otto, *Bismarck and the Development of Germany, 1815–1871*, Princeton, N.J., 1963. An impressive analysis of Bismarck's aims and policies.

• Robertson, Priscilla, *The Revolutions of 1848: A Social History*, Princeton, N.J., 1952.

• Rosenberg, Hans, *Bureaucracy, Aristocracy, and Autocracy: The Prussian Experience, 1660–1815*, Cambridge, Mass., 1958. A difficult but valuable book explaining the forces that molded the modern Prussian state.

• Stearns, Peter N., *1848: The Revolutionary Tide in Europe*, New York, 1974.

• Taylor, A. J. P., *The Hapsburg Monarchy, 1809–1918*, rev. ed., London, 1960. An idiosyncratic account by an eminent historian.

SOURCE MATERIALS

Bismarck, Otto von, *Bismarck, the Man and the Statesman, Written and Dictated by Himself*, London, 1899. Bismarck's memoirs, written after his fall from power.

• Clausewitz, Karl von, *On War*, London, 1968. Published posthumously in 1831, this work, in reality a philosophy of war, was perceived by the Prussian military bureaucracy as a mandate for total war—for the subjugation of all interests of the state to war.

Fichte, Johann Gottlieb, *Addresses to the German Nation*, New York, 1968. Presented in 1808 while French armies occupied Prussia, these lectures helped stir a German nationalist spirit.

Schurz, Carl, *The Reminiscences of Carl Schurz*, 3 vols., New York, 1907–8. Especially valuable is Vol. I. A young German liberal in 1848 and a delegate to the Frankfurt Assembly, Schurz spent the rest of his life as an exile in the United States.

Part Six

THE WEST AT THE
WORLD'S CENTER

The years between 1870 and 1945 found the West at the center of global affairs. The industrial supremacy of western Europe and the United States gave them a combined power greater than that possessed by any nation or empire in previous times. Yet world domination was by no means accompanied by any sense of general world order. The economic might of the Western nations, while it resulted in their ability to dominate the less developed quarters of the globe, resulted, as well, in their concern lest one of their number overpower the others. The old system of the balance of power, designed to preserve peace by insuring that no one country achieved overwhelming predominance at the expense of its neighbors, was strained to the breaking point by economic rivalries that stretched around the world. Meanwhile, tensions mounted within each nation, as landed and middle classes, threatened by the possibility of social turmoil, tried to balance the mounting clamor for political concessions against their desire to retain power in their own hands. Twice during the period, in 1914 and 1939, international and domestic pressures exploded into global wars. Those wars and their results, generated by the rivalries and miscalculations of the Western nations, so sapped the strength of those nations as to depose them thereafter as the sole arbiters of the world's destinies. The Nations of the Far East, subjected to the high tide of Western expansionism, reacted in different ways.

China, under a decrepit dynasty and exhausted by rebellion, was reduced for several decades to a condition of economic dependence, while Japan displayed new vigor when forced out of isolation. Both nations adapted elements of Western civilization to their own basic culture patterns. The great lords of Japan, in drawing up a constitution in 1889, saw fit to establish the forms of cabinet government. The leader of the Chinese Revolution of 1911 made "democracy" one of his shibboleths. But the most powerful current reaching its climax between 1870 and 1945 was undoubtedly nationalism. New states multiplied especially in Europe and in Latin America, and the peoples of the Middle and Far East struck out boldly for control of their own destinies. The peoples of Africa were condemned to a longer struggle for independence. Although the notorious slave trade was gradually ended, the political and technological advantages accruing to the leading Western nations were utilized by them to strengthen their hold on the resources of disunited Africa.

THE FAR EAST	AFRICA	
	British occupation of Cape Colony, 1795	
	House-Canoe system in Niger Delta, c. 1800	**1800**
	Expansion of East African trade, 1800–1875	
	Sultan Sayyid, Zanzibar, 1805–1856	
	Sierra Leone founded, 1808	
	Liberia founded, 1821	
		1825
	British consulates in coastal states, 1830–1860	
	Exploration of interior of continent, 1830–1875	
Anglo-Chinese War (Opium War), 1839–1842		
	Decline of slave trade, 1840–1863	
		1850
Taiping Rebellion, 1851–1864		
Opening of Japan, 1854		
Sun Yat-sen, 1866–1925		
Meiji Restoration in Japan, 1867–1868		
End of feudalism in Japan, 1871	Opening of Suez Canal, 1869	
		1875
	Destruction of Zulu empire, 1879	
	British invasion of Egypt, 1882	
Adoption of constitution in Japan, 1889	Berlin West African Conference, 1884	
Sino-Japanese War, 1894–1895	European Settlement of Rhodesia, 1890	
	Boer War, 1899–1902	
Boxer Uprising, 1900		**1900**
Russo-Japanese War, 1904–1905		
Revolution in China, 1911		

POLITICS	SCIENCE & INDUSTRY

1870

First commercially practical electrical generator, 1870

Gilcrist-Thomas steel process, 1870s

Paris Commune, 1871
Kulturkampf, Germany, 1872
League of Three Emperors, 1873
Constitution for Third French Republic, 1875
End of First International, 1876
Congress of Berlin, 1878

Germ theory of disease, 1875
Invention of telephone, 1876

Triple Alliance, 1882
Berlin conference on imperialism, 1885
Second International formed, 1889
Pan-Slavism, 1890–1914

Dreyfus affair, 1894–1899

Discovery of the X-ray, 1895
Spanish-American War, 1898
Marie Curie, discovery of radium, 1898

Boer War, 1899–1902
Invention of wireless telegraph, 1899

1900

V. Lenin, *What Is to Be Done?,* 1902

First airplane flight, 1903
Russo-Japanese War, 1904–1905
Ivan Pavlov, Nobel Prize for physiology, 1904
Revolution in Russia, 1905
Albert Einstein, development of relativity theory, 1905–1910

Triple Entente, 1907
Bosnian Crisis, 1908
Model T Ford, 1908
Revolt of the Young Turks, 1908

Balkan Wars, 1912–1913

First World War, 1914–1918
Russian Revolution, 1917

Treaty of Versailles, 1919
Socialist revolution, Germany, 1919
1920
League of Nations, 1920–1946

NEP, Russia, 1921

Mussolini's March on Rome, 1922

Hitler's beer-hall putsch, 1923
New constitution, Soviet Union, 1924
Locarno agreements, 1925

Discovery of viruses, sulfa drugs, and penicillin, 1930s
Hitler, chancellor of Germany, 1933
World economic conference, 1933
New Deal, United States, 1933–1940

ECONOMICS & SOCIETY	ARTS & LETTERS	
	Impressionism in art, 1870–1900	*1870*
Growth of finance capitalism, 1880s		
Social welfare legislation, Germany, 1882–1884		
	Émile Zola, *Germinal,* 1885	
Sherman Anti-Trust Act, United States, 1890	Henrik Ibsen, *Hedda Gabler,* 1890	
Meline tariff, 1892	Paul Cézanne, *The Card Players,* 1890–1892	
	George Bernard Shaw, *Plays Pleasant* and *Unpleasant,* 1898	
Women's suffrage movement, England, 1900–1914	Sigmund Freud, *The Interpretation of Dreams,* 1900	*1900*
Social welfare legislation, France, 1904; 1910		
	Cubism in art 1905–1930	
Social welfare legislation, England, 1906–1912		
	Marcel Proust, *Remembrance of Things Past,* 1913–1918	
	Oswald Spengler, *The Decline of the West,* 1918	
	Bauhaus established, 1919	
German inflation, 1920s	Writers of the "Lost Generation," 1920–1930	*1920*
	Surrealism and Dadaism, 1920s	
	Ludwig Wittgenstein, *Tractatus Logico-philosophicus,* 1921	
	T. S. Eliot, *The Waste Land,* 1922	
	James Joyce, *Ulysses,* 1922	
Great Depression, 1929–1940		
	Neo-realism in art, 1930s	

POLITICS	SCIENCE & INDUSTRY
Italy conquers Ethiopia, 1935–1936 Rome-Berlin Axis, 1936	National rearmament programs, 1935
Spanish Civil War, 1936–1939 Germany annexes Austria, 1938 Munich conference, 1938 Nazi-Soviet pact, 1939 Second World War, 1939–1941 United States enters war, 1941	Discovery of atomic fission, 1939
Allied invasion of Normandy, 1944 Bombing of Hiroshima and Nagasaki, 1945 United Nations founded, 1946	First atomic bomb test, 1945

1940

ECONOMICS & SOCIETY	ARTS & LETTERS

J. M. Keynes, *General Theory of Employment, Interest, and Money,* 1936

1940

Jean-Paul Sartre, *Being and Nothingness,* 1943

Chapter 29

THE PROGRESS OF INDUSTRIALIZATION (1870–1914)

We have conquered for ourselves a place in the sun. It will now be my task to see to it that this place in the sun shall remain our undisputed possession . . .

—Kaiser William II, speech, 1901

I f most historians now speak of a second industrial revolution oc-curring during the years after 1870, they are quick to qualify the term. Whatever the changes in technique and in scope—and they were significant—they do not compare to those which characterized the first revolution—*the* Industrial Revolution. There is, however, good reason to distinguish a second period of industrial development and advance from the first. Successful nation-building meant that the years 1870–1914 would be characterized by sharply increased interna-tional economic rivalries, culminating in a scramble after imperial ter-ritories in Africa and Asia. Britain, if it did not actually surrender its industrial lead during this period, failed to counter with any real suc-cess the energetic and determined challenges from Germany and the United States to its constantly decreasing lead. New technology, par-ticularly in the fields of metals, chemicals, and electricity, resulted in new products. Improving standards of living produced greater de-mand, which, in turn, increased the volume of production. And the need for increased production called forth significant reorganization to provide a freer supply of capital and to ensure a more efficient labor force. It is these changes that distinguish the second stage of indus-trialization from the first, and therefore warrant its separate treatment. Yet they must be perceived as stemming not only from those eco-nomic conditions which were the result of the first stage, but also from the more general political, social, and cultural climate whose his-tory we have been tracing.

A second industrial revolution

In analyzing the progress of industrialization, we shall deal with changes in three major areas: in technology; in scope and scale of production; and in the reorganization of the capitalist system. Finally we shall examine the phenomenon of late–nineteenth-century imperialism, and consider the extent to which that phenomenon can be attributed to increasing economic and industrial rivalries.

1. NEW TECHNOLOGIES

Technology in steel

A most important technological change in this period resulted in the mass production of steel. The advantages of steel over iron—a result of steel's lower carbon content—are its hardness, its malleability, and its strength. Steel can keep its cutting edge, where iron cannot; it can be worked more easily than iron, which is brittle and which, if it is to be used industrially, must almost always be cast (that is, poured into molds). And steel, because of its strength in proportion to its weight and volume, makes a particularly adaptable construction material. These advantages had been recognized by craftsmen for centuries. Until steel could be produced both cheaply and in mass, however, the advantages remained more theoretical than real. Two inventions, during the earlier years of the Industrial Revolution, had reduced the price and increased the output of steel to some degree. The crucible technique, discovered in the eighteenth century in England, called for the heating of relatively small amounts of iron ore to a point at which foreign matter could be removed by skimming, the carbon content reduced, and a proper proportion of carbon distributed evenly throughout the finished product. Although individual crucibles were not large, holding on the average no more than forty-five to sixty pounds, they could be poured together to produce steel ingots of several tons. A century later, in the early 1840s, two Germans adapted the puddling process, used in the production of iron, to the manufacture of steel. While it did not produce steel as hard as that made in crucibles, it reduced its price considerably.

*Bessemer, Siemens-
Martin, and Gilchrist-
Thomas systems*

Not until the invention of the Bessemer and Siemens-Martin processes, however, could steel begin to compete with iron. In the 1850s, an Englishman, Henry Bessemer, discovered that by blowing air into and through the molten metal he could achieve a more exact degree of decarbonization in much shorter time, and with far larger quantities of ore, than was possible with either the crucible or puddling methods. Bessemer soon found, however, that his "converters" were incapable of burning off sufficient quantities of phosphorous; and phosphorous in anything but the smallest quantities made the metal unworkable. A partial solution was achieved with the introduction of non-phosphoric hematite ores. Yet this was of little long-term use in most European countries, where supplies of hematite ore were not

The Manufacture of Steel by the Bessemer Process. An 1875 engraving.

abundant. This same problem plagued the German inventors Frederick and William Siemens, whose furnace made use of waste gases to increase heat. Not until Pierre Martin, a Frenchman, discovered that the introduction of scrap iron into the mix would induce proper decarbonization, could the Siemens furnace be used to make steel commercially. And not until the late 1870s was the problem of phosphoresence solved for both the Bessemer and the Siemens-Martin processes. The solution was a simple one, discovered by two Englishmen, a clerk and a chemist: Sidney Gilchrist Thomas and his cousin Sidney Gilchrist. They introduced limestone into the molten iron to combine with the phosphorous, which was then siphoned from the mix. And they lined the converter in such a way that the slag was prevented from eating away the walls and releasing phosphorous back into the molten metal.

Together, these three processes revolutionized the production of steel. Although the use of iron did not end overnight, steel soon moved into the lead. In the British shipbuilding industry, for example, steel had overtaken iron by 1890. In part because Siemens-Martin was particularly suited to the manufacture of steel plates used in shipbuilding, that process dominated the manufacture of steel in Britain, where shipbuilding was a major industry. Bessemer steel, which could be manufactured more cheaply and in larger plants, was more commonly produced on the Continent and in America. The result was a particular increase in the production of German steel: by 1901, German converters were capable of pouring an average of 34,000 tons, compared to Britain's 21,750. By 1914 Germany was producing twice as much steel as Britain, and the United States twice as much as Germany.

A second and equally important technological development resulted in the availability of electric power for industrial, commercial, and domestic use. Electricity's particular advantages result from the fact

Increased steel production

that it can be easily transmitted as energy over long distances, and from the fact that it can be converted into other forms of energy—heat and light, for example. Although electricity had, of course, been discovered prior to the first Industrial Revolution, its advantages could not have been put to general use without a series of inventions which occurred during the nineteenth century. Of these, some of the most important were the invention of the chemical battery by the Italian Alessandro Volta in 1800; of electromagnetic induction by the Englishman Michael Faraday in 1831; of the electromagnetic generator in 1866; of the first commercially practical generator of direct current in 1870; and of alternators and transformers capable of producing high-voltage alternating current in the 1880s. These inventions meant that by the end of the century it was possible to send electric current from large power stations over comparatively long distances. Electric power could be manufactured by water—hence cheaply—and delivered from its source to the place where it was needed.

Once it had been delivered to its destination, the power was converted and put to use in myriad ways. Households quickly became one of the major users of electrical power. The invention by Thomas Edison of the incandescent filament lamp—or light bulb—was crucial in this regard. As individual houses were electrified to receive the power that was to be transformed into light, consumer demand for electricity resulted in further expansion of the electrical industry. Demand for electrical power was increasing in the industrial sector as well. Electric motors soon began to power subways, tramways, and, eventually, long-distance railways. Electricity made possible the development of new techniques in the chemical and metallurgical industries. Most important, electricity helped to transform the work patterns of the factory. Heavy steam engines had made equipment and machinery stationary; electric motors meant that comparatively lightweight power tools could be moved—often by hand—to the site of a particular piece of work. The result was far greater flexibility in terms of factory organization. Smaller workshop industries benefited as well; they could accommodate themselves to electrically powered motors and tools in a way they could not to steam.

An Early Dynamo Used for Lighting

Steel and electricity were only two of the most important areas where technological changes were taking place. The chemical industry was significantly advanced by developments in the manufacture of alkali and organic compounds. Demand for alkali had increased with the demand for soaps and textiles, and with the changes in the manufacturing process of paper, which required large amounts of bleach. An older, more expensive and wasteful technique used extensively by the British was superseded after 1880 by a new process perfected by the Belgian Ernest Solvay. The result was, again, a rapid overtaking of the British by the Germans in the production not only of alkalis but of sulphuric acid, a by-product recoverable in the Solvay process, and used in the manufacture of fertilizers, petroleum refining, iron, steel, and textiles. In the field of organic compounds, the impetus for further discovery came as a result of demand for synthetic dyes. Although the British and French were the first successful pioneers in this area, the Germans once more moved ahead to a commanding lead by 1900. At the turn of the century German firms controlled about 90 percent of the world market.

The need for more and more power to meet increasing industrial demands resulted not only in developments in the field of electricity, already noted, but in the improved design and expanded capacity of steam engines. The most noteworthy invention in this area was the steam turbine, which permitted steam engines to run at speeds heretofore unobtainable. Internal combustion engines made their appearance during this period as well. Their major advantage lay in their efficiency; i.e., they could be powered automatically, and did not need to be stoked by hand like steam engines. Once liquid fuels—petroleum and distilled gasoline—became available, as they did increasingly with the discovery of oil-fields in Russia, Borneo, and Texas about 1900, the internal combustion engine took hold as a serious competitor to steam. By 1914 most navies had converted from coal to oil, as had domestic steamship companies. The automobile and the airplane, both still in their infancies, made little impact upon the industrial world, however, before 1914.

2. CHANGES IN SCOPE AND SCALE

These technological changes must be understood as occurring against a background of—indeed in part as a result of—a generally increased standard of living for the majority of men and women in the Western

Improved engines

The First Successful Airplane Flight

The Interior of a Berlin Department Store, 1882

Increase in domestic consumption

world. There were, of course, still a great many very poor people, both in cities and in the country: casual laborers, the unemployed, those in declining industries and trades. Those skilled workers and their families whose real incomes did rise as a result of deflation and higher wage rates did not experience anything like the rate of increase enjoyed by most of the middle class. Nor could they expect to avoid altogether the stretches of unemployment that made life so chaotic for so many of their unskilled co-workers. Yet despite these qualifications, it is fair to say that more people enjoyed a higher standard of living than ever before. And a higher standard of living produced the demand for an increase in consumer goods.

New consumers

Increased consumption of manufactured goods was by no means uniform; it was higher in urban and industrialized areas than in the country. But even in the country, traditional thrift was challenged as farmers and their wives journeyed by train into the cities, saw what they had not imagined they could have, and then decided they must spend their savings to have it. To accommodate the new and largely middle-class consumers, department stores and chain stores designed their products and their advertising to make shopping as easy and inviting as possible. Behind large plate-glass windows goods were displayed attractively and temptingly; periodic sales encouraged householders to purchase "bargains"; catalogues and charge accounts made it easy for customers to spend money without leaving home. The result was an enormous increase in the volume of manufactured consumer goods produced for this rapidly expanding consumer market. Bicycles, clocks, appliances, furnishings—these and a great many other things were now being made in large quantities, and with new materials (cheap steel) and new techniques (electrical power). Many of these products were designed according to the correct assumption that women were more and more responsible for household purchases. Therefore, goods were fashioned to appeal directly to women, or to the children for whom women were responsible. The foot-powered sewing machine was a particular case in point—the first domestic appliance. Isaac Singer, the American responsible for the development of the treadle and straight needle in the 1850s, was as much an entrepreneur as an inventor. He was a pioneer in the field of advertising and promotion, encouraging purchase on the installment plan and providing courses for would-be domestic seamstresses.

Sewing machines changed far more than the sewing habits of housewives, however. They were cheap, lightweight tools, easily installed and easily operated. Workshop masters could set up several, employ a handful of young women at very low wages, and make a profit turning out cheap ready-made clothing in response to increasing markets. Here is just one of the ways in which the scale of manufacturing altered during the latter part of the nineteenth century, both demand and technology conspiring to produce the change. In metal-working, hard-edged steel allowed for the rapid cutting of patterns, which reduced price, which, in turn, encouraged the manufacture of a variety of inexpensive metal goods—kitchenware, for example. The sewing machine led to the development of other new tools that helped cut costs in the clothing industry: button-holers, lace-makers, leather-stitchers. Whereas it took one cobbler ten hours to make a pair of shoes in 1850 by hand, by the end of the century it took a team of cobblers but a few hours to produce ten pairs using machinery. In

The web of industrial change

Advertisement for a German Sewing Machine. The company proclaims the machine's versatility: unsurpassed for use in the home as well as in the workshop or factory.

textiles, improved engines doubled the pace of mules and looms. In heavy industry, steam hammers performed the work of many men more precisely and with greater speed than before. New equipment of this sort was expensive. As a result, in heavy industry, it was the larger companies that prospered, and in the course of their prosperity, they grew even larger.

Industrial expansion and consolidation

In all the countries of Europe, and in the United States, the pattern is one of expansion and consolidation. This was especially the case in Germany, where in the iron and steel industry nearly 75 percent of those employed worked in factories of a thousand or more, and where over 90 percent of the electrical equipment manufactured was made in factories with over fifty employees. Machinery was thus altering the scale of manufacturing in two directions at once. In the clothing industry, entrepreneurs could use inexpensive machines to make small workshops turn a profit. In steel foundries, the cost of new equipment forced small competitors to the wall, with the result that the foundries grew very much bigger.

Effects of increase in scale on workers: (1) relearning

The increase in the scale of manufacturing had important and often disturbing consequences for workers. The most obvious was the need for men and women to relearn their trades. They were compelled to adapt their older skills to the new machines. Very often this adaptation resulted in a loss of either pay or prestige, or both. Most machine work was not skilled work. A trainee could "pick up" a trade in a week or so. Workers who had prided themselves on a particular skill and had been paid according to their ability to perform it, had to face the fact that industrial change was not only forcing them to relearn, but was compelling them to tell themselves that their new "skills"—if they could be called that—did not amount to very much. For example, when the machine itself could cut metal with infinitesimal accuracy, there was far less need than there had been previously for the skills of a human "fitter." Even if workers were not forced to relearn in these ways in order to accommodate to increased scale, they often had at least to accommodate to factory reorganization and rationalization. In workplaces where the hand-carrying of materials had been a major factor in their final cost, mechanization to reduce that cost would produce a bewildering series of changes. Electric cranes, used together with huge magnets in the iron and steel industries, increased the speed with which goods could be moved, and demanded that workers defer to whatever changes their introduction might entail.

(2) efficiency

A second—and even more important—effect of the change in scale was the constant demand for further efficiency. The greater the scale of the operation, the more important it became to eliminate waste. One minute lost in the production of every ten pairs of shoes might not make much difference if only fifty pairs were produced in a day. But if hundreds were being made, it became crucial, in the eyes of management, to see that those minutes were no longer lost. In facto-

Technological Change and Production Speed-Up. An early assembly line of the Ford Motor Company, United States, 1913. Car bodies slid down the ramp and were attached to the chassis as they passed through the line below. One thousand cars were produced each day.

ries where capital had been spent on new machinery, the owners, conscious of the cost of their investment, increased output in order to realize a profit on their recent investment. In factories where older machinery was still in use, owners believed that the only way they could remain competitive with modernized operations was by extracting all they could from their less productive equipment. In both cases, workers were pressed to produce more and more. One result of this drive for efficiency was a restructuring of wage scales. Prior to this period, although there had been serious wage disputes, both management and labor appeared content to bargain from the traditional notion of "a fair day's wage for a fair day's work." Definitions of what was fair naturally varied. But the level of individual performance was generally set by custom. What workers produced in the course of a day continued to determine what they were expected to produce. From about 1870 onward, however, expectations and procedures began to change. Periodic economic depressions in the last quarter of the nineteenth century saw profits fall before wages. This pattern caused employers to insist on greater individual productivity from their employees. It was no longer enough to work at a job with customary speed. Workers were now asked to produce as much as the owners thought they were potentially capable of producing.

But who was to determine that potential? That question plagued industrial relations during these years. Employers, who were adopting precision tools in order to increase production, grew more and more convinced that worker output could be gauged with a like precision as well. The foremost theoretician of worker efficiency and what was called scientific management of labor was the American Frederick W.

Scientific management

Taylor (1865–1915). Taylor devised a three-step system whereby a worker's output could be "scientifically" measured, a system which, he argued, would provide a precise method for the determination of wage scales. First, he observed, timed, and analyzed workers' movements on the job, in order to determine how long a particular task should take. Second, he figured the labor costs of these movements. Third, he produced "norms," or general standards, which all workers were expected to maintain. These norms were invariably higher than those which had prevailed under traditional conditions.

Piece rates

In order to encourage workers to accept these increased standards, Taylor urged all factory-owners to adopt piece rates (i.e., payment to workers according to the specific amount produced) rather than hourly or daily wages. Payment by piece rate was already a growing practice in many European and American factories. In theory, at least, workers were not opposed to this method of payment; they reasoned that their only hope for a share in increasing output lay in their chance to be paid directly for what they made. But when they were told that their pay would not increase unless they measured up to predetermined—and, to their mind, unrealistic—norms, they rebelled. They argued that rates were set according to the performance of the speediest workers. Even though workers might earn more money if they agreed to the new rates, they resented the intrusion of management upon the pace of their working lives. Despite this opposition, scientific management spread throughout the industrialized West. In England, the United States, and on the Continent, particularly in the engineering trades, factory after factory subscribed to the new gospel. Where it could not entirely succeed in introducing "efficiency" on the shop floor, management proceeded to rationalize its own procedures. Accounting departments were expanded, and encouraged to attend closely to the problem of cost control in all areas of production and distribution. These reforms were no more than a reflection of the general move in the direction of greater efficiency. They were brought on by the vastly increased scale of production, the need to reduce waste wherever possible, and the desire to derive maximum profits from the elimination of unnecessary motions and unproductive habits.

3. THE NEW CAPITALISM

The growth of incorporation

Responding to the increased scope of production and to the consequent pressures for further efficiency, the institutions of capitalism began to reorganize toward the end of the nineteenth century. Hitherto, most firms had been small or at most middle-sized; now, as firms grew and their need for capital increased, they began to incorporate. Limited liability laws, enacted by most countries in the course of the century, worked to encourage this incorporation. "Limited liability" meant that an individual owning stock in a particular corporation

could be held liable only for the amount of his or her shares, should
that corporation bankrupt itself. Once insured in this way, many thousands of middle-class men and women considered corporate investment a safe and financially promising way of making money for
themselves. A stockholding, "rentier" class emerged, brought into
existence by the willingness of governments to encourage capitalism
through friendly legislation, and by the desire of capitalist businessmen to expand their industrial undertakings to meet increased demands. More and more companies incorporated. In doing so, their
management tended to be removed from the direct control of family
founders or of company-based boards of directors. The influence of
bankers and financiers, often situated in cities far removed from the
factories they invested in, grew accordingly. These men were not investing their own money but the money of their clients; their power
to stimulate or to discourage the growth of particular industries and
enterprises encouraged a kind of impersonal "finance" capital.

Corporate organization on a large scale facilitated the spread of industrial unification. Some industries—steel, for example—combined
vertically. Steel companies, to ensure uninterrupted production, acquired their own coal and iron mines. By doing so, they could guarantee themselves a supply of raw materials at attractive prices. Often the
same steel companies would obtain control of companies whose products were made of steel: for example, shipyards or railway factories.
Now they would not only possess a ready stock of raw materials but
an equally ready market for their manufactured products—steel plates,
steel rails, whatever they might be. Such vertical integration was only

Vertical organization

The New York Stock Exchange, 1893

Horizontal organization:
cartels and trusts

possible as a result of the money available for investment through the institutions of finance capital.

A second form of corporate organization was a horizontal formation: the cartel. These were combinations of individual companies producing the same kind of goods, joined for the purpose of controlling, if not eliminating, competition. Since their products were identical, an identical price could be charged. Companies involved in the production of coal and steel were especially suited to the organization of cartels because of the costs of initial capitalization. It is very expensive to build, equip, and man a steel foundry; thus there were relatively few of them. And because there were few, they were the more easily organized into a combine. Cartels were particularly strong in Germany; less so in France, where there was not as much heavy industry, where the tradition of the small family firm was particularly entrenched, and where there was long-standing opposition to competition in the form of price-cutting and general intra-industrial warfare. In Britain, though some cartels were formed, continuing subscription to the policy of free trade meant that companies would find it difficult to maintain fixed prices. How could they do so if they could not exclude, by means of a tariff, foreign competitors who wanted to undersell them? Germany had abandoned the policy of free trade in 1879; the United States, where cartels were known as trusts, did the same after the Civil War, though not all at once. Britain, however, clung to free trade until well into the twentieth century.

Opposition to cartels and
trusts

Defenders of the cartel argued that the elimination of competition brought more stable prices and more continuous employment. They pointed out as well that cartels almost always reduced the cost of production. Opponents questioned, however, whether those reduced costs were reflected in lower prices, or, as they charged, in higher stockholder profits. Critics of cartels were vocal in the United States, where the so-called captains of industry, most prominently the financier J. P. Morgan (1837–1913), were attacked as a new breed of feudal barons. The Sherman Anti-Trust Act was passed by Congress in 1890 to curb the practice of industrial combination. It had little effect in retarding the process, however, until the trust-busting presidency of Theodore Roosevelt (1901–1906). Elsewhere in the West, corporate cartels and combines of various sorts were either encouraged or at least tolerated as a natural stage in the growth of a capitalist system that, it was argued, was showering benefits on all classes of society.

J. P. Morgan

4. INTERNATIONAL COMPETITION: BRITAIN VS. GERMANY

Throughout the period we have been examining, Britain and Germany were locked in industrial competition. By 1914, both the United States and Germany were outproducing Britain in a number of areas. Yet the German challenge was, for the British, the more significant. Industrial competition with Germany helped reshape international political alliances at the end of the century. Britain, moving to align itself with its ancient enemy France against the Germans, found itself engaged in a contest of naval superiority with the latter, determined that in that field the British would not lose their age-old advantage to the upstart challenger.

To what degree did the Germans succeed in overtaking the British? By 1914, Britain's industrial-commercial day was by no means over. The volume of German trade at the turn of the century was no more than 60 percent as great. Britain, more mature industrially than Germany, was shifting resources to the service sector of the economy, into areas such as the wider distribution of goods. If Britain's output of manufactured goods did no more than double between 1870 and 1913, as compared to Germany's sixfold increase, it was in part for this reason. Nor should one suppose that all areas of German industry were functioning as efficient, modernized, and technologically advanced units. For every up-to-date chemical plant, for every thriving steel mill, there were many smaller workshops where manufacturing took place on little more than a domestic scale. Having said this, however, the fact remains that the Germans *were* a powerful threat to the British. Even before 1870, Germany had ceased to provide a ready market for British manufactures; the Germans were supplying their own needs. After 1870, Germany began to export to the rest of the world. Moving into markets that the British had considered exclusively their own, German salesmen promoted German goods in Australia, South America, China, and in Britain itself. In fields such as the manufacture of organic chemicals and electrical equipment, Germany outsold Britain across the globe.

The extent of Germany's achievement

How can Germany's success and, perhaps more important, Britain's inability to counter it be explained? To attempt an answer to the latter question first: Britain was handicapped because it had been the first nation to industrialize. Because of the capital they had invested in older factories and equipment, the British were reluctant to enter new fields or to exploit new methods. For example, because the British had constructed plants to manufacture alkali by an earlier, less efficient process, they found themselves trapped into continuing to produce in that way after the Solvay process had been discovered. Rather than make the expensive switch, British manufacturers attempted to make their alkali more competitive by cutting costs and improving worker efficiency. But when further refinements were introduced in the 1890s, British output not only failed to keep pace with German and also American increases, but actually decreased. The same difficulties arose with steel. Here again Britain was hampered by the problem of priority. Because the British were the first to industrialize, their manufacturing centers took shape in accordance with the scale of early- and mid–nineteenth-century production. Now there was need for

*Reasons for Britain's lag:
(1) the problem of priority*

Interior of a Krupp Steel Mill, Essen, Germany

large tracts of land, close to transportation, to accommodate steel mills. Because of the cramped layout of Britain's industrial cities, it could not build mills as large as those in Germany or the United States. The result was that by 1900 the largest British steel mills were no bigger than the average-sized mills in Germany. Even new plants built for other manufacturing purposes in Britain were only a third as large as those constructed by its major rival. Because German plants were big, and because, therefore, they represented a large investment of capital, those who managed them did all they could to ensure their efficient operation. They rationalized design and standardized parts to an extent the British, with their smaller plants, continued to believe unnecessary. Smaller firms tended to receive smaller and more specialized orders which did not encourage standardization. Although standardization was accomplished by 1914 in Britain in some industries—notably iron and steel—in many others it remained more the exception than the rule.

(2) attitudes Britain's industrial lead, which froze its urban areas into obsolete patterns and thus prevented growth, froze British attitudes as well. Because they had come so far so fast, the British had grown complacent. Nowhere is this fact more clearly reflected than in the British attitude toward education. If the achievements of the first Industrial Revolution—for example, the steam engine, the spinning jenny—were the result of what might be called creative tinkering, those of the second revolution were the product of a close and fruitful union of pure science with technology. Achievement now depended on a generally literate work-force, a trained body of mechanics, a scientifically grounded body of technicians, and a corps of highly trained, creative scientists. Germany was producing these cadres; Britain was not.

Only in 1870 was a system of public elementary education instituted in Britain, and not until ten years later was it made compulsory. In Germany, compulsory education dated from the eighteenth century. The British governing class believed the primary purpose of education was social control: teaching a boy or girl not only how to read and write, but to accept his or her particular place within the social structure. Though German elementary education was authoritarian in many respects as well, the fact that it had begun earlier and was directly joined to systems of secondary education encouraged the development of abilities; it was in this respect far less wasteful than the British. As Britain lagged in the area of elementary education, it lagged in the development of scientific and technological laboratories and training centers. In Germany, the state established an elaborate network of such technical institutions; in Britain there were almost none before the First World War.

Complacency

Complacency was the major reason for this lack. The British tended to believe, wrongly, that practical experience and on-the-job training would produce the skills necessary to keep abreast of change. In addition, the British upper middle class convinced itself that the goal of education was not the production of creative technologists but of "gentlemen." Fathers who had made their fortunes as entrepreneurs during the first Industrial Revolution sent their sons to private boarding schools and to the ancient universities of Oxford and Cambridge to receive a "gentleman's" education—training in Greek and Latin, primarily. Those sons, whose creative talents might otherwise have been channeled into science and technology, chose careers in politics, or in the imperial or domestic bureaucracies instead. The result was a severe narrowing of the pool of creative technologists and dynamic entrepreneurs. There were fewer men than in either Germany or the United States interested in organizing the increasingly large amounts of capital necessary to engage in industrial expansion. It was easier to invest money overseas than to undertake the revitalization of various enterprises at home. A suspicion of what was new, encouraged by the British tendency to rely upon practical experience of the past, prevented Britain from rising in more than a fitful way to the German challenge.

5. INTERNATIONAL COMPETITION: IMPERIALISM

A global economy

The rivalry between Britain and Germany was only the most intense aspect of international competitiveness during the last decades of the nineteenth century. As nations proceeded with the business of industrialization, their search for markets brought them into direct opposition with one another. One result was that the dogma of free trade was abandoned by all save Britain. As we have seen, the Germans rejected the policy of low tariffs in 1879. Austria and Russia had already done so. Spain instituted new scales of import duties in 1877 and again in 1891. In France, two decades of gradual abandonment were climaxed by the passage of the Méline Tariff in 1892. Although individual nations attempted to isolate themselves from each other in this way, developments in international economics mandated the continuing growth and development of an interlocking, worldwide system of manufacturing, trade, and finance. For example, the general adoption by western Europe and the United States of the gold standard meant that the currencies of the so-called civilized world could be readily exchanged with each other against the measure of a common standard—the international price of gold. Hence countries needing to import from the United States, for example, did not have to sell goods directly to that country. They could sell to South America, exchange the money they received for gold, and then buy from America.

"Invisible" exports

Almost all European countries, dependent on vast supplies of raw materials to sustain their rate of industrial production, imported more than they exported. To avoid the mounting deficits that would otherwise have resulted from this practice, they relied upon "invisible" exports: i.e., shipping, insurance, and interest on money lent or invested. The extent of Britain's exportations in these areas was far greater than that of any other country. London was the money market of the world, to which would-be borrowers looked for assistance before turning elsewhere. By 1914, Britain had $20 billion invested overseas, compared with the $8.7 of the French and the $6 billion of the Germans. The insurance firm of Lloyds of London serviced clients around the world. The British merchant fleet transported the manufactured goods and raw materials of every trading nation. It was the volume of its "invisible" exports that permitted Britain to remain faithful to the doctrine of free trade while other European nations were forced to institute tariffs.

Effects on Africa and Asia

The competition between the principal economic powers of this worldwide marketplace affected not only their relationships with each other but also with those less developed areas upon which they were increasingly dependent for both raw materials and markets. Some of those areas, such as India and China, were the seats of ancient empires. Others, such as central Africa, sheltered less complex tribal soicieties. No matter what the nature of the indigenous civilization, the intrusion upon it of modern science and technology, systematic wage labor, financial and legal institutions caused enormous disruption. Though drawn into the world economy, these areas did not draw from it the benefits that the West did. Native industries such as Indian textile spinning and weaving stood no chance in competition with the factory-made products of Manchester. African herdsmen and hunters endured the disruption of their living habits by the activities of European ranchers and miners. Men who had made their living as boatmen and carters lost their livelihood to the railways constructed by Western nations. New jobs there might be; but they were jobs worked according to a Western style, dictated by Western economic demands, and threatened by Western economic disorders. In great measure the workers of this emerging world were assuming the role of a global unskilled working class under the hegemony of Western capitalism.

With this global background before us it is easier to understand the patterns of late–nineteenth-century imperialism. Imperialism we shall define simply as the domination of one people by another. So defined, imperialism had existed throughout the nineteenth century. The French had penetrated Algeria and the British, India. In other parts of the world, where Western powers did not govern directly, they often exercised an indirect influence so powerful as to preclude "native" defiance. When the West "opened" China beginning in 1834, it left the Chinese in nominal charge of their state. But it insured that affairs would be conducted to its advantage and within its "sphere of influence." Britain added to its "informal" empire in this way in South America, Africa, and south and east Asia.

Imperialism defined

As time passed, and rivalries increased, European powers moved with greater frequency and determination to control both the government and the economy of underdeveloped nations and territories. Although the primary reasons for the new imperialism were political and economic, support for imperial policy was motivated by a variety of sentiments. Some argued that it was Europe's duty to civilize—or to Christianize—the "barbaric" and "heathen" quarters of the globe. To combat slave-trading, famine, filth, and illiteracy seemed to many legitimate reason for invading the heart of Africa and the jungles of Asia. Hundreds of Europeans gave up comfortable middle-class lives to participate in what was without question a selfless mission. Others supported imperialism because the policy allowed them to celebrate their country's power. Men, women, and children took pleasure in pointing to those remote areas on the map colored with their particular hue. It was somehow reassuring to know that the sun never set on the British Empire.

*Reasons for the new
imperialism*

Those in charge of the imperial building process, however, although they welcomed support from whatever quarter and for whatever reason, decided policy in response to a combination of political and economic considerations, and as a corollary to the process of nation-building. National security and the preservation of a general balance of power were issues never far from the forefront of politicians' thinking and planning. Britain's domination of Egypt in the 1880s was the result, in large measure, of its fear of what might occur in the Near East should large portions of the decaying Ottoman Empire fall into Russian hands. Britain had purchased 44 percent of the shares in the Suez Canal Company in 1875, and considered the waterway a strategic lifeline to the east. The canal had been built by the French under the direction of the engineer Ferdinand de Lesseps. Begun in 1859 and completed in 1869, it was expected to assist France in its bid for com-

*The politics of
imperialism*

mercial expansion to the East. Britain obtained its shares from the spendthrift khedive (viceroy) of Egypt at a time when he was threatened with bankruptcy. When, in 1882, nationalist rebels protested continuing British intervention in the internal affairs of Egypt, the British claimed they had no choice but to bombard the port of Alexandria and place the Egyptian ruler under their protection. A continuing British presence in Egypt, and the willingness of the British government to support Egyptian claims to the Upper Nile, worried the French, who were growing to fear Britain's political domination of the entire African continent. Moving to correct what they perceived as a severe political imbalance, the French challenged the British and at Fashoda, in the Sudan, came close to war in 1898. The British called the French bluff, however, and war was averted. The power struggle over the Suez, Egypt, and the Sudan provides an excellent example of the manner in which international politics was directly related to the advancement of imperialism.

*The economics of
imperialism*

Equally important as an explanation for imperialism are the facts of late–nineteenth-century world economics. There are those who have argued that imperialism was the result of the need for industrial Europe to invest surplus capital. This argument makes some sense when applied to Britain, about half of whose total of $20 billion in foreign investments was at work within its empire. But it fails to explain the imperial ambitions of the Germans and the French, who had much less capital to invest, and who invested that which they had in non-imperial enterprises. Only a very small portion of German capital was invested in German colonies by 1914; about one-fifth of French capital was so invested. The French had more capital in Russia, hoping to stabilize that ally against the Germans, than in all their colonial possessions.

A more important economic reason for imperial expansion lay in Europe's continuing need for imports. Demand for raw materials, far

*Dredges and Elevators at Work
on the Construction of the Suez
Canal, 1869*

IMPERIALISM IN AFRICA TO THE EVE OF WORLD WAR II

more than the need to spend surplus capital, made colonies a necessary investment and imperialism, therefore, a worthwhile policy. Certainly Europe, and particularly Britain, continued to need more and more markets for manufactured goods. Yet those areas into which the imperially minded nations penetrated after 1870, though they afforded their colonial masters an opportunity to increase exports to some degree, were generally too poor to answer fully the market needs of Europe's manufacturers. In 1914, despite imperialism, the industrial

The need for imports

countries remained their own best customers. Economics, although an important explanation for the rise of imperialism, is by no means the only one.

Imperial competition centered in Africa. Germans pressed inward from the east; Frenchmen from the west. The Portuguese schemed to connect the ancient colonies of Angola, on the west, with Mozambique, on the east. Most active among the European powers during this initial period of late–nineteenth-century colonization was a privately financed group of Belgians under the leadership of that country's king, Leopold II. In association with H. M. Stanley, an American newspaperman and explorer, Leopold and a group of financiers founded the International Congo Association in 1878, which negotiated treaties with chieftains that opened the Congo River basin to commercial exploitation. A conference, called in Berlin in 1885 and attended by most European nations and the United States, attempted to establish certain ground rules for the game of imperial acquisition. The Congo was declared a Free State, under the trusteeship of Leopold (the first example of this later familiar device of protecting "backward" peoples). A European nation with holdings on the African coast was declared to have first rights to territory in the interior behind those coastal regions. Those rights, however, could be sustained only by what was termed "real" occupation—that is, the presence on the ground of either administrators or troops. The scramble was on! Occupation was accompanied by the exploitation of native labor. Agreements reached with local chieftains, whom the Europeans courted, authorized the employment of men and women as laborers under conditions little better than slavery. Often forced to live in compounds apart from their families, Africans were victimized by a system which rooted out prevailing custom without attempting to establish anything like a new civilization in its place.

The division of the geographical spoils proceeded apace. The Portuguese increased their hold in Angola and Mozambique. The Italians invaded Somaliland and Eritrea. They attempted to extend their controls to Ethiopia, but were repulsed by an army of 80,000 Ethiopians, the first instance of a major victory by native Africans over whites. Germany came relatively late to the game. Bismarck was reluctant to engage in an enterprise which, he believed, would do little to profit the empire either politically or economically. Eventually concluding, however, that they could not afford to let other powers divide the continent between them, the Germans established colonies in German East Africa, in the Cameroons and Togo on the west coast, and in the desertlike and economically valueless territory of South West Africa. The French controlled large areas in West Africa and, in the Red Sea, the port of Obok. It was to further their plan for an east-west link that the French had risked challenging the British at Fashoda. That scheme, however, fell afoul of Britain's need to dominate Egypt, and

"The Rhodes Colossus." The ambitions of Cecil Rhodes, the driving force behind British imperialism in South Africa, is satirized in this cartoon, which appeared in *Punch*.

of its plans for a north-south connection through the African continent.

Cecil Rhodes, the English entrepreneur and imperial visionary, promoted the notion of a Capetown-to-Cairo railway both before and after his assumption of the prime-ministership of the Cape Colony in 1890. His plans were thwarted in the south, however, by the presence of two independent neighboring republics, the Transvaal and the Orange Free State, both inhabited by descendents of the original Dutch settlers in South Africa. These Boers—the Dutch word for "farmers"—had fled from the British in the Cape Colony and established themselves in their agricultural states in defiant opposition to the freebooting and exploitationist spirit of the British economic adventurers who had driven them from the Cape. When diamonds and gold were discovered in the Transvaal in 1886, the tension between the British and the Boers grew. As British prospectors and entrepreneurs moved in, the Boers refused to pass laws permitting the exploitation of their resources by foreign firms. They also taxed the interlopers heavily. Rhodes retaliated by attempting to force a war with the republics. His first try, the dispatching of a force of irregular volunteers under the command of Dr. L. S. Jameson in 1895, failed to

Boer Commandos Under Louis Botha. Botha became the first prime minister of the Union of South Africa following the Boer War.

provoke a conflict, but precipitated general censure on the British for harassing a peaceful neighbor. Rhodes was forced to resign as prime minister of the Cape Colony in 1896. War broke out in 1899. Its course, however, did not run according to British plans. The Boers proved tough fighters. It took three years to secure an armistice; it took further long months and resort to brutal policies such as detention camps and farm-burning to bring the resilient republicans to heel. The major consequence of the Boer War was to reduce Britain's stature in the eyes of its own citizens and in the eyes of the world.

Britain in India

Britain's imperial record in India was more distinguished than it was in Africa. The "informal" rule of the commercially motivated East India Company had proved ineffective in 1857, when native Indian troops and a large number of other disaffected elements within the subcontinent rebelled in what the British chose to call "The Indian Mutiny," but which was in fact a far more serious and deep-seated challenge to foreign control. Henceforth the British determined to rule directly. But at the same time, they decided to rule through the Indian upper classes, and not, as in the past, in opposition to them. Although instruction in British-sponsored schools continued in English, Indian customs were tolerated as they had not been before, and princes and their bureaucracies were incorporated as protectorates into the general scheme of government. A class of westernized, and yet devotedly Indian, civil servants and businessmen thus emerged by the end of the nineteenth century, trained by the British yet burdened by no sense of obligation to their tutors. This group provided the leader-

THE GREAT POWERS AND IMPERIALISM IN ASIA TO SEPT. 1, 1940

Imperialism. Left: Germans traveling in East Africa, 1907. Right: A British officer in India, c. 1900.

ship for the nationalist movement that was to challenge British rule in India in the mid–twentieth century.

Imperialism elsewhere

Elsewhere in the world, Western nations hastened to plant their colors upon those territories that promised rewards, either economic or strategic. Britain, France, Germany, and the Netherlands all staked claims in the East Indies, the Dutch achieving an overall hegemony there by 1900. China allowed itself to be victimized by a series of commercial treaties; among the predators was China's neighbor Japan, the only non-Western nation able to modernize in the nineteenth century. The United States played a double game. It acted as champion of the underdeveloped countries in the Western Hemisphere when they were threatened from Europe. Yet the Americans were willing, whenever it suited them, to prey on their neighbors, either "informally" or formally. When, at the end of the century, Spain's feeble hold on its Caribbean and Pacific colonies encouraged talk of rebellion, the United States stepped in to protect its investments and guarantee its maritime security. It declared and won a war against Spain in 1898 on trumped-up grounds. In the same year, the United States annexed Puerto Rico and the Philippines, and established a "protectorate" over Cuba. When Colombia's colony, Panama, threatened to rebel in 1903, the Americans quickly backed the rebels, recognized Panama as a republic, and then proceeded to grant it protection while Americans built the Panama Canal on land leased from the new government. Intervention in Santo Domingo and in Hawaii proved that the United States was no less an imperial power than the nations of western Europe. Together, by the end of the century, those countries had succeeded in binding the world together as it had never been before. The military and economic power with which they had accomplished that achievement meant that, for the time being at any rate, they would be the world's masters.

- *Items so designated are available in paperback editions.*
- Ashworth, W., *A Short History of the International Economy since 1850,* rev. ed., London, 1975.

  Barkin, Kenneth D., *The Controversy Over German Industrialization, 1890–1902,* Chicago, 1970. The political and social struggles between agricultural and industrial interests. An important monograph.

  Betts, Raymond F., *Europe Overseas: Phases of Imperialism,* New York, 1968.

  Branschwig, H., *French Colonialism, 1871–1914,* New York, 1966.

  Cameron, Rondo E., *France and the Economic Development of Europe, 1800–1914,* Princeton, N.J., 1961. Emphasizes the export of French capital and skill in the economic growth of Europe.

  Clapham, John, *The Bank of England: A History,* Cambridge, 1944. The best history of this important institution.

  Cooke, James J., *The New French Imperialism, 1880–1910; The Third Republic and Colonial Expansion,* Hamden, Conn., 1973.

- Fieldhouse, D. K., *The Colonial Empires,* London, 1966. A general survey from the eighteenth to the twentieth centuries.

- Gollwitzer, Heinz, *Europe in the Age of Imperialism, 1880–1914,* London, 1969.

  Henderson, W. O., *Studies in German Colonial History,* Chicago, 1962.

- Hobsbawm, Eric, *Industry and Empire: The Making of Modern English Society, 1750 to the Present Day,* New York, 1968.

- Hodgart, Alan, *The Economics of European Imperialism,* New York, 1978.

- Kindleberger, C. P., *Economic Growth in France and Britain, 1851–1950,* Cambridge, Mass., 1963. A technical account.

- Landes, David S., *The Unbound Prometheus,* London, 1969. Particularly good on the Anglo-German rivalry.

  Langer, William L., *The Diplomacy of Imperialism, 1890–1902,* New York, 1960.

  Louis, William Roger, ed., *Imperialism: The Robinson and Gallagher Controversy,* New York, 1976. The best introduction to recent debate over the nature and causes of imperialism.

  May, E. R., *American Imperialism,* New York, 1968.

  Milward, Alan S., and S. B. Saul, *The Development of the Economies of Continental Europe, 1850–1914,* Cambridge, Mass., 1977. An excellent, comprehensive text, particularly good on the smaller European nations.

  Platt, D. C. M., *Finance, Trade, and Politics in British Foreign Policy, 1815–1914,* Oxford, 1968.

  Price, Roger, *The Economic Modernization of France,* New York, 1975. Rejects conventional periodizations; stresses the advent of railroads which transformed the market structure of France.

  Robinson, Ronald, and J. Gallagher, *Africa and the Victorians: The Official Mind of Imperialism,* London, 1961. Contains their famous thesis that imperialism was not deliberately pursued as a policy of state, but rather was a response to events in colonial areas. The modern debate over imperialism begins with this work.

- Shannon, Richard, *The Crisis of Imperialism, 1865–1915,* St. Albans, Eng., 1976. An excellent survey of the transformation of British society in the wake of modern industrialization.

Stolper, Gustav, et al., *The German Economy, 1870 to the Present,* New York, 1967. A good introduction.

Thornton, A. P., *Doctrines of Imperialism,* New York, 1965.

SOURCE MATERIALS

Court, W. H. B., *British Economic History, 1870–1914: Commentary and Documents,* Cambridge, 1965. An excellent collection of documents.

Lenin, Vladimir, *Imperialism: The Highest Stage of Capitalism,* 1916. (Many English editions.) Lenin's most significant contribution to Marxist ideology. He saw the essence of imperialism as the export of capital rather than goods which led to worldwide competition, of which World War I was an inevitable result.

• ———, *The Lenin Anthology,* ed. by R. C. Tucker, New York, 1975.

Reitz, Deneys, *Commando: A Boer Journal of the Boer War,* London, 1929. A superb memoir of the Boer War.

Chapter 30

THE MIDDLE CLASS CHALLENGED

The time of surprise attacks, of revolutions carried through by small conscious minorities at the head of unconscious masses, is past. Where it is a question of a complete transformation of the social organization, the masses themselves must also be in it, must themselves already have grasped what is at stake, what they are going in for, with body and soul.

—Friedrich Engels, *The Class Struggles in France, 1848–50*

Capitalism's continuing expansion encouraged middle-class men and women at the end of the nineteenth century to believe themselves the necessary key to the progress of the human race. At the same time, however, that belief was being challenged from several directions. In each case, the challenges called into question assumptions close to the core of middle-class consciousness. Socialist doctrine, which was for the first time receiving a widespread hearing, pronounced capitalism a threat, rather than a boon, to society. New scientific theories—particularly the theory of evolution—declared that the key to progress was not the well-laid schemes of humanity, but chance. Psychologists discovered the irrationality of human beings and philosophers their ultimate helplessness. Paintings, poetry, and music proclaimed an artists' revolution on behalf of the idea of art for its own sake, not for the edification of a middle-class public. Together, these various intellectual and cultural currents threatened the notion that society would most successfully advance under middle-class auspices, setting its course in accordance with middle-class moral and economic precepts, and placing its faith in a belief in the importance and inevitability of continued material progress.

The dimensions of the challenge

I. THE CHALLENGE OF SOCIALISM

Marx in England

The history of socialism in the latter half of nineteenth century is, to a great degree, the biography of its most famous propagandist and theoretician, Karl Marx (1818–1883). Marx was both a social thinker and a political leader. At certain times theory dictated his actions; at others, political events led him to alter doctrine. But always he was at the center of the socialist movement, his moral passion, as much as his scholarly research, shaping the course of its events. The fact of his continuing influence is particularly remarkable for two reasons. First, although a German, he lived from 1849 until his death in London, an exile from the mainstream of continental socialism, in a country whose toleration of socialists was a mark of its comparative immunity from their doctrines. Second, Marx was not a leader who readily took others into his confidence. His antisocial nature was due, in part, to the poverty in which he was forced to live. He and his family were kept alive by gifts of money from his faithful friend and collaborator, Friedrich Engels, who had gone to work for his father's Manchester textile firm, and by occasional stints as a political journalist—for a time Marx was a correspondent for the *New York Tribune*.

Capital

During the 1850s and 1860s Marx labored to produce his definitive analysis of capitalist economics, *Capital,* the first volume of which was published in 1867. In it Marx elaborated upon the theories first enunciated in his earlier economic tracts. He described in detail the processes of production, exchange, and distribution as they operated within the capitalist system. He argued that under capitalism, workers were denied their rightful share of profits. The value of any manufactured item, Marx claimed, was determined by the amount of labor necessary to produce it. Yet workers were hired at wages whose value was far less than the value of the goods they produced. The difference between the value of workers' wages and the value of their work as sold was pocketed by members of the capitalist class, who, according to Marx, made off with far more than a justifiable portion of the sale price. This so-called labor theory of value, borrowed from a somewhat similar doctrine held by Ricardo and other classical economists, was the basis for Marx's claim that the working class was compelled to suffer under the capitalist system. Because workers were forced to sell their labor they became nothing more than commodities in the economic market.

So long as capitalists refused to pay wages more nearly equal to the labor value of their employees' work, those employees would remain exploited. Marx preached that the only class which, under capitalism, produced more wealth than it enjoyed was the working class, the proletariat. The bourgeoisie, which owned the means of production and was therefore able to appropriate that which was rightfully the work-

Karl Marx

ers', had a vested interest in maintaining the status quo; hence its willingness to make use of political, social, religious, and legal institutions to keep the proletariat in its place.

Marx predicted that capitalism would eventually do itself in. He argued that as time passed, market competition would compel the formation of ever-larger industrial and financial combinations. As the smaller enterpreneurial class—the petty bourgeoisie—was squeezed out by more powerful combines, its members would join with the proletariat, until society resembled a vast pyramid, with a much-enlarged proletariat at its base and an opposing force of a few powerful capitalists at its tip. At this point, Marx declared, the proletariat would rise in revolution against what was left of the bourgeoisie.

Marx as prophet

After capitalism had received its death blow at the hands of the workers, it would be followed by a stage of socialism. This would have three characteristics: the dictatorship of the proletariat; payment in accordance with work performed; and ownership and operation by the state of all means of production, distribution, and exchange. But socialism was intended to be merely a transition to something higher. In time it would be succeeded by communism, the goal of historical evolution. Communism would mean, first of all, the classless society. No one would live by owning, but solely by working. The state would now disappear, relegated to the museum of antiquities, "along with the bronze ax and the spinning wheel." Nothing would replace it except voluntary associations to operate the means of production and provide for social necessities. The *essence* of communism was payment in accordance with needs. The wage system would be completely abolished, and citizens would be expected to work in accordance with their faculties, entitled to receive from the total fund of wealth produced an amount in proportion to their needs.

The advent of communism

In the ten years after its publication, *Capital* was translated into English (Marx had written it in German), French, Russian, and Italian. It became the theoretical rallying point for a growing band of socialists who stood opposed to the world the middle class had made. For a time it breathed life into an organization of continental and British workers that had been founded in London in 1864: the International Workingmen's Association, usually referred to as the International. This body had been formed with the declared purpose of forging an international working-class alliance to overthrow capitalism and abolish private property. Marx delivered its inaugural address, in which he preached that workers must win political power for themselves if they were ever to escape their industrial bondage. Various difficulties had prevented the formation of a radically oriented workers' organization prior to this time. There was, first of all, fear of official reprisal. Second, the irregular pace of industrialization across Europe meant that workers in one country could have little understanding of the particular plight of their fellow-workers elsewhere. Finally, the period after

The First International

1850 had witnessed an increase in general prosperity which encouraged the more highly skilled—and more politically conscious—workers to forsake revolutionary goals and to pursue the more immediate end of accommodation with middle-class politicians. The German socialists' dealings with Bismarck (see below, p. 789), were a case in point. Meanwhile, however, the determination of a small band of dedicated radical socialists temporarily surmounted the problems to permit the formation of the first international workers' association.

Lassalle and Bakunin

Marx immediately assumed the direction of the International. He labored to exclude moderates from its councils and denounced the German socialists, and their leader Ferdinand Lassalle (1825–1864), for striking bargains with Bismarck. The duty of socialists, Marx argued, was not partnership with the state, but rather its overthrow. At the same time Marx battled the doctrines of the Russian anarchist Michael Bakunin (1814–1876), who opposed the socialist notion that social evil was the product of capitalism. Bakunin argued that the state was the ultimate villain, and preached its immediate destruction through isolated acts of terrorism. He also opposed centralization within the International, urging instead a kind of federal autonomy for each national workers' group. To Marx, these individualist notions represented nothing more than reversion to a kind of primitive rebellion, heroic but ultimately fruitless. He succeeded in having Bakunin banished from the International in 1872. The International prospered for a time during the 1860s. Individual trade unions in various countries were persuaded to join in this united campaign which preached revolution and, through the application of pressure both at the ballot box and in the factory, seemed to promise at least higher wages and shorter hours. Under Marx's direction the International was a highly organized and tightly controlled body, far more effective in this respect than any previous socialist organization.

The troubled International

Yet by 1876 it had faded from existence. Despite Marx's abilities as an authoritarian chief of staff, the International throughout its existence had to battle those same circumstances which delayed its foundation. In addition, Marx's insistence upon control from the center thwarted a growing desire on the part of individual socialist organizations to pursue programs of immediate benefit to themselves. These factors weakened the International. What probably brought about its demise was its association with events occurring in Paris after the defeat of France by Germany in 1870 in the Franco-Prussian War.

The Paris Commune

Following the collapse of Napoleon III, a new republic, generally conservative in tone, had been established by the French. In March 1871, the government attempted to disarm the Paris National Guard, a volunteer citizen army with radical political sympathies. The guard refused to surrender, declared its autonomy, deposed officials of the new government, and proclaimed a revolutionary committee—the Commune—as the true government of France. Though this move-

The Aftermath of the Paris Commune. A view of Champs Élysées showing damage resulting from the 1871 uprising. The Arc de Triomphe may be seen in the distance.

ment is commonly described as a rebellion of dangerous radicals intent upon the destruction of law and order, most of its members resembled the Jacobins of the first French Revolution and belonged largely to the lower middle class. They did not advocate the abolition of private property but rather its wider distribution. The movement was precipitated by bitterness over the defeat of Napoleon III and exhaustion by the long siege of Paris that followed. Added to these factors were fears that the central government would be dominated by the rural population to the disadvantage of the urban masses in the capital. After several weeks of frustrating disputation, the conflict turned into a bloody civil war. The Communards killed about sixty hostages, including the archbishop of Paris. The government numbered its victims by the thousands. The courts-martial which were set up executed twenty-six. Thousands of others were sentenced to imprisonment or banishment in New Caledonia, in the South Pacific.

While middle-class Europe reacted in horror at what it perceived as a second Reign of Terror, Marx, in the name of the International, extolled the courage of the Communards, who, he wrote, had fought the first pitched battle in the class war he had predicted. In a pamphlet entitled *The Civil War in France* (1871), Marx claimed that the Commune was an example of the transitional form of government through which the working class would have to pass on its way to emancipation. But many of the less radical members of the International were frightened and disturbed not only by the events of the Commune itself, but by the possibility of reprisals against members of an organization that openly praised men and women who were considered by the middle class to be little more than murderers. In 1872 Marx acknowl-

The Commune and the International

The Assassination of Hostages by the Communards in Paris, 1871

edged defeat by moving the seat of the International's council to the United States, a country far removed from the organization's affairs and from the criticisms that had begun to be heaped upon Marx for his misdirection. In 1876, the First International expired.

The spread of socialism

Although the International collapsed, socialism continued to gain ground as both a theory and a program. The German Social Democratic party was founded in 1875; a Belgian Socialist party in 1879; and in France, despite the disasters of the Commune, a Socialist party was established in 1905. In England, although socialism was much debated and discussed, no party proclaiming itself socialist emerged. When the Labour party came into being in 1901, however, various socialist societies were represented on its executive council, along with less radical, nonsocialist trade union groups. On the periphery of Europe—in Spain, Italy, and Russia—socialism made less headway. There the absence of widespread industrialization and the educational backwardness of large elements within the population retarded the development of a working-class consciousness, and of socialism as its political expression.

"Purists" vs. "revisionists"

During the years before the First World War, socialists continously and often bitterly debated the course they should follow as they attempted to achieve their goal of radical change. One group, led by Marx himself until his death, urged socialists to avoid collaboration with other parties to achieve such immediate ends as higher wages, shorter working hours, unemployment insurance, etc. These reforms, the "purists" declared, were the means by which the bourgeoisie could buy off the proletariat and hence indefinitely postpone revolution. On the other hand, "revisionist" socialists urged their followers to take advantage of the fact that many of them now could vote for socialist candidates in elections. They argued that those candidates, if elected, could help them obtain a better life in the immediate future. Socialist theory might proclaim a worldwide struggle of the proletariat against the bourgeoisie; but was this any reason to turn one's back on a chance to make real headway through the ballot box in achieving reforms that would put a better life within reach of workers and their families?

Revisionism spread despite efforts of the "purists" to put a stop to it. In Germany the pattern had been established by Lassalle, whose opportunism had led him to bargain with Bismarck. Following his death, his place as theorist was taken by Eduard Bernstein, a Social Democrat and member of the German parliament, the Reichstag. Bernstein argued that capitalism could be gradually transformed to benefit the working class, and that revolution might not be necessary to achieve this end. Bernstein's most outspoken opponent in Germany was his fellow socialist Karl Kautsky, an orthodox Marxist who warned that collaboration would end in the total corruption and demoralization of the proletariat. In France, the same battle was waged by the "purist" Jules Guesde, who preached that the Socialist party's primary goal should be the development of proletarian class consciousness, and Jean Jaurès, socialist leader in the Chamber of Deputies, who advocated a revisionist course. In both Germany and France, revisionists outnumbered purists by a wide margin. This was, to an even greater degree, the case in Britain. There, Fabian socialists—so named from their policy of delay, in imitation of the tactics of Fabius, a Roman general—preached what they called "the inevitability of gradualism." They believed their country would evolve towards socialism by means of parliamentary democracy. Prominent among the Fabians were the social investigators Sidney and Beatrice Webb, the novelist H. G. Wells, and the playwright George Bernard Shaw.

Revisionist gains

The continued success of revisionism led its opponents to sharpen their attack and to advocate increasingly violent means to achieve their ends. Their campaigns, though they never managed to convince a majority of the working class, nevertheless attracted an increasing number of adherents. Some who had originally supported the revisionists grew disappointed when reforms did not come as quickly as expected. At the same time, in much of Europe, the cost of living began to rise for many workers. The comparative prosperity that some members of the working class had experienced vanished in the face of price rises that were not matched by wage increases. The result was a frustration which encouraged the adoption of a more militant stance. Germans rallied to the side of the radical socialists Rosa Luxemburg and Karl Liebknecht, while in France a new revolutionary socialist party disowned the reformist leader Alexandre Millerand, after he agreed to serve as cabinet member in a nonsocialist government.

Jean Jaurès

*Anarchism and
syndicalism*

The Second International, which had been founded in 1889, demanded at a conference in 1906 that affiliated parties declare their goal to be the destruction of the bourgeois order and the state which served its interests.

This militant mood encouraged acceptance of the doctrines of anarchists and syndicalists. Anarchists preached the overthrow of capitalism by violence. They differed from socialists, however, in their hatred of the machinery of the state or any government based upon coercion. Socialists argued that until the communist millennium promised by Marx, the state would remain a necessary means to the achievement of that eventual end. Anarchists worked to see the immediate abolition of a state bureaucracy which, no matter who controlled it, they believed would result in tyranny. Bakunin, whom Marx had succeeded in expelling from the First International, was anarchism's most popular propagandist. Syndicalism, like anarchism, demanded the abolition of both capitalism and the state. It resembled socialism in its demand that workers share in the ownership of the means of production. Instead of making the state the owner and operator of the means of production, however, the syndicalist would delegate these functions to syndicates of producers. Thus all the steel mills would be owned and operated by the workers in the steel industry, the coal mines by the workers in the coal industry, and so on. These associations would take the place of the state, each one governing its own members in all of their activities as producers. In all other matters workers would be free from interference.

Sorel

Syndicalism received its most sympathetic hearing in France, where a General Confederation of Labour, after 1902, resolved to seek solutions to economic problems outside the legally constituted framework of French politics. The most effective spokesman for syndicalism was the Frenchman Georges Sorel (1847–1922). Sorel, in his *Reflections on Violence,* published in 1908, argued that workers should be made to believe in the possibility of a general strike by the proletariat which would result in the end of bourgeois civilization. The general strike might be nothing more than myth, Sorel acknowledged. Yet, as myth, it remained a powerful weapon in the hands of those whose goal was the destruction of society and who must not shy from the employment of violent means to achieve that end.

Socialism before the First World War, then, was not a unified force. It was divided by quarrels between purists and revisionists, and challenged by the even more radical proposals of anarchists and syndicalists. Socialists, intent on their goal of international solidarity among working classes, ignored the appeal that nationalism and imperialism might make to workers in France, Germany, and Britain. Yet despite its divisions and weaknesses, socialism appeared to the middle classes of Europe as a real threat to their continued prosperity. Capitalism had provided the machinery by which the bourgeoisie had

Georges Sorel

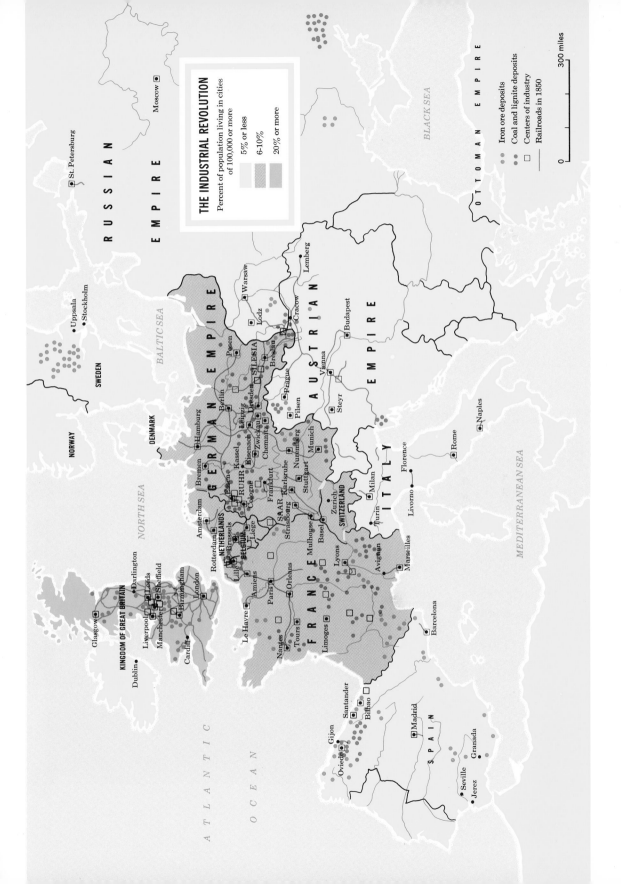

THE INDUSTRIAL REVOLUTION
Percent of population living in cities
of 100,000 or more

5% or less
6-10%
20% or more

● Iron ore deposits
● Coal and lignite deposits
□ Centers of industry
— Railroads in 1850

300 miles

0

RUSSIAN EMPIRE

• Moscow

• St. Petersburg

BLACK SEA

OTTOMAN EMPIRE

• Uppsala
• Stockholm

SWEDEN

NORWAY

DENMARK

BALTIC SEA

• Warsaw

• Lodz

GERMAN EMPIRE

• Posen

SILESIA
• Breslau

• Cracow

• Lemberg

• Budapest

AUSTRIAN EMPIRE

• Berlin

□ Leipzig
□ Dresden
• Zwickau
• Chemnitz

• Prague

• Pilsen

Vienna

• Steyr

• Hamburg

• Bremen

Hannover

RUHR
• Kassel
Eisenach

• Cologne

Frankfurt

Nuremberg

Munich

• Zurich

SWITZERLAND

• Milan

• Turin

ITALY

• Florence

• Livorno

• Rome

• Naples

MEDITERRANEAN SEA

• Amsterdam

Rotterdam

NETHERLANDS

BELGIUM
• Brussels
• Liège

Lille

SAAR
Strasbourg
Karlsruhe
Stuttgart
Basel

Mulhouse

• Lyons

• Avignon

• Marseilles

FRANCE

Amiens

• Paris

• Orleans

Tours

Limoges

• Nantes

Le Havre

NORTH SEA

KINGDOM OF GREAT BRITAIN

• Glasgow

• Dublin

• Darlington

• Leeds
□ Sheffield

□ Liverpool
□ Manchester

□ Birmingham

• London

Cardiff

ATLANTIC

OCEAN

• Barcelona

• Santander

• Bilbao

• Madrid

• Gijon

Oviedo

SPAIN

• Seville

• Jerez

• Granada

The Massacre of Chios, Eugène Delacroix (1798–1863). During the Greek war for independence, Turks slaughtered more than 20,000 Greeks in 1822, depicted in this famous painting. (Louvre)

Liberty Leading the People, Eugène Delacroix (1798–1863). Delacroix was a colorful painter of dramatic and emotional themes, as exemplified by this imaginary scene from the Revolution of 1830. (Louvre)

The Last of England, Ford Madox Brown (1821–1893). A haunting scene of a couple emigrating from England by one of the most noted pre-Raphaelites. (The City Museum and Art Gallery, Birmingham, England)

Valley of Aosta—Snowstorm, Avalanche, and Thunderstorm, Joseph M. W. Turner (1775–1851). Turner's complete absorption in light, color, and atmosphere helped to prepare the way for the French impressionists. (MMA)

Portrait of a Gentleman, Jean Auguste Ingres (1780–1867). A student of David, Ingres was a devoted admirer of classical antiquities. But he was also influenced by romanticism. (MMA)

A Woman Reading, Camille Corot (1796–1875). Corot was predominantly a naturalist, a painter of lifelike scenes of innocence and simplicity. He shared the romanticists' sentimental worship of woods and fields. (MMA)

The Port of La Rochelle, Corot. (Louvre)

Beatrice and Dante, William Blake (1757–1827). This painting is from Blake's series for *The Divine Comedy*. (The Tate Gallery, London)

The Gleaners, Jean François Millet (1814–1875). Sensuous colors and love of natural settings typifies Millet's work. (Louvre)

Above: *The Guitarist*, Édouard Manet (1832–1883). Right: *Émile Zola*, Manet. Though Manet is called the "father of impressionism," he was also a rebel against the traditions of sweetness and artificiality that dominated the XIX cent. He liberated painting, as his friend Zola emancipated literature. (MMA) (Louvre)

Village Girls, Gustave Courbet (1819–1877). One of the first of the realists, Courbet often portrayed life in a bitter and disparaging light. He eschewed imagination and painted only what he saw. (MMA)

The Third-Class Carriage, Honoré Daumier (1808–1879). Though Daumier was noted for his realistic caricatures and satires, his attitude toward common folk was one of sympathy and understanding. (MMA)

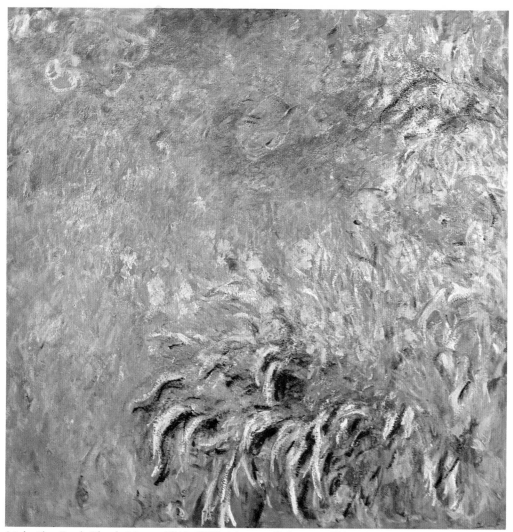

Iris beside a Pond, Claude Monet (1840–1926). Monet called some of his paintings Impressions, and the name soon came to designate a school. (Art Institute of Chicago)

Pink and Green, Edgar Degas (1834–1917). Degas was an impressionist to the extent of his interest in fleeting motion. But as an admirer of the classicist Ingres, he emphasized line and careful composition. (MMA)

Still Life, Cézanne. It has been said that when the impressionists painted a haystack, there was light, but there was no haystack. When Cézanne painted an apple, there was the play of light; there was also the apple. (MMA)

Montagne Sainte-Victoire with Aqueduct, Paul Cézanne (1839–1906). This landscape has been a source of inspiration for many of the tendencies of so-called "modern" art. The composition is as structurally balanced and proportioned as a Greek temple. (MMA)

The Card Players, Cézanne. Here are exemplified Cézanne's skill in composition, his discriminating sense of color, and the sculptured qualities of solidity and depth he gave to his figures. (Stephen C. Clark)

The Japanese Divan, Henri de Toulouse-Lautrec (1864–1901). Toulouse-Lautrec found his chief source of inspiration in the night life of Paris. *Divan Japonais* was a noted Paris café. (MMA)

Portrait of the Artist, Vincent van Gogh (1853–1890). This self-portrait shows a deep seriousness and intense concentration. (V. W. van Gogh)

Ia Orana Maria, Paul Gauguin (1848–1903). Gauguin revolted not only against the complexity and artificiality of European life, but against civilization itself. He finally fled to Tahiti to paint the lush, colorful life of an uncorrupted society. (MMA)

The Starry Night, van Gogh. This painting gives vivid expression to van Gogh's bold conceptions. (Museum of Modern Art)

Sunflowers in a Vase, van Gogh. The feverish technique seems to have endowed the flowers with rhythmic motion. (V. W. van Gogh)

Balzac, Auguste Rodin (1840–1917). Rodin was the great realist of XIX-cent. sculpture. He concentrated most of his attention upon facial detail, no matter how unflattering the result might be. (MMA)

A Young Woman in the Sun, Auguste Renoir (1841–1919). Though Renoir used impressionist techniques, the results sometimes bore little resemblance to the work of other impressionists. He believed that "a picture ought to be a lovable thing, joyous and pretty." (Jeu de Paume)

Luncheon of the Boating Party, Renoir. (Phillips Memorial Gallery)

Portrait of Gertrude Stein, Pablo Picasso (1881–1973). Picasso seems to have given this portrait of the great experimenter in poetry some elements of the distortion of form characteristic of the work of both. (Museum of Modern Art)

The Piano Lesson, Henri Matisse (1869–1954). Matisse conveyed a freshness of approach and a vitality of line and color. (Museum of Modern Art)

Three Musicians, Pablo Picasso. This painting, regarded by many as the masterpiece of cubism, sums up the final stage of the movement. (Museum of Modern Art)

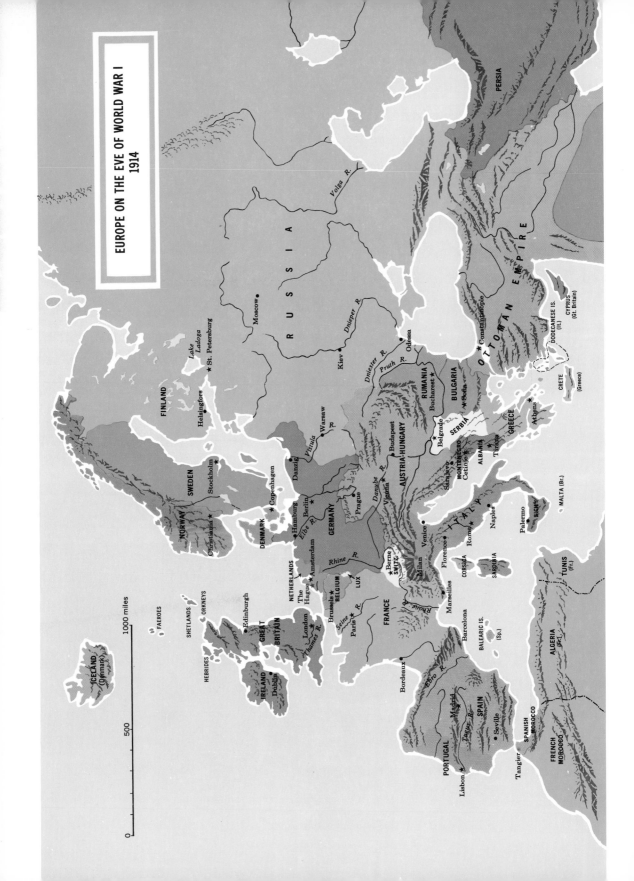

EUROPE ON THE EVE OF WORLD WAR I
1914

Darwin

ria and other microscopic organisms originated from water or from other decaying vegetable and animal matter. By locating the source of bacteria, Pasteur's discovery opened the way for major improvements in the areas of public sanitation and health, among others, the process of ridding food of objectionable bacteria by sterilization—pasteurization—that was named for him. Pasteur, along with the German Robert Koch (1843–1910), also proved conclusively that germs were not, as was commonly supposed, the result but rather the cause of disease. The discovery of the X-ray by the German Wilhelm von Röntgen in 1895 and of radium by the Polish scientist Marie Curie in 1898 not only altered perceptions as to the nature of energy, but suggested ways in which energy could be put to use for medical purposes. These discoveries—along with similarly important ones in the areas of cell theory, anesthetics, and antiseptics—worked to convince the educated public that science was a friend of humanity, and that it was also predictable, operating in accordance with laws which had only to be discovered in order to be put to use. Isaac Newton's law of gravitation continued to reign supreme, arguing that the universe was orderly, and essentially timeless, and that the passage of time brought with it no fundamental change.

Against this psychologically reassuring fortress of a harmonious universe, biological scientists hurled the bomb of evolutionary theory. We have seen that this theory was at least as old as Anaximander in the sixth century B.C., and that it was accepted by many of the great minds of antiquity. We have learned also that it was revived in the eighteenth century by the scientists Buffon and Linnaeus. But neither of these men offered much proof or explained how the process of evolution works. The first to develop a systematic hypothesis of evolution was the French biologist, Jean Lamarck (1744–1829). The essential principle in Lamarck's hypothesis, published in 1809, was the inheritance of acquired characteristics. He maintained that an animal, subjected to a change in environment, acquired new habits, which in turn were reflected in structural changes. These acquired characteristics of body structure, he believed, were transmissible to the offspring, with the result that after a series of generations a new species of animal was eventually produced. Lamarck's successors found little evidence to confirm this hypothesis, but it dominated biological thought for nearly fifty years.

A much more convincing hypothesis of organic evolution was that of the English naturalist Charles Darwin (1809–1882), published in 1859. The son of a small-town physician, Darwin began the study of medicine at the University of Edinburgh, but soon withdrew and entered Cambridge to prepare for the ministry. Here he gave most of his time to natural history. In 1831 Darwin obtained an appointment as naturalist without pay on H.M.S. *Beagle,* which had been chartered for a scientific expedition around the world. The voyage lasted nearly five years and gave Darwin an unparalleled opportunity to become

The Haymarket Riots, Chicago, 1886. A comtemporary illustration depicting the results of attempts to unionize workers at the McCormick Harvester works.

achieved power. Socialism attacked capitalism and hence those who were its direct beneficiaries. Although most socialists disapproved of violence, violent acts were attributed by middle-class men and women to an amorphous, anticapitalist body easily labeled "socialist." Riots by trade unionists in Chicago's Haymarket Square in 1886 and in London's Trafalgar Square in 1887; the assassinations of President Sadi Carnot of France in 1894, of King Humbert of Italy in 1900, and of President William McKinley of the United States in 1901; strikes which grew in number and violence throughout Europe and America after 1900—all these events were perceived by members of the middle class as part of a larger movement whose professed goal was to tear from them their economic, political, and social security.

Sociali
the mid

2. THE CHALLENGE OF SCIENCE AND PHILOSOPHY

While socialism challenged middle-class self-confidence from one quarter, science and philosophy threatened from another. The fact that science might undermine, rather than sustain, certainty was all the more difficult to comprehend, given the manner in which science and technology had together assisted in the birth and continued development of industrialization. This is not to say that science abandoned its role as an instrument for the solving of human problems and as a vital aid to continuing progress. There were striking improvements in the field of medicine, for example. The Frenchman Louis Pasteur (1822–1895) proved that all forms of life, no matter how small, are reproduced only by living beings. Hitherto, according to the theory of spontaneous generation, it had commonly been supposed that bacte-

Science an

acquainted at first hand with the manifold variations of animal life. He noted the differences between animals inhabiting islands and related species on nearby continents, and observed the resemblances between living animals and the fossilized remains of extinct species in the same locality. It was a magnificent preparation for his life's work. Upon returning from the voyage he read Malthus's essay on population, and was struck by the author's contention that throughout the world of nature many more individuals are born than can ever survive, and that consequently the weaker ones must perish in the struggle for food. Finally, after twenty more years of careful and extensive research, he issued his *Origin of Species* (1859).

Darwin's hypothesis was that of natural selection. He argued that it is nature, or the environment, which selects those variants among offspring that are to survive and reproduce. Darwin pointed out, first of all, that the parents of every species beget more offspring than can possibly survive. He maintained that, consequently, a struggle takes place among these offspring for food, shelter, warmth, and other conditions necessary for life. In this struggle for existence certain individuals have the advantage because of the factor of *variation,* which means that no two of the offspring are exactly alike. Some are born strong, others weak; some have longer horns or sharper claws than their brothers and sisters or perhaps a body coloration which enables them better to blend with their surroundings and thus to evade their enemies. It is these favored members of the species that win out in the struggle for existence and survive as the "fittest" of their generation; the others are eliminated generally before they have lived long enough to reproduce. Darwin regarded variation and natural selection as the primary factors in the origin of new species. In other words, he taught that individuals with favorable characteristics would transmit their inherited qualities to their descendants through countless generations, and that successive eliminations of the least fit would eventually produce a new species. Darwin applied his concept of evolution not only to plant and animal species but also to humans. In his second great work, *The Descent of Man* (1871), he attempted to show that the human race originally sprang from some apelike ancestor, long since extinct, but probably a common forebear of the existing anthropoid apes and humans.

The Darwinian hypothesis was elaborated and improved by several later biologists. The German August Weismann (1834–1914) flatly rejected the idea that acquired characteristics could be inherited. He conducted experiments to show that body cells and reproductive cells are entirely distinct, and that there is no way in which changes in the former can effect the latter. He concluded, therefore, that the only qualities transmissible to the offspring are those which have always been present in the reproductive cells of the parents. In 1901 the Dutch botanist Hugo De Vries (1848–1935) published his celebrated mutation hypothesis, based upon Darwin's original hypothesis and, in

Charles Darwin

Illustrations from Darwin's First Edition of *The Descent of Man.* The drawings were used to point up the similarities between a human embryo *(top)* and that of a dog *(bottom).*

large part, upon laws of heredity discovered by the Austrian monk Gregor Mendel (1822–1884). De Vries asserted that evolution results not from minor variations, as Darwin had assumed, but from radical differences or mutations, which appear in more or less definite ratio among the offspring. When any of these mutations are favorable to survival in a given environment, the individuals possessing them naturally emerge triumphant in the struggle for existence. Not only do their descendants inherit these qualities, but from time to time new mutants appear, some of which are even better adapted for survival than their parents. Thus in a limited number of generations a new species may be brought into existence. The mutation theory of De Vries corrected one of the chief weaknesses in the Darwinian hypothesis. The variations which Darwin assumed to be the source of evolutionary changes are so small that an incredibly long time would be necessary to produce a new species. De Vries made it possible to conceive of evolution as proceeding by sudden leaps.

Evolution and chance

Clearly, the implications of this new theory were deeply disturbing for those who had until now believed in an orderly universe, or had taken as literal the words of the Bible. For the latter the task of reconciling Darwin's account of creation with the first chapter of Genesis, though troublesome, was often not insuperable. Outside fundamentalist sects, the Bible was, at this time, perceived by growing numbers as containing a combination of myths, legends, history, and profoundly important moral truths. The work of the German theologian David Friedrich Strauss (1808–1874) and of the French historian Ernest Renan (1832–1892) had cast doubt on the historical accuracy of the Bible, and dealt with its inconsistencies. These writers had defended the intentions of the Bible's various authors, while firmly insisting upon their human fallibilities. Their searching yet nevertheless sensitive critiques helped people understand that they need not abandon their Christian faith simply because Darwin insisted that the world and all that lived within it had been created over millions of years and not in six days. Far more difficult to deal with was the notion, explicit in Darwin, that nature was not a changeless harmony, but instead a constant and apparently undirected struggle. Chance, and not order, ruled the universe. Nothing was fixed, nothing perfect, all was in a state of flux. Good and bad were defined only in terms of an ability to survive. The "best" of a species were those that triumphed over their weaker rivals. All of a sudden, the universe had become a harsh and uncompromising place, deprived of pre-Darwinian certainties; belief in a benevolent God was now much harder to sustain.

Thomas Henry Huxley

Darwin's most vigorous defender, the philosopher Thomas Henry Huxley (1825–1895), was one of those who could no longer reconcile science with a belief in God. While he did not reject the possibility of a supernatural power, Huxley averred that "there is no evidence of the existence of such a being as the God of the theologians." He pronounced Christianity to be "a compound of some of the best and some of the worst elements of Paganism and Judaism, moulded in practice by the innate character of certain people of the Western World."[1] Huxley coined the word *agnosticism* to express his contempt for the attitude of dogmatic certainty symbolized by the beliefs of the ancient Gnostics.[2] As propounded by Huxley, agnosticism is the doctrine that neither the existence nor the nature of God nor the ultimate character of the universe is knowable.

Huxley

The most uncompromising of the evolutionist philosophers was Ernst Heinrich Haeckel (1834–1919). Originally a physician, later a professor of biology, Haeckel was the first outstanding scientist on the Continent to subscribe wholeheartedly to Darwinism. At the age of sixty-five he summarized his conclusions in a book entitled *The Riddle of the Universe*. The philosophy of Haeckel comprised three main doctrines: atheism, materialism, and mechanism. He would have nothing to do with Huxley's agnosticism; on the contrary, he dogmatically affirmed that nothing spiritual exists. The universe, he maintained, was composed of matter alone, in a process of constant change from one form into another. Life, Haeckel stated, originated from the spontaneous combination of the essential elements of protoplasm. From these earliest forms of protoplasm all the complex species of the present gradually evolved through the process of natural selection. Haeckel regarded the mind of humans as just as much a product of evolution as the body. The human mind differs only in degree from the minds of the lower animals. Memory, imagination, perception, and thinking are mere functions of matter; psychology should be considered a branch of physiology. Such was the compact philosophy of materialism and determinism which appeared to Haeckel and his followers to be a logical deduction from the new biology.

Haeckel

The middle classes of western Europe and the United States, disoriented by the antireligious implications of evolutionary theory, received some comfort from the writings of those who adapted Darwinian thought to the analysis of society—the so-called Social Darwinists. These thinkers argued that the apparent "success" of Western civilization was the result of its special fitness. The white race, they boasted, had proved itself superior to the black; non-Jews superior to Jews; rich superior to poor; the British Empire superior to the subject territories it controlled. If nature was a matter of competition, so was society, with the victory going to that race or nation which could demonstrate its fitness to survive by subduing others.

The Social Darwinists

Though he never expressed his ideas that crudely, the English philosopher Herbert Spencer (1820–1903) extolled the virtues of competition in a way that made it easier for others to do so. Spencer grounded

---

[1] T. H. Huxley, *Collected Essays,* V (London, 1902), 142.
[2] See above, p. 72.

Herbert Spencer

Anthropology

Friedrich Nietzsche

his philosophy upon evolutionary theory. His keynote was his idea of evolution as a universal law. He was deeply impressed by Darwin's *Origin of Species* and enriched the hypothesis of natural selection with a phrase that has clung to it ever since—"the survival of the fittest." He contended that not only species and individuals are subject to evolutionary change, but also planets, solar systems, customs, institutions, and religious and ethical ideas. Everything in the universe completes a cycle of origin, development, decay, and extinction. When the end of the cycle has been reached, the process begins once more and is repeated eternally. As a political philosopher, Spencer was a vigorous champion of individualism. He condemned collectivism as a relic of primitive society, as a feature of the earliest stage of social evolution. Any so-called assistance individuals might receive from the state, Spencer argued, would result not only in their own degeneration, but in that of society as well.

If Social Darwinists could reassure some by implying the biological right of Western civilization to survive as the "fittest" within the contemporary world, anthropologists—pioneers in what was essentially a new scientific discipline—argued, on the contrary, that no culture could be perceived as "better" than any other. All societies were adaptations to a particular environment. Each society produced its own customs, which could not be declared "good" or "bad," but only successful or unsuccessful, according to the degree to which they helped that society survive. This notion of cultural "relativism" was a theme in the influential work of the English anthropologist Sir James Frazer (1854–1941). In his masterpiece, *The Golden Bough,* he demonstrated the relationship of Christianity to primitive practices and magical rites. Christianity was nothing more or less than one society's response to the craving for an explanation of the apparently inexplicable.

Christianity was challenged far more directly in the writings of the German philosopher Friedrich Nietzsche (1844–1900). Nietzsche was not a scientist, nor was he interested in the nature of matter or in the problem of religious truth. He was essentially a romantic poet glorifying the struggle for existence to compensate for his own life of weakness and misery. Born in 1844, the son of a Lutheran minister, he was educated in the classics at Leipzig and Bonn and at the age of twenty-five was made a professor of philology at the University of Basel. Ten years later repeated and severe attacks of nerves forced his retirement. He spent the next decade of his life in agony, wandering from one resort to another in a fruitless quest for relief. If we can believe his own statement, each year was made up of two hundred days of pain. In 1888 he lapsed into hopeless insanity, which continued until his death in 1900.

Nietzsche's philosophy is contained in such works as *Thus Spake Zarathustra, A Genealogy of Morals,* and *The Will to Power.* His cardinal idea was the notion that natural selection should be permitted to operate unhindered in the case of human beings as it does with plants and animals. He believed that such a constant weeding out of the unfit would eventually produce a race of supermen—not merely a race of physical giants but men distinguished above all for their moral courage, for their strength of character. Those who should be allowed to perish in the struggle were the moral weaklings, who had neither the strength nor the courage to battle nobly for a place in the sun. Before any such process of natural selection could operate, however, religious obstacles would have to be removed. Nietzsche therefore demanded that the moral supremacy of Christianity and Judaism be overthrown. Both of these religions, he alleged, glorified the virtues of the downtrodden. They exalted into virtues qualities which ought to be considered vices—humility, nonresistance, mortification of the flesh, and pity for the weak and incompetent. The enthronement of these qualities prevented the elimination of the unfit and preserved them to pour their degenerate blood into the veins of the race.

His philosophy

Scientists and philosophers, as they continued to explore the various and sometimes contradictory implications of evolutionary theory, helped to undermine the comforting notion of humankind's essential superiority to the rest of the animal kingdom. The work of the Russian psychologist Ivan Pavlov (1849–1936) resulted in the discovery of the conditioned reflex. Although Pavlov experimented with animals, he insisted that his conclusions applied equally to human beings. The conditioned reflex is a form of behavior in which natural reactions are produced by an artificial stimulus. Pavlov showed that if dogs were fed immediately following the ringing of a bell, they would eventually respond to the sound of the bell alone and secrete saliva exactly as if confronted by the sight and smell of the food. This discovery suggested the conclusion that the conditioned reflex is an important element in human behavior and encouraged psychologists to center their attention upon physiological experiment as a key to understanding the mind.

Pavlov

Pavlovians inaugurated a type of physiological psychology known as behaviorism. Behaviorism is an attempt to study the human being as a purely physiological organism—to reduce all human behavior to a series of physical responses. Such concepts as *mind* and *consciousness* are relegated to the scrap heap as vague and meaningless terms. For the behaviorist nothing is important except the reactions of muscles, nerves, glands, and visceral organs. There is no such thing as an independent psychic behavior; all that humans do is physical. Thinking is essentially a form of talking to oneself. Every complex emotion and idea is simply a group of physiological responses produced by some stimulus in the environment. Such was the extremely mechanistic interpretation of human actions offered by followers of Pavlov.

Behaviorism

The other important school of psychology to make its appearance

Freud and psychoanalysis

Sigmund Freud

Science and religion

after the turn of the century was psychoanalysis, founded by Sigmund Freud (1856–1939), an Austrian physician. Psychoanalysis interprets human behavior mainly in terms of the unconscious mind. Freud admitted the existence of the conscious mind (the ego), but he avowed that the unconscious (the id) is much more important in determining the actions of the individual. He considered humans as egoistic creatures propelled by basic urges of power, self-preservation, and sex. These urges are much too strong to be overcome; but inasmuch as society (the superego) has branded their unrestrained fulfillment as sinful, they are commonly driven into the unconscious, where they linger indefinitely as suppressed desires. Yet they are seldom completely submerged; they rise to the surface in dreams, or they manifest themselves in lapses of memory, in fears and obsessions, and in various forms of abnormal behavior. Freud believed that most cases of mental and nervous disorders result from violent conflicts between natural instincts and the restraints imposed by an unfortunate environment. Freud hoped that by elucidating his theory of the unconscious he could impose predictable patterns upon the irrationality that seemed to characterize so much human activity. His search for order, however, resembled that of the behaviorists by continuing to stress the extent to which men and women, like animals, were prey to drives, impulses, and reflexes over which they could exercise at best only minimal control.

Under the impact of these various scientific and philosophical challenges, the institutions responsible for the maintenance of traditional faith found themselves hard pressed. Protestantism had based its revolt against Roman Catholic orthodoxy upon the belief that men and women should seek to understand God with the aid of not much more than the Bible and a willing conscience. In consequence, Protestants had little in the way of authoritarian doctrine to support them when their faith was challenged. Some—the fundamentalists—chose to ignore the implications of scientific and philosophical inquiry altogether, and continued to believe in the literal truth of the Bible. Some were willing to agree with the school of American philosophers known as Pragmatists (Charles Pierce, William James), that if belief in a personal God produced mental peace or spiritual satisfaction, that belief must therefore be true. Truth, for the Pragmatists, was whatever provided useful, practical results. Other Protestants sought solace from religious doubt in religious activity, founding missions, and laboring among the poor. Many adherents to this "Social Gospel" were also "Modernists," determined to accept the ethical teachings of Christianity while discarding belief in miracles and the doctrines of original sin and the Incarnation.

The Roman Catholic Church was compelled by its tradition of dogmatic assertion to assist its followers in their response to the modern world. In 1864 Pope Pius IX issued a *Syllabus of Errors* condemning what he regarded as the principal religious and philosophical "errors" of the time. Among them were materialism, free thought, and "indifferentism," or the idea that one religion is as good as another. Though the *Syllabus* was generally accepted by the Church, it was condemned by some critics as a "crusade against civilization." While heated discussions continued over the *Syllabus of Errors* Pope Pius convoked a Church council in 1869, the first to be summoned since the Catholic Reformation. The most noted pronouncement of the Vatican Council was the dogma of papal infallibility. In the language of this dogma the pope, when he speaks *ex cathedra*—that is in his capacity "as pastor and doctor of all Christians"—is infallible in regard to all matters of faith and morals. Though generally accepted by pious Catholics, the dogma of papal infallibility evoked a storm of protest in many circles. Governments of several Catholic countries denounced it, including France, Spain, and Italy. The death of Pius IX in 1878 and the accession of Pope Leo XIII brought a more accomodating climate to the Church. The new pope was ready to concede that there was "good" as well as "evil" in modern civilization. He added a scientific staff to the Vatican and opened archives and observatories. However, he made no concessions to "liberalism" or "anticlericalism" in the political sphere. He would go no farther than to urge capitalists and employers to be more generous in recognizing the rights of organized labor.

The effect of various scientific and philosophical challenges upon the men and women who lived at the end of the nineteenth century cannot be measured in any exact way. Millions undoubtedly went about the business of life untroubled by the implications of evolutionary theory, content to believe as they had believed. Certainly, for most members of the middle class, the challenge of socialism was understood as "real" in a way that the challenge of science and philosophy probably was not. Socialism was a threat to livelihood. Darwinism, relativism, materialism, and behaviorism, though "in the air" and troublesome to those who breathed that air, did not impinge upon consciousness to the same degree. Men and women can postpone thoughts about their origins and ultimate destiny in a way that they cannot postpone thoughts about their daily bread. And yet the impact of the changes we have been discussing was eventually profound. Darwin's theory was not so complicated as to prevent its popularization. If educated men and women had neither the time nor inclination to read the *Origin of Species,* they read magazines and newspapers which spelled out for them its implications. Those implications induced an uncertainty that tempered the optimism of capitalist expansion.

Men and women who had never read the German philosopher Arthur Schopenhauer (1788–1860) might well have agreed with his assessment of this world as one condemned to witness the devouring of the weak by the strong. Yet their commitment to the ways of the

Roman Catholicism

Pope Pius IX

Pope Leo XIII

world prevented their acceptance of Schopenhauer's particular remedy: an escape into a life of personal asceticism and self-denial. Like the English poet and essayist Matthew Arnold, sensitive men and women might feel themselves trapped in a world resembling no more than "a darkling plain," where there was "neither joy, nor love, nor light, nor certitude, nor peace, nor help for pain."

3. THE CHALLENGE OF LITERATURE AND THE ARTS

The revolt against art as morality

Literature and the arts in the late nineteenth century continued to challenge the middle-class worldview by drawing attention to the shortcomings as well as the achievements of industrial society. By 1900, however, many artists and writers were working according to a precept even more disturbing in its implications to the educated public than a critique of social values and realities. They agreed with the writers who were protesting middle-class values that the purpose of art was not to pander or to sentimentalize. They disagreed with them, however, by declaring that art had no business preaching morality—attempting to "improve" by example. This generation of artists and writers argued that one did not look at a painting or read a poem to be instructed in the difference between good and evil, but to understand what was eternally true and beautiful—to appreciate art for its own sake. They were not so much interested in reaching a wider audience, whose standards of taste they generally deplored, as they were in addressing each other. This self-conscious desire not only to live apart but to think apart from society was reflected in their work. In 1850, educated men and women could read a Dickens novel or examine a Daumier print and understand it, even if they did not admire it or agree with its message. In 1900, men and women found it much harder to understand, let alone admire, a painting by Paul Cézanne or a poem by Paul Valéry. Artists and public were ceasing to speak the same language, a fact which contributed, as did the ideas of Darwin and Nietzsche, Pavlov and Freud, to the further confusion and fragmentation of Western culture.

Realism

These new perceptions of the artist's relationship to society did not surface to any measurable degree before the very end of the century. Until that time, the arts were dominated by what has come to be called *realism*. Realists were predominantly critics of contemporary society. Swayed by a fervor for social reform, they depicted the inequities of the human condition against the sordid background of industrial society. Like the romantics, the realists affirmed the possibility of human freedom, although realists emphasized more than romantics the obstacles that prevented its achievement. Realists differed most markedly from romantics in their disdain of sentiment and emotional extravagance. Adopting from natural science the idea of life as a struggle for survival, they tried to portray human existence in accordance with hard facts, often insisting that their characters were the irresponsible victims of heredity, environment, or their own animal passions.

Realism as a literary movement made its initial appearance in France. Its leading exponents included the novelists Honoré de Balzac and Gustave Flaubert,[3] whose work, as we have already noted, contained a stinging assessment of the dullness and greed of modern life. Émile Zola (1840–1902), another Frenchman, is often called a naturalist rather than a realist, to convey the idea that he was interested in an exact, scientific presentation of the facts of nature without the intrusion of personal philosophy. Naturalism was expected to dismiss moral values in a way that realism was not. Zola did have a definite moral viewpoint, however. His early years of wretched poverty imbued him with a deep sympathy for the common people and with a passion for social justice. Though he portrayed human nature as weak and prone to vice and crime, he was not without hope that a decided improvement might come from the creation of a better society. Many of his novels dealt with such social problems as alcoholism, poverty, and disease.

Realism in the writings of the Englishman Charles Dickens was overlaid with layers of sentimentality. Dickens was a master at depicting the evils of industrial society, but the invariable happy endings of his novels testify to his determined—and unrealistic—unwillingness to allow wrong to triumph over right. No such ambivalence marked the works of the later English novelist Thomas Hardy (1840–1928), however. In such well-known narratives as *The Return of the Native, Jude the Obscure,* and *Tess of the D'Urbervilles,* he expressed his conception that humans are the playthings of an inexorable fate. The universe, though beautiful, was depicted as in no sense friendly, and the struggle of individuals with nature was a pitiable battle against almost impossible odds. If any such being as God existed, he watched with indifference while the helpless denizens of the human ant-heap crawled toward suffering and death. Hardy pitied his fellow creatures, regarding them not as depraved animals but as specks of dust caught in the wheels of a cosmic machine.

Pity for humanity was a central theme in the work of the German Gerhard Hauptmann (1862–1946). Calling himself a naturalist, Hauptmann nevertheless reflected the realists' concern for suffering. His plays show the influence of Darwin in their emphasis upon determinism and environment. *The Weavers,* which depicts the suffering of Silesian weavers in the 1840s, is probably his most outstanding work. Doubtless the most eminent playwright among realists and naturalists was the Norwegian Henrik Ibsen (1828–1906). Ibsen's early dramas were not favorably received, and while still a young man he decided to abandon his native country. Residing first in Italy and then in Ger-

[3] See above, p. 854.

Russian literature:
Turgenev and Dostoevsky

Henrik Ibsen

Tolstoy

many, he did not return permanently to Norway until 1891. His writings were characterized most of all by bitter rebellion against the tyranny and ignorance of society. In such plays as *The Wild Duck, A Doll's House, Hedda Gabler,* and *An Enemy of the People,* he mercilessly satirized the conventions and institutions of respectable life, and showed, with great insight, how these oppressed women in particular. Along with his scorn for hypocrisy and social tyranny went a profound distrust of majority rule. Ibsen despised democracy as the enthronement of unprincipled leaders who would do anything for the sake of votes to perpetuate themselves in power. As one of his characters in *An Enemy of the People* says: "A minority may be right—a majority is always wrong."

The literature of the Russians, while it came into its own during the period of realism, includes within it themes that are both romantic and idealist as well. Russia's three most outstanding novelists of this period were Ivan Turgenev (1818–1883), Feodor Dostoevsky (1821–1881), and Leo Tolstoy (1828–1910). Turgenev, who spent much of his life in France, was the first of the Russian novelists to become known to western Europe. His chief work, *Fathers and Sons,* describes in brooding terms the struggle between the older and younger generations. The hero is a nihilist (a term first used by Turgenev), who is convinced that the whole social order has nothing in it worth preserving. Dostoevsky was almost as tragic a figure as any he projected in his novels. Condemned at the age of twenty-eight on a charge of revolutionary activity, he was exiled to Siberia, where he endured four horrible years. His later life was harrowed by poverty, family troubles, and epileptic fits. As a novelist, he chose to explore the anguish of people driven to shameful deeds by their raw, animal emotions and by the intolerable meanness of their lives. He was a master of psychological analysis, probing into the motives of distorted minds with an intensity that was almost morbid. At the same time he filled his novels with a broad sympathy and with a mystic conviction that humanity can be purified only through suffering. His best-known works are *Crime and Punishment* and *The Brothers Karamazov.*

It is generally conceded that the honor of being Russia's greatest novelist must be divided between Dostoevsky and Tolstoy. As an earnest champion of the simple life of the peasant, Tolstoy was somewhat less deterministic than the author of *Crime and Punishment.* Yet in his *War and Peace,* a majestic epic of Russian conditions during the period of the Napoleonic invasion, he expounds the theme that individuals are at the mercy of fate when powerful elemental forces are unleashed. His other most celebrated novel, *Anna Karenina,* is a study of the tragedy which lurks in the pursuit of individual desire. The hero, Levin, is really Tolstoy himself, who eventually finds refuge from doubt and from the vanities of worldly existence in a mystic love

Leo Tolstoy in His Study Dictating to His Secretary

of humanity. As Tolstoy grew older he became more and more an evangelist preaching a social gospel. In such novels as *The Kreutzer Sonata* and *Resurrection* he condemned most of the institutions of civilized society and called upon men and women to renounce selfishness and greed, to earn their living by manual toil, and to cultivate the virtues of poverty, meekness, and nonresistance. His last years were devoted mainly to attacks upon such evils as war and capital punishment and to the defense of victims of persecution.

The works of all these realists and naturalists, whatever their individual differences, shared two things in common: they contained vigorous moral criticism of present-day middle-class society, and they were written in direct and forceful language that the middle class could understand, if it chose to read or listen. The same can be said of realist painters such as Courbet and Daumier, discussed previously, and of the sculptor Auguste Rodin (1840–1917), whose style and message were neither difficult to comprehend nor easy to ignore. Realist artists were still anxious to address the public, if only to attack its members for their shallowness and insensitivity. The advent of the *impressionist* movement in painting in the 1870s marks the first significant break in this tradition. It is at this point that artists began to turn away from the public and toward each other. The movement started in France, among a group of young artists whose work had been refused a place in the annual exhibitions of the traditionally minded French Royal Academy. They had been labeled "impressionists" in derision by critics who took them to task for painting not an object itself, but only their impression of that object. The name in fact suited the personal, private nature of their work. They were painting only to please themselves, to realize their own potential as artists.

In a sense, impressionists were realists, for they were determined to paint only what they saw, and they were vitally interested in the

Realism in art

Impressionism

Monet and Renoir

See color plates following
page 960

Expressionism: Cézanne

scientific interpretation of nature. But impressionist technique was different from that of the older realist painters. Scenes from the world around them were not depicted as if the results of careful study. On the contrary, the works of impressionists sought to reveal immediate sense impressions, leaving it to the mind of the observer to fill in additional details. This often resulted in a type of work appearing at first glance to be nonnaturalistic. Figures were commonly distorted; a few significant details were made to represent an entire object; and dabs of primary color were placed side by side without a trace of blending. Convinced that light is the principal factor in determining the appearance of objects, the impressionists fled from the studio to the woods and fields in an attempt to capture the fleeting alterations of a natural scene with each transitory shift of sunlight and shadow. From science they had learned that light is composed of a fusion of primary colors visible in the spectrum. Accordingly, they decided to use these colors almost exclusively. They chose, for example, to achieve the effect of the green in nature by placing daubs of pure blue and yellow side by side, allowing the eye to mix them.

Impressionism differed from realism in one other very important respect. In these new paintings artists remained detached from their subject. They did not paint to evoke pity, or to teach a lesson. They painted to proclaim the value and importance of painting *as painting*. In doing so, the artist was not deliberately setting out to exclude the viewers. It was clear, however, that the viewer must not expect to understand a painting except on the artist's terms. Probably the greatest of the impressionists were the Frenchmen Claude Monet (1840–1926) and Auguste Renoir (1841–1919). Monet was perhaps the leading exponent of the new mode of interpreting landscapes. His paintings have no structure or design in the conventional sense; they suggest, rather than depict, the outlines of cliffs, trees, mountains, and fields. Intensely interested in the problem of light, Monet would go out at sunrise with an armful of canvases in order to paint the same subject in a dozen momentary appearances. It has been said of one of his masterpieces that "light is the only important person in the picture." Renoir's subjects include not only landscapes but portraits and scenes from contemporary life. He is famous most of all for his pink and ivory nudes, which, as expressions of frank sexuality, represented a threat to middle-class sensibilities.

The freedom explicit in the work of the impressionists encouraged other painters to pursue fresh techniques and to define different goals. The *expressionists* turned upon the impressionists, objecting to their preoccupation with the momentary aspects of nature and their indifference to meaning. Expressionists were not arguing a return to meaning in the sense of "message." They were instead insisting that a painting must represent the artist's particular intellect. Here again, they were making art a private matter, removing it yet another step from the public. The artist who laid the foundations of expressionism was Paul Cézanne (1839–1906), now recognized as one of the greatest painters who ever lived. A native of southern France, Cézanne labored to express a sense of order in nature that he believed the impressionists had ignored. To achieve this end, he painted objects as a series of planes, each plane expressed in terms of a color change. While Cézanne was in this way equating form with color, he also began to reduce natural forms to their geometrical equivalents, hoping thereby to express the basic shapes of existence itself. He distorted form into geometrical regularity until abstraction became reality. In all this Cézanne was declaring the painter's right to recreate nature in such a way as to express an intensely personal vision.

Art as personal expression was the hallmark of two other painters in the so-called post-impressionist period, the Frenchman Paul Gauguin (1848–1903) and the Dutchman Vincent Van Gogh (1853–1890). Both, by their life as well as their art, declared war on traditional nineteenth-century values. Dismayed by the artificiality and complexity of civilization, Gauguin fled to the South Sea Islands and spent the last decade of his life painting the hot and luscious colors of an unspoiled, primitive society. Van Gogh, whose passionate sympathy for the sufferings of his fellow humans led him to attempt the life of a minister to poor mining families and undoubtedly contributed to his eventual insanity and ultimate suicide, poured out the full intensity of his feelings in paintings such as *The Starry Night,* which seem to swirl off the canvas.

In the years between 1900 and the First World War, art underwent still further revolutionary development. Henri Matisse (1869–1954) greatly extended Cézanne's use of distortion, thereby declaring once again the painter's right to create according to an individual definition of aesthetic merit. This declaration was given its most ringing prewar endorsement by Pablo Picasso (1881–1973). Picasso, a Catalan Spaniard who came to Paris in 1903, developed a style, *cubism,* that takes its name from an attempt to carry Cézanne's fascination with geometrical form to its logical conclusion. Influenced both by the work of Cézanne and by African sculpture, cubism results not only in distortion but in some cases in actual dismemberment. The artist may separate the various parts of a figure and rearrange them in other than their natural pattern. The purpose is partly to symbolize the chaos of modern life but also to express defiance of traditional notions of form—to repudiate once and for all the conception of art as representational prettiness.

The artistic declaration of independence from middle-class society was enunciated most dramatically by painters, but was heard also in the realms of literature and music. In France, the work of a group calling itself the symbolists, and centered upon the poetry of Paul Verlaine, Arthur Rimbaud, Stéphane Mallarmé, and Paul Valéry at-

Self-Portrait by Paul Gauguin

Cubism: Picasso

See color plates following page 960

New directions in literature and music

Girl Before a Mirror by Pablo
Picasso

tempted to intensify the personal while transcending reality in a way
reminiscent of the impressionists, expressionists, and cubists. In
music, as well, there was a break from the romantic tradition that
dominated the nineteenth century and was expressed in the works of
composers such as Robert Schumann (1810–1856), Felix Mendelssohn
(1809–1847), and Franz Liszt (1811–1886). Already the late romantic
operas of Richard Wagner had taken vast liberties with harmony and
departed from stereotypical melodic patterns, producing music that
was not subject to the tyranny of form but sensitive to personal expression.

Self-imposed isolation   Whether in painting, in literature, or in music, artists sought to escape to a position from which they could learn and then express what
was closest to their own consciousness. Their direct, calculated dismissal of conventional form and content declared their fundamental
disdain for—more important, their complete lack of interest in—the
problems of the world at large. Their self-imposed isolation served
only to increase the general sense of a fragmented world that, despite
its material prosperity, was at war with itself.

SELECTED READINGS

• *Items so designated are available in paperback editions.*

SOCIALISM

• Avineri, S., *The Social and Political Thought of Karl Marx,* London, 1968.
• Cole, G. D. H., *A History of Socialist Thought,* Vols. I–III, London, 1953–56.
   A comprehensive treatment of the period 1789–1914.

Gay, Peter, *The Dilemma of Democratic Socialism: Eduard Bernstein's Challenge to Marx,* New York, 1952.

Goldberg, Harvey, *A Life of Jean Jaurès,* Madison, Wisc., 1962. A good biography of the eminent French socialist.

Joll, James, *The Anarchists,* London, 1964.

Landauer, C., and E. Valkenier, *European Socialism,* Berkeley, Calif., 1959.

Lichtheim, G., *A Short History of Socialism,* New York, 1970.

• McBriar, A. M., *Fabian Socialism and English Politics, 1884–1918,* Cambridge, 1966. An extensive study of this important circle: their composition, their ideology, their methods.

Noland, Aaron, *The Founding of the French Socialist Party, 1893–1905,* Cambridge, Mass., 1956. Primarily a narrative account of the translation of ideology into political reality.

Schorske, Carl E., *German Social Democracy, 1905–1917,* Cambridge, Mass., 1955. A magnificent study of the problems of the Social Democrats in a time of imperialism and war.

SCIENTIFIC THOUGHT

• Butterfield, Herbert B., *The Origins of Modern Science,* rev. ed., New York, 1957.

Eiseley, Loren C., *Darwin's Century: Evolution and the Men Who Discovered It,* New York, 1961.

Fothergill, P., *Historical Aspects of Organic Evolution,* London, 1952.

Gillespie, C. C., *The Edge of Objectivity,* Princeton, N.J., 1960. A history of scientific ideas.

• Hughes, H. Stuart, *Consciousness and Society,* New York, 1958. Examines the reaction to Positivism and the growing interest in the irrational by considering the work of Freud, Max Weber, and others.

• Jones, Ernest, *The Life and Work of Freud,* 3 vols., New York, 1953–57. The official biography, by a close collaborator and eminent psychoanalyst.

• McKenzie, A. E. E., *The Major Achievements of Science,* Cambridge, 1960.

Singer, Charles, and A. E. Underwood, *A Short History of Medicine,* rev. ed., New York, 1962.

Wightman, W. P. D., *The Growth of Scientific Ideas,* Edinburgh, 1951.

THE ARTS

Barzun, Jacques, *Darwin, Marx, and Wagner,* Boston, 1941. Argues that these men were not so much originators of new ideas, as founders of systems which are mechanistic and pseudoscientific and therefore threatening to the human cultural heritage.

Kaufmann, Walter A., *Nietzsche: Philosopher, Psychologist, Anti-Christ,* Princeton, N.J., 1974.

Lang, Paul, *Music in Western Civilization,* New York, 1941.

Mosse, G. L., *The Culture of Western Europe: The Nineteenth and Twentieth Centuries,* Chicago, 1961.

Shattuck, Roger, *The Banquet Years: The Arts in France, 1885–1918,* New York, 1958. The emergence of modernism in French art, literature, and music.

SOURCE MATERIALS

- Arnold, Matthew, *Culture and Anarchy,* New York, 1971. Originally published in 1867. A perceptive criticism of English society and a call for an authoritarian principle in an increasingly democratic society.
- Darwin, Charles, *The Descent of Man,* Cambridge, Mass., 1964. See especially Chapter XXI.
- ———, *Origin of Species,* Cambridge, Mass., 1964. See especially Chapters IV, XV.
  Edwards, Stewart, ed., *The Communards of Paris, 1871,* New York, 1976. Annotated eyewitness reports, documents, and accounts of the Paris Commune.
- Gosse, Edmund, *Father and Son,* New York, 1963. A moving autobiography by a distinguished Victorian literary critic, this work reveals the conflict between the religious fundamentalism of the father and the skepticism of the son in the wake of Darwinian theory.
  Kohn, Hans, *The Mind of Modern Russia,* New Brunswick, N.J., 1955. An edited collection of historical, literary, and philosophical works of nineteenth- and twentieth-century Russian authors, designed to reveal the conflict between traditional and Western thought in Russia.
- Marx, Karl, *Capital,* intro. by G. D. H. Cole, New York, 1974.
  Webb, Beatrice, *My Apprenticeship,* London, 1926. Beatrice Webb was one of the leading Fabian Socialists, and in this first volume of her autobiography she explains how she, as a member of one of England's wealthier families, was converted to a socialist creed.
  Zola, Émile, *L'Assommoir,* London, 1970. Written in 1877 and set in the Paris of the 1860s, this bitterly realistic novel portrays the brutalization of the French working class by the forces of industrial change, poverty, and alcohol.

Chapter 31

THE SEARCH FOR STABILITY
(1870–1914)

Ah! What a seething there has been, . . . customs worthy of the inquisition and despotism, the pleasure of a few gold-braided individuals setting their heels on the nation, and stifling its cry for truth and justice, under the mendacious and sacrilegious pretext of the interest of the State!

—Émile Zola, "J'accuse"

Between 1870 and 1914, the major powers of Europe worked to maintain both domestic and international stability. Accomplishment of this goal was facilitated by continuing industrialization. Despite periodic trade depressions, general prosperity increased for almost all classes of society at least until 1900. And prosperity, in its turn, helped to produce stability, allowing for the establishment in many countries of social welfare systems designed to benefit workers and their families, and thus to gain their political allegiance. At the same time, various factors operated to make the achievement of a generally stable Western world difficult, and ultimately impossible. First, the process of nation-building, which had resulted in the dramatic creation of a modern Germany and Italy, left potential conflict in its wake. Second, although the majority of citizens in most western European countries participated at least indirectly in the governance of their country and enjoyed certain guaranteed rights, heated debate continued as to the political usefulness of such arrangements. In France, monarchists threatened the republic; in Germany, democrats battled imperial and bureaucratic oligarchy; in Russia, liberals rose against tsarist autocracy. And across Europe, socialists contended against the political strength of the middle classes. Finally, the international rivalries that we have seen growing between nations as they reached out to build empires became more heated with the coming of the new century. Nations grouped into alliances, hoping that a

The roots of instability

balance between power blocs might continue to provide the international stability that Europe had enjoyed since 1815, and that had prevented general war. Instead, the alliances produced only further tensions, and ultimately general world conflict.

1. GERMANY: THE SEARCH FOR IMPERIAL UNITY

The structure of the empire

During the years immediately following the foundation of the German Empire, Bismarck was particularly anxious to achieve imperial unity under Prussian domination. In this he was aided by the economic and military predominance of the Prussian state, and by the organizational framework upon which the empire had been constructed. All powers not granted to the central government were reserved to the individual states. Each had control over its own form of government, public education, highways, police, and other local agencies. Even the enforcement of the laws was left primarily in the hands of the state governments, since the empire had no machinery for applying its laws against individuals. Despite their apparent autonomy, however, the states were in fact subordinate to the empire, and to the emperor himself, the Prussian William I. President A. Laurence Lowell of Harvard once accurately described the German imperial units as comprised of "a lion, a half-dozen foxes, and a score of mice." The Prussian "lion" exercised authority through the person of the emperor and his chancellor. The empire was not governed by a cabinet system, in which ministers of state were responsible to a popularly elected legislature. Instead, the chancellor and other ministers were responsible solely to the emperor. And William was no mere figurehead; he was vested with extensive authority over the army and navy, over foreign relations, and over the general enactment and execution of imperial laws. He had the authority to declare war if the coasts or territory of the empire were attacked. And as king of Prussia, he controlled that country's block of one-third of the votes in the generally conservative upper house, or Bundesrat, of the imperial parliament.

The parliament was by no means a mere rubber stamp, however. All treaties had to be approved by the Bundesrat. Money for the imperial treasury had to be voted by the lower house, the Reichstag, which was elected by universal manhood suffrage and whose membership was primarily middle class. Yet these powers were essentially negative. Although the parliament could veto proposals of the kaiser (emperor) and his ministers, it could not initiate legislation on its own. Hence, although Bismarck often found himself temporarily stymied by the activities of an unsympathetic legislature, he could expect, in the end, to have his way. That way was directed toward the goal of a unified Germany under Prussian domination: essentially conservative; antisocialist, though not necessarily opposed to social welfare schemes; protectionist, and thus sympathetic to the interests of Ger-

William I of Germany

man industrialists; and, in foreign affairs, anti-French, standing firm against any threat from that longtime antagonist.

Bismarck's first campaign on behalf of imperial unity was launched against the Roman Catholic Church. Called the *Kulturkampf*, or "struggle for civilization," the attack was initiated, with some help from intellectual liberals, in 1872. Bismarck's motives were almost exclusively nationalistic. He perceived in some Catholic activities a threat to the power and stability of the empire he had just created. He resented, first of all, the support Catholic priests continued to give to the states'-rights movement in southern Germany and to the grievances of Alsatians and Poles. He was alarmed also by recent assertions of the authority of the pope to intervene in secular matters and by the promulgation in 1870 of the dogma of papal infallibility. For these reasons he resolved to deal such a blow to Catholic influence in Germany that it would never again be a factor in national or local politics. His weapons were a series of laws and decrees issued between 1872 and 1875. First, he induced the Reichstag to expel all the Jesuits from the country. Next, he forced through the so-called May Laws, which placed theological seminaries under state control and permitted the government to regulate the appointment of bishops and priests. No one was allowed to be appointed to any position in the Church unless a German citizen, and then only after a state examination. At the same time civil marriage was made compulsory, even though a religious ceremony had already been performed. In the enforcement of these measures, six of the ten Catholic bishops in Prussia were imprisoned, and hundreds of priests were driven from the country.

The Kulturkampf

Although Bismarck won some of the chief battles of the *Kulturkampf*, he lost the war. The Catholic or Center party appealed so effectively on behalf of the persecuted clergy, and adopted so enlightened an economic program, that it grew into the largest political party in Germany. In the elections of 1874 it captured nearly a fourth of the seats in the Reichstag. Recognizing that he needed this party to support other elements of his program, Bismarck gradually relaxed his persecution of the Catholics. Between 1878 and 1886 nearly all of the obnoxious legislation was repealed, and the Catholic Church restored practically to its former position in Germany.

The failure of the Kulturkampf

By the late 1870s Bismarck had declared war on German socialism, now perceived by him as a far more immediate threat to the empire than Catholicism. The Social Democratic party, under the reformist leadership of the politician Wilhelm Liebknecht (1829–1900), successor to Ferdinand Lassalle, was building a substantial following. Bismarck, his memory of the Paris Commune (see above, pp. 957) still fresh, feared socialism as anarchy, and therefore as a direct challenge to the stability and unity he was attempting to achieve within the empire. Forgetting for the moment the manner in which he had courted the socialists when he needed their support in the 1860s, Bismarck now appeared determined to extinguish them. His attack was motivated

Bismarck's antisocialism

not only by his personal perception of the socialist threat; he was by now anxious to continue to court the favor of industrialists whom he had won to his side by his policy of protective tariffs. In 1878, two separate attempts were made by unbalanced zealots on the life of the emperor. Although neither would-be assassin had anything but the most tenuous connection with the socialists, Bismarck used their actions as an excuse to secure legislation abolishing workers' rights to meet and to publish. The legislature also agreed to a law which gave the government the right to expel socialists from major cities, as was later done in Berlin, Breslau, and Leipzig.

Social welfare legislation

Bismarck was too clever a politician to suppose that he could abolish socialism solely by means of repression. He was prepared to steal at least a portion of the socialists' thunder by adopting parts of their legislative program as his own. In a speech in the Reichstag he frankly avowed his purpose of insuring the worker against sickness and old age so that "these gentlemen [the Social Democrats] will sound their bird call in vain." In addition, he had military purposes in mind. He was desirous of making the German worker a loyal soldier by safeguarding his health in some measure from the debilitating effects of factory labor. Bismarck's program of social legislation was initiated in 1883–1884 with the adoption of laws insuring workers against sickness and accidents. These acts were soon followed by others providing for rigid factory inspection, limiting the employment of women and children, fixing maximum hours of labor, establishing public employment agencies, and insuring workers against incapacity on account of old age. By 1890, when Bismarck was dismissed by the young Emperor William II, Germany had adopted nearly all the elements, with the exception of unemployment insurance, in the pattern of social legislation that later became familiar in the majority of Western nations.

Continuing spread of German socialism

Neither Bismarck's repressive nor his progressive legislation succeeded in killing German socialism, however. The Social Democratic party continued to grow. Bismarck's dismissal came in part over William's insistence that the antisocialist legislation was achieving nothing. The disagreement between the two men extended beyond the question of socialism, however. William II was determined to be his own master. Unity and stability would be the result of his personal initiative, not that of his chancellor. In this, William was expressing his belief in the divinely ordained prerogatives of the Hohenzollerns, the royal house of Prussia. He was asserting claims that—though they sat well enough with the federated princes, the large landowners, the military, and the big industrialists—were increasingly anathema to the democratic forces of the lower middle and working classes. Social Democrats and Progressives were demanding a new constitution guaranteeing control over the chancellor by the majority party in the Reichstag. To these demands the intransigent emperor remained deaf,

Bismarck and William II of Germany

further threatening the fragile stability which Bismarck's policies had attempted to encourage. In the election of 1912 the Social Democrats polled 4,250,000 votes and elected 110 members—the largest single bloc—to the Reichstag. National unity was on a collision course with class conflict. Germany was spared a domestic constitutional crisis only by the infinitely more profound international crisis of the First World War.

2. FRANCE: THE EMBATTLED THIRD REPUBLIC

Politically divided France

Although France, in 1870, was not a newly constructed nation, like the German Empire, it was a nation sorely in need of reunification and dedication to a common set of political purposes. Its history for the past century had left it torn between various factions. Monarchists were divided between supporters of the Bourbon and Orleanist dynasties, their allegiance sustained by loyalties either to the descendents of Louis XVIII or of Louis Philippe. Bonapartists looked for political salvation to Napoleon III's son and heir Louis Napoleon. Republicans recalled the short-lived triumphs of their revolutionary ancestors. Socialists called down plagues on all political houses but their own. The result of this deep division was that not until 1875 did France have a constitution under which it could function.

Following the collapse of Napoleon III's empire a provisional government was organized to rule the country until a new constitution could be drafted. Elections held in 1871 for a national constituent assembly resulted in the choice of some 500 monarchists and only about

200 republicans. Conservative political sentiment was further rein-forced by the events of the Paris Commune, which occurred during the period immediately following the elections. But the apparent win-ners, the monarchists, could not agree among themselves as to whether their king should be a Bourbon or an Orleanist. This stale-mate led to the eventual passage in 1875—by one vote—of a series of constitutive laws which made France a republic. These laws es-tablished a parliament with a lower house elected by universal man-hood suffrage (the Chamber of Deputies) and an upper house elected indirectly (the Senate); a cabinet of ministers presided over by a pre-mier; and a president. Although at first the relative powers of presi-dent and premier were not clearly established, within two years the nation had declared itself in favor of a premier at the head of a govern-ment answerable to the Chamber of Deputies. An early president, Marshal MacMahon, attempted in 1877 to dismiss a premier with whom he disagreed but who was supported by a majority in the chamber. When new elections were held, MacMahon's policy was repudiated. Henceforth, premiers of the Third Republic were answer-able to the chamber and not to the president, who became a figure-head. Yet the resolution of this constitutional question failed to pro-duce political stability, since the premier had no authority to dissolve the legislature. This meant that members of the chamber could vote a premier and his fellow ministers out of office at will, with no risk of being forced to stand for reelection. If defeated on a vote, the premier and his colleagues had no alternative but to resign. The result was no fewer than fifty ministries in the years between 1870 and 1914. The Third Republic, for all its constitutional shortcomings, nevertheless managed to last until 1940—far longer than any system of French gov-ernment since 1789. Its longevity was due, as much as anything, to the stability of other French institutions—the family, the law courts, and the police, for example.

In the years after 1875, the republicans, who had been feared at first as dangerous radicals, proved themselves to be generally moderate. It was the discontented monarchists and authoritarian sympathizers within the army, the Roman Catholic Church, and among the families of the aristocracy who took to plotting the overthrow of duly consti-tuted governmental authority. Much of the time of successive republi-can governments was taken up defending the country from these reac-tionary radicals. In the late 1880s, a general, Georges Boulanger, gathered about him a following not only of Bonapartists, monar-chists, and aristocrats, but of workingmen who were generally dis-gruntled with their lot and who believed, with Boulanger, that a war of revenge against Germany would put an end to all their troubles. Thanks to the general's own indecisiveness, the threatened coup d'état came to nothing. But Boulanger was a symptom of deep discontents; he appealed, like Napoleon III, to disparate groups of disenchanted citizens, promising quick, dramatic solutions to tedious problems.

One further symptom of the divisions which plagued the republic during the later years of the nineteenth century was the campaign of anti-Semitism which the reactionaries adopted to advance their aims. The fact that certain Jewish bankers were involved in scandalous dealings with politicians lent color to the monarchist insistence that the government was shot through with corruption and that Jews were largely to blame. In the face of those charges it is not strange that anti-Semitism should have flared into a violent outbreak. In 1894 a Jewish captain of artillery, Alfred Dreyfus, was accused by a clique of monarchist officers of selling military secrets to Germany. Tried by court-martial, he was convicted and sentenced for life to Devil's Island, a ghastly prison camp in the Caribbean. At first the verdict was accepted as the merited punishment of a traitor; but in 1897 Colonel Picquart, a new head of the Intelligence Division, announced his conclusion that the documents upon which Dreyfus had been convicted were forgeries. A movement was launched for a new trial, which the War Department promptly refused. Soon the whole nation was divided into friends and opponents of Dreyfus. On his side were the radical republicans, socialists, people of liberal and humanitarian sympathies, and such prominent literary figures as Émile Zola and Anatole France. The anti-Dreyfusards included monarchists, clerics, anti-Semites, militarists, and a considerable number of conservative workingmen. Dreyfus was finally set free by executive order in 1899, and six years later was cleared of all guilt by the Supreme Court and restored to the army. He was immediately promoted to the rank of major and decorated with the emblem of the Legion of Honor.

The Dreyfus affair

The history of the Dreyfus affair gave the republicans the solid ground they had lacked in order to end the plottings of the radical reactionaries once and for all. The leaders of the republic chose to attack their enemies by effectively destroying the political power of the Roman Catholic Church in France. The anticlericalism expressed in

Anticlericalism

*Alfred Dreyfus Leaving His Court-
Martial*

this campaign was probably in part the product of a materialistic age, and of a long-standing mistrust by French republicans of the institution of the Church. Its main source, however, was the nationalism which we have already seen fueling Bismarck's *Kulturkampf.*

Anticlericalism in France reached its peak between 1875 and 1914. The great majority of the leaders of the Third Republic were hostile to the Church; and naturally so, for the Catholic hierarchy was aiding the monarchists at every turn. Clerics had conspired with monarchists, militarists, and anti-Semites in attempting to discredit the republic during the Dreyfus affair. But in the end they had overreached themselves. In 1901 the government passed a series of acts prohibiting the existence of religious orders not authorized by the state, forbidding members of religious orders to teach in either public or private schools, and finally, in 1905, dissolving the union of Church and State. For the first time since 1801 the adherents of all creeds were placed on an equal basis. No longer were the Catholic clergy to receive their salaries from the public purse. Although some of these measures were modified in later years, the Church remained in the minds of most Frenchmen under a heavy cloud of suspicion.

The republic was, during these years, pressed from the Left as well as the Right. Socialism was a political force in France, as it was in Germany. Yet the response of republicans in France to socialist pressure differed markedly from that of Bismarck. There was no antisocialist legislation. Indeed, a law was passed in 1881 abolishing "crimes of opinion," thereby extending the freedom of the press considerably. In the same year, another law authorized public meetings without prior official approval. But if there was no attempt at repression, there was little positive social reform. The largest single party in the republic, the Radicals or Radical Socialists, was really a party representing small shopkeepers and lesser propertied interests. The Radicals were willing to found and maintain a democratic compulsory educational system, but they were reluctant to respond to demands for labor legislation such as had been granted to German workers. Those laws which were passed—establishing a ten-hour workday in 1904 and old-age pensions in 1910—were passed grudgingly and only after socialist pressure. The result was a growing belief among socialists and other workers that parliamentary democracy was worthless, that progress, if it was to be made, would be made only as a result of direct industrial action: the strike. A wave of strikes swept the country for several years before 1914, including one by postal workers in 1909 and by teachers and railwaymen in 1910. The government suppressed these actions by ruthless intervention. By 1914, the republic, though hardly on the brink of revolution, remained divided and uncertain. If the threat from the radical Right had been quelled, the challenge from the Left was only just being faced.

Legislation to curb the Church

Pressure from the Left

3. GREAT BRITAIN: FROM MODERATION TO MILITANCE

During the half-century before 1914, the British prided themselves on what they believed to be a reasonable, orderly, and workable system of government. Following the passage of the Second Reform Bill in 1867, which extended suffrage to over a third of the nation's adult males, the two major political parties, Liberal and Conservative, vied with each other in adopting legislation designed to provide an increasingly larger proportion of the population the chance to lead fuller and healthier lives. Laws which recognized the legality of trade unions, allowed male religious dissenters to participate fully in the life of the ancient universities of Oxford and Cambridge, provided elementary education for the first time to all children, and facilitated the clearance and rebuilding of large urban areas, were among those placed on the books during the administrations of the two leading politicians of the period, the Conservative Benjamin Disraeli (1804–1881) and the Liberal, William Gladstone (1809–1898). In 1884, suffrage was once more widened, to include over three-fourths of the adult males, and to allow rural workingmen the chance to vote for the first time. Coupled with a previous act which instituted the secret ballot, this electoral reform bill brought Britain nearer to representative democracy.

Benjamin Disraeli

Yet Britain continued to be governed almost exclusively by a small ruling class of men drawn either from landed society or from the upper reaches of the middle class. As members of successive governmental cabinets they recognized their responsibility to Parliament and, in particular, to its lower House of Commons. It was their task, as cabinet ministers, to impose a legislative program upon the Commons. And if the House refused to agree to that program, they recognized, as well, their obligation either to resign forthwith—to make way for a cabinet of opposing party members—or to "go to the country," that is, to dissolve Parliament and order a new election to test the opinion of the voters. This system of "ministerial responsibility" meant that the cabinet retained full responsibility for the management of public affairs, subject, however, to the will of the people as represented by the House of Commons. It produced a generally stable government: Although ministries had to answer to Parliament, Parliament would think twice before voting a ministry out of office when it knew that the ministry might well appeal to the voters for support in a general election. (The lack of this particular feature was what had condemned the French Third Republic to its succession of short-lived governments.) Political stability was insured by more than the device of ministerial responsibility, however. Since both the Conservative and Liberal political leadership was drawn in large part from similar social and economic strata, there was little chance for violent change during these years. One party might espouse a particular cause—the

William Gladstone

"Ministerial responsibility"

Conservatives imperialism, the Liberals more self-government for Ireland, for example. But both parties generally agreed upon a course steered by men whose similar background and temperament promised programs that were neither radical nor reactionary. This moderation suited the electorate, which was content to defer to politicians whose leadership was secured by the undoubted fact of Britain's general prosperity.

By 1914, however, that leadership was being seriously challenged. Prosperity, though widespread enough, did not extend to the unskilled: dock workers, transport workers, and the like. These groups formed trade unions to press their claims. Their determination encouraged other unions to assume a more militant and demanding stance. In the 1890s this activity produced a reaction in the form of anti–trade union employers' associations and a series of legal decisions limiting the right of unions to strike. Workers, in turn, reacted by associating with middle-class socialist societies to form an independent Labour party, which was born in 1901 and five years later managed to send twenty-nine members to the House of Commons. Sensitive to this pressure from the Left, the Liberals, during their ministry which began in 1906, passed a series of reforms they hoped would insure a minimum standard of living for those who had heretofore known little security. Sickness, accident, old-age, and unemployment insurance schemes were adopted. A minimum wage was decreed in certain industries. Labor exchanges, designed to help unemployed men and women find new jobs, were established. Restrictions on strikes and on the right of trade unions to raise money for political purposes were relaxed.

Much of this legislation was the work of David Lloyd George (1863–1945), chancellor of the exchequer (finance minister) in the Liberal cabinet of Prime Minister Herbert Asquith. Together with another young Liberal, Winston Churchill (1874–1965), Lloyd George had hammered together legislation that was both a reflection of his own political philosophy and a practical response to the growing political power of the working class. To pay for these programs—and for a larger navy to counter a German build-up—Lloyd George proposed a budget in 1909 that included progressive income and inheritance taxes, designed to make wealthier taxpayers pay at higher rates. His proposals so enraged the aristocratic members of the House of Lords that they declared themselves prepared to throw out the budget, an action contrary to constitutional precedent. Asquith countered with a threat to create enough new peers (titled noblemen) sympathetic to the budget to insure its passage.[1] The House of Lords eventu-

*Liberal reforms,
1906–1914*

Lloyd George's budget

[1] In Britain the monarch had the authority to elevate an unlimited number of men to the peerage. But since the crown acts only on the advice of the prime minister, it is this official who has the actual power to create new members of the House of Lords. If necessary, he could use this power to pack the upper house with his own followers.

Lloyd George and Winston Churchill on Their Way to the House of Commons on Budget Day, 1910

ally surrendered; the result of the crisis was an act of Parliament which provided that the House of Lords could not veto legislation passed by the House of Commons.

The rancor aroused by this constitutional conflict was intense. Self-proclaimed defenders of the House of Lords screamed threats in a chamber unused to anything but gentlemanly debate. Angry threats were by no means confined to the Houses of Parliament during these years, however. Throughout Britain, men and women threw moderation to the winds as they disputed issues in an atmosphere little short of anarchic. The reasons for this continued agitation were various. A decline in real wages after 1900 kept the working class in a militant mood, despite Liberal reforms, and produced an unusually severe series of strikes in 1911 and 1912. A liberal plan to grant Home Rule (self-government) to Ireland produced not only panic in the Protestant minority counties of the north (Ulster) but arming and drilling of private militias with an intensity that seemed to forecast civil war.

Increased militance

Perhaps the most alarming—because the most unexpected—of the militant revolts that seized Britain in the years before 1914 was the campaign for women's suffrage. The middle-class women who engaged in this struggle enjoyed more freedom of opportunity than their mothers had known. Laws had been passed easing the process of divorce and permitting married women control of their own property. Some universities had started to grant degrees to women. Contraceptive devices—and feminist propaganda defending their use—had begun to result in changed attitudes toward sexuality within the middle class. Perhaps because of these gains, many women felt their lack

Suffragettes

London Dock Strike, 1911.
Police move to clear demonstrators from shops where
they have taken refuge after
having been fired upon.

of the vote all the more acutely. Although the movement began
among middle-class women, it soon included some female members
of the working class and the aristocracy. Agitation reached a peak after
1900, when militant suffragettes—under the leadership of Emmeline
Pankhurst, her daughters Christabel and Sylvia, and others—resorted
to violence in order to impress upon the nation the seriousness of their
commitment. Women chained themselves to the visitors' gallery in
the House of Commons; slashed paintings in museums; invaded that
male sanctum, the golf course, and inscribed VOTES FOR WOMEN in acid
on the greens; disrupted political meetings; burned politicians' houses;
and smashed department store windows. The government countered
violence with repression. When women, arrested for their disruptive
activities, went on hunger strikes in prisons, wardens proceeded to
feed them forcibly, tying them down, holding their mouths open with
wooden and metal clamps, and running tubes down their throats.
When hunger strikes threatened to produce deaths and thus martyrs
for the cause, the government passed the constitutionally dubious Cat
and Mouse Act, which sanctioned the freeing of prisoners to halt their
starvation and then, once they had regained their health, authorized
their rearrest. The movement was not to see the achievement of its
goal until after World War I, when reform came largely because of
women's contributions to the war effort.

  Whether Britain's militant mood might have led to some sort of
general conflict had not the war begun in 1914, is a question historians
Instability continue to debate. Suffice it to say that national sentiment in the last
few years before the outbreak of general hostilities was a far different

Violent Suffragette Protest. Emily Davison was killed when she threw herself in front of the king's racehorse at the Epsom Derby, June 4, 1913. Her purpose was to call attention to the suffragette cause.

one from that of the 1870s. Britain, so confident of itself and of its moderation, was proving no less a prey to instability than other European nations.

4. RUSSIA: THE ROAD TO REVOLUTION

In only one European country, Russia, did conditions pass from instability to insurrection during these prewar years. The Russian revolutionary movement had numerous forerunners. Waves of discontent broke out several times during the nineteenth century. Threatened uprisings between 1850–1860 persuaded Tsar Alexander II to grant local self-government, to reform the judicial system, and, most important of all, to liberate the serfs. Yet his government failed to sustain all these reforms; a wave of reaction followed. Radicalism revived and the number of revolutionary sects increased. Allied with them were the nihilists, who tended to condemn the whole political and social system. Although nihilism originated about 1860 as a movement to solve Russian problems by spreading enlightenment among the peasants, its failure to win general support by propagandist methods turned its leadership more and more to terrorism. The culmination of this terrorism was the assassination of the tsar in 1881.

The years that followed the death of Alexander II marked the flood-tide of reaction against the entire policy of reform. The new tsar, Alexander III (1881–1894), governed under the theory that Russia had nothing in common with western Europe, that its people had been

Reform and reaction in nineteenth century Russia

nurtured on despotism and mystical piety for centuries and would be utterly lost without them. Such Western ideals as rationalism and individualism would undermine the childlike faith of the Russian masses and would plunge the nation into the dark abyss of anarchy and crime. In like manner, Western institutions of trial by jury, parliamentary government, and free education could never bear fruit if planted in Russian soil. With such doctrines as his guiding principles, Alexander III enforced a regime of stern and vengeful repression. He curtailed in every way possible the powers of the local assemblies, increased the authority of the secret police, and subjected villages to government by wealthy nobles selected by the state. These policies were continued, though in somewhat less rigorous form, by his son, Nicholas II (1894–1918), a much less effective ruler. Both tsars were ardent proponents of Russification and used it with a vengeance to strengthen their power. Russification was simply the more ruthless counterpart of similar nationalistic movements in various countries. Its purpose was to extend the language, religion, and culture of Great Russia, or Russia proper, over all of the subjects of the tsar and thereby to simplify the problem of governing them. It was aimed primarily at the Poles, Finns, and Jews, since these were the nationalities considered most dangerous. Inevitably it resulted in oppression. The Finns were deprived of their constitution; the Poles were compelled to study their own literature in Russian translations; and high officials in the tsar's government connived at *pogroms,* i.e., wholesale massacres, against the Jews.

   Despite these attempts to turn Russia's back to the West, however, the nation was being drawn more closely than it had ever been before into the general European orbit. Russia was industrializing, and making use of European capital to do so. Economic policies during the

A Railroad Yard in Eastern Russia, 1896

1890s, when Count Sergei Witte was the tsar's leading minister, resulted in the adoption of the gold standard, which made Russian currency easily convertible. Railways and telegraph lines were constructed; exports and imports multiplied by factors of seven and five respectively from 1880 to 1913. In addition, Russian writers and musicians contributed in a major way to the enriching of Western culture. We have already noted the singular contributions of Tolstoy, Turgenev, and Dostoevsky. The musical works of Peter Tchaikovsky (1840–1893) and Nikolai Rimsky-Korsakov (1844–1908), while expressing a peculiarly Russian temperament and tradition, were recognized as important additions to the general body of first-rate contemporary composition.

With Westernization came the growth of both the business and wage-earning classes. And with an increase in class consciousness new political parties emerged. Middle-class businessmen and professionals combined with enterprising landowners in 1903 to form a Constitutional Democratic party, whose program included the creation of a nationally elected parliament or Duma to determine and carry out policies which would further the twin goals of liberalization and Westernization. Meanwhile, two essentially working-class parties, the Social Revolutionaries and the Social Democrats, began to agitate for far more radical solutions to the problems of Russian autocracy. The Social Revolutionaries concerned themselves with the continued plight of the peasants, who, when serfdom was abolished, were compelled to purchase their land, and who were burdened with high taxes. The Social Revolutionaries wanted to equalize the landholdings of peasants within their local agricultural communes or *mirs,* and to increase the power of the *mirs* in their continuing competition with large landowners. The Social Democrats were Marxists, who saw themselves as westerners and as part of the international working-class movement. In 1903 the leadership of the Social Democratic party split in an important disagreement over revolutionary strategy. The Mensheviks, who took their name from the Russian word for minority, argued unsuccessfully for a broadly based party which, while remaining revolutionary, would nonetheless accept assistance from progressives and democrats. The Bolsheviks—the majority of the Social Democrats—favored a strongly centralized party controlled by a committee whose "party line" would be accepted at all organizational levels. The Bolsheviks reorganized the Social Democrats under the leadership of the young, dynamic, and dedicated revolutionary Vladimir Ulanov (1870–1924), who wrote under the pseudonym of N. Lenin.

Lenin was a member of the middle class, his father having served as an inspector of schools and minor political functionary. He had been expelled from the University of Kazan for engaging in radical activity, following the execution of his elder brother for his involvement in a

Growth of political parties

The Young Lenin, 1897

Lenin

plot to assassinate Alexander III. Lenin spent three years as a political prisoner in Siberia; from 1900 until 1917 he lived as a political exile in western Europe. His zeal and abilities as both a theoretician and a political activist are evidenced by the fact that he retained leadership of the Social Democrats even while residing abroad. Lenin continued to preach the gospel of Marxism and of a relentless class struggle. His treatise *What Is to Be Done?* was a stinging response to revisionists who were urging collaboration with less radical parties. Revolution was what was to be done, Lenin argued, revolution "made" as soon as possible by an elitist group of agitators working through the agency of a disciplined party. Lenin and his followers, by merging the tradition of Russian revolutionism with Western Marxism, and by endowing the result with a sense of immediate possibility, fused the Russian situation in such a way as to make eventual explosion almost inevitable.

The revolution that came in 1905, however, took even the Bolsheviks by surprise. Its unexpected occurrence was the result of a war between Russia and Japan, which broke out in 1904, and in which the Russians were soundly beaten. Both countries had conflicting interests in Manchuria and Korea; this fact was the immediate cause of the conflict. On land and sea the Japanese proved themselves the military superiors of the Russians. As dispatches continued to report the defeats of the tsar's army and navy, the Russian people were presented with dramatic evidence of the inefficiency of autocracy.

Members of the middle class who had hitherto refrained from association with the revolutionists, now joined in the clamor for change. Radical workingmen organized strikes and held demonstrations in every important city. Led by a priest, Father Gapon, a group of 200,000 workers and their families went to demonstrate their grievances at the tsar's winter palace in St. Petersburg on January 22, 1905—ever after known as Bloody Sunday. The demonstrators were met by guard troops and many of them were shot dead. By the autumn of 1905 nearly the entire urban population had enlisted in a strike of protest. Merchants closed their stores, factory-owners shut down their plants, lawyers refused to plead cases in court, and even valets and cooks deserted their wealthy employers. It was soon evident to Tsar Nicholas that the government would have to yield. On October 30, he issued his October Manifesto, pledging guarantees of individual liberties, promising a moderately liberal franchise for the election of a Duma, and affirming that henceforth no law would be valid unless it had the Duma's approval. This was the high-water mark of the revolutionary movement. During the next two years Nicholas issued a series of sweeping decrees which negated most of the promises made in the October Manifesto. He deprived the Duma of many of its powers, and decreed that it be elected indirectly on a class basis by a number of electoral colleges. Thereafter the legislative body contained a majority of obedient followers of the tsar.

The Russo-Japanese War

The Revolution of 1905

Bloody Sunday. Demonstrating workers who sought to bring their grievances to the attention of the tsar are met and gunned down by government troops, January 1905.

The reasons for this setback to the revolutionary movement are not hard to discover. In the first place, the army remained loyal to its commander-in-chief. Consequently, after the termination of the war with Japan in 1905, the tsar had a large body of troops that could be counted upon if necessary to decimate the ranks of the revolutionists. An even more important reason was the split in the ranks of the revolutionists themselves. After the issuance of the October Manifesto, large numbers of the bourgeoisie became frightened at threats of the radicals and declared their conviction that the revolution had gone far enough. Withdrawing their support altogether, they became known henceforth as Octobrists. The more radical merchants and professional men, organized into the Constitutional Democratic party, maintained that opposition should continue until the tsar had been forced to establish a government modeled after that of Great Britain. This fatal division rendered the middle class politically impotent. Finally, disaffection appeared within the ranks of the workers. Further attempts to employ the general strike as a weapon against the government ended in disaster.

The reasons for setback

But the Russian revolutionary movement of 1905 was not a total failure. The cruel vengeance taken by the tsar convinced many people that their government was not a benevolent autocracy, as they had been led to believe, but a stubborn and brutal tyranny. The uprising revealed to the masses their principal mistakes and taught them what sources of strength they should rely upon for success in the future. Moreover, some of the concessions actually obtained were not completely wiped out. The Duma was not abolished. It continued to serve

Gains from the revolutionary movement

as a means by which at least scattered opponents of reaction could make themselves heard. In addition, the revolt of 1905 persuaded some of the more sagacious advisors of the tsar that last-ditch conservatism was none too safe. The result was the enactment of a number of reforms designed to conciliate the troublesome classes. Among the most significant were the agrarian reforms sponsored by the government's leading minister, Peter Stolypin, between 1906 and 1911. These included: (1) the transfer of 5 million acres of royal land to the peasants for a price; (2) permission for the peasant to withdraw from the *mir* and set up as an independent farmer; and (3) cancellation of the remaining installments owed by the peasants for their land. Nor were the working classes altogether forgotten. Decrees were issued permitting the formation of labor unions, providing for a reduction of the working day (to not more than ten hours in most cases), and establishing sickness and accident insurance. Yet the hopes of some liberals that Russia was on the way to becoming a progressive nation on the Western model proved illusory. The tsar remained stubbornly autocratic. Few peasants had enough money to buy the lands offered for purchase. In view of the rising cost of living, the factory workers considered their modest gains insufficient. A new revolutionary outbreak merely awaited a convenient spark.

5. THE SEARCH FOR STABILITY ELSEWHERE IN THE WEST

Reforms in Italy

Other European countries generally found it just as difficult to attain internal tranquility in the late nineteenth century as did those whose history we have surveyed. Italy was plagued by squabbles among its political leaders, aggravated by the festering quarrel with the papacy over the seizure of ecclesiastical territories. Illiteracy and poverty, particular problems in the agrarian south, contributed to unrest, as did working-class radicalism in the industrial cities of the north. Attempts were made to relieve distress by the passage of social welfare legislation, including provision for nationalized life insurance. In 1912 a law tripled the electorate, instituting something approximating universal manhood suffrage. Relatively few of the newly enfranchised exercised their right to vote, choosing to register their discontent by more direct means such as strikes.

Nationalism in Austria-Hungary

Nationalist aspirations continued to be a major problem in eastern Europe. In 1867 an attempt had been made to resolve national differences in Austria by dividing the empire in two—an Austrian empire west of the river Leith, and a kingdom of Hungary to its east. Each of the two components in this so-called Dual Monarchy was to be the equal of the other, though the two were joined by the same Hapsburg monarch, by several common ministries, and by a kind of superparliament. This solution failed to put an end to nationalist divisions, however. Czechs and other Slav minorities in both of the new terri-

EUROPE AFTER THE CONGRESS OF BERLIN · 1878

tories nursed resentment against what they perceived as domination by alien German or Magyar culture. Despite the division of responsibilities between Austria and Hungary, the government remained centralized under the rule of the Emperor-King Francis Joseph. Social agitation was countered, as in Germany, by repression coupled with welfare measures. Universal male suffrage was introduced into Austria in 1907; in Hungary it was opposed by the Magyar majority which saw it as a device whereby the Slavic minority might increase its power.

In southeastern Europe nationalist agitation continued to rend the ever-disintegrating Ottoman Empire. Before 1829 the entire Balkan peninsula—bounded by the Aegean, Black, and Adriatic Seas—was controlled by the Turks. But during the next eighty-five years a gradual dismemberment of the Turkish Empire occurred. In some instances the slicing away of territories had been perpetrated by rival European powers, especially by Russia and Austria; but generally it

The Ottoman Empire

was the result of nationalist revolts by the sultan's Christian subjects. In 1829, at the conclusion of a war between Russia and Turkey, the Ottoman Empire was compelled to acknowledge the independence of Greece and to grant autonomy to Serbia and to the provinces which later became Rumania. As the years passed, resentment against Ottoman rule spread through other Balkan territories. In 1875–1876 there were uprisings in Bosnia, Herzegovina, and Bulgaria, which the sultan suppressed with murderous vengeance. Reports of atrocities against Christians gave Russia an excuse for renewal of its age-long struggle for domination of the Balkans. In this second Russo-Turkish War (1877–1878) the armies of the tsar won a smashing victory. The Treaty of San Stefano, which terminated the conflict, provided that the sultan surrender nearly all of his territory in Europe, except for a remnant around Constantinople. But at this juncture the great powers intervened. Austria and Great Britain, especially, were opposed to letting Russia assume jurisdiction over so large a portion of the Near East. In 1878 a congress of the great powers, meeting in Berlin, transferred Bessarabia to Russia, Thessaly to Greece, and Bosnia and Herzegovina to the control of Austria. Seven years later the Bulgars, who had been granted some degree of autonomy by the Congress of Berlin, seized the province of Eastern Rumelia from Turkey and in 1908 established the independent Kingdom of Bulgaria.

*The Young Turk
revolution*

In the very year when this last dismemberment occurred, Turkey itself was engulfed by the tidal wave of nationalism. For some time the more enlightened Turkish citizens had been growing increasingly disgusted with the weakness and incompetence of the sultan's government. In particular, those who had been educated in European universities were growing more and more convinced that their country should be rejuvenated by the introduction of Western ideas of science, patriotism, and democracy. Organizing themselves into a society known as the Young Turks, they forced the sultan in 1908 to establish constitutional government. The following year, when a reactionary movement set in, they deposed the reigning sultan, Abdul Hamid II, and placed on the throne his brother, Mohammed V, as a titular sovereign. The real powers of government were now entrusted to a grand vizier and ministers responsible to an elected parliament. This revolution did not mean increased liberty for the non-Turkish inhabitants of the empire. Instead, the Young Turks launched a vigorous movement to Ottomanize all of the Christian subjects of the sultan. At the same time the disturbances preceding and accompanying the revolution opened the way for still further dismemberment. In 1908 Austria annexed the provinces of Bosnia and Herzegovina, which the Treaty of Berlin had allowed it merely to administer, and in 1911–1912 Italy entered into war with Turkey for the conquest of Tripoli.

Of all the major nations of the West, the United States probably underwent the least domestic turmoil during the several decades before

THE DISMEMBERMENT OF THE OTTOMAN EMPIRE · 1683-1923

1914. The Civil War had exhausted the country; until the end of the century the ever-expanding frontier provided an alternative for those discontented with their present lot. Yet the United States also felt, to some degree, the pressures that made stability so hard to sustain in Europe. Though the Civil War had ended, the complex moral problem of racism remained to block all attempts to truly heal the nation. Severe economic crises, particularly an economic depression in the 1890s, accompanied by the collapse of agricultural prices and the closing of factories, caused great suffering and aroused anger at capitalist adventurers who seemed to be profiting at the expense of the country as a whole. Many grew convinced that a restricted money supply had produced the depression. Demand for the issuance of paper money

Unrest in the United States

Eugene Debs

and the increased coinage of silver were at the heart of the programs of the Greenback and the Populist parties, which attracted large followings, and which campaigned as well for an income tax and government ownership of railways, and telephone and telegraph lines. Socialism of a reformist brand was espoused by Eugene V. Debs (1855–1926), leader of a mildly Marxist Socialist party. It failed to appeal to the generally un–class-conscious American worker, who continued to have faith in the dream of economic mobility. More radical was the membership of the Industrial Workers of the World, a general union whose goal was to organize the unskilled and immigrant worker. Perceived as a device of foreign agitators, the IWW was repressed both by the government and by industrial management. Characteristic of the generally moderate tone of American reformism was the Progressive movement, which captured both the imagination and votes of a vocal minority of middle-class Americans whose hostility over the accumulation of private economic power and the political corruption of urban "bosses" was balanced by their belief in the democratic process and in the possibility of continuing human progress. The movement, many of whose ideas were embodied in the programs of Presidents Theodore Roosevelt and Woodrow Wilson, was halted by the First World War, which fostered an environment hostile to the democratic process.

6. INTERNATIONAL RIVALRIES: THE ROAD TO THE FIRST WORLD WAR

The end of a century of peace

Despite the domestic instabilities and uncertainties that characterized the Western world in the years before 1914, a great many men and women retained a faith in the notion of peaceful progress. There had been an absence of multinational armed conflict—with the exception of the Crimean War—for a century. European countries—even autocratic Russia—had been moving gradually towards what most agreed was the worthy goal of democracy. Indeed, instability could be understood as the result of either an overzealous or an overdelayed movement in that direction. Above all, industrialization seemed to be providing a better standard of living for all—or at least all within the Western world. There is little wonder, therefore, that men and women reacted with disbelief as they saw their world crumbling during the days of frantic diplomatic maneuvering just prior to the outbreak of war in August 1914.

The balance of power

The key to an understanding of the coming of World War I lies in an understanding of international diplomacy during the years after 1870. Europe had prided itself on the establishment of a balance of power, which had kept any one nation from assuming a position so powerful as to threaten the general peace. During his years as chancellor, Bismarck played a diplomatic variation upon this general theme, in order to ensure that France would not engage in a war of revenge against the German victors of 1870. There was little prospect that the French would attempt war singlehanded. Therefore, Bismarck determined to isolate France by attaching all of its potential allies to Germany. In 1873 he managed to form an alliance with both Austria and Russia, the so-called League of the Three Emperors, a precarious combination that soon went on the rocks. With the League of the Three Emperors defunct, Bismarck cemented a new and much stronger alliance with Austria. In 1882 this partnership was expanded into the celebrated Triple Alliance when Italy was added as a member. The Italians did not join out of love for either Germany or Austria but from motives of anger and fear. They resented the French occupation of Tunisia (1881), a territory which they regarded as properly theirs. Moreover, Italian politicians were still at odds with the Church, and they feared that supporters of the papacy in France might gain the upper hand and send a French army to defend the pope. In the meantime, the Three Emperors' League had been revived. Though it lasted for only six years (1881–1887), Germany managed to hold the friendship of Russia until 1890.

Thus after little more than a decade of diplomatic maneuvering, Bismarck had achieved his ambition. By 1882 France was cut off from nearly every possibility of obtaining aid from powerful friends. Austria and Italy were united with Germany in the Triple Alliance, and Russia after a three-year lapse was back once more in the Bismarckian

Bismarck's diplomatic success

Grand Palace, Paris Exposition, 1900. European nations continued to promote exhibitions of this sort, patterned after the Crystal Palace exhibition of 1851. Designed to celebrate the growth of Western industrialism, they also served to promote international rivalry.

camp. The only conceivable quarter from which help might come was Great Britain; but, with respect to continental affairs, the British were maintaining a policy of "splendid isolation." Therefore, so far as the danger of a war of revenge was concerned, Germany had little to fear. Bismarck's complicated structure of alliances appeared to answer the purpose for which he claimed it had been built—to keep the peace. But the alliance system was a weapon that could cut two ways. In Bismarck's hands, it kept the peace. In hands less diplomatically capable, it might become less an asset than a liability, as was the case after 1890.

A diplomatic revolution

During the years between 1890 and 1907, European nations, competing against each other across the globe for trade and territory, became more suspicious of the intentions of each other. This general international insecurity produced a diplomatic revolution that obliterated Bismarck's handiwork, and resulted in a new alignment which threatened the Germans. To be sure, the Germans had Austria still on their side; but they lost the friendship of both Russia and Italy, while Britain abandoned its isolation to enter into agreements with Russia and France. This shift in the balance of power had fateful results. It convinced the Germans that they were surrounded by a ring of enemies, and that consequently they must do everything in their power to retain the loyalty of Austria-Hungary—even to the extent of supporting that country's foreign adventures.

The Triple Entente

The first of the major results of this diplomatic revolution was the formation of the Triple Entente. In 1890 Russia and France began a political flirtation which gradually turned into a binding alliance. The secret military convention signed by the two countries in 1894 provided that each should come to the aid of the other in case of an attack by Germany, or by Austria or Italy supported by Germany. This Dual Alliance of Russia and France was followed by an Entente Cordiale between France and Great Britain. During the last two decades of the nineteenth century, the British and the French had frequently been involved in sharp altercations over colonies and trade, as in the Sudan. By 1904, however, France, fearing Germany, had buried its differences with Britain and in that year signed the Entente Cordiale. This was not a formal alliance but a friendly agreement, covering a variety of subjects. The final step in the formation of the Triple Entente was the conclusion of a mutual understanding between Great Britain and Russia. Again there was no formal alliance. The two powers simply came to an agreement in 1907 concerning their ambitions in Asia.

Two opposing camps

Thus by 1907 the great powers of Europe had come to be arrayed in two opposing combinations, the Triple Alliance of Germany, Italy, and Austria-Hungary, and the Triple Entente of Britain, France, and Russia. Had these combinations remained stable and more or less evenly matched, they might well have promoted the cause of peace. But no such condition prevailed. Each grew weaker and less stable with the passage of time. And it was this instability, rather than the al-

The Baghdad Railroad. German and Turkish officials celebrate the launching of the enterprise.

liance system itself, which was perhaps the most important contributing factor leading to the outbreak of war.

The tensions within the new alliances become more comprehensible if one considers the national aims of each of the principal European states. By 1900 six great powers in Europe—Germany, France, Russia, Italy, Austria-Hungary, and Great Britain—were competing for power, security, and economic advantage. Each had specific objectives, the fulfillment of which it regarded as essential to its national interest. Germany built its ambitions around eastward expansion. After 1890 German capitalists and imperialists dreamed of a *Drang nach Osten* (drive to the east) and planned the construction of a railway from Berlin to Baghdad to facilitate economic control of the Ottoman Empire. Austria also looked to the east, but to the Balkans rather than to any part of western Asia. Austria's hold on Trieste and other portions of the Adriatic coast was precarious, since much of this territory was inhabited by Italians. If it could carve a highway through the Balkans to the Aegean, its access to the sea would be more secure.

Aims of the great powers: Germany and Austria-Hungary

To a large degree the objectives of France were dictated by a desire to curb or counterbalance the growing might of Germany. France hoped to recover Alsace and Lorraine. But recovery of these lost provinces was not the only French objective. The French were also determined to add Morocco to their African empire regardless of the interests of other powers. The motives of the French were both economic and political. Morocco contained rich mineral deposits, and would be also valuable for strategic reasons and as a reservoir from which troops might be drawn.

Ambitions of France

A paramount ambition of Russia was to gain control of the Bosporus and the Dardanelles. Achievement of this long-desired goal would prevent the Russian fleet from being bottled up in the Black Sea in the event of war. Besides, it would give unquestioned access to the Mediterranean and probably possession of Constantin-

Ambitions of Russia

ople. Turkey would be eliminated from Europe, and Russia would fall heir to the Balkans. In addition, if the tsar's agents could get to Constantinople before the Germans, they could turn the Berlin-to-Baghdad railway into an empty dream. But the Russians had other ambitions. They coveted access to the Persian Gulf and Indian Ocean and tried for years to make Persia a Russian protectorate. They also strove for better outlets to the Pacific and attempted to extend their control over Manchuria. That each of these ambitions constituted a threat to the status quo scarcely needs emphasis.

Ambitions of Great Britain and Italy

The power policies of Great Britain and Italy were somewhat less closely related to the specific actions of other countries. The policy of Britain, in fact, was directed against almost everyone. It was no less suspicious of the Russian ambitions at Constantinople than it was of the German. Until after the beginning of the twentieth century the British distrusted France. Their cardinal aims were (1) to maintain the lifelines of their empire; (2) to keep open the sea lanes to their sources of imports and foreign markets; and (3) to preserve a balance among the nations on the Continent so that no one of them would ever become strong enough to attack Great Britain. If the actions of any other country threatened to interfere with these cardinal aims (as they often did), the hostility of Britain would instantly be aroused. The offending nation would be put in its place by diplomatic pressure, by forming an alliance against it, or by going to war, as the British finally did against Germany in 1914. Italian policy was mainly based on hopes of aggrandizement at the expense of Austria and Turkey. Austria continued to hold territories which the Italians regarded as rightfully theirs—the so-called *Italia Irredenta* (unredeemed Italy) as late as 1915—while Turkey blocked Italy's acquisition of Tripoli and other territories in North Africa.

Resulting conflicts

These often conflicting ambitions naturally placed strains on the alliances between the great powers. The Triple Alliance declined in strength because of a growing coolness between Italy and Austria. Moreover, Italian nationalists coveted territory in North Africa, notably Tripoli, which they believed they could obtain only by supporting French ambitions in Morocco. Meanwhile, the Triple Entente was threatened by discord between Britain and Russia. Because their lifeline to the East might be imperiled, the British could not view with equanimity the cardinal aim of Russia to gain control of the Bosporus and the Dardanelles and thus of Constantinople. Disharmony in the Triple Entente also increased when Britain and France refused to support Russia in its dispute with Austria over the latter's annexation of Bosnia and Herzegovina. In short, conflicts were so numerous that the members of neither alliance could be quite sure where their opposite numbers might stand in case of a real threat of a European war.

If diplomatic instability was the major cause of the war, two others must nevertheless be emphasized as well. Nationalism, particularly in eastern Europe, played an important role in heightening international conflict. Since the beginning of the twentieth century, Serbia wanted to extend its jurisdiction over all the peoples alleged to be similar to its own citizens in race and in culture. Some of these peoples inhabited what were then the two Turkish provinces of Bosnia and Herzegovina. Others included Croatians and Slovenes in the southern provinces of Austria-Hungary. After 1908, when Austria suddenly annexed Bosnia and Herzegovina, the Serbian scheme was directed exclusively against the Hapsburg Empire. It took the form of agitation to provoke discontent among the Slav subjects of Austria, in the hope of drawing them away and uniting the territories they inhabited with Serbia. It resulted in a series of dangerous plots against the peace and integrity of the Dual Monarchy.

Other causes: nationalism

In many of their activities the Serbian nationalists were aided and abetted by the Pan-Slavists in Russia. The Pan-Slav movement was founded upon the theory that all of the Slavs of eastern Europe constituted one great family. Therefore, it was argued that Russia as the most powerful Slavic state should act as the guide and protector of the smaller Slavic nations of the Balkans. Pan-Slavism was not merely the wishful sentiment of a few ardent nationalists, but was a part of the official policy of the Russian government. It went far toward explaining Russia's aggressive stand in every quarrel that arose between Serbia and Austria.

Pan-Slavism

One further expression of the growth of international instability, and hence one further cause of war, was the spread of militarism. Uncertainty as to the reliability of alliances encouraged the belief that national security depended upon the extent of military and naval preparedness. War scares produced a compulsion to build larger armies and navies. After 1870, every major European power, with the exception of Britain, had adopted conscription and universal military training. Germany and Britain strained their resources either to achieve or to maintain naval superiority. Accompanying this arms race was a growing willingness to acknowledge the place of international aggression in the conduct of world affairs. The American President Theodore Roosevelt had argued that training for war was necessary to preserve the "manly and adventurous qualities" in a nation. The German Field Marshal von Moltke and historian Heinrich von Treitschke saw in military conflict one of the divine elements of the universe and a "terrible medicine" for the human race. The French philosopher Ernest Renan justified war as a condition of progress, "the sting which prevents a country from going to sleep."

Militarism

Field Marshal von Moltke

All these factors—diplomatic instability, nationalism, and militarism—combined to produce a series of crises between 1905 and 1913. They were not so much causes as they were symptoms of international animosity. Yet each left a heritage of suspicion and bitterness that made war all the more probable. In some cases hostilities were averted only because one of the parties was too weak at the time to offer resistance. The result was a sense of humiliation, a smoldering resentment that was almost bound to burst into flame in the future. Two of the crises were generated by disputes over Morocco. Both Germany and France wanted to control Morocco; and in 1905 and 1911 the two powers stood on the brink of war. Each time the dispute was smoothed over, but not without the usual legacy of suspicion.

Moroccan crises

In addition to the clash over Morocco, two crises occurred in the Near East. The first was the Bosnian crisis of 1908. At the Congress of Berlin in 1878 the two Turkish provinces of Bosnia and Herzegovina had been placed under the administrative control of Austria, though actual sovereignty was still to be vested in the Ottoman Empire. Serbia also coveted the territories, since they would double its kingdom and place it within striking distance of the Adriatic. Suddenly, in October 1908, Austria annexed the two provinces, in flat violation of the Treaty of Berlin. The Serbs were furious and appealed to Russia. The tsar's government threatened war, until Germany addressed a sharp note to St. Petersburg announcing its firm intention to back Austria. Since Russia had not yet fully recovered from its war with Japan and was plagued by internal troubles, Russian intervention was postponed.

Serbian crisis

Still more bad blood between the nations of eastern Europe was created by the Balkan Wars. In 1912 Serbia, Bulgaria, Montenegro, and Greece, with encouragement from Russia, joined in a Balkan alliance for the conquest of the Turkish province of Macedonia. The war started in October 1912, and in less than two months the resistance of the Turks was shattered. Then came the problem of dividing the spoils. In secret treaties negotiated before hostilities began, Serbia had been promised Albania, in addition to a generous slice of Macedonia. But now Austria, fearful as always of any increase in Serbian power, intervened at the peace conference and obtained the establishment of Albania as an independent state. For the Serbs this was the last straw. It seemed that at every turn their path to western expansion was certain to be blocked by the Hapsburg government. From this time on, anti-Austrian agitation in Serbia and in the neighboring province of Bosnia became ever more venomous.

Balkan Wars

It was the assassination of the Austrian Archduke Francis Ferdinand by a Serbian sympathizer on June 28, 1914, that ignited the conflict. The four-year war that ensued altered the Western world immeasurably. Yet many changes which came either during or after World War I were the result, not of the war itself, but of pressures and forces we have seen at work during the prewar years. Then European power, at its height, was challenged by forces which that power had unleashed and which it proved unable to contain.

A world at war

SELECTED READINGS

- *Items so designated are available in paperback editions.*
- Berghahn, Victor, *Germany and the Approach of War in 1914,* New York, 1973. Examines the domestic background of German foreign policy, especially the naval program.

  Brogan, D. W., *France under the Republic, 1870–1930,* New York, 1940. An excellent survey, comprehensive and analytical.
- Dangerfield, George, *The Damnable Question: One Hundred and Twenty Years of Anglo-Irish Conflict,* Boston, 1976. A sensitive and judicious assessment of the Irish question.
- ———, *The Strange Death of Liberal England,* New York, 1935. Examines England's three major crises of the prewar period: women's suffrage, labor unrest, and Irish home rule.

  Dansette, Adrien, *A Religious History of Modern France,* Vol. II, New York, 1961. Covers the period 1870–1940.

  Ensor, R. C. K., *England, 1870–1914,* Oxford, 1949. From the Oxford History of England series.
- Eyck, Erich, *Bismarck and the German Empire,* New York, 1968.
- Haimson, L., *The Russian Marxists and the Origins of Bolshevism,* Cambridge, Mass., 1955.

  Halèvy, Elie, *A History of the English People,* Vols. IV–VI, London, 1949–52. The best survey of the period.

  Hoffman, Ross, *Great Britain and the German Trade Rivalry, 1875–1914,* Philadelphia, 1933. A perceptive account.

  Jenks, William A., *Austria under the Iron Ring, 1879–1893,* Charlottesville, Va., 1965. An examination of Austria's attempts at political and social reform, set in the context of a struggle for autonomy from German domination.

  Johnson, Douglas, *France and the Dreyfus Affair,* London, 1966.
- Jones, Gareth Stedman, *Outcast London,* Oxford, 1971. A remarkable book which examines the breakdown in the relationship between classes in London during the latter half of the nineteenth century.

  Mack Smith, Dennis, *Italy: A Modern History,* rev. ed., Ann Arbor, Mich. 1969. An excellent survey.
- McManners, John, *Church and State in France, 1870–1914,* New York, 1972. Particularly good on the question of education and the final separation of Church and State.
- May, Arthur J., *The Hapsburg Monarchy, 1867–1914,* Cambridge, Mass., 1951.
- Mosse, W. E., *Alexander II and the Modernization of Russia,* New York, 1958.

  Nichols, John Alden, *Germany After Bismarck,* New York, 1959.

  Rémond, Rene, *The Right Wing in France from 1815 to De Gaulle,* Philadelphia, 1969. Traces the survival of royalism and Bonapartism in French thought and politics.

  Seton-Watson, Hugh, *The Russian Empire, 1801–1917,* Oxford, 1967.
- Simon, Walter M., ed., *Germany in the Age of Bismarck,* New York, 1968.

• Taylor, A. J. P., *The Struggle for Mastery in Europe, 1848–1918*, Oxford, 1954. An excellent diplomatic history.

Thompson, Paul R., *The Edwardians: The Remaking of British Society*, Bloomington, Ind., 1975. Examines social change in England at the turn of the century and the instruments of that change.

• Thomson, David, *Democracy in France since 1870*, rev. ed., New York, 1969.

Weber, Eugen, *Peasants into Frenchmen: The Modernization of France, 1870–1914*, Stanford, Calif., 1977. Argues that the great achievement of the Third Republic was the consolidation of France, accomplished by bringing rural areas into the mainstream of modern life.

• Williams, Roger L., *The French Revolution of 1870–1871*, New York, 1969. A good narrative account.

SOURCE MATERIALS

Booth, Charles, ed., *Life and Labour of the People in London*, 9 vols., London, 1892–97. A remarkable document for its time. A street-by-street survey of London's labor and poverty. One of the most comprehensive social surveys ever.

Childers, Erskine, *The Riddle of the Sands*, New York, 1978. A best-seller in England in 1903, this novel concerns a future war between England and Germany. Its reception gives evidence of the rise of anti-German sentiment prior to World War I.

• Hamerow, Theodore S., ed., *The Age of Bismarck: Documents and Interpretations*, New York, 1973.

• Lenin, Vladimir, *What Is to Be Done?* London, 1918. Written in 1902, this is Lenin's most famous pamphlet. In it he called for the proletarian revolution to be led by elite cadres of bourgeois intellectuals, like himself.

• Mackenzie, Midge, ed., *Shoulder to Shoulder*, New York, 1975. A richly illustrated documentary history of the British movement for women's suffrage.

• Pankhurst, Emmeline, *My Own Story*, New York, 1914. The memoirs of one of the leaders of England's militant suffragettes.

• Turgenev, Ivan, *Fathers and Sons*, New York, 1966. Turgenev's greatest novel is set in Russia in the 1860s and portrays the ideological conflict between generations at the time of the emancipation of the serfs and the rise of nihilism.

• Zola, Émile, *Germinal*, New York, 1964. Zola's realistic novel describes class conflict in France's coal mining region.

Chapter 32

CHINA, JAPAN, AND AFRICA UNDER THE IMPACT OF THE WEST (1800-1914)

The virtue and prestige of the Celestial Dynasty having spread far and wide, the kings of the myriad nations come by land and sea with all sorts of precious things. Consequently there is nothing we lack, as your principal envoy and others have themselves observed. We have never set much store on strange or ingenious objects, nor do we need any more of your country's manufactures.

> —Edict of the Ch'ien Lung Manchu emperor to King George III of England, 1793

During the nineteenth century, for the first time in history the most advanced western states, through the dynamic effects of the Industrial Revolution, became strong enough to alter the destinies of Far Eastern and African nations by direct intervention. Consequently, the chief problems affecting these Eastern and African nations in this period revolved around the readjustments necessitated by Western expansion. Cultural phenomena were subordinated to political objectives, and international relations became of crucial importance. Because China, Japan, and the African states responded quite differently to the changing world conditions that confronted them, the contrasts among these countries became greater than ever before.

Increased Western intervention

1. IMPERIALISM AND REVOLUTION IN CHINA

The nineteenth century, which witnessed tremendous economic, political, and intellectual progress in the Western world, was a period of trouble for China. The central factor in China's distress was the decadence of the Manchu Dynasty and the incompetence of its admin-

The misfortunes of China under the impact of imperialism

istration, but all her problems were aggravated by the pressure that Western powers were now exerting in the Far East. As in the case of India the objectives of the Westerners at the outset were almost exclusively commercial, and in China as in India the British played the leading role. Although China escaped complete subjugation, her institutions were greatly altered under the Western impact; she suffered the humiliation of seeing her territory and sovereignty infringed upon by Europeans; and for the first time in history Japan displaced China as the leading Asian state.

How Western traders gained a foothold

It was unfortunate that increasing interest in the China trade on the part of Western nations came at a time when the imperial government was almost moribund, undermined by corruption, and lacking in imaginative leadership. During many earlier periods of their history the Chinese had shown themselves to be not only enterprising traders but also capable of profiting from the stimulation offered by contacts with the outside world. By the nineteenth century the eyes of officials were closed to the desirability of any change and to the danger of having unwelcome changes forced upon them. Both the Manchu aristocracy and the Chinese class of scholar-officials that supported it were schooled in the tradition that trade was a contemptible business, unworthy of a gentleman's attention. The Westerners who came to China specifically for purposes of trade were looked down upon as a low order of humanity, and the power they were able to exert in enforcing their demands was slow to be recognized. The policy of the Manchu government was to avoid contamination from the Western hucksters by keeping them at a safe distance and requiring them to have relations only with Chinese merchants, not with government officials. At the same time the government expected to derive profit from levying taxes on whatever trade was permitted, and members of the bureaucracy from top to bottom also exacted commissions for extending privileges to merchants.

Restrictions upon Western traders

At the opening of the nineteenth century, although Western trade had reached fairly large proportions, it was still carried on under cumbersome restrictions which in many ways were disadvantageous to the Chinese as well as to foreigners. Aside from the Portuguese settlement at Macao, the only authorized port of exchange was Canton (by an imperial edict of 1757), at the opposite extremity of the empire from Peking, the seat of government. Silk and tea, the leading Chinese exports, had to be carried overland a distance of at least 500 miles to Canton; their transportation by boat along the coast was not permitted for fear that payment of the excise tax might be evaded. The trade at Canton was under the general supervision of a Manchu official known to foreigners as the "Hoppo" and was handled through a guild of Chinese merchants called the Co-hong. While the Co-hong merchants enjoyed a monopoly of foreign trade, they were taxed and "squeezed" by numerous officials and also were held personally

River View of Canton in the Early Twentieth Century. Canton was the only authorized port of exchange, other than Macao, where the Portuguese had special privileges, until the mid-nineteenth century.

responsible for the conduct of the foreigners with whom they dealt. Beginning about the middle of the eighteenth century a system of "security merchants" had been instituted, whereby every incoming foreign vessel was assigned to the supervision of a particular member of the Chinese guild during its entire stay in port. Foreign merchants were permitted to come to Canton only during the designated trading season (the winter months) and their activities were highly circumscribed. They were forbidden to bring their women or families with them, to ride in sedan chairs, or to employ Chinese servants. They were, theoretically at least, confined to the special area set aside for the "factories," and they could make no request to a government officer except through a Co-hong merchant as intermediary.

That the Canton trade was profitable both to the Chinese and to the foreigners is evidenced by the fact that it continued to grow in spite of the annoying regulations surrounding it and in spite of fluctuations in the assessments upon it. Foreigners were often kept in ignorance of the schedule of duties fixed by the Peking government. The Co-hong merchants—under pressure from the Hoppo, who in turn had to satisfy various other greedy bureaucrats and recover the expenses he had incurred in getting himself appointed to office—were inclined to charge what the traffic would bear. The foreign traders, if fleeced unduly, could of course threaten to break off intercourse altogether.

Methods of trade

"Factories" of the Foreign Powers in Canton, c. 1800. Chinese painting on glass. Western merchants were obliged to confine their activities to this prescribed area of the city. The "factories" were actually trading centers.

Actually, remarkably stable relations were established between Chinese and foreign merchants at Canton. Large transactions were handled, sometimes on a credit basis, with only oral agreements between the two parties, and by communication through a vernacular known as "pidgin English."[1]

The development of friction between Chinese and Westerners

As the volume of Western trade increased, however, friction was bound to arise. Two fundamentally different civilizations were coming into contact with each other. There were wide gaps between the Western and the Chinese concepts of justice and legal procedure. Westerners regarded as barbarous the Chinese view of group, rather than individual, responsibility for misbehavior and the use of torture in obtaining confessions. Consequently, misunderstandings occurred over the apprehension and punishment of criminals. Perhaps even more serious was the fact that the character of the trade began to change in a direction that was disadvantageous to China. In early days Chinese exports—tea, silk, and cotton cloth in lesser quantities—had far exceeded the value of imports into China; and the difference was made up in silver payments to Chinese merchants. Western traders would have preferred to make the exchange in goods, but they had difficulty in discovering any appreciable Chinese demand for commodities which they could supply. The Chinese attitude, as expressed by the Ch'ien Lung emperor to the British in 1793, was: "The Celestial Empire possesses all things in prolific abundance and lacks no product within its borders. There is therefore no need to import the

---

[1]Some large fortunes were accumulated in the process. In 1834, one member of the Co-hong estimated his personal estate at $26,000,000. H. B. Morse and H. F. MacNair, *Far Eastern International Relations*, p. 68.

manufacturers of outside barbarians in exchange for our own products."[2]

Eventually, a means of altering the balance of trade was supplied by the increase of opium consumption in China. Opium had long been used in China as a medicine and as a drug, and the practice of smoking it was introduced along with tobacco-smoking in the seventeenth century. In spite of imperial edicts against it, traffic in the drug grew steadily, with the bulk of the shipments coming from India. So ineffective was an imperial order of 1800 prohibiting this trade that by 1839 more than 4 million pounds of opium were being shipped in annually. Thoroughly aroused to the gravity of the situation, the imperial government resolved to take stronger measures, both for moral and for economic reasons. The traffic was draining specie out of China and, because it was illegal, it brought no revenue to the state while lining the pockets of smugglers and conniving officials.

Although traders of various nationalities, including Americans, participated in the China trade, the greater share had been in the hands of the British East India Company. When, in 1834, the company was divested entirely of its trading functions and the traffic was thrown open to all comers,[3] the situation in China became more critical than ever. As British mercantile interests in the Far East continued to expand, the demand arose in England for the establishment of regular diplomatic relations with the Chinese government. In 1834 Lord Napier was sent as chief superintendent for British trade, under instructions to announce his arrival directly to the viceroy, the highest Chinese functionary at Canton. Napier was unable to carry out his instructions because the viceroy refused to see him on the ground that the "barbarian headman" must conduct his business through the Co-hong merchants, in keeping with law and custom. According to the

[2] C. P. Fitzgerald, *China, a Short Cultural History*, 3d ed., pp. 557–558.
[3] See p. 1209.

Chinese Silk Factory, c. 1800. (Illustration from a French treatise on the silk industry.)

viceroy: "The petty affairs of commerce are to be directed by the merchants themselves. The officials are not concerned with such matters. . . . To sum up the whole matter: the nation has its laws; it is so everywhere. Even England has its laws; how much more the Celestial Empire!"

The vigorous attempts of a special Chinese commissioner to enforce the prohibitions against the opium traffic created a series of incidents which culminated in the Anglo-Chinese War of 1839–1842. This conflict, which was confined to the coastal regions near Canton and the lower Yangtze ports, is known as the Opium War because of the dispute that precipitated it. Actually the British objectives were broader and more ambitious than this title suggests. The real importance of the war is that it served as an entering wedge for the expansion of commercial intercourse and marked the beginning of the subjection of China to conditions imposed by the Western powers. By the treaty of Nanking in 1842 (supplemented the following year) the Chinese government ceded the island of Hong Kong to the British, promised an indemnity and compensation for the opium chests which had been confiscated, and agreed to treat Britain as a most favored nation in any future concessions that might be made. Four ports besides Canton were opened to trade, the Co-hong monopoly was abolished, and the right of residence was granted to foreigners in the treaty ports. Other nations, which had followed the course of the war with interest, were quick to follow the example of Britain in demanding similar privileges, confirmed in separate treaties. A significant feature of the treaty negotiated by the American minister, Caleb Cushing, was that it specifically included the principle of extraterritoriality, which conceded to foreigners accused of crime the right to be tried in their own national courts rather than by Chinese tribunals. These initial treaties omitted reference to the opium traffic but provided that the Chinese tariff on exports and imports should be "uniform and moderate," a

The Emperor Tao Kuang Reviewing His Guard inside the Forbidden City of Peking at the Time of the Opium War. From a painting by Thomas Allom.

The Signing of the Treaty of Tientsin. The treaties of Tientsin and Peking (1858, 1860) formalized the Chinese government's acceptance of the demands of the Western powers trading with China.

phrase interpreted as denying the Chinese government the right to raise the tariff without consent of the Western commercial powers. Thus by 1844 China was saddled with "unequal treaties," depriving her of control over her tariffs and limiting the powers of her courts over foreigners.

The results of the first Anglo-Chinese war were to intensify friction instead of removing it. Much of the fault lay with the foreigners, who took advantage of the weakness and corruption in the Chinese administration to enlarge their own interests. The privilege of extraterritoriality was abused, being extended to cover Chinese servants in the employ of foreigners, and inadequate punishment was given by the foreign powers to their own nationals who were convicted of crime. Portuguese vessels, and some others, engaged in "convoying," nominally to protect coastal shipping against piracy but actually to extort tribute from legitimate traders. Another reprehensible practice, carried on by Europeans and Americans during the middle of the century, was the recruiting of Chinese contract labor for export to plantations in the New World under conditions reminiscent of the old African slave trade. On the other hand, Westerners complained that the Chinese were evading both the spirit and the letter of the treaties. The attempt to establish foreign settlements at Canton led to rioting, because the Cantonese interpreted the treaties as granting foreigners the right of residence only outside the city walls. Less trouble was encountered in the new trading ports, where local sentiment was eager to attract commerce away from Canton now that Canton's monopoly had been broken. In Shanghai, the influx of foreigners resulted in the creating of an "International Settlement"—controlled jointly by British and Americans—and a separate French Settlement in the same city.

In all disputes with China the Western powers had the advantage of superior force, which they did not hesitate to use upon occasion. For

Results of the war and the treaties

The war of 1858–1860

a time, pressure was applied only locally, in the particular district where an untoward incident had occured. In 1858, however, the British and French cooperated in large-scale hostilities against the Peking government. After negotiations at Tientsin (the port of Peking), a misunderstanding arose as to the route for the foreign representatives to follow en route to Peking, whereupon the British and French forced their way up the river to the capital, drove the emperor in flight into Manchuria, and burned the beautiful summer palace of the Manchus. This war of 1858–1860 opened China more widely than ever before to Western penetration. The treaties of Tientsin and Peking added eleven ports to the list of authorized trading centers, legalized and imposed a tax upon the opium traffic, granted foreigners the right to travel in all parts of China, and promised that diplomatic representatives of the Western nations would be received in Peking. Largely because of the interest of the French in missionary activity, the Chinese government, compelled to acknowledge that "the Christian religion inculcates the practice of virtue," undertook to protect missionaries and their property.

*Short-sighted policies of
the Chinese government*

Although by 1860 the ineffectiveness of China as a sovereign state had been clearly demonstrated, the Manchu government showed no inclination to take a realistic view of the situation or to profit from its own mistakes. The heavily staffed bureaucracy numbered some men of genuine ability among its ranks, but it was practically paralyzed by its own inertia. Local officials had acquired the habit of minimizing or concealing problems rather than attacking them, and the top authorities provided no incentive for the drastic renovation that was needed to make the country strong enough to stop the intrusion of European powers. Unwilling to contemplate the necessity or the desirability of change, they tended to regard the Western pressure as a temporary affliction that would disappear in the course of time, as had other calamities in the past. Unable any longer to repel the ocean-borne "barbarians" the government nevertheless indulged in annoying and dilatory tactics, exhausting the patience of Westerners (not a very difficult task) without gaining any real advantage in return. The Manchu rulers were reluctant to give up the illusion that foreign emissaries were merely tribute-bearers from vassal states who should perform the *kowtow* (ceremonial prostration) before the throne. In spite of the pledges given in 1860, no imperial audience was granted to the foreign diplomatic corps at Peking before 1873, and not until twenty years later was it conducted in a manner acceptable to the Western ministers. Oddly enough, while the Manchu rulers persisted in an attitude of irresponsible and haughty superiority toward the Western nations, they were coming to rely upon these nations to carry out some of the normal functions of government within the Chinese empire and even to protect their regime when it was menaced by rebellion.

While the Western powers were tightening their grip on China's commerce and installing their agents in her coastal cities, internal upheavals created havoc and threatened to overthrow the dynasty. The most famous example, although actually only one of a number of contemporary revolts, was the movement known as the Taiping Rebellion, which began in 1851 and was not suppressed until more than a decade later. Its originator and leader, Hung Hsiu-ch'üan, was a native of the region near Canton in Kwangtung province who had shown promise as a scholar but had thrice failed in the provincial civil-service examinations. Frustrated in office-seeking, he nourished a bitter grudge against the Manchu government (which, with some justice, was suspected of discriminating against southern Chinese), and gradually his resentment became fused with a conviction that he had a divine mission to perform. He had received instruction for a short period from a Baptist missionary in Canton and, after an illness and a series of visions which he interpreted as revelations from God Almighty, he undertook to win his countrymen to the true faith. Hung's religion was largely Christian in ideology but with peculiar variations. He recognized God the Father as supreme deity, revered Christ as Elder Brother, and described himself as "Heavenly King and Younger Brother of Jesus." He also identified God with the ancient deity Shang Ti whom the Chinese had worshipped in pre-Chou times, and therefore believed that in propagating his version of Christianity he was actually urging the Chinese to return to their own original faith. Taoism, Buddhism, and ancestor worship he regarded as idolatry, and his followers first attracted the attention of authorities by their zeal in desecrating temples. Eventually Hung conceived his destiny to be to lead the "Association for Worshiping God" in a movement to overthrow the Manchus and inaugurate the "Heavenly Kingdom of Great Peace." Thus the Taiping Rebellion was both an antidynastic revolt and a religious crusade.

Originating in the extreme south, the rebellion spread northward and in 1853 the Taiping leaders captured Nanking, which they retained as their capital for eleven years, entirely cutting off the rich Yangtze valley from the control of the Peking government. Fighting occurred in fourteen out of China's eighteen provinces, and in 1853 rebel troops came within twelve miles of Tientsin. That the Taiping regime ultimately collapsed in spite of the inability of the Manchus to suppress it was due partly to inherent limitations in the movement and partly to the attitude of the great powers. Fundamentally a peasant uprising, the rebellion failed to win the support of the Chinese intelligentsia and actually antagonized this class by repudiating not only popular religions but the whole Confucian tradition as well. In addition, the Chinese gentry realized that the Taipings would institute radical economic changes, jeopardizing private property rights. Some foreign residents, especially Protestants, were at first inclined to view the revolt with sympathy because of its association with Christian

CHINA AND JAPAN IN THE NINETEENTH CENTURY

teaching, but they soon became aware that a triumph of the Taipings would not serve the interests of Christian missionaries. Hung evidently believed that all Christians in China should accept his authority because his revelations were more recent than any described in the Bible, and the rebel leaders became increasingly fanatical. Undoubtedly also, a factor influencing the decision of the Western powers not to support the Taiping movement was that these powers had already successfully pressed demands upon the imperial government and preferred a weak but compliant regime to an aggressive one founded upon revolution.

Without formal intervention in the Taiping wars, the Western powers assisted the Manchus in suppressing the rebellion—even while the British and French were conducting their own war against the Peking authorities in 1858–1860. In view of the confused state of Chinese affairs, perhaps it is not strange that one of the military heroes in the imperial service was Frederick T. Ward, a sea captain from Salem, Massachusetts, who raised a volunteer corps for the protection of Shanghai contrary to the wishes of his own government and over the protest of British naval authorities. General Ward adopted Chinese citizenship, and, in gratitude for the exploits of his "Ever-Victorious Army," the emperor commanded that altars should be erected and perpetual sacrifices offered to his spirit. Ward's most distinguished successor was an Englishman, Major Charles ("Chinese") Gordon. Meanwhile several able Chinese, from the civilian gentry rather than from the professional military clique, had come to the rescue of the hapless Manchus and earned the major credit for suppressing the rebellion. In 1864, the combined Chinese, French, and British forces captured Nanking, the last Taiping stronghold.

The liquidation of Hung's "Heavenly Peace" movement did not bring peace even of an earthly variety to China. Muslim rebellions in the southwest and the northwest remained unsubdued until considerably later. During the thirteen years of Taiping intransigence two-thirds of the provinces had been devastated, the whole country impoverished, and probably no less than 20 million people killed by battle, massacre, and famine. The Manchu Dynasty had been saved only through the efforts of its Chinese subjects and by grace of the foreign powers. Furthermore, the injury to China's intellectual heritage through the destruction of libraries and academies in the Yangtze valley was incalculable. In reaction against Taiping fanaticism the bureaucracy became more uncompromisingly conservative than ever.

The story of China from 1869 to 1911 is the depressing tale of a discredited dynasty clinging to its prerogatives while its people were oppressed and the nation's independence was being gradually whittled away. A little color was added by the career of the famous Empress Dowager, T'zu Hsi, a Manchu woman of great cunning and strong will, who dominated the Peking administration through her control of puppet emperors during much of the period between 1861 and her death in 1908. The "old Buddha," as she was nicknamed, in spite of her irregular and unscrupulous methods, somewhat recouped the prestige of the ruling house, but she neither understood nor contributed to the solution of China's basic problems. Out of the chaos of the Taiping era came a reorganization and centralization of the Chinese maritime customs service. A temporary arrangement, whereby foreigners had collected tariff duties at Shanghai while the authority of the Peking government was paralyzed, was perpetuated and extended to all the treaty ports. The higher personnel of the customs service was composed of foreigners, nominated by their consuls but appointed by Peking, with the understanding that so long as the English predominated in China's foreign trade the inspector general would always be a British subject. Thus the customs administration, while foreign-staffed, was an agency of the Chinese government, maintained its headquarters at Peking, and operated as a unit regardless of provincial divisions. The fact that the foreign inspectorate functioned efficiently emphasized all the more glaringly the general decrepitude of the Manchu administration.

Dividing the Chinese melon

In the last quarter of the nineteenth century China's weakness was further revealed in the loss of some of its outlying possessions. By 1860 it had renounced to Russia all claims to territory beyond the Amur and the Ussuri rivers, thus allowing Russia to surround Manchuria and to control the entire Asiatic seacoast north of Korea. Through a combination of diplomatic and military pressure, culminating in a small-scale war (1884–1885), France acquired a protectorate over virtually all of Indochina except the independent state of Siam. The murder of a British explorer in China's southwestern province of Yunnan led the British to demand, and China to yield, sovereignty over Upper Burma (1886). The Japanese government enforced a claim to suzerainty over the Ryukyu Islands (1881). Not to be outdone, the Portuguese, who had occupied Macao for 300 years, obtained its formal cession in 1887. The full measure of China's humiliation, however, followed the Sino-Japanese War of 1894–1895. Japan, only recently emerged from feudalism and isolation, gave the world a startling demonstration of China's impotence by defeating the Celestial Empire in the short space of eight months. Shortly afterward five great powers—Russia, Great Britain, France, Germany, and Japan—participated in a "battle for concessions," through which the major part of China proper was partitioned into "spheres of interest." The spheres of interest, somewhat vaguely defined and usually radiating from a leased port, theoretically did not impair China's sovereignty; but the concessions as a whole made the country an economic dependency of the great powers.

The "Hundred Days of Reform"

Before the close of the nineteenth century, conditions in China provoked a growing spirit of resentment against both the incompetence of the government and the foreign elements that had taken advantage of it. A group of educated Chinese who were sincerely interested in their country's welfare and also appreciative of Western institutions began to agitate for reform. As might be expected, the reformers were mostly from southern China, especially Kwangtung province. Their first outstanding leader was K'ang Yu-wei, who had been influenced by the Han Learning scholars and wished to utilize Confucian principles in reconstructing the government. On social questions K'ang adopted some decidedly radical views, even contemplating the abolition of the family; but he was not impetuous and set as his immediate goal the attainment of constitutional monarchy for China. For a brief period, known as the "Hundred Days of Reform" (June to September 1898), it looked as if the ideas of K'ang would bear fruit as the young emperor, under K'ang's guidance, issued a series of edicts that indicated a break with the past. The movement came to an unhappy end, however, when the Empress Dowager T'zu Hsi executed a *coup d'état* and forced the emperor into retirement. K'ang Yu-wei escaped arrest and decapitation by fleeing the country.

Having rebuffed the liberal reformers, the Manchu court next gave its blessing to extreme reactionaries. The Empress Dowager shrewdly directed the fulminations of various secret societies—which were potentially a threat to the dynasty—into the channel of antiforeignism. The climax came in 1900 when the so-called Boxers ("Society of Harmonious Fists") unleashed a violent attack upon Christians and foreigners in Shantung and the adjacent northeastern provinces. In view of the fact that the movement was secretly encouraged by the Empress Dowager and was based on extreme anti-Western fanaticism, the number of lives lost was not tremendous even in the critical areas. In other parts of China the provincial authorities, disregarding T'zu Hsi's instructions, generally tried to maintain order and protect the resident foreigners. Thus the Boxer movement was neither a revolution nor

The Boxer uprising

Boxer Uprising. German troops march into the Forbidden City of Peking after the rebels have been driven from the city.

an actual war against the West; but the Western powers cooperated to stifle it with promptness and vigor, allowing their troops to indulge in wanton looting in Tientsin and in Peking, where far more damage was inflicted after the allied forces occupied the capital than while it had been held by the Boxers. Instead of abolishing the Manchu Dynasty as they might easily have done, however, the Western governments decided to shore it up, extracting certain guaranties of good behavior for the future. By the terms of settlement (the Boxer Protocol of 1901) the imperial government was required to pay heavy indemnities and to mete out punishments to certain of its own officials; the civil-service examinations and the importation of arms were suspended temporarily; and the Western powers were granted permission to maintain military units in the Peking area.

Efforts to shore up the old regime

In a final attempt to save the dynasty and partly in response to foreign pressure, the Manchu rulers during the period 1901–1911 projected a series of reforms, which emphasized railroad construction, modernization of the military services, public education, and liberalization of the political structure. These measures, beneficial as they appeared to be, were poorly planned and carried out only half-heartedly, and the reform program actually speeded the coming of revolution. In 1905 the ancient civil-service examinations were formally abolished, preparatory to erecting a modern educational system. But the initiative in implementing the program was left to the provincial governors, most of whom did little about it. Many ambitious Chinese youths went abroad to study, particularly to Japan, where instruction of a very superficial character was supplied to meet the sudden desire for "Western learning." A youth movement began to manifest itself in China, characterized by impatience with the old order but inadequately prepared for leadership in the creation of anything better. The government announced plans for a gradual transition to a constitutional regime with an elected parliament and, as a first step in this direction, established provincial assemblies in 1909. Although these assemblies were not democratically elected and were intended to be only debating societies, they vociferated so loudly that the government deemed it expedient to summon a National Assembly the following year. The National Assembly of 1910 was devised as a bulwark of conservatism, with half its members directly appointed by the emperor. Nevertheless, it proceeded to criticize the government and pressed the demand for more rapid reform.

The Revolution of 1911

Meanwhile resentment was mounting against the policy of the government in regard to railroad construction. The original plan had been to build a unified network of roads by letting the provincial authorities assume responsibility for specific sections, raising the necessary funds by stock subscriptions among the wealthy citizens of each province. It was hoped thus to stimulate national interest in the project and also to avoid recourse to foreign loans. In 1909, however, the Peking government took the whole program into its own hands, partly because it feared that decentralization was dangerous to the imperial authority and partly because mismanagement and graft in the provinces were eating up the funds. The government's decision made it necessary to borrow from foreign capitalists and offended provincial interests. Investors were angered when they learned that their stock would not be redeemed at face value, and in the fall of 1911 outbreaks of violence occurred. The railroad controversy was only one among many factors which brought antidynastic feeling to the point of open rebellion. A bomb explosion in Hankow, on October 10, touched off a general uprising in the Yangtze valley cities, during which Li Yüan-hung, commander of a rebellious imperial garrison, cast in his lot with the revolutionaries.

The revolutionary elements in China, which moved into the foreground with the impromptu insurrections of 1911, were by no means in agreement as to program or tactics. A number of liberal leaders, headed by K'ang Yu-wei, clung to the ideal of a limited monarchy. They would accept the continuation of the dynasty if it was willing to renounce absolutism and promote progress. A more radical group wished to abolish the monarchy altogether and convert China into a republic. The prime figure among the radicals was Dr. Sun Yat-sen (1866–1925), born of a peasant family near Canton, in the province which had produced the leader of the Taipings and countless other opponents of the Manchu regime. At the invitation and expense of an elder brother, Sun had gone to Hawaii to obtain a Western education and had been converted to Christianity. After returning to China he studied medicine, chiefly with Protestant missionary physicians, and received a medical diploma at Hong Kong. He participated in an abortive revolt against the government in 1895, from which he barely escaped with his life. Thereafter Dr. Sun traveled widely, residing in the United States and visiting both England and Continental Europe. During these years he had studied Western institutions, which he became convinced could be successfully adopted in China, and dedicated his energies to stirring up opposition to the Manchus among Chinese at home and abroad. In China his work was carried forward by a secret "Alliance Society," which attracted various disaffected elements in the period preceding the 1911 outbreak.

"Father of the Chinese Republic." Dr. Sun Yat-sen and his second wife, Soong Ching-ling (sister of Mme. Chiang Kai-shek).

Lack of coordination among reformist and revolutionary groups, the distracted and impoverished state of the country, and the persistence of strong sectional loyalties made it impossible for the revolution to follow a clear-cut pattern. Events of the next few years were confused and somewhat paradoxical. Yüan Shih-k'ai, a conservative bureaucrat who had reorganized the army in northern China, was ordered by the Manchu court to suppress the rebellion. Probably because he realized that the dynasty's days were numbered, he avoided decisive engagements with the southern insurgents, even though his

Yüan Shih-k'ai and the Revolution

Yüan Shih-k'ai. Yüan, chosen
provisional president of the Republic of China, ruled as dictator from 1912 until his death in
1916.

*The dictatorship of Yüan
Shih-k'ai*

army was superior to theirs. The National Assembly at Peking, while demanding immediate constitutional reforms and amnesty for the rebels, at the same time nominated Yüan Shih-k'ai—the Manchu's last hope—as prime minister. There was even more confusion in the south than in the north, although a united front was presented against the imperial government by an assembly at Nanking in which central Chinese and Cantonese cooperated. The Nanking assembly elected as president Dr. Sun, who had only recently arrived in China, and declared for a republic. Instead of puncturing this radical trial balloon with one stroke, Yüan arranged with the representatives of Nanking a settlement which embodied a compromise between the northern and southern groups. As a concession to the southern (and radical) factions, China was to be designated a republic with Li Yüan-hung as vice-president and with Nanking as the capital. But to promote harmony, Dr. Sun stepped out of the limelight and recommended that Yüan Shih-k'ai, who was supported by the northern armies, be made provisional president of the republic. Although the Manchu emperor was required to abdicate, Yüan secured an extremely generous settlement for the royal family.

Thus, with comparatively little bloodshed or social upheaval and without interference by the great powers, both the Manchu Dynasty and the institution of monarchy had been overthrown. However, these events proved to be only the beginning of China's revolution; and they were a prelude to one of the most severe periods of distress in China's long history. Obviously, any regime that succeeded the Manchus was confronted with the staggering problems of administrative corruption, economic stagnation, and general demoralization which were the fruits of Manchu misrule. Furthermore, the unequal treaties and foreign spheres of interest that had been imposed upon the country made the attainment of a unified modern state doubly difficult. Progress was bound to be slow at best, but the men who attained power during this stage of the revolution seemed more bent on advancing their own interests than those of the country. Yüan Shih-k'ai, who had not the least sympathy with republican principles, maneuvered himself into the position of a dictator. He refused to transfer the seat of government to the south, and when a parliament met at Peking in 1913 to draw up a constitution he intimidated, tricked, and bribed the delegates. Dr. Sun's Alliance Society had reorganized as the Kuomintang ("Chinese Nationalist Party"), and Kuomintang elements were dominant in the parliament which was attempting to prepare a frame of government. The constitution as drafted placed limits on the executive power; but so successful was Yüan in corrupting the members of parliament that they elected him to the presidency. Yüan then contemptuously dissolved the assembly, outlawed the Kuomintang, and promulgated a "Constitutional Compact" of his own devising, retaining himself as president. From 1914 until his death two years later Yüan Shih-k'ai ruled as a military dictator, backed by the northern army which he had organized for the imperial service. The Western governments, whose attitude toward the Chinese revolution had been remarkably apathetic, were on the whole favorably disposed toward Yüan and extended loans to him through an international banking group. The powers were willing to support a "strong man" in China—so long as China itself remained weak. Russian intrigue combined with Mongol nationalist sentiment to secure autonomy for Outer Mongolia; rebellion in Tibet enabled the British to extend their influence in that dependency; and the Japanese were beginning to cast covetous eyes on the Shantung Peninsula.

Although reactionary, Yüan Shih-k'ai's dictatorship at least demonstrated the fact that monarchy was thoroughly discredited in China. When Yüan committed the mistake of trying to perpetuate the power of his family by ascending the Dragon Throne as the founder of a new dynasty, he met with unexpected opposition. The great powers, particularly Japan, disapproved of his scheme, and fresh rebellions broke out in the southern provinces. The sudden death of the frustrated dictator in the summer of 1916 theoretically restored the republic under its "permanent" constitution. But a clique at Peking carried on Yüan's highhanded methods, while various provincial governors and military commanders were rendering themselves independent of any central authority. China, it seemed, had gotten rid of the Manchus only to fall prey to greedy and unprincipled war lords.

The death of Yüan Shih-k'ai and the rise of the war-lords

2. THE TRANSFORMATION OF JAPAN INTO A MODERN STATE

Japan's policy of isolation, carefully maintained since the early seventeenth century by the Tokugawa Shoguns, was bound to give way when Western nations expanded their trading activities in the Far East. Before the middle of the nineteenth century several attempts, all unsuccessful, had been made by European powers to open Japan to trade. That the United States government finally took the initiative in forcing the issue was due partly to the fact that the British were busily engaged in China. It was also an indication that America's Far Eastern commerce had attained considerable proportions. Since about 1800, United States whaling and clipper ships had passed through Japanese waterways en route to China, and with the rise of steam navigation the need for stations where ships could be refueled and provisioned became more imperative.

The end of Japanese isolation

When Commodore Perry's "black ships" steamed into Tokyo Bay in July 1853, Perry was under instructions from Washington to secure from the Japanese government the promise of protection for shipwrecked United States seamen, permission for merchant ships to

The Arrival of Commodore Perry's Squadron off Uraga, July 8, 1853. This Japanese woodcut was published in 1876.

Commodore Perry and Townsend Harris

obtain repairs and fuel, and the right to trade. Perry's gunboats were sufficiently impressive to induce the Shogun to give a favorable reply when the commodore returned to Edo early the following year. However, the significance of the change in Japan's position was not apparent until a United States consul-general, Townsend Harris, after many vicissitudes negotiated a commercial treaty with the Shogun in 1858. Harris had no gunboats to back his arguments, but he skillfully used the object lesson of European aggression in China to convince the Japanese that they would be better off to yield peaceably to American demands. The Harris Treaty provided for the opening of several ports to traders and for the establishment of diplomatic intercourse, placed limitations on the Japanese tariff, and recognized the principle of extraterritoriality. Following the United States lead, other Western powers secured treaties granting them similar privileges, and it seemed that the pattern that was unfolding in China might be duplicated in Japan. But, as events turned out, Japan's reaction to the Western impact produced results almost the opposite of contemporary developments in China. The reason for this contrast is that the Japanese, after recovering from their initial shock, turned enthusiastically to the task of assimilating Western culture and techniques for the purpose of strengthening their state and winning equal recognition among other nations.

The first important effect of the opening of Japan was that it led to the abolition of the Shogunate, making possible a reorganization of the government along modern lines. The "outer daimyo"—especially the heads of four great domains: Choshu, Satsuma, Hizen, and Tosa—

had long been awaiting an opportunity to displace the Tokugawa family from its dominant position. The action of the Shogun in yielding to the Western powers provided just such an opportunity. Before signing the treaties the Shogun had taken the unprecedented step of going to Kyoto to consult the emperor. The domain lords subsequently demanded that the emperor should be restored to his rightful position as ruler, denounced the Shogun for his weakness in submitting to the foreigners, and raised the cry that the "barbarians" must be expelled. The antiforeignism of the great daimyo was broken by direct action on the part of the "barbarians." In 1863, after an Englishman had been slain by people of the Satsuma daimyo, British vessels bombarded the domain capital. Duly impressed, the Satsuma leaders immediately voiced the desire to acquire a navy like that of Britain. The feudal lords of Choshu were similarly chastened and reoriented in their thinking in 1864 when British, French, Dutch and United States men-of-war unleashed a joint action upon Shimonoseki. In a remarkably short time the key men of the great feudal estates dropped their attitude of uncompromising hostility to the foreigners, meanwhile becoming more determined than ever to end the outmoded dual system of government.

In 1867 the Shogun was prevailed upon to surrender his prerogatives to the emperor. He had expected to be retained as generalissimo, and when he was ordered to lay down his military command also, he resisted. However, the principal clans, acting in concert and in the name of the emperor, quickly defeated the ex-Shogun's forces and relegated the Tokugawa family not to obscurity but to private station. Upon the abolition of the Shogunate, which had existed for almost 700 years, the imperial residence was moved from Kyoto to Edo, renamed Tokyo ("Eastern Capital"), and the old castle of the Shogun was converted into an imperial palace. This series of events constituted what is known as the Meiji Restoration.

It so happened that Emperor Mutsuhito, a lad of fifteen at the time of the Restoration, proved to be an extremely capable person who helped materially in the task of reorganizing Japanese institutions. The years of his reign, known as the Meiji or "Enlightened" era (1868–1912), witnessed the emergence of Japan as a modern and powerful state. Nevertheless, it would be a mistake to attribute Japan's transformation to the initiative of the emperor. As in previous periods of the country's history, effective leadership was supplied by less exalted figures, who used the throne as a symbol to promote a sentiment of national solidarity and to give the sanction of authority to their program. Quite understandably, the leaders in the political field were recruited chiefly from the ranks of feudal society, although they included some members of the old court nobility. In spite of their aristocratic backgrounds, however, the leaders were quick to perceive the necessity of breaking with the past if genuine progress along Western lines was to be achieved. Some of the daimyo voluntarily liquidated feudal institutions within their own jurisdiction, urging others to follow their example, and in 1871 the emperor formally abolished the whole feudal system. The hereditary fiefs reverted to the state and by authority of the emperor were divided into prefectures for administrative purposes; the peasants were made, in theory, free landowners, paying taxes instead of feudal rents. The daimyo and their samurai retainers were granted pensions (later converted into lump-sum payments) amounting to less than the revenues they had formerly claimed.

The last gasp of feudalism

It may seem strange that a feudal nobility would so readily surrender its privileges. The explanation lies partly in the genuine desire of foreward-looking members of the aristocracy to strengthen Japan and partly in the fact that feudal institutions were no longer very profitable and had been largely undermined by the growth of a mercantile economy. Furthermore, able members of the samurai class, who had been the real managers of great domains in Tokugawa times, saw the advantages in establishing a regime in which their talents could be more fully utilized and more adequately recognized. This class did in fact supply many of the leading statesmen during Japan's period of transition. Nevertheless, the abolition of feudalism exacted a real sacrifice of the samurai as a whole. The daimyo received a fairly generous financial settlement and were assigned ranks in a newly created order of nobility. But the samurai found themselves deprived of their incomes while, at the same time, the government forbade them to wear any longer the traditional two swords and ordered them to merge into the ranks of the commonalty. Smoldering discontent among the samurai broke out into open revolt in 1877, presenting the government with a test of strength which it met with complete success. The newly organized concript army, composed of peasants with modern weapons, quickly defeated the proud samurai, and the rebellion of 1877 proved to be "the last gasp of a fast dying feudal society."

The revolution from above

The sweeping political, social, economic, and intellectual changes which took place in Japan during the Meiji era were sufficient to constitute a revolution. However, they were not the result of a mass movement or of any tumultuous upheaval from the bottom of society. The revolution was one directed and carefully controlled from above. The fact that the Tokugawa regime had already unified the country and through its discipline had instilled habits of docility in the population facilitated the work of the Restoration leaders. The majority of the population played only a passive role in the transformation, even though they were profoundly affected by it.

The Constitution of 1889

In carrying out their carefully channeled revolution, Japan's leaders made a painstaking study of the institutions of all the major Western nations and copied, with adaptations, what seemed to be the best features of each. In the political sphere, they reached the conclusion that the principles of constitutional monarchy should be introduced. A bold but somewhat ambiguous statement of policy, known as the Emperor's Charter Oath (1868), had hinted at the establishment of a deliberative assembly; but when plans for the drafting of a constitution were announced, it was made clear that any concessions would be in the nature of a gift from the throne rather than in recognition of inherent popular rights. A hand-picked commission drafted a constitution which, promulgated by the emperor in 1889, was patterned somewhat after the model of the German Imperial Constitution of 1871. It provided for a bicameral parliament or Diet, with a House of Peers (including some representatives of the wealthy taxpayers) and a House of Representatives chosen by an electorate of property owners. The Diet was assigned the normal legislative powers, except that its control over finance was limited, and the constitution included a bill of rights. In spite of some liberal features, the conservative character of the new government was unmistakable. So high was the property qualification for voting that only about 1 percent of the population was enfranchised. The position of the emperor was declared to be inviolable; he retained supreme command of the army and navy, directed foreign affairs, and could veto bills passed by the Diet. Notably lacking was the principle of parliamentary control over the executive; ministers were responsible not to the Diet but to the emperor. Furthermore, although there was a Cabinet of Ministers as well as a Privy Council, both these bodies were created *before* the Constitution went into effect. A peculiarity of the Japanese Cabinet (aside from the fact that it was not responsible to the Diet) was that the Army and

The Opening of the First Japanese Parliament, in November 1890. From a Japanese engraving. Note the Western-style Diet chamber, lighting, decor, and costumes.

Navy ministers could consult with the emperor directly, without the mediation of the premier.

While the Japanese constitution incorporated several important features and much of the nomenclature of Western political institutions, the government remained close to Japanese traditions in its spirit and functioning. These traditions (which had more in common with Confucianism than with Western political concepts) included such fundamental ideas as that men are by nature unequal and the inferior person should be subject to the superior, that society is more important than the individual, that government by man is better than government by law, and that the patriarchal family is the ideal pattern for the state.[4] Political reforms were considered only a means to an end, which was not necessarily to produce the greatest happiness of the greatest number but to promote the efficiency, strength, and prestige of the state. The men who, in consultation with the emperor, introduced the constitution of 1889 had no notion of relinquishing their command at the instigation of parliamentary cliques or under the pressure of public opinion. The guiding personalities were a fairly large group, numbering perhaps a hundred men, chiefly ex-daimyo and ex-samurai, who together composed a sort of oligarchy. Young men at the time of the Restoration, they retained their influence throughout the Meiji period and beyond, and eventually were referred to as the "elder statesmen" (*Genro*). Acting quietly behind the scenes, they frequently made important decisions of policy. Fortunately for Japan, these "elder statesmen" were as a whole realistic in outlook, moderate in judgment, and highminded.

Political parties

In spite of the absence of democratic traditions and in spite of the authoritarian character of the Restoration government, the granting of a constitution led, almost from the outset, to a desire for further political reforms. Members of the Diet at least had the right to criticize the ministers, and voices were raised in favor of the extension of parliamentary control over the ministry. Political parties were organized, leading to a struggle in the Diet between the defenders of bureaucratic government and the advocates of the cabinet system. The germination of political parties actually antedated the constitution. The "Liberal" party, which appeared in 1881, was primarily an outgrowth of an "association for the study of political science" founded several years earlier by Itagaki, a samurai of the Tosa domain. In 1882, Count Okuma of Hizen launched his "Progressive" party. These two "radical" aristocrats were doubtless motivated partly by resentment against the fact that their own affiliates had secured relatively few posts in the bureaucracy, most of which were filled by Choshu or Satsuma men. Nevertheless, the introduction of political parties helped to strengthen the movement for the establishment of representative government.

After the constitution went into effect, the character and the activi-

[4]For an illuminating discussion of these concepts, see R. K. Reischauer, *Japan: Government-Politics,* chapter I.

ties of political parties in Japan were peculiar and not entirely healthy. Emphasizing personalities rather than specific programs, parties came and went, fusing into one another, or changing their names in a bewildering fashion. Their effectiveness was lessened by their lack of a broad popular base, by the government's censorship of press and speech, and by the fact that when party spokesmen became too troublesome they could usually be quieted by offering them patronage or admitting them to the lower ranks of the bureaucracy. But, with all their faults, the parties provided opportunities for acquiring political experience and also forced the bureaucrats to explain and defend their policies to the public. The campaign to achieve party government—that is, to make the Cabinet responsible to the Diet—gained considerable headway on the eve of World War I and was resumed vigorously during the 1920s.

Experiments with constitutional government were only one aspect of Japan's political transformation. A modern and efficient military establishment was a prime objective that was rapidly attained, with a navy modeled after Great Britain's and an army copied from that of Germany, largely because the superiority of the latter had been strikingly demonstrated in the Franco-Prussian War. The principle of universal military service, introduced in 1873, was not a Japanese invention (although conscript peasant armies had been known to both China and Japan in ancient times and had played a part in Japan's feudal wars of the sixteenth century), but was based upon the example of modern European states. The administrative system was revised, and new judiciary and legal codes were adopted which compared favorably with those of Western countries and enabled the Japanese to claim successfully that they were not behind the West in the administration of justice. In 1894 Great Britain voluntarily surrendered extraterritorial rights in Japan, and by 1899 all the other powers had taken the same step. The abrogation of external control over the customs duties required a longer period of negotiation, but tariff autonomy was achieved in 1911. Henceforth Japan was entirely free from the humiliation of "unequal treaties."

*Militarism and the
abolition of foreign
privileges*

The economic changes of the Meiji era were perhaps even more significant than the political. In Tokugawa feudal days Japan was far from being a purely agrarian nation, and before the Restoration of 1867 an urban economy, chiefly mercantile and capitalistic, had come into being. When the new regime undertook to strengthen the state and secure the benefits of Westernization, it launched an ambitious program for the development of industry and a modern system of communications. Because private capital was not available in sufficient quantities to do the job quickly and because of the fear that extensive borrowing from foreign investors would endanger Japan's economic independence, the government assumed the initiative in constructing railroads, telegraph and telephone lines, docks, shipyards, and even manufacturing plants, while it also aided private industry by loans and subsidies. There was no tradition of laissez faire in Japan to stand in the way of government participation in the economic sphere, and public officials were anxious to move ahead as rapidly as possible. However, many enterprises which had been fostered by the state were eventually transferred to private hands, although the state retained control of railways and communications for strategic and security reasons. Hence, in Japan, economic progress led to the growth of a capitalist class, but one which did not correspond exactly with similar classes in the Western industrial nations. The members of the new capitalist class, like the prominent political figures, were drawn largely from the old aristocracy, while not excluding men of bourgeois origin—money-lenders and rice merchants of the Tokugawa era. Daimyo now found a profitable field of investment for the funds they had received upon surrendering their feudal privileges, and the more nimble-witted of the samurai also participated in industrial development.

Mitsui and Mitsubishi

The history of the famous house of Mitsui, which grew to be the largest combination of mercantile, financial, and industrial interests in Japan, illustrates the remarkable success of a samurai family that was shrewd enough to anticipate future developments. In early Tokugawa times the Mistui, defying the prejudices of their class, had abandoned fighting in favor of the more solid rewards of commerce. They opened a store in Kyoto and in its management apparently anticipated the techniques of modern scientific salesmanship, displaying advertising posters and on rainy days giving away to customers paper umbrellas printed with the Mitsui trademark. Before the close of the seventeenth century, the family had established a banking house in Edo. The Mitsui heartily welcomed the opening of Japan to foreign trade, and so confident were they of the success of the Restoration that they lent large sums of money to the emperor and his entourage while the new government was in the process of formation. The Mitsui family also formed a connection with the great Choshu domain whose members filled important government posts, and thus were enabled to participate in various aspects of the economic program.[5] The Mitsubishi group of interests, which was the greatest rival of the Mitsui and, like them, developed under samurai leadership, effected a similar connection with the Satsuma group. In spite of the rapid industrialization of Japan, capitalists were relatively few, and they were generally affiliated with clan bureaucrats who dominated the government.

*Peculiarities of Japanese
capitalism*

Industrial developments in Japan in the late nineteenth and early twentieth centuries differed in several respects from the typical pattern of economic change in the West. In the first place, they were so rapid that in one generation the country was producing a surplus of manufactured goods, and foreign markets had become essential to the

[5] O. D. Russell, *The House of Mitsui.*

national economy. Second, the Industrial Revolution was transported to Japan after it had already reached an advanced stage in the Western nations, and consequently characteristics of the early and late Industrial Revolutions were intermingled. The employment of women in industry at low wages, the lack of organization among the laborers or of legal safeguards to protect them, and the working conditions in factories and mines were parallel to the early stages of the Industrial Revolution in the West. On the other hand, the projection of the government into the business sphere and the appearance of finance capitalism were phenomena that were only beginning to manifest themselves in western Europe and the United States. To a considerable extent in Japan, finance capitalism preceded industrial capitalism, because there had not been time for financial reserves to accumulate from the savings effected by a gradual mechanization of industry. The wealth of the aristocracy and of merchant and banking houses—essentially unproductive classes—was drawn upon to expedite industrial progress, and the fortunate members of these groups were in a position to dominate the productive enterprises of mining, manufacturing, and distribution as these grew to maturity.

Another peculiarity of Japan's industrial development was the fact that, while total production increased rapidly and some large plants were built for heavy industries, the majority of the factories remained small. Even in the 1930s, when Japan's industrial laborers numbered 6 million, almost three-fourths of them worked in small establishments employing fewer than a hundred workers and about one-half of them toiled in plants employing not more than five. The small factories, however, were usually not independent but were controlled by the great financial houses, which resembled trusts in their structure and obtained monopolies of whole fields of production. Workers in the cotton and silk textile mills, for example, might be likened to

The Japanese trusts

Japanese Buddhists Expiate Their Sins. Japanese Buddhists, seen copying sutras in Zojoji Temple in Tokyo, reflect one of the traditional religious means of coping with the stress of modernization.

workers under the domestic system in early modern Europe, even though they tended machines instead of using hand tools. The supplying of raw materials and the distribution and sale of finished products—especially in the export trades—were handled by a few centralized organizations from which a network of controls extended over hundreds of tiny workshops scattered throughout the country. Naturally this system placed the worker at a great disadvantage, and his bargaining position was further weakened by the prevalence of an oversupply of cheap labor. In spite of the growth of huge cities, the larger part of the population remained on the land, which was insufficient in resources to support the peasant families. Hence these families were glad to supplement a meager income by letting some of their members, especially daughters, work in the shops for such wages as they could get. Between the depressed class of small farmers and laborers and the wealthy capitalists, the gulf was as great as that which had separated the upper and lower strata of the old feudal hierarchy.

Extensive social and cultural changes also accompanied the transformation of Japan's economic and political institutions. Some of these changes were brought about deliberately by government action; others were unintended or even unwelcome. To carry out a program of Westernization a system of public education was clearly necessary. A Ministry of Education was established in 1871, careful studies were made of the procedures of Western countries, and schools were built rapidly at state expense. Japan was the first Asian nation to introduce compulsory education and did it so successfully that illiteracy almost disappeared, even among the poorest classes of society. There was also notable progress in instructional facilities at the higher level, providing boys with opportunities for technical and professional as well as academic training, and offering separate and more limited instruction for girls. The program was extremely ambitious and the curricula of the middle and higher schools were exacting. The study of Chinese classics and Confucian philosophy was retained, and to these were added—besides Japanese language, literature, and history—Western scientific and technical subjects as well as foreign languages. Notably lacking, however, was the encouragement of original thought. The system was devised to serve the ends of the government and aimed to produce a nation of loyal, efficient, and disciplined conformists. To that end, all students were required to take so-called "morals classes," which stressed patriotism. Western science and technology were appropriated without the liberal and humanistic traditions which had engendered them; and investigation of the social sciences was almost entirely neglected. Thus, the emphasis was not upon the fullest development of the individual but upon enabling him to fit into a firmly fixed pattern of society without questioning it. The Ministry of Education exercised strict surveillance over teachers and texts, making the schools a powerful agency for indoctrination.

Japanese Agriculture. Left: Transplanting rice in a paddy field early in June. Right: Harvesting rice in a farm village. In the background is Mount Fuji.

The creation of a wide reading public stimulated literary production, some of which was intended for mass circulation. Although Japanese writers were greatly influenced by contemporary Western literature, as reflected in their tendency toward realism, they were by no means mere imitators and produced literary work of great merit. Journalism became a flourishing occupation, and some newspapers of high caliber appeared. The Japanese press, however, labored under disadvantages, the most serious being the arbitrary and often erratic governmental censorship. Editors who dared to criticize officials, or who were merely unlucky enough to publish news which officials desired to keep from the public, were likely to be fined and imprisoned or to have their offices closed. It is significant that a considerable number of journalists, in spite of the risks involved, persisted in giving expression to independent and critical opinion.

Literary production

In passing successfully through the difficult years of the Restoration period, the Japanese gave abundant evidence of vitality, courage, and versatility. In many fields they had come abreast of the Western nations, while they had also retained their own distinctive cultural heritage. At the same time, the accomplishments were not an unmixed good, and social problems had arisen which could not be easily solved. The most dubious aspect of Japan's condition, in spite of its mounting industrial strength, was in the economic sphere. Scientific knowledge, improved sanitation and medical facilities, and especially the impact of the Industrial Revolution induced a terrific increase in a population that had remained almost stationary for over

New social problems

a century. Between 1867 and 1913, the population grew from about 30 million to more than 50 million, and from this time on the rate of growth was still more rapid. There was hardly enough arable land in Japan to produce food for such large numbers, even under the most efficient methods of cultivation. While a brisk foreign trade could correct the deficiency, not only was a sufficient volume of trade difficult to maintain but the profits from manufacturing and commerce were concentrated in the hands of a small group. The standard of living of the farmers—the great majority of the population—remained almost at a standstill while the total national income was rising. With the abolition of feudalism, the peasants had become free landed proprietors, but their economic condition was not greatly improved thereby. Taxation bore far too heavily upon them; they had to compete in a cash market dominated by large landlords and industrialists; and their individual holdings were often insufficient to support a family. Many farmers had to supplement their small plots by renting additional holdings. Tenant farming in place of independent proprietorship became a striking characteristic of Japanese agriculture. The urban laborers were even worse off than the poor farmers; and Japan lacked a strong middle class to redress the balance of society. The revolutions of the Meiji era, unlike their counterparts in the Western world, were not essentially middle-class movements and had not broken the ascendancy of leaders whose ideals and outlook had been shaped in a feudal atmosphere.

Factors contributing to an authoritarian trend

The fundamental attitudes and loyalties of the old Japan passed into the new, even though they wore a somewhat different guise and were associated with more effective implements. It was not difficult for the creed of unswerving loyalty to a feudal superior to be converted into an intense patriotism, for which the emperor served as a symbol of national unity and object of common devotion. Ancient legends and

Japanese Religious Festival. The participants are dressed in costumes of different epochs. Spectacles of this sort served to remind the people of their national heritage and consolidated their devotion to the state.

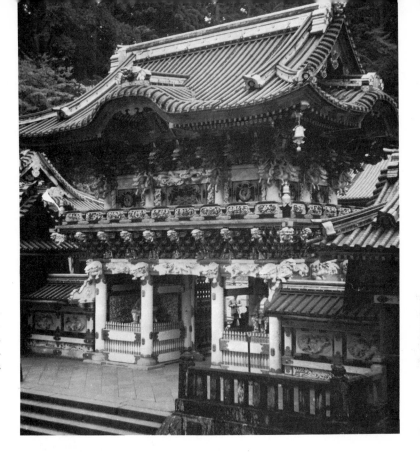

A Gate of the Toshogu Shrine, Nikko National Park. Although the Japanese have adopted Western architectural styles for their public buildings, for their religious edifices they retain the native style, with its curved roofs and lavish ornamentation.

the Shinto cults were refurbished to stimulate patriotic sentiments and to inspire confidence in Japan's unique destiny. As already suggested, an efficient and in many ways progressive educational system was utilized for this same end. The army, also, became an educational agency of a very potent kind. It was made up largely of literate but unsophisticated peasants, who found membership in the military establishment more rewarding financially and more gratifying to the ego than a life of grubbing on a tiny farm. The provincialism, prejudices, and legitimate resentments of the peasant rendered him susceptible to indoctrination by fanatics who preached the superiority of Japan over other nations, the infallibility of the divine emperor, and the subordination of civilians to the military. However, the influences promoting an authoritarian or militaristic regime were never unopposed. Continuous and broadening contacts with the outside world and a gradual reaction to the disturbing consequences of rapid economic change introduced a train of liberal thought, which threatened to collide with the forces of conservatism.

Japan's external relations during the Meiji era were directly related to, and appreciably affected by, internal developments. It is not strange that Japan, in the process of becoming a modern state, adopted a policy of imperialism, in view of its agility in assimilating the tech-

Moderates vs. *extremists*

niques of Western nations and also in view of the stresses created by
the industrialization of the country. As time went on, however, differences of opinion appeared among Japanese statesmen, business and
financial leaders, and intellectuals as to the proper course to pursue in
advancing the interests of the state. Some bureaucrats were conservative or even reactionary, generally unsympathetic to parliamentary
institutions, and inclined to favor an aggressive foreign policy. Others
were primarily interested in building up Japan's economic and financial strength, securing foreign markets by peaceful penetration, and
creating a prosperous and stable society at home. While not genuinely
democratic, they at least accepted the implications of constitutional
government and were anxious to win an honorable position for their
country within the family of nations. Fortunately for Japan, the moderate expansionists were fairly successful during this period in holding
the militant faction in check, although not without making some
concessions to them.

Adventures in imperialism

Japanese expansion in Eastern Asia would almost inevitably be at
the expense of the decadent Chinese Empire. In 1876, the Japanese
government took direct steps to end the isolation of Korea, a "hermit
nation" which had been as tightly sealed against outside influences as
Japan under the Tokugawa Shogunate. Copying a page from the
Western book, the Japanese negotiated a treaty with the Seoul government which accorded them extraterritoriality and other rights, as well
as opening Korea to commercial intercourse. The treaty also recognized Korea as an independent state, in total disregard of the fact that
the Peking government considered the peninsula a tributary dependency of the Manchu Empire. Actually the Manchu officials had
neglected to enforce their claims, and their belated attempt to recover
their position by counterintrigue against the Japanese was almost certain to provoke a clash with Japan. Korea, at this time, was an ideal
breeding ground for war. In spite of brilliant episodes in its past, the
kingdom had degenerated into one of the most backward regions of
Asia. The administration was corrupt and predatory, the peasants
ignorant and wretched, and conditions in general thoroughly belied
the country's poetic name—Chosen ("Land of the Morning Calm").
Japan's interest in Korea was both economic and strategic, the latter
because Russia had acquired the Maritime Province on the Pacific
coast directly north of the Korean border and had already attempted
to intervene in Korea's troubled affairs. After a local rebellion had
furnished the excuse for both China and Japan to rush troops into
Korea, the Sino-Japanese War was precipitated.

Wars with China and
Russia

It could be—and has been—argued that, beginning with its swift
victory over China in 1895, Japan's policy in Asia was one of territorial aggression. In the treaty of Shimonoseki, Japan required from
China not only recognition of Korean independence and the payment
of an indemnity but also the cession of Formosa, the Pescadores

Islands, and the southern projection of Manchuria—the Liaotung Peninsula. Japan joined in the scramble for concessions in China, acquiring a sphere of interest in Fukien province opposite Formosa. When harassed by the advance of Russian imperialism in Korea, Japan attacked Russia in 1904 and, after defeating its forces on land and sea, annexed the southern half of Sakhalin Island and obtained economic concessions in Manchuria. These facts, however, are only part of the story, which in its entirety indicates that the Japanese were adept in mastering the object lessons of European diplomacy and power politics. Following the Sino-Japanese War, under pressure from Russia, France, and Germany, Japan had been forced to relinquish its claim to the Liaotung Peninsula, on the ground that occupation of this region by a foreign power would threaten the safety of the Peking government. Almost immediately afterward, Russia, by a treaty of alliance with China, secured control of the very region it had denied to Japan and converted practically all Manchuria into a Russian sphere of interest. Several attempts on the part of the Japanese government to reach an accommodation with Russia in regard to Korea and Manchuria were frustrated by the recklessness and duplicity of the Tsar's agents. Nevertheless, some influential Japanese considered war with Russia too dangerous an undertaking, and the government would probably not have dared to attack Russia except for the fact that the Anglo-Japanese Alliance of 1902 assured Japan of the friendly backing

The Sino-Japanese War. Japanese troops attack Chinese forces defending Pyongyang in Korea, September 15, 1894.

NAVAL SEE-SAW.—LI HUNG CHANG
GETS A JOLT.

JAPANESE NAVY RESCUING COREA FROM THE
CHINESE DRAGON.

CHINA AND JAPAN WRESTLING OVER THE MAP OF COREA.

A PAGE OF CARTOONS BY A JAPANESE ARTIST.

The Sino-Japanese Struggle over Korea, as Seen by a Japanese Cartoonist (1894)

of the world's greatest naval power. The British welcomed Japan's accession to a position of strength as a means of checking Russian expansion in the Far East. During the Russo-Japanese War, sentiment in both Great Britain and the United States was prevailingly in favor of Japan, largely because of the devious and bullying tactics that the Russians had been pursuing. President Theodore Roosevelt's sympathy for Japan helped in terminating the hostilities, and the peace treaty was negotiated at Portsmouth, New Hampshire.

Japan's victory over Russia seemed for a time to restore a balance of power in the Far East. Russia, shaken by the Revolution of 1905, and Japan, its financial reserves drained by the war, quickly agreed on apportioning their respective spheres in Manchuria—publicly affirming, of course, that they had no intention of violating China's territorial integrity. But the balance of power proved to be unstable. The outbreak of the European war in 1914, necessitating a "retreat of the West" from Asia, provided Japan with a golden opportunity to consolidate and extend her position.

A temporary balance of power in East Asia

3. AFRICA DURING THE CENTURY OF EUROPEAN IMPERIALIST EXPANSION

By the opening of the nineteenth century, the cause for the abolition of the slave trade was winning a growing number of converts among governing circles in Denmark, England, France, and the United States. Humanitarian abolitionist sentiment was strongest among the Quakers, particularly in Great Britian. And in the economic realm, a growing chorus of British merchants and industrialists questioned mercantilism and championed the doctrines of laissez faire and free trade. There was an increasing belief among plantation owners that free, paid labor was more efficient than slave labor. At the same time,

Free trade, abolitionist sentiment grows

sons of the Industrial Revolution were convinced that greater profits could be made from trade in tropical raw materials, especially mineral resources, needed to supply European industries. Moreover, British attitudes toward the establishment and maintenance of colonies had become increasingly negative since the fiasco of the American Revolution. In the first decade of the nineteenth century these sentiments prompted the abolition of the slave trade. Denmark took the lead in 1805, followed by Britain in 1807 and the United States shortly afterward. Henceforth, British naval squadrons in West African waters would protect legitimate traders and attempt to suppress the seaborne trade in slaves.

In West Africa the slave trade had contributed to the growth of autocratic, militaristic institutions in those societies that had profited from it. In some forest states, power had shifted from the elders, priests, and traditional chiefs to kings and their warrior bands. From an economic point of view, the productive capacities of Africans had been severely retarded by the slave trade. Therefore, it was now incumbent upon the Europeans to encourage farming, mining, and legitimate trading, and to stimulate the cultivation of cotton, tobacco, cocoa, and other cash crops which might contribute to an improvement in African living standards while also serving as a resource for European industries. Freed slaves from the ships of illegal slavers would be Westernized, Christianized, and returned to the "Dark Continent." Africa was still considered the "white man's graveyard," and humanitarians confidently assumed that repatriated blacks were better equipped to spread the fruits of Western civilization to their benighted brothers in the bush. All these assumptions, while perhaps well meaning, were deeply rooted in a cultural chauvinism dating back to the heyday of the slave trade. Yet in response to such sentiments, colonies for freed blacks were established by the British in Sierra Leone in 1808, by the Americans in Liberia in 1821, and by the French at Libreville in Gabon in 1849.

A shift in the locus of power

Ironically, the outlawing of the slave trade contributed to an inflation in the price of slaves and a consequent growth in volume of the traffic. Furthermore, Eli Whitney's cotton gin, invented in 1795, created new demands for slaves on the plantations of the southern United States. The growth in illicit trade led to more stringent attempts at suppression after 1820. United States participation in the antislave-trade naval squadrons propelled American legitimate merchants to Africa's shores in large numbers. Between 1850 and 1862, United States merchants, mainly from Salem, Massachusetts, dominated West African transatlantic commerce. From the mid-1840s the Atlantic slave trade declined steadily, and President Lincoln's Emancipation Proclamation of 1863 nearly brought it to an end.

U.S. participation in antislave trade squadrons

The slave trade and the concomitant traffic in European arms contributed to the emergence of a new class of African and mulatto mer-

Middlemen in the African Slave Trade. The nineteenth-century residence of a mulatto merchant who was active in the slave trade. Elmina, Gold Coast.

chants in West African seaports. In their societies, power rested on personality and ability, not birth. A few of these merchants became extremely wealthy capitalists.

The House-Canoe system

The Atlantic trade after 1800 triggered unprecedented political and economic expansion in the palm-oil-rich Niger Delta. Local chiefs and affluent nonroyal entrepreneurs organized a remarkably democratic House-Canoe institution of governance, which acted as a cooperative trading unit and as an institution of local government. The old hierarchical forest empires of Benin and Oyo, unable to adjust to the challenges of legitimate trade and to the rise of this dynamic merchant class, were gradually eclipsed. Asante and Dahomey, on the other hand, survived by culturally assimilating their slaves and organizing them to perform large-scale labor in Asante gold mines or on expansive plantations in Dahomey.

African and European responses to the abolition of the slave trade

Former European slaving nations also had to make painful economic readjustments to the termination of the slave trade. After 1843 it was clear to the British that chartered companies lacked the financial resources to maintain the old coastal fortresses and warehouses. Reluctantly, the Crown assumed these responsibilities. The Dutch and the Danes failed to make the adjustment to the changing nature of trade and transferred their coastal installations to the British in 1850 and 1872 respectively. British treaties with African potentates, aimed initially at restricting the slave trade, gave way in the 1830s to treaties calling for the protection of European commercial interests through the establishment of consulates. British consuls would be responsible for ensuring the free flow of goods from the interior to European warehouses in coastal ports. Because the British treasury, bending to popular opinion at home, refused to undertake the costs of maintaining such enclaves, the consuls had to finance them by levying duties. Beginning in the 1860s, ambitious consuls, on their own initiative, did not hesitate to dispatch military expenditions to inland kingdoms to punish chiefs if they hindered the free flow of trade.

Such interference in the affairs of African governments created a vicious cycle of political disintegration. Recalcitrant chiefs, humiliated and intimidated by the superior firepower of European weapons, lost their ability to hold distant provinces together. In Oyo in the 1860s and in Asante after 1874, this condition released centrifugal tendencies and contributed to a breakdown of law, order, and security. Oyo's economy, crippled from the decline of the slave trade, was further weakened by the rise of a coastal trade in palm oil. As inland states, Benin and Oyo found it impossible to compete effectively with African trading houses located among the oil-rich estuaries of the Niger Delta. From 1821 to 1893 the Oyo empire in particular was torn first by a breakdown in the constitution, then by a destructive Fulani invasion that left its magnificent capital in ruins, and finally by civil war. By 1865 refugees from the countryside had begun to stream into stockaded villages like Ibadan, which swelled into sprawling cities. The Yoruba became an urbanized people almost overnight, and leadership passed into the hands of professional military men who could offer protection.

Political disintegration

Once the British had thrown their weight onto the balance of African rivalries, it became a matter of prestige and commitment for them to remain in Africa. In the Niger Delta in 1854 they exiled the powerful African trader king, Dappa Pepple, for cornering the lucrative palm-oil trade to the detriment of British nationals. In 1861 they established a consulate at Lagos, thus opening a hundred-year chapter of direct interference in Nigerian trade and politics. In 1874 they bombarded the capital of Asante in order to punish the king for closing trade routes to the coast. And after 1874 they squelched an experiment by the Fante people in nation building along Western democratic lines by declaring their territory a "Gold Coast Colony." Likewise, ambitious French governors in Senegal had, since 1854, become involved in the internal affairs of inland Muslim states.

*British interference in
Nigerian trade and politics*

Significantly, these militant gestures were usually initiated not by home governments but rather by men in the field—governors, consuls, and sometimes traders. Before 1875, European powers rarely manifested an impulse to territorial empire in Africa. Nor had any of them formulated a coherent or consistent colonial African policy. The tide of public opinion, especially in Great Britain, ran against imperialist ventures, largely because they were so costly. Other than officials and entrepreneurs, those who came to Africa were usually scientists, privately financed and interested in resolving botanical, ethnographic or geographical questions; or they were missionaries and physicians

*Local initiatives and anti-
imperialist sentiment in
Europe*

*The demystification of
Africa*

*The expansion of East
African trade brings social,
political, economic
reorientations*

*Sayyid Said and the
reassertion of Omani
hegemony*

*Ngoni invasions bring
social upheaval*

*The East African ivory
and slave trade*

like David Livingstone, who sought to root out domestic slavery and the slave trade, introduce modern medical practice, and further Christian proselytization.

By 1875 the major geographical mysteries had been solved: the course of the Niger River (1830), the source of the Nile (1862), Mounts Kilimanjaro and Kenya (1848 and 1849, respectively) and the vast river system of the upper Congo Basin (1860s). European explorers had also made direct contact with the major inland empires: Asante (1817), Sokoto Caliphate (1824), Bunyoro (1872). In 1854 quinine proved to be an effective drug for mitigating the effects of the hitherto deadly malaria. European probes into the interior now became more frequent and less costly in human lives. Fear of malaria had previously discouraged the white man from penetrating the tropical rain forest.

Unlike West Africa, East Africa during the first three quarters of the nineteenth century witnessed a dramatic revival of trade, particularly in slaves, cloves, and ivory. By 1800 Africans in what are today Kenya and Tanzania had begun to organize long-distance caravans and trading networks. Previously, items passed haphazardly from community to community before reaching their destination. Criteria for leadership among these small-scale societies now changed from skills in hunting and expertise in rain making to ability in organizing trade, negotiating business deals, and accumulating European manufactured weapons.

The Omani Arabs, preoccupied with internal strife in southern Arabia for a century, were reunited by 1805 and determined to reassert their authority over the East African coastal towns. Under the cunning leadership of Sultan Sayyid Said, Omani hegemony was restored and the capital was transferred from Muscat in Oman to the fertile and picturesque island of Zanzibar, some twenty miles off the East African coast. On Zanzibar, Sultan Said stimulated the growth of a vast plantation economy, built upon the cultivation of cloves and coconuts and worked by African slaves imported from the mainland. Indians were attracted to the island to serve as financial advisers and moneylenders to Arab and Swahili caravan operators.

Slaves were readily available in the 1840s because of a severe social and demographic upheaval in what are known today as Tanzania, Malawi, and northern Mozambique. Thousands of warrior bands of Ngoni streamed into the region from South Africa. They descended upon the local populations, which had no tradition of fighting and were therefore defenseless. Entire communities were often sold into bondage to Arab, Swahili, and other African slavers.

East Africa by mid-century had become the world's most important source of ivory and the major area for illicit slaving. Dispossessed captives were forced to carry huge quantities of elephant and rhinoceros tusks to the coast. The ivory was shipped to Britain and India while the slaves were sold either to Arab plantation owners on Zan-

Indian Financiers in Zanzibar. An Indian merchant's house in Zanzibar.

zibar, to French planters on the nearby sugar-producing islands of Mauritius and Réunion, or to sheikhs in Arabia.

By the 1870s numerous East African individuals and communities had established their own trading networks and armed themselves to protect their economic spheres. The He-he, taking advantage of an unprecedented growth in the European arms traffic after the Franco-Prussian War, became highly organized warriors. Entrepreneurs like Tippu Tip and Mirambo forged their own extensive trading operations and successfully competed with the Arabs for inland resources. However, the Arabs enjoyed the financial backing of Zanzibar as well as commercial connections with Indian and Arabian overseas markets.

In 1843 Arab traders were received at the court of the king of Buganda on the northwest shore of Lake Victoria. Within another decade they extended their operations west of Lakes Victoria and Tanganyika. They were not interested in the propagation of Islam nor in territorial conquest; their sole concern was for trade. And for that reason they often found a warm reception among East African chiefs, who sought arms and imported luxury items in order to boost their own prestige.

Arab penetration

While the East African interior sank into a condition of almost complete social disintegration, Sayyid Said continued to build a vast commercial empire in the western Indian Ocean. Nearly every important coastal town from Mombasa in Kenya to the Mozambique border fell under Said's commercial sway. Not since the fifteenth century had the Swahili city-states enjoyed such prosperity. But it was a false wealth, based on exploitation of the interior. Fortunes were made in Zanzibar on slaves, cloves, and ivory; and the economic stability and security provided by Sultan Said attracted seafarers from Britain, Germany,

Growing British influence over the Zanzibar Sultanate

Panorama of the Island Town of Zanzibar. Zanzibar, one of the oldest Swahili city-states, may have been flourishing as early as the first century A.D. In the fifteenth century it was minting its own coinage and trading actively with

France, and the United States. While these nations established consulates at Zanzibar, only the British one survived beyond 1850. Indeed, after the opening of the Suez Canal in 1869, the western Indian Ocean, particularly Zanzibar, became strategically more important to British interests in India than it had ever been before.

Since 1822, the British had forced on Sultan Said a series of ordinances restricting his slave-trading activities. In return, the British navy would protect the Sultan's legitimate trade and government from foreign interference. Sayyid Said struck an excellent bargain and kept it until his death in 1856, after more than half a century in power. After his demise, the British quickly split his domain into two parts, Muscat and Zanzibar, with separate sultans over each. Henceforth, ambitious British consuls in Zanzibar used the pretense of slave-trade suppression as a cloak for the expansion of their own control over the Sultanate.

In the 1870s Zanzibar became a springboard for European missionary activity on the mainland. British, German, and French mission-

Zanzibar: springboard for missionary activity in East Africa

cities of the Persian Gulf and beyond. By the nineteenth century there was a significant Western presence. Note that the Sultan's palace, arsenal, and battery are flanked by European and American consulates.

Buganda's ascendancy

aries, Catholic and Protestant, followed the trails blazed only decades earlier by the caravan drivers. They found the interior of Tanzania in social and political chaos. The fabric of civilization had been almost totally destroyed. Yet along the western shores of Lake Victoria, the highly centralized kingdom of Buganda had begun to emerge as the most powerful state in East Africa. Its king, or *kabaka,* was both respected and feared by Europeans and Africans alike. Buganda itself had recently passed from a feudal to a bureaucratic stage of development and was in the process of undertaking an imperialistic policy of territorial expansion.

South Africa and the Dutch East India Company

The nineteenth century in South Africa opened with a change of European rule at the Cape from the Dutch East India Company to the British Crown. The Dutch East India Company had established a refreshment station at Table Bay in 1652 for their ships sailing between the Netherlands and Java. By 1750 it had swelled into a large company colony, consisting not only of Dutch settlers and company employees but also of French Huguenots and Germans. Some merged into the indigenous African population to form a distinct racial group called the "Cape Colored." However, the majority of these predominantly Calvinistic settlers remained racially aloof and clung dogmatically to a fundamentalist interpretation of the Bible. Their religion became a justification for racial separation. Far removed from the European Enlightenment and liberal currents, they remained intensely provincial in outlook. The majority were illiterate farmers and cattlemen whose only socially cohesive force was the Dutch Reformed Church and its preachers, or predikants. As strong individualists, these frontiersmen resented the authority of company rule, emanating from distant Cape Town.

1795: British occupation

In 1795 the British temporarily occupied the Cape to prevent it from falling into the hands of Napoleon's navy. The Netherlands had already been overrun by the French and were in no position to assume responsibilities for the nearly bankrupt Dutch East India Company. British occupation became permanent after 1806. Following the Napoleonic wars, Britain enjoyed mastery of the world's major sea lanes. The Cape Colony was thus taken primarily for its strategic importance in relation to India. Table Bay, at the foot of the African continent, offered one of the finest harbors en route to the Orient.

Dutch settlers' resistance to Anglicization

Britain's attempt to Anglicize the Cape Colony met with fierce resistance from the predominantly Dutch settlers. The settlers hated the liberal, cosmopolitan, nonracial attitudes of these newcomers, many of whom were Anglican missionaries. They also resented the substitution of English for Afrikaans as the official language and the introduction of British-staffed circuit courts, with judges who allowed slaves to testify against their masters. In 1834 the institution of slavery was abolished and Africans were henceforth equal to Europeans before the law.

The Great Trek and Boer racism

The following year, several thousand Dutch settlers, called Boers, reacted to these ordinances by migrating en masse across the Orange River onto the high grassy plains known as the veld. This "Great Trek" culminated in the establishment of a series of autonomous racist republics. However, the so-called Promised Land had been inhabited by politically segmented but culturally related Bantu societies for nearly six hundred years. Their small, defenseless communities were no match for well-armed, determined foreigners. The Boers, however, were not the only group in search of new pastures. Both the savanna people and the Boers had to contend with an expanding Zulu empire moving up from the southern coast. Tragically, the savanna dwellers became caught in this destructive Boer–Zulu vise.

British vacillation

British policy toward the Boers and Bantu had always been one of vacillation. In 1848 the British crushed the new Boer republics, only to restore their independence less than a decade later. Their policy regarding the Bantu swung from noninterference and racial separation to paternalistic cooperation and integration. The only constant ele-

The Zulu City of Umgungundhlovu. All Zulu royal cities followed a consistent elliptical design. These were essentially predatory cities, which thrived not on market or craft activity, but on pillage of the surrounding countryside. At its zenith, Umgungundhlovu contained over 1,700 dwellings, capable of accommodating twenty soldiers in each. This city was burned to the ground by Boer commandos in 1838.

ments in their policy were the prevention of Boer access to the sea and the minimization of Bantu–Boer conflicts.

Clashes between Zulu and Boer east of the Orange River brought havoc to the local Sotho, Nguni, and Ndebele populations and forced them to disperse in all directions. Some refugees coalesced and organized centralized kingdoms in parts of what are today Lesotho, Swaziland, Botswana, Zambia, and Zimbabwe. Others, like the Nguni, became warriors in self-defense against Zulu imperialism and moved northward across the Zambezi River into Tanzania. There these roving bands of Ngoni (as they were called in East Africa) caused the same kind of social disruption that had been inflicted upon them by the Zulu and Boers only decades earlier in their former South African homelands. In 1879, in a gesture of conciliation to the Boers, the British defeated the highly disciplined though ill-equipped Zulu and shattered their proud empire into thirteen weak chieftaincies. The Zulu empire ceased to exist, but Zulu nationalism and culture continued to flourish.

The African diaspora

Of the hundreds of African states, only Ethiopia and Liberia succeeded in withstanding the European imperialist conquest. Ethiopia survived largely because of its modernization programs. Since the 1850s it had begun to emerge from nearly four centuries of isolation. By 1855 a young warrior from the Shoa kingdom had gained control over the nearly independent kingdoms of Gondar, Gojjam, and Tigre, and in so doing had reunited them into an Ethiopian empire. Taking the title of Emperor Theodore II, he laid the foundations of a modern state through administrative reforms and through the creation of a modern national army. For the first time, an effort was made to bring

The new Ethiopian empire

the clergy's extensive feudal estates under government control and to weaken the provincial nobility by establishing districts under Theodore's own appointed governors.

Theodore's work was extended under Emperor Menelik II (1889–1913), who with Italian firearms launched an era of imperial expansion. By the turn of the century, he had through war and diplomacy conquered the Galla in the north, the Gurage and Kaffa in the south, the Muslim state of Harar and Somali-occupied Ogaden in the east, and Wallage in the west. At the Battle of Adowa in 1896 Menelik's 100,000-strong army defeated the invading Italians and saved Ethiopia from European conquest. From his new capital of Addis Ababa in the Abyssinian highlands, he employed European technocrats to construct highways and bridges, hospitals and schools, a postal and telegraphic network, a modern banking system, and a more efficient civil service.

Liberia, independent since 1847, also attempted to modernize, using the United States as a model. But faced with chronic economic stagnation, soaring debts, and gradual frontier encroachments by the British and French, the Liberians turned for survival to the United States in 1912. Though the nation became an economic dependency of American corporate and financial institutions, it was able to maintain its political sovereignty. This was largely due to solidarity among the Americo-Liberian ruling elites, whose ancestors had returned to Africa from America.

SELECTED READINGS

• *Items so designated are available in paperback editions.*

GENERAL

Clyde, P. H., and B. F. Beers, *The Far East,* 4th ed., Englewood Cliffs, N.J., 1966.
• Griswold, A. W., *The Far Eastern Policy of the United States,* New York, 1938.
Peffer, Nathaniel, *The Far East: A Modern History,* Ann Arbor, 1958.
Romein, Jan, *The Asian Century: A History of Modern Nationalism in Asia,* Berkeley, 1962.
Vinacke, H. M., *A History of the Far East in Modern Times,* 6th ed., New York, 1959.

CHINA (*See also Readings for Chapter 23*)

Bays, D. H., *China Enters the Twentieth Century: Chang Chih-tung and the Issues of a New Age, 1895–1909,* Ann Arbor, 1978.
Bland, J. O. P., and E. T. Backhouse, *China under the Empress Dowager,* Philadelphia, 1910.
Chang Chung-li, *The Chinese Gentry,* Seattle, 1955.
Ch'ên, Jerome, *Yuan Shih-k'ai,* 2d ed., Stanford, 1972

• Chesneaux, Jean, *Peasant Revolts in China: 1840–1949,* New York, 1973.

Collis, Maurice, *Foreign Mud,* London, 1964. An account of life among the English merchants at Canton.

• Fairbank, J. K., *The United States and China,* 4th ed., Cambridge, Mass., 1979. Brief but perceptive.

Fleming, Peter, *The Siege at Peking,* New York, 1959. The Boxer uprising and its suppression.

• Franke, Wolfgang, *A Century of Chinese Revolution 1851–1949,* New York, 1971.

Gaster, Michael, *Chinese Intellectuals and the Revolution of 1911,* Seattle, 1969.

Hsü, C. Y., *The Rise of Modern China* 2d ed., New York, 1975. Especially good on the nineteeenh century.

• Levenson, J. R., *Confucian China and Its Modern Fate: A Trilogy,* Berkeley, 1968.

• Michael, Franz, *The Taiping Rebellion: History,* Seattle, 1972.

• Schiffrin, H. Z., *Sun Yat-sen and the Origins of the Chinese Revolution,* Berkeley, 1968.

• Tan, C. C., *The Boxer Catastrophe,* New York, 1955.

Yeng, S. Y., *The Taiping Rebellion and the Western Powers,* New York, 1971. Comprehensive and informative.

JAPAN (*See also Readings for Chapter 23*)

Allen, G. C., *A Short Economic History of Modern Japan, 1867–1937,* rev. ed., New York, 1963.

Barr, Pat, *The Coming of the Barbarians: The Opening of Japan to the West, 1853–1870,* New York, 1967.

Beckmann, G. M., *The Making of the Meiji Constitution: The Oligarchs and the Constitutional Development of Japan, 1868–1891,* Lawrence, Kan., 1957.

Borton, Hugh, *Japan's Modern Century,* 2d ed., New York, 1970.

Brown, D. M., *Nationalism in Japan: An Introductory Historical Analysis,* Berkeley, 1955.

Craig, A. M., *Chōshū in the Meiji Restoration,* Cambridge, Mass., 1961.

Jansen, M. B., *Sakamoto Ryōma and the Meiji Restoration,* Princeton, 1961. A penetrating study of the conflict and confusion in Japanese politics at the end of the Tokugawa period.

• Lockwood, W. W., *The Economic Development of Japan, 1868–1938,* Princeton, 1954.

Reischauer, R. K., *Japan: Government-Politics,* New York, 1939.

Roberts, J. G., *Mitsui: Three Centuries of Japanese Business,* New York, 1974. Carries the story through the American occupation.

Russell, O. D., *The House of Mitsui,* Boston, 1939.

Scalapino, R. A., *Democracy and the Party Movement in Prewar Japan,* Berkeley, 1953.

• Storry, Richard, *A History of Modern Japan,* Baltimore, 1960.

Walworth, Arthur, *Black Ships off Japan,* New York, 1946.

Yanaga Chitoshi, *Japan since Perry,* New York, 1949.

AFRICA

Anstey, Roger, *The Atlantic Slave Trade and British Abolition, 1760–1810,* London, 1975.

Boahen, Adu, *Topics in West African History,* New York, 1968.

Carter, Gwendolen, and Patrick O'Meara, eds., *Southern Africa in Crisis,* Bloomington, 1977.

Curtin, Philip D., *The Image of Africa,* Madison, Wis., 1964.

• Davidson, Basil, *The African Slave Trade,* Boston, 1961.

Duignan, Peter, and L. H. Gann, eds., *Colonialism in Africa, 1860–1960,* London, 1975.

• Fage, J. D., *A History of West Africa,* New York, 1969.

Flint, John, ed., *The Cambridge History of Africa,* Vol. 5, *c. 1790 to c. 1870,* Cambridge, 1976.

Forde, D., and P. M. Kaberry, eds., *West African Kingdoms in the Nineteenth Century,* New York, 1967.

Gailey, H. A., *A History of Africa 1800 to the Present,* New York, 1972.

Konczacki, Z. A., and J. M. Konczacki, eds., *The Economic History of Tropical Africa,* Vol. 1, *The Pre-Colonial Period,* London, 1977.

Miers, Suzanne, *Britain and the Ending of the Slave Trade,* London, 1975.

Miers, Suzanne, and Igor Kopytoff, eds., *Slavery in Africa: Historical and Anthropological Perspectives,* Madison, Wis., 1977.

Munro, J. Forbes, *Africa and the International Economy, 1800–1960,* London, 1976.

Ogot, B. A., and J. A. Kieran, eds., *Zamani: A Survey of East African History,* New York, 1969.

Penrose, E. F., ed., *European Imperialism and the Partition of Africa,* London, 1975.

Pope-Hennessy, John, *A Study of the Atlantic Slave Traders: Sins of the Fathers,* New York, 1969.

Wilson, Henry S., *The Imperial Experience in Sub-Saharan Africa since 1870,* London, 1977.

SOURCE MATERIALS

Crowder, M., and J. F. Ade Ajayi, eds., *History of West Africa,* Vol. I, New York, 1972.

Curtin, Philip D., ed., *Africa Remembered,* Madison, 1967.

• de Bary, W. T., ed., *Sources of Chinese Tradition,* Chaps. XXIV, XXV, XXVI, New York, 1960.

• ———, ed., *Sources of Japanese Tradition,* Chaps. XXIV, XXV, New York, 1958.

• Michael, Franz, *The Taiping Rebellion: Its Sources, Interpretations, and Influences.*

Emerson, Joyce, tr., *The Lotus Pool,* London, 1961. Autobiographical account of struggle against restrictions of the patriarchal family.

The Complete Journal of Townsend Harris, New York, 1930.

• Teng Ssu-yü, and J. K. Fairbank, *China's Response to the West: A Documentary Survey,* 2 vols., Cambridge, Mass., 1954.

Toson, S., *The Broken Commandment,* tr. K. Strong, Tokyo, 1974. A major novel of the Meiji period.

Waley, Arthur, tr., *The Opium War through Chinese Eyes,* London, 1958.

Chapter 33

WORLD WAR I

Nevertheless, except you share
With them in hell the sorrowful dark of hell,
Whose world is but the trembling of a flare,
And heaven but as the highway for a shell,

You shall not hear their mirth:
You shall not think them well content
By any jest of mine. These men are worth
Your tears. You are not worth their merriment.

—Wilfred Owen, "Apologia Pro Poemate Meo"

The war that broke out in 1914 was one of the most extraordinary in history. Though it was not really the "first world war," since such conflicts as the Seven Years' War and the Napoleonic wars had also been global in extent, it had an impact far exceeding either of those. It quickly became a "people's war," in which civilians as well as soldiers in the trenches participated in violent demands for extermination of the enemy. It bore fruit in an epidemic of revolutions and sowed the dragon's teeth of new and even more venomous conflicts in the future. In such ways it set the pattern for an age of violence that has continued through most of the twentieth century.

A world at war

Historians who have studied the evidence are generally of the opinion that no one nation was solely responsible for the outbreak of war. Perhaps none of the combatants really wanted war; they would have preferred to achieve their aims by other means. But in pursuing these aims they followed policies that made war virtually inevitable. The most dangerous of national objectives were probably those of Germany. This was true not because they were more self-serving than those of other Western powers, but because they posed a more serious threat to the balance of power in Europe. As the war progressed it appeared that Germany was attempting to achieve on the Continent objectives that Britain and France had succeeded in attaining in Asia and Africa. From the beginning of the war, Germany's rulers were think-

Responsibility for war

ing in terms of a vastly enlarged German empire that would include as satellite states Poland, Belgium, Holland, the Balkans, and Turkey, establishing a great sphere of influence comparable to that of the United States in the Western Hemisphere and of Russia in the heartland of Eurasia. Fears of what this German scheme would do to the European balance of power frightened diplomats in other European capitals.

I. THE ROAD TO ARMAGEDDON

The assassination of Francis Ferdinand

It has been generally held that the assassination of the Austrian archduke was the immediate cause of World War I. Francis Ferdinand was soon to become emperor of Austria-Hungary. The reigning monarch, Francis Joseph, had reached his eighty-fourth year, and his death was expected momentarily. The murder of the heir to the throne was therefore considered in a very real sense as an attack upon the state.

Motives of the assassins

The actual murderer of Francis Ferdinand was a Bosnian student by the name of Gavrilo Princip, the tool of Serbian nationalists. The murder, though committed in Sarajevo, the capital of Bosnia, was the result of a plot hatched in Belgrade, the Serbian capital. The conspirators were members of a secret society officially known as Union or Death, but commonly called the Black Hand. What were the motives of the conspirators? If there is any one answer, it would seem to lie in the plan which Francis Ferdinand was known to be developing for the reorganization of the Hapsburg Empire. This plan, designated as *trialism,* involved a proposal for changing the Dual Monarchy into a triple monarchy. In addition to German Austria and Magyar Hungary, already practically autonomous, there was to be a third semi-independent unit composed of the Slavs. This plan was exactly what the Serb nationalists did not want. They feared that if it were put into effect, their Slovene and Croatian kinsmen would be content to remain under

The Archduke Francis Ferdinand. He and his wife are leaving the Senate House in Sarajevo shortly before the assassination, June 28, 1914.

Hapsburg rule. They therefore determined to get Francis Ferdinand out of the way before he could become emperor.

In the weeks immediately following the assassination, Austrian officials conducted an investigation which confirmed their suspicions that the plot was of Serbian origin. Consequently, on July 23, they dispatched to the Serbian government a severe ultimatum consisting of eleven demands: among them Serbia was to suppress anti-Austrian newspapers; to crush secret patriotic societies; to eliminate from the government and from the army all persons guilty of anti-Austrian propaganda; and to accept the collaboration of Austrian officials in stamping out the subversive movement against the Hapsburg Empire. On July 25, in accordance with the time limit of forty-eight hours, the Serbian government transmitted its reply. Of the total of eleven demands, only one was emphatically refused, and five were accepted without reservations. The German chancellor regarded it as almost a capitulation, and Emperor William II declared that now all reason for war had dissipated. The Austrians, however, pronounced the Serbian reply unsatisfactory, severed diplomatic relations, and mobilized parts of their army. The Serbs themselves had been under no illusions about pleasing Austria, since, three hours before transmitting their reply, they had issued an order to mobilize the troops.

Austrian ultimatum to Serbia

The Austrian intransigence vis-à-vis the Serbian response was actually the culmination of a belligerence which had been growing among European nations prior to the events which followed the assassination. As early as July 18 Sergei Sazonov, the Russian foreign minister, warned Austria that Russia would not tolerate any effort to humiliate Serbia. On July 24 Sazonov informed the German ambassador: "I do not hate Austria; I despise her. Austria is seeking a pretext to gobble up Serbia; but in that case Russia will make war on Austria."[1] In the adoption of this attitude, Russia had the support of France. About the twentieth of July, Raymond Poincaré, president of France, paid a visit to St. Petersburg. He kept urging Sazonov to "be firm" and to avoid any compromise which might result in a loss of prestige for the Triple Entente. He warned the Austrian ambassador that "Serbia has very warm friends in the Russian people. And Russia has an ally, France."[2]

Russia and France

The attitude of Germany in these critical days was ambiguous. Although the kaiser was shocked and infuriated by the assassination, his government did not make any threats until after the actions of Russia gave cause for alarm. Yet both William II and the chancellor, Theobald von Bethmann-Hollweg, adopted the premise that stern punishment must be meted out to Serbia without delay. They hoped in this way to confront the other powers with an accomplished fact. The kaiser declared on June 30: "Now or never! Matters must be cleared up with the Serbs, *and that soon.*" On July 6 Bethmann-Hollweg gave

The attitude of Germany

[1] S. B. Fay, *The Origins of the World War*, II, 300.
[2] *Ibid.*, II, 281.

Nicholas II and Raymond Poincaré, the President of the French Republic, in St. Petersburg on July 23, 1914

a commitment to the Austrian foreign minister which was interpreted by the latter as a blank check. The Austrian government was informed that the kaiser would "stand true by Austria's side in accordance with his treaty obligations and old friendship." In giving this pledge Bethmann and his imperial master were gambling on the hope that Russia would not intervene for the protection of Serbia, and that therefore the quarrel would remain a mere local squabble.

Russian mobilization

Austria declared war against Serbia on July 28, 1914. For a fleeting, anxious moment there was a possibility that the conflict might be contained. But it was quickly transformed into a war of larger scope by the action of Russia. On July 29 Sazonov and a prowar military clique persuaded Tsar Nicholas II to issue an order mobilizing all troops, not only against Austria but against Germany as well. Their argument was a logical one. Such a vast country as Russia would require considerable time to get its military machine into operation. But before the order could be put into effect, Nicholas changed his mind, having just received an urgent appeal from the kaiser to help preserve the peace.

See color map facing page 961

On July 30 Sazonov and the Russian chief of staff went to work to induce the tsar to change his mind again. For more than an hour they sought to convince the reluctant autocrat that the entire military system should be set in motion. In the end, Nicholas signed an order for immediate mobilization.

There was now no drawing back from the abyss. The Germans were alarmed over Russian preparations for war. The latest action of the tsar's government made the situation far more critical, since in German military circles, and also in French and Russian, general mobilization meant war. Upon learning that the tsar's decree had gone into effect, William II's government sent an ultimatum to St. Petersburg demanding that mobilization cease within twelve hours. On the afternoon of August 1, the German ambassador requested an interview with the Russian foreign minister. He appealed to Sazonov for a favorable answer to the German ultimatum. Sazonov replied that mobilization could not be halted, but that Russia was willing to continue negotiations. The ambassador repeated his question a second and a third time, emphasizing the terrible consequences of a negative answer. Sazonov finally replied: "I have no other answer to give you." The ambassador then handed the foreign minister a declaration of war and, bursting into tears, left the room. In the meantime, the kaiser's ministers had also dispatched an ultimatum to France demanding that its leaders make known their intentions. Premier René Viviani replied on August 1 that France would act "in accordance with her interests," and immediately ordered a general mobilization of the army. On August 3 Germany declared war upon France.

All eyes now turned in the direction of Britain. What would happen, now that the other two members of the Triple Entente had rushed headlong into war? For some time after the situation on the Continent had become critical, Britain vacillated. It is difficult to believe that the British would have long remained out of the war, even if the neutrality of Belgium had never been violated. In fact, as early as July 29, Sir Edward Grey, Britain's foreign secretary, had given the German ambassador in London a warning that if France were drawn into the war, Great Britain would enter also. Nevertheless, it was the invasion of Belgian territory which provided the immediate cause of

*The German ultimatums
to Russia and France*

Britain enters the war

August 1, 1914. A German officer reads the declaration of war in the streets of Berlin.

Britain's entry. In 1839, along with the other great powers, Britain had signed a treaty guaranteeing the neutrality of Belgium. Moreover, it had been British policy for a century or more to try to prevent domination of the Low Countries, lying directly across the Channel, by any powerful continental nation. The Germans planned to attack France through Belgium. Accordingly, they demanded of the Belgian government permission to send troops across its territory, promising to respect the independence of the nation and to pay for any damage to property. When Belgium refused, the kaiser's legions began pouring across the frontier. The British foreign secretary immediately went before Parliament and urged that his country should rally to the defense of international law and to the protection of small nations. He argued that peace under the circumstances would be a moral crime, and declared that if Britain should fail to uphold its obligations of honor in this matter it would forfeit the respect of the civilized world. The next day, August 4, the cabinet sent an ultimatum to Berlin demanding that Germany respect Belgian neutrality, and that the Germans give a satisfactory reply by midnight. The kaiser's ministers offered no answer save military necessity, arguing that it was a matter of life and death for Germany that its soldiers should reach France by the quickest and easiest way. As the clock struck twelve, Great Britain and Germany were at war.

The conflagration spreads

Other nations were quickly drawn into the terrible vortex. On August 7 the Montenegrins joined with their kinsmen, the Serbs, in fighting Austria. Two weeks later the Japanese declared war upon Germany, partly because of their alliance with Great Britain, but mainly for the purpose of conquering German possessions in the Far East. On August 1 Turkey negotiated an alliance with Germany, and in October began the bombardment of Russian ports on the Black Sea. Thus most of the nations definitely bound by alliances entered the conflict in its early stages on one side or the other. Italy, however, though still technically a member of the Triple Alliance, proclaimed neutrality. The Italians insisted that the Germans were not fighting a defensive war, and that consequently they were not bound to go to their aid. Italy remained neutral until May 1915, when Britain and France bribed its leaders with secret promises of Austrian and Turkish territory to engage in the war on the side of the Triple Entente.

2. THE ORDEAL OF BATTLE

The "holy war" of the principal powers

In the Book of Revelation it is related that the forces of good and evil shall be gathered together on "the great day of God" to do battle at Armageddon. The author might almost have been thinking of the titanic conflict which engulfed the nations of Europe in 1914. For World War I was seldom admitted to be a struggle between rival imperialist powers or a product of nationalist jealousy. Instead, it was represented by spokesmen for both sides as a crusade against the forces of evil. No sooner had war begun than social and political leaders in England and France pronounced it a gallant effort to safeguard the rights of the weak and to preserve the supremacy of international law and morality. Prime Minister Asquith on August 6, 1914, declared that Britain had entered the conflict to vindicate "the principle that smaller nationalities are not to be crushed by the arbitrary will of a strong and overmastering Power." Across the Channel, President Poincaré was assuring his fellow citizens that France had no other purpose than to stand "before the universe for Liberty, Justice and Reason." Socialists who had, in the past, proclaimed their international solidarity and their opposition to the wars of capitalism, now in almost all cases declared themselves national patriots. Later, as a consequence of the preaching of such writers and orators as H. G. Wells, Gilbert Murray, and the American president, Woodrow Wilson, the crusade of the Entente powers became a war to redeem mankind from the curse of militarism. In the opposing camp, the subordinates of the kaiser were doing all in their power to justify Germany's military efforts. The struggle against the Entente powers was represented to the German people as a crusade on behalf of a superior *Kultur* and as a battle to protect the fatherland against the wicked encirclement policy of the Entente nations. German socialist politicians were persuaded to vote for the war on the grounds that a German war with Russia would help liberate the Russian people from the tsarist yoke.

World War I fooled military experts who believed it would end quickly. Open warfare soon disappeared from the Western Front—the battle line that stretched across France from Switzerland to the North Sea, where the fighting was concentrated for four years. Following

War of attrition

Modern Warfare. After the first few battles, the war on the Western Front settled into static or position warfare. During the four-year period, veritable cities of mud, stone, and timber sprang up behind the trenches.

Left: *British armored trucks move toward the front.* Above: *A British tank and field ambulance.*

Germany's initial advance into France, the opposing armies settled down in a vast network of trenches, from which attacks to dislodge the enemy were launched, usually in the murky hours just before dawn. These attacks always failed to achieve more than very limited gains. Protected by barbed wire and machine-guns—both making their first major appearance in a European war—defenders had the advantage. The one weapon with the potential to break the stalemate, the tank, was not introduced into battle until 1916, and then with such reluctance by tradition-bound commanders that its half-hearted employment made almost no difference. Airplanes were used almost exclusively for reconnaissance, though occasional "dog-fights" did occur between German and Allied pilots. The Germans sent Zeppelins to raid London, but they did little significant damage. Commanding officers continued to believe that the war would have to be won on the ground. Only by battering their enemies first with artillery and then with thousands of men armed with rifles, grenades, and bayonets, did they believe they could achieve the always elusive "breakthrough." On more than one occasion those in charge of the war attempted to end the stalemate by opening military fronts in other areas of the world. In 1915, Britain and France attempted a landing at Gallipoli, in Asia Minor, in the hope of driving Turkey from the war. The campaign was a disaster for the Entente powers, however, failing, as did others, to refocus the fighting or to free it from the immobility of the trenches.

Life for the common soldier on the Western Front alternated between the daily boredom and extreme unpleasantness of weeks spent in muddy and vermin-ridden trench communities, and the occasional and horrifying experience of battle, a nightmare not only of artillery, machine-guns, and barbed wire, but of exploding bullets, liquid fire, and poison gas. Battles that accomplished almost nothing devoured

The toll

Wartime Leaders. Left: Haig, Joffre, and Lloyd George discuss strategy. Right: Reviewing a map are Hindenburg, William II, and Ludendorff, members of the German high command.

the men who fought them. Over 600,000 soldiers were killed and wounded when the Germans unsuccessfully besieged the French stronghold of Verdun, near France's eastern border, for six months in the spring of 1916. In the battle along the Somme River, which lasted from July to October 1916, and which gained the British and French no more than a few miles, the Germans lost 500,000 men, the British 400,000, and the French 200,000. Although the war, because of its stationary nature, took a relatively light civilian toll, the total numbers of dead and wounded were staggering: out of an estimated 65 million men who fought under the flags of the various belligerents, 10 million were killed and another 20 million wounded. The struggle was an endurance contest. The victory of the Entente powers came as a result of their continued control of the seas and of their ability to obtain almost unlimited supplies of money, food, and munitions from allies and neutral countries around the world.

As the conflict dragged on, more and more nations entered the war on one side or the other. Italy postponed its entry until the spring of 1915. Bulgaria joined Germany and its allies, known as the Central Powers, in September 1915, and Rumania entered on the opposite side about a year later. The event which helped greatly to tip the scales in favor of an Entente victory was the declaration of war against Germany by the United States on April 6, 1917. The United States entered the war for a variety of reasons. All sorts of moral arguments were avowed by President Wilson and other high officials of the government—to "make the world safe for democracy," to banish autocracy and militarism, and to establish a league or society of nations in place of the old diplomatic maneuvering. Undoubtedly, the primary reason, though, was the concern of the American government to maintain the balance of power in Europe. For years it had been a cardinal doctrine in the State Department and among military and naval

World War I Posters Held Back Little in Their Appeal to Emotions

The Lusitania *Leaving New York Harbor.* In February 1915 the *Lusitania* was torpedoed and sunk by a German U-boat. Among the 1,200 people drowned were 119 Americans. The disaster was one step in the chain of events which led to the entry of the United States into the war on the side of Britain and France.

officers that the security of the United States depended upon a balance of forces in the Old World. No one power must be allowed to establish its supremacy over all of Europe. So long as Great Britain was strong enough to prevent that supremacy, the United States was safe. Some authorities believe that American officials had grown so accustomed to thinking of the British navy as the shield of American security that they could hardly tolerate the thought of any different situation. Germany, however, presented not merely a challenge to British naval supremacy, but threatened to starve the British nation into surrender and to establish a hegemony over all of Europe.

Submarine warfare

The direct cause of United States participation in World War I was the U-boat, or submarine, warfare of the Germans. Once it became clear that the war would be one of attrition, the Germans recognized that unless they could break the Entente's stranglehold on their shipping, they would be defeated. The result was a campaign of submarine warfare. In February 1915, the kaiser's government announced that neutral vessels headed for British ports would be torpedoed without warning. President Wilson replied by declaring that the United States would hold Germany to a "strict accountability" if any harm should come to American lives or property. The warning had little effect. The Germans were convinced that the U-boat was one of their most valuable weapons, and they considered themselves justified in using it against the British blockade. They also believed, correctly, that the British were receiving war materiel clandestinely shipped aboard passenger ships from the United States, and continued to sink them, thus appearing to violate United States neutrality. When the kaiser's ministers announced that, on February 1, 1917, they would launch a campaign of unrestricted submarine warfare, Wilson cut off diplomatic relations with the Berlin government. On April 2 he went before a joint session of the two houses of Congress and requested and received a declaration of war.

3. REVOLUTION IN THE MIDST OF WAR

In the midst of world war came revolution. Russia, already severely weakened by internal conflicts before 1914, found itself unable to sustain the additional burden of continuous warfare. In a nation ruled as autocratically as was Russia, a successful war effort depended greatly on the determination and talents of its ruler, the tsar. Nicholas II was, by nature, irresolute and weak. His limited capabilities were further undermined by the irrationality of his wife, Alexandra, a religious fanatic, and of her spiritual mentor, the monk Rasputin. The latter had gained the tsarina's sympathy by his ability to alleviate the sufferings of her hemophiliac son, and used his influence over her to shape policy to his own self-aggrandizing ends. The tsar's incompetent direction meant that Russia's armies could not win battles, and suffered a series of humiliating defeats by the Germans. In some instances soldiers were sent to the front without rifles; their clothing supplies were also inadequate. Medical facilities were scarce. The railway system broke down, producing a shortage of food not only in the army but in the cities as well. By the end of 1916, Russia's power to resist had practically collapsed.

Incompetence of the tsar

The revolution in Russia followed a succession of stages somewhat similar to those of the French Revolution of 1789. The first of these began in March 1917 with the forced abdication of the tsar. For this the immediate cause was disgust with the conduct of the war. But there were many other factors—inflation and consequent high prices, and scarcity of food and coal in urban areas. With the overthrow of the

The March 1917 revolution

Tsar Nicholas II and His Family on the Eve of the Revolution

tsar, the authority of the government passed into the hands of a provisional ministry organized by leaders in the Duma in conjunction with representatives of workers in Petrograd, calling themselves a *soviet,* or government council. (The city had abandoned the supposedly Germanic name of St. Petersburg at the beginning of the war.) With the exception of Alexander Kerensky (1881–1970), who was a member of the rurally based Social Revolutionary party, nearly all of the ministers were bourgeois liberals. Their hope was to transform the Russian autocracy into a constitutional monarchy modeled after that of Great Britain. In accordance with this aim, they issued a proclamation of civil liberties, released thousands of prisoners, and made plans for the election of a constituent assembly.

The provisional government

The provisional government proved itself inadequate to deal with the problems it faced. Its leaders did not seem to understand the new conditions created by the war, or even some of those arising in the prewar period. Among these were overcrowding in the cities, the emergence of an urban working class, and the inevitable harshness of the class conflict in the initial stages of industrialization. Further, the heads of this provisional government made the mistake of attempting to continue the war on the basis of previous imperialist aims. They hoped to obtain Constantinople and everything else that had been promised to Russia in its secret treaties. But the masses of the Russian people were desperately weary of the years of hardship and struggle. What they wanted was peace and a chance to return to a normal life. Consequently, in May, when the leaders renewed their pledge of support for the Entente powers, opposition was so strong that they were forced to resign. A new government was organized which managed to stay in power until September. Led by Kerensky, it consisted

Scenes from the Russian Revolution. Left: Street Fighting in Petrograd, 1917. Right: Russian soldiers join the Bolsheviks in front of the Winter Palace.

Strife in Ireland, 1916. British troops raiding the office of a Dublin printer who supported the rebellion.

primarily of moderate socialists. The ultimate failure of this regime may be ascribed chiefly to the insignificant role played by the middle class in Russia at the time. In no sense can it be compared as a revolutionary force with the bourgeoisie in France in 1789. It was much smaller in size and lacked the prestige and wealth of the elements that destroyed the absolute monarchy of Louis XVI. Moreover, it had little support from the mass of the Russian people.

The downfall of Kerensky's regime marked the end of the first stage of the Russian Revolution. The second began immediately after, with the accession of the Bolsheviks to power under the leadership of Lenin on November 7, 1917. Soon after the overthrow of the tsar the Bolsheviks had begun to plan for a socialist revolution. They worked their way into the Petrograd Soviet, the Council of Workers' and Soldiers' Deputies, and quickly gained control of it from the Mensheviks and Social Revolutionaries. They organized an armed Red Guard and took possession of strategic points throughout the city. By November 7 everything was ready for a coup d'état. Red Guards occupied nearly all the public buildings and finally arrested the members of the government, though Kerensky himself escaped. Thus the Bolsheviks climbed to power with scarcely a struggle. Their slogan of "Peace, Land, and Bread" made them heroes to the soldiers disgusted with the war, to the peasants hungry for land, and to the urban population suffering from various shortages. As soon as possible, the Bolsheviks sued for peace with the Germans, accepting terms that included the surrender of Poland, the Ukraine, and Finland. The treaty was signed at Brest-Litovsk in March 1918.

Triumph of the Bolsheviks

Yet another outbreak of revolution in this period was the so-called Easter Rebellion in Ireland. At the beginning of World War I, Irish nationalists, who resented the rule of their country by the British, were ripe for revolt. They had been promised self-rule on the eve of the war, but the British later reneged on the ground that a national

The Easter Rebellion in Ireland

emergency must take preeminence over everything else. This greatly angered the Roman Catholic majority of southern Ireland. They scheduled Easter Monday, 1916, as a day for revolt. British forces quelled the uprising, but not until after a hundred people had been killed. Sporadic outbreaks kept the island in turmoil for years thereafter, but were finally brought to a temporary end by an agreement constituting southern Ireland as a free republic. The northern counties, or the province of Ulster, were to continue subject to the British crown.

4. ARMISTICE AND PEACE

Peace proposals

While fighting on the several fronts raged through four horrible years, various attempts were made to bring about the negotiation of peace. In the spring of 1917, Dutch and Scandinavian socialists decided to summon an international socialist conference to meet at Stockholm in the hope of drafting plans for ending the fighting which would be acceptable to all the belligerents. The Petrograd Soviet embraced the idea and on May 15 issued an appeal to socialists of all nations to send delegates to the conference and to induce their governments to agree to a peace "without annexations and indemnities, on the basis of the self-determination of peoples." The socialist parties in all the principal countries on both sides of the war accepted this formula and were eager to send delegates to the conference, but when the British and French governments refused to permit any of their subjects to attend, the project was abandoned. That the rulers of the Entente states were not afraid of these proposals merely because they emanated from socialists is indicated by the fact that a similar formula suggested by the pope was just as emphatically rejected. Nowhere was there a disposition to take peace proposals seriously. Woodrow Wilson, as spokesman for the Allies, declared that negotiation of peace under any conditions was impossible so long as Germany was ruled by the kaiser. The Central Powers professed to regard with favor the general import of the papal suggestions, but they refused to commit themselves on indemnities and restorations, especially the restoration of Belgium.

The Fourteen Points

The best-known of all the peace proposals was President Wilson's program of Fourteen Points, which he incorporated in an address to Congress on January 8, 1918. Summarized as briefly as possible, this program included: (1) "open covenants openly arrived at," i.e., the abolition of secret diplomacy; (2) freedom of the seas; (3) removal of economic barriers between nations; (4) reduction of national armaments "to the lowest point consistent with safety"; (5) impartial adjustment of colonial claims, with consideration for the interests of the peoples involved; (6) evacuation of Russia by foreign armies; (7) restoration of the independence of Belgium; (8) restoration of Alsace and Lorraine to France; (9) a readjustment of Italian frontiers "along clearly recognizable lines of nationality''; (10) autonomous development for the peoples of Austria-Hungary; (11) restoration of Rumania, Serbia, and Montenegro, with access to the sea for Serbia; (12) autonomous development for the peoples of Turkey, with the straits from the Black Sea to the Mediterranean "permanently opened"; (13) an independent Poland, "inhabited by indisputably Polish populations," and with access to the sea; (14) establishment of a League of Nations. On several other occasions throughout 1918 Wilson reiterated in public addresses that this program would be the basis of the peace for which he would work. Thousands of copies of the Fourteen Points were scattered by Allied planes over the German trenches and behind the lines, in an effort to convince both soldiers and civilians that the Entente nations were striving for a just and durable peace.

By the close of the summer of 1918 the long nightmare of bloodshed was approaching its end. A great offensive launched by the British, French, and United States forces in July dealt one shattering blow after another to the German battalions and forced them back almost to the Belgian frontier. By the end of September the cause of the Central Powers was hopeless. Bulgaria withdrew from the war on September 30. Early in October the new chancellor of Germany, the liberal Prince Max of Baden, appealed to President Wilson for a negotiated peace on the basis of the Fourteen Points. But the fighting went on, for Wilson had returned to his original demand that Germany must agree to depose the kaiser. Germany's remaining allies tottered on the verge of collapse. Turkey surrendered at the end of October. The Hapsburg Empire was cracked open by rebellions on the part of the empire's subject nationalities. Moreover, an Austrian offensive against Italy had not only failed but had incited the Italians to a counteroffensive, with the consequent loss to Austria of the city of Trieste and 300,000 prisoners. On November 3 the Emperor Charles, who had succeeded Francis Joseph in 1916, signed an armistice which took Austria out of the war.

Germany was now left with the impossible task of carrying on the struggle alone. The morale of its troops was rapidly breaking. The

The collapse of the Central Powers

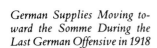

German Supplies Moving toward the Somme During the Last German Offensive in 1918

blockade was causing such a shortage of food that there was real danger of starvation. The revolutionary tremors that had been felt for some time swelled into a mighty earthquake. On November 8 a republic was proclaimed in Bavaria. The next day nearly all of Germany was in the throes of revolution. A decree was published in Berlin announcing the kaiser's abdication, and early the next morning he was moved across the frontier into Holland. In the meantime. the government of the nation had passed into the hands of a provisional council headed by Friedrich Ebert, leader of the socialists in the Reichstag. Ebert and his colleagues immediately took steps to conclude negotiations for an armistice. The terms as now laid down by the Entente powers provided for acceptance of the Fourteen Points with three amendments. First, the item on freedom of the seas was to be stricken (in accordance with the request of the British). Second, restoration of invaded areas was to be interpreted in such a way as to include reparations, that is, payment to the victors to compensate them for their losses. Third, the demand for autonomy for the subject peoples of Austria-Hungary was to be changed to a demand for independence. In addition, troops of the Entente nations were to occupy cities in the Rhine valley; the blockade was to be continued in force; and Germany was to hand over 5,000 locomotives, 150,000 railway cars, and 5,000 trucks, all in good condition. There was nothing that the Germans could do but accept these terms. At five o'clock in the morning of November 11, two delegates of the defeated nation met with the commander of the Entente armies, Marshal Foch, in the dark Compiègne forest and signed the papers officially ending the war. Six hours later the order, "cease fire," was given to the troops. That night thousands of people danced through the streets of London, Paris, and Rome in the same delirium of excitement with which they had greeted the declarations of war.

The peace concluded at the various conferences in 1919 and 1920 more closely resembled a sentence from a court than a negotiated settlement. Propaganda had encouraged victorious soldiers and civilians to suppose that their sacrifices to the war effort would be compensated for by payments extracted from the "wicked" Germans. The British prime minister, David Lloyd George, campaigned during the election of 1918 on the slogan, "Hang the Kaiser!", while one of his partisans demanded "Squeeze the German lemon until the pips squeak!". In all the Allied countries nationalism and democracy combined to make compromise impossible and to reassert the claim that the war was a crusade of good against evil. The peace settlement drafted by the victors inevitably reflected these feelings.

The conference convoked in Paris[3] to draft a peace with Germany

---

[3] The conference did most of its work in Paris. The treaty of peace with Germany, however, takes its name from Versailles, the suburb of Paris in which it was signed.

The Council of Four. Meeting to draft a peace treaty in Paris were Orlando of Italy, Lloyd George of Britain, Clemenceau of France, and Wilson of the United States.

was technically in session from January until June of 1919, but only six plenary meetings were ever held. All of the important business of the conference was transacted by small committees. At first there was the Council of Ten, made up of the president and secretary of state of the United States, and the premiers and foreign ministers of Great Britain, France, Italy, and Japan. By the middle of March this body had been found too unwieldy and was reduced to the Council of Four, consisting of the American president and the English, Italian, and French premiers. A month later the Council of Four became the Council of Three when Premier Vittorio Orlando withdrew from the conference in a huff because Wilson refused to give Italy all it demanded.

The Paris Conference

The final character of the Treaty of Versailles was determined almost entirely by the so-called Big Three—Wilson, Lloyd George, and Clemenceau. These men were about as different in personality as any three rulers who could ever have been brought together for a common purpose. Wilson was an inflexible idealist, accustomed to dictating to subordinates and convinced that the hosts of righteousness were on his side. When confronted with unpleasant realities, such as the secret treaties among the Entente governments for division of the spoils, he had a habit of dismissing them as unimportant and eventually forgetting that he had ever heard of them. Though he knew little of the devious maneuvers of European diplomacy, his unbending temperament made it difficult for him to take advice or to adjust his views to those of his colleagues. Lloyd George, the canny Welshman who had succeeded Asquith as prime minister of Britain in 1916, possessed a cleverness and Celtic humor that enabled him to succeed, on occasions, where Wilson failed; but he was above all a politician—shifty and not particularly sympathetic to particular European problems such as nationalism.

The Big Three: Wilson and Lloyd George

The third member of the great triumvirate was the aged and cynical

Clemenceau

French premier, Georges Clemenceau. Born in 1841, Clemenceau had been a journalist in the United States just after the Civil War. Later he had won his nickname of "the Tiger" as a relentless foe of clericals and monarchists. He had fought for the republic during the stormy days of the Boulangist episode, the Dreyfus affair, and the struggle for separation of Church and State. Twice in his lifetime he had seen France invaded and its existence gravely imperiled. Now the tables were turned, and the French, he believed, should take full advantage of their opportunity. Only by keeping a strict control over a prostrate Germany could the security of France be preserved.

Emasculating the Fourteen Points

From the beginning a number of embarrassing problems confronted the chief architects of the Versailles treaty. The most important was what to do about the Fourteen Points. There could be no doubt that they had been the basis of the German surrender on November 11. It was beyond question also that Wilson had represented them as the Entente program for a permanent peace. Consequently there was every reason for the peoples of the world to expect that the Fourteen Points would be the model for the Versailles settlement—subject only to the three amendments made before the armistice was signed. In actuality, however, no one among the highest dignitaries at the conference, with the exception of Wilson himself, gave more than lip service to the Fourteen Points. In the end, the American president was able to salvage, in unmodified form, only four of the parts of his famous program; point seven, requiring the restoration of Belgium; point eight, demanding the return of Alsace and Lorraine to France; point ten, providing for independence for the peoples of Austria-Hungary; and the final provision calling for a League of Nations. The others were ignored or modified to such an extent as to change their original meanings.

Germany sentenced

By the end of April 1919 the terms of the Versailles treaty were ready for submission to the enemy, and Germany was ordered to send delegates to receive them. On April 29, a delegation headed by Count von Brockdorff-Rantzau, foreign minister of the provisional republic, arrived in Versailles. A week later the members of the delegation were commanded to appear before the Allied representatives to receive the sentence of their nation. When Brockdorff-Rantzau protested that the terms were too harsh, he was informed by Clemenceau that Germany would have exactly three weeks to decide whether or not to sign. Eventually the time had to be extended, for the heads of the German government resigned their positions rather than accept the treaty. Their attitude was summed up by Chancellor Philip Scheidemann in the pointed statement: "What hand would not wither that sought to lay itself and us in those chains?" The Big Three now made a few minor adjustments, mainly at the insistence of Lloyd George, and Germany was notified that seven o'clock on the evening of June 23 would bring either acceptance or invasion. Shortly after five a new government of the provisional republic announced that it would yield to "overwhelming force" and accede to the victors' terms. On June 28, the fifth anniversary of the murder of the Austrian archduke, representatives of the German and Allied governments assembled in the Hall of Mirrors at Versailles and affixed their signatures to the treaty.

The provisions of the Treaty of Versailles can be outlined briefly. Germany was required to surrender Alsace and Lorraine to France, northern Schleswig to Denmark, and most of Posen and West Prussia to Poland. The coal mines of the Saar Basin were to be ceded to France, to be exploited by the French for fifteen years. At the end of this time the German government would be permitted to buy them back. The Saar territory itself was to be administered by the League of Nations until 1935, when a plebiscite would be held to determine whether it should remain under the league, be returned to Germany, or be awarded to France. Germany's province of East Prussia was cut off from the rest of its territory, and the port of Danzig, almost wholly German, was subjected to the political control of the League of Nations and the the economic domination of Poland. Germany was disarmed, surrendering all its submarines and navy of surface vessels, with the exception of six small battleships, six light cruisers, six destroyers, and twelve torpedo boats. The Germans were forbidden to have any airplanes, either military or naval, and their army was limited to 100,000 officers and men, to be recruited by voluntary enlistment. To make sure that Germany would not launch any new attack upon France or Belgium, it was forbidden to keep soldiers or maintain fortifications in the Rhine valley. Lastly, Germany and its allies were held responsible for all the loss and damage suffered by the Entente governments and their citizens, "as a consequence of the war imposed upon them by the aggression of Germany and her allies." This was the so-called war-guilt provision of the treaty (Article 231), but it was also the basis for German reparations. The exact amount that Germany should pay was left to a Reparations Commission. In 1921 the total was set at 33 billion dollars.

The main provisions of the Treaty of Versailles

For the most part, the Treaty of Versailles applied only to Germany. Separate pacts were drawn up to settle accounts with Germany's allies—Austria-Hungary, Bulgaria, and Turkey. The final form of these treaties was determined primarily by a Council of Five, composed of Clemenceau as chairman and one delegate from the United States, Great Britain, France, and Italy. The treaties reflected a desire on the part of their drafters to recognize the principle of national self-determination. The experience of the prewar years convinced diplomats that they must draw national boundaries to conform as closely as possible to the ethnic, linguistic, and historical traditions of the people they were to contain. Yet practical, political difficulties made such divisions impossible.

The goal of self-determination

The settlement with Austria, completed in September 1919, is

ICELAND
(Denmark)

FAEROES
(Denmark)

SHETLANDS

ORKNEYS

HEBRIDES

SCOTLAND

NORTH

SEA

GREAT BRITAIN

IRELAND

Dublin

ENGLAND

London

ATLANTIC

OCEAN

English Channel

NETHERLANDS

Amsterdam

Brussels

BELG.

LUXEMBURG

Paris

LORRAINE

ALSACE

BAY OF
BISCAY

FRANCE

Berne
SWITZ.

NORWAY

Christiania

SWEDEN

Stockholm

Skagerrak

Kattegat

DENMARK

Copenhagen

GOTLAND

ÖLAND

GULF OF BOTHNIA

FINLAND

Helsingfors

Leningrad

G. of Finland

Tallinn
ESTONIA

Riga
LATVIA

BALTIC

SEA

LITHUANIA

Kaunas

Danzig

E. PRUSSIA
(Germany)

Berlin

GERMANY

Rhine
R.

Warsaw

Brest-Litovsk

POLAND

Prague

CZECHOSLOVAKIA

Danube *R.*

Vienna

AUSTRIA

Budapest

HUNGARY

RUMANIA

Bucharest

ADRIATIC

SEA

YUGOSLAVIA

Belgrade

SERBIA

MONTENEGRO

Sofia
BUL-

ITALY

Rome

Tirana

ALBANIA

GREECE

Aegean

Athens

PORTUGAL

Lisbon

Madrid

SPAIN

BALEARIC IS.

(Spain)

CORSICA
(France)

SARDINIA
(Italy)

Strait of
Gibraltar

Tangier

SP. MOROCCO

Rabat

Algiers

Tunis

SICILY
(Italy)

MEDITERRANEAN

MALTA
(Gt. Britain)

CRETE
(Greece)

MOROCCO

ALGERIA

TUNISIA

Tripoli

LIBYA

0   1000 miles

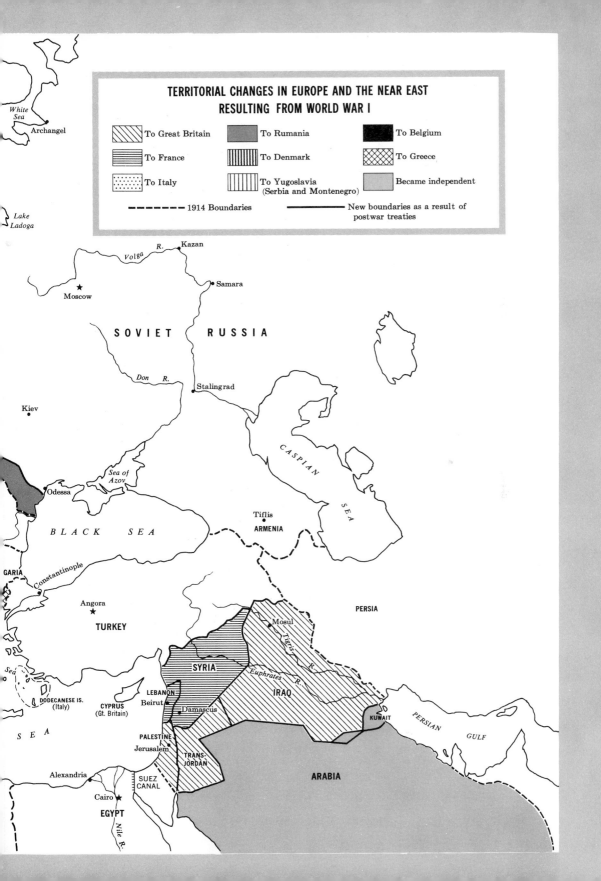

TERRITORIAL CHANGES IN EUROPE AND THE NEAR EAST
RESULTING FROM WORLD WAR I

To Great Britain	To Rumania	To Belgium
To France	To Denmark	To Greece
To Italy	To Yugoslavia (Serbia and Montenegro)	Became independent

- - - - - 1914 Boundaries ———— New boundaries as a result of postwar treaties

White Sea

Archangel

Lake Ladoga

Kazan

Volga R.

Samara

Moscow

SOVIET   RUSSIA

Don   R.

Stalingrad

Kiev

CASPIAN   SEA

Sea of Azov

Odessa

Tiflis

BLACK   SEA

ARMENIA

GARIA

Constantinople

Angora

TURKEY

PERSIA

Mosul

Tigris R.

SYRIA

Euphrates R.

Sea

DODECANESE IS.
(Italy)

CYPRUS
(Gt. Britain)

LEBANON

Beirut

Damascus

IRAQ

KUWAIT

PERSIAN   GULF

SEA

PALESTINE

Jerusalem

TRANS-
JORDAN

Alexandria

SUEZ
CANAL

Cairo

EGYPT

Nile R.

ARABIA

The treaty with Austria:
The compromising of
national self-determination

known as the Treaty of St. Germain. Austria was required to recognize the independence of Hungary, Czechoslovakia, Yugoslavia, and Poland and to cede to them large portions of its territory. In addition, Austria had to surrender Trieste, the south Tyrol, and the Istrian peninsula to Italy. Altogether the Austrian portion of the Dual Monarchy was deprived of three-fourths of its area and three-fourths of its people. Contrary to the principles of self-determination, in several of the territories surrendered the inhabitants were largely German-speaking—for example, in the Tyrol, and the region of the Sudeten mountains awarded to Czechoslovakia. The Austrian nation itself was reduced to a small, land-locked state, with nearly one-third of its population concentrated in the city of Vienna.

The second of the treaties with lesser belligerents was that with Bulgaria, which was signed in November 1919 and called the Treaty of Neuilly. Bulgaria was forced to give up nearly all of the territory it had gained since the First Balkan War. Land was ceded to Rumania, to the new kingdom of Yugoslavia, and to Greece. Here again, self-determination was compromised. All of these regions were inhabited by large Bulgarian minorities. Since Hungary was now an independent state, it was necessary that a separate treaty be imposed upon it. This was the Treaty of the Trianon Palace, signed in June 1920. It required that Slovakia should be ceded to Czechoslovakia, Transylvania to Rumania, and Croatia-Slovenia to Yugoslavia. In few cases was the principle of self-determination of peoples more flagrantly violated. Numerous sections of Transylvania had populations that were more than half Hungarian. Included in the region of Slovakia were not only Slovaks but almost a million Magyars and about 500,000 Ruthenians. As a consequence, a fanatical irredentist movement flourished in Hungary after the war, directed toward the recovery of these lost provinces. The Treaty of the Trianon Palace slashed the area of Hungary from 125,000 square miles to 35,000, and its population from 22 million to 8 million.

The settlement with Turkey was a product of unusual circumstances. The secret treaties had contemplated the transfer of Constantinople and Armenia to Russia and the division of most of the remainder of Turkey between Britain and France. But Russia's withdrawal from the war after the Bolshevik Revolution, together with insistence by Italy and Greece upon fulfillment of promises made to them, necessitated considerable revision of the original scheme. Finally, in August 1920, a treaty was signed at Sèvres, near Paris, and submitted to the government of the sultan. It provided that Armenia be organized as a Christian republic; that most of Turkey in Europe be given to Greece; that Palestine and Mesopotamia become British "mandates," i.e., to remain under League of Nations control but to be administered by Britain; that Syria become a mandate of France; and that southern Anatolia be set apart as a sphere of influence for Italy. About all that would be left of the Ottoman Empire would be the city of Constantinople and the northern and central portions of Asia Minor. The decrepit government of the sultan, overawed by Allied military forces, agreed to accept this treaty. But a revolutionary government of Turkish nationalists, which had been organized at Ankara under the leadership of Mustapha Kemal (later called Atatürk), determined to prevent the settlement of Sèvres from being put into effect. The forces of Kemal obliterated the republic of Armenia, frightened the Italians into withdrawing from Anatolia, and conquered most of the territory in Europe which had been given to Greece. At last, in November 1922, they occupied Constantinople, deposed the sultan, and proclaimed Turkey a republic. The Allies now consented to a revision of the peace. A new treaty was concluded at Lausanne in Switzerland in 1923, which permitted the Turks to retain practically all of the territory they had conquered. Though much reduced in size compared with the old Ottoman Empire, the Turkish republic still had an area of about 300,000 square miles and a population of 13 million.

Incorporated in each of the five treaties which liquidated the war with the Central Powers was the Covenant of the League of Nations. The establishment of a league in which the states of the world, both great and small, would cooperate for the preservation of peace had long been the cherished dream of President Wilson. Indeed, that had been one of his chief reasons for taking the United States into the war. He believed that the defeat of Germany would mean the deathblow of militarism, and that the road would thenceforth be clear for setting up the control of international relations by a community of power instead of by the cumbersome and ineffective balance of power. But in order to get the league accepted at all, he felt himself compelled to make numerous compromises. He permitted his original idea of providing for a reduction of armaments "to the lowest point consistent with domestic safety" to be changed into the altogether different phrasing of "consistent with national safety." To induce the Japanese to accept the league he allowed them to keep the former German concessions in China. To please the French, he sanctioned the exclusion of both Germany and Russia from his proposed federation, despite his long insistence that it should be a combination of all the nations. These handicaps were serious enough. But the league received an even more deadly blow when it was repudiated by the very nation whose president had proposed it.

Established under such unfavorable auspices, the league never succeeded in achieving the aims of its founder. In only a few cases did it succeed in allaying the specter of war, and in each of these the parties to the dispute were small nations. But in every dispute involving one or more major powers, the league failed. It did nothing about the seizure of Vilna by Poland in 1920, because Lithuania, the victimized nation, was friendless, while Poland had the powerful backing of France. When, in 1923, war threatened between Italy and Greece, the

Kemal Atatürk

The League of Nations

Successes and failures of the league

League of Nations Buildings, Geneva, Switzerland

Italians refused to submit to the intervention of the league, and the
dispute had to be settled by direct mediation of Great Britain and
France. Thereafter, in every great crisis the league was either defied or
ignored. Its authority was flouted by Japan in seizing Manchuria in
1931 and by Italy in conquering Ethiopia in 1936. By September 1938,
when the Czechoslovakian crisis arose, the prestige of the league had
sunk so low that scarcely anyone thought of appealing to it. On the
other hand, the point must be made that Wilson's great project justified its existence in other, less spectacular, ways. It reduced the international opium traffic and aided poor and backward countries in controlling the spread of disease. Its agencies collected invaluable statistics
on labor and business conditions throughout the world. It conducted
plebiscites in disputed areas, supervised the administration of interna-
tionalized cities, helped in finding homes for racial and political refugees, and made a notable beginning in codifying international law.
Such achievements may well be regarded as providing a substantial
groundwork for a later effort at international organization, the United
Nations, formed after World War II.

The league, with all its failings, was seen as the one promising result
of the war that many soon recognized as a hideously wasteful carnage.

A war of waste

The price would have been enormous even if all the results which were
supposed to flow from an Entente victory had really been achieved.
But few indeed were the permanent gains. In fact, the war which
was to "end all wars" sowed the seeds of a new and more terrible
conflict in the future. The autocracy of the kaiser was indeed destroyed, but the ground was prepared for new despotisms. World War
I did nothing to abate either militarism or nationalism. Twenty years
after the fighting had ended, there were nearly twice as many men

under arms as in 1913; and national and ethnic rivalries and hatreds were as deeply ingrained as ever.

If the war failed to make the world less of an armed camp, it nevertheless altered it drastically in other ways. In the first place, it strengthened a belief in the efficacy of central planning and coordination. To sustain the war effort, the governments of all the major belligerents were forced to manage their economies by regulating industrial output, exercising a close control over imports and exports, and making the most effective use of manpower—both civilian and military. Second, the war upset the world trade balance. With few manufactured goods coming from Europe, Japanese, Indian, and South American capitalists were free to develop industries in their own countries. When the war was over, Europe found it had lost many of its previously guaranteed markets. Third, while war was altering the patterns of world trade, it was also producing worldwide inflation. To finance their fighting, governments resorted to policies of deficit financing (spending above their income) and increased paper money which, with the shortage of goods, inflated their price. Inflation hit hardest at the middle class, those men and women who had lived on their income from invested money, and now saw that money worth far less than it once had been. Fourth, the war, while it brought hardships to most, brought freedom to many. Women were emancipated by their governments' need for them in factories and on farms. The contribution of women to the war effort undoubtedly explains the granting of female suffrage in both Great Britain and the United States in 1918 and 1920. Finally, despite this legacy of liberation, the war's most permanent contribution to the spirit of the postwar years was

Changes brought by the war

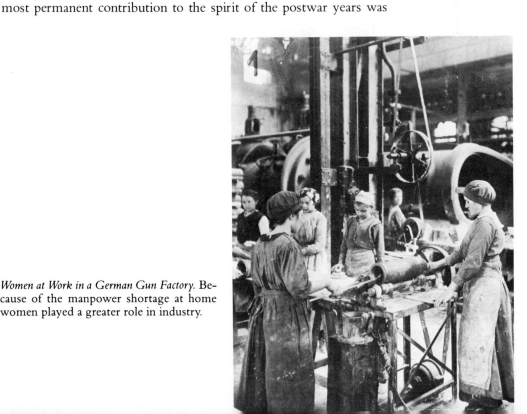

Women at Work in a German Gun Factory. Because of the manpower shortage at home women played a greater role in industry.

disillusion—particularly within the middle classes. A generation of men had been sacrificed—"lost"—to no apparent end. Many of those left alive were sickened by the useless slaughter, to which they knew they had contributed and for which they believed they must share at least part of the guilt. They were disgusted by the greedy abandonment of principles by the politicians at Versailles. Hatred and mistrust of the "old men" who had dragged the world into an unnecessary conflict, who had then mismanaged its direction with such ghastly results, and who had betrayed the cause of international peace for national gain soured the minds of many younger men and women in the postwar period. The British poet Edmund Blunden expressed this profound disillusionment when he took as the title for a poem, written to celebrate New Year's Day 1921, the Biblical verse: "The dog is turned to his own vomit again, and the sow that was washed to her wallowing in the mire."

SELECTED READINGS

• *Items so designated are available in paperback editions.*

THE WORLD WAR AND THE PEACE SETTLEMENT

• Falls, Cyril, *The Great War*, New York, 1959. A military history.
• Fay, Sidney B., *The Origins of the World War*, 2 vols., New York, 1928–30. Comprehensive.
  Feldman, Gerald D., *Army, Industry, and Labor in Germany, 1914–1918*, Princeton, N.J., 1966.
• Fischer, Fritz, *Germany's Aims in the First World War*, New York, 1967. One of the most significant historical works of the twentieth century. Thoroughly documents Germany's goal of world domination in World War I and reopens the question of war guilt.
• ———, *World Power or Decline*, New York, 1974.
• Fussell, Paul, *The Great War and Modern Memory*, New York, 1975. A brilliant examination of British intellectuals' attitudes toward the war.
  Gatzke, Hans, *Germany's Drive to the West*, Baltimore, 1950.
  Guinn, Paul, *British Strategy and Politics, 1914–1918*, Oxford, 1965.
  Hardach, Gerd, *The First World War, 1914–1918*, Berkeley, Calif., 1977. An excellent economic history of the war.
  Horne, Alastair, *The Price of Glory: Verdun, 1916*, New York, 1963.
• Lafore, Laurence D., *The Long Fuse: An Interpretation of the Origins of World War I*, Philadelphia, 1971. Argues that the war was the result of obsolete institutions and ideas.
  Lacqueur, Walter, and G. L. Mosse, eds., *1914: The Coming of the First World War*, New York, 1969. An excellent series of essays by modern scholars.
  Liddell Hart, B. H., *The War in Outline*, London, 1936. A good introduction to the military history of World War I.
  Mayer, Arno, *Political Origins of the New Diplomacy, 1917–1918*, New York,

1969. An important work which examines the advent of Wilson and Lenin into world diplomacy.

————, *Politics and Diplomacy of Peacemaking: Containment and Counter-revolution at Versailles, 1918–1919*, New York, 1967.

Moorehead, Alan, *Gallipoli*, London, 1956. A study of the British campaign.

Nicolson, Harold, *Peacemaking, 1919*, Boston, 1933. Written by a participant, provides a good account of the atmosphere of Versailles.

• Steiner, Zara S., *Britain and the Origins of the First World War*, New York, 1977. Argues that external rather than internal strains brought Britain into the war.

• Taylor, A. J. P., *English History, 1914–1945*, New York, 1965. An excellent treatment of the war and its impact on British society.

• Turner, L. C. F., *Origins of the First World War*, New York, 1970.

• Tuchman, Barbara, *The Guns of August*, New York, 1962. A popular account of the outbreak of war.

• Wheeler-Bennett, J. W., *The Forgotten Peace: Brest-Litovsk, March 1918*, London, 1939. An excellent study of personalities involved in the Russo-German peace treaty.

Zeeman, Z. A. B., *The Break-up of the Hapsburg Empire, 1914–1918*, New York, 1961.

THE RUSSIAN REVOLUTION

Carr, E. H., *A History of Soviet Russia*, Vols. I–III, London, 1950 ff. A comprehensive treatment of the Russian Revolution from 1917–1923.

• Deutscher, Isaac, *The Prophet Armed*, New York, 1954. The first volume of a magnificent biography of Trotsky; covers the years 1879–1921.

Fischer, Louis, *The Life of Lenin*, New York, 1964. A lengthy, somewhat popularized biography by a journalist who was present during the revolution.

Keep, John L. H., *The Russian Revolution*, New York, 1977.

• Pares, Bernard, *A History of Russia*, rev. ed., New York, 1953.

• Rabinowitch, Alexander, *The Bolsheviks Come to Power*, New York, 1976.

• Tucker, Robert C., *Stalin as Revolutionary*, New York, 1973. Stalin's life to 1929; a psychobiography.

• Ulam, Adam, *The Bolsheviks: The Intellectual and Political History of the Triumph of Communism in Russia*, New York, 1965.

• Von Laue, T. H., *Why Lenin? Why Stalin? A Reappraisal of the Russian Revolution, 1900–1930*, Philadelphia, 1964.

• Wolfe, Bertram D., *Three Who Made a Revolution*, rev. ed., New York, 1964. A study of Lenin, Trotsky, and Stalin.

SOURCE MATERIALS

Carnegie Foundation, Endowment for International Peace, *The Treaties of Peace, 1919–1923*, 2 vols., New York, 1924.

Gooch, G. P., and H. Temperley, eds., *British Documents on the Origins of the War, 1898–1914*, London.

Keynes, John Maynard, *The Economic Consequences of the Peace,* London, 1919. A contemporary attack upon the peace settlement, particularly the reparations agreements, by the brilliant economist who served on the British delegation to the peace conference.

Trotsky, Leon, *History of the Russian Revolution,* 3 vols., Ann Arbor, Mich., 1957.

Chapter 34

THE WEST BETWEEN THE WARS

Democracy of the West today is the forerunner of Marxism, which would
be inconceivable without it. It is democracy alone which furnishes this
universal plague with the soil in which it spreads. In parliamentarianism,
its outward form of expression, democracy created a monstrosity of filth
and fire . . .

—Adolf Hitler, *Mein Kampf*

The First World War had been waged in hopes of making the
world "safe for democracy." And for a short time after 1918,
despite the shortcomings of the Versailles settlement, it
seemed as if that elusive goal might stand a chance of success. Germany began the postwar era as a republic. Most of the new states
created by the Treaty of Versailles attempted to function under representative governments. Yet by 1939 only three of the chief powers—
Great Britain, France, and the United States—remained on the list of
democratic countries. Among the lesser states democracy survived in
Switzerland, the Netherlands, Belgium, the Scandinavian countries, a
few republics of Latin America, and the self-governing dominions of
the British Commonwealth. Nearly all of the rest of the world had
succumbed to despotism of one form or another. Italy, Germany, and
Spain were fascist; Hungary was dominated by a landowning oligarchy; Poland, Turkey, China, and Japan were essentially under military
rule. Russia, although professing to be a communist utopia, was in
fact a dictatorship.

Decline of democracy

The reasons for the decline of democracy in the West varied according to particular national circumstances. Generally, however, democracy's failure can be attributed to several major causes. First, class
conflict increased in many countries during the interwar years. The
real issue in most parts of continental Europe was whether control of
the government and economic system would continue in the possession of aristocracies, industrialists, and financiers, or some combina-

Reasons for its decline

tion of these elements. None of them were willing to surrender more than a fraction of their considerable power to the less privileged majorities which, at great sacrifice, had made major contributions to the war effort. The common people expected and had been promised that those contributions would be rewarded by greater attention to their political rights and economic needs. When they were ignored, they were naturally embittered, and hence prey to the blandishments of political extremists. Second, economic conditions worked against the establishment of stable democracies. The creation of new nations encouraged debilitating economic rivalries. War had disoriented the world's economy, leaving in its wake first inflation and then depression. Finally, nationalist sentiment encouraged discontent among minorities in the newly established states of central Europe. Countries weakened by conflicts between national minorities were an unlikely proving ground for democracy, a political system which functions best in an atmosphere of unified national purpose. Instead they turned, along with others, to totalitarianism, a system which holds out the promise of efficiency and strength of purpose, achieved by centralized authority in return for the surrender of individual liberties.

1. TOTALITARIANISM IN COMMUNIST RUSSIA

Soon after the November 1917 revolution Russia began to succumb to totalitarian rule. The country's desperate plight—the result of wartime *Lenin* devastation and governmental corruption and mismanagement—compelled the Bolshevik leaders to centralize power in the hands of a few. During this transformation, Lenin assumed ultimate control of the government. He had all of the qualities necessary for success as a revolutionary figure. He was an able politician and an exceedingly effective orator. Absolutely convinced of the righteousness of his cause, he could strike down his opponents with the zeal and savagery of a Robespierre. On the other hand, he cared nothing for the luxuries of wealth or personal glory. He lived in two rooms in the Kremlin and dressed little better than an ordinary workman.

The most prominent of Lenin's lieutenants was the brilliant but erratic Leon Trotsky (1879–1940). Originally named Lev Bronstein, Trot- *Trotsky* sky was born of middle-class Jewish parents in the Ukraine. He was a stormy petrel of revolutionary politics during most of his life. Before the revolution he refused to identify himself with any particular faction, preferring to remain an independent Marxist. For his part in the revolutionary movement of 1905 he was exiled to Siberia; but he escaped, and for some years led a roving existence in various European capitals. He was expelled from Paris in 1916 for pacifist activity and took refuge in the United States. Upon learning of the overthrow of the tsar, he attempted to return to Russia. Captured by British

Lenin Speaking to Crowds in Moscow. To the right of the platform, in uniform, is Trotsky.

agents at Halifax, Nova Scotia, he was eventually released through the intervention of Kerensky. He arrived in Russia in April 1917 and immediately began plotting for the overthrow of the provisional government and later of Kerensky himself. He became minister of foreign affairs in the government headed by Lenin, and later, commissar for war.

No sooner had the Bolsheviks come to power than they proceeded to effect drastic alterations in the political and economic system. On November 8, 1917, Lenin decreed nationalization of the land and gave the peasants the exclusive right to use it. On November 29 control of the factories was transferred to the workers, and a month later it was announced that all except the smallest industrial establishments would be taken over by the government. Banks also were nationalized soon after the Bolshevik victory. Scarcely had the Bolsheviks concluded the war with the Central Powers, than they were confronted with a desperate civil war at home. Landlords and capitalists did not take kindly to the loss of their property. The result was a prolonged and bloody combat between the Reds, or Bolsheviks, and the Whites, including not only reactionary tsarists but also disaffected liberals, Social Revolutionaries, Mensheviks, and some peasants. The Whites were assisted for a time by expeditionary forces of British, French, and Japanese troops—hoping to defeat the Bolsheviks in order to bring Russia back into the war against Germany—and later by the armies of the newly created republic of Poland. Under the direction of Trotsky, who appealed to the Russian people both in the name of revolution and the fatherland, the Red army was mobilized to a degree that allowed it to withstand both the foreign invaders and the Russian insurgents. By 1922, the Bolsheviks had managed to stabilize their boundaries, although to do so they were forced to cede former Russian territory to the Finns, to the Baltic states of Latvia and Estonia, to Poland, and to Rumania. Internally, the Bolsheviks responded to the White counter-

The civil war

See color map following page 1088

The Red Army, 1919. This scene near the southern front was the celebration of the victory over the counter-revolutionary forces.

revolution by instituting a "Terror" far more extensive than the repression that had earned that name during the French Revolution. A secret police force shot thousands as suspects or merely as hostages. The tsar and tsarina and their children were executed by local Bolsheviks in July 1918 as White forces advanced on the town of Ekaterinburg, where the family was held prisoner. That same year, a Social Revolutionary attempted to assassinate Lenin; what followed in Petrograd can only be described as a massacre. The Terror abated when the regime had satisfied itself that it had destroyed its internal opposition.

Economic and constitutional changes

The civil war was accompanied by an appalling economic breakdown. In 1920 the total industrial production was only 13 percent of what it had been in 1913. To make up for the shortage of goods, the government abolished the payment of wages and distributed supplies among the workers in the cities in proportion to their need. All private trade was prohibited, and everything produced by the peasants above what they required to keep from starving was requisitioned by the state. This system was an expedient to crush the bourgeoisie and to obtain as much food as possible for the army in the field. It was soon abandoned after the war had ended. In 1921 it was superseded by the New Economic Policy (NEP), which Lenin described as "one step backward in order to take two steps forward." The NEP authorized private manufacturing and private trade on a small scale, reintroduced the payment of wages, and permitted peasants to sell their grain in the open market. In 1924 a constitution was adopted, replacing imperial Russia with the Union of Soviet Socialist Republics. The union represented an attempt to unite the various nationalities and territories that had constituted the old empire. Each separate republic was, in theory, granted certain autonomous rights. In fact, government remained centralized in the hands of a few leaders. Further, central authority was maintained by means of the one legal political party—the Communist party—whose Central Committee was the directing force behind both politics and government, and whose organizational apparatus reached out into all areas of the vast country.

The philosophy of Bolshevism, now more popularly known as communism, was developed primarily by Lenin during these years. It was proclaimed, not as a new body of thought, but as a strict interpretation of Marx's writings. Nevertheless, from the beginning there were various departures from Marx's teachings. These changes were the necessary result of the fact that Marx had expected revolution to occur first in highly industrialized countries, whereas it had in fact broken out and succeeded in one of the least industralized nations in Europe. Marx had assumed that a capitalist stage must prepare the way for socialism; Lenin denied that this was necessary and insisted that Russia could leap directly from a manorial to a socialist economy. In the second place, Lenin emphasized the revolutionary character of socialism much more than did its original founder. Marx did believe that in most cases revolution would be necessary, but he was inclined to deplore the fact rather than to welcome it. Further, he had stated that "there are certain countries such as England and the United States in which the workers may hope to secure their ends by peaceful means." Last of all, Bolshevism differed from Marxism in its conception of proletarian rule. There is nothing to indicate that Marx ever envisaged a totalitarian state. True, he did speak of the "dictatorship of the proletariat," but he meant by this a dictatorship of the whole working class over the remnants of the bourgeoisie. Within the ranks of this class, democratic forms would prevail. Lenin, however, set up the ideal of the dictatorship of an elite, a select minority, wielding supremacy not only over the bourgeoisie but over the bulk of the proletarians themselves. In Russia this elite has remained the Communist party, whose membership has varied from 1,500,000 to 15,700,000.

The tenets of communism

The death of Lenin in January 1924 precipitated a titanic struggle between two of his lieutenants to inherit his mantle of power. Outside of Russia it was generally assumed that Trotsky would be the man to succeed the fallen leader. But the fiery commander of the Red army had a formidable rival in the tough and mysterious Joseph Stalin (1879–1953). The son of a peasant shoemaker in the province of Georgia, Stalin received part of his education in a theological seminary. Expelled at the age of seventeen for "lack of religious vocation," he thereafter dedicated his career to revolutionary activity. In 1917 he became secretary-general of the Communist party, a position through which he was able to build up a political machine. The battle between Stalin and Trotsky was not simply a struggle for personal power; fundamental issues of political policy were also involved. Trotsky maintained that socialism in Russia could never be entirely successful until capitalism was overthrown in surrounding countries. Therefore, he in-

The struggles between Trotsky and Stalin

Left: *Lenin's Casket Is Carried Through the Streets of Moscow.* It was not known with certainty until 1956 that, prior to his death, Lenin had discredited Stalin. Right: *Lenin and Stalin.* Under Stalin this picture was used to show his close relationship with Lenin. In fact, the photograph has been doctored.

sisted upon a continuous crusade for world revolution. Stalin was willing to abandon the program of world revolution, for the time being, in order to concentrate on building socialism in Russia itself. His strategy for the immediate future was essentially nationalist. The outcome of the duel was a complete triumph for Stalin. In 1927 Trotsky was expelled from the Communist party, and two years later he was driven from the country. In 1940 he was murdered in Mexico City by Stalinist agents. Lenin did not hold either Stalin or Trotsky in lofty esteem. In a "testament" written shortly before his death, he criticized Trotsky for "far-reaching self-confidence" and for being too much preoccupied with administrative detail. But he dealt far less gently with Stalin, condemning him as "too rough" and "capricious" and urging that the comrades "find a way" to remove him from his position at the head of the party.

In his struggle with Trotsky, Stalin had insisted that Russia's first priority was economic well-being. In line with this doctrine, one of *Five-Year Plan*   Stalin's first major reforms was the introduction of the so-called Five-Year Plan. Based upon the conviction that the Soviet Union had to take drastic steps to industrialize and thereby achieve economic parity among the nations of the world, the plan instituted an elaborate system of national priorities. It decreed how much of each major industrial and agricultural commodity the nation should produce, the amount of wages workers should receive, and the prices that should be charged for all that was sold at home and abroad. The first plan, instituted in 1928, was succeeded by others during the 1930s. In some areas goals were met, in a few they were exceeded, in some they fell

short. One of the major results of the Five-Year Plans was the creation
of an extensive state bureaucracy, charged with the task of organization
and supervision at all levels.

Included in the first plan was a program for agricultural collectivization. The scheme was designed to bring rural farms together into
larger units of several thousand acres, under the communal proprietorship of peasants. Only with this sort of reorganization, Russia's rulers declared, could the new and expensive processes of mechanization
be introduced, and the country's agricultural yield thereby increased.
Not surprisingly, the argument failed to win the support of the
more prosperous farmers—the kulaks—who had been allowed to retain
ownership of their land despite the revolution. Their opposition led to
another Terror, made all the more deadly by a famine which occurred
in southeast Russia in 1932. The kulaks were liquidated, either killed
or transported to distant labor camps—i.e., the rural bourgeoisie was
eliminated, to be replaced by a rural proletariat. Collectivization was
an accomplished fact by 1939. It represented to a vast number of Russians a revolution far more immediate than that of 1917. Twenty
million people were moved off the land, which, once it had been
reorganized into larger units, and production mechanized, required
fewer laborers. They were sent to cities, where most went to work in
factories. Agricultural output did not increase during the early years of
collectivization. But the scheme was nevertheless of benefit to the
government. By controlling production, the central bureaucracy was
able to regulate the distribution of agricultural products, allocating
them for export, where necessary, to pay for the importation of
much-needed industrial machinery.

Collectivization

As part of Stalin's campaign to put the interests of Russia ahead of
those of international communism, the Bolshevik regime adopted a
new and more conservative foreign policy during the 1930s. Its international goals contradicted the militant socialist internationalism of
the 1920s. Lenin had supported revolutionary leftist movements in
Europe, sending money and lending moral support to the radical German Marxists Karl Liebknecht and Rosa Luxemburg in 1919, and to
the short-lived Soviet regime of the Bolshevik Béla Kun in Hungary
in the same year. Shortly thereafter, the Third International—later
called the Comintern—was formed. It declared its allegiance to international communism; its policy was to oppose cooperation or collaboration with the capitalist governments of the West and to work for
their overthrow.

The Third International

With Stalin's suppression of the internationalism advocated by
Lenin and Trotsky, however, came a change in tactics and a revival of
militarism, or nationalism, and of an interest in playing the game of
power politics. The Russian army was more than doubled in size and
was reorganized in accordance with the western European model. Patriotism, which the older strict Marxists despised as a form of capital-

Stalinist conservatism

ist propaganda, was exalted into a Soviet virtue. When Germany once again appeared to threaten Russian security, as it did in the 1930s, the rulers of the Kremlin decided that Russia needed friends. Along with their efforts to build up a great army and to make their own country self-sufficient, they adopted a policy of cooperation with the western European powers. In 1934 they entered the League of Nations, and in 1934 they ratified a military alliance with France.

Constitution of 1936

In 1936, the rulers of Communist Russia drafted a new constitution. It was adopted by popular vote and went into effect January 1, 1938. It continued to provide for a union of eleven (later fifteen) republics, each supposedly autonomous and free to secede if it chose. The constitution established universal suffrage for all citizens eighteen years of age and over. They were to vote not only for the local soviets but for members of a national parliament. The highest organ of state power was declared to be the Supreme Soviet of the USSR, composed of two chambers, both given equal legislative powers. To represent it when it was not meeting, the Supreme Soviet was to elect a committee of thirty-seven members known as the Presidium. This body was also empowered to issue decrees, to declare war, and to annul the acts of administrative officials which did not conform to law. The highest executive and administrative agency was to be the Council of Ministers, likewise elected by the Supreme Soviet. The constitution contained a bill of rights. Citizens were guaranteed the right to employment, the right to leisure, the right to maintenance in case of old age or disability, and even the traditional privileges of freedom of speech, of the press, of assemblage, and of religion. The constitution of 1936 was, and still is, more of a sham than a reality. Its provisions for universal suffrage, for the secret ballot, and for a bill of rights had little meaning. The explanation lies in the fact that the real power in the Soviet Union rests with the Communist party, the only party allowed to exist. The organs of the government are little more than the vocal mechanisms through which the party expresses its will.

The purges

It is noteworthy that the very period in which the constitution was being put into effect witnessed an eruption of mass arrests and executions of persons alleged to be "Trotskyists, spies, and wreckers." Collectivization and industrialization had not been achieved without bitter disagreement among Russia's political leadership. Critics on the Left and Right were disturbed by both the ends and means of Stalin's programs, and by his obvious craving for personal power. Before his critics could strike at him, Stalin struck at them. Between 1936 and 1938 more than a score of prominent Old Bolsheviks were tried, confessed publicly to having plotted against the state, were condemned either as Trotskyites or bourgeois collaborators, and put to death. Their confessions, which surprised the world at the time, were obtained, it was later learned, by means of physical and psychological torture. Some 9 million further victims of these purges were arrested, impri-

Panel (3), Wassily Kandinsky (1866–1944). The Expressionist painters carried their explorations of the psychological properties of color and line to the point where subject matter was deemed unnecessary and even undesirable. (Museum of Modern Art)

Nude Descending a Staircase, Marcel Duchamp (1887–1968). An example of the impact of film on painting. The effect is that of a series of closely spaced photographs coalescing to create motion. (Philadelphia Museum of Art)

I and the Village, Marc Chagall (1889–   ). The subject refers to the artist's childhood and youth in Vitebsk, Russia. The profile on the right is probably that of the artist himself. (Museum of Modern Art)

The Table, Georges Braque (1881–1963). An example of later cubism showing the predominance of curvilinear form and line instead of geometric structure. (Museum of Modern Art)

The Persistence of Memory, Salvador Dali (1904–   ). The Spaniard Dali is the outstanding representative of the surrealist school. Many objects in his paintings are Freudian images. (Museum of Modern Art)

Barricade, José Clemente Orozco (1883–1949). The Mexican muralist Orozco was one of the most celebrated of contemporary painters with a social message. His themes were revolutionary fervor, satire of aristocracy and the Church, and deification of the common man. (Museum of Modern Art)

Sea and Gulls, John Marin (1870–1953). A native of New Jersey, Marin was a gifted abstract painter. His objects are sometimes recognizable, sometimes not. He painted not the likeness of nature, but *about* nature. (Museum of Modern Art)

Around the Fish, Paul Klee (1879–1940). Klee is recognized as the most subtle humorist of XX-cent. art. The central motif of a fish on a platter suggests a banquet, but many of the surrounding objects appear to be products of fantasy. (Museum of Modern Art)

Above: *Little Big Painting*, Roy Lichtenstein (born 1923). Oil on canvas. (The Whitney Museum of American Art). In the 1960's and early 1970's, American artists dominated the new movements, particularly "Pop," "Op," and "the New Realism." The works on this and the following page are by some of the best-known contemporary artists.

Left: *Summer Rental No. 2*, Robert Rauschenberg (born 1925). Oil on canvas. (Collection Whitney Museum of American Art). Gift of the Friends of the Whitney Museum of American Art.

Top Left: *Girl in Doorway*, George Segal (born 1924). A life-size construction in plaster, wood, glass, and aluminum paint. (Collection Whitney Museum of American Art). Top Right: *Green Coca Cola Bottles*, Andy Warhol (born 1931). Oil on canvas. (Collection Whitney Museum of American Art). Gift of the Friends of the Whitney Museum of American Art. Left: *Gran Cairo*, Frank Stella (born 1936). Synthetic polymer paint on canvas. (Collection Whitney Museum of American Art). Gift of the Friends of the Whitney Museum of American Art.

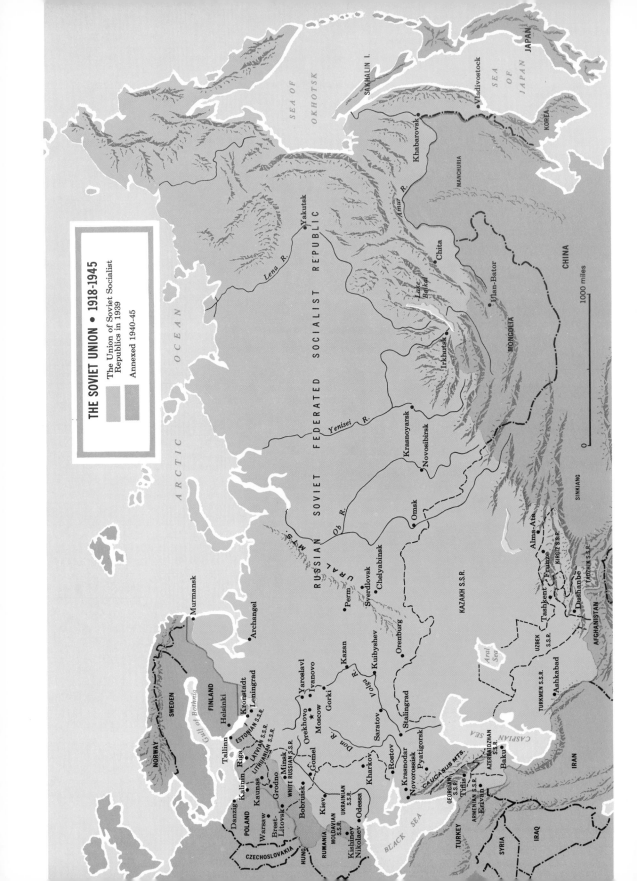

THE SOVIET UNION • 1918-1945

The Union of Soviet Socialist
Republics in 1939

Annexed 1940-45

ARCTIC OCEAN

NORWAY

SWEDEN

FINLAND

Helsinki

Murmansk

Archangel

Gulf of Bothnia

Tallinn
ESTONIAN S.S.R.

Kronstadt
Leningrad
Kalinin
Riga
LATVIAN S.S.R.
Kaunas
LITHUANIAN S.S.R.
Grodno
WHITE RUSSIAN S.S.R.
Minsk
Danzig
POLAND
Warsaw
Brest-
Litovsk
Bobruisk
Gomel
Kiev
UKRAINIAN S.S.R.
Odessa
Nikolaev
MOLDAVIAN
S.S.R.
Kishinev
RUMANIA
HUNG.
CZECHOSLOVAKIA

Orekhovo
Yaroslavl
Ivanovo
Moscow
Gorki
Kazan
Kuibyshev
Saratov
Volga R.
Stalingrad
Don R.
Rostov
Kharkov
Krasnodar
Novorossiak
Pyatigorsk
CAUCASUS MTS.
BLACK SEA

Perm
Sverdlovsk
Chelyabinsk
URAL MTS.
Orenburg

Kama R.

RUSSIAN SOVIET FEDERATED SOCIALIST REPUBLIC

Yakutsk

Lena R.

Krasnoyarsk
Novosibirsk
Yenisei R.
Omsk
Ob R.

KAZAKH S.S.R.

Aral
Sea

UZBEK
S.S.R.
Tashkent
Frunze
KIRGIZ S.S.R.
Alma-Ata
TADZHIK S.S.R.
Dushanbe
Ashkabad
TURKMEN S.S.R.

AFGHANISTAN

SINKIANG

CHINA

MONGOLIA
Ulan-Bator

Lake
Baikal
Irkutsk

Chita

Khabarovsk

Amur R.

SEA OF OKHOTSK

SAKHALIN I.

Vladivostock
KOREA
SEA OF JAPAN
JAPAN

MANCHURIA

CASPIAN
SEA
Baku
AZERBAIDZHAN
S.S.R.
GEORGIAN
S.S.R.
Tiflis
ARMENIAN S.S.R.
Erivan
TURKEY

IRAN

Ashkabad

SYRIA
IRAQ

1000 miles
0

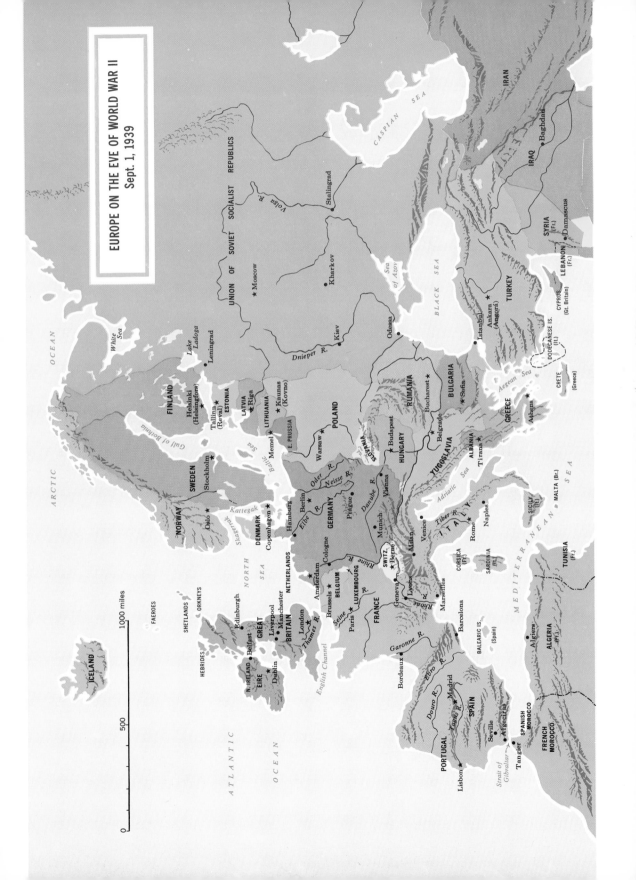

EUROPE ON THE EVE OF WORLD WAR II
Sept. 1, 1939

EUROPE · 1979

Members of the North Atlantic Treaty
Organization (NATO)

Members of the Warsaw Pact

Non-aligned States

Other Communist States

miles

0   100   200   300   400   500

soned, or sent to Siberia. By ridding the country of his opposition Stalin forestalled further revolution—not an unlikely possibility, given discontent with his policies—and solidified his position as virtual dictator of Russia.

The Soviet revolution achieved profound results. By 1939 private manufacturing and private trade had been almost entirely abolished. Factories, mines, railroads, and public utilities were exclusively owned by the state. Stores were either government enterprises or co-operatives in which consumers owned shares. Agriculture also had been almost completely socialized. No less revolutionary were the developments in the social sphere. Religion as a factor in the lives of the people declined to a place of small importance. Christianity was still tolerated, but churches were reduced in number, and were not permitted to engage in any charitable or educational activities. Furthermore, members of the Communist party were required to be atheists. Post-revolutionary communism not only renounced all belief in the supernatural but attempted to cultivate a new ethics. The cardinal virtues in this positive morality are industry, respect for public property, willingness to sacrifice individual interests for the good of society, and loyalty to the Soviet fatherland and to the socialist ideal.

Results of the Soviet upheaval

By the outbreak of World War II the Soviet regime had undeniable accomplishments to its credit. Among the principal ones were: (1) the reduction of illiteracy from at least 50 percent to less than 20 percent; (2) a notable expansion of industrialization; (3) the establishment of a planned economy, which operated successfully enough to prevent unemployment; (4) the opening of educational and cultural opportunities to larger numbers of the common people; and (5) the establishment of a system of government assistance for working mothers and their infants and free medical care and hospitalization for most citizens.

Accomplishments of the Bolshevik regime

But these accomplishments were purchased at a very high price. The program of socialization and industrialization was pushed at so frantic a pace that the good of individual citizens was overlooked. The Stalinist regime fastened upon Russia a tyranny as extreme as that of the tsar. Indeed, the number of its victims sentenced to slave-labor camps—estimated to be as high as 20 million—probably exceeded the number consigned by the tsars to exile in Siberia.

The price of revolution

2. THE EMERGENCE OF FASCISM IN ITALY

That Italy turned to totalitarianism may seem strange in view of the fact that the Italians emerged from World War I on the winning side. Italy had been the victim of frustrated nationalism for many years. Its aspirations for power and for empire had been shattered. The effect was to produce a sense of humiliation and shame, especially in the minds of the younger generation, and to foster an attitude of contempt

Frustrated nationalism in Italy

for the existing political regime. Members of the old ruling class were held up to scorn as cynical, vacillating, defeatist, and corrupt. Even before World War I there was talk of revolution, of the need for a drastic housecleaning that would deliver the country from its incompetent rulers.

The demoralizing and humiliating effects of the war

But the establishment of a dictatorship in Italy would never have been possible without the demoralizing and humiliating effects of World War I. The chief business of the Italian armies had been to keep the Austrians occupied on the Southern Front while the British, French, and Americans hammered Germany into submission along the battle lines on the Western Front. To accomplish its purpose Italy had to mobilize more than 5,500,000 men; of these nearly 700,000 were killed. The direct financial cost of Italian participation in the struggle was over 15 billion dollars. These sacrifices were no greater than those made by the British and the French, but Italy was a poor country. Moreover, in the division of the spoils after the fighting was over, the Italians got less than they expected. While Italy did receive most of the Austrian territories promised in the secret treaties, the Italians maintained that these were inadequate rewards for their sacrifices and for their valuable contribution to an Entente victory. At first the nationalists vented their spleen for the "humiliation of Versailles" upon President Wilson, but after a short time they returned to their old habit of castigating Italy's rulers. They alleged that such men as Premier Orlando had been so cravenly weak and inept that they had allowed their own country to be cheated.

Inflation, radicalism, and economic chaos

The war contributed to the revolution in a multitude of other ways. It resulted in inflation of the currency, with consequent high prices, speculation, and profiteering. Normally wages would have risen also, but the labor market was glutted on account of the return to civilian life of millions of soldiers. Furthermore, business was demoralized, owing to extensive and frequent strikes and to the closing of foreign markets. Perhaps the most serious consequence of the war, to the upper and middle classes at least, was the growth of socialism. As hardship and chaos increased, the Italian socialists embraced a philosophy akin to Bolshevism. They voted as a party to join the Third International. In the elections of November 1919, they won about a third of the seats in the Chamber of Deputies. During the following winter socialist workers took over about a hundred factories and attempted to run them for the benefit of the workers. Radicalism also spread through the rural areas, where so-called Red Leagues were organized to break up large estates and to force landlords to reduce their rents. The landowning classes were badly frightened and were therefore ready to accept Fascist totalitarianism as a less dangerous form of radicalism that might save at least part of their property from confiscation.

How much the Fascist movement depended for its success upon the leadership of Benito Mussolini is impossible to say. Mussolini was born in 1883, the son of a socialist blacksmith. His mother was a schoolteacher, and in deference to her wishes he eventually became a teacher. But he was restless and dissatisfied and soon left Italy for further study in Switzerland. Here he gave part of his time to his books and the rest of it to writing articles for socialist newspapers. He was finally expelled from the country for fomenting strikes in factories. Upon returning to Italy he took up journalism as a definite career and eventually became editor of *Avanti,* the leading socialist daily. His ideas in the years before the war were a mixture of contradictory forms of radicalism. He professed to be a Marxist socialist, but he mingled his socialism with doctrines of corporatism, adapted from the French syndicalists.

The career of Mussolini

Mussolini in fact believed in no particular set of doctrines. No man with a definite philosophy could have reversed himself so often. When war broke out in August 1914, Mussolini insisted that Italy should remain neutral. But he had scarcely adopted this position when he began urging participation on the Entente side. Deprived of his position as editor of *Avanti,* he founded a new paper, *Il Popolo d'Italia,* and dedicated its columns to arousing enthusiasm for war. He regarded the decision of the government the following spring to go in on the side of the Entente allies as a personal victory.

Mussolini's contradictory ideas

The word *fascism* derives from the Latin *fasces,* the ax surrounded by a bundle of sticks representing the authority of the Roman state; the Italian *fascio,* means group or band. *Fasci* were organized as early as October 1914, as units of agitation to swing Italy over to the Entente cause. Their membership was made up of young idealists, fanatical nationalists, and bored white-collar workers. The original platform of the Fascist movement was drafted by Mussolini in 1919. It was a surprisingly radical document, which demanded, among other things, universal suffrage; abolition of the conservative Senate; the establishment by law of an eight-hour day; a heavy capital levy; a heavy tax on inheritances; confiscation of 85 percent of war profits; acceptance of the League of Nations; and "opposition to all imperialisms." This platform was accepted more or less officially by the movement until May 1920, when it was supplanted by another of a more conservative character. Indeed, the new program omitted all reference to economic reform. On neither of these platforms did the Fascists achieve much political success.

The evolution of fascism

The Fascists made up for their initial lack of numbers by disciplined aggressiveness and strong determination. As the old regime crumbled, they prepared to take over the government. In September 1922, Mussolini began to talk openly of revolution and raised the cry, "On to Rome." On October 28 an army of about 50,000 Fascist militia, in blackshirted uniforms, occupied the capital. The premier resigned, and the following day the king, Victor Emmanuel III, invited Mussolini to form a cabinet. Thus, without firing a shot the blackshirts had

The march on Rome

Left: *"On to Rome."* Mussolini (wearing a suit) and uniformed Fascists march into Rome in October 1922. Right: *Mussolini Addressing a Crowd of His Followers from the Balcony of the Palazzo Venezia in Rome*

gained control of the Italian government. The explanation is to be found not in the strength of fascism, but in the chaos created by the war and in the weakness and irresolution of the old ruling classes. By the end of the next three years Mussolini's revolution was virtually complete. He had abolished the cabinet system, made the political system a one-party system, and reduced the functions of the parliament to ratifying decrees.

The leading doctrines of Italian fascism may be summarized as follows:

Major doctrines of fascism

(1) Totalitarianism. The state incorporates every interest and every loyalty of its members. There must be "nothing above the state, nothing outside the state, nothing against the state."

(2) Nationalism. The nation is the highest form of society ever evolved by the human race. It has a life and a soul of its own apart from the lives and souls of the individuals who compose it. There can never be a real harmony of interests between two or more distinct peoples. Internationalism is therefore a perversion of human progress.

(3) Militarism. Strife is the origin of all things. Nations which do not expand eventually wither and die. War exalts and ennobles man and regenerates sluggish and decadent peoples.

Corporatism

Declaring his allegiance to these principles, Mussolini began to build what he called the corporatist state. The Italian economy was placed under the management of twenty-two corporations, each responsible for a major industrial enterprise. In each corporation were representatives of trade unions, whose members were organized by the Fascist party, the employers, and the government. Together, the members of these corporations were given the task of determining working conditions, wages, and prices. In fact, however, the decisions of these bodies were closely managed by the government. In 1938 the last vestiges of democratic control were removed in Italy. The Chamber of Deputies was replaced by the Chamber of Fasces and Corporations, whose members were appointed by the government.

Corporatism did little to lessen Italy's plight during the years of worldwide depression which occurred in the 1930s. Although he managed to make his country appear more efficient—his admirers often bragged that he had at last "made the trains run on time"— Mussolini failed to solve its major problems, particularly those of the peasantry, whose standard of living remained desperately low. Mussolini's fascism was little more than illusion. It is a measure of the Italians' disgust with their past leaders that they were so ready to be taken in.

Its failure

3. THE RISE OF NAZI GERMANY

Germany succumbed to totalitarianism later than Italy. For a brief period following World War I, events seemed to be moving the country to the Left. Most of the leading politicians in the immediate postarmistice government were socialists, members of the Social Democratic party. Their reformist policies, which had seemed radical enough to many prior to the war, now appeared too mild to a group of extreme Marxists who had been encouraged by the revolution in Russia. Calling themselves Spartacists,[1] and led by the able Rosa Luxemburg and Karl Liebknecht, they attempted an uprising in 1919 designed to bring the proletarian revolution to Germany. Despite assistance from the Russian Bolsheviks, the rebellion was crushed; Liebknecht and Luxemburg were killed by soldiers while being taken to prison. In engineering the Spartacists' defeat, the German government had recourse to private vigilante groups headed by disillusioned former army officers, men whose true sympathies lay no more with democratic socialism than with Russian communism, and whose discontent would soon focus on the government they had helped to salvage.

Germany: the Spartacists

With the Spartacist revolt only just behind them, the leaders of a coalition of socialists, Catholic Centrists, and liberal democrats in 1919 drafted a constitution for the new German republic reflecting a generally progressive political and social philosophy. It provided for universal suffrage, for women as well as men; the cabinet system of government; and for a bill of rights, guaranteeing not only civil liberties but the right of the citizen to employment, to an education, and to protection against the hazards of an industrial society. But the republic set up under this constitution was beset with troubles from the start.

The Weimar Republic

[1] After the Roman, Spartacus, who led a slave revolt.

Karl Liebknecht (center) *and Rosa Luxemburg*

Reactionaries and other extremists plotted against it. Moreover, the German people had had little experience with democratic government. The Weimar Republic (named for the city where its constitution was drafted) did not spring from the desires of a majority of the nation. It was born of change forced upon Germany in its hour of defeat. Its instability made it a likely victim of the forces it was desperately attempting to tame.

The factors which led to the eventual triumph of German totalitarianism were many and various. First was the sense of humiliation arising from defeat in the war. Between 1871 and 1914 Germany had risen to lofty heights of political and cultural prestige. German universities, science, philosophy, and music were known and admired all over the world. The country had likewise attained a remarkable prosperity, by 1914 surpassing Britain and the United States in several fields of industrial production. Then came the crushing blow of 1918. Germany was toppled from its pinnacle and left at the mercy of its powerful enemies. It was too much for the German people to understand. They could not believe that their invincible armies had really been worsted in battle. Quickly the legend grew that the nation had been "stabbed in the back" by socialists and Jews in the government. Though there was no truth in this charge, it helped to salve the wounded pride of German patriots. Those in search of a scapegoat also blamed the laxity and irresponsibility that appeared to distinguish the republican regime. It was alleged that Berlin had displaced Paris as the most frivolous and decadent city of Europe. What the country seemed to need was authoritative leadership to spearhead a campaign to regain the world's respect.

Causes of German totalitarianism: (1) defeat in war

Another major reason for the appeal of totalitarianism was the inflation that Germany suffered in the 1920s. When the country began to experience severe unemployment, the government increased the supply of paper money—eventually to a flood—in order to finance programs of unemployment insurance and to try to provide its citizenry with the economic wherewithal to stay alive. The result was a period of wild inflation, particularly demoralizing to the middle class. Salaries could not keep up with the vast increase in the cost of living. Those who existed on fixed incomes—pensioners, stockholders—saw their security vanish. As they lost their faith in the ability of the government to come to their aid, these men and women began, as well, to lose whatever faith they may have had in the republic. Germany recovered from inflation in the late 1920s, thanks, largely, to the scaling down of reparations payments and to foreign loans and investments. But the middle class, traumatized by its experience of inflation, continued its search for a government that promised attention to its needs and sympathy with its problems. That search intensified with the advent of the Great Depression of 1929. As we shall see, the depression was a major disaster for most of the world. In few countries, however, were its effects more keenly felt than in Germany. Farmers were angered by the collapse of agricultural prices and by their burden of debts and taxes. University students saw little prospect of gaining a place in already overcrowded professions. Six million workers were unemployed. Once again the middle class saw its savings vanish.

(2) economics

One political result was a swing on the part of many workers to the German Communist party. The Spartacist failure had, for a time, quelled middle-class fears of a leftist takeover. But in the presidential election of 1932, the Communist party polled about 6 million votes, or over one-seventh of the total. As had happened in Italy, a number of capitalists and property-owners were alarmed at what they regarded as a growing danger of Bolshevik revolution and lent their support to a different sort of totalitarianism as the lesser of two evils.

(3) fear of Bolshevism

The origins of German totalitarianism go back to 1919 when a group of seven men met in Munich and founded the National Socialist

Depression in Germany. Following the defeat in World War I, inflation was rampant and food in short supply. Here a fallen horse is torn to shreds by hungry citizens.

The founding of the Nazi party; the early career of Hitler

German Workers' party.[2] Presently the most obscure of the seven emerged as their leader. He was Adolf Hitler, born in 1889, the son of a petty customs official in the Austrian civil service. Hitler's early life was unhappy and maladjusted. Rebellious and undisciplined from childhood, he seems always to have been burdened with a sense of frustration. He was a failure in school and decided that he would become an artist. With this purpose in view he went to Vienna in 1909, hoping to enter the Academy. But he failed the required examinations; for the next four years he was compelled to eke out a dismal existence as a casual laborer and a painter of little sketches and watercolors. Meanwhile he developed some violent political prejudices. He became an ardent admirer of certain vociferously anti-Semitic politicians in Vienna; and since he associated Judaism with Marxism, he hated that philosophy also. When World War I broke out, Hitler was living in Munich, and though an Austrian citizen, he immediately enlisted in the German army. Following the war, he joined with other disaffected Germans to denounce the Weimar Republic. In 1923, Hitler led an attempt in Munich by the Nazis' private army, the Brownshirts, to stage a "putsch," or sudden overthrow of the government. The revolution was proclaimed in a beer hall, with Hitler firing a revolver into the ceiling. The Brownshirts were quickly dispersed, and Hitler sentenced to a term in prison, where he composed a declaration of his beliefs, *Mein Kampf* (My Struggle). In this rambling treatise he expressed his hatred of Jews and communists, his sense of Germany's betrayal by its World War I enemies, and his belief that only with strong leadership could the country regain its rightful place within the European concert of nations.

The Nazi revolution

Hitler's message appealed to an ever-growing number of his disillusioned and economically threatened countrymen and women. In the election of 1928 the Nazis won 12 seats in the Reichstag. In 1930, they won 107 seats, their popular vote increasing from 800,000 to 6,500,000. During the summer of 1932 the parliamentary system broke down. No chancellor could retain a majority in the Reichstag, for the Nazis declined to support any cabinet not headed by Hitler, and the communists refused to collaborate with the socialists. In January 1933, a group of reactionaries—industrialists, bankers, and Junkers—prevailed upon President Paul von Hindenburg to designate Hitler as chancellor, evidently in the belief that they could control him. It was arranged that there should be only three Nazis in the cabinet, and that Franz von Papen, a Catholic aristocrat, should hold the position of vice-chancellor. But the sponsors of this plan failed to appreciate the tremendous resurgence of mass feeling behind the Nazi movement. Hitler was not slow in making the most of his new opportunity. He persuaded von Hindenburg to dissolve the Reichstag and to

---

[2] The name of the party was soon abbreviated in popular usage to Nazi.

One Step Away from Power. President von Hindenburg followed by Hitler, Göring on the extreme right, and other Nazi party members.

order a new election on March 5. When the new Reichstag assembled, it voted to confer upon Hitler practically unlimited powers. Soon afterward the flag of the Weimar Republic was hauled down and replaced by the swastika banner of the National Socialists. The new Germany was proclaimed to be the Third Reich, the successor of the Hohenstaufen Empire of the Middle Ages and of the Hohenzollern Empire of the kaisers.

Within a few months, other and more sweeping changes occurred. Germany was converted into a highly centralized state with the destruction of the federal principle that had been a feature of Bismarck's imperial scheme. All political parties except the Nazi party were declared illegal. Totalitarian control was extended over the press, over education, the theater, the cinema, radio, and many branches of production and trade. Drastic penalties were imposed upon the Jews: they were eliminated from government positions, deprived of citizenship, and practically excluded from the universities. With the passing of the years, the entire regime seemed to shift more and more in a radical direction. The new tendency approached its climax in 1938 with the extension of party control over the army and with the institution of a fanatical crusade against the Jews to expel them from the Reich or to annihilate them entirely.

Consolidation of Nazi rule

So far as its ideology was concerned, German totalitarianism resembled the Italian variety in a great many of its essentials. Both were collectivistic, authoritarian, nationalistic, militaristic, and anti-intellectual. Yet there were some outstanding differences. Italian fascism never had a racial basis. True, after the formation of the Rome-Berlin Axis, an alliance made in 1936, Mussolini issued anti-Jewish decrees.

Nazi racism

But race was not a central theoretical pillar of Italian fascism as it was of German National Socialism. The Nazis argued that the so-called Aryan race, which was supposed to include the Nordics as its most perfect specimens, was the only one ever to have made any notable contributions to human progress. They contended further that the accomplishments and mental qualities of a people were determined by blood. Thus the achievements of the Jew forever remained Jewish, or Oriental, no matter how long he or she might live in a Western country. It followed that no Jewish science or Jewish literature or Jewish music could ever truly represent the German nation. Obviously, most of this racial doctrine was mere rationalization. The Nazis persecuted the Jews because Hitler was himself rabidly anti-Semitic and because they needed a scapegoat upon whom they could place the blame for their nation's troubles. Before this extremism had run its course, millions of Jews had been rounded up, tortured, and murdered in concentration camps. Other representatives of "imperfect" racial and social groups—homosexuals, gypsies, and anti-Nazi intellectuals—met a similar fate. The extremism of Hitler's anti-Semitic campaigns underscores the fact that National Socialism was more fanatical than Italian fascism. It was comparable to a new religion, not only in its dogmatism and its ritual, but in its fierce intolerance and its zeal for expansion.

Dissimilarities with Italian fascism

Despite the fact that Germany was one of the most highly industrialized countries in the world, National Socialism had a peculiar peasant flavor which Italian fascism did not possess. The key to Nazi theory was contained in the phrase *Blut und Boden* (blood and soil). The word *soil* typified not only a deep reverence for the homeland but an abiding affection for the peasants, who were considered to embody the finest qualities of the German race. No class of the population was more generously treated by the Nazi government. This high regard for country folk came partly no doubt from the circumstance that they had the highest birthrate of the nation's citizens and therefore were

A Nazi Party Rally. Hitler at the height of his power, followed by other Nazi party officials.

most valuable for military reasons. It was explainable also by the reaction of the Nazi leaders against everything that the city stood for—not only intellectualism and radicalism but high finance and the complicated problems of industrial society. In its attempt to control all aspects of national life, Nazism resembled not only Italian fascism but all totalitarian regimes. Trade unions were replaced by the government-controlled National Labor Front. Public works programs—including reforestation and housing and highway construction—were begun. A policy of rearmament led to further industrial organization, and helped reduce unemployment.

The significance of German and Italian totalitarianism is still a subject of controversy among students of modern history. Some argue that it was simply the enthronement of force by big capitalists in an effort to save their dying system from destruction. It is true that the success of both movements in gaining control of the government depended in some measure upon support from great landowners and captains of industry. A second interpretation would explain German and Italian totalitarianism as a reaction of debtors against creditors, of farmers against bankers and manufacturers, and of small businessmen against high finance and monopolistic practices. Still other students of the movement interpret it as a revolt against communism, a reversion to primitivism, a result of the despair of the masses, a protest against the weaknesses of democracy, or a supreme manifestation of nationalism. Undoubtedly it was all of these things combined. An increasingly popular view in recent years holds that fascism and Nazism were extreme expressions of tendencies prevalent in all industrialized countries. If official policies in most Western countries in the 1930s took on more and more of an authoritarian semblance—a tightly controlled economy, limitation of production to maintain prices, and expansion of armaments to promote prosperity—it was because nearly all nations in that period were beset with similar problems.

The complex significance of German and Italian totalitarianism

4. THE DEMOCRACIES BETWEEN THE WARS

The histories of the three Western democracies—Great Britain, France, and the United States—run roughly parallel during the years after the First World War. In all three countries there was an attempt by governments to trust to policies and assumptions that had prevailed before the war. The French, not surprisingly, continued to fear Germany and to take whatever steps they could to keep their traditional enemy as weak as possible. Under the leadership of the moderate conservative, Raymond Poincaré, who held office from 1922 to 1924, and again from 1926 to 1929, the French pursued a policy of deflation, which attempted to keep the price of manufactured goods low, by restraining wages. This policy pleased businessmen, but was hard on the working class. Edouard Herriot, a Radical Socialist who

Class conflict in France

served as premier from 1924 to 1926 was, despite his party's name, a spokesman for the small businessman, farmer, and lower middle class. Herriot declared himself in favor of social reform, but he refused to raise taxes in order to pay for it. Class conflict lay close to the surface of French national affairs throughout the 1920s. While industries prospered, employers rejected trade unionists' demands to bargain collectively. A period of major strikes immediately after the war was followed by a sharp decline in union activity. Workers remained dissatisfied, even after the government passed a modified social insurance program in 1930, insuring against sickness, old age, and death.

Britain's economic difficulties

Class conflict flared in Britain as well. Anxious to regain its now irretrievably lost position as the major industrial and financial power in the world, Britain, like France, pursued a policy of deflation, designed to lower the price of manufactured goods and thus make them more attractive on the world market. The result was a reduction in wages which undermined the standard of living of many British workers. Their resentment helped to elect a Labour party government in 1924 and 1929. But its minority position in Parliament left it little chance to accomplish much of consequence, even had its leader, Prime Minister J. Ramsay MacDonald, been a more adventurous socialist than he was. In 1926 British trade unions grew increasingly militant because of the particularly distressing wage levels in the coal mining industry, and because the Conservative government, returned to power under Prime Minister Stanley Baldwin in 1925, refused to be deflected from its deflationary stance. The unions staged a nationwide general strike which, though it failed as an industrial strategy, turned the middle class more than ever against the workers.

Conservatism in the U.S.

The United States was undoubtedly the most impregnable fortress of conservative power among the democracies. The presidents elected during the 1920s—Warren G. Harding, Calvin Coolidge, and Herbert Hoover—upheld a social philosophy formulated by the barons of big business in the nineteenth century, and the Supreme Court used its power of judicial review to nullify progressive legislation enacted by state governments and occasionally by Congress.

Labor Troubles in Britain. Mounted police escorting delivery wagons through a mob of angry strikers during the general strike of 1926.

The Stock Market Crash, October 24, 1929. Crowds milling outside the New York Stock Exchange on the day of the big crash.

The course of Western history was dramatically altered by the advent of worldwide depression in 1929. We have already mentioned this event as it contributed to the rise of Nazism. But all countries were forced to come to terms with the economic and social devastation it produced. The Great Depression had its roots in a general agricultural slump in the 1920s, the result of increased postwar production which drove down the price of grain and other commodities to the point of bankrupting farmers, though not far enough to benefit the urban poor. To chronic agricultural distress was added the financial crisis that began with the collapse of prices on the New York stock exchange in 1929. With a drop in the value of stocks, banks found themselves short of capital and forced to close. International investors called in their debts. Industries, unable to sell, stopped manufacturing and started laying off workers. Unemployment further contracted markets—fewer people had money with which to buy goods or services—and that contraction led to more unemployment.

The Great Depression

The results of the depression took varied forms throughout the West. In 1931 Great Britain abandoned the gold standard, and the government of the United States followed suit in 1933. By no longer pegging their currencies to the price of gold, these countries hoped to make money cheaper, and thus more available for programs of public and private economic recovery. This action was the forerunner of a broad program of currency management, which became an important element in a general policy of economic nationalism. By way of illustration, President Franklin D. Roosevelt informed the London Economic Conference of 1933 that "the sound internal economic system of a nation is a greater factor in its well-being than the price of its currency in changing terms of the currencies of other nations." As early as 1932 Great Britain abandoned its time-honored policy of free trade. Protective tariffs were raised in some instances as high as 100 percent.

Results of depression: economic nationalism

Léon Blum

Domestic policies

The New Deal

Its achievements

Domestically, Britain moved cautiously to alleviate the effects of the depression. A national government, which came to power in 1931 with a ministry composed of members from the Conservative, Liberal, and Labour parties, was reluctant to spend beyond its income, as it would have to in order to underwrite effective programs of public assistance. Of the European democracies, France adopted the most advanced set of policies to combat the inequalities and distress that followed in the wake of the depression. In 1936, responding to a threat from ultraconservatives to overthrow the republic, a Popular Front government, under the leadership of the socialist Léon Blum (1872–1950), was formed by the Radical, Radical Socialist, and Communist parties, and lasted for two years. The Popular Front nationalized the munitions industry and reorganized the Bank of France so as to deprive the 200 largest stockholders of their monopolistic control over credit. In addition, it decreed a forty-hour week for all urban workers and initiated a program of public works. For the benefit of the farmers it established a wheat office to fix the price and regulate the distribution of grain. Although the threat from the political Right had for a time been quelled by the Popular Front, conservatives were generally uncooperative and unimpressed by its attempts to ameliorate the conditions of the French working class. The anti-Semitism that had surfaced at the time of the Dreyfus affair resurfaced; Blum was both a socialist and a Jew. Businessmen saw him as the forerunner of a French Lenin, and were heard to opine, "better Hitler than Blum." They got their wish before the decade was out.

The most dramatic changes in policy after the depression occurred, not in Europe, but in the United States. The explanation was twofold. The United States had clung longer to the economic philosophy of the nineteenth century. Prior to the depression the business classes had adhered firmly to the dogma of freedom of contract and insisted upon their right to form monopolies and to use the government as their agent in frustrating the demands of both workers and consumers. The depression in the United States was also more severe than in the European democracies. Industrial production shrank by about two-thirds. The structure of agricultural prices and of common stocks collapsed. Thousands of banks were forced to close their doors. Unemployment rose to 15 million, or to approximately 33 percent of the total labor force. An attempt to alleviate distress was contained in a program of reform and reconstruction known as the New Deal. The chief architect and motivator of this program was Franklin D. Roosevelt (1882–1945), who succeeded Herbert Hoover in the presidency on March 4, 1933.

The aim of the New Deal was to preserve the capitalist system, by managing the economy and undertaking programs of relief and public works to increase mass purchasing power. Although the New Deal did assist in the recovery both of individual citizens and of the country, through programs of currency management and social security, it left the crucial problem of unemployment unsolved. In 1939, after six years of the New Deal, the United States still had more than 9 million jobless workers—a figure which exceeded the combined unemployment of the rest of the world. Ironically, only the outbreak of a new world war could provide the full recovery that the New Deal had failed to assure, by directing millions from the labor market into the army and by creating jobs in the countless factories that turned to the manufacture of war materiel.

5. INTELLECTUAL AND CULTURAL TRENDS IN THE INTERWAR YEARS

The First World War, which proved so disillusioning to so many, and the generally dispiriting political events which followed in its train, made it difficult to hold fast to any notion of a purposeful universe. Philosophers, to a greater degree than their predecessors, declared that there was little point in attempting to discover answers to questions about the nature of ultimate reality. These antimetaphysicians discarded the search for God or for the "meaning" of life as a hopeless and therefore pointless task. Probably the most influential of these thinkers was the Viennese Ludwig Wittgenstein (1889–1951), founder, with the Englishman Bertrand Russell (1872–1970), of the school of Logical Positivism. Developed further by the so-called Vienna Circle, whose leader was Rudolf Carnap, Logical Positivism emerged as an uncompromisingly scientific philosophy. It is not concerned with values or ideals except to the extent that they may be demonstrable by mathematics or physics. In general, the Logical Positivists reject as "meaningless" everything that cannot be reduced to a "one-to-one correspondence" with something in the physical universe. In other words, they reduce philosophy to a mere instrument for the discovery of truth in harmony with the facts of the physical environment. They divest it almost entirely of its traditional content and use it as a medium for answering questions and solving problems. They are concerned especially with political theory, regarding that subject as particularly burdened with unproved assumptions and questionable dogmas.

Antimetaphysics

Sociologists reinforced philosophers in denying the value of metaphysics. One of the most important was the German Max Weber (1864–1920), who, in his book *The Protestant Ethic and the Spirit of Capitalism* (1905), argued that religion must be understood as a cultural force, in this case assisting directly in the spread of capitalism. By making work a cardinal virtue and idleness a supreme vice, Protestantism had encouraged the work ethic, which, in turn, had fueled the energies of early capitalist entrepreneurs. When he turned to a study of

Bertrand Russell

the contemporary world, Weber concluded that societies would inevitably fall more and more under the sway of ever-expanding and potentially totalitarian bureaucracies. Recognizing the extent to which such a development might threaten human freedom, Weber posited the notion of "charismatic" leadership as a means of escaping the deadening tyranny of state control. A term derived from the Greek word for gift, "charisma" was, according to Weber, an almost magic quality which could induce hero worship and which, if properly directed by its possessor, might produce an authority to challenge bureaucracy. Weber himself recognized the dangers as well as the attractions of charismatic authority, dangers which the careers of Hitler and Mussolini soon made all too apparent. Another thinker who treated religion as a powerful social and psychological force, rather than as a branch of metaphysics, was the Swiss psychologist Carl Jung (1875–1961). Originally a student and disciple of Freud, Jung broke with his intellectual mentor by proclaiming the existence of a force behind individual id, ego, and superego: the "collective unconscious." Jung's literary background and his personal penchant for mysticism helped persuade him of the enduring psychological and therapeutic value of myth and religion, something Freud refused to acknowledge.

Antirationalist and antidemocratic philosophies

The writings of some philosophers during the interwar years not only reflected a sense of crisis and despair but, because of the influence of those works, contributed to it as well. Foremost among these were the Italian Vilfredo Pareto (1848–1923) and the German Oswald Spengler (1880–1936), who agreed in their contempt for the masses, in their belief that democracy was impossible, in their anti-intellectual viewpoint, and in their admiration for strong and aggressive leaders. Spengler was, in many respects, more extreme than Pareto. Although he completed in about 1918 an erudite and in some respects brilliant philosophy of history, which he entitled *The Decline of the West,* his later writings reflected totalitarian prejudices. In his *Hour of Decision,* published in 1933, he fulminated against democracy, pacifism, internationalism, the lower classes, and nonwhite peoples. He sang the praises of those "who feel themselves born and called to be masters," of "healthy instincts, race, the will to possession and power." Spengler despised the old, analytical reasoning of urban intellectuals and called upon men to admire the "deep wisdom of old peasant families." Human beings, he maintained, are "beasts of prey," and those who deny this conclusion are simply "beasts of prey with broken teeth."

Literary disillusion

Literary movements during the interwar period showed tendencies similar to those in philosophy. The major novelists, poets, and dramatists were deeply concerned about social and political problems and about the hope and destiny of humanity. Like the philosophers, they were disillusioned by the brute facts of World War I and by the failure of victory to fulfill its promises. Many were profoundly affected also by revolutionary developments in science and especially by the probings of the new science of psychoanalysis into the hidden secrets of the mind. Much of the literature of the interwar period expressed themes of frustration, cynicism, and disenchantment. It was an era dominated by those whose ideals had been shattered by the events of their time. Its mood was set by the early novels of the American Ernest Hemingway (1899–1961), by the poetry of the Anglo-American T. S. Eliot (1888–1965), and by the plays of the German Bertolt Brecht (1898–1956). In *The Sun Also Rises,* Hemingway gave the public a powerful description of the essential tragedy of the so-called lost generation and set a pattern which other writers, like the American F. Scott Fitzgerald, were soon to follow. In his poem *The Waste Land* (1922), T. S. Eliot presented a philosophy that was close to despair. Once you are born, he seemed to be saying, life is a living death, to be ground out in boredom and frustration. The German, Brecht, in plays written to be performed before the proletarian patrons of cabarets, proclaimed the corruption of the bourgeois state and the pointlessness of war.

T. S. Eliot

The works of many writers in the interwar period reflected to an increasing extent the isolation of self-conscious intellectuals and the constricting of their audience that, as we have seen, characterized the years before the First World War. While Brecht carried his revolutionary messages into the streets of Berlin, other writers wrote primarily for each other or for the small elite group who could understand what they were saying. Eliot crammed his poetry with esoteric allusions. The Irishman James Joyce (1882–1941), whose ability to enter his characters' minds and to reproduce their "stream-of-consciousness" on paper made him a writer of the very first order, nevertheless wrote with a complexity that only few could appreciate. The same was true, though to a lesser extent, of the novels of the Frenchman Marcel Proust (1871–1922) and the Englishwoman Virginia Woolf (1882–1941). In her novels and essays, Woolf was an eloquent and biting critic of the ruling class of Britain, focusing in part on the enforced oppression of women even in that class.

Intellectual isolation

Virginia Woolf

The Great Depression of the 1930s forced a reexamination of the methods and purposes of literature. In the midst of economic stagnation and threats of totalitarianism and war, the theory evolved that literature must have a political purpose, that it should indict meanness, cruelty, and barbarism, and point the way to a more just society. It should also be a literature addressed not to fellow intellectuals, but to common men and women. The new trend was reflected in the works of a diversity of writers. The American John Steinbeck (1902–1968), in *The Grapes of Wrath,* depicted the sorry plight of impoverished farmers fleeing from the "dust bowl" to California only to find that all the land had been monopolized by companies that exploited their workers. Pervading the novels of the Frenchman André Malraux

Influence of the depression

Jean-Paul Sartre

Existentialism

George Orwell

John Maynard Keynes

(1901–   ) was the strong suggestion that the human struggle against tyranny and injustice is that which gives meaning and value to life. Young British writers such as W. H. Auden, Stephen Spender, and Christopher Isherwood declared, as communist sympathizers, that artists had an obligation to politicize their art for the benefit of the revolution. They rejected the pessimism of their immediate literary forebears for the optimism of political commitment to a common cause.

In this they differed radically from their French contemporary, Jean-Paul Sartre (1905–1980), whose pessimistic philosophy of Existentialism was receiving its first hearing at this time. Sartre was a teacher of philosophy in a Paris *lycée* and subsequently a leader of the French resistance movement against the Germans. His philosophy takes its name from its doctrine that the *existence* of human beings as free individuals is the fundamental fact of life. But this freedom is of no help to humanity; instead it is a source of anguish and terror. Realizing, however vaguely, that they are free agents, morally responsible for all their acts, individuals feel themselves strangers in an alien world. They can have no confidence in a benevolent God or in a universe guided by purpose, for, according to Sartre, all such ideas have been reduced to fictions by modern science. The only way of escape from despair is the path of "involvement," or active participation in human affairs. It should be noted that in addition to the atheistic Existentialism of Sartre, there was also a prior Christian version, which had its origin in the teachings of Søren Kierkegaard (1813–1855), a Danish theologian of the mid–nineteenth century. Like its atheistic counterpart, Christian Existentialism also teaches that the chief cause of human agony and terror is freedom, but it finds the source of this freedom in original sin.

Another writer who refused to allow himself the luxury of political optimism was the Englishman George Orwell (1903–1950). Although sympathetic to the cause of international socialism, Orwell continued to insist that all political movements were to some degree corrupted. He urged writers to recognize a duty to write only on the basis of what they had themselves experienced. Above all, writers should never simply parrot party propaganda. Orwell's last two novels, *Animal Farm* and *1984,* written during and immediately after the Second World War, are powerful expressions of his mistrust of political regimes—whether of the Left or the Right—that profess democracy but in fact destroy human freedom.

Optimism during the 1930s was generally the property of those writers who were prepared to advocate a violent change in the social order, most notably men and women sympathetic to the doctrines of communism and the achievements of Soviet Russia. An exception to this rule was the British economist John Maynard Keynes (1883–1946), who argued that capitalism could be made to work if governments would play a part in its management, and whose theories helped shape the economic policies of the New Deal. Keynes had served as an economic adviser to the British government during the 1919 treaty-making at Paris. He was disgusted with the harsh terms imposed upon the Germans, recognizing that they would serve only to keep alive the hatreds and uncertainties that breed war. His dismay did not induce him to turn his back on the world and its problems, however. Keynes was very much a man of the world, among other things a successful financial speculator in his own right. Keynes believed that capitalism with its inner faults corrected could provide all the justice and efficiency reasonable people could expect. Capitalism, though, would require a "face-lifting" that some of its more conservative defenders would consider drastic. First, the idea of a perpetually balanced budget would need to be abandoned. Keynes never advocated continuous deficit financing. He would have the government deliberately operate in the red whenever private investment was too scanty to provide for the needs of the country. But when depression gave way to recovery, private financing could take the place for most purposes of deficit spending. He favored the accumulation and investment of large amounts of venture capital, which he declared to be the only socially productive form of capital. Finally, Keynes recommended monetary control as a means of promoting prosperity and full employment. He would establish what is commonly called a "managed currency," regulating its value by a process of contraction or expansion in accordance with the needs of the economy. Prosperity would thus be assured in terms of the condition of the home market, and no nation would be tempted to "beggar its neighbor" in the foolish pursuit of a favorable balance of trade.

Trends in art tended to parallel those in literature. For much of the period, visual artists continued to explore aesthetic frontiers far re-

John Maynard Keynes

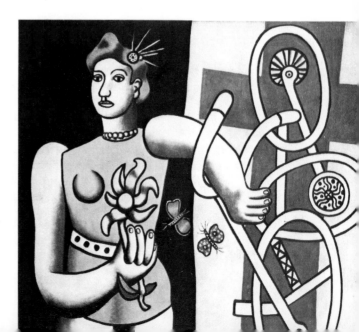

Big Julie by Fernand Léger. Note the artist's fascination with industrial shapes and images.

Mountain, Table, Anchors, Navel
by Jean Arp

Trends in art

See color plates following
page 1088

Art and the depression

moved from the conventional taste of average men and women. Picasso followed his particular genius as it led him further into cubist variations and inventions. So did others, such as the Frenchman Fernand Léger (1881–1955), who combined devotion to cubist principles and a fascination with the artifacts of industrial civilization. A group more advanced, perhaps, than the cubists, the expressionists argued that since color and line express inherent psychological qualities which can be represented without reference to subject matter, a painting need not have a "subject" at all. The Russian Wassily Kandinsky (1866–1944) carried the logic of this position to its conclusion by calling his untitled paintings "improvisations," and insisting that they meant nothing. A second group of expressionists rejected intellectuality for what they called "objectivity," by which they meant a candid appraisal of the state of the human mind. Their analysis took the form of an attack upon the greed and decadence of postwar Europe. Chief among this group was the German George Grosz (1893–1959), whose cruel, satiric line has been likened to a "razor lancing a carbuncle." Another school expressed its disgust with the world by declaring that there was in fact no such thing as aesthetic principle, since aesthetic principle was based on reason and the world had conclusively proved by fighting itself to death that reason did not exist. Calling themselves dada-ists (after a name picked at random, allegedly, from the dictionary) these artists, led by the Frenchman Marcel Duchamp (1887–1968), the German Max Ernst (1891–   ), and the Alsatian Jean Hans Arp (1887–1966), concocted "fabrications" from cut-outs and juxtapositions of wood, glass, and metal, and gave them bizarre names: *The Bride stripped bare by her Bachelors, even* (Duchamp), for example. These works were declared by critics, however, to belie their professed meaninglessness, to be, in fact, expressions of the subconscious. Such certainly were the paintings of the surrealists, artists such as the Italian Giorgio de Chirico (1888–1978) and the Spaniard Salvador Dali (1904–   ), whose explorations of the interior of the mind produced irrational, fantastic, and generally melancholy images.

For a time in the 1930s artists, like writers, responded to the sense of international crisis by painting to express their pain and outrage directly to a mass audience. Among the chief representatives of the new movement were the Mexicans Diego Rivera and Jose Clemente Orozco, and the Americans Thomas Hart Benton, Reginald Marsh, Edward Hopper, and Grant Wood. The fundamental aim of these artists was to depict the social conditions of the modern world and to present in graphic detail the hopes and struggles of peasants and workers. While they scarcely adhered to any of the conventions of the past, there was nothing unintelligible about their work; it was intended to be art that anyone could understand. Much of it bore the sting or thrust of social satire. Orozco, in particular, delighted in pillorying the hypocrisy of the Church and the greed and cruelty of plutocrats and plunderers.

Mural of Kansas City, Missouri by Thomas Hart Benton. The mural protests the corruption of American politics and the depression misery and degradation of farm workers and industrial laborers. The man in the armchair is the political boss of Kansas City in the 1930s, Tom Pendergast.

It was inevitable that music should reflect the spirit of disillusionment that reached a climax following World War I. The more original developments were closely parallel to those in painting. Most fundamental of all was the revolt against the romantic tradition, especially as it had culminated in Wagner. Many, although by no means all, composers went so far as to repudiate the aesthetic ideal entirely, relying upon complexity and novelty of structure or on a sheer display of energy to supply interest to their works.

The chief trends in contemporary music

Deviations from the classical and romantic formulas have been generally of two types, designated broadly as impressionism and expressionism. The former seeks to exploit the qualities of musical sound to suggest feelings or images. The latter is concerned more with form than with sensuous effects and tends toward abstraction. The most perfect exponent of impressionism was Claude Debussy (1862–1918), its originator. Even in France impressionism did not prove to be an enduring school. With Maurice Ravel (1875–1937), most celebrated of the composers who reflected Debussy's influence, it became less poetic and picturesque and acquired a degree of cold impassivity together with greater firmness of texture.

Musical impressionism

Expressionism, more radical and more influential than impressionism, comprises two main schools: atonality, founded by the Viennese Arnold Schoenberg (1874–1951), and polytonality, best typified by the Russian Igor Stravinsky (1882–1971). Atonality abolishes key. In this type of music, dissonances are the rule rather than the excep-

Musical expressionism: atonality

Igor Stravinsky

Development of functional architecture

tion, and the melodic line commonly alternates between chromatic manipulation and strange unsingable leaps. In short, the ordinary principles of composition are reversed. The atonalists attempt, with some success, to let musical sound become a vehicle for expressing the inner meaning and elemental structure of things.

Polytonality, of which Stravinsky is the most famous exponent, is essentially a radical kind of counterpoint, deriving its inspiration partly from baroque practices of counterpoint that were placed in the service of new ideas. However, it does not simply interweave independent melodies which together form concord, but undertakes to combine separate keys and unrelated harmonic systems, with results that are highly discordant. While the atonalists have retained elements of romanticism, the polytonalists have tried to resurrect the architectural qualities of pure form, movement, and rhythm, stripping away all sentimentality and sensuous connotations.

Architects during this period were also intent upon denying sentimentality. Between 1880 and 1890 certain architects in Europe and America awoke to the fact that the prevailing styles of building construction were far out of harmony with the facts of modern civilization. The result was the launching of a new architectural movement known as functionalism. Its chief pioneers were Otto Wagner (1841–1918) in Germany and Louis Sullivan (1856–1924) and Frank Lloyd Wright (1869–1959) in the United States. The basic principle of functionalism is the idea that the appearance of a building shall proclaim its actual use and purpose. There must be no addition of friezes, columns, tracery, or battlements merely because some people consider such ornaments beautiful. True beauty consists in sincerity, in an honest adaptation of materials to the purpose they are intended to serve. Functionalism also includes the idea that architecture shall express either directly or symbolically the distinguishing features of contemporary culture. Ornamentation must therefore be restricted to such elements as will reflect an age of science and machines. Modern men and women do not believe in the Greek ideas of harmony, bal-

Taliesin East by Frank Lloyd Wright. A famous example of the functional style, with the pattern of the house conforming to the natural surroundings.

Contrasting Architectural Styles in Germany Between the Wars. Left: The Bauhaus by Walter Gropius. This school in Dessau, Germany, is a starkly functional prototype of the interwar "international style." Right: The Chancellery in Berlin by Albert Speer. Note the massive qualities of the Nazi state style.

ance, and restraint or in the medieval virtues of piety and chivalry, but in power, efficiency, speed, and comfort. These are the ideals which should find a place in architecture.

The functional style of building construction is one of the most significant architectural developments since the Renaissance. Among all of the styles which have been adopted during the last 300 years, it is the only one that is really original. Known also as modern architecture or the international style, it is the best approach that has yet been made to an efficient use of the tremendous mechanical and scientific resources of the contemporary world. It permits an honest application of new materials—chromium, glass, steel, concrete—and tempts the builder's ingenuity in devising others. One of the pioneer practitioners of the functional or international style was the German Walter Gropius (1883–1969), who, in 1919, established a school—the *Bauhaus*—to serve as a center for the theory and practice of modern architecture. Gropius and his followers declared, as good functionalists, that the aesthetic content of a building can only be expressed legitimately in terms of its purpose.

Gropius was one of the multitude of German intellectuals—both Jewish and non-Jewish—to leave their country after Hitler's rise to

The significance of functional architecture

power. Nazism had its own cultural aesthetic, which it imposed upon Germany. Functionalism, which celebrated the qualities of material, line, and proportion, had no place in a totalitarian regime, where the arts were obliged to advertise the virtues of the state, its tradition, and the aspirations of its people. Instead of Gropius, Hitler had Albert Speer, an architect of unimpressive talents, who produced for him grandiose designs whose vacuous pretentiousness was an unconscious parody of Nazi ideology. Atonality in music was banished along with functionalism in architecture, to be replaced by the mystical and heroic nationalism of Wagner.

Art was an important part of the new and cultural arm of totalitarianism: propaganda. Never before had so many of the world's people been able to read. Nineteenth- and twentieth-century governments had encouraged literacy, fearing an ignorant working class as a revolutionary threat. Now totalitarian regimes used education unashamedly as a means of indoctrination. Books critical of the state were banned, their places on school and library shelves taken by others specifically written to glorify the present leadership. Youth programs instructed children in the virtues of discipline and loyalty to the state. Mass gymnastic displays suggested the ease with which well-trained bodies could be made to respond to the military needs of the nation. Propagandizing was made more effective by the advent of mass-circulation publishing, the radio, and the motion picture. Newspapers which printed only what the state wanted printed reached a wider audience than ever before. Party political broadcasts, beamed into homes or blared through loudspeakers in town squares, by their constant repetitiveness made people begin to accept—if not believe—what they knew to be untrue. Films could transform German youths into Aryan gods and goddesses, as they could Russian collective farms into a worker's paradise. Sergei Eisenstein (1898–1948) the Russian director, rewrote Russian history on film to serve the ends of the Soviet state. Hitler commissioned the filmmaker Leni Riefenstahl to record a political rally staged by herself and Speer. The film, entitled *Triumph of the Will,* was a visual hymn to the Nordic race and the Nazi regime. (And the comedian Charlie Chaplin riposted in his celebrated lampoon, *The Great Dictator,* an enormously successful parody of totalitarian pomposities.)

In Western democracies, although the media were not manipulated by the state as they were elsewhere, their effectiveness as propagandizers was nevertheless recognized and exploited. Advertising became an industry when manufacturers realized the mass markets that newspapers, magazines, and radio represented. Much that was printed and aired was trivialized by writers and editors who feared that serious or difficult material would antagonize the readers or listeners upon whom they depended for their livelihood. This is not to say that the new media were uniformly banal, or that artists and per-

A Scene from John Ford's film of
Steinbeck's *The Grapes of Wrath*

formers were unable to use them to make thoughtful protests. The
film version of Steinbeck's *Grapes of Wrath,* directed by John Ford,
though an exception to the normal run of escapist Hollywood come-
dies and adventures, was perhaps as stinging an indictment of capitalism as the novel, and it reached far more people. During these years
popular culture, whatever else it was, remained a powerful and alarming new fact of life: powerful in terms of its vast audience; alarming
because of its particular applicability as a means of controlling the
minds of men and women.

SELECTED READINGS

• *Items so designated are available in paperback editions.*

GENERAL

Galbraith, John Kenneth, *The Great Crash, 1929,* Boston, 1955. An enter-
taining and informative account by the celebrated economist.
• Hamilton, George Heard, *Painting and Sculpture in Europe, 1880–1940,* Bal-
timore, 1967. An excellent survey.
Hughes, H. Stuart. *Contemporary Europe: A History,* Englewood Cliffs,
N.J., 1971. A good general text.
Laqueur, W., and G. L. Mosse, eds., *The Left-Wing Intellectuals between the
Wars, 1919–1939,* New York, 1966. Recent essays by modern historians.

• Passmore, John A., *A Hundred Years of Philosophy*, New York, 1968.
• Rothschild, Joseph, *East Central Europe between the Two World Wars*, Seattle, 1975. An authoritative survey; does not include Austria.
  Shapiro, Theda, *Painters and Politics: The European Avant-Garde and Society, 1900–1925*, New York, 1976. An analysis of the political and social attitudes of a revolutionary generation in the arts.

THE SOVIET UNION

  Carr, E. H., *A History of Soviet Russia*, Vols. IV–VII, London, 1950 ff. Comprehensive analysis of the period 1923–26.
• Daniels, Robert U., *The Conscience of the Revolution*, Cambridge, Mass., 1960. Discusses the opposition to Bolshevism in the 1920s.
• Deutscher, Isaac, *The Prophet Unarmed*, London, 1959. Trotsky, 1921–1929.
• ———, *The Prophet Outcast*, London, 1963. Trotsky in exile, 1929–1940.
  ———, *Stalin: A Political Biography*, New York, 1949.
  Fainsod, Merle, *How Russia Is Ruled*, Cambridge, Mass., 1967.
  Nettl, J. P., *The Soviet Achievement*, New York, 1967.

FASCISM

• Bracher, Karl Dietrich, *The German Dictatorship: The Origins, Structure, and Effects of National Socialism*, New York, 1970. A penetrating and exhaustive study of the Nazi state by a political scientist.
• Bullock, Alan, *Hitler: A Study in Tyranny*, rev. ed., New York, 1962. The standard biography.
  Conway, John S., *The Nazi Persecution of the Churches*, London, 1968. A thorough and judicious account.
• Dahrendorf, R., *Society and Democracy in Germany*, Garden City, N.Y., 1967.
  Delzell, Charles F., *Mussolini's Enemies: The Italian Anti-Fascist Resistance,* Princeton, N.J., 1961.
• Eyck, Erich, *History of the Weimar Republic*, 2 vols., Cambridge, Mass., 1962. A sympathetic account by a prominent German liberal.
• Gatzke, Hans, *Stresemann and the Rearmament of Germany*, Baltimore, 1954. Details German rearmament in violation of the Treaty of Versailles and secret agreements between Weimar Germany and Soviet Russia in the 1920s.
  Gay, Peter, *Weimar Culture: The Outsider as Insider*, New York, 1968. Examines the failure of commitment to the Weimar Republic by German intellectuals.
  Kirkpatrick, Ivone, *Mussolini: A Study in Power*, New York, 1964. The standard biography.
• Mosse, G. L., ed., *Nazi Culture*, New York, 1966.
• Nolte, Ernst, *The Three Faces of Fascism*, New York, 1966. A difficult but rewarding study of Germany, Italy, and France, from a philosophical perspective.
• Schoenbaum, David, *Hitler's Social Revolution: Class and Status in Nazi Germany, 1933–39*, Garden City, N.Y., 1966.
• Waite, R. G. L., *The Psychopathic God*, New York, 1977. An intriguing if not always successful attempt to explain Hitler's character and actions with the aid of psychoanalytic theory.

• ———, *Vanguard of Nazism: The Free Corps Movement in Postwar Germany, 1918–1923,* New York, 1952. An important monograph which describes the mentality of violence within elements of German society.
• Weiss, John, *The Fascist Tradition: Radical Right-Wing Extremism in Modern Europe,* New York, 1967.
• Wiskemann, Elizabeth, *Fascism in Italy: Its Development and Influence,* New York, 1969.
• Zeman, Z. A. B., *Nazi Propaganda,* New York, 1973. Examines an important bulwark of the authoritarian state.

THE DEMOCRACIES

Bullock, Alan, *The Life and Times of Ernest Bevin: Trade Union Leader, 1881–1940,* London, 1960. An excellent study of the British trade unionist and the political and social history of Britain between the wars.
• Burns, James M., *Roosevelt: The Lion and the Fox,* New York, 1956.
Curtis, Michael, *Three Against the Third Republic: Sorel, Barres, and Maurras,* Princeton, N.J., 1959. The attack from the French Right.
• Graves, Robert, and Alan Hodge, *The Long Week-End: A Social History of Great Britain, 1918–1939,* London, 1940. A striking portrait of England in the interwar years.
• Greene, N., *From Versailles to Vichy: The Third Republic, 1919–1940,* New York, 1970.
Harrod, R. F., *The Life of John Maynard Keynes,* New York, 1951.
Hughes, H. Stuart, *The Obstructed Path: French Social Thought in the Years of Desperation, 1930–1960,* New York, 1968.
Joll, J., *Intellectuals in Politics: Three Biographical Essays,* London, 1960. Léon Blum, Walther Rathenau, and Filippo Marinetti.
• Leuchtenburg, W. E., *Franklin Roosevelt and the New Deal, 1932–1940,* New York, 1964. A good introduction.
Lorwin, V. R., *The French Labor Movement,* Cambridge, Mass., 1954.
Lyman, Richard W., *The First Labour Government,* London, 1957.
• Mitchell, Broadus, *Depression Decade: From New Era through New Deal, 1929 to 1941,* New York, 1947.
Mowat, Charles L., *Britain between the Wars, 1918–1940,* Chicago, 1955. A detailed political and social history, especially valuable for its extensive biographical footnotes.
• Schlesinger, Arthur M., Jr., *The Age of Roosevelt,* 3 vols., Boston, 1957–1964. An extensive biography by an admirer of Roosevelt.
• Taylor, A. J. P., *English History, 1914–1945,* New York, 1965. The best survey of the period. Witty, provocative, insightful.
• Thomson, David, *Democracy in France since 1870,* rev. ed., New York, 1969.
• Weber, Eugen, *Action Française: Royalism and Reaction in Twentieth-Century France,* Stamford, Conn., 1962. The best study of this protofascist movement.

SOURCE MATERIALS

Cole, G. D. H., and M. I. Cole, *The Condition of Britain,* London, 1937. A contemporary analysis by English socialists.

Greene, Nathanael, comp., *European Socialism Since World War I,* Chicago, 1971. A collection of contemporary accounts.

Hitler, Adolf, *Mein Kampf,* New York, 1962. Hitler's autobiography, written in 1925. Contains his version of history and his vision for the future. Especially important for his insight into the nature of the masses and the use of propaganda.

Noakes, Jeremy, and Geoffrey Pridham, *Documents on Nazism, 1919–1945,* New York, 1975. An excellent sourcebook. Comprehensive and annotated.

• Speer, Albert, *Inside the Third Reich,* New York, 1964. The self-serving but informative memoirs of one of the leaders of Nazi Germany.

Tucker, Robert C., ed., *The Great Purge Trial,* New York, 1965. An annotated edition of the transcript of one of the Soviet "show-trials" that so puzzled Western observers.

• Woolf, Virginia, *Three Guineas,* New York, 1938. The brilliant analytical work in which Woolf takes apart both the motivation for war and the oppression of women in modern society.

Chapter 35

WORLD WAR II

The President [Roosevelt] and the Prime Minister [Churchill], after a complete survey of the world situation, are more than ever determined that peace can come to the world only by a total elimination of German and Japanese war power. This involves the simple formula of placing the objective of this war in terms of an unconditional surrender by Germany, Italy, and Japan.

—Franklin D. Roosevelt, Casablanca, January 24, 1943

I n September 1939, Europe plunged again into war. The peace of 1919–1920 turned out to be no more than an armistice; once more millions of people were locked in a conflict that surpassed any that had occurred heretofore. As had happened in 1914–1918, the new struggle soon became worldwide. Although World War II was not merely a continuation of, or a sequel to, World War I, the similarity in causes and characteristics was more than superficial. Both were precipitated by threats to the balance of power, and both were conflicts between peoples, entire nations, rather than between governments. On the other hand, there were notable differences. The methods of warfare in World War II had little in common with those of the earlier conflict. Trench warfare was largely superseded by bombing and by sudden aerial (Blitzkrieg) attacks, with highly mobile armies, on both civilian populations and military installations. Because so many were now vulnerable to the ravages of warfare, it seems safe to say that the distinction between soldiers and civilians was more completely obliterated in the second conflict than it had been in the first.

A comparison of the two world wars

1. THE CAUSES OF THE WAR

The causes of World War II were related to the failure of the peace terms of 1919–1920. Those terms, while understandable in view of the passions and hatreds engendered by the First World War, created almost as many problems as they solved. By yielding to the demands of the victors for annexation of territory and the creation of satellite states, the peacemakers sowed new seeds of bitterness and conflict. By proclaiming the principle of self-determination while acquiescing in the distribution of national minorities behind alien frontiers, the treaties raised expectations while at the same time frustrating them. Perhaps most important, by imposing harsh terms on Germany, the treaty-makers gave the Germans what seemed to many to be legitimate grievances, by depriving them of their rightful share of international power and saddling them with the entire burden of war "guilt."

The role of power politics in causing World War II is undeniable. Although Woodrow Wilson and other sponsors of the League of Nations had acclaimed the league as a means of eliminating power struggles, it did nothing of the sort. It merely substituted a new and more precarious balance for the old. The signatures on the peace treaties had scarcely dried when the victors began the construction of new alliances to maintain their supremacy. A neutralized zone consisting of the Baltic states, Poland, and Rumania was created as a buffer against Soviet Russia. A Little Entente composed of Czechoslovakia, Yugoslavia, and Rumania was established to prevent a revival of Austrian power. These combinations, together with a Franco-Belgian alliance and a Franco-Polish alliance, would also serve to isolate Germany. Thus the old system of power politics was reconstituted along essentially the same lines it had had before World War I. Even the league itself was fundamentally an alliance of the victors against the vanquished. That there would be fears and anxieties over a disturbance of the new power arrangement could hardly be unexpected. The first sign of such a disturbance appeared in 1922 when Germany and Russia negotiated the Treaty of Rapallo. Though disguised as a mere trade agreement, it opened the way for political and, according to some accounts, even military collaboration between the two states.

Diplomats made various attempts to preserve or restore international amity during the 1920s and 1930s. Some saw in disarmament the most promising means of achieving their purpose. Accordingly, a succession of conferences was called in the hope of limiting at least the competition in armaments. The results were negligible. In 1925 representatives of the chief European powers met at Locarno and acted on the suggestion of the German foreign minister, Gustav Stresemann, that Germany and France pledge themselves to respect the Rhine frontiers as established in the Versailles treaty. They agreed also that they would never go to war against each other except in "legitimate defense." More widely celebrated than the Locarno Agreements was the Pact of Paris, or Kellogg-Briand Pact of 1928. Its purpose was to outlaw war as an international crime. Eventually, nearly all the nations of the world signed an agreement renouncing war as "an instrument

Members of the Council of the League of Nations. In the front row, from the right, are Chamberlain of Britain, Vandervelde of Belgium, Stresemann of Germany, and Briand of France

of national policy" and providing that the settlement of international disputes "of whatever nature or of whatever origin" should never be sought "except by peaceful means." Neither the Locarno Agreements nor the Pact of Paris was much more than a pious gesture. The signatory nations adopted them with so many reservations and exceptions in favor of "vital interests" that they could never be effective instruments for preserving peace. Had the League of Nations they set up been better organized, it might have relieved some of the tensions and prevented clashes between nations still unwilling to relinquish their absolute sovereignty. It was not a league of all nations, however. Both Germany and Russia were excluded, at least for a time, thereby pushing them into the role of outsiders.

Economic conditions were a third important cause of the outbreak of war. The huge reparations imposed upon the Germans, and the French occupation of much of Germany's industrial heartland, helped, as we have seen, to retard Germany's economic recovery and bring on the debilitating inflation of the 1920s. The depression of the 1930s contributed to the coming of the war in several ways. It intensified economic nationalism. Baffled by problems of unemployment and business stagnation, governments resorted to high tariffs in an attempt to preserve the home market for their own producers. The depression was also responsible for a marked increase in armaments production, which was seen as a means of reducing unemployment. Despite the misgivings of some within the governments of Britain and France, Germany was allowed to rearm. Armaments expansion, on a large scale, was first undertaken by Germany about 1935. The results in a few years were such as to dazzle the rest of the world. Unemployment disappeared and business boomed. It would have been too much to expect that other dissatisfied nations would not copy the German example. Similarly, the depression resulted in a new wave of militant expansionism directed toward the conquest of neighboring territories as

Economic conditions

The Krupp Shipworks in Germany.
Seen here are German submarines
in the final stages of assembly.

a means of solving economic problems. Japan took the lead in 1931
with the invasion of Manchuria. The decline of Japanese exports of
raw silk and cotton cloth meant that the nation as a consequence was
unable to pay for needed imports of coal, iron, and other minerals.
Japanese militarists were thus furnished with a convenient pretext for
seizing Manchuria, where supplies of these commodities could then be
purchased for Japanese currency. Mussolini, in part to distract the Italians from the domestic problems brought on by economic depression,
invaded and annexed Ethiopia in 1936. Finally, the depression was
primarily responsible for the triumph of Nazism, whose expansionist
policies contributed directly to the outbreak of war.

Nationalism

Nationalism was a further cause of the general discontent that
helped increase the chances for world war. In eastern Europe, national
and ethnic minorities remained alienated from the sovereign states
into which the treaty-makers had placed them. This was particularly
the case of the Sudetenland Germans, who had been included in the
newly created state of Czechoslovakia. That country could in fact
boast no national majority, including as it did Czechs, Slovaks, Poles,
Ruthenians, and Hungarians, as well as Germans. Although it possessed an enlightened policy of minority self-government, the
patchwork state of Czechoslovakia remained unstable. And its instability was to prove a key factor as the tensions mounted in the late
1930s.

Appeasement

A final cause of war was the policy of "appeasement" which was
pursued by the Western democracies in the face of German, Italian,
and Japanese aggression. The appeasers' strategy was grounded in
three commonly held assumptions. The first was that the outbreak of
another war was unthinkable. With the memory of the slaughter of
1918 fresh in their minds, many in the West embraced pacifism, or at
any rate adopted an attitude that kept them from realistically addressing the implications of Nazi and fascist policies and programs. Sec-
ondly, many in Britain and the United States argued, as the years

passed, that Germany had been mistreated in the Versailles treaty, that the Germans had legitimate grievances which should be acknowledged and resolved. Finally, the appeasers were, for the most part, staunch anticommunists. They believed that by assisting Germany to regain its former military and economic power, they were constructing a bulwark to halt the westward advance of Soviet communism. When Japan invaded Manchuria, the West refused to impose sanctions against the Japanese through the League of Nations, arguing that Japan, too, could serve as a counterweight to Russia.

Hitler took advantage of this generally tolerant attitude to advance the expansionist ambitions of Germany. As the country rearmed, Hitler played upon his people's sense of shame and betrayal, proclaiming their right to regain their former power within the world. In 1933, he removed Germany from the League of Nations—and thus from any obligation to adhere to its declarations. In 1935 Hitler tore up the disarmament provisions of the Treaty of Versailles, announcing the revival of conscription and the return to universal military training. In 1936 he repudiated the Locarno Agreements and invaded the Rhineland. Britain and France did nothing to stop him, as they had done nothing to prevent Mussolini's invasion and conquest of Ethiopia the previous year.

Hitler's aggressive moves

In 1936 civil war broke out in Spain; a series of weak republican governments had proved unable to prevent the country's political disintegration. Although they had signed a pact of nonintervention with the other Western powers, Hitler and Mussolini both sent troops and equipment to assist the forces of the rebel fascist commander, Francisco Franco. Russia countered with aid to the communist troops serving under the banner of the Spanish republic. Again, Britain and France did nothing. The Spanish Civil War lasted three years, with the forces of the fascists finally victorious over those of the republicans. The conflict engaged the commitment of many young European and American leftists and intellectuals, who saw it as a test of the West's determination to resist totalitarianism. The fighting was brutal; aerial bombardment of civilians and troops was employed for the first time on a large scale. Hence the Spanish war has often been seen as a "dress rehearsal" for the much larger struggle that was shortly to follow.

The Spanish Civil War

In March of 1938, Hitler annexed Austria, declaring it his intention to bring all Germans into his Reich. Once more, there was no official reaction from the West. Hitler's next target was the Sudetenland in Czechoslovakia. With Austria now a part of Germany, Czechoslovakia was almost entirely surrounded by its hostile and rapacious neighbor. Hitler declared that the Sudetenland was a natural part of the Reich and that he intended to occupy it. The British prime minister, Neville Chamberlain, determined to negotiate, but on Hitler's terms. On September 28, Hitler agreed to meet with Chamberlain, Premier Édouard Daladier of France, and Mussolini in a four-power

Munich and after

The Munich Conference, 1938. Left: Prime Minister Chamberlain of Britain and Hitler during the Munich conference. Right: Chamberlain addressing a crowd on his return from the Munich conference. In his speech, September 30, 1938, he proclaimed that "peace in our time" would result from the agreement.

conference in Munich. The result was another capitulation by France and Britain. During the next few months Hitler not only annexed the Sudetenland (as the Munich agreement had permitted him to do), but he annihilated the entire Czech republic. This action intensified the crisis. The Soviet government was convinced that the Munich settlement was a plot by Britain and France to save their own skins by diverting Nazi expansion eastward. In August 1939, Stalin and his colleagues, having failed to persuade Britain and France to ally with them on their terms, entered into a pact of their own with the Nazi government. Its effect was to give Hitler the green light for an attack on Poland. There was an understanding that the two dictators would divide Poland between them. In going to Munich, Britain and France had thought of their own interests; Russia would now look after its own.

See color map following page 1088

2. THE OUTBREAK OF HOSTILITIES

Beginning of the war

Following the extinction of Czechoslovakia, Hitler demanded the abolition of the Polish Corridor, a narrow strip of territory connecting Poland with the Baltic Sea. The corridor contained a large German population, which Hitler declared must be reunited with the Fatherland. Convinced finally that Hitler's appetite for power was insatiable, Chamberlain announced that Britain would give Poland armed assistance. Soon afterward he declared that his government would come to the aid of any country that felt itself menaced by Hitler's ambitions. In the weeks that followed, both Britain and France gave definite guarantees not only to Poland but to Greece, Rumania, and Turkey. Hitler, judging Britain and France by past performance, believed these pledges were worthless. With the Soviets drawn into his camp, he expected that Poland would quickly capitulate, and that the Western allies would back down once more as they had done at Munich. When Poland stood firm, Hitler decided to attack. On September 1, 1939, a long column of German tanks crossed the Polish border. Upon learning of the attack, Britain and France sent a joint warning to Germany to cease its aggression. To this there was no reply. September 3 brought a radio announcement by Neville Chamberlain that Britain was at war with Germany. He spoke of the "bitter blow" it was to him that his "long struggle for peace" had failed. He asserted that it was evil the British nation would be fighting against—"brute force, bad faith, injustice, oppression, and persecution." Later the same day France also entered the war.

The conflict with Poland proved to be a brief encounter. In less than three weeks the Polish armies had been routed, Warsaw had been captured, and the chiefs of the Polish government had fled to Rumania. For some months after that the war resolved itself into a kind of siege, a "phony war" or "sitzkrieg," as it was sometimes called. Such fighting as did occur was largely confined to submarine warfare, aerial raids on naval bases, and occasional battles between naval vessels. In the spring of 1940 the sitzkrieg was suddenly transformed into a Blitzkrieg, or "lightning war." The Germans struck blows at Norway, Denmark, Belgium, the Netherlands, and France, conquering them one after another. In France a puppet government loyal to the Germans was established at Vichy under the leadership of the aged World War I hero, Marshal Henri-Philippe Petain.

The "phony war"

Following these conquests the war entered a new stage, the so-called Battle of Britain. Before launching an invasion across the Channel, the Nazis decided to attempt the reduction of Britain's military strength and civilian will by air raids. From August 1940 to June 1941

The Battle of Britain

The Beginning of World War II. A long line of German tanks crossing into Poland.

A German V-2 Rocket. Used in the later years of the war, it was the forerunner of the early space launch vehicles.

thousands of planes smashed at British ports, industrial centers, and air defenses throughout the country. Despite the fact that whole sections of cities were laid in ruins and more than 40,000 civilians killed, the British held firm. Winston Churchill had by this time succeeded Neville Chamberlain as prime minister of Britain. A maverick Conservative, who had served in Britain's World War I government as a Liberal, Churchill was not trusted by his party's leadership, particularly since he had been one of the few who had spoken out in favor of British rearmament during the years of appeasement. Now that his warnings had proved true, he was given direction of the war as head of a national government composed of ministers from the Conservative, Liberal, and Labour parties. Churchill, an exceedingly compelling orator, used the radio to persuade his countrymen and women—and the rest of the free world—that Britain must not, and would not, surrender to the Nazis. His friendship with President Roosevelt, and the latter's conviction that the United States must come to Britain's aid, resulted in the shipment of military equipment and ships to the British under the so-called Lend-Lease Act passed by the U.S. Congress in 1941.

Meanwhile, Germany moved eastward into the Balkans, subduing the Rumanians, Hungarians, Bulgarians, and Yugoslavs. The Italians, less successful in their campaigns in Greece and North Africa, required German assistance to accomplish their missions. Scornful of Mussolini's military inadequacies, Churchill called him Hitler's "jackal." Frustrated in his attempt to subjugate Britain, Hitler broke with his erstwhile ally Russia, and turned eastward, on June 22, 1941, with a massive invasion. Before the end of the year his armies had smashed

Left: *London During the Blitz*. This picture conveys a vivid impression of the agony which the British capital suffered during the Battle of Britain, which lasted from August 1940 to June 1941. Behind the tumbling ruins brought down by firebombs is St. Paul's Cathedral. Right: *French Refugees Driven from Their Homes During the Early Years of the Nazi Occupation*.

Pearl Harbor, December 7, 1941. This photo shows American battleships sunk at their moorings, following the Japanese raid on what President Franklin D. Roosevelt declared was "the day that will live in infamy."

their way to the gates of Moscow but never actually succeeded in capturing it.

The war was converted into a global conflict when Japan struck a deadly blow at Pearl Harbor on December 7 of the same year. The Japanese had been involved in a costly war with China since 1937. To wage it successfully they needed the oil, rubber, and extensive food resources of the Netherlands Indies, the Malay Peninsula, and Southeast Asia. They had allied with Germany in 1940. Now, before attacking south, they considered it necessary to lock the back door by crushing American naval and air power on the base of Pearl Harbor. The next day the United States Congress recognized a state of war with Japan, and on December 11 Germany and its allies declared war upon the United States.

Pearl Harbor

The course of the war was marked by several turning points. The first was the stubborn defense of Moscow by Stalin's armies in November and December 1941. The second was the defeat of the Germans under General Erwin Rommel in North Africa in 1942, which opened the way for the Allied invasion of Italy and the overthrow of Mussolini in the following year. The third was the Battle of Stalingrad in 1943, when the Germans failed in their attempt to cut northern Russia off from the food-producing region of the Ukraine and from the oil resources north and south of the Caucasus. The turning points in the Pacific war came during the spring of 1942 with the defeat by the United States Navy of Japanese forces in the battles of the Coral Sea and of Midway. These defeats spelled the doom of Japanese attempts to capture Australia and the Hawaiian Islands and thereby deprive the United States of advance bases for a counteroffensive against Japan.

The war's turning points

By the winter of 1944–1945 World War II was nearing its end. On June 6, 1944 (D-Day), Allied forces had crossed the English Channel and landed successfully in northern France. On August 25 Paris was liberated. In September advance detachments drove to the Rhine, and

Left: *D-Day.* Cargo ships are seen pouring supplies ashore during the invasion of France. Balloon barrages float overhead to protect the ships from low-flying enemy planes. Right: *Signing the German Surrender, May 7, 1945.*

eventually whole armies penetrated to the heart of Germany, an advance necessitated by Hitler's refusal to surrender unconditionally. At the same time, Soviet troops were approaching from the east. On April 21, 1945, they hammered their way into the suburbs of Berlin. During the next ten days a savage battle raged amid the ruins and heaps of rubble. On May 2 the heart of the city was captured, and the Soviet red banner flew from the Brandenburg Gate. A few hours earlier Adolf Hitler killed himself in the bomb-proof shelter of the Chancellery. On May 8 representatives of the German High Command signed a document of unconditional surrender. Peace had come at last to an exhausted Europe after five years and eight months of slaughter.

It was only then that the world began to learn the extent of German tyranny. When Allied armies opened the concentration camps in Germany and elsewhere in what had been German-occupied Europe, they found the starved, diseased, and brutalized remnants of a total of six million prisoners, those who had been able to survive the ghastly experience of Nazi persecutions. Most of the men, women, and children who had been imprisoned, tortured, and killed, were Jews, although Poles, Russians, gypsies, homosexuals, and other "traitors" to the Reich had been incarcerated, used for forced labor, and executed also.

The end of the war in the Pacific was delayed for another four months. Victory over the Japanese Empire had to be achieved by savage naval battles and by bloody assaults upon almost impregnable islands. In June 1945, Okinawa was taken, after eighty-two days of desperate fighting. The Americans now had footholds less than 500 miles from the Japanese homeland. The government in Tokyo was nervously anticipating an invasion and calling upon the citizens for supreme endeavors to meet the crisis. On July 26 the heads of the United States, British, and Chinese governments issued a joint proclamation calling upon Japan to surrender or be destroyed. In the absence of a reply the highest officials of the United States government resolved to make use of a new and revolutionary weapon to end the war quickly. This weapon was the atomic bomb, recently developed in secrecy by Allied scientists. Many high military and naval officers contended that use of the bomb was not necessary, on the assumption that Japan was already beaten. Harry Truman, who had succeeded Roosevelt following the latter's death in April 1945, decided otherwise. On August 6, a single atomic bomb was dropped on Hiroshima, completely obliterating about 60 percent of the city. Three days later a second bomb was dropped, this time on Nagasaki. These actions, like the fire-bombing of Dresden and Tokyo, insured that the Allies would share the responsibility for the carnage of the war, and that, unlike the First World War, this one would take a heavy toll of civilian lives. President Truman warned that the United States would continue to use the atom bomb as long as might be necessary to bring Japan to its knees. On August 14, Tokyo transmitted to Washington an unconditional acceptance of Allied demands.

3. THE PEACE SETTLEMENT

The war was over. To fight it, governments had been compelled, to an even greater degree than during the First World War, to mobilize their entire populations. Both sides used mass propaganda techniques to maintain popular commitment to their cause. As Wilson had spoken of a war "to end wars," so the Western leaders promised a peace that would rid the world of conflict. The first statement of Allied objectives in the event of victory was the Atlantic Charter,

The Atlantic Charter and the United Nations declaration

Victims of the Nazi Concentration Camp at Belsen, Germany. Photographed in 1945.

View of Hiroshima After the First Atom Bomb Was Dropped, August 6, 1945. This photo, taken one month later, shows the utter devastation of the city. Only a few steel and concrete buildings remained intact.

issued by Roosevelt and Churchill on August 14, 1941. Its essential principles were as follows: (1) no territorial changes that do not accord with the wishes of the people concerned; (2) the right of all peoples to choose the form of government under which they will live; (3) all states to enjoy access, on equal terms, to the trade and raw materials of the world; (4) freedom to traverse the seas without hindrance; (5) disarmament of all nations that threaten aggression. The Atlantic Charter acquired a broad significance when it was reaffirmed by the United Nations declaration on January 2, 1942. Twenty-six nations signed this declaration, including Great Britain, the United States, the Soviet Union, and the Republic of China. Subsequently about fourteen others added their signatures. The declaration resembled Wilson's Fourteen Points: both were ringing affirmations of international peace and freedom; both were designed to bolster Allied morale; and both fell victim to the realities of power politics.

As the war progressed, high officials of the leading United Nations met in various conferences for the purpose of determining the conditions of peace. The first of outstanding importance was the conference that met in Cairo in November 1943, to discuss the fate of the Japanese Empire. The participants were Roosevelt, Churchill, and the Chinese leader, Generalissimo Chiang Kai-Shek. They agreed that all of the territories taken by Japan from China, with the exception of Korea, were to be restored to the Chinese Republic. Korea was to become free and independent. They agreed, further, that Japan was to be stripped of all the islands in the Pacific which it had seized or occupied since 1914 and of "all other territories which she had taken by violence

The Cairo Declaration

or greed." What disposition was to be made of these islands and territories was not specified.

The second important conference to determine the conditions of peace met at Yalta, in the Crimea, in February 1945. This time the chief participants were Roosevelt, Churchill, and Stalin. A formal report issued at the close of the conference declared that the Big Three had agreed upon plans for the unconditional surrender of Germany, upon methods of controlling Germany and its allies after the war, and upon the establishment of a United Nations Organization to keep the peace. In addition, it was announced that Poland would surrender its eastern provinces to Russia and be compensated by "substantial accessions of territory" in the north and west—to be taken, of course, from Germany. The existing government of Poland, set up under Soviet auspices, was to be reorganized with the inclusion of democratic leaders from among the Poles. The government of Yugoslavia was also to be broadened in similar fashion. Regarding the Far East, it was agreed that Russia should enter the war against Japan and receive as its reward all the territories taken from it by Japan in the Russo-Japanese war of 1904–1905.

The Yalta agreement reflected the idealism of the Atlantic Charter in its provision for a United Nations. It also foreshadowed the tension between East and West which in a few years, would take the shape of a "cold war" between Russia and its political satellites, on the one side, and the Western powers, on the other. Stalin, a determined power politician, was anxious to protect Russian interests. Hence his insistence on a Polish settlement that would insure a strong, pro-Soviet bulwark against Germany. Although Stalin promised free elections there, he refused to agree to an international commission to supervise them.

The surrender of Germany required yet another conference of the victorious powers. On July 17, 1945, Stalin, Churchill, and Truman, met in Potsdam, a suburb of Berlin. Before the Potsdam Conference had finished its work, Churchill had been replaced by Clement Attlee,

The Yalta agreement

The implications of the Yalta agreement

The Yalta Conference. Churchill, Molotov, Secretary of State Stettinius, at the left, and Stalin, in the center, with glasses raised in a toast. Roosevelt is also to Stalin's left.

The Potsdam Conference.
Churchill, a cigar in his
mouth, is seated in the
back to the left; Stalin is
at the right; Truman is
seated with his back to
the camera.

The Potsdam agreement

the new Labour prime minister of Great Britain. The most important provisions of the formal declaration, issued on August 2, were as follows: (1) the territory formerly known as East Prussia was to be divided into two parts, the northern part to go to the Soviet Union, and the southern part to be assigned to Poland; (2) Poland was to receive the former free city of Danzig; (3) all German territory east of the Oder and Neisse rivers would be administered by Poland, pending a final settlement; (4) the military power of Germany would be totally destroyed; and (5) Germany would be divided into four occupation zones, to be governed, respectively, by the Soviet Union, Great Britain, the United States, and France. In November 1945, a trial of major Nazi leaders, conducted by an inter-Allied tribunal, began in Nuremberg, Germany. In September of the following year, eighteen of the twenty-two defendants were found guilty of "war crimes," receiving sentences ranging from ten-years' imprisonment to death.

The peace treaties

After the end of the war the victorious states drafted peace treaties with Japan and with Germany's satellites. The treaty with Japan deprived the Japanese of all the territory they had acquired since 1854—in other words, their entire overseas empire. They gave up the southern half of Sakhalin Island and the Kuril Islands to Soviet Russia, and the Bonins and Ryukyus to control by the United States. They also renounced all rights to Formosa, which was left in a status still undefined. They yielded to the United States the right to continue maintaining military installations in Japan until the latter was able to defend itself. The treaty went into effect in April 1952, against the opposition of the Russians, who had hoped that Japan would be crippled by more drastic punishments and thereby left an easy convert to communism.

As in the case of the Versailles treaty one of the most significant elements in the World War II settlement was its provision for an international organization. The old League of Nations had failed to avert the outbreak of war in 1939, and in April 1946 it was formally dissolved. Allied statesmen had long recognized the need for a new organization. In February 1945, they agreed at Yalta that a conference to implement that need should be convoked for April 25 in San Francisco. Despite the sudden death of Roosevelt two weeks earlier, the conference met as scheduled. A charter was adopted on June 26, providing for a world organization to be known as the United Nations and to be founded upon the principle of "the sovereign equality of all peace-loving states." Its important agencies were to be (1) a General Assembly composed of representatives of all the member states; (2) a Security Council composed of representatives of the United States, Great Britain, the Soviet Union, the Republic of China, and France, with permanent seats, and of six other states chosen by the General Assembly to fill the nonpermanent seats; (3) a Secretariat consisting of a secretary-general and a staff of subordinates; (4) an Economic and Social Council composed ot eighteen members chosen by the General Assembly; (5) a Trusteeship Council; and (6) an International Court of Justice.

Establishment of the United Nations

Although the United Nations has failed to live up to the hopes of its founders, it continues to function as the world's longest-lived international assembly of nations. By far the most important functions of the new organization were assigned by the charter to the Security Council. This agency has the "primary responsibility for the maintenance of international peace and security." It has authority to investigate any dispute between nations, to recommend methods for settlement, and, if necessary to preserve the peace, to employ diplomatic or economic measures against an aggressor. If, in its judgment, these have proved, or are likely to prove, inadequate, it may "take such action by air, naval, or land forces" as may be required to maintain or restore international order. The member states are required by the charter to make available to the Security Council, on its call, armed forces for the maintenance of peace.

The Security Council

The Security Council was so organized as to give almost a monopoly of authority to its permanent members. It was the belief of the Big Three who assembled at Yalta, and of President Roosevelt especially, that the peace of the world depended upon harmony among the states primarily responsible for winning the war. Accordingly, they agreed that when the Security Council should be set up, no action of any kind could be taken without the unanimous consent of Great Britain, France, the United States, the Republic of China, the Soviet Union, and two other members besides. This absolute veto given to each of

The veto power of the Big Five

the principal states had none of the hoped-for effects. Instead of bolstering the peace of the world, its chief result was to cripple the council and to render it helpless in the face of emergencies. The primary cause of this was the growth of distrust between Soviet Russia and the West.

Other agencies of the U.N.

The remaining agencies of the U.N. were given a wide variety of functions. The Secretariat, composed of a secretary-general and a numerous staff, is chiefly an administrative authority. Its duties, though, are by no means routine, for the secretary-general may bring to the attention of the Security Council any matter which, in his opinion, may threaten international peace. The functions of the Economic and Social Council are the most varied of all. Composed of eighteen members elected by the General Assembly, it has authority to initiate studies and make recommendations with respect to international social, economic, health, educational, cultural, and related matters, and may perform services within such fields at the request of U.N. members. Under its jurisdiction are such specialized agencies as the World Health Organization (WHO), which works to control epidemics and to assist underdeveloped nations in stamping out cholera, typhus, and veneral disease, and in raising standards of health and sanitation; and the Food and Agriculture Organization (FAO), which seeks to promote increases in food production by finding remedies for agricultural depressions, for plant and animal diseases and insect pests, and by projecting plans for mechanizing small farms and for the more efficient distribution of food.

Failures of the U.N.

During the first three decades the work of these agencies helped the U.N. achieve a modestly impressive record of accomplishment. But against its successes must be recorded major failures as well. The U.N. failed in its efforts to establish control of nuclear weapons. And it was powerless in the face of any determined effort by a major power to have its own way, as in the case of the Soviet suppression of a revolt in Hungary in 1956; or the massive intervention by the United States in Vietnam. If the United Nations acted upon occasion to defuse potentially explosive world situations, it failed to achieve the lofty peacemaking and peace-keeping goals set for it by its ambitious and idealistic founders.

SELECTED READINGS

• *Items so designated are available in paperback editions.*
Aron, Raymond, *The Century of Total War,* New York, 1954.
Carr, E. H., *The Twenty-Years Crisis,* London, 1942. Stimulating, though somewhat dogmatic.
• Carr, Raymond, *The Spanish Tragedy: The Civil War in Perspective,* London, 1977. A thoughtful introduction to the Spanish Civil War and the evolution of Franco's Spain.

- Churchill, Winston S., *The Second World War*, 6 vols., London, 1948–1954. His history and apologia. Particularly useful is Volume I, *The Gathering Storm*.
- Divine, Robert A., *Roosevelt and World War II*, Baltimore, 1969. A diplomatic history.
- Feis, Herbert, *Churchill-Roosevelt-Stalin: The War They Waged and the Peace They Sought*, Princeton, N.J., 1957.

  Géraud, André, *The Gravediggers of France*, Garden City, N.Y., 1944. A critical and impassioned account of the fall of France.

  Gilbert, Martin, and R. Gott, *The Appeasers*, Boston, 1963.
- Hersey, John, *Hiroshima*, New York, 1946.

  Hilberg, Raul, *The Destruction of the European Jews*, Chicago, 1961. Exhaustive.

  Holborn, Hajo, *The Political Collapse of Europe*, New York, 1951. Examines Europe's position in light of the rise of Russia and the United States as superpowers.
- Jackson, Gabriel, *The Spanish Republic and the Civil War, 1931–1939*, Princeton, N.J., 1965.
- Lafore, Laurence D., *The End of Glory: An Interpretation of the Origins of World War II*, New York, 1970.

  Milward, Alan S., *War, Economy, and Society, 1939–1945*, Berkeley, Calif., 1977. Analyzes the impact of the war on the world economy and the ways in which economic resources of the belligerents determined strategies.

  Neumann, W. L., *After Victory: Churchill, Roosevelt, Stalin, and the Making of the Peace*, New York, 1967.
- Paxton, Robert D., *Vichy France: Old Guard and New Order*, New York, 1972. A bitter account.
- Payne, Stanley, *The Spanish Revolution*, New York, 1970.
- Reitlinger, G., *The Final Solution: The Attempt to Exterminate the Jews of Europe, 1939–1945*, New York, 1968.

  Snell, J. L., *Illusion and Necessity: The Diplomacy of Global War, 1939–1945*, Boston, 1963.
- Taylor, A. J. P., *The Origins of the Second World War*, New York, 1962. A controversial but provocative attempt to prove that Hitler did not want a world war.
- Wright, Gordon, *The Ordeal of Total War, 1939–1945*, New York, 1968. Particularly good on the domestic response to war and the mobilization of the resources of the modern state.

SOURCE MATERIALS

- Bloch, Marc, *Strange Defeat: A Statement of Evidence Written in 1940*, London, 1949. An analysis of the fall of France, written by one of France's greatest historians, who later died fighting for the resistance.
- Churchill, Winston, *Churchill in His Own Words: Years of Greatness; The Memorable Wartime Speeches of the Man of the Century*, New York, 1966.
- De Gaulle, Charles, *The Complete War Memoirs*, New York, 1964.

  Noakes, Jeremy, and Geoffrey Pridham, *Documents on Nazism, 1919–1945*, New York, 1975.

Part Seven

THE EMERGENCE OF
WORLD CIVILIZATION

*Western civilization, as we have described and analyzed it, no longer
exists today. Instead, we speak in terms of a world civilization, one that
owes much of its history and many of its most perplexing problems to the
West, but one which is no longer shaped by those few nations that for so
many centuries dominated the globe.*

*The great powers of the nineteenth century—Britain, France, and Ger-
many—are powers now only insofar as they have agreed to pool their interests in an all-European Common Market. The mid–twentieth century
superpowers, the United States and the Soviet Union, after two decades of
confrontation, have begun to understand the limitations of their power and
to adjust their expectations accordingly. Power, and with it the attention of
the world, is shifting from the West to the emerging nations of Africa, the
Middle East, Asia, and Latin America. Their vast natural resources are
affording many of them the chance to play the old Western game of power politics, and in a world arena wider than ever before. The equally vast dimensions
of their internal problems—economic, racial, nutritional, and political—suggest that their solution will have to be worldwide as well. We are all,
as the American designer Buckminster Fuller has said, partners for better or
worse on "spaceship earth."*

The Emergence of World Civilization

THE AMERICAS	INDIA AND THE MIDDLE EAST

1800

Latin American wars of independence, 1808–1826
Independence of Argentina, 1816
Independence of Brazil, 1822
Independence of Mexico, 1822
U.S. Monroe Doctrine, 1823

1850

Great Indian Mutiny, 1857–1858

Empire of Maximilian, 1862–1867
Dominion of Canada established, 1867

Mahatma Gandhi, 1869–1948

Organization of Indian National Congress, 1885
Republic of Brazil, 1889
Jawaharlal Nehru, 1889–1964

1900

Organization of Australian Commonwealth, 1901

Madero Revolution in Mexico, 1911

New Constitution in Mexico, 1917

Amritsar Massacre (India), 1919
Intensification of Indian nationalism, 1919–1947
Republic of Turkey proclaimed, 1923
Mustafa Kemal Atatürk, president of Turkey, 1922–1938

Perón regime in Argentina, 1946–1955

Independence of India and Pakistan, 1947
State of Israel proclaimed, 1948

Egypt becomes a republic, 1952–1953
Suez crisis, 1956

1950

Establishment of Castro regime in Cuba, 1959
Military dictatorship in Brazil, 1964–

Second Turkish Republic, 1961

Indira Gandhi prime minister of India, 1966–1977; 1980–
Six-Day War, 1967

Separatist movement in Quebec, 1967–

Military dictatorship in Chile, 1973–

ASEAN, 1967
India-Pakistan war, 1971
Republic of Bangladesh, 1972
"Yom Kippur War," 1973

Panama Canal treaties, 1977
Revolutions in Nicaragua and El Salvador, 1979

Egyptian-Israeli peace treaty, 1979
Revolution in Iran, deposing the Shah, 1979
Soviet military intervention in Afghanistan, 1979–

1980

THE FAR EAST	AFRICA	
	Expansion of East African trade, 1800–1875 Sierra Leone founded, 1808 Liberia founded, 1821	**1800**
	British consulates in coastal states, 1830–1860 Exploration of interior of continent, 1830–1875	
Anglo-Chinese War (Opium War), 1839–1842	Decline of slave trade, 1840–1863	
		1850
Taiping Rebellion, 1852–1864 Opening of Japan, 1854 Sun Yat-sen, 1866–1925 Meiji Restoration in Japan, 1867–1868	Opening of Suez Canal, 1869	
	Destruction of Zulu empire, 1879	
Adoption of constitution in Japan, 1889 Sino-Japanese War, 1894–1895 Boxer Uprising, 1900 Russo-Japanese War, 1904–1905	Boer War, 1899–1902	**1900**
Revolution in China, 1911 Dictatorship of Yüan Shih-k'ai, 1914–1916 Era of warlords in China, 1916–1928	Union of South Africa, 1909	
Nationalist regime in China, 1928–1949 Triumph of militarists in Japan, 1936 War in Far East, 1937–1945		
Vietnam War, French phase, 1947–1954 Communist regime in China, 1949– Independence of Indonesia, 1949 Korean War, 1950–1953	Apartheid policy in South Africa, 1948– Independence of Libya, 1949	**1950**
Bandung Conference, 1955	Mau Mau revolts in Kenya, 1952–1958 Algerian war of independence, 1954–1962 Conflict in the Congo, 1960 Organization of African Unity, 1963–	
Vietnam War, American phase, 1963–1973		
Great Proletarian Cultural Revolution in China, 1966–1969	Civil war in Nigeria, 1967–1970	
	Guerrilla war in Rhodesia, 1972–1980	
Vietnam-Cambodia war, 1978–1979 Chinese invasion of Vietnam, 1979		
	Rhodesia becomes independent state of Zimbabwe, 1980	**1980**

POLITICS	SCIENCE & INDUSTRY

1945

Truman Doctrine, 1947
Communist regimes established in eastern Europe,
   1947–1948
Marshall Plan, 1948
Division of Germany, 1949
NATO, 1949
Korean war, 1950–1953

                                Hydrogen bomb, 1952

Death of Stalin, 1953   Discovery of polio vaccine, 1953
                                  Discovery of DNA, 1953
Hungarian revolt, 1956
Suez crisis, 1956

                                  Sputnik launched, 1957

1960

Berlin wall, 1961

Cuban missile crisis, 1962
Assassination of John F. Kennedy, 1963
War in Vietnam, 1964–1975 (U.S. phase)
Assassination of Malcolm X, 1965

Assassination of Martin Luther King, Jr., 1968

                                  Manned U.S. spacecraft lands on moon, 1969

1970   Advent of automation, 1970s

First SALT agreements signed, 1972

ECONOMICS & SOCIETY	ARTS & LETTERS	
	Abstract expressionism in art, mid-1940s Albert Camus, *The Plague,* 1947	**1945**
	Simone de Beauvoir, *The Second Sex,* 1949–1950	
	Samuel Beckett, *Waiting for Godot,* 1952	
European Common Market established, 1958 Black civil rights movement, United States, 1960–1968 Frantz Fanon, *Wretched of the Earth,* 1961 Youth "revolution," 1960s Women's liberation movement, 1960s–1970s	Lorraine Hansberry, *A Raisin in the Sun,* 1959 "Pop" art, 1960s	**1960**
		1970
	Arthur Penn, *Bonnie and Clyde,* 1972 Alexsandr Solzhenitsyn, *The Gulag Archipelago,* 1973	

Chapter 36

THE EMERGENCE OF LATIN AMERICA

What is the oligarchy? It consists of the great landowners—the *"latifun-distas"*—their political and military henchmen, and their financial allies (the bankers and the capitalists, in the old sense of the word). . . . The oligarchs form a true caste, with aristocratic impulses, racist attitudes, and a profound contempt for their own countries.

—Victor Alba, *Alliance without Allies: The Mythology of Progress in Latin America*

The Hemisphere is coming apart. The Monroe Doctrine is dead, and the era of American paternalism is ended.

—O. Edmund Clubb

I. CONQUISTADORES AND COLONISTS OF LATIN AMERICA

By far the oldest civilization in the Western Hemisphere is that of Latin America. Here the first settlements were made by the Spanish and Portuguese explorers and conquerors who followed in the path of Columbus. But centuries before any white men set foot on American soil, Indians in Guatemala, Mexico, and the Andean Highland had developed superior cultures which bore almost all the characteristics of civilizations. Had they not been conquered, they might well have provided the basis for a native cultural growth in Central and South America equal to that of any of the other continents. The reasons for this superiority appear to lie almost exclusively in geographic conditions favorable to the progress of agriculture. The lush fertility and benign climate of the valleys of Central America and the northwest portion of South America made possible the production of surplus food. As a result, population increased rapidly, a diversification of trade and industry occurred, cities and towns multiplied, and

Native civilizations of Latin America

The Public Entry of Cortés into the Aztec Capital. Hernando Cortés arrived in Mexico in 1519 and within four years had overrun the entire area of high culture in central Mexico.

a priestly class came into existence devoted to the cultivation of sacred lore. Such developments facilitated the growth of science and other branches of learning and the invention of new crafts and skills. By contrast, the Indians of the greater part of the United States and Canada were forced to continue their existence as nomads and hunters. Their homelands were either so densely forested or so arid as to make agriculture discouraging and profitless.

Civilized Indians in Latin America: (1) the Aztecs

The principal discoverers of Latin America—Christopher Columbus, Amerigo Vespucci, Juan de Solis, and Vasco de Balboa—were quickly followed by a horde of conquerors. Best known among them were Hernando Cortés and Francisco Pizarro. Restless, greedy, and zealous for adventure, they endured incredible hardships, dragging their men through jungles and swamps and over snow-capped mountains in quest of plunder. The former won fame of a sort as the subjugator of Mexico and the latter as the conqueror of Peru. At the time they made their conquests both countries were occupied by various peoples in advanced stages of cultural development. Mexico was inhabited by the Aztecs and Mayas, while Peru was the home of the Incas. The Aztecs were relative newcomers on the scene of civilization. They established themselves in central Mexico about the thirteenth century A.D. and founded their capital, Tenochtitlán (Mexico City), a short time later. Their achievements included a system of pictographic writing, some knowledge of astronomy and engineering, an elaborate architecture, and the building of roads and aqueducts. Their capital city had a population of some 200,000. Its streets were paved with stone and were kept scrupulously clean by an efficient public-works department. The ruler of the country was a hereditary monarch whose powers were limited to those of commander of the army and chief justice. Aztec religion can only be described as a maze of superstitions and cruel practices. Its distinguishing feature was the sacrifice of war captives and, on occasions, of Aztecs themselves on the altars of the gods. Pouring out the blood of human beings was believed to be especially effective in winning the divine favor.

Representing higher stages of cultural achievement were the Mayas and Incas. The former originated in Guatemala and Honduras and reached the climax of their progress in the eighth and ninth centuries A.D. About 1000 A.D. most of them migrated to Yucatán and were concentrated there when conquered by the Spaniards. Mayan culture seems to have been developed primarily by a leisure class of nobles and priests. It revealed a high level of progress in many fields. A system of writing, in which some of the symbols apparently had phonetic value, was extensively used for religious purposes. Writing materials included stone, deer skin, and a kind of paper made from the maguey plant. A calendar, with a year of 365 days, enabled the priests to determine lucky and unlucky days and the appropriate periods for planting and harvesting crops. Mathematical calculations were refined to the extent of having a vigesimal system (with twenty instead of ten as the basic unit) and a conception of zero as a device for giving different values to the same number. Notable also was progress in the arts. The Mayas excelled in making gold and silver ornaments and in the erection of truncated pyramids with temples on top. Tastes in personal adornment included the curious practice of filing and chipping teeth to give them sharp points and sometimes inlaying them with precious stones. Beards were removed by a scorching process instead of by shaving. Religion was no more highly developed than that of the Aztecs and included the same barbarities of human sacrifice.

Of more recent origin than the culture of the Mayas was that of the Incas, who were at the zenith of their progress when conquered by the Spaniards. Extending into Ecuador, Bolivia, northern Chile, and

(2) the Mayas

Detail of an Aztec Pyramid in Central Mexico. The serpent was an object of worship for the Aztecs.

Machu Picchu. The "Lost City of the Incas" is located in the Andes Mountains, Peru.

(3) the Incas

northwestern Argentina, the Inca empire had its center in southeastern Peru. It was organized on the basis of collectivist paternalism. All the land belonged to the emperor, to the priests, or to the tribe, and was cultivated by males of the common classes between the ages of twenty-five and fifty. In good years the surplus production was stored by the emperor to provide for his subjects in time of famine. From the produce on its lands the tribe took care of the young and the aged, the disabled and the sick. It was a paradise of security but with little freedom. In intellectual achievements the Incas did not equal the Mayas. They had no system of writing but used knotted strings of many colors to record numbers and sets of facts. On the other hand, they had an extensive knowledge of medicine and surgery and built excellent roads and suspension bridges. They understood also the principles of fertilization and irrigation and knew how to terrace hillsides to prevent erosion.

Division of Latin America between Spain and Portugal

During the sixteenth and seventeenth centuries the entire area of Mexico and Central and South America passed under the domination of Spain and Portugal. Three-fifths of it was taken by Spain, and the remainder probably would have been also, had not the pope intervened in an attempt to give an equal recognition to the claims of both countries. In 1493 he issued a Bull of Demarcation, drawing a line from north to south 100 leagues west of the Azores. All territory that might be discovered east of the line was to belong to Portugal, and everything west of the line to Spain. In 1494 the two countries signed a treaty relocating the line 370 leagues west of the Cape Verde Islands. Portugal thereby acquired a foothold on the eastern bulge of South America, which was later expanded into Brazil.

The methods of colonization and colonial administration followed by both Spain and Portugal were of such a character as to influence profoundly the entire history of Latin America. This was particularly true of Spain, which also set the pattern for her neighboring state since both were united under a common sovereign between 1580 and 1640. The cardinal elements in Spanish colonial policy were despotism and paternalism. The highest authorities in the empire were the viceroys, who ruled as the personal representatives of the Spanish king. At first there were two, one in New Spain, including Mexico and Central America, and the other in Peru. In the eighteenth century two additional viceroyalties were created: New Granada (Panama, Colombia, Venezuela, Ecuador) and La Plata, or Buenos Aires. The viceroys were paid magnificent salaries, amounting at one time to the equivalent of $200,000 a year. The purpose behind such generosity was to prevent corruption, an objective by no means universally attained. At the same time their royal master took precautions to prevent the viceroys from becoming too powerful. The authority they exercised was to be that of the Spanish crown, not their own. For this reason they had to tolerate the existence of an advisory council, or *audiencia,* which also served as a court of appeal against their decisions. Members of the *audiencia* had the right to communicate with the king regarding the acts of the viceroy without the latter's knowledge. At the end of his term, and occasionally during it, the viceroy must submit to a searching inquiry or investigation in which a royal judge heard the complaints of all and sundry as to official misconduct.

Spanish colonial policy

As an adjunct to despotic rule in the colonies, the Spanish kings made use of the Church. The priests gave valuable help in teaching the population to obey the king and his agents and in opposing new ideas and expressions of discontent. In almost any emergency the hierarchy could be counted upon to give loyal support to the govern-

The Church as an arm of the government

Portuguese Chart of the South Atlantic. Miller Atlas, 1519.

ment. By the middle of the sixteenth century the Inquisition had been extended to Latin America as an instrument for maintaining absolute rule. Headquarters were established in Mexico City and Lima from which inquisitors were sent out to all parts of the continent to discover and punish unorthodox belief. Public executions were occasionally staged in the principal cities to provide object lessons of the fearful punishment in store for any who might waver in the faith. To such exhibitions the public was regularly invited in the hope that the deterrent effect would be complete. That the penalties of the Inquisition were sometimes invoked for political and personal reasons goes almost without saying.

Paternalism and mercantilism

The keynote of economic administration in the colonies was paternalism. Actually, nothing else could have been expected, since, according to the theory, the land of the Americas was the personal possession of the king. It was his private estate which he could dispose of as he saw fit. But economic administration in the Spanish colonies was also shaped to a large extent by the theory of mercantilism, which was beginning to dominate the thinking of all Western nations. Mercantilism demanded that colonies should exist for the benefit of the mother country; they should bring bullion into her treasury and contribute in every way possible toward making her rich and powerful. It followed that the government of the mother country had the right to regulate and control the economic activities of the colonies in her

Brazilian Colonial Church in the Portuguese Baroque Style. Baroque workmanship in colonial Latin America is thought by some authorities to be finer than that in Spain and Portugal.

Silver Mining at Potosi. By an unknown artist, about 1584. The discovery of silver at Potosi in the Bolivian highlands in 1545 marked the beginning of a greatly accelerated flow of bullion from the New World to Spain.

own interest—to dictate what they should produce and from whom they should buy and to whom they should sell. In substance this meant a monopoly of colonial trade for the merchants of the mother country and a strict prohibition of manufactures.

The economic policies described had unfortunate effects upon both the Spanish colonies and the homeland. The resources of the former were poorly developed, and some lay unused or undiscovered for centuries. With attention focused upon gold and silver and with manufacturing prohibited, there was little incentive to exploit the deposits of copper, manganese, and other minerals which might well have supported a considerable industry. Some branches of agriculture were also discouraged in order that the colonies might produce vast quantities of sugar, cotton, and tobacco which would help the mother country in maintaining a favorable balance of trade, since these products would not have to be purchased for gold outside the empire. The whole system of restrictive policies was stupid and vicious and retarded the development not only of the colonies but of the country that owned them. As late as the end of the sixteenth century Spain was an economically backward nation, with a large portion of her

Effects of economic policies

wealth concentrated in cattle and sheep, with no powerful commercial or industrial class, and with manual labor frowned upon as unworthy of a good Spaniard.

Early in the eighteenth century the Hapsburg dynasty in Spain was supplanted by Bourbon rulers. Recognizing the corruptions and inefficiency of the system of colonial administration, the Bourbon kings initiated reforms. They were no more interested in the welfare of the colonies than their predecessors had been, but they did perceive the danger that a disgruntled colonial population might become a prey to foreign conquest. They hoped, moreover, to increase the flow of revenue into the royal treasury. With these ends in view they modified trade restrictions, encouraged industry and a more varied agriculture, and even granted commercial concessions to foreigners. The most noted of these was the *asiento* of 1701, which conferred upon France the privilege of supplying the Spanish colonies with Negro slaves. In 1713, at the end of the War of the Spanish Succession, it was transferred to Britain. By the close of the eighteenth century the Spanish-American trade as a whole was the richest in the world, and had more than tripled in fifty years.

2. REVOLUTIONS FOR INDEPENDENCE

Between 1808 and 1826 Latin America was engulfed by a tidal wave of revolutions. The underlying causes did not differ greatly from the factors which had produced the North American Revolution of 1775. Pre-eminent among them was dissatisfaction with the mercantilist policies of the home government. Despite the reforms of the Bourbons, many relics of oppression and discrimination survived. A rigid censorship was imposed. Books of European and North American radicals could be obtained only by smuggling. As late as 1773 a Colombian scientist was condemned for giving lectures on the Copernican system. Taxes were numerous and excessive, and monopoly and favoritism flourished. Prosperous Creoles, or colonial whites, resented their exclusion from the highest and most lucrative positions in the government and the Church, which were reserved for Spanish-born aristocrats. The former were not starving, any more than were the members of the bourgeoisie in France on the eve of that country's revolution. What rankled in their breasts was being deprived of privileges that they believed should rightly belong to them on the basis of their wealth and intelligence.

It is possible that the discontent of Spain's colonies would never have reached revolutionary proportions had it not been for the examples already set by the revolutions in France and in North America. The colonists' grievances had abated rather than increased and probably would have lessened still further. But revolutions are contagious.

An outbreak in one country is almost certain to spread to other countries where similar conditions exist even if in much smaller degree. This is especially true when a philosophy of discontent is propagated on an international scale. During the latter half of the eighteenth century hundreds of Creoles had adopted revolutionary doctrines from the writings of Voltaire, Rousseau, Jefferson, and Paine. Some had been educated or had traveled in Europe or in the United States. The discovery that intellectual leaders in other countries were boldly attacking despotic government and superstitious religion made a profound impression and led Spanish colonials to ask themselves why such things should be tolerated in their own lands.

Influence of the French and North American revolutions

Just as in North America a period of indifference and "salutary neglect" by the British government fostered a spirit of independence in the colonies, so in Latin America a similar period weakened the ties between Spain and her possessions. Between 1803 and 1808 Spain as a satellite of France took part in the wars of Napoleon to make himself master of Europe. In 1805 the British defeated Napoleon's fleet at Trafalgar and virtually destroyed the sea power of France and her allies. Spain, in particular, experienced great difficulty in maintaining communications with her empire. As a result her colonies in Latin America acquired habits of self-reliance. More and more they depended upon their own efforts in solving political and economic problems. So great was their isolation from Spain that they cultivated a profitable trade with the British. For the mother country to have forced them back under the yoke of mercantilist restrictions would have been difficult indeed.

Spain's neglect of her colonies during the wars of Napoleon

The spark that ignited colonial unrest into actual revolution burst forth in 1808. A quarrel had developed between the weak Bourbon king of Spain, Charles IV, and his son Ferdinand. Napoleon forced

Spanish Colonial Patio. Examples of the cultural heritage of old Spain have been adapted by the wealthier citizens of Latin America.

CANADA
(British)

UNITED STATES
OF AMERICA

A T L A N T I C

O C E A N

GULF OF
MEXICO

Mexico
City

BR.
HONDURAS

CUBA
(Spain)

SAINT DOMINGUE (France)

JAMAICA
(British)

SANTO DOMINGO (Spain)

C A R I B B E A N   S E A

P A C I F I C

Bogotá

Orinoco R.

(British after 1803)

FRENCH GUIANA

NEW
GRANADA

DUTCH
GUIANA

Equator

0°

GALAPAGOS IS.

O C E A N

Amazon R.

B R A Z I L

A N D E S

Lima

P E R U

M O U N T A I N S

B U E N O S
A I R E S
O R
L A   P L A T A

Rio de Janeiro

0   1000   2000 miles

Santiago

Buenos Aires

Montevideo

La Plata R.

P A T A G O N I A

FALKLAND
ISLANDS

Spanish

Portuguese

British

CAPE HORN

LATIN AMERICA ON THE EVE OF INDEPENDENCE ca. 1800

both to abdicate and gave the Spanish crown to his brother Joseph. When news of these highhanded proceedings reached the colonies, there was general indignation. At first the colonies vented their wrath against the French, but gradually they came to realize that here was an opportunity to get rid of all foreign oppressors. Agitation took an anti-Spanish turn and was ultimately followed by declarations of independence and revolutionary wars. Wealthy Creoles took the lead, especially in Caracas, Buenos Aires, Quito, Bogotá, and Santiago.

The first of the larger Spanish colonies to proclaim its independence was Venezuela. Here a revolutionary pattern had been developing for a number of years. In 1806 the impetuous Creole, Francisco de Miranda, attempted with the help of foreigners to land expeditions in his native country and wrest control of it from Spain. He obtained aid from English and American sources but failed to gain more than a temporary foothold on the territory of Venezuela. Five years later representatives from a nubmer of provinces met in a revolutionary assembly and declared Venezuela an independent republic. Learning of the revolutionists' activities, Miranda sailed from England to enlist in the cause. Appointed commander-in-chief of the patriot armies, he launched a campaign to conquer the remainder of the country. Misfortune stalked his efforts. Reverses suffered by his armies were turned into disaster when an earthquake shook the provinces controlled by the revolutionists and snuffed out the lives of 20,000. Equal to the occasion, the Spanish government sent priests with instructions to tell the people that the catastrophe was a divine punishment for their sin of rebellion. The patriot armies disintegrated, and their commander was seized and thrown into the dungeon.

With the defeat of Miranda, the revolution in Venezuela was left to be completed by his erstwhile friend, Simón Bolívar. A wealthy Creole rancher, Bolívar had finally turned against Miranda, accusing him of deserting the revolution, and had been partly responsible for his capture by the Spaniards. Concluding thereafter that the revolutionary cause in Venezuela was hopeless, he went to Colombia and joined the patriot forces there. He returned to Venezuela in 1813 and captured Caracas. In January 1814, the Second Venezuelan Republic was proclaimed with Bolívar as its head with the title of "Liberator." In six months the new government had been crushed by the Spaniards, and its founder fled to Jamaica. He did not return for three years. In 1817 he began the rebuilding of a stronger patriot force in Venezuela, and two years later, with the help of 4,000 soldiers of fortune from Great Britain, completed a spectacular foray into Colombia. Inflicting a decisive defeat upon the Spaniards and their collaborators, he proclaimed the Republic of Colombia on August 10, 1819. Three months later a constitution was issued for the United States of Colombia, including Venezuela, with Bolívar as president. Thereafter the great Liberator devoted his efforts to freeing the remainder of the northern

Equestrian Statue of Simón Bolívar (1783–1830), Soldier, Statesman, and Revolutionary Leader. On Plaza Bolívar, Caracas, Venezuela.

portion of the continent from Spanish rule. By 1821 he had liquidated the royalist forces in Venezuela. Meanwhile, his able lieutenant Antonio José de Sucre, had begun the liberation of Ecuador, and in 1822 won a brilliant victory against the Spaniards, which assured the independence of the country. Soon afterward Bolívar arrived in Quito and persuaded the Ecuadorean revolutionists to unite with Colombia and Venezuela in a republic of Gran Colombia.

Concurrently with these events in the northern areas, an independence movement was growing apace in the south. As early as 1790 businessmen in the port of Buenos Aires had developed a profitable trade with Spain and an even more profitable one with Great Britain. They longed for relief of these ventures from monopolistic restrictions imposed by the Spanish government. During the Napoleonic Wars their demands were encouraged by the British government. In 1810 a band of Creoles in Buenos Aires overthrew the vice-regal government of Joseph Bonaparte and appointed a supreme governing council to rule in the name of Ferdinand VII. While the urban Creoles were debating how far they should go in the direction of complete independence, and what form of government would best suit their needs, delegates from the outlying provinces assembled at Tucumán in 1816 and declared absolute independence from the mother country. Thenceforth rivalry between the capital and the rural provinces impeded the progress of the revolution.

At least one native of Argentina perceived that internal squabbles would lead to nothing but ultimate defeat. This man was José San Martín, who had served in the Spanish army from the age of eleven and had fought the French invaders in the Peninsular campaign. With Spain under the heel of Napoleon, he had returned to his native country. Ignoring local quarrels, he determined to give positive direction to the Argentine revolution by attacking the royalists in Peru, their principal stronghold on the continent. He obtained an appointment as governor of the province of Cuyo, on the eastern slope of the Andes, where he planned to organize and equip an army for an incursion into Chile, which would then be used as a base for operations against Peru. In his preparations he was assisted by Bernardo O'Higgins, a Chilean revolutionary of Irish descent. By 1817 everything was ready for the daring expedition. Scrambling over the rocky slopes of the continental divide, the invaders came down into Chile, fell upon the royalists near Santiago, and won a spectacular triumph. The grateful Chileans offered San Martín a dictatorship, which he declined, insisting that it be conferred upon his Chilean collaborator, O'Higgins. San Martín then turned his attention to completing plans for the attack on Peru. The expedition got under way in September 1820. Less than a year later the redoubtable patriot entered Lima, issued a declaration of independence from Spain, and was vested with the title of "Protector" of the new Peruvian government. Although a dictator in theory, he exercised little power. He seemed to feel that his mission as a revolutionist was now fulfilled. Moreover, he was unable to agree with Bolívar as to the form of government to be established when the time should come to unite the countries they had liberated from Spanish rule. In 1822 he left Peru, sojourned briefly in Chile and Argentina, and then left for France, where he died in 1850.

The struggle for independence in Brazil followed a less violent course than that in most other South American countries. Revolutionary feeling was not strong, perhaps for the reason that Brazil was more backward than most of her neighbors. Two-thirds of her population were slaves. There was no large middle class, and there were no cities worthy of the name. Schools were few, and scarcely more than a tenth of the people could read and write. Even more than in the Spanish colonies, the impetus for revolution in Brazil came from the Napoleonic Wars. When Napoleon's troops drove the Portuguese rulers from Lisbon in 1807, they sailed to Brazil, arriving in Rio de Janeiro in March 1808. The Regent, Prince John, was chagrined to find his colony so backward and launched an immediate program of reform and improvement. He established schools, a bank, hospitals, and a library. He reorganized the administration of the colony, sponsored new methods of agriculture, and abolished the restrictions on colonial manufacturing. He raised the status of the colony to that of a kingdom on a par with Portugal itself. But upon becoming king of both countries after the death of his deranged mother in 1816, he surrounded himself with a royal court in Brazil and gave a virtual monopoly of high offices in Church and state to his Portuguese favorites. The effect was to antagonize many of his Creole subjects. Although the majority confined the expression of their discontent to grumbling, a group in the north attempted unsuccessfully to establish an independent republic (1817).

In 1820 a liberal revolution broke out in Portugal. King John sailed for Lisbon and left his young son Pedro as Regent in Brazil. Scarcely had the new government gained power in Portugal than it turned to a reactionary policy, particularly with regard to the empire. Brazil was reduced once more to a mere colony, and Pedro was ordered to return to Portugal to "complete his political education." The Brazilians implored him to remain as their ruler, and he agreed to do so. When all attempts to compromise with the Portuguese failed, a revolt broke out in Brazil. In 1822 Pedro was raised to the status of emperor, and within a year the Portuguese troops had been driven from the country.

By 1826 all the South American countries had thrown off the yoke of European rule. Uruguay remained a province of Brazil, however, until 1828, and Argentina was unable to solve the problem of unity between Buenos Aires and her rural provinces until 1861. Meanwhile another section of Latin America was striving for the goal of independence. This was the viceroyalty of New Spain, which included Mexico, Central America, portions of the West Indies, and the Spanish territory within the present limits of the United States. The island of Haiti was the first to raise the standard of revolt. During the eighteenth century it had become a colony of France—her most lucrative, by the way. It was a seething volcano of discontent, however. Its population had a three-class structure. At the top were a few thousand whites, mostly French planters and officials. At the bottom were 500,000 miserably exploited Negro slaves. A middle layer comprised the mulattoes, torn into mutually hostile factions and despised by both blacks and whites. In 1791 Toussaint L'Ouverture, a slave but the grandson of an African king, emerged as the leader of the Negroes. Under the influence of the French Revolutionary policy of abolishing slavery in the colonies, he led the Negroes in a prolonged revolt against their masters. With some accuracy he can be regarded as a forerunner of twentieth-century guerrilla leaders. His followers were a straggling force of irregulars, poorly armed and equipped, who followed a tactic of strike and run. In ten years they gained control of the entire island. Toussaint issued a constitution and assumed dictatorial powers.

Failure of the revolution

When Napoleon had established himself as master of France, he resolved to put an end to the rule of the upstart rebel. Avowing that he would never "leave an epaulette on the shoulder of a Negro," he sent a huge expedition under the command of his brother-in-law, General Le Clerc, to overthrow Toussaint's government. Nearly two years and an act of treachery were required to accomplish the task. Informing Toussaint that he would "not find a more sincere friend than myself," Le Clerc invited the Negro to his quarters for negotiations. He then seized him and shipped him off in chains to a prison in France. Angered by this treachery, the slaves again rose in rebellion and with new and equally capable leaders soon forced the French to withdraw. In 1803 Haiti was proclaimed an independent kingdom. Curiously, the precedent set by the Haitians seemed to exert little influence upon the other principal islands of the West Indies. Cuba and Puerto Rico, for example, remained under Spanish rule until 1898.

The first Mexican revolutions

Scarcely anywhere in Latin America did the revolution present a more discouraging aspect than in Mexico. Here the Creoles did not constitute so powerful a middle class as in some parts of South America. Moreover, the antagonism of the Indians and the poorer *mestizos,* or half-breeds, against the whites hindered combined action to oust the Spaniards. A revolt was finally launched in 1810, however, in the rural provinces. Its leader was a Creole priest, Father Hidalgo. The son of a poor farmer, he had obtained a good education and had become rector of the Colegio de San Nicolàs. But he was an ardent admirer of Rousseau and was reputed to have questioned the Virgin

Birth and the authority of the pope. His original plan was to lead the Indians in a rebellion against the Spanish-born aristocrats, but when his scheme was exposed he turned upon the government itself. He captured the important towns of Guanajuato and Guadalajara and then advanced with 80,000 men upon Mexico City. Ultimately defeated, he was captured, condemned by the Inquisition, and shot. One of his followers, José Morelos, continued the revolution for four more years and attempted to set up an independent government. But like Hidalgo, he eventually fell into the hands of the royalists and was condemned to death. The destinies of the revolution then passed into the hands of a crafty adventurer, Agustín de Iturbide. A soldier by profession, who had hitherto fought on the side of the royalists, Iturbide saw a chance to further his ambitions by joining the patriots. Openly espousing independence and racial equality, he attracted formidable support and, in September 1821, entered Mexico City in triumph. The following year he proclaimed himself emperor of an independent Mexican empire. But since the basic economic and social problems remained unsolved, the future of the nation continued to be fraught with anxiety and turmoil.

3. PROBLEMS OF GROWTH AND DEVELOPMENT

Following their achievement of independence, the Latin American states went through a long struggle for national maturity. It could scarcely be said that many of them attained this goal before the end of the nineteenth century. A score of difficulties beset them on every hand. To begin with, the population was heterogeneous. The former Spanish colonies were composed of 45 percent Indians, 30 percent *mestizos* or half-breeds, 20 percent whites, and 5 percent Negroes. In Brazil half the people were Negroes, a fourth were whites, and the remainder Indians and half-breeds. Over the continent as a whole the nonwhites outnumbered the Caucasians 4 to 1; yet the latter fought tooth and nail to maintain a dominant position. The success achieved in this struggle was purchased at the price of class hatred and the perpetuation of social and economic backwardness.

Obstacles to national maturity: (1) heterogeneous population

A second obstacle, related to the first, was the wide disparity of economic condition among the classes. At the top was a tiny minority of rich Spaniards and prosperous Creoles. At the bottom was a vast multitude of half-starved peasants, eking out a precarious livelihood on lands no one wanted or compelled to become laborers on the estates of the rich. The inevitable consequence was periodic revolts of the masses to force a redistribution of the land. Since land comprised the bulk of the wealth, capital accumulated slowly. In the main, the deficiency was made up by foreign investors, who frequently demanded political concessions and were eager to fish in troubled

(2) the gulf between rich and poor

waters for their own advantage. Few causes contributed more toward encouraging unscrupulous adventurers to overturn governments at the behest of their foreign sponsors.

Still a third difficulty was the political inexperience of the Latin American peoples. More than 90 percent, of course, were uneducated, and consequently both ignorant and indifferent with respect to political problems. But even many of the educated ones were ill prepared to assume the tasks of governing. Their knowledge of politics came not from experience but from reading the books of theorists. Enthusiasm for this or that form of government burned with white-hot intensity, and factions vied with each other to put their ideas into effect overnight, frequently by revolutionary action. Worse yet, as a result of the long and sanguinary struggles for independence, a military tradition was firmly implanted in most of the states, and swaggering generals overshadowed civilian leaders.

Although Latin Americans are often reproached with their failure to achieve political maturity and stability as soon as did the English-speaking inhabitants of North America, such comparisons have little validity. They leave out of reckoning the fact that the United States went through a long period of sectional conflict, culminating in civil war, before its people could decide whether they were one nation or a confederation of nations. But aside from this, the circumstances affecting Latin America were so different from those obtaining in Canada and the United States that any conception of the two regions as parallel entities is bound to be inaccurate.

Perhaps the most important difference resided in the fact that Canada and the United States comprised millions of acres of practically unoccupied land. The native peoples were so few in numbers and so widely scattered that they could easily be pushed aside or exterminated. In Latin America the Indians were more numerous, in many cases more highly civilized, and therefore more successful in resisting the encroachments of the whites. The policy of the Spaniards, moreover, was to convert the natives to Christianity, not to exterminate them. It did not seem inconsistent with this that they should also be exploited and oppressed. As a consequence, there quickly developed a class system based upon race, with a prosperous minority of Spaniards and Creoles monopolizing the good things of life and a subject population composed of Indians and half-breeds living in squalor and toiling for the barest subsistence.

As a second difference, the Spanish colonies were founded by one of the most unprogressive nations in Europe. The economic system of Spain was outmoded. Her government was despotic and corrupt. Spanish Catholicism reeked with intolerance and superstition. The Church was used by the government as an instrument of repression, and the fanaticism of the Spanish Inquisition was notorious. On the eve of the discovery of America the most enterprising of Spain's inhabitants—the Moors and the Jews—had been driven from the country. England had the advantage of not beginning her colonization of the New World until the seventeenth century. By that time the power of her middle class was well consolidated and able to set up obstacles to despotic government. Instead of one church having a monopoly of religious authority, the Christians of England were divided into competing sects, and no one of them was strong enough to impose its will upon the others. The country, moreover, had been a haven of refuge for persecuted religionists from other nations, for the Huguenots in particular. Many of these were enterprising merchants and artisans who brought their initiative and skills with them, adding no small amount to the intellectual wealth of England. Long before the end of the seventeenth century, the "tight little island" was the most progressive nation in Europe. And while the Spanish colonists brought with them the customs and institutions of the Middle Ages, those who went out from England carried the ideas of the modern world. They believed in education, in equality of opportunity, and in the application of ambition and intelligence to the solution of human problems. These viewpoints helped immensely in promoting a free and dynamic society in North America in contrast with the static, semifeudal society of Central and South America.

The last three quarters of the nineteenth century unfolded a record of developments in Latin America similar in some respects to that in the United States. There was the same feverish activity in railroad building and in the construction of telegraph and telephone lines. There was the same rapid growth of population, owing largely to the influx of immigrants from Europe. The population of Argentina, for example, grew from 2 million in 1870 to about 4 million in 1900; and more than half of this increase was the result of immigration from Italy, Spain, France, Germany, and the British Isles. In Latin America as in the United States there were bitter struggles over centralization versus states' rights. There was sharp rivalry also between liberals and conservatives over extension of the suffrage and over economic reform for the benefit of the lower classes.

Growth and development during the nineteenth century

But the differences were quite as significant. Nearly every country of Latin America was torn by revolutions, many of them resulting in the enthronement of military dictators. The history of Colombia was almost unique in that only twice during the century following independence was her government overthrown by violence. In neighboring Venezuela revolutions occurred with such frequency as to reduce economic development virtually to a standstill. Only the accession in 1909 of a man on horseback, Juan Vicente Gómez, who ruled for twenty-six years, brought a semblance of stability to the country. In many states of both Central and South America, religion complicated the struggle between factions. The conservatives, made up of the landholding and aristocratic elements, invariably supported the

Political instability

Church. The liberals, who drew their following mainly from the business classes, were anticlerical. On occasion the latter allied themselves with the landless peasants in attacks upon the extensive holdings of the clergy.

The major difference, however, consists in the numerous wars fought by the Latin American states against each other. The longest was the struggle between Uruguay and Argentina, which lasted for fourteen years (1838–1852). The most famous was the War of the Pacific (1879–1883), in which Chile, Peru, and Bolivia fought over the desert region of Atacama. The bloodiest was the war of 1865–1870, in which the dictator of Paraguay (Francisco López) resisted the combined onslaughts of Brazil, Uruguay, and Argentina for five years. The Paraguayans fought almost literally to the last man. Only a handful of adult males survived, and more than half of the total population was wiped out. The only element of justice in the outcome was the fact that López himself was numbered among those killed. It was this dictator's imperialist ambitions which had precipitated the conflict in the first place.

Wars of the Latin American states

Two states of Latin America went through experiences during the nineteenth century in a number of respects distinctive. One was Brazil and the other was Mexico. The former was almost unique in its political stability. A constitution drafted by a commission under Emperor Pedro I in 1824 remained in effect for sixty-five years. It was a moderately liberal document, guaranteeing freedom of speech, of the press, and of religion, and providing for a legislative assembly, but it left the emperor above the law and exempt from responsibility for the acts of his ministers. Disaffection against the monarchy mounted under Pedro II and culminated in revolution after his government enacted a measure emancipating all the slaves without compensation to their owners. An armed uprising forced the emperor to abdicate in 1889, and a republic was proclaimed under a provisional government headed by the victorious general. A constitution drafted in 1891 by a committee of lawyers for the Republic of Brazil continued in effect, with few changes, until the suspension of constitutional government by the Vargas dictatorship in 1937.

Emperor Pedro II of Brazil

Iturbide and Juárez as rulers of Mexico

The history of Mexico in the nineteenth century resembled the history of Brazil in that both countries wavered between monarchy and republicanism and had similar conflicts over church and state. But Mexico was one of the few Latin American countries in which the *mestizos* and Indians (the former especially) played an active part in determining the course of political developments. Her first ruler after independence, Iturbide, who became Emperor Agustín I, was of mixed white and Indian parentage. As a statesman he was a failure and in little more than a year was driven from the throne and forced into exile. In 1824 a republic was set up with a constitution similar to that of the United States, except that the Roman Catholic faith was made the established religion. Between 1833 and 1855 Mexico was ruled most of the time by the redoubtable Antonio López de Santa Anna, famous as the opponent of the United States in the dispute over Texas and in the war that followed. Although holding the title of president, he governed as a dictator with the support of a clerico-military oligarchy. Cruel, treacherous, and greedy for power, he exemplified that *personalismo* which has been the curse of so many Latin-American countries. His downfall was achieved by a coalition of radicals and liberals led by two full-blooded Indians, Juan Álvarez and Benito Juárez, and a Creole, Ignacio Comonfort. Although Comonfort became president, the real leader of the coalition was Juárez. He and his followers inaugurated a program aimed at the destruction of clerical and military privilege, the suppression of the Church, and the distribution of Church lands to the people. These reforms were eventually incorporated in a new constitution adopted in 1857.

The clericals and conservatives did not take kindly to the Constitution of 1857. The consequence was civil war, the so-called War of the Reform, from 1858 to 1861. It ended in a complete victory for Juárez and his followers, with the result that more drastic anticlerical laws were enacted to supplement the provisions of the constitution. Religious orders were suppressed, Church property was nationalized, and civil marriage was established. But the triumph of the liberals did not obliterate the nation's troubles. The government was so desperate for money that it sold some of the confiscated Church lands to secular landlords. The peasants were merely transferred from one exploiter to another. The war disrupted economic conditions to such an extent that payments on foreign debts were suspended. This gave the wily Napoleon III an excuse to intervene. In 1862 he sent a French army to Vera Cruz, which finally battered its way to Mexico City and took possession of the government. Meanwhile an assembly of Mexican conservatives went through the sham of "offering" the Mexican throne to Archduke Maximilian of Austria, who had already been selected by Napoleon III as his puppet ruler.

As emperor of Mexico, Maximilian was worse than a failure. Although he was kindly, idealistic, and sympathetic with the plight of most of his new subjects, he was amateurish and dominated by an overly ambitious wife. Moreover, he antagonized the conservatives by his acid criticisms of corruption and indifference in the Church and in the army. The followers of Juárez had distrusted him from the beginning. The primary cause of his downfall, however, was a shift in the power struggle in Europe. The Austro-Prussian War of 1866 put Napoleon in a position where he could no longer afford to give military support to Maximilian. As a result of her victory in that war Prussia now loomed as a dangerous rival of France. Soon afterward, therefore, the French emperor withdrew his troops. He was impelled to take this action partly, of course, by vigorous protests from the

Antonio López de Santa Anna

The War of the Reform and the overthrow of the republic

Maximilian, Emperor of Mexico

government of the United States against French violation of the Monroe Doctrine. But even without these protests, his decision could not have been long delayed.

In the absence of French military support, Maximilian's empire in Mexico speedily collapsed. The liberal forces of Juárez closed in upon him, and he was captured, court-martialed, and executed by a firing squad. Juárez was quickly elected president and re-elected in 1871, but death overtook him the following year. He had time to accomplish only a few of his aims for making Mexico a modern, progressive state. He drastically reduced the size of the army, eliminated waste and extravagance in the government, and initiated steps for a wide extension of public education. But the troubles of the nation were far from ended. It was impossible to repair overnight the damage caused by twenty years of civil strife. The national debt continued to increase, economic activity had shrunk, and the country seemed almost on the verge of exhaustion. In 1877 the government of Juárez's successor was overthrown, and a dictatorship was established that was destined to remain in power for more than thirty years. The new ruler was Porfirio Díaz, the son of a Creole father and an Indian mother. Originally a pupil and follower of Juárez, he repudiated his master when the latter was re-elected president in 1871. Thereafter he pursued his own ambitions and strove with an iron will to mold his country in accordance with his cherished schemes.

The regime of Díaz brought Mexico prosperity but nothing that resembled democracy. For the most part he ruled benevolently but always with an eye to the perpetuation of his own power. He soon controlled the electoral machinery and used government funds to buy off potential opponents. Those who couldn't be bought he dealt with in more summary fashion. For disposing of suspected revolutionaries his general order to the army and the public was: "When caught in the act, kill in cold blood." Yet under his rule the nation made rapid progress, and the business classes at least luxuriated in dividends and profits. Foreign trade multiplied six times over, and railroad mileage increased from 400 to 16,000. Mines were brought up to unprecedented levels of production, smuggling was eliminated, the national budget was balanced, and interstate tariffs were abolished to the substantial benefit of industry and commerce. Many of these improvements were made possible, however, by the importation of foreign capital. The suppliers of these funds frequently drove unscrupulous bargains as part of the terms of the investment. They exacted concessions to buy land at ridiculous prices, including full title to all minerals beneath the surface. Prosperity at the price of so large a part of the nation's heritage eventually proved to be too much for the middle classes to endure. By 1900 the reputation of Díaz had lost its luster. By 1911 when his government collapsed and the aged dictator sailed for France, the Mexican republic was ripe for revolution to undo the evils of three decades.

Porfirio Díaz. The Díaz rule in Mexico from 1877 to 1911 was characterized by political dictatorship and economic development.

It would scarcely be an exaggeration to say that Latin America witnessed more social and political changes from 1900 to 1980 than in the previous four centuries of her history. Two significant developments distinguish the record of the twentieth century thus far. The first is a phenomenal increase in population. Around 1800, Central and South America had a population of about 17 million; by 1900 this had grown to about 70 million and by 1979 to 350 million. The population of Brazil more than trebled between 1900 and 1960. Argentina surpassed even this ratio, with a growth in numbers from 4,200,000 in 1900 to 20 million sixty years later. The number of Mexicans rose from 20 million in 1940 to 47 million in 1968 and 67 million by the later 1970s. With an average annual growth rate of about 3 percent, the Latin American countries seem destined to more than double their present population before the year 2000 when, according to predictions, it would total 650 million. Nearly everywhere population was beginning to exert terrific pressure upon available resources. Since 1950 there has been a steady migration of people from rural districts to the cities, but the expansion of industry and commerce has been too limited to absorb them into profitable employment.

Phenomenal increase in population

Closely related to the growth of population was the increasing tension inherent in a sharply polarized society. A small elite controlled both the economy and the political structure, while the great majority remained impoverished and unprivileged, and a genuine middle class failed to develop. At the turn of the century, 90 percent of Latin Americans lived a hand-to-mouth existence of squalor and wretchedness. Most of them were peons, or laborers on large estates, doomed to a kind of slavery by debts they could never repay. Their families were crowded together in one-room shacks with no stove or fireplace, no running water, and no sanitary facilities. Wages received for a day's toil scarcely equaled the hourly pay for comparable work in the United States. As the twentieth century approached, the picture was very much the same, in spite of political rhetoric and promises of reform. The progress of industrialization, though significant, had done little to relieve the inequities in society; in some ways it had intensified them. Most of the fertile lands were still owned by a few wealthy families who ruled their great estates, or *haciendas,* in semifeudal fashion. Though less than 10 percent of the population, this powerful landlord class, together with its allies in banking and industry, monopolized the professions, government positions, and the officer ranks in the army.

Polarization of society

The country which seemed most likely to move forward along the path of social progress was the Republic of Mexico. A revolt in 1911, which overthrew the dictatorship of Porfirio Díaz, inspired hope for reform. But the years ahead were filled with domestic turmoil and troubled by unfriendly relations with the United States. The great

Revolution in Mexico

CANADA

UNITED STATES
OF AMERICA

A T L A N T I C

O C E A N

*GULF OF
MEXICO*

MEXICO
(1821)

Havana

Nassau

BAHAMAS
(Brit.)

HAITI (1804)

DOMINICAN REP. (1844)

Mexico City ★

CUBA
(1898)

San Juan

PUERTO RICO (U.S.)

JAMAICA
(1962)

Port au Prince

Santo
Domingo

SEE INSET
BELOW

CENTRAL AMERICA

CARIBBEAN SEA

BARBADOS (1967)

TRINIDAD AND
TOBAGO (1962)

Caracas

Port of Spain

Georgetown

Paramaribo

P A C I F I C

Bogotá

VENEZUELA
(1811)

Orinoco R.

GUYANA (1966)

SURINAM (Du.)

FRENCH GUIANA
Cayenne

COLOMBIA
(1821)

Equator

Quito

ECUADOR (1822)

Amazon

R.

O C E A N

GALAPAGOS IS.
(Ecuador)

*A
N
D
E
S

M
T
S.*

PERU
(1821)

BRAZIL   (1822)

★ Brasília

Lima ★

BOLIVIA
(1825)

★ La Paz

| 0 | 1000 | 2000 miles |

Sucre

PARAGUAY
(1811)

Rio de Janeiro

CHILE
(1818)

★ Asunción

*A
N
D
E
S

M
O
U
N
T
A
I
N
S*

Santiago

Buenos Aires ★

URUGUAY (1828)

★ Montevideo

ARGENTINA
(1816)

La Plata R.

FALKLAND ISLANDS
(Br.)

*CAPE
HORN*

Dates indicate year
of independence

CENTRAL AMERICA

JAMAICA
(1962)

★ Belize

BRITISH HONDURAS

Kingston

GUATEMALA
(1821)

*CARIBBEAN

SEA*

HONDURAS (1821)

Tegucigalpa ★

Guatemala ★

Salvador

EL SALVADOR (1821)

NICARAGUA
(1821)

Managua ★

San José ★

PANAMA
CANAL

Panama ★

COSTA RICA
(1821)

PANAMA (1903)

PACIFIC OCEAN

LATIN AMERICA TODAY

neighbor to the north had annexed about half of Mexico's territory following the war of 1846–1848 and in the early twentieth century appeared quite willing to intervene in behalf of North American interests. In 1916 the United States government sent an expeditionary force across the border in pursuit of the revolutionary general Pancho Villa and backed Villa's rival, Carranza, for the presidency. Under President Carranza a constitutional convention in 1917 drafted a new constitution which went into effect in May of that year.

The Constitution of 1917 had several objectives in line with the revolutionary ideals of those who had been struggling to remake the country ever since the end of the Díaz regime: (1) to democratize the government; (2) to reduce the influence of the Church; and (3) to give to the nation control over its economic resources and to provide for the masses a more equitable share of the wealth they produced. In pursuance of the first, the Constitution bestowed the suffrage upon all male citizens twenty-one years of age and over and subjected the powers of the president to a measure of control by Congress. In keeping with the second, freedom of religion was guaranteed, the Church was forbidden to conduct primary schools, and the state legislatures were empowered to limit the number of priests in each district. But the most significant provisions of the Constitution were probably those dealing with economic reform. Peonage was abolished. An eight-hour day with one day's rest in seven was proclaimed the standard for industrial workers. The right to strike was recognized, and the government was given the authority to provide for social insurance. Mineral resources were declared to be the property of the nation. No foreigners were to be granted concessions to develop them unless they agreed to be treated as Mexican citizens. Private property of any kind might be expropriated by the government after the payment of just compensation.

*The Mexican
Constitution of 1917*

Pancho Villa (Center) and General John J. Pershing of the United States Army. In 1916 Pershing commanded the United States expeditionary force sent to Mexico to apprehend Villa.

Inadequate reforms

Political and economic flaws

Echeverría

In spite of its liberal constitution and success in avoiding military dictatorships, Mexico has not yet fulfilled the promise of an equitable and democratic society. The failure is partly due to problems which have grown to such proportions that they frustrate efforts to resolve them. Several presidents strove earnestly to complete the revolutionary aims of the Constitution of 1917. They expropriated millions of acres of land and redistributed them to the peasants. They instituted teacher-training programs, built new schools, and made primary education free and compulsory. Legislation was enacted guaranteeing old-age pensions and providing insurance for illness, accidents, and unemployment. Mexico became the first country in the world to nationalize its oil industry (in 1938, with compensation to the former owners). Nevertheless, changes have been more in form than in substance, and they have not eliminated the sources of social unrest.

For the past fifty years the government of Mexico has been dominated by a single political party, the Institutional Revolutionary Party (PRI). The PRI chooses the presidential candidate, the legislature, the state governors, and most of the judges. The president in turn exercises practically unlimited authority over all branches of government. This system has bred complacency, inefficiency, and corruption. Although Mexico achieved a high economic growth rate, industrial progress did not benefit those most in need of help. Agrarian reform, the core of the revolutionary program, has been limited and sporadic. With only 12 percent of the land under cultivation or grazing, rapid population increase forced a migration of unemployed peasants into the towns, with the consequent creation of large urban slums. Mexico City has been called the "largest poor city" in the world. The rural areas, lacking adequate schools and medical care, remain neglected and exploited. In 1968 only 175,000 students were enrolled in public universities—out of a population of close to 50 million. Repressive policies provoked a student insurrection at the University of Mexico in 1968, which was brutally suppressed by President Díaz Ordaz's special troops. Although officially denied, the jails hold many political prisoners, some of whom have been tortured.

Luis Echeverría Alvarez, president from 1970 to 1976, promised the people social justice and a more equitable distribution of wealth. A flamboyant figure who courted popularity with Third World nations and brashly offered to settle the Middle East crisis, he put forward a program of "shared growth," increasing both industrial production and social services and expropriating more than a million acres for distribution to landless peasants. His reforms, though not radical, antagonized large property owners and business interests, and were also expensive. The government deficit mounted alarmingly, the consumer price index rose 90 percent within five years, and when the peso was devalued in 1976 it suffered a 50 percent decline.

Echeverría's successor, José López Portillo, political scientist, novelist, and former finance minister, reverted to a more conservative course and attempted to regain the confidence of influential groups his predecessor had alienated, including foreign investors. By a stroke of good fortune the beginning of his term of office coincided with the discovery of enormous oil and gas reserves along and off the western shore of the Gulf of Mexico. As recently as 1973 Mexico had been an oil importing country, and suffered severely in that year when the price of oil quadrupled. Recent surveys indicate that Mexico's petroleum reserves are among the world's largest. It remained to be seen whether this potential source of prosperity would merely speed the growth of capitalist enterprise or be devoted to fulfilling the long postponed promise of the Mexican Revolution. Seventy percent of the nation's wealth was controlled by 20 percent of its people; unemployment or underemployment victimized half of the population; three-fifths of the adult population was still illiterate. To an increasing extent oil exports had to be drawn upon to offset the country's deficiency in the production of foodstuffs. At the same time, Mexico's newly discovered mineral resources had given it an improved bargaining position with the United States and the means for pursuing an independent foreign policy. President López Portillo declared his government's intention to assist struggling revolutionary regimes in Central America and the Caribbean.

President López Portillo of Mexico

Progress in the 1950s

Brazil—the largest Latin American country, with a land area greater than that of the forty-eight continental United States—made only limited advances toward democracy, and these were halted in the 1930s. Constitutional changes adopted in 1934 provided for the secret ballot and the enfranchisement of both men and women, though a literacy qualification debarred many from voting. Three years later President Getulio Vargas, using economic depression and the growth of communism as an excuse, made himself dictator and issued a new constitution which gave him practically absolute authority. Forced to resign by a bloodless revolution in 1945, he was again chosen president in 1950 but was ousted by the military four years later. For several years a bitter struggle raged between Vargas's followers and their opponents.

In spite of factional wrangling, the later 1950s showed stirrings of progress in Brazil. President Juscelino Kubitschek planned an ambitious program of economic development, but because he avoided tax increases, his policy of government spending was highly inflationary. At the same time, volunteer reformers, supported by trade unions, political radicals, a Catholic Action Movement, and even some bishops of the Church hierarchy, brought help to the depressed rural area of northeastern Brazil, organizing peasant cooperatives, starting schools and health clinics, and offering technical assistance. Such radical activity at the grass roots, added to the mild reformism of the government, was too much for the oligarchy that controlled most of the land and the army. Kubitschek's successors had been no more successful than he in stabilizing the economy, and in April 1964 Pres-

President Getulio Vargas of Brazil

Modern Brazil. Left: A slum on the outskirts of Rio de Janeiro contrasts sharply with Brasília, Brazil's capital, on the right.

Specious prosperity under a military dictatorship

ident João Goulart, a leader of the Labor party, was overthrown by a coup d'état. A military dictatorship has held Brazil in its grip ever since.

In the 1960s the country seemed to be caught in the surge of an economic boom. A resplendent new capital, Brasília, was constructed deep in the interior, and São Paulo on the coast grew from a sleepy provincial town to become the largest industrial city in the Southern Hemisphere. Proponents of a trans-Amazonian highway boasted that the gigantic project would be visible to the naked eye from the moon, although ecologists warned that destruction of the Amazon rain forests would endanger the oxygen supply and lead to soil exhaustion. Industry expanded and diversified, to free the economy from dependence upon its single staple, coffee. Manufactures—including shipbuilding, automobiles, steel products, and precision instruments—increased sufficiently to contribute 20 percent of Brazil's exports. By 1971 the overall annual growth rate approached 11 percent. Prosperity, however, was somewhat fictitious and was obtained at the risk of eventual disaster. The increasingly industrialized economy depended precariously on outside support—chiefly from the United States, Canada, Japan, and West Germany—for 40 percent of capital investment and 60 percent of foreign trade. During the mid-1970s the growth rate slumped to below 5 percent, and there were signs that the "economic miracle" was coming to an end. Because imports supplied 80 percent of its oil, Brazil was badly jolted by the sharp rise in the price of this commodity. By 1978 the national debt had reached $40 billion, and inflation was running at an annual rate of over 40 percent. While the value of agricultural exports—chiefly coffee and sugar—declined, the government attempted to improve industrial output by offering generous concessions to multinational corporations. It also invested heavily in arms production and succeeded in making Brazil one of the world's leading exporters of armaments. While national income rose substantially between 1964 and 1969 and the earnings of university graduates went up by 50 percent, real wages for the great body of workers declined in about the same proportion and, a decade later, more than one-fifth of them were unemployed. Brazil's prosperity has done little to improve health care and social services; the infant mortality rate is one of the highest in Latin America.

Leaders of the junta

The military junta that has governed Brazil for the past fifteen years suppressed not only the democratic process but every vestige of civil liberty, imposing tight censorship, incarcerating citizens without trial, and torturing suspected opponents of the regime. President Ernesto Geisel, who described his government as a "relative democracy," partially relaxed the censorship and granted limited responsibility to a Congress chosen by general election in November 1978. General João Baptista Figueiredo, handpicked by Geisel to succeed him as president in March 1979, declared: "I intend to open this country up to democracy. And anyone who is against that, I will jail, I will crush." Disdainful of opposition from within or without, recent presidents have displayed an independent stance in foreign relations. President Geisel abruptly terminated a military-aid agreement with the United States and, defying remonstrances from Washington, signed a pact with West Germany for the purchase of nuclear reactors and uranium enrichment technology. Proclaiming that Brazil was no longer an emerging nation but a full-fledged power, the ruling generals appeared ready to disclaim the "special relationship" with the United States on which they had previously relied.

The Chilean tragedy

The recent history of Chile adds a somber chapter to the story of the misfortunes and frustrations enveloping the countries of Latin America. From the time of independence in 1818, Chile had been remarkably free from internal upheavals. As in most other parts of the continent the economy was dominated by large landowners and foreign investors, while peasants and industrial workers—together constituting 70 percent of the population—lived in poverty. Yet the political structure seemed relatively stable, committed to democratic principles, and—with a few brief interruptions—controlled by civilians. Following the authoritarian presidency of Carlos Ibañez in the early 1930s, constitutional rule continued unbroken for four decades. In 1973 it was destroyed in a blood bath precipitated by a combination of domestic traitors, fascist-minded generals, and international conspirators.

In 1964 Eduardo Frei, a lawyer of German extraction, was chosen

El Teniente Copper Mine, Chile. El Teniente Mining Company had been jointly owned by the Kennecott Copper Corporation and the Chilean government until the Allende government expropriated it in 1971. Chile ranks third in world copper production, after the United States and Zambia.

Allende's Popular Unity coalition and its opponents

president. His party, the Christian Democrats, advocated social welfare measures and his administration accomplished some reforms, including agreements for a gradual transfer of the copper mines from foreign to national ownership. It made little progress, however, with the basic problem of land ownership and distribution. The presidential election of 1970, with 86 percent of the registered voters participating, brought Salvador Allende into office at the head of a Popular Unity coalition of Socialists, Communists, and other leftists. A long-time member of the Chilean Socialist party, Allende sought radical changes but was determined to achieve them by democratic methods. His government broke the control of monopolies, enacted a substantial program of agrarian reform, improved health care sufficiently to cut the infant mortality rate in half, and brought relief to the workers by reducing unemployment. His determination to pursue a "Chilean way to socialism"—democratic and nonviolent—aroused the fears of both native and foreign business interests, who resolved to fight him with all the resources they could command. Economic crises, aggravated by a simultaneous rise in food costs and a drop in the price of copper, Chile's main export, plagued Allende's government. What was not generally known at the time is that an economic breakdown—attributed by critics to Allende's ineptitude and Marxist ideology—was deliberately engineered by Chilean far-right elements, with the support of multinational corporations and the United States government. The CIA, at the urging of the International Telephone and Telegraph Company, had tried to prevent Allende's installation as president in

1970. Failing in this the CIA, with the approval of President Nixon and Henry Kissinger's "Forty Committee" of the National Security Council, secretly spent some $8 million in an attempt to "destabilize" the Chilean government. A black market disrupted trade, acts of sabotage and strikes instigated by agents provacateurs crippled key industries, and an avalanche of propaganda attempted to convince all classes that Allende was violating the constitution while he was wrecking the economy.

In spite of a well-financed scare-and-smear campaign, the congressional elections of March 1973 gave Allende's Popular Unity coalition almost 44 percent of the vote, actually increasing its representation in the legislature although not to the point of holding a majority. Infuriated by this popular vote of confidence in the president, his opponents resorted to extreme measures. After several abortive attempts to incite a popular uprising against the government, the military high command mobilized a force of 100,000 men and on September 11, 1973, launched attacks on key centers throughout the country. The operation was less a coup d'état than an undeclared civil war, though such an uneven contest that there could be little doubt as to the outcome. Although disorganized and poorly armed, civilian resistance proved much stiffer than had been expected. A small band led by Allende defended the Presidential Palace for five hours against tanks and aerial bombardment. Allende was machine-gunned by his captors (who announced his death as suicide) and the slaughter continued for weeks. Some 15,000 civilians were killed outright; thousands more were imprisoned, tortured, or exiled.

The overthrow of one of the few constitutional democracies in Latin America transferred power to a four-man junta headed by General Augusto Pinochet Ugarte, an unappealing figure who liked to compare himself to Spain's Generalissimo Franco and who vowed to replace discredited "liberal democracy" with something more suitable to the times. His methods evoked memories of the horrendous days of Hitler and Stalin. Secret police, the DINA, caused people to "disappear" without a trace and abused prisoners in torture chambers bearing such sardonic titles as "Discothèque" and "Palace of Laughter." An International Commission of Jurists has estimated that during the first eighteen months after the military takeover 95,000 persons—about 1 percent of the population—were arrested for at least a twenty-four-hour period. Unrelenting repression and terror failed to break all internal resistance, while reports of violations of human rights pushed Chile toward a position of international isolation. The United States Congress ended military aid in 1976, but private banks continued to provide financial assistance to the junta. Uneasy relations between Santiago and Washington were severely strained when Orlando Letelier, formerly Allende's ambassador to the United States and an outspoken critic of the junta, was murdered on the streets of Washington, D.C., by DINA agents in September 1976. President

Forceful overthrow of democratic government in Chile

Salvadore Allende, President of Chile, 1970–1973

Rule of the junta

Pinochet made a few cosmetic changes intended to mollify his critics. In 1977 he dissolved the dreaded DINA, but it immediately reappeared under a new name—National Information Center (CNI). The following year he granted permission for a May Day demonstration, following which his police only mildly abused the 500 dissidents they rounded up. Going further, the general tentatively scheduled parliamentary elections for the mid-1980s, while warning that there could be no relaxation of military rule and no presidential election before 1991.

Internal opposition

General Pinochet described Chile under his regime as an island of peace in a troubled world and boasted that he had laid a sound economic base for future development, but there was reason to doubt the durability of his "new democracy." Chile's productive enterprises were heavily mortgaged to foreign corporations, while small industrial concerns faced the prospect of bankruptcy. Eduardo Frei's Christian Democrats, who had helped overthrow Allende only to be outlawed along with other political parties, were having second thoughts. Divisions within the armed forces threatened to erode the power base. Workers were daring not only to grumble but to revive union activity, including resort to strikes and boycotts. They had ample ground for dissatisfaction. In 1977 Chile's industrial production was lower than in 1970, construction had fallen off 20 percent in the same period, real wages were down by more than 18 percent, and the incidence of unemployment was as high as Brazil's.

Obstacles to democracy in Argentina

Amply endowed with agricultural and pastoral resources, though weak in oil and minerals, Argentina is potentially the richest of Latin American countries, but it has made little progress toward either political or economic democracy. Universal manhood suffrage and the secret ballot were adopted in 1912, but voting has typically been manipulated by powerful cliques for their own advantage. Argentina's political history is marked not only by addiction to authoritarian gov-

Agriculture in Argentina. A harvesting scene at the end of the nineteenth century. The nation's booming wheat industry contributed substantially to its prosperity early in the twentieth century.

ernment but also by extraordinary instability. Since 1930 only one president has completed his mandated term of office. Seemingly, the ingredients for a homogeneous society are present. The Indian minority has always been small, and a liberal immigration policy has given the nation a predominantly European character. Argentina is the most urbanized Latin American country, and its people are among the best educated. Yet deep-seated animosities persist which jeopardize democratic progress and political stability. They can be traced in part to rapid industrialization and to the fierce antagonism between urban and rural classes. More than 50 percent of the population is employed in industry, and a wide gulf separates the interests and attitudes of Buenos Aires—where a third of the population is concentrated—from those of the outlying provinces. A second and related source of conflict has been the role of the trade unions. Originating under the leadership of Spanish and Italian immigrants tinged with syndicalist ideology, they developed a strong sense of labor solidarity and militancy. A national confederation of organized workers (CGT), eventually encompassing half of the labor force, became a power within the state, alternately supporting and combating the recurring military dictatorships. Still another factor tending to foster autocratic government has been an intense national pride. Argentinians believe their country should be the leader of Latin America and particularly resent interference by the United States in the affairs of the southern continent.

Much of Argentine political history in the twentieth century has revolved around a small number of dominating personalities. One such was Hipólita Irigoyen, who inspired fanatical loyalty among his followers and was elected president in 1916 for a six-year term and again in 1928. His popularity stemmed partly from the fact that he managed to keep Argentina neutral during World War I and later gained for her a place of recognition in world affairs. But he ruled as an autocrat, enforcing a vicious antistrike policy against labor, and, during his second term, permitting widespread corruption. He was overthrown by a bloodless revolution in 1930 engineered by conservatives and high-ranking officers of the armed forces. For several years conservatives and bourgeois liberals alternated in the possession of power. With the outbreak of World War II a sinister fascist movement began to develop in Argentina. Sympathy with the Axis, based in part upon fear of communism, was widely prevalent. Large numbers of the business classes were of German or Italian extraction, and many army officers were German trained. The nation was already in the throes of economic crises, the government was almost bankrupt, and inflation and overcrowding in the cities inflicted cruel hardships on people with meager resources. The official policy of paying low wages as a means of boosting exports created a surly, rebellious class of workers ready to follow any demagogue who promised to better their condition. The man who stepped into this role was Juan D.

*The road to fascism: Juan
Perón*

Juan Perón, President of Argentina

Perón. Leader of a movement to force the resignation of the incumbent president, he ran for the office himself in 1946. By promising wage increases, rent controls, and partitioning of great estates, he won enough support among the *descamisados* ("shirtless ones") in addition to that of the military and business elements to ensure his election. By recruiting peasants he enlarged the trade unions and made them his power base, using them to intimidate the industrial oligarchy and to hold the military in check. His colorful personality and bold, unscrupulous actions attracted a devoted mass following, but his methods of governing resembled the familiar pattern of fascist dictatorship—censorship, saber rattling, antiforeignism, and economic nationalism.

Perón antagonized the Catholics by legalizing divorce and by attempting the separation of church and state. And while he did little for the peasants, he incurred the enmity of the middle class by conferring expensive benefits upon his followers in the General Confederation of Labor and by expanding the national debt. Though a revolt which broke out in June 1955 was suppressed, it flared up again in September. The rebels won the support of the navy and finally threatened to bombard the city of Buenos Aires if Perón did not surrender. A military junta persuaded him to relinquish his rule and go into exile. He fled to Paraguay and later found refuge in Madrid. In May 1956 the constitution was restored and the great liberal newspaper *La Prensa* was given back to its rightful owners.

The persistence of the Peronist heritage

The restoration of constitutional government proved to be short-lived and did not end the threat to democracy in Argentina. It was impossible to eradicate overnight the influence of 2 million *peronistas* who longed for a revival of the dictatorship that had conferred favors upon the working classes. It was also impossible to suppress the ambitions of the generals and colonels, who demanded strong government until Peronism and communism could be completely eliminated as effective instruments of class legislation. In 1962 and again in 1966 the army removed an elected president from office. Meanwhile economic ills remained, dating from the depression of the 1930s as well as from the Perón regime—a foreign-trade deficit, chronic unemployment, a mountain of public debt, and a steadily advancing cost of living. The military junta that seized power in 1966 dissolved all political parties, purged the universities, and tightened control over the trade unions, but it was unable to resolve the economic crises. Three army generals ruled successively, the third of whom was Alejandro Lanusse, chosen by the joint chiefs of staff as head of the nation in March 1971. Abler than his predecessors, Lanusse also showed himself to be more conciliatory. He legalized political parties, restored some confiscated property, and announced his intention of holding elections for the office of president within two years. This seemed a bold plan in view of the dissensions within the country. Lanusse faced two military uprisings against him and opposition from both the right and the left, including labor unions, middle-class terrorists, and even a revolutionary faction of the Catholic clergy. Though he had himself once been imprisoned by Perón, Lanusse invited the exiled dictator to return for a month's visit, and unregenerate *peronistas* nominated their aging hero as the presidential candidate of their Justicialist Liberation Front. Perón chose not to run, but when the elections were held as scheduled in March 1973, his stand-in, Dr. Héctor Cámpora, a sixty-four-year-old former dentist, outdistanced his closest rival by better than two to one. Accepting the unexpected verdict, Lanusse relinquished the presidential office in May. But Cámpora's inauguration as the first civilian president in seven years did not halt the bloody violence and terrorism that racked the country, and in July Cámpora stepped down in favor of Perón. Upon the death of the ex-dictator the following summer, his widow Isabel, a former cabaret dancer, attempted to fill the post of chief executive. Her disastrous administration of twenty months witnessed the spread of corruption throughout the bureaucracy, black marketing, debasement of the currency, and the world's highest rate of inflation, bringing the government to the brink of ruin. She was deposed by a smoothly executed coup in March 1976, and a three-man junta, headed by General Jorge Videla, acceded to power.

The military junta that has ruled Argentina since the overthrow of Señora Perón retrieved the economy from chaos, but at the expense of every trace of civil liberty. The trade deficit was erased and the rate of inflation reduced—from over 500 percent in 1976 to about 100 percent in 1978. While not abolishing trade unions, the junta seized control of the powerful CGT and froze wages, but not prices. The unions represent a potential threat to the regime and have ventured to call strikes. The generals vowed to exterminate the guerrilla terrorist bands that had shaken the country over a period of many years. Determined to suppress even subversive thoughts, the government unleashed a terror of its own, employing more than a dozen different agencies to stifle dissidents by fright, torture, and execution. Domestic violence increased significantly after the coup of March 1976. Two years later Amnesty International estimated that 15,000 persons had disappeared, between 8,000 and 10,000 more were held in official prisons, while unnumbered victims were suffering in secret detention camps.

The Argentine military junta

Nearly 60 percent of the people of Latin America live under direct military rule or under governments responsible to the military. These regimes are notoriously unstable. Bolivia, an extreme example, has had more than 200 coups during the past century and a half, three of them since 1978. A civilian administration, elected in 1979 after ten years of army rule, lasted less than three months. Democratic prospects brightened that fall when, following the expulsion of a coup leader, the presidency was entrusted to Lydia Gueiler, an elderly

Prevalence of military governments: Bolivia an extreme example

grandmother, who kept the generals in their barracks until she had carried out plans for a free general election, held in June 1980. But when the voters chose as president an elder statesman who had enacted popular reforms during his tenure of office in the 1950s, the military, led by General Luis Garcia Meza, struck swiftly, arresting Gueiler and her cabinet and preventing the newly elected president from taking office. The coup was encouraged and actively assisted by General Videla, dictator of Argentina, who declared that an elected government in Bolivia posed "a high degree of risk."

Most of the Latin American military governments are both repressive and reactionary, depleting resources through excessive defense budgets and employing specially trained counterinsurgency forces to quell any opposition within their own countries. They are generally allied with local oligarchs and assisted by foreign capital. An exception to the norm is Peru, where in 1968 the army installed a regime that was both authoritarian and progressive. Under the leadership of General Juan Velásco Alvarado some 8 million acres of land were redistributed, workers' cooperatives set up, educational opportunities extended for both men and women, and large foreign properties nationalized. These reforms for the benefit of the poor antagonized the rich, while a depressed economy and steadily increasing cost of living aroused general discontent, leading in the mid-1970s to riots, which the government forcefully suppressed. When Velásco was overthrown by another officer in 1975, his successor promised a return to civilian rule. A general election in May 1975 resulted in a clear victory for ex-President Fernando Belaúnde Terry, an architect, city planner, and political moderate.

Uruguay, smallest of the South American republics with a population of less than 3 million, had a better record of educational and political progress than most of its neighbors for many years. A constitution, modeled upon that of Switzerland, provided for equal suffrage, the secret ballot, and minority representation. José Batlle y Ordóñez, an outstanding statesman, president from 1903 to 1907 and from 1911 to 1915, created a type of welfare state. His reforms, which included the eight-hour day and minimum wages, old-age pensions and social insurance, benefited city workers but, unfortunately, did less for the peasants because they left the monopolistic land system unchanged. After several decades of relative prosperity and a rising standard of living, since mid-century the country has suffered economic decline, attributable partly to falling prices for its exports of wool, meat, and hides, but partly to such internal factors as a narrow concentration of wealth, inefficiency in both agriculture and industry, and bureaucratic waste in government. Demoralized by a runaway inflation, Uruguay was torn by strikes and riots and terrorized by bands of desperate guerrillas. Yielding to pressure from the army, President Juan Bordaberry, in June 1973, dissolved Congress and announced that he would govern by decree. His coup was accompanied by harsh repression and the wholesale arrest of trade union leaders. Subsequently, the constitution was suspended, parliament replaced by a National Security Council, political parties and trade unions suppressed, and censorship imposed. The military dictatorship, following the gruesome pattern of intimidation and torture, set a new record for political imprisonment. By the end of 1975, 2 percent of the population was under detention. Uruguay—a state once hailed as the "Switzerland of South America" and a model of democracy—had become one of the worst offenders against human rights.

Most of the small banana and sugar republics of Central America and the West Indies have been denied the advantages of democratic government. Guatemala, for instance, has been the victim of foreign intervention and dictatorship. When President Jacobo Arbenz of Guatemala attempted to expropriate idle lands and transfer them to landless peasants in 1954, the oligarchy of large estate owners overthrew his government by an armed invasion, staged in neighboring Honduras with the support of the United Fruit Company and the CIA. Internal violence, endemic in Guatemala since the 1954 coup, has cost the lives of at least 40,000 people. Despite acceptable constitutions, the Dominican and Haitian republics passed under personal dictatorships tempered by assassination or the threat thereof. The Dominican Republic suffered under the misrule of General Rafael L. Trujillo for nearly thirty years until he was blotted out by assassins' bullets in 1961. Graft, nepotism, and police terrorism had been the instruments of his power. Elections held in 1962 resulted in the choice of Juan Bosch, a liberal intellectual, as president. After less than a year he was overthrown, and a military clique assumed power. In 1965 Bosch and his followers, including some Communists, launched a counterrevolt. Bloody strife ensued followed by prompt United States intervention. President Johnson professed an obligation to protect American lives and to save the island from communism. Eventually, upon pleas from Washington, the Organization of American States sent a joint expedition to maintain order in the Dominican Republic, but unrest continued. The inauguration in August 1978 of Antonio Guzmán as president marked the first peaceful transfer of power between constitutionally elected governments in the nation's history.

Political turbulence in Central America and the West Indies

Similar troubles beset the republic of Haiti. Beginning in 1945 a series of revolutions alternating with chaos culminated in 1957 in the dictatorship of François Duvalier. Though he ruled with the title of president, his power rested upon the armed forces. In 1964 he was made president for life. Relying on repression as harsh as that of General Trujillo, he faced the constant possibility of revolution, for Haiti is poorer and culturally more backward than the Dominican Republic. It has the highest rate of illiteracy, the deepest poverty, and the most primitive economic development of all the countries of Latin America. Nevertheless, its government had one advantage over the governments of some neighboring states: it enjoyed the support of

The Duvalier dictatorship in Haiti

Washington. The State Department evidently considered Duvalier the least of a number of possible evils. When "Papa Doc" died in 1971, his twenty-year-old playboy son, Jean-Claude Duvalier, succeeded him as president for life. Although "Baby Doc" freed a few political prisoners and gave the appearance of relaxing the terror, he only made it less open; conditions remained the same as before. Farmers, comprising 80 percent of the population, barely subsist on soil depleted in fertility and impaired by erosion. Three-fourths of Haiti's children suffer from malnutrition; the infant mortality rate is more than ten times that of the United States. Factory workers, for near-starvation wages, produce underwear, wigs, stuffed toys, and baseballs for export to American markets. One proof of the desperate plight of these people of the "Fourth World" is that thousands of them have attempted to escape by boat, hoping to be granted political asylum in the United States. Upon reaching Miami, many have been jailed for illegal entry or forced to return to Haiti.

The Cuban revolution

Among the smaller Latin American nations, Cuba occupies a unique position because of the transformation it has undergone and because of the controversy it has aroused. Freed from Spanish rule in 1898, Cuba became nominally independent but actually a semicolony of the United States. By treaty and by a clause inserted in the Cuban Constitution of 1901, the United States was given the right to intervene in the internal affairs of the new republic, and did so several times before the so-called Platt Amendment was revoked in 1934 under President Franklin Roosevelt's "good neighbor" policy. The United States, however, retained a naval base at Guantánamo Bay. A rising spirit of nationalism, resentment against a narrow concentration of wealth, and the weakness of a two-crop economy left the country a prey to disorder. Events reached a crisis during the world depression of the 1930s. In 1936 a ruthless army sergeant, Fulgencio Batista, with aid from the United States and the support of the army, gained control of the government. In 1940 he was elected president. With the titular as well as the actual authority in his hands, he maintained a dictatorial rule until 1959. In that year he was overthrown by a coterie of young revolutionists under the leadership of Fidel Castro. Castro's program was essentially a patchwork and his followers a motley assortment. Some were anti-Communists, some were democratic socialists, and several had definite commitments to communism. Calling their bid for power the Twenty-sixth of July Movement because it had been launched on July 26, 1953, Castro and his comrades eventually demanded a complete revolution in Cuba. They would obliterate all traces of United States imperialism, expropriating American owners of banks, industries, and hotels. They would nationalize these properties and some others in order to provide jobs for the unemployed. They proposed also an extensive land reform for the benefit of the peasants. As the movement extended its power over the country and

Fidel Castro

gained full control in 1959, it took on a more radical character. In 1961 Castro announced himself "a Marxist-Leninist."

Following their dramatic victory in 1959 the revolutionaries faced difficult years as they attempted to transform Cuba's social and economic base while struggling to survive and to win international recognition. Alarmed at the prospect of profit losses to investors if foreign holdings were nationalized, the United States severed relations with Cuba in 1961, later persuaded the Organization of American States to expel Cuba from membership, and imposed a trade embargo. Unable to isolate the wayward island republic completely, the Washington government in April 1961 planned and assisted an invasion of Cuba by embittered Cuban exiles. An attempted landing at the Bay of Pigs was a total failure. Stung by this rebuff the Kennedy administration permitted anti-Castro saboteurs and terrorists to operate out of Miami and urged the CIA to "get rid of" Castro. A Senate investigating committee later reported that between 1961 and 1963 eight separate assassination plots against the Cuban prime minister had been considered. The threat of invasion or subversion from the Colossus of the North helped to unify the islanders behind their revolutionary leaders. It also forced Castro to seek allies outside the Western Hemisphere and, ultimately, to become dependent on the Soviet Union for financial, military, and diplomatic support. Although the U.S.S.R. has kept Cuba in line by absorbing half of its sugar crop and providing free military assistance, the relationship has been an uneasy one. The discovery by United States intelligence agencies that the Soviets had stationed bombers and established missile bases in Cuba led to a critical confrontation between the two superpowers in October 1962. After exchanges with President Kennedy, Premier Khrushchev agreed to remove the missiles and dismantle the bases, but Cubans resented the fact that they had not been consulted during the crisis, even though the nuclear war so narrowly averted would have begun on their soil. Castro's government has sought, with growing success in recent years, to establish ties with other Latin American countries and with distant nations of the Third World. It has sent technicians, military instructors, and troops to several fledgling African states, not always with the blessing of the Soviet Union.

Years of crisis

The Cuba of Fidel Castro's revolution presents strange contradictions. The revolution has accomplished needed reforms and, in spite of erratic changes in government policy, has bettered living conditions for classes that had always been impoverished. It has lifted the country out of the stagnation that paralyzes most Latin American societies. Improved sanitation, hygiene, medical and hospital facilities raised the level of public health, as evidenced by a decline in deaths from tuberculosis, malaria, typhoid, and polio. The infant mortality rate is the lowest in Latin America, as is illiteracy, now down to about 4 percent of the population. Women, given legal equality with men, have

*The contradictions of
Castro's Cuba*

advanced in all the professions; 52 percent of the doctors are women. Beaches and resorts have been opened to the public, and the administration of justice—except for political offenders—is evenhanded. Economically, Cuba has remained dependent on a few exports, such as nickel and especially sugar, and the price of these declined sharply in the 1970s. There are shortages of many commodities; even necessities are rationed. Belying Castro's boast that by 1980 every family would own a house or an apartment and that every farmer would have an air-conditioned tractor, plans for industrial development have been drastically curtailed. But Cuba possesses fertile farmlands and with more efficient management could become a prosperous agricultural country. Aside from serious blunders in economic planning, the picture is shadowed by the suppression of personal freedom, censorship, and constant indoctrination—"government by oratory." By 1960 Castro was holding more political prisoners than had been jailed by Batista. Over 700,000 Cubans have left the country and other hundreds of thousands undoubtedly would do so if they could. The strong and weak points of the regime reflect the complex personality of its ruler, a man of tremendous charisma, courage, and drive but essentially an improviser, who drifted ideologically from constitutional democrat and anti-Communist "humanist" to "socialist" and then to "Marxist-Leninist" and Communist. Conceivably, with changing circumstances he might shift again. In 1978 he initiated a dialogue with leaders of his exiled countrymen, promised to free political prisoners and permit emigration, and welcomed foreign visitors to Havana. Having proved that a small country on the United States' doorstep could make itself independent of its mighty neighbor, he seemed eager to mend broken ties.

The "boatlift" of 1979–1980

Cuban efforts to improve relations with the United States have generally been rebuffed, and American animosity was reinforced when, beginning in the spring of 1979, a flood of Cuban emigrants crowded into vessels of every description and descended upon the Florida coast. Castro's motive for permitting this exodus was partly a desire to embarrass the United States government, which had failed to act upon an agreement negotiated in 1965 to admit to the United States 130,000 Cuban residents holding dual citizenship. Castro also saw an opportunity to get rid of undesirable elements, including mental patients and criminals, although these were a small minority of the more than 125,000 who came to American shores in 1979–1980. The "boatlift" operation was abetted by the 800,000-strong community of Cuban exiles living in the Miami area, and the sudden influx into southern Florida put a severe strain upon communities already overcrowded and afflicted by racial tensions.

Major changes in Latin America are needed before its people can approach the degree of well-being enjoyed by developed nations of the Western Hemisphere. Significant changes began during the 1970s. A step toward regional federation was taken in 1969 with the forma-

The Cuban "Boatlift." Between 800 and 900 Cuban refugees crammed on board the ocean-going tug *Dr. Daniels* on this day in early 1980 for the perilous trip from Cuba to Key West, Florida. Thousands of Cubans seized the opportunity to leave Cuba on any boat that would take them to the United States. The Cuban government sought to use this embarrassing situation to rid itself of individuals it identified as "undesirables."

tion of an Andean Pact comprising Bolivia, Chile, Colombia, Ecuador, and Peru, and joined by Venezuela in 1973. Chile, however, withdrew three years later; Bolivia's brutal July 1980 coup alienated other pact members; and the association has made little headway toward its goal of creating a common market. For an indefinite future Latin America will require financial and technical assistance, but the effectiveness of outside help depends upon the type of aid and the terms under which it is granted. Multinational corporations with large Latin American investments have used local capital for development projects while displacing local management and siphoning off most of the profits. United States corporations control upward of 75 percent of Latin America's raw materials and approximately half of its modern industry, banking, and foreign trade. President Kennedy's Alliance for Progress, initiated in 1961, disbursed aid chiefly in the form of loans, tied to United States exports and primarily benefiting the groups that already had a stranglehold on the Latin American economies. Designed to usher in a "Development Decade," the Alliance for Progress actually widened the gap between rich and poor and kept governments dependent upon foreign investors. The desire for economic independence has sparked a demand for restructuring the Organization of American States (OAS). A call for revision of the OAS, with exclusion of the United States, came from Venezuela, a country whose large petroleum reserves gave its economy the highest growth rate on the continent by the mid-1970s and upon which the United States relied for one-third of their crude oil imports. A seemingly minor but by no means negligible challenge to Washington's hegemony appeared in tiny Puerto Rico, a colony that had advanced

Problems and prospects

The Panama Canal under Construction. The Miraflores Lower Locks, November 12, 1912.

in 1952 to a partially self-governing commonwealth, but which after a period of rapid economic development was nearing financial collapse. While disagreeing on the solution for their problems, the islanders were nearly unanimous in desiring a change in the status quo.

The effects of Carter's human rights policy

The human-rights policy enunciated by President Jimmy Carter produced slight but potentially significant changes in the relationship between the United States and Latin America. Soon after taking office in 1977 President Carter pledged support to "political systems that allow their people to participate freely and democratically in the decisions that affect their lives." His administration cut off or reduced military aid to such flagrantly oppressive Latin American regimes as Argentina, Chile, and Bolivia; welcomed democratic tendencies discernible in Ecuador, Honduras, Peru, and even Brazil; and actually prevented a military coup in the Dominican Republic in 1978. After pressuring the Dominican president Joaquin Balaguer to honor his pledge to hold free elections, Washington, with the backing of the Organization of American States, warned Balaguer that serious consequences would follow any interference with the electoral process. The result was a victory for a popular coalition, the peaceful accession to office of a civilian president, Antonio Guzmán, and a softening of the traditional image of "Yankee imperialism."

The Panama Canal treaties

A notable departure in United States policy, marking perhaps the beginning of a new era in interhemisphere relations, was the settling, through patient negotiation, of a long and bitter dispute over the Panama Canal. Under United States control since 1903, the canal had declined in both economic and strategic importance. The surrounding zone, however, held fourteen military bases, used by the U.S. Southern Command and by the School of the Americas which trained counterinsurgency forces for Latin American military governments. In September 1977 President Jimmy Carter and General Omar Torrijos of Panama signed treaties providing for United States withdrawal from the zone, the gradual phasing out of the military bases, and the transfer of canal operation to Panama by the end of the century. In their first free election in nearly a decade, Panamanians ratified the treaties by plebiscite in October 1977.

Solid and lasting progress for Latin America requires transformation of the political and economic structure. In El Salvador, fiefdom of a coffee oligarchy, 2 percent of the population owns 60 percent of the land; illiteracy in the rural areas runs as high as 67 percent. Ecuador is owned by a Spanish landed aristocracy constituting 5 percent of the population, and by foreign corporations—Pepsi Cola, General Electric, Texaco, and United Fruit. Native Indians have been driven from their lands or reduced to a state of serfdom; 70 percent of Ecuador's children die before the age of three. More than half of Guatemala's arable land is owned by 2 percent of the farmers. Bolivia has the tin, silver, gold, and natural gas resources to make it a prosperous country, but a majority of its 5.5 million people—two thirds of them Indians—exist at or below the poverty level. While these illustrations are extreme cases, they are not too far from the norm. If reform does not come, revolution inevitably will. This fact was convincingly demonstrated in 1979 when a ragged band of guerrillas toppled Nicaragua's Anastasio Somoza, one of the most notorious dictators in Latin America. Somoza's father, commanding a national guard trained by United States Marines, had made himself president of Nicaragua in 1937, and his family henceforth treated the country as its private possession, acquiring ownership of practically the whole economy while forcibly

*The Nicaraguan
revolution*

The Nicaraguan Revolution. Sandinista commandos and elated citizens celebrate the fall of the Somoza government by toppling a huge statue of Anastasio Somoza Garcia, the father of the ousted president, in Managua, the nation's capital.

stifling opposition. Somoza's corruption and insatiable greed eventually lost him support of the business community, but effective resistance awaited the rise of the Sandinista National Liberation Front (named after a guerrilla leader who had been treacherously murdered by the elder Somoza) from the ranks of the dispossessed. In August 1978 twenty-five Sandinista commandos stormed the national palace, seized 1,500 hostages, and held them for ransom. By the following July the rebels had enlisted support throughout the country and, after forcing Somoza to flee to Miami, they set up a National Reconstruction Government, representing a wide spectrum of political opinion and including several Catholic priests. The junta undertook the staggering task of rebuilding a shattered economy, of wiping out illiteracy (within two years reducing it from 50 percent to 12 percent), and of developing democratic institutions. Although the revolutionary government nationalized the Somoza family's holdings, it adopted the goal of a mixed capitalist-socialist economy in which private enterprise would retain an important role. Affirming its commitment to human rights, the ruling group abolished the death penalty. It also pursued an independent foreign policy, attempting to cultivate friendly relations with Nicaragua's neighbors and with the United States.

The successful Nicaraguan revolution sent tremors through neighboring Honduras, Guatemala, and El Salvador, all under harsh military regimes. The woefully undeveloped country of Honduras was returned to civilian rule with the election of a constituent assembly in April 1980. In October 1979 a coup led by younger army officers ousted the hard-line dictator of El Salvador. A joint military-civilian junta that came to power with the coup enunciated a far-reaching reform program, including nationalization of banks and land redistribution. Opposition from large landowners and conservative business interests crippled the reform process and infuriated the radical left, resulting in rapidly escalating outbreaks of violence. The ruling junta allied itself more and more closely with the extreme right, tolerating right-wing death squads that kidnaped, tortured, and executed their opponents. Battle lines were drawn between the National Guard and the Democratic Revolutionary Front, which had been formed by representatives of some 150 organizations. In 1980 the death toll exceeded 10,000 and an equal number of families fled from their homes. In March Archbishop Oscar Romero, who had protested the shipment of U.S. arms to El Salvador, was assassinated. The following December four American missionary women were murdered in the countryside. In January 1981 two more Americans, including the head of El Salvador's Agrarian Reform Institute, were killed. Although evidence pointed to the National Guard's complicity in these outrages, the United States government early in 1981 decided to increase military aid to the junta. As U.S. intervention was countered by Cuban help to the guerrillas by way of Nicaragua, the tiny country faced the prospect of a long and devastating civil war.

Revolutionary movements in Latin America have won substantial support from segments of the Catholic church and from Protestant denominations. Beginning in the 1960s, groups of young priests became outspoken advocates of social justice and sought to relieve mass poverty by direct action, a stand that brought them increasingly into conflict with their governments. Some 850 bishops, priests, and nuns have been murdered, arrested, or tortured during the past ten years; church publications have been seized and presses destroyed. In El Salvador Jesuits were denounced as "agents of international communism." In light of the church's historic role as ally and staunch support of dominant Latin American oligarchies, the shift during the last two decades is truly dramatic.

The church and revolution

SELECTED READINGS

• *Items so designated are available in paperback editions.*

Alexander, R. J., *The Perón Era,* New York, 1951.

——, *Prophets of the Revolution: Profiles of Latin American Leaders,* New York, 1962.

——, The Tragedy of Chile, Westport, Conn., 1978. A detached political narrative.

Arciniegas, Germán, *Latin America: A Cultural History,* New York, 1967.

Bailey, Helen, and A. P. Nasatir, *Latin America: The Development of Its Civilization,* 2d ed., Englewood Cliffs, N.J., 1968.

• Boorstein, Edward, *Allende's Chile: An Inside View,* New York, 1977. By Allende's economic adviser.

Burnell, Elaine, ed., *One Spark from Holocaust: The Crisis in Latin America,* Santa Barbara, 1972. A valuable and provocative symposium.

• Cardoso, F. H., and E. Faletto, *Dependency and Development in Latin America,* tr. M. M. Urquidi, Berkeley, 1979.

• Cline, H. F., *The United States and Mexico,* Cambridge, Mass., 1953.

Crawford, W. Rex, *A Century of Latin American Thought,* Cambridge, Mass., 1944.

• Cumberland, C. C., *The Meaning of the Mexican Revolution,* New York, 1967.

DeVylder, Stefan, *Allende's Chile: The Political Economy of the Rise and Fall of the Unidad Popular,* New York, 1976.

• Dobyns, H. F., and P. L. Doughty, *Peru: A Cultural History,* New York, 1977.

Draper, Theodore, *Castroism, Theory and Practice,* New York, 1965. Highly critical.

Fagg, J. E., *Latin America, a General History,* 3d ed., New York, 1977.

Fiechter, G. A., *Brazil since 1964: Modernization under a Military Regime,* tr. Alan Braley, New York, 1975. A judicious account by a Swiss author.

• González Casanova, Pablo, *Democracy in Mexico,* 2d ed., tr. Danielle Salti, New York, 1972. A brief study by a distinguished Mexican scholar.

Gordon, W. C., *The Political Economy of Latin America,* New York, 1965.

• Halperin, Maurice, *The Rise and Decline of Fidel Castro,* Berkeley, 1972. A critical account of the years 1959–1964.

Hanke, Lewis, *Latin America, a Historical Reader,* Boston, 1974.

• Hellman, J. A., *Mexico in Crisis,* New York, 1978. Assesses developments since the 1910 Revolution.

Hemming, John *Red Gold: The Conquest of the Brazilian Indians,* Cambridge, Mass., 1978. Depicts the tragic results of European expansionism.

LaFeber, Walter, *The Panama Canal: The Crisis in Historical Perspective,* New York, 1978. An informative study of U.S.-Panamanian relations.

Lambert, Jacques, *Latin America: Social Structure and Political Institutions,* tr. Helen Katel, Berkeley, 1967.

Llerena, Mario, *The Unsuspected Revolution: The Birth and Rise of Castroism,* Ithaca, 1978.

• Loveman, Brian, *Chile: The Legacy of Hispanic Capitalism,* New York, 1979. A social and economic history to the overthrow of Allende.

• Lynch, John, *The Spanish American Revolutions, 1808–1826,* New York, 1973.

MacEoin, Gary, *Revolution Next Door: Latin America in the 1970s,* New York, 1971. A profoundly disturbing view of Latin American realities.

• Picón-Salas, Mariano, *A Cultural History of Spanish America: From Conquest to Independence,* tr. I. A. Leonard, Berkeley, 1962.

• Pike, Frederick B., *Spanish America 1900–1970: Traditional and Social Innovation,* New York, 1973.

• Poppino, R. E., *Brazil: The Land and People,* 2d ed., New York, 1973.

Rotberg, R. I., with C. K. Clague, *Haiti: The Politics of Squalor,* Boston, 1971.

Sandford, R. R., *The Murder of Allende and the End of the Chilean Way to Socialism,* tr. Andrée Conrad, New York, 1975. A harrowing narrative by a Chilean political journalist.

• Skidmore, T. E., *Politics in Brazil, 1930–1964: An Experiment in Democracy,* New York, 1969.

• Smith, P. H., *Labyrinths of Power: Political Recruitment in Twentieth-Century Mexico,* Princeton, 1979. A careful analysis of the Mexican political power structure.

Steenland, Kyle, *Agrarian Reform under Allende: Peasant Revolt in the South,* Albuquerque, 1978.

Thomas, Hugh, *Cuba: The Pursuit of Freedom,* New York, 1971. A monumental, well-documented history of Cuba from 1762 to 1970.

• Waddell, D. A. G., *The West Indies and the Guianas,* Englewood Cliffs, N.J., 1967.

Weaver, Muriel, *The Aztecs, Maya, and Their Predecessors: Archaeology of Mesoamerica,* New York, 1972.

Weinstein, Martin, *Uruguay: The Politics of Failure,* Westport, Conn., 1975. A compact, informative analysis.

Wilgus, A. C., ed., *South American Dictators during the First Century of Independence,* Washington, 1937.

Chapter 37

THE COMMONWEALTH OF NATIONS

We are fortunate to witness the emergence of the Republic of India and our successors may well envy us this day, but fortune is a hostage which has to be zealously guarded by our own good work and which has a tendency to slip away if we slacken in our efforts or if we look in wrong directions.

—Jawaharlal Nehru, 1951

Millions of our countrymen filled the jails again and again to attain freedom, but after twenty-seven years of that freedom the people are groaning. Hunger, soaring prices and corruption stalk everywhere. The people are being crushed under all sorts of injustice.

—Jayaprakash Narayan, 1974

O ne of the most significant developments in the history of democracy in the modern world has been the evolution of the Commonwealth of Nations. Originally called the British Commonwealth of Nations, it now includes a number of states which repudiate any suggestion of allegiance to Britain. All members of the Commonwealth are self-governing, but many of them recognize the British monarch, represented by a governor-general, as their head of state. This group includes—in addition to the United Kingdom—the large Dominions of Canada, Australia, and New Zealand, and such small ones as Barbados, Jamaica, Malta, Mauritius, Sierra Leone, and Trinidad and Tobago. Political changes within the last few years have resulted in the creation within the Commonwealth of many republics, with no ties to the British Crown. The most conspicuous example is India, but the Commonwealth embraces more than a dozen republics, ranging in size from medium to tiny: Bangladesh, Botswana, Cyprus, Sri Lanka (Ceylon), Fiji, Gambia, Ghana, Guyana, Kenya, Malawi, Malaysia, Nigeria, Singapore, Tanzania, Uganda, and Zambia. The little African state of Lesotho (an enclave within the Republic of South Africa) has the distinction of being a separate kingdom within the

The Commonwealth defined

Commonwealth, under the headship of its Paramount Chief. Evidently the only requisite for membership in the Commonwealth is the desire to belong. Because members may secede at any time and new states may join, the Commonwealth is an evolving organization. Ireland withdrew in 1949 and South Africa in 1961. Pakistan—shaken by a disastrous war with India and angered by the recognition accorded to Bangladesh—terminated its membership in the Commonwealth in 1972. The newly independent Republic of Bangladesh joined the next year. The status of Rhodesia was in dispute for fifteen years following a declaration of independence in 1965 by Ian Smith, leader of Rhodesia's white minority. Britain is no longer the focal point of the Commonwealth, whose membership is spread around the globe. Since 1965 the organization has had its own Secretariat headed by a secretary-general. In recent years the area of most active political change has been the Caribbean, where all of Britain's former colonies are preparing for, or have already achieved, independence. The dozen or so ministates resulting from this movement seek economic aid outside the Commonwealth and also wish to establish closer ties with their non-English-speaking neighbors. Dominica, a tiny island of the Lesser Antilles, which progressed from an "associated state" to an independent republic in 1978, elected to remain in the Commonwealth but also planned to join the Organization of American States and other international organizations. Jamaica (which retains as nominal head of state a governor-general appointed by the British Crown rather than an elected president), under Prime Minister Michael Manley (1972–1980), experimented with close ties to Castro's Cuba.

The history of the United Kingdom and of the principal African states is discussed elsewhere. The purpose of this chapter is to give an account of the major Asian republics that arose within the Commonwealth and of the self-governing dominions settled primarily by emigrants from Britain.[1]

The growth of the Commonwealth

The Commonwealth of Nations as an association of independent or virtually independent states has a history of about seven decades. At an Imperial Conference in 1887, attended by prime ministers of the principal British possessions, suggestions were made that the colonies furthest advanced ought to have the right to participate in the government of the Empire. The idea was revived at subsequent Imperial Conferences, in 1897, in 1902, and in 1907. It was not, however, until World War I that the proposal gave much promise of becoming a reality. The free and liberal assistance given to the mother country by the dominions in that struggle fortified their claims not only to a direct

[1] The Commonwealth of Nations must be distinguished clearly from the British Empire. The latter consists of two parts: the independent empire and the dependent empire. The independent empire includes those members of the Commonwealth of Nations which still render some tenuous allegiance to Great Britain. The dependent empire comprises a diminishing number of colonies ruled directly from London.

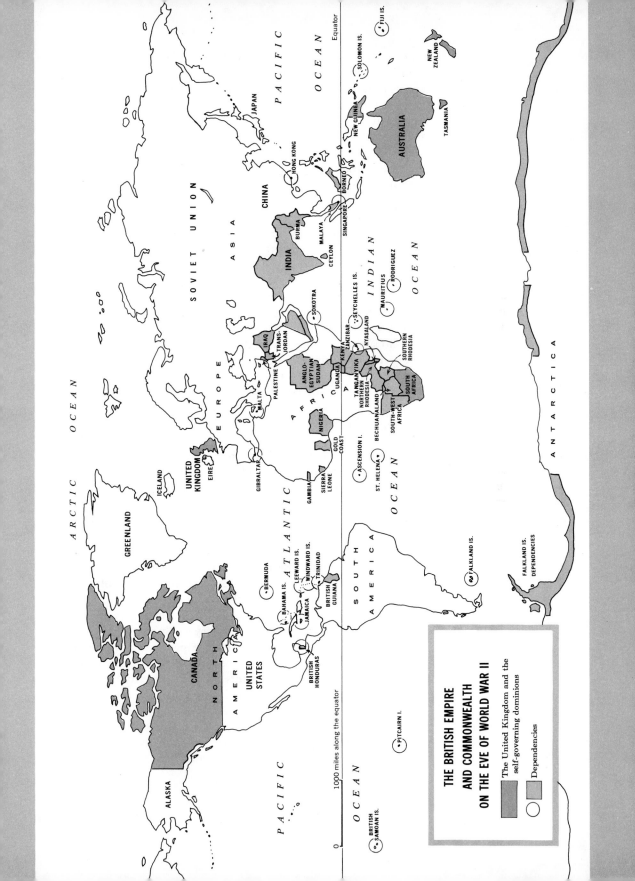

THE BRITISH EMPIRE
AND COMMONWEALTH
ON THE EVE OF WORLD WAR II

The United Kingdom and the
self-governing dominions

Dependencies

voice in imperial affairs but to a more definite recognition of their own independence. The Imperial Conference of 1921 agreed that the events of the war had clearly established the right of the self-governing dominions to be considered coequals with the mother country in foreign affairs. The Conference of 1926 adopted a report prepared by Arthur James Balfour, former prime minister of Great Britain. The report described the self-governing areas under the British flag (including the United Kingdom) as "autonomous communities within the British Empire, equal in status, in no way subordinate one to another in any aspect of their domestic or external affairs, though united by a common allegiance to the crown, and freely associated as members of the British Commonwealth of Nations." In 1931 the substance of the Balfour Report was enacted by Parliament in a memorable law known as the Statute of Westminster.

The Statute of Westminster

Since the enactment of the Statute of Westminster the several states of the Commonwealth of Nations have functioned as practically independent republics. No longer may any law passed by a dominion parliament be disallowed by the Parliament in London or vetoed by the British Cabinet, and no law of the British Parliament may be applied to any dominion unless its government specifically requests that this be done. The prime minister of each dominion has an equal right with the prime minister of Britain to "advise" the king directly. The king himself serves as a mere symbol of the unity of the Commonwealth. Although he is represented in each dominion (but not in the Republics) by a governor-general, the latter has no real authority. His primary function is to receive the resignation of an outgoing prime minister and to designate the leader of the opposition party as his successor. This involves no more freedom of choice than is exercised by the monarch himself when the head of the British Cabinet loses the support of the majority in the House of Commons and gives way to the leader of His (Her) Majesty's Loyal Opposition.

Deficiencies of the Commonwealth

The Commonwealth is no longer the boon to Great Britain that it formerly was. Even those members that acknowledge allegiance to the British monarch have shown an increasing spirit of economic independence and indifference to the welfare of the United Kingdom. It has been said that most of the Old World members are about as beneficial to the former mother country as "poor relations on pay day." Though they continue to look for generous contributions of British aid, they show little disposition to confer any benefits in return. Ghana, for example, grants no preference to British goods. While Australian industrial products enter New Zealand duty free, British goods are subject to tariffs. Air India not only competes with British Airways, but equips its fleet with commercial airliners purchased from the United States. In 1965 Britain had a total trade deficit with the Commonwealth nations of over $1 billion.

The recorded history of Canada dates from 1608 when Samuel Champlain, a French naval officer with an interest in the fur trade, founded a settlement at Quebec. For thirty years thereafter he continued his activities in the St. Lawrence valley, staking claims for the French king as far west as Lake Huron. Later in the seventeenth century the French government granted monopolies to trading companies to colonize and develop "New France." Although the companies ultimately failed, they did establish a few forts and trading posts and brought over a few thousand of their countrymen as permanent settlers. Finally, Jesuit missionaries contributed their part toward opening up the country and enlarging knowledge of its resources and attractions. By the middle of the eighteenth century the population of Canada included about 60,000 Frenchmen.

The founding of Canada

France lost Canada to Great Britain in the French and Indian War, but for some years thereafter the British continued to assume that their newly acquired possession would remain French. When the British Parliament passed the Quebec Act in 1774 to correct certain defects in the organization of the Empire, Canada was not given a representative assembly, since it was taken for granted that the people could neither understand nor be loyal to British institutions. But after the American War for Independence so many Loyalist refugees from the United States, together with immigrants from Great Britain, settled in Ontario that William Pitt thought it advisable to have Parliament enact a law in 1791 separating Upper Canada (Ontario), which was almost entirely British, from Lower Canada (Quebec), which was overwhelmingly French, and providing for an elective assembly in each of the two provinces. The scheme ended in failure. The French and British distrusted each other, and conflicts soon arose between the elective assemblies and the royal governors sent out from London. In 1837 the antagonism flared into an open rebellion. Although quickly suppressed, it called attention to Canada's grievances and impressed upon the British government the necessity of doing something about them. The result was the appointment of a High Commissioner, Lord Durham, with authority to investigate conditions and to institute reforms. When he proceeded to act in too arbitrary a fashion, the government in London withdrew its support and revoked some of his decrees. Durham resigned in anger and returned to England, but subsequently published a report which was destined to become famous in the history of dominion government.

Troubles between French and British Canada

The Durham Report enunciated two principles, which may be regarded as the cornerstone of the dominion system. First, its author declared that colonies already possessing representative institutions should be granted "responsible government." This meant that they

The beginning of responsible government

should be permitted to manage their local affairs through cabinets or ministries responsible to their own legislatures. In the second place, Lord Durham urged the principle that similar colonies in the same geographic area should be federated into one large unit. Applying this to Canada, he pleaded for the unification of the British and French portions into a single dominion. In accordance with this recommendation Upper and Lower Canada were presently united. In 1847 Lord Durham's son-in-law, Lord Elgin, became governor of Canada and put into effect the principle of choosing his cabinet from the party that controlled a majority of seats in the assembly. He allowed it to be inferred that the cabinet would remain in office only so long as it received the support of the majority party. In addition he signed bills sponsored by the cabinet, despite the fact that they conflicted with the interests of the mother country. By these means he conferred upon Canada for all practical purposes a system of responsible government similar to that of Great Britain.

Establishment of the Dominion of Canada

But the dominion government as we now know it dates only from 1867. In that year the hitherto separate colonies of New Brunswick and Nova Scotia united with Quebec and Ontario to form a confederation under the name of the Dominion of Canada. A frame of government was provided for them by the British North America Act passed by the London Parliament in the same year. This act embodied a constitution which the Canadians themselves had adopted in 1864. It established a federal system with a division of powers between the central government and the governments of the provinces. All powers not delegated to the governments of the provinces were declared to be reserved to the central government, with its capital at Ottawa in Ontario Province. This departure from the federal pattern in the United States was inspired in part by the fact that the claims of the seceding southern states to full sovereignty had helped to bring on the American War between the States.

The British North America Act

The British North America Act confirmed the principle of responsible government. A governor-general, appointed technically by the king but actually by the British Cabinet, was made the nominal head of the Dominion. The real power over local affairs was placed in the hands of a Dominion cabinet, nominally appointed by the governor-general but actually responsible to the lower house of the legislature for its official acts and its tenure of office. Legislative power was vested in a Parliament of two houses, a Senate appointed by the governor-general for life, and a House of Commons elected by the people. Except for the fact that cabinet responsibility was to be enforced by the House of Commons exclusively and that money bills must originate therein, both houses were given equal powers. In practice, however, the Senate has retired into a kind of dignified obsolescence, performing no functions except those of an unambitious revising chamber. The Canadian constitution also provided for responsible government in the provinces. The nominal head of each province is a

The Fathers of Confederation. Painting by R. Harris. The constitution that established the confederation was based on the British system of parliamentary government. The British system had to be adapted to satisfy the need for a federal rather than a unitary structure and the framers of the constitution and the confederation inevitably looked to the Constitution of the United States for guidance. The result was a uniquely Canadian achievement designed to address Canada's particular requirements.

lieutenant-governor appointed by the Dominion cabinet. The effective authority is exercised by a cabinet responsible to the provincial legislature. Except in Quebec the legislative bodies in the provinces have only one house.

Since 1867 the growth of Canada has roughly paralleled that of the United States. When the British North America Act was passed, Canada had a population of 3½ million. By 1966 it had grown to 20 million. During the same period the population of the United States increased from 38 million to 196 million. The growth in area of the Dominion of Canada was equally phenomenal. In 1869 the province of Manitoba was carved out of territory purchased from the Hudson's Bay Company. In 1871–1873 British Columbia and Prince Edward Island were added to the Dominion. By 1905 the completion of the Canadian Pacific Railway made possible the creation of two new prairie provinces, Alberta and Saskatchewan. But the growth of Canada cannot be measured in terms of area and population alone. The latter half of the nineteenth century and the early years of the twentieth witnessed the establishment of a sound banking and currency system, a civil service, and a protective tariff for the benefit of Canadian industry. Marked progress occurred also in the exploitation of mineral and forest resources. Canada became the chief supplier of nickel, asbestos, cobalt, and wood pulp to the United States.

Growth of the Dominion

But the Dominion had not yet attained national maturity. It could not amend its own constitution, which in form was an act of the British Parliament, and it was dependent upon the mother country for the conduct of its foreign relations. Perhaps more significant, its population was not being welded into homogeneity. With the opening up of the West, thousands of Ruthenians, Russians, Poles, Scandinavians, and Germans flooded the prairie provinces. Between 1903 and 1914 nearly 2,700,000 such immigrants made their way into Canada. As late as 1941 more than 40 percent of the population of the prairie provinces was of Central or East European origin. But by far the largest minority population was to be found in Quebec. It comprised the French Canadians, whose settlement in the country went back to the earliest beginnings. Fearful of domination by the English-speaking majority and unable to exert much influence on the policies of the central government, they fortified their independent spirit by an increase in numbers—the "revenge of the nursery." Until well into the twentieth century French Canadians had one of the highest birth rates in the world, and today they constitute more than 25 percent of Canada's total population of 23 million. Since 1954, however, their birth rate has been declining, and Quebec now has the lowest rate of population increase in the Dominion. A growing disadvantage in numbers strengthened the French Canadians' determination to resist assimilation.

It is generally asserted that Canada achieved maturity as a nation during World War I. Although interested but little in the tortuous diplomacy leading up to the conflict, the Ottawa government accepted Britain's declaration as an automatic commitment for the whole Empire. The Dominion pledged itself to unlimited support and made sacrifices proportionately equal to those of the mother country itself. Out of a population of only 9 million at the time, 600,000 joined the armed forces, and more than 50,000 gave up their lives on the fighting front. Proud of their efforts in what was generally regarded as a noble cause, Canadians lost their sense of colonial inferiority and came forth as leading champions of Western ideals of democracy and peace. After 1917 the Canadian prime minister sat in the Imperial War Cabinet as an equal of the prime minister of Great Britain in formulating policy. When the war ended, Canada demanded and received a seat at the Peace Conference and subsequently was admitted to the League of Nations. In the years that followed, the Dominion asserted its independence in foreign policy by refusing to accept commitments under treaties negotiated by the British without Canadian participation. Nevertheless, when World War II broke out, Canada plunged into the fray with hardly a moment's hesitation. The threat to the survival of Britain was almost universally regarded as a threat to the interests of Canada. Although the Dominion might legally have remained neutral, it pledged its wealth and the lives of its youth in the same unstinted measure as had characterized its action in World War I.

By the end of World War II Canada, with a greatly strengthened economy, had won a prominent place in world affairs. The Dominion made loans to Great Britain and played a significant role in the development of the United Nations and in the establishment of NATO. At the same time, many old problems remained unsolved. As a nation Canada was still underpopulated. With an area almost equal to that of Europe, it had fewer inhabitants than New York State. Forty-five percent of its people dwelt in the St. Lawrence valley in an area covering but 2 percent of the country. The Yukon and Northwest territories, equal in size to half of the United States, contained only 14,000 inhabitants. At least 50 percent of the land of the Dominion remained unsuitable for agriculture or for almost any other occupation except fur trading and mining. Worse still, the population was sharply divided on the basis of sectional and ethnic interests. Ontario was dominated by industrial and financial ambitions, which gave to the province a conservative outlook in economic affairs and at the same time a determination to achieve independence from British and American influences. The prairie provinces, inhabited largely by immigrants from the United States and from Continental European countries, were the stronghold of agrarian collectivism and of radical innovations for currency inflation and cheap credit. French Canada, embraced by the province of Quebec, continued its devotion to the culture and religion of its ancestors and its resistance to domination from Ottawa.

Old problems remaining unsolved

The geographic position of Canada was also a source of uneasiness. It had the misfortune to lie directly athwart the air routes between Russia and the United States. As the Cold War between these two giants waxed in intensity, Canada had reason to fear that the United States might attempt to dictate an increasing number of its military and economic policies. Many Canadian businessmen disliked the influx of capital investment from the United States, the control of branch factories by foreign head offices, and the excess of imports from the United States over Canadian exports purchased by the States. So strong was the ill feeling that President Eisenhower paid a visit to Ottawa in 1958 and arranged for the setting up of a joint governmental committee to promote cooperation and a better understanding between the two countries. Any results the committee may have achieved were nullified by sharp criticism by the United States government, early in 1963, of Canada's unwillingness to equip its armed forces with nuclear weapons. In the ensuing controversy the Conservative prime minister, John Diefenbaker, lost the support of a majority in the House of Commons and yielded his office to Lester Pearson, leader of the Liberal party. In 1968 Pearson resigned on account of ill health and was succeeded by Pierre Trudeau.

Canada's crucial position

Prime Minister Pierre Trudeau of Canada

The eleven-year ministry of Canada's Liberal party under Pierre Trudeau was a colorful but hardly a tranquil period. Endowed with a lively intellect and considerable personal charm, Trudeau, even with a substantial following, was unable to solve Canada's basic problems. In spite of economic growth and the stimulus of profitable grain exports during the 1970s, nearly 8 percent of the work force was unemployed, and the Canadian dollar slumped below the exchange value of the United States dollar, which was also declining. Confidence in Trudeau's leadership was weakened by his wife's erratic conduct and also by the revelation of surreptitious activities carried on by the Royal Canadian Mounted Police. This revered police force, it was discovered, had for many years secretly opened mail, committed burglaries, and falsified records in combating suspected subversives. Like President Nixon when confronted with Watergate, Trudeau attempted—but failed—to block a judicial investigation of the affair, invoking the claim of "national security." An even deeper source of dissatisfaction lay in the opposition of Canada's provinces to the tightened control exercised by the central government ever since World War II. In Quebec, discontent threatened to disrupt the Dominion.

The French-speaking Québecois, comprising five-sixths of the province's 6 million inhabitants, had long-standing economic and ciate of Frank Lloyd Wright. In 1927 the seat of government of the Commonwealth was formally transferred to the new federal city. resented being conscripted to fight wars they regarded as English and imperialist. They wanted their own educational system to preserve their language and culture. In 1967 René Lévesque organized the *Parti Québecois,* which set as its goal the separation of Quebec from the Canadian federation. Steadily gathering support, the separatist party won a sizable majority of the provincial legislature in the election of 1976 and Lévesque became Quebec's premier. The Parti Québecois's victory made the question of separation a foremost national issue, and tralia policy has been motivated both by feelings of race superiority a French-speaking mother, Trudeau in 1969 had secured passage of the Official Languages Act, making the nation bilingual in public announcements and throughout the civil service. On the other hand, he had used extreme repression after the murder of a Quebec cabinet minister in 1970, and he was adamantly committed to maintaining the unity of Canada.

The Parti Québecois *and separatism*

The May 1979 general election toppled Trudeau's government but produced no clear mandate fot the Progressive Conservative party which took office without a majority in the House of Commons. The returns revealed the indifference of the majority of Canadians to the problem of Quebec. Curiously, the antiseparatist Trudeau carried Quebec while losing heavily throughout English-speaking Canada. The election also reflected the discontent of the western provinces. Joe Clark, the new prime minister and the youngest in Canadian history, was a native of the plains of Alberta. Canadians soon wearied of

A short-lived Conservative ministry

Clark, especially when he proposed an austerity program of steep tax increases and curtailed government spending, and his ministry was overthrown by an adverse vote on budgetary measures. In a special election in February 1980 the Liberal party won a clear majority, and the resilient Trudeau again became prime minister. Among the still unresolved problems confronting his government was the issue of Quebec separatism, which Trudeau, in common with the Conservative opposition, continued to oppose. It seemed doubtful that an independent Quebec could survive even if permitted to secede. Its industry has depended on access to a protected market within Canada. The province receives more in federal aid than it pays in taxes to the central government, yet it has a sizable budgetary deficit. A referendum that Lévesque held in the spring of 1980 indicated that two thirds of Quebec's voters opposed separation from the Canadian federation.

Serious disputes persisted between Ottawa and the sparsely inhabited but richly endowed and rapidly developing western provinces of Manitoba, Saskatchewan, Alberta, and British Columbia, toward which the balance of political power was shifting. Westerners complained that their interests were subordinated to those of populous Ontario and the Atlantic provinces. Trudeau resolved to replace the British North America Act of 1867 with a new constitution that would not only eliminate any hint of dependence on Great Britain, but would also give the central government greater control over natural resources and enable it to redress the inequitable distribution of wealth among the provinces. A conference of provincial premiers in the fall of 1980 failed to agree on constitutional changes. Western oil producers demanded the right to raise the price of oil, which had been kept at about half the current world price, and bridled at suggestions that the oil and gas industries might be nationalized.

Growing discontent of the Western provinces

Relations between Canada and the United States have long been close though sometimes strained. With investments of some $35 billion, by 1970 United States capital controlled the greater part of Canada's rubber and petroleum industries and about 45 percent of total manufacturing and mining capacity. The United States absorbed two-thirds of the Dominion's exports and supplied even more of its imports. Although Ottawa in 1976 established a contractual link with the European Common Market and entered into trade negotiations with Japan, trade between Canada and the United States increased even further. The two countries are each other's most important trade partner and seem likely to remain so. Beginning in 1968 the balance of trade shifted in Canada's favor, and Canada now has heavy capital investments in the United States. In the fall of 1980 the Canadian government took a number of controversial steps designed to reduce foreign control of its mineral and energy resources.

Relations with the United States

With full allowance for Canada's difficulties, there is little doubt that its future holds bright promise. Canada is one of the world's most richly endowed countries in natural resources. With a population hardly more than one-tenth that of the United States, the Dominion's foreign trade is almost one-third as large. Canada leads the world in the production of asbestos, nickel, platinum, zinc, and wood pulp. The nation ranks second in the production of aluminum, cobalt, and uranium, third in the production of gold and titanium, and fourth in the production of wheat. Extensive deposits of iron ore have been discovered in Labrador. Rich deposits of natural gas and oil (some of it under Arctic ice) are a particularly valuable asset when the world's energy sources are shrinking.

2. THE COMMONWEALTH OF AUSTRALIA

The second largest island[2] in the world and the smallest of the continents, Australia began its recorded history under inauspicious circumstances. Discovered by the Dutch in the seventeenth cenury and rediscovered and claimed for England by Captain James Cook in 1770, it was too remote from the homeland to offer attractions for settlement. When the American Revolution eliminated the thirteen colonies in the Western Hemisphere as dumping grounds for British convicts, the government in London turned to Australia. The first convict ship sailed for the island continent in 1787, and Australia remained a penal colony for fifty years. It should be noted, however, that not all the prisoners transported were burglars and cutthroats. The criminal laws of England at that time provided drastic penalties for trivial offenses, such as petty larceny or hunting partridges on

[2] Australia has an area of 2,967,000 square miles. Antarctica, also an island and a continent, has an estimated area of 6,000,000 square miles.

The Landing of Captain Cook at Botany Bay, 1770. This painting, by E. Phillips Fox, depicts the first landing by Englishmen on the east coast of the Australian continent.

Commissioner Hardy Collecting License Fees in the Victoria Gold Fields in the 1850s. Diggers scatter in order to evade paying the fees.

some noble's estate. We can reasonably assume, therefore, that many of the original colonists in Australia were far from being what we would now call hardened ciminals.

Convicts and settlers

The first settlers were convicts exclusively, except for 200 soldiers sent to guard them. This continued to be the case for some time. Gradually a few adventurous free citizens learned of the possibilities of sheep raising and filtered into the colony to establish ranches or "stations." Convicts were released to them as shepherds, with the provision that after the expiration of their terms of sentence they would continue to live in Australia. By 1830 the wool industry had become the backbone of the Australian economy. Ten years later the number of free settlers had grown sufficiently large to justify a decision by the British government to abandon the practice of dumping prisoners in most parts of the continent.

The discovery of gold

In 1848 the trend of Australian development was abruptly changed by the discovery of gold in New South Wales and Victoria. Fortune hunters and adventurers from all over the world followed the magic lure of the yellow metal. Between 1850 and 1860 the population of the continent almost trebled. Inevitably more people came than could find a livelihood in prospecting and mining. When the excitement died away, and the hills and streams no longer yielded gold in easy abundance, the problem arose of what to do with the surplus population. The logical solution seemed to be to encourage them to become farmers. Efforts to establish themselves in this occupation involved a desperate struggle. Scanty rainfall, inadequate transportation facilities, and refusal of the wool growers to "unlock" their vast estates dogged the footsteps of all but the most fortunate farmers with disaster. Not

Effects of the gold rushes

The growth of democracy in the Australian states

Establishment of the Commonwealth of Australia

until the building of railways to the ports, the perfection of dry-farming techniques, the development of suitable strains of wheat, and the improvement of chemical fertilizers was agriculture in Australia placed on a sound foundation.

A considerable number of the basic political and social policies of Australia as a nation can be traced to the gold rushes of the 1850s and their aftermath. First was the White Australia policy, designed to exclude black, brown, and yellow races from settlement on the continent. This policy was an outgrowth of conflicts between Chinese and Caucasian miners in the gold fields. A second was the attempt to build up a manufacturing industry through the use of protective tariffs. Originally adopted by the colony of Victoria in the 1860s, tariffs were later extended to the Commonwealth as a whole. Their use was motivated in part at least by the need for domestic industry to absorb the surplus miners. A third policy was the adoption of heavy governmental borrowing for the construction of public works. Obviously, the need for public works construction could be justified for many reasons: to provide irrigation projects for the benefit of farmers in arid regions; to speed up the development of transportation facilities; to furnish employment opportunities for the influx of immigrants brought in by the discovery of gold.

The Australian Commonwealth as an organized state did not come into existence until 1901. Prior to that time the continent was divided into separate colonies, most of which had split off from the original colony of New South Wales. Movements to federate them made slow progress, mainly because the weak feared domination by the strong and prosperous. But such fears did not prevent a rapid growth of local democracy. By 1850 each of the colonies had its legislative council as a check upon the governor, and had obtained the right to alter its own constitution. Soon afterward the eastern colonies achieved responsible government. Universal manhood suffrage was introduced in South Australia in 1855, in Victoria in 1857, and in New South Wales a year later. About the same time the secret ballot was adopted in Victoria, South Australia, New South Wales, and Queensland. Before 1900 two colonies had begun payment of salaries to members of their legislatures, and several had given women the privilege of voting.

The stage was eventually reached where the arguments for federation outweighed the objections. Foremost among them was the need for a common defense against the militant imperialism of the Great Powers. Important also was the growing inconvenience of tariffs levied by the various colonies against each other. The first step for a union of the continent was taken in 1885 with the establishment of the Australasian Federal Council. Possessing only legislative power with no executive or financial authority, this agency was reduced to impotence by the noncooperation of New South Wales. Its chief significance lay in the renewed impetus it gave to the demand for effective

Establishment of the Seat of Government at Canberra. The Duke and Duchess of York in the Senate at the official opening of the Federal Parliament House in Canberra on May 9, 1927. The Duke reads King George V's commission for the establishment of the seat of government at Canberra.

union. In 1897–1898 a series of conferences resulted in the drafting of a plan of federation which in 1901 was approved by the British Parliament and became the Constitution of the Commonwealth of Australia. The Commonwealth was organized as a federal union comprising the six states of New South Wales, Victoria, Queensland, South Australia, Western Australia, and Tasmania. The capital was temporarily established at Melbourne, but the Constitution contained a provision that a permanent capital should be built in the state of New South Wales, not less than 100 miles from Sydney. In the course of a decade the government invited city planners from all over the world to submit blueprints for a garden municipality to be known as Canberra. The award was given to W. B. Griffin of Chicago, an associate of Frank Lloyd Wright. In 1927 the seat of government of the Commonwealth was formally transferred to the new federal city.

The government of Australia bears a closer resemblance to that of the United States than does the government of Canada. Such a development was rendered inevitable by the spirit of independence existing within the states of Australia and by their distrust of each other. Consequently, when the division of powers was made by the Constitution, it was logical that the government of the Commonwealth should be given only specified powers, and that all powers not thus delegated should be reserved to the states. In some other respects also the Australian system resembles, superficially at least, the American. The Australian Parliament consists of two houses, a Senate and a House of Representatives. The former is composed of six members from each state, elected directly by the people for six years. Membership in the House is proportionate to population. Like several other members of the Commonwealth, Australia has a governor-general representing

The government of Australia

the British Crown, but his powers are insignificant. As in all of the dominions, executive authority as well as the primary control over legislation is vested in the cabinet headed by the prime minister.

One of the most interesting facts of Australian history is the extent to which the country has pursued a policy of social and economic planning. Even during the nineteenth century when the mother country was worshiping the slogans of free competition and free trade, Australia was steadily enlarging the sphere of governmental action to promote social cohesion and maintain a high standard of living. The reasons for this policy are numerous and varied. Geography alone provides a large part of the explanation. One-third of the continent has an average annual rainfall of less than 10 inches, and most of the remainder has less than 20. But even these averages do not reflect the poor distribution of the rain that does fall. In many areas the precipitation may be concentrated within a short period of the year, with months or years of subsequent drought. As a result, only about 8 percent of the total area can be utilized for farming or orchard purposes. About 40 percent is waste, and 50 percent is used for pasture. Under such conditions, it has been impossible for Australia to develop into a nation of independent proprietors cultivating small plots as family farms. In the pasture areas rainfall is so scanty or unreliable that sheep and cattle must be grazed over thousands of acres. This has necessitated the development of vast estates or pastoral "stations" established by owners with considerable capital. They provide employment for what is essentially an agricultural proletariat: shepherds, shearers, and "boundary riders," who have no hope of ever becoming proprietors. Conscious of their grievances, they have been drawn since the later nineteenth century into militant trade unions to struggle for old-age pensions, unemployment insurance, and minimum wages. They have been among the most consistent supporters of government intervention in economic affairs.

A second factor contributing to governmental control and regulation was the gold rushes of the 1850s. As previously noted, these produced a surplus of prospectors and miners who had to be channeled into new occupations. The result was positive action by the colonial governments to promote the development of industry and to extend agriculture into all parts of the limited area where rainfall would permit. The discovery of gold also gave rise to racial problems. In the 1850s thousands of Chinese poured into Victoria and New South Wales and threatened the wage scales and living standards of the white miners. Rapidly the Australians became obsessed with the idea that their country was a "white island in a vast colored ocean." Having already expropriated and partially exterminated the native black population, they pointed to the hundreds of millions of dark-skinned inhabitants of India, the Netherlands Indies, China, and Japan as a flood tide which would overwhelm them unless they built dikes in the form of rigid exclusion laws. Even the tropical regions of northern Australia were to be kept uncontaminated by Oriental labor. Queensland, for example, has taken pride in recent years in the ability of its white inhabitants to cultivate its sugar plantations without being defeated by the moral and physical diseases that have commonly wreaked such havoc upon Caucasians in the tropics.[3] The White Australia policy has been motivated both by feelings of race superiority and by fear of economic competition. Some of its sponsors argue that it is essential to democracy. Racial divisions, they say, would create tensions and conflicts and destroy the spirit of compromise which can exist only in a community of equals. After World War II immigration policy was modified somewhat. Yet as late as 1960 only 5 percent of Australians were of non-British origin. A few of these were Asians, but most had migrated from European countries other than Britain.

One of the earliest forms of government intervention in Australia was control of international trade. The methods employed have included tariffs, bounties, quotas, and marketing restrictions. From the middle of the nineteenth century the several Australian colonies imposed protective tariffs on intercolonial trade. They did so not merely for the benefit of the business classes but to provide employment and to maintain as high a standard of living as possible for farmers and workers. When the Commonwealth was established in 1901, the tariff policy was continued, and the rates have been steadily increased. Sentiment in favor of protection is almost universal. Labor as well as capital insists upon the importance of controlling economic forces for the general welfare. Neither has any respect for the laissez-faire philosophy or is willing to trust the fate of Australia to the shifting trends of the international market.

Protectionism

A second form of government intervention for which Australia has been particularly noted is public ownership of a wide variety of economic enterprises. Ventures brought under government ownership include railways, shipping lines, power plants, hotels, banks, insurance companies, lumber mills, and coal mines. Because of the federal structure of the government, most of such enterprises are conducted by the states rather than by the Commonwealth. Government ownership in Australia is the result in part of the strong influence which labor wields in both state and national politics. Owing to a rigid control of immigration, the supply of labor has been kept from exceeding the demand. This has fostered the growth of a unionism surpassing in strength that of most other countries. In Australia at the present time about 40 percent of all wage earners are enrolled in labor unions, compared with little more than 25 percent in the United States. But orga-

Government ownership

---

[3] It is an ironical fact, however, that in the nineteenth century thousands of Melanesians and Polynesians were brought in from the Pacific islands and shamelessly exploited. They were deported in 1906.

Australia's Nuclear Power Project. A 350-megawatt turbo-generator was commissioned in August 1973 at Yallourn, 90 miles east of Melbourne. The Yallourn complex is the main source of power for the highly industrialized state of Victoria. The plant, built by a Japanese firm, is dominated by the two giant cooling towers. In the background are the old Yallourn power station and an open cut coal field.

nized labor has not been the only force supporting state ownership. The geography of Australia has impelled many capitalists and landowners to look with favor upon government operation of railways and public utilities, at least. Scanty rainfall over most of the continent has limited the growth of cities and towns in the hinterland. But the construction of railroads to bring out the grain, wool, meat, and minerals has been none the less important. With few private corporations bold enough to incur the risks involved, there was no alternative but for governments to shoulder the burden. As a consequence, in these and in some other lines, public ownership of economic ventures has been welcomed as an aid and support of private business.

Other forms of collectivism

In social-welfare legislation Australian achievements have been little more distinctive than those of most other democracies. In a number of cases Australia (together with New Zealand) pioneered in this type of regulation. Other cases merely duplicated the pattern of Great Britain. Old-age pensions, widows' allowances, unemployment and health insurance, slum clearance, and child subsidies stand out as the principal examples. A bonus is paid for every infant born in Australia, and an endowment is provided for every child under sixteen. A National Health System furnishes free drugs, subsidizes hospital and medical expenses, and provides pensions for the blind and victims of tuberculosis. One other element of Australian collectivism, however, has had no counterpart in the mother country. This is a system of compulsory arbitration and wage fixing, designed to maintain industrial peace and safeguard standards of living for industrial workers. In sharp contrast with the attitude of organized labor in most countries, Australian workers have accepted, and for the most part actually welcomed, compulsory arbitration. They regard it as a means to security and as a source of strength for the labor movement, since it tends to bring more members into the union. Moreover, the political strength of the workers is so great that they look upon the government as an agency they can hope to control. Therefore, they do not fear compulsory arbitration as a device which antilabor elements might use against them.

During the past three decades, except for a brief interlude in 1972–1975, Australian politics have been dominated by a coalition of two parties, the Liberal party and the Country party, each of which is actually conservative. A split in the ranks of the Labor party and apprenhension over national security, aggravated by the Cold War, helped give the conservatives their long tenure of power. During this era the government generally followed the lead of the United States in foreign affairs. It sent troops to fight in Korea and in Vietnam, and permitted the United States to install defense bases and electronic communications stations on Australian soil. Growing dissatisfaction with these commitments, together with inflation and the threat of rising unemployment, undermined the popularity of the conservative administration of Prime Minister William McMahon. The national election of December 1972 returned the Labor party to office with a majority in the House of Representatives, and the new prime minister, Gough Whitlam, embarked on an active policy in both domestic and external affairs. He introduced new social-welfare measures, including free university education and the promise—long overdue—of humane treatment of the black aborigines who had been oppressed, neglected, and forced to live in the desolate "Outback" or in city slums. While not repudiating the tripartite security treaty which bound Australia and New Zealand to the United States, Whitlam sought a more independent role for his country. He withdrew Australian troops from the Vietnam War, of which he had long been a critic, ended the military draft, and normalized relations with North Vietnam, North Korea, and the People's Republic of China.

The Labor government under Whitlam's innovative leadership lasted only three years. The high cost of his welfare measures aroused resentment, particularly in business circles, and his display of independence in foreign policy displeased Washington. In October 1975 the Australian Senate, for the first time in the Commonwealth's history, refused to pass the government's budget bill, and the governor-general took the unprecedented step of dismissing the prime minister. Whitlam denounced the governor-general's action as unconstitutional, and Labor demonstrated support for its ousted leader by staging strikes and mass rallies, but in the national election of December 1975 the conservative coalition of Liberal and Country parties won by a landslide. The new prime minister, Malcolm Fraser, a wealthy farmer, promised to combat inflation, cut welfare spending, and restore business confidence.

Australia's defense and intelligence systems are heavily dependent

The Labor Ministry of Gough Whitlam

E. Gough Whitlam, Prime Minister of Australia (1972–1975)

Return of the Conservative Coalition

upon the United States, which country is also an important trading partner. The Commonwealth's economic relationships, however, have shifted considerably during the past twenty years and probably will continue to change. In 1960 Australia sent Great Britain 27 percent of its exports and received in return 36 percent of its imports. A decade later its chief market was Japan. By 1971 30 percent of Australia's exports went to Japan and more than 60 percent of its mineral exports. For coking coal the figure was close to 100 percent. And while Australians had become Japan's chief supplier of raw materials other than oil, they might also expect to develop eventually a profitable market in China, especially for their wheat.

3. THE DOMINION OF NEW ZEALAND

Located about 1,100 miles southeast of Australia, New Zealand was also discovered by the Dutch but explored and claimed for the British by Captain James Cook. At the time of discovery (1769) it was inhabited exclusively by Maoris, an intelligent but warlike people of Polynesian stock. For three-quarters of a century thereafter the only white settlers were missionaries, who labored with modest success to convert the Maoris to Christianity. In 1840 the first boatload of British colonists entered the harbor of what is now Wellington. They had been sent out by the New Zealand Company, founded by Edward Gibbon Wakefield, leader of the new British school of systematic colonizers. While completing a prison term for abducting a schoolgirl heiress, Wakefield came to the conclusion that Britain would be engulfed by civil war unless new economic opportunities could be found for the distressed population of its industrial cities. Caught in the maelstrom of depression and unemployment, workers by the thousands were turning to Chartism and sundry varieties of socialism. A conflict with the privileged classes was inevitable. Eventually Wakefield hit upon the idea that colonization would banish the specter of civil war. The company he founded would transport selected colonists to New Zealand. They would be provided with land at prices sufficiently high to discourage easy accumulation. Only the more prosperous and enterprising colonists would attain the status of owners. The others would have to content themselves for years with jobs as farm laborers. In time they too would buy land, and the proceeds from the sale would be used to finance further immigration.[4]

Wakefield's scheme attracted so much attention that the British government decided to take action. A governor was appointed, and

---

[4] The scheme had already been tried in South Australia, but with limited success. Wakefield subsequently turned to New Zealand in the hope that his theories would be vindicated.

the islands were formally annexed to the British Empire. The announced purpose was to protect the Maoris against unscrupulous white settlers. A week after the first colonists landed at Wellington the newly appointed governor arrived. He proceeded to negotiate a treaty with the native chiefs recognizing the sovereignty of the British Crown over all New Zealand. In return the British guaranteed to the Maoris full possession of their lands, "except as the Crown might wish to purchase them," and granted to the natives the rights and privileges of British subjects. Perhaps it was well that the government acted as it did, for a broadening stream of colonists continued to flow to the islands. By 1856 New Zealand had a white population of 45,000.

In 1852 the British government endowed New Zealand with a constitution. It conferred the executive power upon a governor-general representing the king, and acting with the advice of an Executive Council. Legislative authority was vested in a House of Representatives elected by the people and a Legislative Council appointed by the governor-general. In 1856 the Executive Council was formally recognized as a cabinet, exercising its functions under the principle of responsible government, and in 1951 the appointive upper house was abolished. Other steps in the direction of political democracy came easily. In 1879 universal manhood suffrage was adopted, and a few years later plural voting was abolished. In 1893 New Zealand led the Commonwealth of Nations in bestowing the suffrage upon women in national elections.

Economic reform followed in the wake of political democracy. When the Liberals came into power in 1891 they dedicated their efforts to making New Zealand a nation of small, independent farmers and herdsmen. Measures were adopted to break up large holdings, the formation of which had previously been encouraged by the sale of Maori lands to wealthy individuals. To combat the power of the big landowners required the support not only of landless agriculturists but also of workers in the cities. The Liberals therefore espoused a program of combined agrarian and labor reform which won the allegiance of both classes. The agrarian measures took the form primarily of special taxes on land held for speculative purposes and limitation of the size of holdings in the future. For the benefit of the workers the Liberals provided old-age pensions, factory inspection, regulation of working hours, and compulsory arbitration of industrial disputes. The accession of the Labor party to power in 1935 brought an extension of these measures, with increased benefits to the urban workers.

New Zealand has followed policies of collectivization quite similar to those of Australia. The reasons also have been similar. Lacking the capital to take advantage of new inventions, especially the railroad and the telegraph, the Dominion turned to foreign sources. Money proved to be more easily obtainable when the government itself was the borrower. Moreover, there was a deeply rooted fear among the colonists themselves of private monopoly. The beginning of collectivism occurred about 1870, when the Dominion government entered the London capital market for funds to construct roads, trunk railways, and telegraph lines. About the same time a state life-insurance system was established, and later state fire and accident insurance. A few coal mines also were added to the list of public enterprises, and finally a Bank of New Zealand. Important as a principle of collectivization has been the use of state-owned enterprises for "yardstick" purposes. Government purchase of coal mines, for example, was dictated by the theory that private companies needed the restraint of state competition to keep them from charging excessive prices.

Comparison of New Zealand and Australia

It is not an exaggeration to say that New Zealand enjoys all the advantages for future progress possessed by Australia with none of Australia's disadvantages. The two dominions have homogeneous populations overwhelmingly British in origin. In Australia 99.2 percent of the people are of European extraction, and 97 percent of these are of British ancestry. In New Zealand the percentages are 93 and 96, respectively. In both dominions systematic efforts have been made to preserve perpetually the British character of the nation. The early emigrants to New Zealand brought with them not merely the social customs and political institutions but the flowers, trees, birds, and even animal pests of their native England. New Zealand, like Australia, was populated in considerable measure by people of liberal and even radical tendencies. Both dominions received inundations of immigrants attracted thither by the discovery of gold. Coming from the landless and unemployed elements of Britain, many were infected with Chartism and even traces of socialism. As a consequence, they developed in the colonies institutions of political and economic democracy surpassing those of the mother country.

Upper Takaka Valley, Nelson, New Zealand. New Zealand enjoys the advantages of beautiful scenery, an ideal climate, and an abundance of space for its population.

Geographically, New Zealand has a wide margin of superiority over Australia. Although a mountainous region, with peaks that rise to 12,000 feet, extends the entire length of the southern island, there are no deserts and few areas unsuited to agriculture or grazing. Almost everywhere rainfall is adequate and permits an intensive use of the land. North Island, which contains over 60 percent of the population, has an average of about 50 inches of rain annually. Throughout the Dominion temperatures fluctuate within a comparatively narrow range. Extremes of over 100 degrees or below zero have never been recorded, and in both islands 75 degrees is considered unpleasantly high and 40 degrees uncomfortably low. Such favorable geographic conditions have given to New Zealand a character quite different from that of Australia. For one thing, the distribution of population is much more even. Instead of a few large cities along the seacoast and an almost unoccupied hinterland, there are hundreds of towns of moderate size and not a single city exceeding 400,000. The mean density of population is slightly over 15 persons per square mile compared with 2 for Australia. Geography, more than anything else, has made New Zealand a democracy of small, independent agrarians.

Other notable advantages of New Zealand

New Zealand has remained more closely connected with its British antecedents than has Australia. For one reason, the British and New Zealand economies are complementary rather than competitive. New Zealand is predominantly agricultural. Two-thirds of its land is suitable for farming and grazing. Its only important manufactures are meat and dairy products, fertilizer, pulp and paper. Two-thirds of New Zealand's exports are sold to Great Britain, and half of its imports come from British sources. However, with the recent British trend toward withdrawal from responsibilities east of Suez, New Zealand's ties with Great Britain appear to be loosening. Also Britain's entry into the European Common Market in 1973—ending the protected market in the mother country for the Dominion's butter, cheese, and lamb—affected New Zealand more seriously than it did Australia.

Close ties with Britain

4. INDIA UNDER COMPANY AND CROWN

In securing outposts in India, the British were motivated solely by an interest in trade and had no intention either of colonizing or of ruling territories. Gradually and quite unsystematically, their trading posts were transformed into centers of political administration. The absorption or conquest of native states, even though it ultimately involved large-scale military operations, was carried out not by the British government but by the British East India Company—a privately owned joint-stock corporation, chartered by the Crown and increasingly subjected to control by Parliament. When finally, in 1858, the com-

Foundations of the British East India Company

pany was dissolved and the British government assumed full responsibility for Indian affairs, the administrative and financial system developed by the company was continued in essential features. Another distinctive aspect of the British position in India was the fact that the country was never conquered in its entirety. The British seized strategic regions until their possessions formed a ring around the whole subcontinent (and included substantial portions of the interior as well), but they left hundreds of native states nominally independent. Nevertheless, although Britain's control over India was acquired piecemeal and indirectly, it became as thorough as if it had been imposed by a conquering horde capable of beating down all resistance.

The British East India Company as sovereign

As the trading posts of the East India Company expanded, they gradually took on the nature of colonies. This process had begun even before the close of the seventeenth century and increased rapidly during the eighteenth century. The assumption by the company of sovereign power over various territories created a need for efficient administration, a need which was not met promptly or adequately. In the early days company agents had been selected without regard to their knowledge of Indian affairs (proficiency in Latin and Greek literature was considered much more important), and most of the agents did not remain in India long enough to become well acquainted with the country or its people. There was little integration between the administration of the separate British holdings, although the acquisition of the great province of Bengal (by Robert Clive, in 1757) made Calcutta eventually the company's most important center of administration. Furthermore, the governing body of the company, the court of directors in London, was so far away that its members could not be adequately informed as to what was going on in India. The governors, sent out as servants of the company, in practice often modified

The Modest Beginning of British Rule in India. An early "factory" or trading station, with a walled enclosure containing a warehouse, promenade area, and church. From a copper engraving.

Tipu's Tiger. Wooden model of a tiger mauling a British East India Company officer. This monstrosity (fitted inside with a bellows and miniature organ pipes to simulate groans) was made for Sultan Tipu, ruler of Mysore. Tipu was defeated and killed by Governor Wellesley's troops in 1799.

or even formulated its policies. They negotiated treaties with native rulers, fought wars, and annexed territories.

An act of Parliament in 1814, which renewed the company's charter for twenty years, threw open the commerce of India to all British subjects but allowed the company to retain its monopoly in China and the Far East. By 1834 free-trade sentiment had become so influential in England that the Charter Act of that year deprived the company of all its trading privileges, in China as well as in India. Since it had originally been founded for the purpose of engaging in trade and had now lost that function altogether, the British East India Company might logically have expired in 1834. Instead of doing so, it was permitted to continue administering patronage in the British portions of India, serving as a governmental agency although ultimately subject to parliamentary check. Furthermore, to satisfy the English stockholders, dividends of the company were fixed by law at 10½ percent annually, to be derived no longer from the profits of commerce but levied as a permanent charge upon the revenues of India.

Changes in the status of the company

British territorial expansion inevitably led to conflicts with states beyond the Indian borders. Two Burmese wars made possible the annexation of Lower Burma (1852) and gave the British control of the Bay of Bengal. Less fortunate in sequel was an intervention in the independent state of Afghanistan in 1838–1839, a project unjustified in the first place and so thoroughly bungled that out of an invading force of 16,000 troops only one man escaped death or capture. The fiasco of the Afghan war, however, was a prelude to one of the boldest strokes in the history of British imperialism—the conquest and annexation of Sind. In violation of a signed treaty, the British, during the Afghan war, marched their troops through this independent and neu-

Expansion and conquest

Indian Mutineers Surprised by the Ninth Lancers Unit. A drawing from the book *Campaign in India, 1857–1858.*

tral state and used the country as a military base. Shortly afterward the British government sent Sir Charles Napier with an army into Sind to impose new demands upon the ruling princes. Without even a declaration of war Napier razed a fortress, exiled the rulers, and transferred their sovereignty to the company (1843). Apparently Sir Charles, whose share of the plunder was £70,000, believed that the benefits of British rule outweighed any irregularities in the methods used to establish it. He referred to his own conduct in Sind as "a very advantageous, useful, humane piece of rascality."[5] After two wars against the Sikhs in the Punjab, the governor-general, acting on his own responsibility, annexed the Punjab in 1849. Thus, by the middle of the century, most of the sovereign units in India capable of offering a serious military threat to the British position had been neutralized or brought under the jurisdiction of the company.

The Great Mutiny of 1857

In 1857 an armed uprising, known as the Great Mutiny, produced a crisis in Anglo-Indian relations and necessitated significant changes in British policy. Although the revolt was technically a mutiny because it originated among the native troops (sepoys) employed by the British, it received some popular support and it reflected the political aspirations both of Muslim and of Hindu elements. The underlying causes of the Mutiny lay in general discontent and in suspicions which British policies had aroused. The immediate cause can be attributed to carelessness and gross errors of judgment on the part of

[5] P. E. Roberts, *History of British India*, p. 330.

the military commanders. The British officials were caught quite unprepared for the revolt, which began near Delhi in May 1857, raged intensively for a few months in parts of northern and central India, and was not entirely suppressed until the following year. Many Europeans were slaughtered indiscriminately by the rebel troops, and sickening atrocities were committed on both sides, but the uprising never assumed the character of a mass movement or a genuine revolution. Its leaders were divided in purpose from the beginning. While Muslims dreamed of rehabilitating the Mogul Empire, the Marathas hoped to recover their ascendancy as a powerful Hindu state. The great majority of native princes remained aloof from the rebellion, probably because they recognized the superiority of British military resources.

The most important political result of the Mutiny was the termination of the East India Company and the transfer of full responsibility for the government of India to the British Crown and Parliament.[6] *The termination of the East India Company* The Government of India Act of 1858 created a secretary of state for India with an advisory council to assist him and bestowed upon the governor-general the title of viceroy. There was no immediate change in the details of the administrative system, but a royal proclamation issued by Queen Victoria offered conciliatory assurances in regard to religious toleration, material improvements, and the admission of native Indians to government service.

After 1858, in contrast to the earlier period, the policy of the British government in India was one of caution and conservatism. To minimize the danger of rebellion in the future, the bulk of the people were disarmed and the army was reorganized. *The government's policy of conservatism and caution* The recruited troops were carefully trained, instilled with pride in the service, and grouped in accordance with sectarian, tribal, or local divisions so that there would be little feeling of common interest among the different units. Although Europeans formed a minority of the military personnel, they monopolized the ranks of commissioned officers and retained possession of the heavy artillery. At the same time the government sought to avoid antagonizing any powerful element or prejudice within the population. Notably, the British authorities refrained from further territorial aggression. By treaties with the remaining native princes, the British government guaranteed to these rulers their hereditary rights and possessions but required them to relinquish all control over external affairs. Henceforth a clear division was maintained between the five or six hundred native states and the British provinces. The states ranged in size from Hyderabad—with an area almost equal to that of Great Britain—to tiny principalities, and included altogether about 40 percent of the land area of India. A few of the rulers were more progressive than the British, but most of them were

---

[6] The company stockholders were still treated with tender consideration. The guaranteed annual dividends of 10½ percent continued to be paid until 1874, at which time the stock was redeemed by a government purchase in the amount of £12,000,000.

uninspiring survivals from an age of despotism, quite content to enjoy the protection of the "paramount" power, Great Britain.

The several changes introduced into the government of British India between 1858 and 1919 were more in form than in substance. While the governor-general retained full authority, the door was gradually opened for Indian participation in the administrative machinery by the development of the Indian civil service. From the 1880s on, Indians were allowed to compete in examinations for the selection of civil servants, and they eventually came to supply most of the personnel for the lower and intermediate positions. The Indian civil service grew to be one of the most remarkable institutions of its kind in the world and a source of great pride to the British because of the integrity, efficiency, and loyalty of its members. It exhibited, however, the typical faults of a bureaucracy—inflexibility, conservatism, and lack of imagination. Because there was always an oversupply of educated Indians seeking government posts, and the lucky ones who obtained appointments found their modest salaries considerably above the average income of their countrymen, the civil servants usually developed an attitude of subservience to their superiors. In spite of its beneficent aspects, the Indian civil service became—like the native states—a bulwark of English supremacy and of the status quo.

Widely divergent views have been expressed concerning the overall effects which British administration had upon India and her people, particularly in the nineteenth century. Indisputably, a number of material benefits resulted from British rule. English authorities were generally effective in checking the more violent types of crime, suppressing organized bands of marauders, reducing the hazards of travel, and protecting property. They also attempted to eliminate such cruel customs as suttee, which was outlawed in 1829, and infanticide. Under British rule the population of India expanded greatly, rising from 150 million in 1850 to 250 million in 1881. By 1921 it exceeded 300 million, and another 100 million was added by 1945. This impressive increase is attributable largely to the curbing of internal warfare and to improvements in sanitation and medical facilities under British auspices. Irrigation works were constructed sufficient to provide for 30 million acres of land. Modern communications were introduced, including an extensive network of railroads totaling eventually more than 40,000 miles, a figure far in excess of the railroad mileage of any other Asian country.

Almost all the improvements, however, had their darker side. The rapid increase in population depressed the living conditions of large numbers of the people, and the problem of an adequate food supply was never solved. Severe famines had been known in India long before the British arrived, but some of the worst occurred during the period of British control. Ironically, the proclamation of Queen Victoria as empress of India in 1877 coincided with the greatest famine in

India's history, which took a toll of 5 million lives. It is estimated that between 1877 and 1900 no fewer than 15 million people died of famine. A basic cause of these disasters was the fact that a majority of the population lived close to the starvation level even in normal times and had no savings and no reserves of physical stamina to carry them through an emergency.

Although British rule did not introduce poverty into India, it did little to alleviate it and in some areas intensified it. The taxation system contributed heavily to the poverty of India's population. The principle generally followed by the government was to demand one-half the rental value of the land. British officials pointed to the fact that the tax schedules were somewhat less extortionate than those of earlier autocratic regimes. An important difference, however, was that the British assessments were not theoretical; they were actually collected. Also, in contrast to the situation under earlier empires, much of the revenue raised was drained out of India—in salaries to the higher administrative officials and to European army officers, in dividends to the East India Company stockholders, and in interest on the public debt, most of which was held by Englishmen. Not only did taxation bear too heavily upon the poorest classes but only a small fraction of the government's budget was allotted to relief, social welfare, or education. The major portion was expended on the police, the courts, and especially the Indian army, a professional body which was sometimes used in imperial wars outside of India—in Afghanistan, Burma, or China. In spite of the introduction of sanitation measures, the Indian death rate remained appallingly high, augmented by such diseases as cholera, malaria, and bubonic plague, which can be controlled by modern medical science and have been almost eliminated in Western countries.

Inequities in the system of taxation

Probably the aspect of British rule in India most open to criticism was its economic policy. In the early days of the East India Company there had been a great demand for Indian handmade goods of superior quality, especially silks, cottons, and muslins, which were generally paid for in specie. With the coming of the Industrial Revolution in England, the character of Far Eastern commerce changed. The British became interested in India as a source of raw materials and, even more, as a market for manufactured goods. The Indians were forced to accept "free trade" as applied to British manufactures but were effectively denied the right to export their own manufactures either to England or other countries. An inevitable result of this policy was the decline of village handicrafts which had for centuries constituted a vital element in the whole Indian economy. During the period of British rule, in spite of the growth of some large cities, the proportion of India's population dependent on the land for sustenance actually increased, until by the opening of the twentieth century it constituted more than 80 percent of the total. Excessive ruralization, small tenant holdings, oppressive taxes, and the unchecked extortions of money-

Other evils of economic policy

Social and cultural effects of British rule

Indian National Congress

lenders go far to explain why India remained a land of poverty and famine. The introduction of factory industries in the late nineteenth century offered a new source of employment, but only for a tiny fraction of the population. An oversupply of labor kept wages extremely low, and the sordid conditions of English mill towns during the early Industrial Revolution were repeated and far exceeded in India.

Somewhat more difficult to assess are the effects of the British occupation upon Indian society, culture, and mentality. Quite early the English rulers recognized an obligation to promote educational facilities. Several European scholars became intensely interested in the study of Sanskrit and the related ancient languages and advocated the promotion of a fuller knowledge of India's intellectual heritage. The printing press, introduced by missionaries, was utilized for works in the vernacular. The first newspaper, published in the Bengali dialect, appeared in 1818. A fundamental change in English educational policy in India came in 1833 with the decision to devote all educational funds henceforth to instruction solely in the English language. Lord Macaulay, the famous essayist and historian, who was a member of the governor's council at this time and was primarily responsible for the decision, regarded Hindu literature as nothing but "false history, false astronomy, false metaphysics, false religion."[7] As a matter of fact, the government did very little to carry out the educational plans which had been announced, and it is probable that, with the economic and political decline of the formerly autonomous villages, instructional facilities in India actually deteriorated. Some village schools were still flourishing in the early nineteenth century, but with the decay of village life education gradually fell into neglect and illiteracy increased accordingly. Nevertheless, the official emphasis upon Western studies familiarized Indian intellectuals with nineteenth-century liberal traditions and in the long run intensified their desire for self-government.

Toward the close of the nineteenth century the growth of an Indian nationalist sentiment manifested itself in various ways. The event of greatest import for the future was the formation of the Indian National Congress in 1885 under the initiative of educated Hindus and English sympathizers. The objectives of the organization were ambitious if somewhat vague, and embodied the hope that it would "form the germ of a Native Parliament and . . . constitute in a few years an unanswerable reply to the assertion that India is still wholly unfit for any form of representative institutions." The Congress was never exclusively a Hindu body. It attracted a number of Muslims, and during the first thirty years of its existence five Englishmen were elected to its presidency.

Government officials had at first looked upon the Indian National Congress with benevolence, regarding it as a harmless debating soci-

---

[7]H. G. Rawlinson, *India, a Short Cultural History*, p. 409.

ety or as a safety valve for upper-class discontent. However, as the Congress—which met every December in a different Indian city—pressed more insistently for reform measures, the official attitude became cool or hostile. The result was that the nationalist movement entered a more radical phase about the turn of the century. A contributing factor to this trend was the shattering of the myth of European invincibility by the Italian defeat in Ethiopia in 1896, by the difficulty which Britain encountered in subduing the small Boer states of South Africa, and by Japan's dramatic victory over the great Russian empire in 1905. Incensed by the dictatorial policy of the viceroy, Lord Curzon, some Indian patriots began to demand *swaraj* (independence) and also launched a *swadeshi* campaign, which was an attempt to injure Britain economically by boycotting the sale of British goods and reviving native industries. Outbreaks of violence in western Bengal and in the Punjab merely strengthened the determination of the government to stand firm. The vernacular press was muzzled; agitators were arrested and some of them were deported.

Factors accounting for the growth of Indian nationalism

The growth of a militant opposition to British rule led to dissension within the Indian National Congress and to a cleavage between the moderates and the extremists. The 1907 meeting of the Indian Congress was disrupted by rioting, but the moderate faction succeeded in retaining control of the organization. The nationalist movement, hampered by disagreement among the Hindu leaders, was also weakened somewhat by the establishment of a Muslim organization which stood in rivalry to the Indian National Congress. The Muslim League, founded in 1905, was inspired partly by the fear of the Muslim minority that they might be subjected to Hindu domination if popular government was established in India—a fear heightened by the truculence and the appeal to religious prejudice which some radical Hindu nationalists had displayed. The league also reflected an attempt to reawaken interest in the whole community of Islam, which seemed to be jeopardized by the decline of the Ottoman Empire. In contrast to the Indian Congress the Muslim League was a communal (sectarian) organization; further, it was founded under conservative rather than liberal auspices.

The conflicts between moderates and extremists and the rise of the Muslim League

During World War I only minor disturbances occurred in India. Representatives of all important organizations expressed their sympathy for the British cause and offered assistance. Indian contributions in behalf of Britain and its allies were tremendous. Indian troops fought on the Western front, in East Africa, in the Middle East, and in the Far East; and the country furnished vast supplies of raw materials, foodstuffs, and even manufactures, as cotton, jute, and steel production was intensified. The cooperative attitude of the Indian people during the war was induced by the belief that a victory for Britain and its allies would bring benefits to the world's colonial areas. Woodrow Wilson's utterances on war aims and peace objectives aroused enthu-

Indian cooperation during World War I, in hope of reward from a grateful Britain siasm in India as elsewhere, and from the beginning of the war British spokesmen had intimated that generous reforms would be forthcoming in recognition of Indian loyalty. In 1917 Edwin Montagu, secretary of state for India, announced in the House of Commons that England's policy toward India was "the increasing association of Indians in every branch of the administration and the gradual development of self-governing institutions with a view to . . . responsible government as an integral part of the British Empire."

Although the close of the war found India in a state of high expectancy, the prevailing mood quickly changed to disappointment for several reasons. First, the period was one of widespread suffering, caused by inflated prices, a severe famine, and the ravages of disease, including an influenza epidemic that wiped out 13 million people in 1918–1919. Second, the political reforms embodied in the Government of India Act of 1919 fell far short of responsible government. The franchise was still restricted to a tiny minority of property owners numbering about 3 percent of the population of British India. In addition, the electorate was split up into communal groups, with separate constituencies for Hindus, Muslims, Sikhs, landholders, and other special interests. To Indian nationalists, the constitution of 1919 appeared to be a breach of promise on England's part.

The bitter fruit of disillusionment

British repression; the Amritsar massacre

Probably an even greater factor than the Act of 1919 in arousing resentment was the repressive policy which the British government of India adopted at the close of the war. Punitive measures against rioting led to angry protests and to open violence, climaxed by one of the most shocking affairs in the annals of British rule in India—the Amritsar massacre of 1919. To check a series of outrages in the Punjab, the government had sent troops into the province under the command of Brigadier-General Dyer. At Amritsar on April 13, learning that a large crowd of people was assembling for a public demonstration, General Dyer took a detachment of soldiers to the meeting place and immediately ordered his men to open fire. The crowd, which was listening to speeches and was unarmed, had gathered in an enclosed space, of which Dyer blocked the exit. After ten minutes of steady rifle fire, almost 400 people were killed and more than a thousand wounded. News of this cold-blooded butchery—perpetrated in the name of upholding the "rule of law"—inflamed public indignation throughout India and elsewhere. General Dyer was deprived of his commission but received no other punishment, and English admirers raised a purse in his behalf. The Amritsar massacre, and the indulgent attitude of the government toward those responsible for it, antagonized many Indian leaders who had previously been consistent defenders of Britain. The great poet and educator, Rabindranath Tagore, returned the commission of knighthood with which he had been honored. Another Hindu and friend of Tagore who now became the enemy of British rule and threw himself into the nationalist cause was Mohandas K. Gandhi.

The man who was destined to make the greatest single contribution to the movement for Indian independence gave little evidence in his early life that such would be his role. Gandhi was born in 1869 in a small native state on the western coast of India. He came from a middle-class family which had supplied prime ministers to the prince, and his mother, a pious Hindu, endeavored to instill in him fidelity to the traditions of their caste. His family sent him to England to study law, and after his return home he was offered a position with an Indian firm in South Africa, where he spent some twenty years and had a successful legal practice. His chief interest in South Africa, however, became a deep concern for the unfair treatment to which his countrymen were subjected in that color-conscious region. At the risk of his life and in disregard of insults and humiliation, he campaigned continually against economic and social discrimination, encouraging the timid Indian laborers to organize and calling upon the government to remove flagrant injustices. In this campaign he eventually met with considerable success, but even more important to his later career was his discovery of a technique of mass action that could be effectively employed in defending a moral principle against superior physical force. Gandhi called this technique *satyagraha,* which is loosely translated as "nonviolent resistance" but which means literally "soul force" or "the power of truth." With a keen sensitivity to social injustice, he also became convinced that social and political evils could never be eliminated through violence. He believed these evils should be fought against, but with such weapons as refusal to cooperate with oppressors, no matter what the price; attempting to change the evildoer by force of example; and, above all, developing in oneself the attitudes and the disciplines which are essential to an improved social order. While arriving at these ideas by the route of religion, Gandhi also applied them to the political sphere.

Returning to India in 1914, Gandhi warmly endorsed the cause of Britain in the war against the Central Powers, even putting aside his pacifist principles to urge people to enlist, so confident was he that the struggle was against autocracy and militarism. But disillusioned by the government's behavior and shocked by the Amritsar massacre, he repudiated the new Indian constitution of 1919 and persuaded the Indian National Congress to adopt a program of noncooperation with the government. In 1922, he launched his first mass campaign of nonviolent resistance or "civil disobedience," but suspended the movement after a few weeks when he found that it was being used by terrorists to injure life and property. The program of the Indian National Congress and of the associated Gandhian movement already had begun to attract wide support and cut across sectarian lines. The Muslim League supported it for a while, and Gandhi was unswerving in his insistence upon Hindu-Muslim cooperation.

During the 1920s, as the nationalist movement acquired momen-

Nehru

tum, a number of new personalities came to the fore, of whom the most prominent was Jawaharlal Nehru. The Nehrus were a distinguished Brahman family, wealthy and influential. They had everything to lose, from the purely material standpoint, by casting their lot with a revolutionary movement; but such was the choice they made. Both father and son, and other members of the family, became admirers of Gandhi and joined the National Congress. The father adhered generally to the moderate faction, while his son, who was elected president of the Congress several times, became a leader of the militant and radical wing. The son, Jawaharlal (1889–1964), was educated at the best English schools, taking a B.A. degree at Cambridge University, and became thoroughly Westernized in his tastes and personal interests. Unlike Gandhi, he was by temperament rational and scientific and approached India's problems from a secular standpoint, welcoming industrial development and material progress. While he revered India's cultural heritage, he was emancipated from the dogmas and taboos of traditional Hinduism and—like most of the educated nationalist reformers—opposed the institution of caste. Nehru also became intensely concerned with the need for social reform. He did not embrace Marxism, but he advocated government intervention to alleviate poverty, rehabilitate the peasants, and protect industrial workers. Under Nehru's influence a substantial segment of the National Congress adopted as its two major objectives the winning of complete independence for India and the establishment of a democratic and moderately socialistic regime.

Civil disobedience

The Indian National Congress at its 1928 session had adopted a resolution demanding that Britain grant dominion status within one year. At a lively and unusually large conclave of the Congress in December 1929, the dynamic triumvirate of Gandhi and the two Nehrus persuaded members to take the pledge of *Purna Swaraj* ("Complete Independence"). They announced that January 26 would be celebrated

Leaders of Indian Nationalism—Nehru and Gandhi. Gandhi was assassinated in 1948. Nehru served as Prime Minister of India from 1947 to his death in 1964.

as "Independence Day," reinforced by the threat of civil disobedience. Accordingly, Gandhi's second mass campaign of civil disobedience was launched in the spring of 1930. Indians resigned from public office, stopped buying foreign goods, picketed shops and courts, and even refused to pay taxes. The most dramatic event was Gandhi's famous "march to the sea," in which he led a large body of followers on foot through village after village until they reached the coast. There they filled pans with sea water and let it evaporate to make salt, breaking the law by evading the salt tax and defying a government monopoly. In the salt episode as in the boycotting of state liquor shops, Gandhi shrewdly combined a political issue with a moral principle, thus putting his opponents in an embarrassing position. Widespread arrests accompanied the disobedience campaign. Gandhi was imprisoned in May, and the total number of Congress members jailed at this time has been estimated as high as 60,000.

Modifying his strategy but not his objectives, Gandhi next attempted to reach an understanding with the British authorities. Released from prison early in 1931, he obtained a series of interviews with the viceroy, Lord Irwin (much to the disgust of Winston Churchill, who was "nauseated" at the thought of "a seditious fakir striding half-naked up the steps of the Viceregal Palace"), and he agreed to participate in a round table conference in London, which proved unproductive.

At the close of the civil-disobedience campaign of 1931–1934, Gandhi retired temporarily from politics. He had proved to be the most powerful political figure in the Congress; he was a factor to reckon with at Whitehall and Westminster as well as at Delhi, and he had thousands of followers who would carry out his will almost blindly. Furthermore, he had developed, in the technique of nonviolent resistance, an instrument of mass action of immeasurable potency. In stepping out of the political arena Gandhi was not unaware of the effectiveness of the political weapons he had forged. He recognized, however, the dangers in any form of mass action, and he believed that the Indian people, including himself, needed to perfect their self-control. He said openly that he would prefer for India to remain subject to Britain than for her to attain freedom through a violent revolution. At the opposite pole from Machiavelli, Lenin, and many others, Gandhi denied that the end justifies the means. He believed instead that the means largely determine what the end will be.

Another factor which influenced Gandhi to disassociate himself from the Congress temporarily was that he did not consider himself primarily as a political leader. He disavowed the title of Mahatma ("Great Soul") by which he was known and strenuously discouraged the tendency of ignorant admirers to deify him. Still, he was essentially a religious figure in his personal convictions and in his world

Gandhi en Route to Meetings with Viceroy Lord Irwin in March 1931. Gandhi had recently been released from prison, where he had been interned after his dramatic "march to the sea" in 1930.

The religious motivation of Gandhi's philosophy

The Round Table Conference on the Indian Constitution in Session in London, 1931. Gandhi, the sole delegate from the Indian National Congress, sits at the chairman's left.

view. His beliefs were derived partly from the *Bhagavad-Gita* (which he first read in London in an English translation), partly from the writings of Tolstoi and Ruskin, and partly from the New Testament. He considered himself a Hindu and retained many traditional notions, but he embraced much of the spirit of Christianity, and his real interest lay in the development of religious and ethical values in human society. He had no faith in any political or economic formula and believed that the only real hope for India—or for the world—lay in the cultivation of spiritual resources.

Finally, Gandhi wished to devote the remaining years of his life to helping the downtrodden peasants. He established his *ashram* (disciplined community) in one of the poorest regions of Central India and attempted to educate the villagers in better methods of cultivation and sanitation and in the use of subsidiary industries, especially home spinning and weaving, to improve their living standards. He gave impetus to a widespread movement to rehabilitate the ancient village economy which had long been in decay. He hoped to inaugurate a nonviolent agrarian revolution, carried out by the Indian people without benefit of capital or government, to create a society free from misery while retaining simplicity and closeness to nature. Gandhi became the special champion of the Untouchables, whom he called *Harijan,* or "children of God." His campaign on their behalf illustrates his ability to relate an ideal goal to immediate and practical objectives. Full social acceptance of Untouchables was a necessary act of justice. But Gandhi also perceived that only by breaking the taboo against handling dirt and filth—traditionally the exclusive responsibility of

Gandhi's constructive program

the despised lowest class—could hygienic habits be instilled among the general population. The comprehensive "Constructive Program," to which Gandhi dedicated years of effort, was largely forgotten after India achieved political independence.

A new constitution embodied in the Government of India Act of 1935 disappointed Indian nationalists, both radicals and moderates. It made provincial ministries responsible to elected assemblies which could discuss and act upon any matter not reserved to the central authority. But the provincial governor retained "special responsibilities" and "discretionary powers," which raised doubts as to whether the new system would be much different from the old. The franchise was considerably extended to include about 30 million voters, roughly one-fourth of the adult population of British India, but the device of communal electorates was carried to an excess. Not only religious groups but also special economic classes were given separate representation, and the constitution seemed to be weighted in favor of religious minorities and the propertied interests. The act also provided for letting the native states enter a federation with the central government under terms which would have given the states (most of which were autocracies) an excessive representation.

The Indian National Congress strongly condemned the new constitution, but decided to run candidates in elections, first with the intention of obstructing the processes of government, and later, as the Congress party gained sweeping victories at the polls, with the idea of forming ministries and enacting legislation. By 1937, the Indian Congress had working majorities in seven of the eleven provinces of British India, and during the next two years these provinces enjoyed a taste of responsible parliamentary government. Most remarkable was the novel sight of English civil servants dutifully executing the policies of Indian ministers.

In spite of the good omen of Anglo-Indian cooperation, there were signs of trouble in the offing. A cleavage was growing between the moderate and radical wings of the National Congress, and even more serious was the increased friction between the Congress and the Muslim League. The Hindu-Muslim tension was caused partly by occasional outbreaks of violence incited by religious fanatics; partly by a fear among Muslims that if India became self-governing they would be at a disadvantage as a minority group; and partly by the fact that the Muslim League had come under the aggressive leadership of Mohammed Ali Jinnah and began to revive as a definite political force.

Muhammad Ali Jinnah, President of the Muslim League

That M. A. Jinnah (1876–1948) should become the guiding figure of a militant sectarian organization was somewhat ironic. Jinnah, a successful lawyer, had received a Western education and was decidedly secular in temperament. He did not observe the code of pious Muslims, and he had married a Parsee. Jinnah joined the Indian National Congress, in which he took an active part, but he resigned when Gandhi began to come into ascendancy. After withdrawing from political activity for a while, Jinnah undertook to vitalize the Muslim League and succeeded in making it, for the first time, the mouthpiece of the majority of Indian Muslims and a political party which would have to be bargained with in the future. Jinnah insisted that special guaranties were necessary to protect the Muslim minority, and finally, by 1940, went so far as to claim that the Indian Muslims were not merely a minority or a religious community but a distinct nation. The claim was dubious. Most Muslims in India were the descendants of natives who had been converted to Islam (Jinnah's family belonged to a group of recent converts) and were as truly Indian as the Hindus. If religious affiliation were to be made the basis of nationhood, then India would have to be split into many fragments and a united state would be impossible. The championing by the Muslim League of the interests of the Islamic community finally culminated in the demand for a separate state—Pakistan—an idea not original with Jinnah but which he at last adopted.

India and World War II

The outbreak of World War II brought matters to a critical juncture in India. The Congress took the blunt position that India would fight only as a free nation and demanded self-government with permission to draw up a new constitution. The viceroy could only promise that the 1935 Constitution would be reconsidered after the war and that, for the time being, he would welcome greater "consultation" with representative groups. In October 1940, the Congress authorized the Mahatma to inaugurate a nonviolent civil-disobedience campaign, which began at once. It was not a mass movement, though, and took the form of having individuals make speeches against the war. In each instance the authorities were duly notified in advance, the speaker was arrested quietly, and the jails began to swell again. There was no active interference with the civil or military administration. Actually, Indian contributions to the war against the Axis were enormous—far greater than in World War I—because Indian manufactures had now become important. Two million men were recruited for the Indian army and many Indian officers were commissioned.

The Cripps Offer

With the Japanese invasion of Malaya and Burma, the British government determined on a new effort to rally Indian public opinion to its support and sent Sir Stafford Cripps to India in March 1942 to present an offer of full dominion status under a constitution to be drafted by Indians, including representatives of the native states. The plan called for a federation rather than a unitary state and would have allowed any province that so desired to remain outside the union and retain a separate connection with Britain. It was to become effective only after the war ended, and it made no provision for immediate transfer of responsibility to Indians in the viceroy's council. For these reasons, combined with distrust of the Churchill government, the proposal was rejected by practically all articulate Indian groups.

The failure of the Cripps Offer of 1942 revealed that Indian nation-

Indian Railway Workshop Producing Munitions during World War II

alist sentiment had reached such a degree of agitation that it could no longer be smoothed over. Events moved rapidly when the Churchill government was replaced by a Labor cabinet under Clement Attlee. In March 1946 Attlee announced that the choice of a new constitution would be India's alone and that, while he hoped the Indian people would remain within the Commonwealth, this must be by their own free will. A Cabinet Mission accordingly was sent to India to work with Indian leaders in arranging the transfer of authority.

Now that the British government was prepared to grant independence, the chief stumbling block was found to lie in the Hindu-Muslim controversy, which had grown to large proportions as a political issue only during the preceding decade. For a while it looked as if the partition of India could be avoided. The Cabinet Mission drafted a scheme for a federal union with safeguards to protect minorities and with provisions for considerable regional autonomy. Both the Congress and the League at first accepted this general plan, but in July 1946 Jinnah, reversing his earlier position, rejected the mission proposal, demanded a separate Muslim state, and summoned his followers to engage in "direct action." The consequence was bloody communal rioting in which about 12,000 lives were lost. When a constituent assembly met in December to draft a constitution, the Muslim League sent no representatives, nor could it be persuaded to do so. Although Jinnah's intransigence was evident, some of the blame must rest with Congress members, who made it clear that they would not be bound by any pledges emanating from the British Cabinet Mission. So much ill will had been aroused on both sides that compromise was very difficult. A few extreme Hindu nationalists viewed the prospect of partition with indifference, rashly assuming that a separate Muslim state would sooner or later have to seek reunion with India on India's terms. The British government's determination to relinquish its responsibilities as quickly as possible—in striking contrast to the cau-

The Hindu-Muslim controversy and the decision for partition

Riot in Calcutta, 1946. A dead Hindu surrounded by Muslims armed with lathis. Such scenes were not uncommon on the eve of Indian independence, when extreme tension developed between Hindu and Muslim segments of the population.

The end of British Raj

tious and dilatory policy of the preceding 90 years—doubtless also lessened the chances of resolving the deadlock between the Hindu and Muslim communities. Attlee had served notice that England would leave India by June of 1948. Seeing no other alternative, the new viceroy (Lord Mountbatten) prepared to transfer British authority to two governments instead of one, a delicate and difficult operation. Not only were the Hindu and Muslim provinces separated, but three provinces—Bengal, the Punjab, and Assam—had to be split in order to prevent large Hindu minorities from being assigned to Pakistan. Although Pakistan did not include all the areas demanded by the Muslim League, the division was accepted by both sides in the controversy. Indian independence was formally granted by act of Parliament in July 1947, and in August all authority was surrendered to the two new dominions.

5. INDEPENDENT INDIA, PAKISTAN, AND BANGLADESH

It was a tragic circumstance that the Indian struggle for independence, characterized more by patience than by slaughter, should conclude with the country divided and in an atmosphere of hostility. The partition of India, from the standpoints of geography and economics, was highly artificial. Pakistan included the areas producing jute, cotton, and rice. India, with an insufficient food supply, had the factories needed to process Pakistan's raw materials. Important canals and river systems were bisected by the political boundaries. Nor did partition solve the minority problem. Approximately 15 percent of Pakistan's inhabitants are non-Muslims, chiefly Hindus. The Republic of India has a Muslim minority of approximately 11 percent. Even before partition was completed, refugees began to stream across the borders— Hindus and Sikhs fleeing from Muslim domination and Muslims fearing Hindu persecution. More than 10 million people were involved in the mass exodus during the latter part of 1947, and their suffering was indescribable. The governments of India and Pakistan could not prevent the outrages committed by frenzied fanatics on both sides. It was in connection with this religious strife that Gandhi, a frail old man in his late seventies, performed his last service to India. By appealing to the Hindus and by threatening to fast, he stopped riots in Calcutta. Early in 1948 he went to Delhi and began a fast which ended when the key spokesmen for the Congress pledged protection for the lives and property of Muslims. On January 30, on his way to evening prayers, Gandhi was shot to death by a member of a chauvinistic Hindu society. He was mourned all over India and in Pakistan, and the shock of his assassination had at least a temporarily sobering effect upon the public temper.

*The tragic division of
India; the assassination of
Gandhi*

A prime source of controversy between India and Pakistan was the disposition of the native states. Since the states were no longer protected by the British Raj, it was assumed that they would voluntarily join either India or Pakistan. Most of them did so, the greater number of course going to India, but in a few instances there was trouble. Hyderabad in the Deccan, the largest state in India, had a Hindu population ruled over by a Muslim prince, the Nizam. The Indian government refused to let the Nizam remain independent, as he apparently planned to do. It dispatched an army into Hyderabad and quickly took over the administration (September 1948). In this instance the Indian government claimed to be acting on behalf of the Nizam's Hindu subjects, but it had already taken a somewhat different position in the Kashmir dispute. In this northern state a Hindu prince ruled over subjects who were predominantly Muslims. In 1947 the New Delhi government announced that Kashmir had acceded to the Indian Union at the request of the Maharaja, who, it was argued, had the legal right to transfer his sovereignty. The Maharaja, faced with an invasion of Muslim tribesmen, had appealed to India for military support, and the Indian government had insisted upon the accession of Kashmir to India as a prior condition to granting his request. Fighting between Indian and Pakistani troops was halted in 1949 by a cease-

The Republic of India

fire agreement arranged through a United Nations commission. The cease-fire, however, proved to be only a truce and left Kashmir divided into two parts, occupied respectively by Pakistan and India, with the larger portion under Indian control.

India retained the status of a dominion only until 1950, when a new constitution made it an independent republic, replacing the governor-general by an elected president and severing all ties with the British Crown. Nevertheless, India voluntarily remained within the Commonwealth of Nations (with the term "British" deleted) and thus became the first completely independent republic to hold membership in the association. The Constitution provides for an independent judiciary and a president chosen by an electoral college, but follows the English system of parliamentary government, with the chief power vested in a prime minister responsible to the lower house of the central legislature. The subordinate states, with unicameral legislatures, have the same type of ministerial government. Both the state and national legislative bodies are elected by universal adult suffrage for five-year terms. The Constitution includes a comprehensive bill of rights, outlawing untouchability and discrimination based on caste, and providing for legal equality of the sexes. Although federal in structure, the government has been handicapped by a distribution of power between the center and the states which is both rigid and ambiguous. The Constitution gives the president power to suspend a state government in an emergency, but some very critical areas of jurisdiction are reposed in the states, including education, agriculture, and taxes on land.

Obstacles to Indian unity: linguistic differences

Many difficulties confronted the Republic of India from the very beginning. The absorption of more than 500 princely states into the new political structure, a formidable task in itself, was handled with relative dispatch. Some of the dethroned rajas were retained as governors for a time, but by 1957 all of them were removed from office.

Republic of India Declared. Prime Minister Jawaharlal Nehru moves the resolution for an independent sovereign republic before the constituent assembly in New Delhi in 1950.

They were compensated for their loss of power by the award of generous pensions which continued until 1971, when a constitutional amendment reduced the maharajas to the rank of commoners. Other problems proved more obstinate, revealing dangerous sectional and social cleavages. One of them had to do with linguistic rivalries. In the interest of promoting national unity, the government announced that Hindi, the principal tongue of northern India but spoken by only about one-third of the total population, was to become the official language of the country by 1965. Resistance on the part of other regional linguistic groups proved so strong, however, that on the date when the change was to go into effect, in January 1965, bloody riots broke out in the south, two cabinet ministers resigned, and the government felt constrained to announce that English would remain an "associate official language." as long as non-Hindi-speaking Indians desired.

Prime Minister Nehru with His Daughter, Mrs. Indira Gandhi, in 1956

The independent states of India and Pakistan were bequeathed many things of value by the British: the rudiments of parliamentary government, trained civil servants, an excellent network of railroads, the nuclei of effective military forces, and an educated elite versed in Western institutions and practices. The new states also inherited the unsolved problems of the era of colonial rule, chief of which is the backwardness and crushing poverty of most of the population. Steady and substantial economic progress is necessary if India and Pakistan are to make their way as successful modern states—or even to survive as political entities. The Indian government, committed to material progress, created a Planning Commission and launched a series of Five-Year Plans, beginning in 1951. In many fields impressive results were achieved. Food production has grown by almost 90 percent; power generation increased sevenfold in less than a decade, while irrigation facilities doubled. By 1970 India was exporting heavy machinery and manufacturing 85,000 motor vehicles a year. Two nuclear power plants were in operation by August 1972, but in 1979 they still had only a 640 megawatt capacity. Even in the vital area of agriculture, improvements did not suffice to offset an inexorable growth in the numbers of people. Widely publicized campaigns in support of birth control failed to check the rate of increase, which has doubled since independence. By 1970 India's population of about 550 million was receiving an increment of 13 million each year and was expected to approach 695 million within the next decade. Consequently, per capita annual income has remained at a level of about $100. Social services are lacking for the bulk of the population, 75 percent of whom are still illiterate.

Economic problems; the Five-Year Plans

Nature has not condemned India to be a land of poverty forever. The country holds extensive resources—the world's largest iron-ore reserves, estimated at nearly 22 billion tons, manganese and other valuable minerals, substantial deposits of coal and probably of oil, and

INDIA TODAY

India's great but unrealized potential

great potential for hydroelectric development. Under effective leadership India could doubtless support a prosperous, industrialized, and educated society. The Five-Year Plans fell short of their objectives for a variety of reasons. An overgrown and inept bureaucracy mangled well-intentioned projects, but considerable blame must be placed on the Congress party and its leader Nehru for failure to press vigorously for necessary changes. Long on rhetoric but short on performance, they continually postponed action or compromised with vested interests.

While India is predominantly a country of landowners and cultivators, the poor peasants at the bottom have not shared in agricultural progress as have the upper strata of large landowners who control the farm cooperatives and wield a disproportionate influence over the state and national legislatures. This fortunate minority, possessing considerable capital, has almost entirely escaped taxation. Consequently the government has lacked funds to implement its ambitious development and welfare programs. Even scientifically designed projects for the modernization of agriculture through mechanization, intensive fertilization, and diversified cropping have thus far proved disappointing. The widely acclaimed "green revolution," launched in the late 1960s with the help of international experts, brought a spectacular increase in the per-acre yield of grains, particularly wheat. But the benefits accrued to relatively prosperous landowners, rather than to small farmers, tenants, and laborers unable to afford the new techniques. With 5 percent of rural householders possessing 35 percent of the cultivable land and about half of all agricultural families owning no land at all, the basic need is for a thorough reorganization of land ownership, something the government has never undertaken in spite of its promises.

The need for basic reforms

Within the framework of democratic institutions India, during its first thirty years of independence, operated under what was in effect a one-party system. The Congress party, instead of dissolving as Gandhi had recommended, dominated all branches of the government, and Jawaharlal Nehru served continuously as prime minister until his death in May 1964. This long tenure of power was not an unmixed blessing either for the party or for the country. Once the focal point of an indomitable struggle for freedom, the Congress developed into an Establishment, entrenched behind its monopoly of patronage and the administrative services (vastly larger than the old British Indian civil service), and its vigor and integrity became corroded. Even the

*Preponderance of the
Congress party under
Nehru*

Coke Ovens at the Tata Iron and Steel Company, Jamshedpur, Behar. Tata is the largest steel producer in India. India has the world's largest iron-ore reserves.

luster of Nehru—generally revered as a revolutionary hero and Gandhi's heir—dimmed in later years. Endowed with qualities of mind and heart that entitle him to high rank among popular leaders of this century, Nehru was not entirely successful as a statesman. His own idealism was unquestionable but fuzzy in application, his policies vacillating and impulsive. As an avowed enemy of colonialism, in 1961 he authorized the forcible occupation of Goa, Diu, and Damão, the last remnants of Portugal's empire on the subcontinent; but the next year he blundered into a border clash with Communist China with humiliating results. In the long controversy with Pakistan over Kashmir he was both unyielding and inconsistent. Although publicly admitting the right of the Kashmiris to determine their own destiny, he deposed and imprisoned without trial Sheikh Muhammad Abdullah, the premier of Kashmir, when Abdullah advocated independence for the country. In 1957 he announced the formal annexation of Kashmir to India and subsequently took the position that Kashmir was a domestic issue not subject to mediation by any outside agency.[8] Nehru appeared blind to the corruption and incompetence of his trusted associates, and he neglected to press for the reform program that he himself recognized as essential to India's welfare. His chief asset as a leader was his personality, which combined intellectual faculties of a high order with a charisma that won and held the allegiance even of the unlettered masses.

Difficulties following Nehru's death; Indira Gandhi's new Congress party

Nehru's death left the party with no leader of sufficient stature to hold its dissident factions together; rivalries broke out into the open, while India's internal condition deteriorated. In 1966 the party chiefs picked as prime minister Nehru's daughter, Mrs. Indira Gandhi, hoping that the prestige of the family name would restore public confidence. Disenchantment with the administration was amply demonstrated in India's fourth general election (February 1967), the first one to be marred by tumult and violence. Although the Congress party retained a slim majority in the central parliament, it lost control in half of the state governments. Threatened by opposition from elements of both the extreme right and the extreme left, the Congress party in 1969 split into two factions, and a struggle for power ensued between established leaders of the "old Congress" and Mrs. Gandhi's "new Congress party." Squarely accepting the challenge, Nehru's daughter exhibited a tenacity equal to her father's and a superior talent for practical politics. She took the bold step of calling for general elections in March 1971—a year ahead of schedule—and she campaigned throughout the country, sometimes making fourteen speeches in a single day. The result was a personal triumph for Indira

[8] Sheikh Abdullah, after being twice imprisoned for championing self-determination for Kashmir, accepted union with India as a political and economic necessity and resumed the prime ministership in February 1975. This helped relax tension between India and Pakistan but did not end Kashmiri discontent.

Gandhi and a sweeping victory for her party, which won a two-thirds majority in the national legislature (Lok Sabha).

In the light of Mrs. Gandhi's campaign promises, the 1971 election was a mandate for social reform—to abolish poverty and promote "the fullest internal democracy." In reality it was the beginning of a period of personal rule culminating in dictatorship. Emboldened by the popular enthusiasm she had aroused—the "Indira wave," which reached its apogee with India's smashing defeat of Pakistan in the brief December war—Mrs. Gandhi became increasingly arbitrary and inflexible. She blamed her political opponents for the failure of the economy to improve, while her own administration was, like its predecessors, inefficient and tainted with corruption. In 1974 she used troops to break a strike of railway workers and arrested union leaders. As discontent grew she attempted to quiet it by spectacular diversions. In May 1974 her government announced it had exploded a 10-kiloton nuclear device—proof of technological progress but alarming to neighboring countries despite assurances of "purely peaceful" intent. A year later she annexed the tiny protectorate of Sikkim after Indian troops, on the pretext of quelling a rebellion, arrested the monarch.

A period of personal rule

A crisis in the summer of 1975 led to a coup—not against the government, but by Mrs. Gandhi against the Constitution and the political opposition. On June 12 a state court pronounced her guilty of illegal campaign practices. Instead of resigning the prime ministership, she ordered wholesale arrests of political opponents of all shades of opinion, including members of her own party. The nature of her crackdown was dramatized by the night arrest of "the People's Hero," ailing seventy-two-year-old Jayaprakash Narayan, one of the few remaining uncompromising disciples of Mahatma Gandhi. On June 26 Mrs. Gandhi had the president of India proclaim a state of national emergency. Then she induced a compliant parliament to amend the Constitution to free the executive from any restraint by the judiciary, suspended civil liberties, and imposed a rigid censorship. Indira Gandhi's "emergency" rule—which lasted twenty-one months—was far more repressive than any the British had fastened upon the country. By 1976 the number of arrests and detentions was in the neighborhood of 100,000.

The emergency rule of Indira Gandhi

Mrs. Gandhi justified her extreme measures as necessary to contain a widespread conspiracy that threatened to subvert law and order. Many observers inside and outside India questioned whether turning the "world's largest democracy" into a dictatorship (which she called "disciplined democracy") was not too high a price to pay for suppressing a conspiracy, even if one had been proven to exist. In the long run, Mrs. Gandhi's methods defeated her objectives, however laudable, and failed to bring the benefits she had promised. She cleared out slums in Delhi, reduced smuggling, prodded the industrial sector to a burst of productivity, and halted inflation temporarily. Food

Achievements and failures of the emergency rule

Slums in Bombay. The Indian government has struggled to provide better housing for the poor, but frequently the net effect is to supplement old slums with new slums.

prices dropped in 1975–1976, thanks to a bumper crop in that year which brought a surplus of grain. Meanwhile a land distribution program failed to change the structure of rural society, which was still dominated by a minority of wealthy peasants and commercial farmers. Rural unemployment continued to rise; city workers, forbidden to strike, benefitted little if any from the slight increase in industrial production.

End of the emergency government

Resentment against the emergency government was intensified by a sterilization campaign carried out with such zealous insensitivity that it created a strong backlash. Mrs. Gandhi's son Sanjay, who subjected 7 million men to vasectomies with or without their consent, became a special object of hatred. With no official position in either the Congress party or the government, Sanjay attained the prominence of an heir apparent, and he symbolized the favoritism and corruption that infected the regime. India's sixth general election, after being postponed for a year, was held in March 1977. To the surprise of many, and to Mrs. Gandhi's credit, she accepted the verdict of a free election, which repudiated her authoritarian rule, and she stepped down from office. The decisive factor in her defeat was her alienation of the Muslim community and the Untouchables, two important minorities which had originally been the core of her support.

With Mrs. Gandhi ousted and the Congress party fragmented, political responsibility in 1977 passed to the recently formed Janata party, a shaky coalition of diverse groups, including Muslims, Untouchables, and some elements of the Hindu extreme right. Recruited from competing factions, lacking a positive program, and led by quarreling old men, the Janata party could accomplish little. Although Mrs. Gandhi's defeat in 1977 had been celebrated as a day of national liberation, the ineffectiveness of her successors was so apparent that her star soon began to rise. She regained a seat in parliament in November 1978. Fourteen months later, backed by a two-thirds majority in the Lok Sabha, she became prime minister for the second time. The enthusiasm that greeted her return to power did not remove the stubborn problems confronting the nation. Hindu-Muslim conflicts erupted into violence, strikes and rioting in Assam disrupted oil production, industrial productivity declined while inflation mounted. Mrs. Gandhi suffered a severe personal blow in June 1980 when her son Sanjay, on whom she had relied increasingly for distribution of patronage and party management, was killed in an airplane crash. The following September her government enacted a National Security Ordinance giving police officers extraordinary powers and reminiscent of the repressive measures of the Emergency Rule of 1975–1977. In campaigning for office Indira Gandhi had deplored the plight of the "backward masses," and the evils of "caste-ism, capitalism, and communalism." Whatever her ability to conquer these evils, there was no doubt that they existed. Belying its liberal constitution and democratic electoral process, India's society has remained undemocratic. Caste is still a potent factor, intensifying regional and linguistic jealousies, class conflicts, and political divisions. The outlawing of untouchability has not improved the lot of the Harijans, who suffer from discrimination, segregation, and even physical abuse. And—Indira Gandhi's dazzling career notwithstanding—women are subjected to the traditional restrictions of a male-dominated society.

Failure of the Janata party; Mrs. Gandhi's political comeback

Indira Gandhi Campaigning on the Eve of Her Return to Power in Early 1980

Under Jawaharlal Nehru's guidance India's foreign policy initially was one of nonalignment, stemming from a distaste for military alliances and from a desire to cultivate a spirit of friendship with other Asian countries, including the Communist. Sino-Indian relations, which had been marked by expressions of cordiality on both sides, suffered a rude shock following China's provocative action in Tibet. The New Delhi government gave asylum to the Dalai Lama, who escaped from his country while Chinese troops were suppressing a Tibetan rebellion in 1959. A brief border war between India and China in 1962, although accompanied by acrimonious debate, apparently stemmed more from the absence of clearly defined geographical boundaries in the snow-capped Himalayas than from planned aggression by either party. The abrupt rout of ill-equipped Indian troops

Indian foreign policy

induced the government to upgrade and expand its military forces, which proved more effective in a three weeks' war against Pakistan in 1965. These summer hostilities, provoked by friction over Kashmir, accomplished nothing except to aggravate bad feelings between the two nations and to draw India away from the United States and into the orbit of the Soviet Union, with whom the Delhi government signed a twenty-year treaty of friendship and cooperation in August 1971. India relied on Moscow's backing during a two weeks' war with Pakistan the following December, when both China and the United States supported Pakistan and refused to denounce the brutalities committed by Pakistani troops in East Bengal. If the conflict over Bangladesh was something less than the "holy war for democracy and human rights" acclaimed by a Calcutta journalist, India's smashing victory at least heightened national self-confidence. India had attained an identity—not as the exemplar of nonviolence that Gandhi envisioned—but as a military power.

The problems confronting Pakistan have been similar to India's and even more acute. Pakistan began not as a nation but as a collection of heterogeneous racial and linguistic communities dominated by the Urdu-speaking Punjabis. The country's West and East wings—separated geographically by 1,000 miles—were equally far apart in terms of economics, language, and cultural traditions, with religion serving as the only common bond. Separatist movements within a state which was itself the fruit of separatism threatened to disrupt it and finally succeeded, with the secession of East Pakistan in 1971.

Political democracy has been almost nonexistent in Pakistan, where the creation of any kind of viable government proved an arduous task. Against a background of dissension and without effective leadership (M. A. Jinnah died in 1948 and the Muslim League gradually disintegrated), two successive constituent assemblies struggled with the drafting of a constitution, which was declared in effect in March 1956. Pakistan, while remaining a member of the Commonwealth, was defined as an "Islamic Republic" under a president who was required to be a Muslim. Elections were never held under this constitution. The ensuing period was one of unbridled political bickering, racketeering, and corruption, terminated only when General Muhammad Ayub Khan in October 1958 seized control of the government and imposed martial law. Although Ayub had acted at the instigation of the president, he soon removed him from office along with other prominent party officials, offering them a choice between jail sentences or retirement from politics (most of them chose the latter). Ayub's avowed purpose was to "clean up the mess," and in this he temporarily succeeded, by direct and peremptory measures.

Ayub Khan's military rule brought some improvement over the conditions prevalent during the politicians' paradise of the preceding decade. Inflation was halted, a few modest reforms were enacted, and

General Muhammad Ayub Khan, Pakistan's Head of State, 1958–1969

a new capital, Islamabad, was built near the Northwest Frontier. Most impressive was the economic development of West Pakistan, whose economy during the 1960s seemed to be booming. Agricultural expansion exceeded the rise in population, and manufactures showed one of the highest growth rates in the world. But rapid industrialization, producing a prosperity more apparent than real, was accompanied by questionable and potentially damaging policies. It depended on heavy doses of foreign aid, both economic and military, from the United States. To a large extent it was accomplished at the expense of the peasants. Wages and food prices were kept low while the profits from manufacture soared, creating capital to provide a high rate of reinvestment for further growth but widening the gap between the upper and lower segments of society. Most of the wealth remained concentrated in a plutocracy of "twenty-two families," which controlled 65 percent of Pakistan's industry and 80 percent of its banking assets, as well as the best farmland. Finally, the progress of West Pakistan rested on the exploitation of the eastern wing, which the government treated like a colony. East Pakistan (formerly East Bengal and now Bangladesh) with only one-sixth of the nation's area contained more than half of the population. Its jute industry earned most of Pakistan's foreign exchange, but the larger share of this was diverted to development in the West, and the disparity in per capita income between the two sections increased steadily. Economic oppression—coupled with political discrimination, social neglect, and undisguised contempt for Bengalis—prepared the ground for revolt in East Pakistan.

Although President Ayub gave the country the appearance of stability, public confidence in his rule deteriorated, especially after his futile war with India in 1965. Widespread poverty and the government's suppression of civil rights fostered opposition. Ayub had introduced a new constitution in 1962 incorporating what he called "Basic Democracy," but its operation was strictly authoritarian. The regime that had justified its seizure of power in 1958 as an attack on corruption became itself riddled with corruption from top to bottom. Demonstrations by workers and students erupted into bloody riots, and when the army refused any longer to support him, Ayub resigned in March 1969. His successor was another general, Yahya Khan, who proclaimed martial law, rooted out corruption, and restored order, filling much the same role as had his ousted predecessor a decade earlier. But he was no more able than Ayub to resolve the country's troubles, which centered more and more insistently in the rebellious mood of the East Pakistanis. Seemingly inclined to a policy of reconciliation, President Yahya Khan agreed to hold general elections for a national assembly to draft a new constitution as a step toward parliamentary government resting on universal suffrage. The elections, held in December 1970, brought a resounding victory in East Pakistan to

General Ayub Khan's regime: basic defects

General Yahya Khan: disaffection and revolt in East Pakistan

Sheikh Mujibur Rahman and his Awami League, a party demanding regional autonomy. Even with no support in the West, Mujibur had won the largest representation in the national assembly and was acknowledged by President Yahya as "the next prime minister of Pakistan." But the hard-liner Zulfikar Ali Bhutto, whose Pakistan People's party had gained a majority of West Pakistan's seats, obstructed attempts to work out a settlement. President Yahya postponed the opening of the assembly; yet he agreed to negotiate with Sheikh Mujibur and, accompanied by Bhutto, went to Dacca in March 1971. Apparently the talks served to screen more drastic action. Yahya's troops, with reinforcements secretly flown in, suddenly struck in Bengal, and Mujibur was imprisoned.

The India-Pakistan war of 1971

The murderous events in East Bengal from March to December 1971, resulting in a full-scale war between India and Pakistan, were among the most horrible in a century of unprecedented horrors. Atrocities may have been initiated by the Bengalis, and were perpetrated by them on the Bihari minority after the war had ended; but the most revolting excesses were committed by government troops. West Pakistani soldiers, who began their attack by shooting helpless university students, raped some 200,000 women and slaughtered whole communities of civilians. Their program of genocide was apparently aimed at exterminating every potential leader among the population they despised as rebels and racial inferiors. The government of India admitted 10 million refugees into West Bengal, assisted East Pakistani guerrillas, and early in December entered the war as an active belligerent. The brief combat, conducted on western and eastern fronts, demonstrated India's decisive military superiority over its rival, whose forces surrendered on December 16.

Sheik Mujibur Rahman, Prime Minister of Bangladesh, 1971–1975

Bangladesh ("Bengal Nation") was born from the ashes of victory as an independent state, but whether its 80 million people could survive as a political entity—or survive at all—was a difficult question to determine. With a population density of 1,400 per square mile, it is a land of poverty, and one frequently subject to disastrous storms and floods. To the normal level of misery was now added the problems of repairing the ravages of war, finding food and shelter for returning refugees, disarming guerrilla bands that still roamed the countryside, and creating a government out of chaos. Sheikh Mujibur Rahman, given a hero's welcome when he entered Dacca in January 1972 after nine months in West Pakistani jails, set up a provisional government with himself as prime minister and vowed that Bangladesh would be "a secular, democratic socialist state."

The downfall of Sheikh Mujibur

Although he was able to attract $3 billion in foreign aid, Sheikh Mujib failed completely to achieve his objectives for Bangladesh. The hostility of his countrymen to the idea of a secular state—added to friction between the Muslim majority and minority groups, especially the 10 million Hindus—made the attainment of democracy seemingly

Victims of the Indian-Pakistani War of 1971. Left: Refugees from East Bengal seeking sanctuary in India. Right: Prime Minister Indira Gandhi of India visiting a refugee camp in West Bengal, offering reassurance to homeless East Bengalis.

impossible. As a step toward socialism the jute industry, banks, and major corporations were nationalized, but they were run for the benefit of a clique of Awami League bureaucrats. Mujib's regime became increasingly corrupt and increasingly autocratic until, discarding even the forms of democracy, he dissolved parliament and imposed presidential rule. In August 1975 the discredited hero of Bangladesh's struggle for independence was overthrown and brutally murdered in a coup led by young military officers. A year later the army chief of staff, Ziaur Rahman, assumed the position of martial-law administrator and imposed strict measures to check disorder, including press censorship and thousands of arrests. After taking over the office of president in 1977, General Ziaur amended the constitution to bring it into conformity with the religion of Islam. "Re-elected" president in June 1978, he relaxed the press censorship and lifted martial law. In a parliamentary election of February 1979 his Nationalist party won a comfortable majority of the elected representatives. General Ziaur's accession to power strained the already deteriorating relations with Bangladesh's erstwhile ally, India, but it improved prospects for obtaining financial assistance from other quarters, including the United States. In 1976 Bangladesh restored diplomatic ties with Pakistan, where it found a market for exports of tea and jute. However, any appearance of stability in Bangladesh was jeopardized by the assassination of General Ziaur in May 1981.

*The return to military rule
in Pakistan*

Pakistan, reduced in territory and resources, was left with 60 million people, mostly illiterate and increasing their numbers at the alarming rate of 3 percent a year. Humiliated by defeat, the mood of the nation was resentment against the leaders responsible for a policy of disaster. Yahya Khan resigned the presidency in December 1971, and for the first time in thirteen years Pakistan had a civilian head of state when Zulfikar Ali Bhutto took the oath as president and immediately assumed most of the other important cabinet posts as well. A graduate of the University of California and of Oxford, Bhutto was a colorful figure, with a talent for arousing mass enthusiasm. He chose as motto for his Pakistan People's party, "Islam is our faith, democracy is our policy, socialism is our economy, all power to the people." His six-year rule did little credit to these ideals. It followed the familiar path of corruption and tyranny, marked by arrests, kidnaping, and torture of opponents. Elections held in March 1977 were so obviously rigged in Bhutto's favor that they provoked widespread rioting, and the country seemed on the brink of civil war. In July the army removed Bhutto in a coup led by the chief of staff, General Muhammad Zia ul-Haq, who imposed a second era of military rule upon Pakistan. In response to popular clamor, Zia ul-Haq had the deposed president brought to trial. Convicted of conspiracy to commit murder, he was sentenced to death and hanged in April 1979. To his dedicated followers, who hailed him as a "Martyr King," Bhutto's grave became a shrine. Although Zia had promised to hold elections within three months of his accession to power, he repeatedly postponed them and governed by martial law. Furthermore, he took steps intended to transform Pakistan into a fundamentalist Islamic society, rewriting the legal code and giving judicial and political authority to a body of religious scholars known as the *ulema*. A devout Sunnite Muslim, Zia apparently believed that Pakistan, where Western-style democracy had fared so badly, could survive only under a firm leader capable of enforcing religious orthodoxy and a program of austerity. The government's sanction of an Islamic code that legalized such punishments as flogging and hanging aroused discontent, which was aggravated by economic stagnation and rising prices. In spite of opposition from the Pakistan People's party, revived by Bhutto's energetic daughter Benazir, and from the Shiite Muslim minority, by the fall of 1980 an improved economy and the loyalty of his troops made Zia's position appear secure.

*Changes in Pakistan's
foreign policy*

Pakistan's international position has been materially affected by a disillusioning experience with alliances. While India was pursuing the path of neutralism, Pakistan became a member both of SEATO and of CENTO, thus identifying itself with the Western power bloc. Under a military-aid pact of 1954, the United States agreed to provide supersonic aircraft and other modern weapons, and in turn received permission to use Pakistan territory for strategic intelligence activities.

This military partnership intensified India's mistrust and hostility but did nothing to mitigate Pakistan's disastrous defeat in the Bangladesh war. In 1972 President Bhutto announced his country's withdrawal from the Commonwealth of Nations and also from SEATO. A factor contributing further to Pakistan's isolation was the discovery that its government had for some time been secretly developing atomic weapons—the "Islamic bomb"—to offset India's nuclear capacity. The international situation was altered suddenly when Russian troops invaded Afghanistan in December 1979 to install a Soviet puppet in Kabul. Western powers—and China—turned hopefully to Islamabad as a possible buffer against Russian expansion. The United States offered Zia military aid and sent advisers to plan the upgrading of his forces. General Zia, however, avoided any binding alliance. Possibly a greater threat to the stability of his regime than the presence of Russian troops on his doorstep was posed by the Baluch and Pushtun peoples who inhabited both sides of the Pakistan-Afghanistan border. Their common ethnic and linguistic ties and their solidarity in opposing the Communist military occupation of Afghanistan proved very helpful to Afghan guerrilla fighters and very troublesome to the Russian invaders. Conceivably though, an active role by such minority groups, with loyalties extending beyond Pakistan's artificial frontiers, could hasten the state's dismemberment. In the Northwest Frontier and in Baluchistan—where Bhutto fought a four-year war against insurgents—the demand for autonomy or independence has been a recurrent theme.

Pakistan's international position

SELECTED READINGS

• *Items so designated are available in paperback editions.*

THE COMMONWEALTH

Belshaw, Horace, *New Zealand*, Berkeley, 1947.

Brady, Alexander, *Democracy in the Dominions*, Toronto, 1958.

Cameron, Roderick, *Australia: History and Horizons*, New York, 1971.

Creighton, Donald G., *Dominion of the North, a History of Canada*, Boston, 1944.

Dawson, R. M., *The Government of Canada*, Toronto, 1963.

Fitzpatrick, Brian, *The Australian People, 1788–1945*, Melbourne, 1946. An analytical and revealing account.

Grattan, C. H., *Australia*, Berkeley, 1947.

Lipson, Leslie, *The Politics of Equality: New Zealand's Adventures in Democracy*, Chicago, 1948.

MacInnes, Colin, *Australia and New Zealand*, New York, 1966.

McInnis, E. W., *Canada: A Political and Social History*, New York, 1959.

McIntyre, W. D., *The Commonwealth of Nations: Origins and Impact, 1869–1971*, Minneapolis, 1977.

Millar, T. B., *Australia in Peace and War: External Relations, 1788–1977*, New York, 1978. Emphasizes the recent period.

Shaw, A. G. L., *Convicts and the Colonies*, New York, 1966.

• Siegfried, André, *The Race Question in Canada*, New York, 1907. A perceptive study.

Wade, Mason, *The French Canadians*, New York, 1955.

INDIA, PAKISTAN, AND BANGLADESH (*See also Readings for Chapter 23*)

Bhatia, Krishan, *Indira: A Biography of Prime Minister Gandhi*, New York, 1974.

———., *The Ordeal of Nationhood: A Social Study of India since Independence, 1947–1970*, New York, 1971. Informed and objective account of India's problems.

Bonarjee, N. B., *Under Two Masters*, New York, 1970. By a former civil servant; highly critical.

• Bondurant, Joan, *Conquest of Violence: The Gandhian Philosophy of Conflict*, rev. ed., Berkeley, 1965.

Brecher, Michael, *Nehru: A Political Biography*, New York, 1959.

• Brown, D. M., *The Nationalist Movement: Indian Political Thought from Ranade to Bhave*, Berkeley, 1961.

Brown, W. N., *The United States and India, Pakistan, Bangladesh*, 3d ed., Cambridge, Mass., 1972.

Edwardes, Michael, *Nehru: A Political Biography*, New York, 1972.

Embree, A. T., *India's Search for National Identity*, New York, 1972. An analysis of Indian nationalism to 1947.

• Erikson, E. H., *Gandhi's Truth: On the Origins of Militant Nonviolence*, New York, 1969.

Fischer, Louis, *The Life of Mahatma Gandhi*, New York, 1950. An admirable biography.

Frankel, Francine, *India's Green Revolution: Economic Gains and Political Costs*, Princeton, 1971. A significant and challenging study.

• ———, *India's Political Economy, 1947–1977: The Gradual Revolution*, Princeton, 1979.

Hardgrave, R. L., Jr., *India: Government and Politics in a Developing Nation*, New York, 1970. Well balanced and clear.

Heimsath, C. H., *Indian Nationalism and Hindu Social Reform*, Princeton, 1964.

Hodson, H. V., *The Great Divide: India-Britain-Pakistan*, New York, 1971. An examination of events leading to Partition.

Ikram, S., and P. Spear, eds., *The Cultural Heritage of Pakistan*, London, 1956.

• Iyer, R. N., *The Moral and Political Thought of Mahatma Gandhi*, New York, 1973. A stimulating analysis.

Kothari, Rajni, *Politics in India*, Boston, 1970. Throws light on relationship between caste and politics.

Malik, Hafeez, *Moslem Nationalism in India and Pakistan,* Washington, 1963.

• Maxwell, Neville, *India's China War,* Garden City, N.Y., 1972. Scathingly critical of India's role in the 1962 clash.

Mehta, Ved, *Mahatma Gandhi and His Apostles,* New York, 1977. Emphasizes India's failure to realize Gandhi's ideals.

Menon, V. P., *The Transfer of Power in India,* Princeton, 1957.

Metcalf, T. R., *The Aftermath of Revolt: India, 1857–1870,* Princeton, 1964.

Moore, R. J., *Churchill, Cripps, and India 1939–1945,* New York, 1979. Attributes the partition of India to the failure of the Cripps mission of 1942.

• Morris-Jones, W. H., *The Government and Politics of India,* London, 1964.

• Nehru, Jawaharlal, *The Discovery of India,* New York, 1946.

• Palmer, N. D., *The Indian Political System,* Boston, 1961.

Roberts, P. E., *History of British India under the Company and the Crown,* 3d ed., New York, 1952. An excellent political text.

Sayeed, K. B., *Pakistan: The Formative Phase, 1857–1948,* 2d ed., New York, 1968.

• Sen Gupta, Bhabani, *Communism in Indian Politics,* New York, 1972.

Siddiqui, Kalim, *Conflict, Crisis, and War in Pakistan,* New York, 1972. An indictment of Pakistan's civilian and military elites.

• Srinivas, M. N., *Social Change in Modern India,* Berkeley, 1966.

von Vorys, Karl, *Political Development in Pakistan,* Princeton, 1965. Pessimistic.

Weekes, R. V., *Pakistan: Birth and Growth of a Muslim Nation,* Princeton, 1964.

• Woodruff, Philip, *The Men Who Ruled India,* 2 vols., New York, 1954.

Ziring, Lawrence, *The Ayub Khan Era: Politics in Pakistan 1958–1969,* Syracuse, N.Y., 1971. Generally favorable to Ayub.

SOURCE MATERIALS

Birla, G. D., *In the Shadow of the Mahatma: A Personal Memoir,* Bombay, 1953. Selections from Gandhi's correspondence, interviews and conversations.

Chakravarty, A., ed., *A Tagore Reader,* New York, 1961.

• Gandhi, M. K., *The Story of My Experiments with Truth,* Boston, 1957. Autobiography.

• Jack, H. A., ed., *The Gandhi Reader: A Source Book of His Life and Writings,* Bloomington, Ind., 1956.

McLane, J. R., ed., *The Political Awakening in India,* Englewood Cliffs, N.J., 1970.

Narayan, Jayaprakash, *Prison Diary,* ed. A. B. Shah, Seattle, 1978. Secret diary of Mrs. Gandhi's most famous prisoner.

• Nehru, Jawaharlal, *Toward Freedom,* New York 1951. Autobiography.

———, *Independence and After* (speeches, 1946–1949), New York, 1950.

———, *Jawaharlal Nehru's Speeches, 1949–1953,* Delhi, 1954.

Philips, C. H., *The Evolution of India and Pakistan, 1858 to 1947: Select Documents,* New York, 1962.

Russell, W. H., *My India Mutiny Diary,* London, 1957. Contemporary account by the London *Times* correspondent.

Tagore, Rabindranath, *My Reminiscences,* New York, 1917.

Chapter 38

THE MIDDLE EAST AND AFRICA

All secular power, no matter what form it takes, is the work of Satan. It is our duty to stop it in its tracks and to combat its effects. . . . It is not only our duty in Iran, but it is also the duty of all the Muslims of the world, to carry the revolutionary Islamic policy to its final victory.

—Ayatollah Ruholla Khomeini, *Islamic Government*

I. THE MIDDLE EAST

Few areas of the earth have witnessed more turbulence and rapidity of change than have the countries of the Middle East in recent times. The pattern of their history has been much the same. Before World War I most of them stagnated and slumbered under the rule of the Ottoman Turks. With the breakup of the Ottoman Empire they saw visions of independence and a chance to throw off all traces of foreign domination. Nationalist movements sprang up to prod governments into vigorous action. In many instances they gained control of governments, often in defiance of the religious authorities. They proceeded then with attempts to launch programs of modernization, for building highways, railroads, and schools, subsidizing industries, and sponsoring scientific agriculture and land reform. The problems they encountered, however, in the form of ignorance, corruption, vested interests, and foreign meddling were often too great to be overcome. To this day illiteracy, disease, and high death rates persist in many parts of the Middle East, and poverty is all but universal.

The pattern of Middle Eastern history

A survey of the Middle East may properly begin with Turkey, since it ranks first in population and since nearly the whole region at one time was subject to Turkish rule. We have already seen that the dismemberment of the Turkish Empire began as early as 1829 when the Sultan's government was forced to acknowledge the independence of Greece. Thenceforth one after another of the European provinces

Establishment of the Turkish republic

broke away. By 1914 Turkey in Europe had been reduced to nothing but Istanbul (Constantinople) and a corner of eastern Thrace. But Turkey in Asia still included a vast area from the western border of Persia to the Mediterranean Sea. At the end of World War I, the Turkish government, which had fought on the losing side, accepted a treaty depriving the empire of virtually everything except Istanbul and the northern and central portions of Asia Minor. But before this treaty could be put into effect a group of nationalists, under the leadership of Mustafa Kemal, reconquered much of the lost territory. In 1922 they marched on Istanbul, deposed the Sultan, and in 1923 proclaimed Turkey a republic. The Allies, in the meantime, consented to the making of a new treaty at Lausanne, Switzerland, which permitted the Turks to retain practically all the lands they had reconquered. The new state included Anatolia, Armenia, and eastern Thrace, but none of the outlying territories of Mesopotamia, Arabia, Palestine, or Syria.

Mustafa Kemal: political and educational reforms

For two decades the history of the Turkish republic was almost synonymous with the personal history of Mustafa Kemal. It was his imagination and determination that made the country over from a corrupt and somnolent Oriental despotism into a modern, progressive state with most of the forms if not the substance of democratic government. He began by abolishing the Caliphate and secularizing the state. Under the Sultan religion and the state were intertwined. The Sultan himself was the Caliph, or "Successor of the Prophet," and therefore the spiritual ruler of all Muslims. The law was religious law, and the only officially recognized schools were those attached to the mosques. Kemal's decree abolishing the Caliphate declared that the antiquated religious courts and codes must be replaced by "modern scientific civil codes," and that the schools of the mosques must give way to government schools, which all children between the ages of six and sixteen would be required to attend. But before much progress could be made in educational reform, it was necessary to take one further step, and that was to adopt a new system of writing. The Turkish language was still written in Arabic script, which Kemal regarded as an impossible medium for the expression of Western ideas. In 1928 he had a commission prepare an alphabet using the Roman letters, and this was done so successfully that modern Turkish spelling is consistently phonetic. When he had taught himself the new alphabet, Kemal proceeded to teach others, traveling throughout the country with his blackboard, lecturing audiences on how the characters should be formed. Soon he issued a decree forbidding the holding of public office by anyone who was not adept in the new writing.

Social and economic reforms

The achievements of Kemal also included a social and economic revolution. He issued decrees abolishing the fez, discouraging polygamy, and encouraging women to appear unveiled and both sexes to wear Western clothes. He established schools for girls and made women eligible for business careers and for the professions. In 1929 he gave women the suffrage in local elections and five years later in national elections. The initiative shown by Turkish women under the Republic, not only in entering occupations and professions previously reserved for men but in rising to positions of leadership, makes Turkey unique among Muslim countries and an example for others as well. Equally significant were Kemal's economic reforms. He endowed agricultural colleges, established model farms, and founded banks to lend money to farmers. He freed the peasant from the tithe and set up agencies to distribute seed and farm machinery to almost anyone who could offer a guaranty to use them effectively. Although he undoubtedly had the power to do so, he refrained from instituting measures of forced collectivization such as those of the Russians. He chose rather to adhere to the tradition of Muhammad in encouraging small holdings, in helping the farmer to buy his land, and in teaching him to work it profitably. At the same time he recognized the importance of promoting industrialization. Agriculture alone could not provide the people with a high standard of living or enable the country to make the best use of all its resources. He therefore built thousands of miles of railways and established state monopolies for the manufacture of tobacco, matches, munitions, salt, alcohol, and sugar. Despite the fact that Turkey has abundant resources of coal, iron, copper, and petroleum, and is the world's largest producer of chrome, three-fourths of its nearly 40 million inhabitants still derive their living from agriculture.

Mustafa Kemal Atatürk

Mustafa Kemal (later called Kemal Atatürk) ruled over Turkey from 1922 until his death in 1938. Whether he was simply another twentieth-century dictator, somewhat more benevolent than his compeers, is a question for debate. Legally, his position was that of an elective president, chosen by the Assembly for a four-year term and indefinitely re-eligible. But he himself was president of the Assembly, and, except for a brief period in 1930, he permitted no opposition party to exist. On the other hand, he always described his regime as temporary and transitional. After ten years he still maintained that the people were not yet ready for self-government. He must continue to rule for another decade or so until the citizens grew in wisdom and a sense of responsibility and liberated themselves from the habits and prejudices of the past. To his credit it can be said that he did not involve his country in war and that he never sought the extermination of racial minorities. Although he suppressed a revolt of the Kurds in 1930 with merciless severity, executing twenty-nine of the leaders, he never maintained a Gestapo or Cheka or any similar agency of irresponsible tyranny.

Under Kemal Atatürk's successors, Ismet Inönü and Celal Bayar, Turkey took steps toward supplanting its benevolent dictatorship with a democratic republic. But after World War II, severe economic difficulties, resulting mainly from extravagant spending and inflation, led the government of Premier Adnan Menderes to impose restric-

Revolution of 1960; The Second Turkish Republic

tions. Freedom of the press was abolished, and members of Parliament opposing the government were arrested. Successive student demonstrations against these repressive measures triggered a revolt in 1960 by army officers, who seized control and established a provisional government. Nearly 600 members of the previous regime were tried on charges of corruption and subversion of the Constitution. Of those convicted by the court, three were executed, including the deposed prime minister Adnan Menderes. In 1961 a new constitution was adopted proclaiming the Second Turkish Republic. It provided for a president elected by a Grand National Assembly (parliament) for a seven-year term and ineligible for re-election, and for a prime minister designated by the president on the basis of party representation in the parliament. It included also guaranties of civil liberties, clauses for the protection of workers' rights, and safeguards against abuse of executive power. When elections were held in October 1961, no party gained a majority. A coalition government was formed with the seventy-seven-year-old Ismet Inönü as prime minister. Faced with vexing difficulties and lacking adequate support in the National Assembly, he resigned in 1965.

Economic progress and social unrest

During the 1960s Turkey made considerable economic progress, accompanied by political instability and ominous social unrest. Although inflation continued at a galloping rate, industry expanded steadily and Turkish oil production almost kept pace with domestic demand. A huge dam constructed on the Euphrates promised electric power to transform the primitive rural area of eastern Anatolia. But while foundations were being laid for a modern industrialized society, both the economy and democratic institutions were threatened by bitter factional strife among opposing political extremists and among rival religious groups. Strikes and riots, violent clashes, and political assassinations produced hundreds of deaths and an atmosphere of terror. In March 1971 the military forces imposed martial law for the second time in the history of the republic. Whereas in the 1960 revolution the army had intervened on the liberal side, in 1971 it backed an ultraconservative and repressive "government of national union," which ruled for twenty-nine months. When parliamentary government was resumed, no party could win a majority, and the prime ministership alternated between Bülent Ecevit, leader of the Republican People's party (custodian of Atatürk's reforms but now divided) and Süleyman Demirel, head of the conservative Justice party. Ecevit garnered popularity as champion of the Turkish minority in Cyprus. But when, during the crisis of 1974, he sent an invading army to occupy the whole northern half of the island, he aroused resentment abroad. Both Demirel and Ecevit found it necessary to woo the Islamic-oriented National Salvation party, which controlled 15 percent of the popular vote.

Because of the economic and strategic importance of the Middle

East, unrelaxed tensions in that volatile region made the role of Turkey a matter of concern to neighboring states and to the superpowers as well. The United States operated military bases and electronic listening posts within Anatolia and regarded the Turks, with their army of half a million men, as a key NATO partner. The Turkish invasion of Cyprus in 1974—which so angered the Athens government that it withdrew Greece from NATO—strained relations with the United States. Although Washington had exerted little or no pressure to restrain Ankara's belligerency during the crisis, the United States subsequently suspended arms sales to Turkey. In retaliation the Turks closed twenty-six United States bases within their country. A few years later, after revolution in Iran and Russian-inspired coups in Afghanistan created fears that Western influence in the Middle East might completely collapse, the United States lifted its arms embargo and negotiated for reopening the bases, over which the Turkish government now insisted it should share control.

Turkey's international position

With a strong secular tradition and Western orientation but desirous of maintaining friendship with neighboring Muslim peoples, Turkey has found its position increasingly difficult. Hoping to keep a United States connection without antagonizing the Soviet Union—whose proffered financial aid they sorely need—the Turks seem determined not to become political pawns in the game of the superpowers. But the nation's desperate internal condition makes its future extremely uncertain. By 1979 there were shortages of most basic commodities, including foodstuffs. Industry was operating at about half its capacity, 20 percent of the labor force was unemployed, the annual inflation rate had reached almost 100 percent, and one-third of the country was under martial law. Rival Muslim factions were feuding, and the Kurdish minority in eastern Anatolia adjacent to Iraq and Iran showed signs of unrest. In September 1980 the army high command, after admonishing politicians to unite to fight "anarchy, terrorism, and separatism," executed an almost bloodless but decisive coup, suspending the constitution and arresting more than one hundred persons, including not only party leaders, but also the heads of labor unions. While enforcing martial law, the generals pledged that after the drafting of a new constitution designed to curb social disorder, they would honor the republic's tradition of a return to civilian rule.

Uncertainty as to the future

Second in population—and fast on its way to becoming first in that category among nations of the Middle East—is the Arab Republic of Egypt. Although technically a part of the Ottoman Empire until 1914, Egypt was for all practical purposes a dependency of Great Britain after 1882. The British kept up the pretense of acknowledging the sovereignty of the Khedive and his overlord the Sultan, but when Turkey joined the Central Powers in 1914 the London government issued a proclamation that Egypt would henceforth constitute a protectorate of the British Empire. When the war ended, the London

The beginning of nationalism in Egypt; the rise of the Wafd

authorities refused to allow Egypt to send a delegation to Paris to lay its case before the peace conference. The upshot was the emergence of an Egyptian nationalist movement known as the *Wafd*. The name means literally "delegation," and the movement had been organized originally to present Egypt's demands and grievances at the peace conference. When the British attempted suppression and deported its leader to Malta, the *Wafd* came forth with an insistence upon nothing less than complete independence.

Abolition of the British protectorate

Following a campaign of sabotage and terrorism waged by the *Wafd,* the British decided to abolish the protectorate and in 1922 proclaimed Egypt an independent and sovereign state. But "independence" was made subject to four reservations, to be left absolutely to the discretion of the British pending adjustment by mutual agreement. The first was the protection of the Suez Canal and other vital links in the lifeline of the British Empire. The second was the defense of Egypt itself against foreign encroachments or interference. The third was the protection of foreign interests and minorities in Egypt. The fourth was the maintenance of the dependent status of the Sudan under the joint rule of Britain and Egypt. For the next three decades the history of Egypt was largely occupied by controversy and conflict over these four points or reservations.

The revival of nationalism after World War II

Although the majority of Egyptians resented the attempts of the British to keep the country in a state of vassalage, they were alarmed by Mussolini's invasion of Ethiopia in 1935, and in 1936 accepted an Anglo-Egyptian Treaty of Frienship and Alliance. Egypt agreed to coordinate its foreign policy with that of Britain in return for British assistance in gaining admission to the League of Nations. Before all the terms of the Anglo-Egyptian Treaty could be put into effect, World War II broke out. The British were reluctant to take any steps that might threaten their communications with the East, and the Egyptians did not press the issue of the removal of British troops from

Suez Canal at the Onset of World War I. Britain's concern for the Suez Canal as a lifeline to the Empire was one of the primary factors behind the establishment of a protectorate over Egypt in 1914 and the "reservations" linked to the proclamation of independence in 1922.

their soil. But when the war ended, the flames of nationalist aspirations were kindled anew. The Egyptians now demanded that the British withdraw entirely from both the Suez Canal area and the Sudan. In 1951 the Egyptian government announced that it was abrogating the Treaty of 1936 and also the condominium or joint rule in the Sudan. In July 1954 Britain agreed to the removal of all British troops from Egyptian territory.

In July 1952, Major General Muhammad Naguib seized control of the Egyptian government and the army. The pleasure-loving King Farouk I, alleged to be subservient to the British, was deposed. A year later Egypt was proclaimed a republic, with General Naguib as its first president and premier. The new ruler announced a program of sweeping economic and social reforms, but before it could be fully effected, conflict developed within the military junta that had overthrown the monarchy. Naguib's rival, Lieutenant-Colonel Gamal Abdul Nasser, secured the office of premier, and in June 1956, in a carefully managed election in which he was the only candidate, Nasser was chosen president. In the same election the Egyptian voters adopted a new constitution proclaiming the country an Islamic-Arab state with a democratic form of government.

Nasser resolved to continue and enlarge the program of economic and social reform. In particular, he was determined to relieve the condition of the impoverished masses. He proceeded with plans to distribute 750,000 acres of land, giving farms to 250,000 landless peasants. He soon realized, however, that on account of Egypt's rapid growth in population, more productive land must be made available. To accomplish this purpose he decided upon the construction of the Aswan High Dam, a gigantic reservoir to back up the waters of the Upper Nile and provide irrigation for 2 million acres of arable land. Since the cost ($1.3 billion) would be more than Egypt could stand, he hoped to borrow large sums of money from the World Bank and from the United States and British governments. Alarmed by the Egyptian purchases of arms from Czechoslovakia (a Communist source), the United States suddenly withdrew its offer of a loan to Nasser, and Great Britain did likewise soon after. Nasser retaliated by expropriating the owners of the Suez Canal, who were chiefly British and French, and declared that he would use the revenues of the canal to build the dam. After months of fruitless negotiation, the British and French encouraged an invasion of Egyptian territory by the Republic of Israel. The Israelis had plenty of grievances, since they had been the victims of border raids from the Sinai Peninsula for many years. The invasion began on October 29, 1956, and the British and French intervened soon afterward. The affair precipitated a crisis which threatened for a time to engulf the world. The Soviet rulers warned Israel that its very existence was in danger and darkly hinted their intention of joining forces with Egypt. The United Nations

Gamal Abdul Nasser, Dynamic Arab Nationalist and President of Egypt, 1956–1970

The Suez crisis; Arab-Israeli wars

finally arranged a cease-fire, and in March 1957 the Nasser government reopened the canal, under its own terms of national ownership, to all users except Israel. Nasser formed alliances with Jordan and Syria and vowed that Israel must be wiped from the map. In 1967, when he closed Aqaba, Israel's only direct outlet to the Red Sea, the Israelis responded with a lightning war against Egypt and its Arab allies. The Egyptian and Syrian forces were routed in six days, and the Syrians accepted a cease-fire a short time later, leaving Israel in occupation of the Sinai peninsula and the West Bank of the Jordan River. Violence erupted again in October 1973 when Egypt and Syria launched a surprise offensive in the Sinai and Golan Heights areas respectively. After seventeen days of fierce fighting a cease-fire was established under pressure from the United States and the U.S.S.R.

Peace negotiations between Egypt and Israel

Following Nasser's death in 1970, Anwar Sadat, a relatively obscure member of the group that had overthrown the monarchy in 1952, became president of Egypt. Confronted with problems at home and abroad, he attempted to continue Nasser's policies while moderating their harshness. A new constitution enacted in 1971 contained democratic features, but political power remained with the one and only legal party, the Arab Socialist Union, which had become bureaucratic and unprogressive. Sadat's most distinctive contribution was the reversal of his predecessor's foreign policy. At the risk of sacrificing leadership of the Arab world, he resolved to end the state of war with Israel which exacted a tremendous economic price and continually posed the threat of a general conflagration. Piecemeal agreements, negotiated with the help of United States Secretary of State Henry Kissinger in 1974 and 1975, provided for mutual disengagement in the Suez Canal area and the return of Sinai oilfields to Egyptian control. In June 1975 the canal—closed since 1967—was reopened to merchant

Aswan High Dam. The dam was designed to serve a twofold purpose: to facilitate the irrgation of vast areas of arid land and to generate electrical power.

Israeli Tanks Move into Jerusalem. A scene during the second Arab-Israeli War, June 1967.

ships of all nations, including Israel. Seizing an even bolder initiative, President Sadat—after requesting an invitation—in November 1977 became the first Arab leader to pay an official visit to the state of Israel, where he met an enthusiastic reception in Tel Aviv and Jerusalem. This surprisingly auspicious weekend visit resolved none of the difficulties between the two states but it opened the door to improved relations. In his speech before the Israeli parliament (Knesset) Sadat affirmed Israel's right to exist, but at the same time he called unequivocally for withdrawal from all occupied Arab lands, for Arab access to the holy city of Jerusalem, and for the creation of an independent Palestinian state. Not until March 1979, after many months of negotiation, was an Egyptian-Israeli peace treaty signed, and it left important issues unresolved, particularly the exact nature of the "full autonomy" promised to the Palestinians, and the status of the city of Jerusalem—sacred to the adherents of three religions but which the Israelis had vowed to retain as their nation's capital.

The movement toward accommodation with Israel brought radical changes in Egypt's international position. In 1972 President Sadat expelled his Soviet advisers, thus rebuffing the country that had been Egypt's chief source of economic and military aid. However, his overtures to Israel, which began shortly after the 1973 war and were strongly encouraged by the United States, won for him access to the world's leading arms emporium. United States diplomatic support was also welcome at a time when Egypt was facing isolation in the Arab and Islamic international community. Following the peace treaty with Israel, sixteen Arab states, the Palestinian Liberation Organization, and Iran severed diplomatic relations with Cairo. Sadat continued to be at odds with Arab leaders and Islamic fundamentalists until he was assassinated in October 1981.

President Anwar Sadat of Egypt Addressing the Israeli Knesset in 1977

Egypt's economic performance failed to match its stellar role in the field of diplomacy. With an annual per capita income of $280, the nation is among the world's poorest. Egypt is the most urbanized of the Arab countries and its population of 39 million is growing so rapidly, especially in the cities, that overcrowding and shortages are inevitable. Cairo, with 2 million inhabitants in 1952, had 9 million twenty-five years later. Housing was so scarce that as many as ten people slept in a single room, and squatters improvised living quarters in Cairo's cemeteries. In one of mankind's oldest agricultural regions, farming methods are still primitive. Yet the economic picture is not utterly bleak. Within two years of the reopening of the Suez Canal in 1975 its annual revenue had reached $500,000. Plans were announced to enlarge the waterway to accommodate 200,000-ton supertankers, and the increase in traffic was stimulating rapid urban growth along the canal route. The Aswan Dam, though it has not produced the economic miracle hoped for on its completion in 1970, could provide water for desert reclamation in the Sinai peninsula. Egypt has appreciable reserves of petroleum and in 1977 began to produce some for export.

When World War I ended, the country now known as Israel was a province of Turkey. Its population was about 70 percent Arab and 30 percent Jewish and Christian. By the defeat of Turkey in 1918, it was made a mandate of the League of Nations under the guardianship of Great Britain. In the meantime, Zionists in Britain and the United States worked zealously to convert Palestine into a national home for the Jewish people. In return for their labors the British government issued the famous Balfour Declaration promising to view with favor the establishment in Palestine of a national home for Jewish people. At the same time provision would be made for safeguarding the rights of non-Jewish communities in Palestine.

On the basis of the Balfour Declaration, Britain accepted the mandate for Palestine, promising not merely to establish a Jewish national home, but "to secure the preservation of an Arab National Home and to apprentice the people of Palestine as a whole in the art of self-government." It was an optimistic ambition, but at the time optimism seemed justified. In fact, for ten years there was every reason to expect that the undertaking would be successful. Palestine prospered as never before in its history. Factories were built, land was reclaimed, irrigation works were constructed, the Jordan River was harnessed for electric power, and unemployment disappeared from the face of the land. Except for rioting in Jaffa in 1921, no incident of violence occurred to disturb the general tranquillity. The aspect of the country was so peaceful that in 1926 the British reduced their armed forces to a single RAF squadron and two companies with armored cars.

By 1929, however, evidences of disharmony had begun to appear in the land that was holy to three great religions. The Jews were too prosperous and well educated and were arousing the envy and fears of the Arabs by their high standard of living and their more strenuous competition. Their purchases of land, in many cases from absentee owners, had resulted in the displacement of thousands of Arab cultivators and had thrown them into the cities at a time when the Great Depression was beginning to make unemployment a serious problem. But the major cause of Arab foreboding was the steady increase in the Jewish population. The opportunity to emigrate to Palestine had offered a greater temptation than the Arabs had expected. As a consequence, some of them foresaw a relentless advance and expansion of Europeans and Americans, backed by foreign capital and flaunting a culture that was alien to the ways of the Arab majority. In 1929, 1930, and 1931 armed attacks were waged upon Jewish settlements followed by terrorist murders.

But these episodes paled into insignificance when compared with the bloody violence that followed. When the mandate was established, no one could have foreseen the desperate plight that was to overtake the European Jews with the accession of the Nazis to power in Germany. As news of the persecutions spread, it was inevitable that pressure should be brought upon the British government to relax the barriers against immigration into Palestine. During the period 1933–1935 the admission of more than 130,000 Jewish immigrants was authorized, and uncounted thousands more came in illicitly. From this time on Palestine was a seething caldron of violence and warfare. The Arabs rose in open rebellion against the mandate. Organized terrorism swept the country. Guerrilla attacks in the rural areas and looting, burning, and sabotage in the towns and cities kept the whole population in turmoil. By 1938 Britain had 20,000 troops in Palestine, and even these were unable to maintain order.

The early years of World War II were characterized by relative quiet in Palestine, but trouble broke out anew when a conference of American Zionists at the Biltmore Hotel in New York, in May 1942,

The development of conflicts between Jews and Arabs

Rebellion of the Arabs against the mandate

Immigration to Palestine. Left: British soldiers guard the shore as a ship loaded with unauthorized refugees attempts to land in 1947. Right: A view of the unbearably crowded conditions aboard ships bringing refugees to Palestine.

adopted the so-called Biltmore Program, demanding the establishment of a Jewish state and a Jewish army in Palestine. Soon afterward both Jews and Arabs prepared for war to the hilt. Fanatical Zionists, as well as Arabs, resorted to the use of terrorist methods. Illegal military organizations sprang up on both sides and devoted their energies to raiding, burning, and assassination.

Termination of the mandate and establishment of the State of Israel

In April 1947 the British government referred the Palestine problem to the United Nations and announced that a year later it would terminate the mandate and withdraw all its troops from the country. On May 15, 1948, the British mandate came to an end, and on the same day a Jewish provisional government proclaimed the establishment of an independent State of Israel. Elections were held for a Constituent Assembly, which met in February of the following year and adopted a temporary constitution for a democratic republic. Its chief features were a weak president, a strong cabinet, and a powerful parliament. The constitution also provided for proportional representation, a unicameral parliament, and universal suffrage for Jews and Arabs alike. A unique element in the system was the close association of religion with the state. Marriage and divorce were placed under the exclusive jurisdiction of religious courts—Jewish, Christian, or Muslim as the affiliation of the parties might require.

The Arab-Israeli wars

Meanwhile, from the day of proclaimed independence until the spring of 1949, Israel and its Arab neighbor countries were at war. United Nations efforts brought about truces several times; Israel and Egypt signed a general armistice agreement in February 1949; Jordan and Syria also signed armistices in April. The status at the cease-fire was regarded as a victory for Israel and a defeat for the Arab powers; neither, however, accepted it as final. Violent incidents continued to occur, including retaliatory massacres.

Agricultural development

Despite troubles with the Arabs, Israel strengthened its economy, and many new industries were created. Large sums of money flowed into the country as a result of West German restitution for the outrages of Nazism. Agriculture advanced to a stage sufficient to supply the needs of the home market while export crops such as olives, melons, and citrus fruits were rapidly developed. Land under cultivation more than doubled between 1955 and 1967. The index of industrial production increased from 100 in 1963 to 185 in 1969. The nation had seven universities, two with more than 10,000 students each. Total enrollment in all state schools had increased from 130,000 in 1948 to approximately 800,000 in 1970.

The heavy burden of defense

Yet the fate of Israel was not a happy one. The state was born in strife and during the first twenty-five years of its existence fought four wars with its Arab neighbor states. In the face of adversity Israel managed not only to endure but to grow in strength—a testimony to the resourcefulness and determination of its citizens but also owing to massive economic and military aid from the United States (currently

On the Path to Peace in the Middle East. From left to right, Egyptian President Anwar Sadat, U.S. President Jimmy Carter, and Israeli Prime Minister Menachem Begin shake hands at the announcement of the Camp David accord which laid the groundwork for a peace treaty between Egypt and Israel.

nearly $2 billion a year). Obsession with the problem of security has exacted a heavy economic and psychological toll. Between 1967 and 1975 defense spending rose to become the highest in the world in proportion to population ($1,040 per capita), consuming half the national budget and 32 percent of the gross national product. Armed to the teeth, Israel became an exporter of arms to some fifty other countries; yet peace seemed as elusive as ever.

The Labor party, after thirty years in office, was defeated in the elections of May 1977 and replaced by the Likud bloc, which drew much of its support from extreme nationalists opposed to any compromise with Israel's enemies. Menachem Begin, the new prime minister, was a veteran of the struggle for independence and known as a hard-liner. Nevertheless, he agreed to exploratory talks with President Sadat of Egypt and accepted the invitation to a summit meeting at Camp David, Maryland, where President Carter's patience and persistence bore fruit in the signing of a basic agreement. The Camp David Accords of September 1978 bound Sadat and Begin to take positive steps toward peace in the Middle East. But the formidable difficulties remaining were scarcely lessened by the Egyptian-Israeli treaty signed the following March. While Arab spokesmen denounced Sadat as a traitor to their cause, the Arab populations of Israeli-occupied lands accused Israel of planning to keep them in permanent subjection. The Israeli government refused to treat with the Palestine Liberation Organization, even though the PLO had won wide recognition as the most articulate champion of the cause of the Palestinian refugees. Since 1967 the Israelis had planted more than sixty new Jewish settlements in the West Bank, the Gaza Strip, and the Golan Heights, and a fervent Zionist faction was demanding permanent

The Camp David Accords

THE MIDDLE EAST TODAY

retention of these territories. Meanwhile, the need for a peace agreement became more imperative, not only because of the constant danger that a major war might break out but for the sake of ensuring Israel's survival. Arab populations were increasing much more rapidly than was Israel's, and Arab armies were improving in military effectiveness, as shown in the October 1973 ("Yom Kippur") war. Also, following that conflict, international support for the Israeli position weakened, partly in reaction to the oil embargo imposed by Arab producers. Recognition of these factors prompted a demand within Israel for a policy of accommodation and compromise. In October 1979 Moshe Dayan, hero of the 1967 war, resigned his post as foreign minister in Begin's government because he disapproved of its adamant stand on the Palestinian issue. Further defections from the cabinet followed, and by January 1981 Begin has lost his majority in the Knesset.

During the first thirty years of Israel's existence as a state, the character of the nation changed considerably. Many early Zionists had visualized Israel as a haven for small farmers or a community of agricultural cooperatives. By the mid-1970s it had become a land of teeming cities, with a society 80 percent urban. Rapid industrial growth was paced by rampant inflation, which by 1980 had reached an annual rate in excess of 100 percent. A potential internal problem centered on the Israeli citizens of Arab descent, who were subjected to the strain of conflicting loyalties in times of controversy between Israel and Arab states. Theoretically equal under the law, Israeli Arabs were discriminated against in practice, and most of them lived in exclusively Arab villages in northern Israel. With the world's highest birth rate, their numbers had tripled since 1948, reaching a figure of half a million and constituting about 15 percent of the total population of Israel. Another factor affecting the character of society was a change in the pattern of immigration—a decline in the influx of Western Jews and an increase in those coming from Arabic and North African countries. By 1977 the Sephardic or "Oriental" elements outnumbered those of Western European or American origin (called Ashkenazi), but they suffered some of the same disadvantages as the Israeli Arabs. The combination of internal pressures and external threats created an identity crisis for Israeli citizens. A prominent intellectual, formerly president of the World Zionist Organization, urged Israel to seek security by fulfilling its destiny as a unique spiritual center rather than striving to be "a state like all other states." He recommended Israel's neutralization—returned to its pre-1967 borders but with independence and sovereignty guaranteed by the two superpowers—and a gradual demilitarization of the states of the Middle East.[1]

Until recently, the most barren and backward of the countries formerly included in the Ottoman Empire was that which is now called

The ethnic problem

---

[1]Nahum Goldmann, "True Neutrality for Israel," *Foreign Policy,* Winter 1979–80, pp. 113–41.

A Meeting of the Arab Kings. In the wake of a war on the Nejd-Iraq border, King Faisal of Iraq (seated fourth from the left) and King Abdul Ibn Saud of Saudi Arabia (seated fifth from the left) negotiated a lasting peace under British auspices in 1930.

The formation of Saudi Arabia

Saudi Arabia. Covering an area more than one-fourth that of the United States, Arabia is almost 100 percent desert. Not a single river or lake exists to relieve the monotonous aridity. Inhabited to this day by only 9½ million people, the country did not become a united state until 1927. Prior to that time it was divided into the two main areas of the Hejaz and Nejd. The king of the Hejaz was Sherif Hussein, Protector of the Holy Cities of Mecca and Medina and, after 1924, self-appointed Caliph of Islam. Hussein was driven from his kingdom by the ruler of Nejd, Abdul ibn Saud (1880–1953), who in January 1926 had himself proclaimed King of the Hejaz in the Great Mosque of Mecca. Soon afterward he united his two kingdoms of Hejaz and Nejd into a theocratic state which he named Saudi Arabia.

Saudi oil and ARAMCO

Ibn Saud was shrewd enough to realize that the Muslim world could not hold its own against Western encroachments without adopting Western improvements. Accordingly, he allowed a few railways to be built and imported motor vehicles for his own court and for the transportation of pilgrims to the Holy Cities, and he instituted plans for free education. By far the greatest impetus was the discovery, in the 1930s, that eastern Arabia contained undreamed of riches in the form of petroleum deposits, amounting to the world's largest known reserves. King ibn Saud granted concessions for the exploitation of this wealth to the Arabian-American Oil Company (Aramco), owned jointly by Texaco and the Standard Oil Company of California. Royalties paid by Aramco provided the funds for electrification of cities and the construction of highways, railroads, and airports, to say nothing of aid to agriculture, education, and public health.

Abdul ibn Saud's son and heir, a wildly reckless spendthrift, was deposed by the royal family in 1964 and replaced by his half brother Faisal. King Faisal, who also retained the prime ministership, proved to be an enlightened and able statesman. He abolished slavery in his kingdom, opened public schools for girls, and won wide respect. His success owed much to the loyal service of Sheikh Ahmed Zaki Yamani. Western-educated (New York University, Columbia, Harvard), brilliant, and level-headed, Yamani had been appointed minister of petroleum and mineral resources in 1962, before Faisal's accession to the throne. Sheikh Yamani negotiated agreements with Aramco providing for the gradual transfer of ownership to Saudi Arabia, directed similar negotiations with Western oil companies for other Arab states, and initiated the formation of the Organization of Petroleum Exporting Countries (OPEC). In April 1978 King Faisal was assassinated by a member of his own family. His brother Khalid, who succeeded to the throne, was conservative, puritanical, and too infirm physically to play an active role, but Khalid's designated successor, Crown Prince Fahd, entertained ambitious plans for modernization and industrial development.

Yamani and OPEC

Saudi Arabia affords a striking illustration of how the impact of advanced technology and an expanding market can telescope centuries and divergent cultures. The government is an absolute monarchy, with power exercised by the king but residing in about 3,000 princes of the Saudi royal household. Abject poverty is still prevalent outside the few rapidly modernizing cities. Society for the most part is bound by the rigid restrictions of Muslim traditionalism, seen typically in the banning of alcoholic beverages and in the seclusion of women. But the citizens, with no elections and no parliament to represent them, nevertheless enjoy welfare benefits that might be envied by socialist democracies: free medical service, free education through the university level, subsidies to farmers, and loans to homeowners. The wealth accruing to Saudi Arabia as the world's largest oil-exporting country has enabled it to finance ambitious domestic projects and also to con-

Modernization

Sheik Ahmed Zaki Yamani, Oil Minister of Saudi Arabia, at an OPEC Conference outside Algiers in March 1975

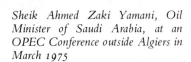

tribute subsidies to Egypt, Jordan, Syria, and the PLO. Since the possession of oil has become not only an economic prize but a potent political weapon as well, Saudi Arabia has acquired a key strategic international position. This was illustrated in 1973–1974 when an Arab oil embargo—instituted by King Faisal against the Western powers—sent shock waves around the globe.

Petrodollars

Saudi Arabia's foreign policy has been anti-Israel, but at the same time anti-Communist and generally aligned with that of the United States. The United States depends on Saudi Arabia for about 20 percent of its oil imports and provides technology and managerial skill in exchange. Through oil royalties the Riyadh government accumulated a huge dollar reserve, amounting by 1975 to more than $70 billion. The investment of the bulk of these "petrodollars" in United States bonds, stocks, and banks provided critical support for the dollar at a time when it was being eroded by the United States' large foreign trade deficit.

The triumph of Iranian nationalism under Riza Khan

The only country of the Middle East which was not under the rule of Turkey at one time or another before 1918 was Persia. But this did not mean freedom from foreign domination. Remote, steeped in languor, and rich in resources, Persia was a constant temptation to ambitious imperialists. In 1907 Great Britain and Russia signed an agreement providing for the division of the country into spheres of influence. The northern sphere was assigned to Russia and the southern to Great Britain. A middle zone was to be left, temporarily at least, under the control of the native Shah. The overthrow of the tsar in 1917 filled the minds of British imperialists with hopes that all Persia might be theirs. By 1919 Lord Curzon had extorted from the Shah

A Saudi Arabian Oil Refinery and Storage Tanks. The Saudis have been producing 10.5 million barrels of oil per day (at least 1 million barrels per day more than they have produced in recent years) in order to make up the shortfall created by the Iranian-Iraqi war that began in the fall of 1980 and to force the OPEC nations to devise a unified policy for the first time in eight years.

an agreement transferring to Great Britain political and military control of the entire country. But the plans of the British were frustrated by Riza Khan, a young army officer who forced the Shah to appoint him minister of war and commander-in-chief of the army. In 1923 he became premier and two years later Shah with the title Riza Pahlavi. In 1932 he canceled the concession of the powerful Anglo-Persian Oil Company and obtained a new contract with terms more advantageous to his own government. In 1935 he changed the name of his country from Persia to Iran, or land of the Aryans.

World War II brought almost as much turmoil and anguish to Iran as if it had been one of the belligerents. Accused of Nazi sympathies, Riza Shah in 1941 was forced to abdicate and was succeeded on the throne by his son Muhammad Riza Pahlavi. Because of its strategic importance, Iran's territory was occupied by the British, Russians, and Americans under pledges to respect its sovereignty and independence and to render economic assistance during and after the war. Despite these pledges, unrest and inflation plagued the country. An internal political conflict led to the temporary expulsion of the Shah. Premier Muhammad Mossadegh, a nationalist leader, precipitated an international crisis in 1951 when he secured authorization from parliament to nationalize the petroleum industry. Western opposition to any assertion of economic independence by an underdeveloped semicolonial country was complicated by Anglo-American rivalry. Averse to prolonged negotiation, the United States government cut off aid to Teheran and persuaded the British to join in enforcing a boycott which denied Iran access to oil tankers and oil markets. The consequent shutdown of the huge Anglo-Iranian refinery at Abadan brought the Iranian government to the point of bankruptcy. In August 1953 a CIA-directed coup overthrew the government, replacing Mossadegh with a former Nazi collaborator and restoring the Shah to his throne. Under a new agreement, 40 percent of Iran's petroleum industry was allotted to five American companies.

Expulsion and restoration of the Shah

Muhammad Riza Pahlavi's reign, spanning nearly four decades, brought his country considerable material progress, an overblown military establishment, brutal repression, and finally a revolution that shook society to its roots. During the 1960s Iran achieved an annual economic growth rate of 9 percent and doubled the gross national product. Revenues from oil, the chief natural resource, made possible highway construction, power-generating dams, and the beginnings of a system of public education. In 1963 The Shah launched what he called a "White Revolution," dedicated to raising living standards of his subjects. However, in spite of the state's ample revenues, "the Shah-People Revolution" produced meager results. A highly touted program of land redistribution reduced the number of tenants but left the majority of farmers on tiny plots, while great landlords retained large estates and the most profitable holdings. In 1979 three out of five

Material progress, but meager social benefits

Muhammad Riza Pahlavi, Shah of Iran

rural families owned either no land or practically none, and millions of uprooted agricultural workers had drifted to the cities in search of work. One-tenth of the population controlled half of the wealth. Social services were inadequate and inferior. In a population of 35 million, 60 percent of adults were illiterate.

While indulging in the trappings of absolute monarchy—exemplified by five palaces maintained for the royal family, and by a multi-million-dollar extravaganza at Persepolis in 1971 to celebrate the 2,500th anniversary of Persian monarchy—the Shah hoped to modernize the nation. Seemingly equating modernization with militarization, between 1959 and 1978 he spent $36 billion on arms, about half of them purchased from the United States. In order to pay for sophisticated planes, missiles, and supporting equipment, he raised the price of oil—contributing to the upward surge that quadrupled oil prices in 1974. Expansion of land, air, and naval forces made Iran the strongest military power in the Persian Gulf area.

An Iranian constitution, dating from 1906 and modeled on that of Belgium, provided for the separation of powers and guaranteed basic rights to the citizens. The Shah, however, suppressed all political parties except one of his own invention and forbade any opposition to his rule. Commander-in-chief of the armed forces, he bolstered his position by keeping an imperial guard and, especially, through the notorious SAVAK, a secret police force trained by the CIA and under the Shah's personal control. SAVAK agents, systematically employing terror and various forms of torture, made the Shah's regime one of the most brutal among the many dictatorships afflicting contemporary civilization. And while repression did not prevent eventual revolution, it eliminated much of the potential leadership needed for reconstruction after the advent of revolution.

Extreme repression

Latent opposition to the Shah's rule had long rankled among Muslim religious leaders, the *mullahs,* both because their influence had been curtailed and because some aspects of modernization were repugnant to them. Intellectuals were alienated by government repression and corruption. Disaffection spread throughout the Iranian population in the late 1970s when an economic slump halted industrial projects and rising unemployment was accompanied by a 50-percent rate of inflation. January 1978 inaugurated a year of riots and bloody clashes. Crowds of millions demonstrated in the streets; some 8,000 people were killed as the police cracked down on protesters. In September the Shah imposed martial law and appointed a military governor, confident that, with the army behind him, he could weather the storm. But strikes in the oil fields and violent eruptions led by university students paralyzed the government and brought the economy to a standstill. When it became evident that the army was not without sympathy for the revolutionaries and might refuse orders to fight against the people, the Shah was forced to vacate his throne. On

Revolution: expulsion of the Shah

January 16, 1979, he left Iran by plane "on a vacation," and a Revolutionary Council was installed in his place. Revolutionary courts sentenced and executed hundreds of the Shah's former supporters, including nearly a third of the military high command.

The Shah's abrupt capitulation left the country in a divided and chaotic state. Western governments had been strangely blind to flaws in Iran's economy and to the nearly universal hatred which Iranians bore toward their ruler. Having praised the Shah as a staunch ally, commanding "an island of stability in one of the most troubled areas of the world," American officials were unprepared to deal effectively with his successors. According to the U.S. ambassador in Teheran, sharp disagreements within the Washington bureaucracy prevented the establishment of links with revolutionary leaders that might have salvaged some United States influence and smoothed the process of transition.[2]

Beyond expulsion of the Shah, the objectives of the popular revolution that swept Iran were not entirely clear. The key revolutionary figure and temporary wielder of power was a seventy-eight-year-old Islamic theologian, Ayatollah Ruholla Khomeini. A life-long enemy of the Pahlavi dynasty, Khomeini had been exiled in 1964, sought refuge in Iraq and later in Paris, and in the French capital gathered around him the nucleus of a revolutionary government. A man of great energy and passionate convictions, Khomeini was idolized upon his re-entry into Iran on February 1 and, with the assistance of a Revolutionary Council, issued decrees for the nation. The Ayatollah's political precepts were derived from theological studies and from his devout Shiite faith, tempered somewhat by the idealism of Plato's *Republic*. Within a few months he drafted a new constitution for Iran, providing for a popularly elected president but making Islamic law binding upon all citizens, and secular officials subject to supervision and removal by the religious authorities. Staggering internal problems confronted the new regime: a crippled economy; tension between religious conservatives and proponents of modernization and secularism; nationalist aspirations among minorities, especially the Kurds of Kurdistan in western Iran. External relations also presented problems. Khomeini, a fervent Islamic nationalist, was not only anti-U.S.A. and anti-Israel but also anti-Communist and anti-Soviet. Iranian resentment toward the United States for its close ties with the Shah's government was aggravated when the ailing exiled monarch was admitted to an American hospital for treatment. In reprisal a group of militants seized the United States embassy in Teheran in November 1979 and held fifty-two hostages captive for 444 days. Their release was

Ayatollah Ruholla Khomeini of Iran

Problems confronting the revolutionary government

[2]William H. Sullivan, "The Road Not Taken," *Foreign Policy*, Fall 1980. pp. 175–86. Sullivan alleges that National Security Adviser Zbigniew Brzezinski tried to promote an army coup in support of the Shah.

obtained only after long, repeatedly stalemated, and humiliating negotiations.

A formidable addition to the troubles afflicting Khomeini's regime was the outbreak of war with Iraq, a neighbor with whom Iran had long-standing disputes. The Iraqis' motives in launching their attack in September 1980 were partly territorial. Repudiating a 1975 agreement made with the Shah, they hoped to gain control of the Shatt al-Arab—the 100-mile-long terminus of the great Tigris-Euphrates river system emptying into the Persian Gulf. The Baghdad government also feared the spread of Islamic fundamentalism and revolutionary fervor which, if it reached beyond Iran's borders, might disaffect Iraq's predominantly Shiite population. Although Iraqi troops were able to penetrate Iran's territory, Iranian defenses proved stronger than anticipated, and Iranian planes bombed Baghdad. Each side claimed to be fighting a holy war (Khomeini added the charge that Iraq was acting at the behest of the "Satan" United States). The conflict imperiled the source of 40 percent of the industrialized West's oil requirements and threatened to ruin the economies of both belligerents.

The ferment agitating the Middle East ever since World War II seemed to reach a critical stage as the 1970s ended. Lands that had nurtured ancient empires and cradled Western civilization were subjected to more rapid change than ever before in their long history. Scarcely anywhere could the assurance of stability be found. Competing pressures from without intensified domestic and regional problems that were already perplexing enough. The most obvious and persistent source of conflict was that between Israel and surrounding Arab peoples, exacerbated by the presence of more than a million Palestinian refugees—bereft of a homeland ever since the Arabic-Jewish war of 1948—and by the disaffection of Arab populations in lands occupied by Israel since the 1967 war. But other rivalries of comparable bitterness divided the region. The "Arab World" was by no means a solid entity. An Arab League, formed in 1945 with Egypt, Saudi Arabia, Jordan, Iraq, Syria, Lebanon, and Yemen as the original members, failed to resolve the differences between conservatives and radicals; nor could it keep its members from being drawn into the power struggle between the United States and the Soviet Union. Egypt, the league's military right arm, was expelled in 1979 in retaliation for Sadat's rapprochement with Israel, and became temporarily a pariah in the eyes of fellow Arabs. A ruinous civil war which racked the tiny state of Lebanon for nineteen months during 1975–1976, pitting Lebanese Christians against Muslims, was symptomatic of the struggle for leadership among Arab states as well as a manifestation of the Israeli-Palestinian conflict. Fighting in Lebanon was halted by the joint intervention of Israel and Israel's official enemy, Syria. President Hafez Assad of Syria was anxious to prevent the complete dismem-

Iranian Demonstrators Outside the U.S. Embassy in Teheran, November 25, 1979. Militants, bearing portraits of Ayatollah Khomeini and cardboard effigies of President Jimmy Carter, protested the American role in Iranian affairs during the previous 26 years while 52 American hostages were held in the embassy.

berment of Lebanon, which he hoped to use as a base for expanding his own influence, and to this end he did not scruple to use force against the Palestinians.

As Egypt's influence waned, Iraq, with a population of only 12 million, appeared a likely candidate for primacy among Muslim countries of the Middle East. Once regarded as highly volatile and unstable, Iraq during the last decade moved rapidly to change its image. In 1968 the Baath Socialist party seized control and established a military dictatorship which was repressive but also introduced positive economic reforms. Huge oil reserves—largest among the Arab states excepting Saudi Arabia, and carefully managed—gave Iraq an advantageous position in foreign trade and its people a relatively high standard of living. Saddam Hussein, leader of the Baath party and, since 1979, president of Iraq, in June 1980 permitted the election of a 250-member assembly to share legislative power with the dominant Revolutionary Council. In the 1970s Hussein loosened ties with Moscow, in spite of a fifteen-year friendship treaty signed in 1972. He repudiated the Iraqi Communist party and dismissed its representatives from his cabinet. Steadily increasing Iraq's armaments, Hussein intended his country to displace Iran as the strongest military power in the Persian Gulf. The exhausting war with Iran put his ambition to a severe test.

Iraq's growing strength

Explosive forces in the Middle East include the nationalist ambitions of ethnic minorities: the Baluchi of Iran, Afghanistan, and Pakistan; the Kurds of Iran, Iraq, and Turkey. Mistrust between the Shiite and Sunnite divisions of Islam is another factor, as is the struggle between advocates and opponents of progressive change. The inherent danger in conflict springing from these issues is multiplied beyond

Dangers inherent in policies of the superpowers

measure by the fact that Middle Eastern nations are heavily armed. For this, responsibility rests mainly with the two superpowers, who sought both profits from arms sales and at the same time the acquisition of client states. They are discovering, however, that client states, sufficiently armed, cannot only bully their neighbors but also turn against their supposed benefactors.

Until recently the Middle East was a region of abject poverty. Among great numbers of the population it still is, but the tapping of its enormous stores of petroleum—totaling two-thirds of the world's proven reserves—has brought wealth and clout to those in control of this natural resource. The result has been to make the Middle East not only the scene of confrontation between the superpower blocs but also a focal point in the growing tension between advanced industrial nations and undeveloped countries of the Third World. The embargo on oil shipments imposed by the Arab states in 1973 demonstrated their ability to regulate supply and manipulate price. By 1980 the Organization of Petroleum Exporting Countries—with the ready compliance of Western oil conglomerates—had raised the price of oil to nine times what it was in October 1973. The revolution in oil prices has brought a parallel revolution in trade relationships. Industrialized nations like the United States face mounting trade deficits, while desert monarchies and Gulf sheikhdoms pile up surpluses of "petrodollars." Whether to devote this accumulating surplus to raising living standards in the desperately poor countries of Africa and Asia or use it to bolster the economies of the industrial states—highly developed but increasingly dependent upon imports for vital raw materials—is a crucial question confronting the OPEC governments. The leverage which they can exert in either direction is evident.

President Paul Kruger of the Transvaal

2. THE REPUBLIC OF SOUTH AFRICA

Perhaps in no other African state have the problems of nation building, tribalism, and racial cooperation proved more difficult than in the Republic of South Africa. Conflicts between Boer, Bantu, and Briton have punctuated the history of South Africa for generations. Each group almost fanatically adheres to its own traditions and conceptions of how society should be organized.

Before the 1870s Great Britain had followed a colonial policy of benign neglect toward South Africa. The interior, long considered barren in natural resources, was of little importance to the British. Indeed, their prime concern lay in protecting the vital sea route to India by controlling the strategically important harbors along the South African coast. But in 1870 diamonds were discovered at Kimberley, and fifteen years later the fabulous gold fields of the Witwatersrand became a mecca for prospectors and adventurers from all over the world. Between 1872 and 1902 the white population of South Africa quadrupled. Congested cities such as Johannesburg and Bloemfontein mushroomed on the veldt. The simple pastoral economy of the old-fashioned Boers had come to an end.

The discovery of diamonds and gold multiplied the political difficulties of the Boer republics. British and other foreigners swarmed in in such numbers that they threatened to overwhelm the white Afrikaner settlers. The latter retaliated by branding the immigrants as outlanders and denying them political privileges except under the most rigorous conditions. The suffrage was refused, the press censored, and public meetings practically forbidden. In desperation the British organized a conspiracy to overthrow the most obstinate of the Boer governments, that of Paul Kruger, president of the Transvaal. Ammunition was collected, with the connivance of Cecil Rhodes, prime minister of the Cape Colony; and on December 29, 1895, 600 Britons and their armed retainers, under the leadership of Rhodes's friend, Dr. Leander Jameson, raided the Transvaal. The invaders were quickly surrounded and captured, but their act greatly magnified the tension between British and Boers. The Afrikaner governments increased the restrictions against foreigners and accumulated arms in preparation for a showdown. In October 1899, war broke out between these republics and the colonies predominantly British.

Prime Minister Cecil Rhodes of the Cape Colony

The Boer War dragged its length through three bloody years. Not until Britain sent sizable reinforcements under the leadership of its best generals was it able to snatch victory from the jaws of defeat. Finally, outnumbered seven to one, the Boers yielded and signed the Treaty of Vereeniging. In return for submitting to British rule, they were exempted from indemnities, promised representative institutions at an early date, and permitted to retain their own language in the courts and schools. The British government provided $15,000,000 to accelerate the process of reconstruction. It was one of the most generous peace settlements in history. At this time the victorious British were in the position to impose on South Africa a universal, nonracial franchise. Tragically, the plight of the African majority was ignored. The question of racial justice was avoided in the name of Boer-British reconciliation.

The Boer War (1899–1902)

In 1909 Cape Colony, Natal, the Orange Free State, and the Transvaal were merged into the Union of South Africa. The National Convention that drafted the Constitution provided for a unitary instead of a federal state. The reasons were several. The need for railway construction and for solving the problems of a large black population seemed to demand unification. More important was the fact that the two white nationalities did not occupy separate provinces as in Canada. In most states the rural population was Afrikaner or Boer, the urban population British. In some additional respects also the government of South Africa differed from that of the other dominions. The

The Union of South Africa

General James B. M. Hertzog, Leader of the Afrikaner National-ist Party

Growth of the nationalist movement

Cabinet did not stand or fall as a unit, but, theoretically at least, disagreements were permitted among the members. Its control over the upper house of Parliament was more effective. In case of a conflict between the Cabinet and the Assembly, or lower house, both houses might be dissolved and their members compelled to stand for re-election. South Africa had a much more conservative attitude toward the suffrage than did the other dominions. Universal manhood suffrage for whites was not adopted until 1930. Woman suffrage was also adopted in the same year, but in the face of stiff opposition. The minister of justice, for example, declared that the female franchise conflicted "with the intentions that the Creator had for women." As for the Africans, who constituted more than 75 percent of the population, all were disfranchised except in the southernmost Cape Province, where Negro and Asian citizens voted under limited conditions.

The sharpest controversies in South African politics since the formation of the Union have been those relating to nationality and race. Although the British made repeated efforts at reconciliation following the Boer War, the old hatreds died hard. In 1912 a faction of extremist Boers broke away from their kinsmen and formed the Nationalist party. Under the leadership of General Hertzog, they strove to preserve the cultural independence of the Afrikaners and to tolerate no fusion with the British. They resented British aggressiveness and regarded it as synonymous with an imperialism which threatened to obliterate the customs and institutions of their revered ancestors. They eventually came to advocate the severance of all ties with the British and the transformation of the Dominion into an Afrikaner republic. Anti-Semitism also emerged as a cardinal policy in the minds of the most fanatical. The finance capitalists who controlled the gold and diamond mines of the Rand[3] were alleged to be mostly Jews who were lightly taxed by the British-dominated government. By 1938 the Nationalists seemed almost as greatly disturbed by the "Jewish Menace" as they were by the "Black Peril" and were demanding the exclusion of all Jewish immigrants.

The two world wars of 1914 and 1939 contributed to the strength of the Nationalist movement. The followers of General Hertzog were determined that South Africa should not be dragged into war at the behest of the London government. The right to remain neutral they considered an indispensable badge of their nation's sovereignty. In 1914 some of them organized a rebellion as an armed protest against enslavement to British objectives. But the policy of their opponent, General Jan Christiaan Smuts, prevailed, and South Africa contributed its share toward winning the war. Eight years after the Armistice the Nationalists, supported by Labor, gained control of the government, but with a watered-down program that did not demand complete

[3] The Rand, or Witwatersrand, is a sixty-mile ridge which constitutes a watershed between the Vaal and Limpopo Rivers.

independence. When Britain again went to war in 1939, the South African government split. Six Cabinet ministers supported the war, five opposed. In the Assembly the vote was 80 in favor of the war to 67 against. It was obvious that the termination of hostilities would leave the country torn asunder and that the difficulties and tensions growing out of the war would widen the cleavage still further. Military production brought thousands of Africans into the towns and created fears of Communist uprisings or some other form of social revolution. In the official census of 1946, blacks for the first time in history outnumbered whites in the urban areas. Following this, the government-appointed Fagan Commission held that the incorporation of blacks in the nation's economic system is an irrevocable reality and that the Africans' progressive integration into the whites' political system should be accepted as a logical consequence.

As an Afrikaner party of the extreme right, the Nationalists played upon the fears engendered by the Fagan Commission and in the 1948 elections they gained control of parliament. The Nationalists not only espoused the idea of an independent republic purged of British influence but demanded a policy of apartheid, or strict legal separation of the races. South Africa would be a republic founded upon the ideals of Paul Kruger, not upon those of Cecil Rhodes or Jan Smuts.

General Jan Christiaan Smuts, Spokesman of South African Moderates

In the decade ahead, the Nationalist-dominated parliament passed a long series of segregationist legislation, affecting every aspect of life. The Prohibition of Mixed Marriages Act (1949) made interracial marriages illegal. In 1950, the Population Registration Act provided for the classification of the population into whites, coloreds (people of mixed race and Indians), and Bantu. The Group Areas Act, passed in the same year, called for the division of the nation into separate areas according to race and tribe. Apartheid in the realm of land ownership was already enshrined in the Native Land Act of 1913, which was aimed at regulating the purchase, ownership, and occupation of land outside urban areas on a racial basis. Only 13 percent of South Africa's total land area was reserved for Africans, even though they made up more than 80 percent of the population. Attempts to control the movement of Africans from place to place, particularly from rural to urban areas, date back to 1760 with the first pass law. Civil and political rights have always been withheld from urban Africans on the pretext that they are "temporary sojourners" with a permanent residence in some far-off tribal reserve.

Segregationist legislation

The Reservation of Separate Amenities Act (1953) provided for the segregation of public amenities, including parks and transportation terminals. In the same year, the Native Labour Act redefined the term "employee" to exclude all blacks, thereby disenfranchising their unions and forbidding strikes. African trade unions, while not prohibited, were denied recognition and severely circumscribed. The Industrial Conciliation Act of 1956 and subsequent amendments banned

Anti-African labor legislation

Apartheid in South Africa. Among the restrictions imposed upon blacks is the requirement that they carry passports. Here a policeman and an interpreter check the papers of an African bound for Johannesburg to work in the mines.

racially mixed labor unions and provided that certain jobs or occupations be reserved for whites only.

Apartheid laws: education and the franchise

A series of Bantu Education Acts brought schools under central government control and extended segregation to university education. Moreover, a constitutional amendment disenfranchised coloreds, who had veen voting in Cape province since the 1850s. Africans had been taken off the voter rolls in 1936. Opposition to these and the plethora of other apartheid laws was stifled through the Suppression of Communism Act (1950), an omnibus law which empowered the government to ban any organization or person suspected of "communism" or of endangering the security of the state.

Policy of divide and rule

In an attempt to control the rising tide of African nationalism by fostering tribalism at the expense of pan-Africanism, the government passed the Promotion of Bantu Self-Government Act (1959). In classical divide-and-rule fashion, it envisioned the consolidation of the 260 scattered native reserves into a series of "independent" Bantu states, or Bantustans, each with its own tribal identity.

The polarization of politics

African reaction to these and the many other segregationist laws, including the pass laws, was manifested in a number of futile passive-resistance and defiance campaigns between 1952 and 1956. Their failure led to a rift within the African National Congress (founded in 1912); and in 1959 a radical group split off under the leadership of Robert Sobukwe and took the name of Pan-Africanist Congress. The white political spectrum had also become more polarized. The United party, mainly English-speaking, over the years had steadily lost ground in parliament to the Afrikaner-dominated Nationalists. In 1959 a small group of antiapartheid white liberals broke from the

United party and formed the Progressive party. Over the next decade and a half they held a single seat in the Assembly.

In 1960 African resistance to apartheid culminated in a passive demonstration at Sharpeville. The South African police panicked in the face of the large, angry gathering and killed sixty-seven peaceful black demonstrators. Following the Sharpeville massacre a state of emergency was declared, the African National Congress and the Pan-Africanist Congress was banned, and their leaders who escaped arrest either fled the country or went underground to engage in terrorist activity. Whites, growing ever more fearful of the "black menace," responded in the 1960s with legislation further eroding the personal liberties of nonwhites. The General Law Amendment Act of 1963 empowered police to arrest and detain people indefinitely without trial or access to legal counsel. A Publications Control Board, created in the same year, imposed censorship over literature and films. Throughout the 1960s police raids resulted in the arrest and imprisonment of militants.

Sharpeville and the white response

In 1961 Prime Minister Hendrik Verwoerd took steps toward implementing these ideals when he ordered the withdrawal of South Africa from the Commonwealth of Nations and proclaimed the country an independent republic. For the time being there would be two capitals, Cape Town and Pretoria, and two languages, English and Afrikaans. It was clear, however, that the ultimate objective was an Afrikaner nation thoroughly purged of British influences.

The emergence of an Afrikaner nation

Verwoerd was assassinated in 1966 and was succeeded by John B. Vorster. In the following year, a severe Terrorism Act was passed, presuming the guilt of everyone accused of terrorism until proven innocent. Two years later, the Bureau of State Security (BOSS) was created to suppress radical movements.

The Terrorism Act

South Africa's economy boomed in the early 1970s, benefiting most racial and ethnic groups. White feelings of security were sufficiently restored for the Vorster government to embark on a futile policy of rapprochement with black African nations to the north. It also moved quickly to devolve more autonomy on the newly created Bantu states within South Africa. In late 1976, the Transkei became the first Bantu homeland to receive its independence.

New policy of rapprochement with black African nations

Economic prosperity led to a shortage of white skilled labor, and as a consequence the job reservation act was eased to enable blacks to move into positions formerly reserved for whites. These moves failed to assuage African nationalism. In 1972 the moderate Black Peoples' Convention was formed, along with the black South African Students' Movement. This reawakening of black consciousness, led by a new and more militant generation of youths, was further stimulated by the articulate speeches of Gatsha Buthelezi, chief of the KwaZulu homeland.

The reawakening of black consciousness

Among white Afrikaners, two schools of thought emerged: the

*The death of détente and
the renewal of suppression*

enlightened, or verlighte, and the narrow-minded, or the verkrampte. The verlightes demanded an easing of the rigid apartheid laws, especially in the areas of sports and culture. But they were not prepared to grant the principle of "one man one vote."

This state of political and social ferment in South Africa subsided almost as quickly as it had begun. In 1975 Portugal, in a surprising about-face, gave independence to Mozambique and Angola, two close neighbors of South Africa. This rekindled the revolution of rising political expectations among South Africa's blacks, coloreds, and Asians. Moreover, in the same year, the nation began to slide into an economic recession, after enjoying a steady annual growth rate of more than 5 percent since 1933. Whites again became fearful of a loss of status; and this fear was exacerbated by the installation of Marxist, militantly anti–South African governments in Mozambique and Angola. South African military intervention in the Angolan civil war in 1975–1976 drew world-wide condemnation and killed Vorster's détente program with black Africa. African student militancy, inspired by such intellectuals as Steve Biko, grew rapidly after a 1974 pro-Mozambique student rally. Feelings exploded in violent riots in June 1976 in Soweto, a sprawling ghetto of nearly 3 million Africans not far from downtown Johannesburg. More than a thousand black youths were killed by the South African police and many more were imprisoned. An intensification of the suppression and liquidation of black opposition came to world attention in September 1977 with the police killing of the jailed Steve Biko, president of the Black Peoples' Convention. Racial tension was mounting and the major African newspaper, the *World,* was banned and its editor detained.

Police Action in Johannesburg. In downtown Johannesburg the authorities disperse a group of black and white demonstrators who were protesting police actions in the huge Soweto ghetto. Over 1,000 blacks were killed by police in Soweto in June 1976.

As world opinion turned against South Africa, the white pendulum swung further to the right. English-speaking and Afrikaans-speaking whites began to close political ranks. The opposition United party disintegrated, with most of its members joining the Nationalist party but a few joining with the Progressives to form the Progressive Federal party. In the November 1977 elections the Nationalist party gained vast new strength, winning 134 of 165 seats in the all-white National Assembly. South Africa was moving toward a one-party state.

October 1978 witnessed the retirement of John Vorster, who became titular president, and the appointment of the Defense Minister Pieter W. Botha as new prime minister. In early 1979, racial and ethnic relations continued their steady deterioration among the 4.3 million whites, 2.4 million coloreds, 765,000 Asians, and 19 million blacks. The South African government became increasingly isolated from the world community of nations.

3. THE UPSURGE OF AFRICA

Modern African nationalism and pan-African sentiment are not post–World War II phenomena. Their roots go back to 1847 with the establishment of the independent Republic of Liberia. Liberia was the first independent state in Africa to support Western-style institutions and to prove that black men were capable of governing themselves along so-called modern lines. Edward Blyden, a leading Liberian intellectual (born in the West Indies), called in the 1860s for racial integrity and solidarity and coined the phrase "Africa for Africans." He exhorted black men to preserve the African essence of their civilizations and to resist Westernization at the hands of European imperialists. Native-born, Western-educated intellectuals on the Gold Coast (now Ghana) and Nigeria were to take up this call in the two decades prior to the first World War. Nevertheless, these protonationalists represented but a thin veneer and were predominantly drawn from among second sons of wealthy traditional nobility. Many of them were torn between their rich African heritage and that of Western civilization and found it difficult to identify with their peasant brethren in the bush. They were willing to work within the colonial framework and to pursue a moderate, gradualist course. After World War II, these early elites were eclipsed by impatient youthful nonaristocratic intellectuals who returned to Africa after many years abroad. Armed with the techniques of political party organization, they reached out to the masses, particularly the urban unemployed.

The 1950s and 1960s witnessed a groundswell of colonial revolts in northern and central Africa. For the most part, they were directed against Great Britain and France, though Belgium, Italy, and Portugal

The war in Algeria

were also involved. The first of the former colonies to gain independence was Libya. Taken by Italy from Turkey in 1912, Libya passed under the control of the United Nations at the end of World War II. In 1949 the U.N. recognized the Libyan demand for freedom, and two years later independence was formally proclaimed.

The most violent of the colonial revolts in northern Africa occurred in Algeria. Algeria had been a part of the French Empire since the middle years of the nineteenth century. The French poured millions of dollars of capital into their colony, and thousands of French nationals came there to settle. Many people of other nationalities, especially Spaniards, also emigrated to Algeria, with the result that by 1960 the European inhabitants numbered about 1 million in a total population of 10,300,000. These Europeans, inaccurately referred to as the "French" population, monopolized not only the government positions but also the best economic opportunities in industry, agriculture, trade, and finance. The Arab and Berber inhabitants were chiefly peasants and laborers, though some, of course, maintained their own shops in the *casbah,* or native quarter, of each of the large cities. In 1954 Arab and Berber (Muslim) nationalists rose in revolt when their demand for equal status with the European population was denied by the French government. The revolt continued its bloody course for seven years. It was complicated by the fact that many of the European settlers (*colons*) hated the government in Paris almost as much as they did the Algerian nationalists. They were determined to keep Algeria "French" and feared a sell-out by President Charles de Gaulle that would make the former colony independent and subject the *colons* to the rule of the Arab and Berber majority. In April 1961, the announcement of a plan by de Gaulle to negotiate a settlement in Algeria that would pave the way for eventual independence led to a revolt in the

Algeria, 1962. After nearly eight years of strife and terror, Algeria was on the threshold of independence.

territory by four French generals. They seized government buildings, arrested loyal French officials, and threatened to invade France. De Gaulle proclaimed a state of emergency and ordered a total blockade of Algeria. In the face of such determined opposition the revolt collapsed. The war of the nationalists, however, continued for another year. On a promise of immediate self-government and eventual independence the nationalists laid down their arms in March 1962. Three months later Algeria entered the ranks of independent states and was admitted to the United Nations. The war had cost the lives of about 40,000 soldiers and civilians and had left a heritage of bitterness that would probably linger for years.

If any one country could be considered the leader of the African colonial revolt, it was Ghana, formerly called the Gold Coast, a colony of Great Britain. In 1954 Britain granted self-government, independence in 1957, and in 1960 Ghana became a republic. Leadership of the Ghana independence movement was at that time supplied by Kwame Nkrumah. The son of an illiterate goldsmith, he obtained an education in the United States and in England. He returned to his homeland in 1948 and became a nationalist agitator. Though he classified himself as a Marxist, he denied being a Communist. Yet he admired Lenin and generally looked to Moscow for support of his policies rather than to London or Washington. Apparently the key to his thinking was opposition to imperialism. He considered it preposterous that the Africans of Central Africa, with their proud traditions of an ancient culture, should be ruled by Europeans. He regaled his followers with stories of a Golden Age in Africa, whose cultural center was in Timbuktu, with a great university manned by distinguished scholars. For a time Nkrumah ruled benevolently even after converting the nation into a one-party state. He established hospitals and schools and raised the literacy standards. Accused of extravagance and corruption, he was deposed by a revolt of army officer in 1966. He was driven from his homeland and forced to take refuge in Guinea where he died in 1972. Nevertheless, Nkrumah's writings on neocolonialism and his pan-African ideas are still widely read by African intellectuals.

Kwame Nkrumah (Center, Seated) and Members of His Government in Ghana

The most violent of the revolts in Central Africa occurred in the Congo, where there was not simply one previous colony but two. The smaller is now the People's Republic of the Congo. Though granted nominal independence in 1960, it is still under the influence of France and the People's Republic of China. Conditions in the larger Congo, now called Zaire, which was at one time a colony of Belgium, have been more serious. Fearing an outbreak of violence among its disaffected colonial subjects, Belgium, in 1960, granted them independence. This was the signal for the beginning of a series of rebellions and assassinations that raged for more than five years. A chief cause of the flaming disorders centered in the southeastern province of

The revolt in the Congo

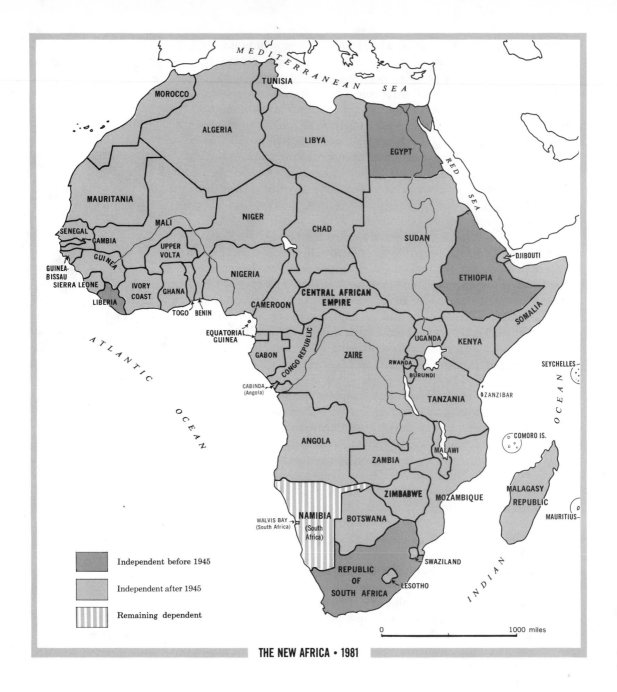

Independent before 1945	
Independent after 1945	
Remaining dependent	

0   1000 miles

THE NEW AFRICA • 1981

Katanga. Here were located rich copper resources controlled by Belgian capitalists. At one time the copper mines of Katanga had produced revenues sufficient to defray one-half the costs of the colonial government. In July 1960, Katanga seceded and attempted to gain control of the entire country. In the revolt several former premiers and other high officers were murdered. The U.N. Security Council sent a contingent to guard against revival of civil war. Strong-man rule was revived by President Mobutu, and a degree of stability was ultimately restored.

In most other sections of Central and Eastern Africa there was at least the illusion of tranquillity. Such countries as Nigeria and Kenya seemed like good examples. Both were former British colonies. Some authorities held that British and French colonial administrations were wiser than that of most other European empires. Whereas the Portuguese and Belgians withheld self-government as long as they could, and then granted it suddenly, the British and French brought their colonies to independence more gradually. Many local leaders were trained in administration and knew how to deal with intricate problems before they actually arose. Yet even in Nigeria the familiar charges of corruption and inefficiency led to the murder of the premier and the overthrow of the government in 1966. After more assassinations a military government seized control. Within a year the Eastern Region seceded and proclaimed itself the Republic of Biafra. Civil war followed and harassed the country for three years. The total of casualties was enormous. More than 1 million people lost their lives. Thousands were killed in battle, but many more died of starvation. The rebels capitulated in 1970. From every standpoint the war was a tragedy. Nigeria is one of the most richly endowed of African countries. Its natural resources include oil and natural gas, coal, and the world's greatest abundance of columbium (used in steel manufacturing).

Civil War in Nigeria

Also hovering on the verge of tragedy has been the recent history of Kenya, a country of East Africa lying athwart the equator. Unlike Nigeria, Kenya is a poor country. The whole northern three-fifths of the territory is barren and almost waterless. Sections can be found in which there is no rainfall whatever for years at a time. The only well-watered sections are in the south and along the coast. It follows that agricultural resources are limited. The staple crops include coffee, sisal, tea, and wheat. Sugar cane, maize, tobacco, and cotton are also grown. Most of the farms are small. The construction of the railroad from the Kenya coast to Uganda at the turn of the century brought in thousands of Indian settlers. They did not become farmers or artisans, but settled in the cities and towns as petty traders. Despite their low standard of living and their meager profits they encouraged the Africans to substitute a money economy for the age-old system of barter. Nevertheless, many Indians in Uganda and Kenya remained aloof, choosing not to become citizens or to allow Africans to enter their trades. This caused serious friction between the two races, and in 1972 led to the mass expulsion of Indians from Uganda.

Conditions in Kenya

The population of Kenya has never been closely unified. Ethnic jealousies are rampant and sometimes break into open conflict. These

The Mau Mau rebellion

Jomo Kenyatta Addressing an All-Africa Congress in London.

Kenyatta's African socialism

jealousies seem not to be based on economic competition or greed. They appear rather to spring from ancient differences rooted in cultural characteristics and hatreds from the past. The most serious of these conflicts broke into the open in 1952 when the Mau Mau rebellion occurred. The Mau Mau were an offshoot of the Kikuyu tribe, who had been forcibly removed from their ancestral lands by European settlers at the turn of the century. By the close of the Second World War, the Kikuyu were experiencing a population explosion and sought to regain their lost territory. They instituted a reign of terror in some parts of the colony against the white settlers and all their kinsmen who sympathized with the colonial government. By 1958 the revolt was suppressed, and five years later the country obtained independence. Basically, Mau Mau was a Kikuyu-inspired nationalist movement aimed at achieving African self-determination over questions of land and governance.

The leader who had done most to promote the growth and progress of Kenya was Jomo Kenyatta, president of his country from 1963 until his death in August 1978, when he was succeeded by his vice president, Daniel Arap Moi. However, his own people, the Kikuyu, continued to dominate the nation's political and economic institutions, despite growing challenges from the large Luo ethnic group. In 1951 he was thrown into prison for seven years, accused as a Mau Mau leader and a dangerous enemy of the state. His imprisonment seems to have done more to educate him in the realities of politics than to imbue him with hatred of his captors. While in prison he developed his philosophy of African socialism. Although for a time Kenyatta had studied at Moscow University, he adopted almost none of the trappings of Soviet communism. Instead his socialism bore a closer resemblance to that of the British or the Scandinavian countries. He urged his followers to forget the wrongs of the past and to concentrate on building a better world for the future. This future would be found in avoiding affiliations with either the East or the West. The African way has little in common with either capitalism or communism. The sharp antagonisms of class that exist in Europe and America have not been conspicuous elements in the African tradition. African socialism, according to Kenyatta, cannot be based on a dictatorship of the proletariat or any other form of class rule. Rather, its aim should be to prevent the seizure of power by individuals or groups armed with economic power. Its aim should be to enable every mature citizen to participate fully and equally in political affairs. Such is the essence of democracy and also of African socialism, according to Kenyatta's conception.

One of the most successful experiments in African nation building has occurred in Tanzania under its president, Julius Nyerere. Unlike neighboring Kenya, Tanzania is not plagued by tribalism. There are not two or three major tribes maneuvering for power. Rather, Tan-

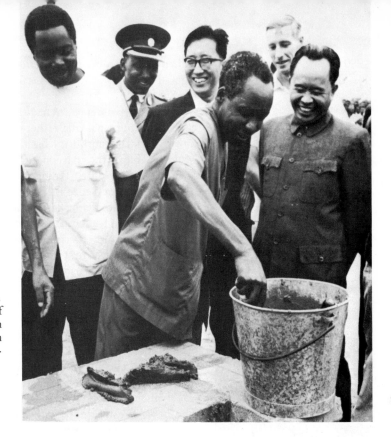

President Julius Nyerere of Tanzania. Nyerere, accompanied by a group of Chinese officials, lays the foundation stone of the New Chinese-Tanzanian Friendship Textile Mill in Dar es Salaam.

zania embraces a multitude of small tribes none of which is strong enough to dominate the political system. Tanzania itself is the result of the merging of two British-administered colonial units: the United Nations Trust Territory of Tanganyika and the Protectorate of Zanzibar. Since their union in 1964, Nyerere has gradually decreased his dependence on British trade and is relying more heavily on foreign assistance from the Communist world, particularly the People's Republic of China, which is completing a rail link between landlocked, copper-rich Zambia and Tanzania's port of Dar es Salaam on the Indian Ocean. Nevertheless, under Nyerere's able and democratic leadership, Tanzania is pursuing a policy of nonalignment. Nyerere, a noted Third World political theorist, has developed a unique brand of African socialism called *Ujamaa* ("familyhood" in Swahili) which is rooted in the traditional communalistic, extended family form of social organization. Yet it also draws heavily upon the experimental Chinese communes and the Israeli kibbutzim. The accent of Nyerere's socialism is upon the dignity of work and national self-reliance. While Nyerere, a practicing Catholic, claims to be a socialist, he is opposed to Marxist doctrinaire socialism. According to Nyerere, modern African socialism "can draw from its traditional heritage the recognition of 'society' as an extension of the basic family unit." While it is

Tanzania and experiments in African socialism

The personalization of authority

Kenneth D. Kaunda, President of the Republic of Zambia

Nation building and pan-Africanism

The growth of centralization in government

still too early to predict the success of Tanzania's model Ujamaa villages, Nyerere's influence is strongly felt throughout Africa south of the Sahara.

Since independence, African systems of government have succumbed to personal rule rather than to sweeping institutional reform. In other words, authority became personalized, not institutionalized. Most notable of the charismatic heads of state were Sese Seko Mobutu of Zaire, Dr. Kamuzu Banda of Malawi, Seko Touré of Guinea, Leopold Senghor of Senegal, Felix Houphouet-Boigny of Ivory Coast, Julius Nyerere of Tanzania, Jomo Kenyatta of Kenya, Seretse Khama of Botswana, Kenneth Kaunda of Zambia, Samora Machel of Mozambique, and Kwame Nkrumah of Ghana. The trend toward personalization was first evident during the struggle for independence. It reached a high in 1977 when Jean-Bedel Bokassa suspended all democratic institutions and crowned himself emperor of the Central African Empire. In some respects, this trend is simply a return to the precolonial situation in which some rulers governed by divine and ancestral right and in which little differentiation existed between executive, judicial, and legislative powers.

Since the eve of independence, the old traditional political elites have been gradually edged out of leadership positions in the central governments. Some countries have abolished chieftaincy altogether. The new, Western-educated and modernizing elites have sought to follow two often contradictory paths: the formation of a national belief system or ethos based on a return to authentic African values, and the fostering of pan-Africanist ideology. Internally, ethnic conflicts continue to impede the process of nation building. And the realization of the pan-African dream, a united states of Africa, is blocked by the colonial legacy. International disputes persist over artificial boundaries drawn during the European scramble for African territory in the late nineteenth century. African diplomacy is hindered by the diversity of European languages, and regional economic integration is made difficult by continuing patterns of dependency on the economic ties to former colonial masters. In many states today, particularly in French-speaking Africa, European technocrats and capitalists continue to play important roles in the political and economic sectors. Some political scientists have called this situation "neocolonialistic." The Organization of African Unity (OAU), established in 1963, has had a dismal record in resolving inter-African disputes and in preventing external Great Power interference.

While the influence of popularly elected legislative bodies has steadily diminished, local government remains remarkably dynamic and responsive to the masses. Nevertheless, the process of government centralization continues in most countries. Corruption and nepotism in many African nations, particularly in Kenya, Nigeria, and Zaire, by 1979 had become major corrosive forces in national life. The contrast of great affluence among bureaucrats and extravagant public spending on the one hand and persistent poverty among the broad masses on the other has bred popular political apathy and cynicism. In an attempt to stem this tide, Presidents Nyerere and Kaunda of Tanzania and Zambia, respectively, have developed strict codes of behavior for their civil servants. Generally, African leaders are less bound by public opinion today than they were in the early years of independence. Nearly everywhere, opposition parties have been suppressed and a large majority of Africans remain outside the decision-making process. Only Nigeria, Gambia, Botswana, and Senegal actively encourage multiparty activity.

Political repression and falling food production in some African nations have created a serious refugee problem. By 1977, nearly one in every two hundred Africans was a refugee. Indeed, Africa suffered the highest ratio of refugees to total population in the world, with more than 2 million displaced persons.

The refugee problem

Military coups have been a major factor in African politics since the mid-1960s. The first military coup in independent Africa occurred in 1952 in Egypt. By 1976, twenty out of forty-one African states were ruled by military elements or by military/civilian coalitions. Between 1965 and 1978 Africa experienced thirty-three military coups, eight in Dahomey (now Benin) alone. By 1979, most African nations had armed forces and military budgets far in excess of their defense needs. This growing militarism has contributed to an escalating incidence of inter-African warfare and internal instability. In 1978 alone, Tanzania and Uganda were at war with each other; Soviet-supplied Ethiopia fought a civil war against the secessionist Eritrean province and a war with Somalia over the Ogaden. Morocco and Mauretania battled in the western Sahara against an Algerian-backed liberation force. In

Militarism

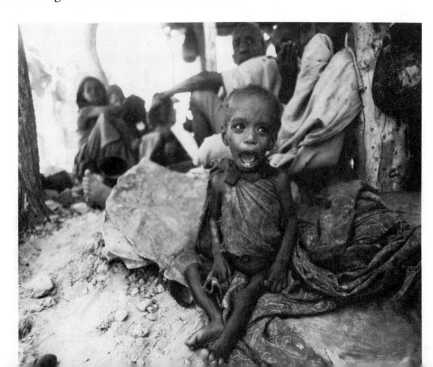

The Refugee Problem. A starving child crying at a feeding center in a village in southern Ethiopia. Due to overpopulation, a number of African nations are facing serious problems which manifest themselves in the form of food shortages, inadequate housing, poor health and educational services, and high unemployment rates.

Reaction to military dictatorships and corruption

Liberia and Zimbabwe

The importance of Africa's mineral wealth

Central Africa, Zaire was assisted by French- and American-equipped Morocco in repelling an Angolan-based invasion of its copper- and cobalt-rich Shaba province. Southward, Soviet- and Chinese-supplied guerrillas struggled against the white-dominated and South African–equipped Rhodesian army.

Growing public disenchantment with military governance led in 1979 to the restoration of free elections and civilian rule in Ghana and Nigeria. Impatience with corruption and nepotism brought down the fascist dictatorships of Presidents for Life Macias Nguema in Equatorial Guinea and Idi Amin in Uganda and Emperor Jean-Bedel Bokassa of the Central African Empire. In a bloodless coup, Bokassa was replaced by David Dacko, who restored the republic and who was himself overthrown in 1966. In neighboring Chad, the Christian-dominated government of President Felix Malloum was toppled, opening the way for a civil war between Christians and Muslims.

Early in 1980, a military coup in Liberia ended the nepotistic regime and the life of President William R. Tolbert, Jr. In the same year, Great Britain ended nearly two centuries of colonial rule in Africa by transforming the Crown colony of Rhodesia into the independent nation of Zimbabwe, under Robert Mugabe, a Marxist and former guerrilla leader.

By mid-1980, only the Republic of South Africa and Namibia remained under white political control. Black majority rule had been achieved everywhere else. Many of these nations are richly endowed with minerals, essential to industrial development in Africa as well as in western Europe, North America, and Japan. Nigeria, a major member of the Organization of Petroleum Exporting Countries (OPEC), had become the United States' second largest source of imported oil. Western Europe depended on Zaire for most of its copper, uranium, and cobalt, and on South Africa for its gold, chrome, and industrial diamonds.

Africa, in turn, continued to rely on the West for advanced technology and development loans. With global inflation and soaring oil prices, many of the developing nations found themselves terribly in debt to Western creditors, especially to the International Monetary Fund. In some respects, these near-bankrupt nations had to surrender a considerable degree of fiscal autonomy to the IMF in order to be eligible for debt rescheduling. These interdependencies will undoubtedly grow in the decades ahead. A few African nations hold great promise for economic growth through the twenty-first century, particularly those endowed with mineral resources. However, most others will suffer from chronic underdevelopment. The challenge of Africa lies in its ability to bargain on a more equitable basis with both the East and West.

Prime Minister Robert Mugabe of Zimbabwe

• *Items so designated are available in paperback editions.*

THE MIDDLE EAST

Ahmed, J. M., *The Intellectual Origins of Egyptian Nationalism,* New York, 1960. Informative and well-documented account.

Bose, T. C., *The Superpowers and the Middle East,* New York, 1972.

• Chaliand, Gérard, *The Palestinian Resistance,* Baltimore, 1972.

Halpern, Manfred, *The Politics of Social Change in the Middle East and North Africa,* Princeton, 1967.

• Hitti, Philip K., *History of the Arabs,* New York, 1940.

Hoskins, H. L., *The Middle East,* New York, 1954. A careful, judicious study.

Issawi, Charles, *Egypt in Revolution: An Economic Analysis,* New York, 1963.

Karpat, Kemal, *Turkey's Politics: The Transition to a Multi-Party System,* Princeton, 1959. Sophisticated account by a Turkish political scientist.

Khouri, Fred J., *The Arab-Israeli Dilemma,* Syracuse, N.Y., 1968.

• Kirk, George E., *A Short History of the Middle East,* London, 1948.

• Laqueur, Jacques, *The Struggle for the Middle East,* Baltimore, 1972.

Lenczowski, George, *The Middle East in World Affairs,* 3d ed., Ithaca, 1962.

———, *Oil and State in the Middle East,* Ithaca, 1960.

• Lewis, Bernard, *The Emergence of Modern Turkey,* 2d ed., New York, 1968.

Lewis, Geoffrey, *Turkey,* 3d ed., London, 1965.

• Prittie, Terence, *Israel: Miracle in the Desert,* rev. ed., Baltimore, 1968.

Quandt, W. B., F. Jabber, and A. M. Lesch, *The Politics of Palestinian Nationalism,* Berkeley, 1973.

• Rodinson, Maxime, *Israel and the Arabs,* Baltimore, 1970.

Segre, V. D., *Israel: A Society in Transition,* New York, 1971.

Stone, I. F., *Underground to Palestine,* New York, 1979. Account of a secret voyage through the British blockade in 1946.

Twitchell, K. S., *Saudi Arabia,* Princeton, 1958.

• Wilber, D. N., *Iran Past and Present,* 7th ed., Princeton, 1975.

AFRICA

Bartlett, Vernon, *Struggle for Africa,* New York, 1953.

Carter, G. M., *The Politics of Inequality,* New York 1958. A penetrating study of South Africa.

Clark, M. K., *Algeria in Turmoil,* New York, 1959.

• Davenport, T. R. H., *South Africa: A Modern History,* London, 1977.

Decalo, Samuel, *Coups and Army Rule in Africa,* New Haven, 1976.

Fasholé-Luke, Edward, and Richard Gray, eds., *Christianity in Independent Africa,* Bloomington, 1977.

• Geiss, Immanuel, *The Pan-African Movement,* New York, 1974.

• Gutkind, Peter C. W., and Immanuel Wallerstein, eds., *The Political Economy of Contemporary Africa,* Beverly Hills, 1976.

Hartwig, Gerald W., and K. David Patterson, eds., *Disease in African History,* Durham, 1978.

Low, D. A., and Alison Smith, eds., *History of East Africa*, Vol. III, London, 1976.

• Macmillan, W. M., *Africa Emergent*, 1949.

• Marquard, L., *The Peoples and Policies of South Africa*, New York, 1952.

Nyerere, Julius, *Ujamaa: Essays on Socialism*, New York, 1971.

• Oliver, Roland, and Anthony Atmore, *Africa since 1800*, New York, 1967.

Owen, Roger, and Robert Sutcliffe, eds., *Studies in the Theory of Imperialism*, London, 1975.

Pannikkar, K. M., *The Afro-Asian States and Their Problems*, New York, 1959. Brief but discerning.

Ranger, T. O., ed., *Aspects of Central African History*, London, 1969.

Thompson, L. M., *Politics in the Republic of South Africa*, Boston, 1966.

Wilson, M., and L. M. Thompson, eds., *The Oxford History of South Africa*, 2 vols., New York, 1971.

SOURCE MATERIALS

Apartheid: Its Effects on Education, Science, Culture and Information (UNESCO).

Ben-Gurion, David. *Israel: A Personal History*, New York, 1971.

Berkes, Niyazi, *Turkish Nationalism and Western Civilization*, tr. Z. Gökalp, London, 1959.

Brookes, Edgar H., *Apartheid: A Documentary Study*, London, 1968.

Edib, Halide, *Memoirs*, London, 1926.

Hobart Houghton, D., and Jennifer Dagut, eds., *Source Material on the South African Economy: 1860–1970*, London, 1972.

Horrell, Muriel, comp., *A Survey of Race Relations in South Africa, 1977*, Johannesburg, 1978.

Meir, Golda, *My Life*, New York, 1975.

Weizmann, Chaim, *Trial and Error*, New York, 1949.

Chapter 39

ERUPTION IN THE FAR EAST

Countries want independence, nations want liberation, and people want revolution.

> —Premier Chou En-lai

The current international situation is excellent; there is great disorder under heaven.

> —Chairman Mao Tse-tung

The contemporary era of the Far Eastern countries began under the stimulation provided by the impact of Western explorers and merchants. By the middle of the twentieth century profound changes had taken place not only within the Eastern countries but also in their relationship to the West. No longer merely peripheral to the main fields of interest of the Western nations, they had become in some measure the pivotal center of world affairs. Japan seized upon a large empire in Asia and the Pacific, which she retained until defeated in a long struggle against the most powerful of the Western states. China, after almost disintegrating and after passing through a cycle of revolution, emerged with radically altered institutions but, once again, as one of the strongest states of Asia. Moreover, China for the first time in her history was in a position to assume a major role in world politics.

The new Far East

I. NATIONALISM AND COMMUNISM IN CHINA

The overthrow of the Manchu Dynasty, accomplished with comparatively little effort in 1911, marked the beginning in China of a long period of instability and disorder that has witnessed a wide displacement of China's traditional institutions and culture. Perhaps never before in the country's history has there occurred such a transforma-

Stages of the Chinese Revolution

tion as during its modern revolutionary era. The Chinese Revolution falls roughly into four overlapping stages: (1) the pseudo-republic of Yüan Shih-k'ai, 1912–1916; (2) the rule of warlords and the weakening of the central government, 1916–1928; (3) the Nationalist revolution, 1923–1949; and (4) the Communist revolution, which gained momentum in the 1930s and, after a military triumph in 1949, brought fundamental external and internal changes to China. The second period, almost purely negative, was the natural result of the decadence that had preceded the downfall of the Manchu Dynasty. The third and fourth stages had some objectives in common and were combined for a time, although they finally came to be directly opposed to each other.

The rise of the warlords

Yüan Shih-k'ai, the first president of the Republic, who tried unsuccessfully to restore the monarchy, maintained at least a semblance of unity in the state. After his death in 1916, much of China passed under the rule of independent military commanders, although a group at Peking preserved the fiction of a republican government. Some of these militarists had been officials under the Manchus; others were ex-soldiers or ex-bandits who had collected an army and taken over the administration of one or more provinces. Most of them were extortionate, and the common people of China suffered deplorably from their tyranny. China's participation in World War I at a time when the central government was unable even to put its own house in order was a factor contributing to internal confusion. At the urging of the Allied powers, the Peking government declared war on Germany in 1917, hoping to gain advantages at the peace settlement. During the war, however, Japan seized the opportunity to "assist" her weak ally, selling war materials and extending loans to China and securing economic concessions within the country. At the Paris Peace Conference the requests of the Chinese delegation were almost completely disregarded, and Japan refused to restore the Shantung Peninsula, which she had taken over from Germany.

The Kuomintang

The third stage of the Revolution is associated with the personality and program of Sun Yat-sen. Dr. Sun's part in the inauguration of the Republic in 1912 had been a brief one, but after returning to Canton, where his following was strongest, he directed a barrage of criticism against the Peking military government. The rise of warlords was not confined to the north, and Sun actually was dependent for support upon militarists in control of the Kwangtung-Kwangsi area. His party, the Kuomintang, was a small faction, and its professed principles of parliamentary democracy seemed utterly unrealistic in a "phantom Republic" ravaged by irresponsible military bands. But with remarkable swiftness the Kuomintang changed into a dynamic organization capable of making a bid for control of the state. The initiative and organizing skill for accomplishing this transformation were largely supplied from outside China, by agents of the revolutionary Communist regime in Russia.

Understandably, the Bolshevik leaders, faced with the task of consolidating their power in Russia and confronted by the hostility of the Great Powers, were eager to win support in revolutionary China. Rebuffed by the Peking government, they turned to Dr. Sun in Canton. The Third (Communist) International had organized a Far Eastern division and established at Moscow a university named after Sun Yat-sen to train Chinese revolutionaries, some of whom joined the Communist party. Although Dr. Sun rejected communism, he had hoped for the support of Western nations and welcomed the offer of Russian cooperation. In 1923 Sun and the Russian emissaries arrived at a working agreement which provided for Russian assistance and for the admission of Chinese Communists to the Kuomintang but left Sun the undisputed head of the Kuomintang party. Acknowledging that China's immediate task was to achieve national unity and free itself from the yoke of foreign imperialism, the Soviet government sent military and political advisers to Canton.

During the Moscow-Canton entente of 1923–1927, the Chinese nationalist movement acquired a disciplined leadership, clear-cut objectives, and considerable popular support. A general dissatisfaction with the dreary and corrupt rule of the military cliques, the humiliation of China at the Paris Peace Conference, and the entrenched position of the Great Powers in their spheres of interest all helped to intensify nationalist sentiment. Disillusionment following the war stimulated a spirit of revolt among young intellectuals and among the lower classes, as evidenced by the growth of labor unions in the Yangtze valley industrial cities, peasant movements, youth movements, and movements for the emancipation of women. The various dissident elements needed only effective leadership to be enlisted in a campaign for the regeneration and strengthening of China under a truly national government. Soviet advisers taught Sun Yat-sen and his associates how to supply this leadership. Under the direction of Michael Borodin, a seasoned revolutionary who had worked as an agitator in Turkey and Mexico, the Kuomintang was revamped on the model of the Russian Communist party. On the propaganda front, posters, pictures, and slogans dramatized the Kuomintang program, which was to unseat the warlords, introduce honest and democratic government, stamp out the opium habit, and promote other reforms.

Consolidation of power by
the Kuomintang at
Canton

By 1925 Canton had become the center of a small but effective government, which collected taxes, regulated commerce, and was developing its own "new model" army, officered by men trained at the Whampoa Academy (near Canton) under supervision of European military experts, and indoctrinated with loyalty to Sun Yat-sen and to his party. This Canton government was actually a Soviet regime without being Communist. Controlled by the high command of the Kuomintang, it provided the first example of a party dictatorship in China. Although the Canton government showed vigor, it was not recognized by foreign powers, not even by Soviet Russia. Russia

Dr. Sun Yat-sen Surrounded by His Military Staff

maintained correct relations with the Peking government, and restored some Russian concessions to its jurisdiction after Peking recognized the Soviet Union in 1924. At the same time, Russian agents were assisting Sun Yat-sen's group in preparations to overthrow the Peking regime.

The doctrines of Sun Yat-sen

Dr. Sun did not live to see the phenomenal success of the organization that he had founded, but he left a body of doctrines as a heritage of the Kuomintang party. His most important writings were put together rather hastily during the period of Communist-Kuomintang collaboration and partly at the urging of Borodin, who recognized their value for propaganda purposes. The gist of Sun's program and political philosophy is contained in the famous *San Min Chu I* ("Three Principles of the People"), which became a sort of Bible for the Kuomintang. The Three Principles, usually translated as "Nationalism," "Democracy," and "Livelihood," have been likened to Abraham Lincoln's "government of the people, by the people, and for the people"; but there is considerable difference between the American and the Chinese interpretations of the terms. By nationalism Sun meant, first, the freeing of China from foreign interference and, second, the development of loyalty among the people to the state instead of to the family or the province. In his second principle, Sun was concerned with popular sovereignty and the ideal of representative government. Recognizing that people are unequal in capacity, he believed that the chief political problem, in both China and the West, was to discover how popular sovereignty could be combined with direction by experts. The principle of livelihood referred to the necessity for material progress and also to social reform, rejecting Marxism but failing to outline any specific program. Sun's ideas as a whole were neither very original nor very radical nor even very clear. Democracy apppeared in his conception as a rather remote goal, to be attained at the end of the revolutionary struggle. The three stages of revolution, according to Sun, would be (1) the military stage, necessary to establish order; (2) the "tutelage" stage, devoted to training the people and with power restricted to the revolutionary leaders (the Kuomintang party); and (3) the constitutional stage, embodying representative popular government.

In view of Dr. Sun's limitations both as a leader and as a thinker, it is remarkable that he came to be revered as the Father of the Revolution. His life ended, characteristically, on a note of futility. He had gone north in the latter part of 1924 to arrange an alliance with two of the war lords against a third, but arrived in Peking to find that a settlement had been made without his knowledge. Already in poor health, he died the following March. But when finally removed from the scene, Sun became a legendary figure to his followers, and "Sun-yatsenism" proved to be a far more potent force than Dr. Sun had ever been. He left behind him a legacy of hope, and he had stirred the imagination of Chinese all over the world with the vision of a strong and free China under a republican constitution which would combine the best thought of ancient sages with modern scientific techniques. By the Kuomintang his writings and speeches were treasured as unalloyed wisdom, while their vagueness made it possible to invoke the master's authority for contradictory policies.

By 1926, when the Canton government had become strong enough to challenge the northern militarists, the Nationalist revolution entered its active phase. Kuomintang forces under command of the young general Chiang Kai-shek (1888–1975) swept rapidly northward into the Yangtze valley and in less than six months overran half the provinces of China. The success of this "punitive expedition," however, brought to the surface a dissension that had been stirring for some time within the party. A conservative faction distrusted the Communist connection and wanted to oust Communists entirely. The radical wing, hoping to base the organization upon the support of the peasant and working classes, stressed the desirability of a concrete reform program and of continued association with the Russian advisers. Temporarily the radicals seemed to have won. Chiang Kai-shek, whose sympathies were conservative and who had suppressed radical demonstrations at Shanghai and executed Communists and suspected Communists when Kuomintang troops occupied this important city, was temporarily deprived of his command. But by midsummer of 1927 the picture had completely changed. Borodin and the other Russian advisers were dismissed; trade unionists and radicals were disciplined or driven out of the party, and some party members went into voluntary exile in Russia.

Dr. Sun Yat-sen (Seated) and Chiang Kai-shek

Although the reversal of direction in 1927 was startling and decisive, actually there had been little likelihood that the radicals could maintain their ascendancy. The Chinese Communists at this time numbered only about 50,000. While there were plenty of discontented peasants and a Chinese Federation of Labor claimed two and a half million members, these groups were not capable of carrying to successful conclusion the fight against the northern militarists. And the Kuomintang army was far from being a radical body. Kuomintang leaders had welcomed and benefited from Russian assistance, but now that they felt strong enough to stand alone they had no desire to serve the interests of a foreign power. There were grounds for suspecting that the Russians intended to convert the Chinese revolution into an outpost of Soviet Communism, and the discovery of a Soviet plot at Peking prompted the northern government to break off relations with Russia. In supporting the Moscow-Canton entente of 1923–1927, the Soviet leaders, hoping for the speedy coming of world revolution, had gambled and lost. But they had provided the spark without which the Kuomintang might never have been fired into action.

After the purge of the radical wing, the Kuomintang leaders proceeded rapidly with their plan to extend their authority throughout the country. From this time forward the dominant figure of the party was Chiang Kai-shek, whose return to a position of influence was automatic with the triumph of the conservatives. In addition to his repute as a military commander, Chiang enjoyed the prestige of belonging to the "ruling family" of the Revolution, through his marriage to the American-educated Soong Mei-ling, a sister of Madame Sun Yat-sen. Kuomintang forces pushed on, without too much difficulty, through the territories of discredited military governors, and occupied Peking in 1928. The Nationalists renamed the city Pei-p'ing ("Northern Peace") and moved their capital to Nanking, in keeping with pledges made in the early period of the Revolution.

The task of national reconstruction confronting the Kuomintang leaders was a far more difficult undertaking than the seizure of power had been. Even the maintenance of power was not easy, as remnants of the war-lord regimes lingered on in various parts of China. Although Kuomintang supremacy still depended upon military support, the party claimed that it had completed the first, or military, stage of Dr. Sun's formula of revolution and had inaugurated the second stage—that of political "tutelage." In spite of its anti-Communist orientation, the structure both of the Kuomintang and of the government which it set up at Nanking followed closely the Soviet pattern. The party was a hierarchy, reaching from the smallest units, or cells, through district and provincial bodies up to the Central Executive Committee at the top. The president of the National Government and the members of his Council of State were selected by the Central Executive Committee of the Kuomintang, of which the key member was Chiang Kai-shek. At the central, provincial, and local levels the government embodied, not democracy, but a party dictatorship.

A number of important accomplishments can be credited to the Nationalist regime at Nanking. The portions of China which were brought under its jurisdiction became more unified than at any time since the eighteenth century, and China's prestige in the eyes of the world was enhanced. The Nationalists promptly secured diplomatic recognition and financial assistance from abroad. Following the lead of the United States, the Great Powers agreed to relinquish their control over customs duties, granting tariff autonomy to China by 1929. It was more difficult to persuade them to surrender their privileges of extraterritoriality, a step not taken by the United States and Great Britain until 1943.

Accomplishments of the Nationalist regime

While progress undeniably occurred during the era of Nationalist rule, the defects of the regime became more and more serious. Radical elements had been expelled before the triumph of the Kuomintang, and even moderate liberals were given scant encouragement. Originating as a party of revolution, the Kuomintang when in power neglected to carry out the social reforms that were necessary to win the allegiance of the common people. Very little was done to improve the condition of poor tenants and farm laborers, even though Sun Yat-sen had specified assistance to these classes as a primary objective of the "Principle of Livelihood." In command of a one-party government and eager to perpetuate its own authority, the Kuomintang employed coercive measures against those who opposed it. It maintained secret police, disguised under the title of "Bureau of Investigation and Statistics." To indoctrinate potential party members it organized a tightly disciplined Youth Corps (ironically named the *San Min Chu I* after Sun's "Three Principles"). The Nationalist regime seemed to be preparing the Chinese people less for constitutional democracy than for a permanent condition of tutelage.

Defects of the Nationalist regime

The downfall of the Kuomintang in China after a rule of twenty years was caused by three factors: (1) failure of the Kuomintang regime to solve the problems of Chinese society; (2) unrelenting opposition from the Chinese Communists, who ultimately set up a rival government; and (3) the long war beginning with the Japanese invasion of 1937, which drained the country's resources, demoralized the people, and promoted the chaotic conditions so favorable to the spread of communism. The struggle against the Communists began almost as soon as the Kuomintang had established its government at Nanking and was a continuous process even during the most successful years of the Nationalist period. Following the rupture with the Kuomintang in 1927, the Communist party had been driven underground but extended its activities in both rural and urban areas of central and southern China, and in Kiangsi province it organized a rival government in the form of a Soviet Republic. Almost annihilated by Kuomintang forces in a series of military campaigns, the Communist leaders turned the desperate struggle to their advantage by inciting revolutionary aspirations among the depressed peasantry and

Causes of the Kuomintang's failure

by developing the technique of guerrilla warfare into a fine art. Mao Tse-tung was the key personality behind both of these policies.

The son of a relatively well-to-do peasant, Mao Tse-tung as a youth had rebelled against landlordism and the tyranny of parental authority. One of a dozen men who founded the Chinese Communist party in 1921, he became a deputy member of the Central Executive Committee of the Kuomintang and was entrusted by the Communists with the task of peasant organization. A report prepared for the Chinese Communist party in 1927 on peasant revolutionary activity in Hunan (south central China) provides the clue to Mao's strategy of revolution and is prophetic of his ultimate program for China. Already he was instigating direct action among the lowliest tenants: (1) forming village co-operative associations; (2) smashing temples and burning the wooden idols for fuel; (3) intimidating and assaulting "bad gentry." "A revolution is not the same as inviting people to dinner," he wrote. "A rural revolution is a revolution by which the peasantry overthrows the authority of the feudal landlord class. . . . several hundred million peasants will rise like a tornado or tempest, a force so extraordinarily swift and violent that no power, however great, will be able to suppress it." In sharp disagreement with both the Chinese and Russian party leaders, Mao was convinced that whoever won the peasants would win China.

Threatened with extinction by Chiang's superior troops, Mao Tse-tung conceived and executed the famous "Long March" of October 1934 to October 1935—a mass migration across 6,000 miles of difficult terrain and one of the most amazing exploits in military history. Of the 90,000 men who slipped through Chiang's lines in southwestern China, not more than 20,000 reached Yenan, in northern Shensi Province, which was to be the Communists' headquarters until their

Chinese Civilians on the Szechuan Road. Chinese residents of Shanghai pour into the International Settlement upon hearing rumors that a Japanese attack on the city was imminent. December 2, 1935.

final victory in the civil war. Shattering as the experience had been, it served to weld the survivors into a solid group of tested loyalty and toughness, relying upon their own ingenuity rather than upon directives from Moscow, and it established Mao Tse-tung as undisputed leader of the party. He had demonstrated his tactics of "retreat in order to advance" and his ability to sustain and renew his forces directly from the countryside while the cities and economic apparatus of the state were in the hands of his enemies. Gradually the Communist region of the northwest acquired the attributes of a separate state, with a fluid political structure and well-organized military units. In expanding the area of their influence, the Communists' chief asset was their introduction of reforms which the Nanking government had promised but never fulfilled. They tackled the land problem directly, breaking up great estates, forcing rent reductions, establishing land banks and cooperative societies, building irrigation works, and educating ignorant peasants in better methods of cultivation and crop control. Their immediate and practical assistance to farmers who had been oppressed by high rents and high taxes and their success in eliminating graft in the region under their administration enabled them to compete successfully with the Kuomintang regime for popular favor. The Communists also strengthened their position by calling for national resistance against Japanese aggression, to which Chiang Kai-shek, intent upon crushing Communism, had offered only half-hearted opposition.

When, in line with the Soviet strategy of fostering antifascist "popular fronts," the Chinese Communists appeared cooperative, pressure within the Kuomintang induced Chiang Kai-shek to enter into an alliance with them to halt the common enemy, Japan. But this had the unfortunate effect of encouraging the Japanese militarists to make

War with Japan

Japanese Troops Enter Peking in July 1937 at the Beginning of the Eight-Year War with China

Chinese Communist Artillery Units in Action near Peking

war. Faced with the prospect of a united China, they goaded their government into launching an attack in the Pei-p'ing area (July 7, 1937). This was the beginning of a fateful conflict which soon expanded into World War II.

China in World War II; prelude to civil war

The course of the war revealed that China was a far stronger nation than it had been forty years earlier. Even though the mighty Japanese military machine eventually occupied the coastal cities and almost all of eastern China and forced the Nationalist government to move its capital far inland to Chungking, it was never able to conquer the entire country. Actually, after the United States entered the war against Japan and began to supply China with substantial military aid, the Nationalist government contributed little to the war effort. Chiang Kai-shek, unsure of the loyalty of his own staff and determined to hoard his military resources, ignored the American advisers who tried to prod him into action. While doing little against the Japanese, he kept an army of half a million men in the northwest to isolate the Communist "Border Region" government at Yenan. American negotiations attempting to bring the Yenan and Chungking regimes into a coalition government failed because Chiang insisted that the Communists give up their separate command and put all military forces at his disposal, a condition they regarded as equivalent to a death sentence. Without the advantage of foreign aid or help from Chungking, Communist guerrillas successfully penetrated Japanese lines and gradually secured control of much of northern China. At the close of the war when the Nationalists, assisted by an American airlift, occupied the principal cities, Communist units held the countryside, and they seized stores of Japanese arms and ammunition that Russian troops withdrawing from Manchuria had conveniently left behind. After the Japanese surrender, China's international conflict gradually turned into a civil war.

The Nationalists had formulated plans for reform and promised to replace the party dictatorship with a democratic representative government. They drafted a constitution and early in 1947 conducted elections for a National Assembly, which dutifully chose Chiang Kai-shek as president of the Republic. But while the Nationalists were inaugurating a democratic constitution for China, they were rapidly being dispossessed from the country by the advance of Communist

The retreat of the Nationalists

"Support for the People's Very Own Army." This woodcut, dating from the 1940s, illustrates the close ties that existed between the peasantry and the Communist army. Such illustrations may have overstated the case, but they did highlight a striking contrast between the Communists and the Nationalists.

armies. So low had the prestige of the Kuomintang party fallen that it could summon very little assistance in its hour of peril. In 1949 the southerly retreat of Nationalist forces turned into a rout that ended with all the mainland in the hands of the Communists. By 1950 the jurisdiction of President Chiang's government was confined to the island of Taiwan (Formosa).

The People's Republic of China; the Constitution of 1954

After their victory over the Nationalists, the Communist leaders moved rapidly to secure their hold upon the vast territory of China. In October 1949 they proclaimed the People's Republic of China with its capital in Peking. In 1954 they enacted a Constitution for the People's Republic, which, like the constitution of Soviet Russia, combines the language and forms of parliamentary democracy with the principle of domination by the Communist party. Nominally, supreme authority is vested in an All-China People's Congress, charged with enacting laws and electing major officials. The Constitution contains a Bill of Rights which covers the whole field of individual liberties, recognizes equality of the sexes, declares all persons over eighteen years of age eligible to vote and to hold office, and even guarantees the ownership of private property. However, it leaves the application of these rights very tentative by giving the government power to punish "traitors, counterrevolutionaries, and bureaucratic capitalists."

Unique features of the Communist revolution

The accession of the Chinese Communists to power was followed by sweeping economic, social, and cultural changes which transformed the country and its people in fundamental ways. The Chinese Revolution, one of the most far-reaching in history and in some ways unique, was stamped by the dominating personality of Party Chairman Mao Tse-tung, who adapted theoretical Marxism to immediate problems and blended it with elements of China's traditional culture pattern. Combining fixity of purpose with flexibility in tactics, Mao was pragmatic and innovative in both thought and action. His oversimplified but stimulating interpretation of history bore a strong flavor of nationalism. Invoking reverence for China's "splendid

Mao Tse-tung at a Desk in His Cave Headquarters during the Communist Advances in 1948

historical heritage" and "glorious revolutionary tradition," he paid tribute to some pre-Communist reformers and to Sun Yat-sen, whose widow—Chaing Kai-shek's sister-in-law—became a vice-chairman of the People's Republic. Although he accepted the Marxist dogma of class struggle, Mao identified it with recurring unsuccessful peasant uprisings, including the nineteenth-century Taiping rebellion. Mao's was the first large-scale and successful revolution anywhere in the world that was founded on peasant support and directed by a leader from the peasant class. In this respect it contrasts with the revolution of Lenin and Stalin, which entailed expropriation and forcible suppression of the peasants. No less than the Soviet revolution, it aimed at creating a new society, but, again in contrast with the Russian example, this radical objective was pursued for nearly thirty years—until Mao's death in 1976.

The Communist regime in China claimed to have achieved a coalition of classes, namely peasants, workers, petty bourgeoisie, and "national bourgeoisie." The inclusion of the last two classes marked a departure from orthodox Marxism and an attempt to win the support of financial and industrial elements whose cooperation was essential to bolstering the economy. Businessmen who qualified as "Communist" or "national" capitalists by being willing to work with the new government were allowed to retain their properties temporarily, but found their affairs subjected to rigid control, and in 1956 the national bourgeoisie were formally expropriated. The Central Committee of the Communist party or Chairman Mao himself determined public policies, the permissible limits of debate, and the operation of organs of government, in keeping with the principles of a "People's Democratic Dictatorship."

The "Democratic Dictatorship"

The economic transformation of China since 1949 is an impressive aspect of the Communist revolution, all the more remarkable when viewed against the previous retarded condition of the country. As in India, industrialization was given high priority and—in contrast to India—the government possessed sufficient coercive power to effect rapid change. Geological surveys have revealed mineral resources far in excess of previous estimates. Oil reserves, including offshore deposits, are enormous. By 1977 China's oil production equaled that of Indonesia. In coal deposits China ranks third among the world's countries and also has large known reserves of natural gas as well as adequate supplies of manganese, tungsten, antimony, tin, copper, and aluminum. In recent years the Chinese have supplemented their energy sources by building 7 million small biogas plants which, at low cost, convert animal and vegetable waste into methane gas and fertilizer. By 1960 China's furnaces were producing almost as much steel as was made in France, and the output of electric power had been increased ten times. The acreage of irrigated land more than doubled between 1949 and 1960, and the same period witnessed an extensive forestation program highly significant for soil and water conservation.

Economic objectives and prospects

Blast Furnaces at Anshan. The major steel-producing center in southern Machuria, it is a testament to China's growing industrial strength.

A complex system of dams and reservoirs in the Yellow River valley, designed to end the danger of flooding in this region and to provide a larger and surer crop yield, has not yet been completed. Railroad mileage has doubled but is still far from adequate, especially since the objective is a wide dispersion of industry hitherto concentrated in Manchuria and the eastern seaboard. With Soviet technical assistance the Chinese trained their own engineers capable of designing precision tools. Their manufactures include such items as cars, trucks, and jet planes; also electronic, surgical, and scientific instruments.

The agrarian revolution and the "Great Leap Forward"

More profound than the changes in the scope and tempo of industrialization has been the agrarian revolution. The character of agriculture and of the society engaged in it has been altered radically, through successive stages. The first phase of land reform was simply expropriation of the landlords, many of whom were killed. Then, the newly created peasant proprietors were urged to form cooperatives, pooling the resources of one or more villages. The next step was a drive for collective farms, communally owned and directed by party members or supporters. This was accomplished with remarkable swiftness between 1955 and 1957, by which time more than 90 percent of the family holdings had been collectivized. Although Chinese farmers undoubtedly "volunteered" to join cooperatives because they were given little choice, the government relied primarily upon psychological and social pressure, employing what Mao has described as "persuasive reasoning," and there was no liquidation of resisting peasants. But Mao attempted to make material and institutional changes serve as instruments for molding the psychology of the masses. More than once his dogged pursuit of ideological goals threatened to jeopardize the positive gains of the revolution. The first example was a program announced as the "Great Leap Forward," launched in 1959. It called for the merging of rural co-operatives and collective farms into large communes, which, it was claimed, embodied the principle of ownership by the whole people rather than by a single community. The purpose of the communes was to provide a mobile labor force to implement an overly ambitious program of rapid industrialization and to increase food production. For a variety of reasons—including the callousness and ineptitude of local directors and a prolonged drought in the Yellow River valley that brought poor harvests in 1959 and 1960—the Great Leap Forward turned out to be a disaster. Food shortages necessitated the importation of grain, and the demoralization of labor and the drainage of capital resources caused a severe industrial depression. Forced to revise its tactics drastically, the government in 1962 announced its intention to give agriculture top priority for the immediate future. While the communes were retained and their number increased (now totaling 190), they were reduced in size, a degree of ownership and management was restored to local production teams, and farmers were permitted to cultivate small private plots and sell on the open market.

The failure of the Great Leap Forward temporarily weakened Mao's position. In 1959 he relinquished the office of state chairman and, continuing as head of the party, worked quietly to consolidate his support within the party and within the army. When he felt his base to be strong enough he made a second major attempt to radicalize the revolution and, at the same time, immobilize his opponents. More ambitious and more effective than the 1958 Leap Forward, this second thrust was embodied in the celebrated Great Proletarian Cultural Revolution, which kept China in turmoil from 1966 to 1969 and was not formally laid to rest until August 1977.

Preparation for a second attempt at radical change

The background and objectives of the Proletarian Cultural Revolution are complex. To some extent it was a power struggle between "moderates," represented by Chief of State Liu Shao-ch'i (Liu Shao-qi), and "radicals," led by Chairman Mao and Defense Minister Lin

A People's Court in Session. The establishment of local community courts such as this served as a self-liberating exercise for the peasantry.

Piao (Lin Biao). It also reflected disagreement concerning China's response to escalation of the Vietnam War by the United States. Liu Shao-ch'i, viewing the United States' massive military intervention as a prelude to an attack on China, called for a united front of all socialist countries in defense of North Vietnam. Mao Tse-tung, backed by Lin Piao, insisted that China should not be drawn into a "people's war of liberation" unless directly attacked. He argued that China, by concentrating on its own internal development, could "bypass the Soviet Union on its way to Communism." By August 1966 the Mao-Lin faction dominated the Central Committee of the party, although it by no means controlled the entire party hierarchy or all units of the army.

Undoubtedly the overriding factor in precipitating the Cultural Revolution was ideological. Mao resolved at all costs to prevent his revolution from subsiding until it had produced an equalitarian society. He chastised Soviet leaders for stopping short of this goal and denounced as "revisionists" all those within his own party who showed signs of succumbing to the fleshpots of capitalism. He feared that the prospect of material success had brought a relaxation of effort, which China could ill afford in view of its unrealized potential and weak military posture. He viewed with misgivings the tendency of a bureaucracy to grow rigid and complacent, producing a managerial class more "expert" than "red." In his determination to reform the party both in personnel and structure he temporarily disrupted it completely.

Before 1965 the Communist movement in China had presented the outward appearance of remarkable harmony. But with the onset of the Cultural Revolution scores of officials were arrested, demoted, or forced to make public confession of such crimes as "hedonism," "revisionism," "antiparty activity," or "taking the road to capitalism." The purge numbered high personnel among its targets, includ-

A Red Guard Demonstration in Peking. Middle-school students display their solidarity with the Cultural Revolution by waving copies of the book of quotations from Chairman Mao. The slogan painted on the wall proclaims: "We are not only able to destroy the old world, we are able to build a new world instead— Mao Tse-tung."

ing Liu Shao-ch'i, president of the Republic since 1959 and long regarded as Mao's heir apparent. As the stepped-up purification campaign met with stubborn resistance, Mao turned to the nation's youth, exhorting them to undertake their own Long March and to "learn revolution-making by making revolution." He closed the schools and urged students to organize themselves into units of Red Guards (formally inaugurated at Peking in August 1966) and devote their energies to ferreting out enemies of the revolution. China was treated to the unprecedented spectacle of mobs of teenage youths denouncing their elders, smashing ancient monuments, invading private homes, and noisily demanding unswerving devotion to the thought of Mao Tsetung. Mao encouraged the formation of Revolutionary Committees combining party and nonparty members, and put them in charge of factories, local and provincial governments, and even important departments of the central government. He hoped to replace the Soviet-style dual system of state and party structures that was developing in China with a flexible but unified system.

The attempt to achieve such radical goals generated a condition of chaos bordering on anarchy. Strikes in major industrial centers, disruption of the transport system, and widespread disorders in rural areas placed China's economic gains in jeopardy. At the same time the Chinese found themselves isolated diplomatically, even in the Communist world. Excesses committed by Red Guards and bands of "Revolutionary Rebels," leading to the outbreak of civil war in some provinces in 1968, made it imperative for Mao and Chou En-lai to stem the revolutionary tide. They called on the People's Liberation Army to restore order, and the party line shifted to a denunciation of extremists. Lin Piao, a prime instrument of the Cultural Revolution and named as Mao's successor in a new party constitution of 1960, fell into disgrace. Reportedly he was killed in an airplane crash while attempting to defect to Russia in September 1971.

Undoubtedly the Cultural Revolution of 1966–1969 exacted a heavy price. It left a residue of suspicion and fear and set a precedent for youthful violence, reflected, perhaps, in recent years in the rampages of hoodlum gangs in several cities. Still, in spite of its ugly aspects, its toll of lives and property, the Cultural Revolution was not the total catastrophe envisioned by some foreign critics. Testifying to rapid economic recovery was a record high output of food grains in 1970–1972 and an annual industrial growth rate of about 10 percent. In the midst of its domestic crisis China managed to produce a hydrogen bomb (June 1967), far earlier than Western experts had thought possible. Also Mao had succeeded in inspiring and energizing his massive following, even though his ideal of permanent revolution seemed unlikely to outlive him.

Chinese society—for centuries one of the most stable in the world—has been profoundly affected by the Communist revolution. A fore-

Chairman Mao Tse-tung. Shown here with his then "closest comrade" Marshal Lin Piao (Defense Minister and Vice Chairman of the Republic who was purged in 1971). Premier Chou En-lai stands behind them.

Effects of the Cultural Revolution

Left: *The Cultural Revolution at the Grass Roots*. Agricultural workers have erected red painted signs with quotations from Chairman Mao and carry copies of his "Quotations" into the fields with them. Right: *A Reservoir and Irrigation Project in Chekiang Province, Eastern China*. Labor-saving machinery is still in short supply.

Changes in society; restrictions on urban growth

most problem, inherited from the past, was how to nourish a large and continually expanding population, especially with an economy disrupted by civil war. Vigorous campaigns were conducted to restrict the birth rate—by providing contraceptives and family-planning courses, by encouraging late marriages, and by offering economic incentives for couples to limit the number of their children to one or two. The result has been a dramatic drop in the rate of increase, with the likelihood that China's population, now in the neighborhood of 900 million, will be stabilized by the end of the century. Although less than 15 percent of China's land area is cultivated, more than 80 percent of its people are rural dwellers. The government has restricted the growth of cities (Shanghai with nearly 11 million is the largest) and has tried to establish a symbiotic relationship between each urban center and the surrounding farm area. Not only has immigration from country to town been controlled, but also some 12 million city-educated youths have been resettled in rural areas since the Cultural Revolution. Economic planning has emphasized decentralization and has allowed considerable autonomy to regional units in development programs. To some extent efficiency has been subordinated to the goals of widely dispersed industry, interdependence between industry and agriculture, and regional "self-reliance."

China is still poor in comparison with developed Western countries or Japan. Annual per capita income—about $340—does not greatly exceed that of India, but a significant difference is that instead of being concentrated at the top, it is fairly evenly distributed. No doubt the majority of the Chinese people are better off in basic material necessities than they have been for many centuries. Improved standards of hygiene and sanitation, expanded medical facilities, and intense educational campaigns succeeded in stamping out opium addiction, curtailing prostitution, and raising the level of public health. By supplementing a scarce supply of skilled professionals with semi-skilled trainees, the Chinese have been able to make generally available such social services as child day-care centers, hospitals, and mobile clinics employing both up-to-date Western and traditional Chinese medicines and techniques. Although wages and farm incomes are low, the individual has the benefit of low rents, free medical service, and disability and retirement pensions.

A significant aspect of social change is the demise of the centuries-old patriarchal family structure and the emancipation—at least in theory—of women. A marriage law of 1950 gave women equal rights with men in respect to choice of spouse, conjugal privileges and obligations, and divorce. Legal equality between the sexes led to enhanced status of the single-unit monogamous family. It is still common for working couples to house their retired elders (and housing space is at a premium), but the tyrannical authority formerly wielded by a clan matriarch over daughters-in-law has been broken, and progress toward bridging the proverbial generation gap has occurred. Women have entered the labor force in large numbers and have been admitted to occupations and professions that formerly were man's preserve. In China as elsewhere women are a decided minority in levels of highest responsibility, and at lower levels it is usually the husband rather than the wife whose job determines a couple's place of residence. But if Chinese women are not yet fully liberated, they are far freer from exploitation by male kindred than they were or than are the women of many other lands.

Some cultural changes promoted by the Communists had their beginnings during the Nationalist era. A "literary revolution" of the 1920s had made vernacular speech an accepted vehicle for modern authors in place of the difficult, archaic language of Chinese literary classics. Linguistic reform under the Communists involved simplification of written characters and adoption of an allegedly more nearly phonetic system of transliteration into languages using the Roman alphabet (*pinyin,* in place of the older "Wade-Giles" system). As in other totalitarian regimes, the Communists undertook to define cultural standards and to make art the handmaiden of ideology, a policy which during the height of the Proletarian Revolution reduced it to a level of mediocrity. Education inevitably was buffeted by shifting revolutionary currents. Mao Tse-tung repudiated completely the classical Chinese tradition of a scholarly elite drawn from the gentry. He stressed the need to combine theory with practice, instituted "half-

Improved living standards

Changes in the family and the position of women

Cultural and educational trends

study, half-work" programs, and sent youths from city classrooms out into the fields to work with and learn from the peasants. The regular schools, closed during the Cultural Revolution, were not restored to normal operation until after Mao's death. In spite of vicissitudes one educational objective has been largely met—about 90 percent of the population has become literate.

Attempts to remake human nature

The dark side of the picture of China's changing society is the high price that has been paid for rapid material progress. The party chiefs used ruthless means to seize power and to keep it. Although violence and terror have not been the typical weapons either of party discipline or of popular coercion and there has been no general liquidation of "kulaks" or of bourgeoisie, psychological pressure, "thought control," and "reform through labor" have been employed regularly in the effort to remold recalcitrants. The whole citizen body is constantly exposed to political indoctrination through the communication media, entirely controlled by the government. Paradoxically, although Mao restricted intellectual freedom and resorted to coercion, his view of human nature was neither cynical nor pessimistic. Rejecting the historical determinism of orthodox Marxism, he insisted that ideas and human will and resolution can play an important part in shaping events. He believed it possible not only to reform institutions but to remake human nature, producing a "new man" who would instinctively put the interests of society foremost. The very chaos of the Cultural Revolution he hoped would further his purpose of creating a direct and permanent working relationship between the party's leaders and the masses, eliminating as far as possible the middle levels of authority. This radically utopian concept did not prevent the rise of a bureaucratic managerial class; actually it served to legitimize the authority of the managers. To some observers the contemporary Chinese Communist regime bears more than a superficial resemblance to the classical imperial tradition of a benevolent government wielding

Workers' School. Railway workers in northern China attend classes as part of the state's attempt to extend education.

absolute power over an obedient and disciplined population. It follows that as long as the rulers enjoy the "mandate of Heaven," their position will not be seriously challenged.

The rapid unification of China under a totalitarian regime has drastically altered the power relationships in Asia and the Far East. With a powerful army at their disposal, the Communists re-established Chinese jurisdiction over important areas that had been lost during the decline of the Manchu Dynasty. They took possession of Manchuria, retained Sinkiang in the far west, and installed their forces in Tibet. And while augmenting China's national prestige they posed as the champions of Asian peoples against Western imperialism, assisting revolutionary movements against the British in Malaya and against the French in Indochina.

China's foreign relations

China's internal developments and policies have been affected by her relations with other countries. At the outset the greatest threat to the Communist regime seemed to lie with the United States, which had supported Chiang Kai-shek throughout the war, continued its alliance with him, and financed his military establishment of 600,000 troops on the island of Taiwan—within 100 miles of the mainland. Stung by charges that liberals in the State Department had "lost" China for the United States, successive Washington administrations clung to an unrealistic and contradictory policy of regarding the People's Republic, on the one hand, as a bungling incompetent unworthy of notice and, on the other, as a dangerous and demonic power bent on world conquest. The United States withheld diplomatic recognition from Peking, blocked its admission to the United Nations, embargoed American trade with the mainland, and installed a ring of military bases around East Asia. Through its "containment" policy, implemented by a network of defensive alliances, the United States sought to isolate China, and effectively isolated its own citizens from contact with an important area of the world.

Hostility of the United States; the "containment" policy

The simultaneous isolation of China and Russia—as the Cold War alienated the U.S.S.R. from her erstwhile Western allies—at first strengthened the fraternal and ideological bonds between the two large Communist states. In 1950 their representatives signed a thirty-year treaty of "friendship, alliance, and mutual assistance," which invalidated the 1945 treaty between the U.S.S.R. and the Chinese Nationalists. The preamble of China's 1954 Constitution reaffirmed "indestructible friendship" with the Soviet Union. China relied heavily upon Russia for technical assistance in economic development. Between 1950 and 1955 China's exchange with the Soviet-bloc countries increased from 26 percent to 75 percent of her total foreign trade. The late 1950s, however, evidenced disaffection between the two Communist giants. Differences led swiftly to deterioration in both diplomatic and economic relations. The Sino-Soviet rift is attributable to a number of causes. The Chinese resented the Russian's failure to

The Sino-Soviet rift and its significance

May Day Parade in Peking. Processions such as this commemorate the success of the revolutionary struggle and serve to reinforce the popular commitment to revolutionary values and to a strong state.

fulfill their aid agreements, including the promise of help in developing atomic weapons. Other factors were the inevitable rivalries of great-power politics and conflicting national territorial ambitions. The Chinese hinted at the eventual rectification of their frontiers at Russia's expense, and both China and the Soviet Union deployed large numbers of troops along their 5,000-mile common border from Central Asia to Manchuria. In 1969 violent clashes occurred between Russian and Chinese troops in Sinkiang in the far west and along the Ussuri River in the northeast. The most fundamental source of disagreement between the two countries was ideological. Peking accused the Russians of abandoning the cause of world revolution against imperialism and condemned Khrushchev's policy of peaceful coexistence. The breach between Peking and Moscow reflected the differences in outlook between the heirs of an old revolution and the directors of one still comparatively young. In Mao Tse-tung's view Soviet Russia, now a have nation, had succumbed to revisionism and was taking the primrose path to accommodation with the capitalist powers for the sake of security and the grantification of consumer demands.

While breaking with much of the past, Mao Tse-tung and his comrades retained the ancient concept of China as a unique and indestructible community, proudly self-sustaining. They strove to avoid close dependence on any other state, Communist or not. (Russian assistance during the 1950s was chiefly in the form of loans and these were repaid.) For many years China was forced into isolation by the hostility of Western nations. The break with the Soviets in the early 1960s and the internal turmoil that followed a few years later made the country's isolation almost complete. But the return to more moderate policies brought decided changes in foreign relations. The Peking government restored diplomatic relations ruptured during the Cultural Revolution and proceeded to win recognition from a rapidly growing number of states. The end of China's isolation was dramatically illustrated in 1971 by rapprochement with the United States and by China's admission to the United Nations and the transfer of a permanent seat in the Security Council from the Chinese Nationalists to the People's Republic.

The end of China's isolation

Ironically, the American president who renewed ties with China had built a political career on strident anti-Communism. President Nixon's decision to cultivate cordial relations with his inveterate ideological enemies was prompted partly by the promise of new trade opportunities and partly by the hope of gaining an advantage in dealing with the Soviets by drawing closer to their repudiated ally. In any case it was no longer possible to ignore the People's Republic, which had become a military power equipped with nuclear bombs and missiles. Summit meetings in 1972 did not produce formal diplomatic recognition of the Peking government by Washington, but a joint communiqué issued at Shanghai on February 28 pledged the two countries to work toward the normalization of relations and the relaxation of tensions in Asia, including Indochina. One crucial question remained unresolved: the Chinese stipulated that "the liberation of Taiwan is China's internal affair"; the Americans affirmed "interest in a peaceful settlement of the Taiwan question by the Chinese themselves," and the "ultimate objective of the withdrawal of all United States forces and military installations from Taiwan."

The Washington-Peking rapprochement

The subject of Taiwan is a story in itself, which cannot be detailed here. Ever since 1949 when Chiang Kai-shek and his defeated forces retreated to the island, it had been a thorn in the side of the Peking government and the chief source of friction with the United States. The United States retained its alliance with Chiang Kai-shek, recognized his government at Taipei as the "Republic of China," supplied him with arms and money, and threatened to "unleash" his forces to reconquer the mainland. On one point the Communists and the Nationalists agreed—that Taiwan was an integral part of China. They disagreed as to whether it was a severed head or a severed foot. In an atmosphere of international tension, Taiwan's economy thrived. The Nationalists had imposed themselves upon the Taiwanese by force; their rule was an extension of the party dictatorship they had devel-

Taiwan under the Nationalist regime

Generalissimo Chiang Kai-shek

oped at Nanking. But while Chiang Kai-shek had botched the governance of China, he scored a major success in Taiwan. Helped by United States investments and by World Bank credits, the Nationalists' republic sustained a high rate of economic growth. Between 1952 and 1978 the gross national product increased nearly twenty-fold and per capita annual income rose from $148 to $1,304, bringing Taiwan to third rank in that category (after Japan and Singapore) among Far Eastern countries. While the native Taiwanese—about 85 percent of the island's 17 million inhabitants—were given very limited political rights and held under martial law, they shared in the material progress of both agriculture and industry. Wealth is fairly evenly distributed and, while women have achieved none of the freedoms enjoyed by their sisters in the People's Republic, the Taiwanese are far better off in material goods than are the mainland Chinese. With sizable military forces as well as a bustling and technologically advanced economy, Taiwan has many characteristics of an independent middle-class power. Yet political independence (which native Taiwanese might prefer) is out of the question because of the fixed policies of both the Taipei and Peking governments.

The U.S. break with Taiwan and restoration of diplomatic relations with China

In December 1978 President Carter abruptly announced his intention to break diplomatic relations and abrogate the 1954 mutual defense treaty with the Taiwan regime, and the following March he restored normal diplomatic relations with Peking. The initial shock of this policy reversal was softened somewhat when Congress passed the Taiwan Relations Act in April 1979. The act stipulated that the United States would regard any attempt to determine the future of Taiwan by other than peaceful means as "of grave concern to the United States." The diplomatic break had no adverse effect on the island's economy. During the first four months of 1979 Taiwan's foreign trade rose 36 percent over the same period of the preceding year, and trade with the United States increased by more than 20 percent. At an annual figure of close to $10 billion, United States trade with Taiwan was ten times as great as with the mainland. Chiang Ching-kuo, who succeeded to the presidency after the death of his father Chiang Kai-shek in 1975, held fast to the claim that his was the only legitimate Chinese government. Peking's present leaders have indicated that they would accept an arrangement allowing full autonomy to Taiwan under its present government, in turn for acknowledgment of China's formal sovereignty.

Death of Mao Tse-tung and conservative reaction

The death in September 1976 of Mao Tse-tung—the most influential Chinese personality since Confucius—marked the end of an era. In the years following the Cultural Revolution, with the aging chairman's health declining, intraparty strife persisted between the "radicals," who stressed revolutionary ideology, and the "moderates," who desired stability and rapid material progress. Premier Chou En-lai's death in January 1976 removed a steadying influence that had repeatedly been effective in bridging the gap between opposing factions. Despite some ominous disturbances, following Mao's death his hand-picked successor to the premiership, Hua Kuo-feng (Hua Guo-feng), was named party chairman (October 1976). But that the political pendulum was swinging to the right was reflected in the increasingly prominent role of a Chou En-lai protégé, Vice-Premier Teng Hsiao-ping (Deng Xiaoping), who had been purged during the Cultural Revolution and purged again as late as April 1976. Hua Kuo-feng gradually receded into the background (he resigned the premiership in September 1980), while the ascendant Teng faction not only undertook to purge the party of radicals, but also repudiated the Cultural Revolution almost completely—villifying its heroes and rehabilitating its victims (a posthumous award in some cases). Though still honoring Mao Tse-tung's memory, the new leaders hinted that even the "Great Helmsman" had made mistakes.

In a sensational sixty-seven-day public trial ending on January 25, 1981, ten defendants were accused of having killed 34,000 people during the Cultural Revolution, of torturing or persecuting hundreds of thousands, and of plotting to poison Chou and eliminate Mao. Pilloried as the archvillain was none other than the widow of Mao Tse-tung, the feared and hated Chiang Ch'ing (Jiang Qing), acknowledged leader of the notorious "gang of four," which had become a scapegoat for the excesses and failures of the Cultural Revolution. Chiang's scornful and defiant outbursts against her accusers and judges injected a note of excitement into an otherwise dismal, and apparently well-coached, performance. She was given a suspended death sentence, subject to commutation to life imprisonment after a two-year probationary term at hard labor.

Vice-Premier Teng Hsiao-ping

More than a reaction against the radicalism of the Cultural Revolution, the policies of China's post-Mao leadership seemed to herald the end of the revolutionary process that had kept the country in ferment throughout a generation. Teng and his associates set as their goals internal order, efficient management, and rapid economic development. Eager to modernize China, they declared that "the proletariat can and must learn from the bourgeoisie," and they called upon industrial nations for technological help, opened their country to tourists, and began cautiously to accept foreign investments and credits. But while condemning the terror tactics of their predecessors and while offering greater material incentives to the populace, the new leaders evidenced a determination to maintain authoritarian control. They tightened discipline in the Communist party, purging about a third of its trained personnel, clamped down on the display of unauthorized wall posters which had become a popular vehicle for airing grievances, and emphasized the goal of political stability, to be achieved through "democratic centralism." To speed technological progress, they were willing to sanction the profit motive and to risk dependence on foreign capital—steps that Mao had steadfastly avoided. These concessions to capitalist ideology suggested that China's "moderni-

Changing goals—toward "modernization"

THE FAR EAST TODAY

zation" might reverse the movement toward an equalitarian society and create a new elite class. The dismissal or sidetracking of Mao's revolutionary dream was by no means universally approved. It would be rash to assume that the dominance of a conservative faction has been fixed for an indefinite future, or that the pendulum—which has swung over such a wide arc—will never swing again.

Changes in foreign relations demonstrated most clearly China's departure from the prescriptions of Mao. According to the "Three-World Thesis"—attributed to Mao but in reality one of Chou's contributions—the two superpowers constituted the first "world," other advanced industrial nations of West and East formed the second, and underdeveloped ex-colonial nations represented the third. While the Chinese claimed affiliation with the last group, they began avidly to cultivate relations with the second, for the twin purposes of speeding their own economic development and of enlisting support against the U.S.S.R., which they had come to regard as the "principal enemy." Along with their predilection for rapid economic growth, the successors of Mao showed themselves much less concerned with ideological purity than with raising China's stakes in the game of power politics. That ideologies come and go while human nature and politics remain much the same could hardly be better illustrated than it was by the sight of a Communist government—one that had for years castigated American "imperialism"—now advocating a stronger NATO and the retention of United States military bases in Japan and the Philippines. Pressing the advantage of cooling relations between Japan and the Soviets, the Chinese, after four years of negotiation, secured a formal peace treaty with Japan, signed in Peking in August 1978. By this time Japan had become China's largest trading partner, contributing one-fourth of the total foreign trade of the People's Republic.

New departures in foreign relations

2. THE CLIMAX OF IMPERIALISM AND THE BEGINNING OF A NEW ERA IN JAPAN

In the early twentieth century, while China was in the throes of revolutionary struggle, Japan was enjoying relative stability and increasing prosperity. The transformations which characterized the Meiji Restoration had been accomplished without seriously disturbing the structure of Japanese society. Before 1914 Japan had enlarged its territories, acquired the basis for a strong industrial economy, and finally found itself in a position to seek hegemony in the Far East.

The ascendancy of Japan by 1914

The Japanese government entered the war against Germany in 1914, nominally out of regard for the Anglo-Japanese alliance but actually from a desire to secure Kiaochow Bay and the German concessions in the Shantung Peninsula. The Japanese also seized the German outposts in the Pacific north of the equator—the Marshall, Caroline, and Mar-

Results of participation in World War I

*Japan's victories and
defeats at the Peace
Conference*

iana Islands. Japan showed little interest in the Western phases of the war, but utilized to the utmost the opportunities presented by China's weakness and by the involvement of the Western powers in the titanic struggle in Europe.

The success of Japan's policy of exerting diplomatic and economic pressure was demonstrated at the Peace Conference of 1919. The Chinese delegation naturally demanded the restoration of Shantung, a request entirely consonant with Wilsonian principles. The Japanese refused to comply, and Wilson did not press the matter vigorously, partly because another Japanese objective of a less questionable character had been defeated. The Japanese had asked for a declaration endorsing the principle of "the equality of nations and the just treatment of their nationals." The fear that such a declaration would conflict with the policy of limiting Oriental immigration led the Americans and British to oppose it when the matter was put to a vote in the League of Nations Commission. At the same time they yielded to Japan on the Shantung question and also allowed Japan to retain, as mandates under the League of Nations, the North Pacific islands taken from Germany.

In spite of having plucked the fruits of imperialism, Japan after World War I seemed to be moving in a liberal direction, both in domestic affairs and in her international relations. The antiwar sentiment prevalent for a short time in much of the Western world was manifest, to a lesser degree, in Japan and provoked a revulsion against military leadership. Japan had been associated with the foremost Western democracies during the war, was one of the "Big Five" at the Paris Peace Conference, and—in contrast to Wilson's own United States—signed the Versailles Treaty and joined the League of Nations. Twice before in their history the Japanese had revealed a capacity for adopting what seemed to be the most effective and up-to-date institutions in the world as they knew it, and many of their leaders were persuaded that democracy was essential for progress in the twentieth century. Japanese statesmen were impressed by the fact that autocratic and militaristic Germany had been defeated and autocratic Russia had collapsed in revolution, while the apparently weaker democratic nations had been victorious. And, although few of these statesmen were convinced democrats in the full sense of the term, they were at least desirous of retaining the good will of the democratic powers which seemed to be in command of the world's destiny at the moment.

During much of the 1920s Japan's international policy was on the whole conciliatory, as illustrated by the Washington Conference of 1921–1922, which produced a Naval Arms Limitation Agreement, a Nine-Power "Open Door" Treaty concerning China, and a Four-Power Pacific Pact. The Japanese accepted a limitation of Japan's battleship tonnage to a figure three-fifths that of the United States and of Britain, and agreed to terminate their alliance of twenty years' standing with Great Britain. The Four-Power Pact which replaced the alliance was based on nothing more substantial than the promise of friendly consultation on problems of the Pacific and pledges to maintain the status quo in regard to fortifications in this area. The Nine-Power Treaty, affirming the principle of the Open Door, actually restored nothing to China, but the Japanese delegates, in private conferences with the Chinese, promised that their government would withdraw its troops from Shantung and return the administration of the province to China, leaving Japanese interests represented only in the form of private capital investments. This action was carried out as promised before the close of 1922. Many Japanese businessmen were convinced that the cultivation of friendly relations with the sprawling mainland state would pay far bigger dividends than would the seizure of territory by force and at the risk of inviting a boycott of Japanese trade.

Promising as the liberal-democratic trends in Japan were, they did not become vigorous enough to extinguish deeply entrenched reactionary forces which eventually led the country to disaster. The failure of the liberal elements must be attributed in part to external factors. The disillusionment and cynicism that became general in the postwar years throughout the West had their counterpart in Japan. The trends of international politics did not indicate a substantial gain for democratic processes. The rise of fascism in Europe demonstrated a powerful movement in the opposite direction. Almost everywhere, virulent nationalism seemed to be in the ascendancy, obscuring the hope of a cooperative world order. With democracy on the defensive or in retreat in the countries of the West, where it was indigenous, it could scarcely be expected to triumph easily in such a nation as Japan, where it was a recent innovation with no cultural or institutional roots.

The counterinfluence of nationalism

The sensibilities of the Japanese were irritated by the discrimination they encountered in the form of tariffs against their goods and immigration laws against their citizens. In 1924 the United States Congress passed an Oriental Exclusion law, placing Asians in a category inferior to that of the most backward Europeans. The United States was not alone in such a policy, and many Japanese began to feel that the great white nations were determined never to treat them as equals. The high tariff policies of the United States and other Western powers were another disturbing factor, producing psychological as well as economic repercussions. By 1930 the larger share of Japan's foreign trade, both export and import, was with the United States, with a trade balance decidedly favorable to the latter country. Protectionists in the United States alleged that American standards were threatened by competition from "cheap" Japanese labor. Yet the chief Japanese import was raw cotton and Japan's leading export to the United States was raw silk, an item hardly competitive with American industry.

Discriminatory polices of Western nations

In the last analysis, the defeat of liberal forces was due to deficiencies in the structure of Japanese society and in the economic system. The fundamental problem of creating a stable economy and satisfactory living standards for the majority of the people was never solved, and the problem became steadily more acute as the population continued to increase at the rate of 1 million a year. In spite of the expansion of commerce and manufacture, Japan's per capita income by 1928 was equal only to about one-eighth of that of the United States. Japan's prosperity, such as it was, depended upon participation in a world market that was subjected to more and more intense competition. Foreign trade received a severe blow when the price of silk, her leading article of export, declined about 75 percent between 1925 and 1934. To compensate for the collapse of the silk market, Japanese manufacturers stepped up the production of cotton cloth, but in this field they were bucking old and strongly established competitors. The Great Depression struck Japan just when the country seemed to be pulling out of a slump. Between 1929 and 1931 Japan's foreign commerce fell off by one-half, while rural and industrial indebtedness swelled to a figure in excess of the national income.

The highly inequitable distribution of wealth within Japan made for an artificial stratification of classes and interests that was unfavorable to the development of a democratic society. The middle class was too small and insecure to be a very effective liberal force. The great body of farmers and laborers had been ushered out of the discipline of Tokugawa feudalism into the discipline of an efficient centralized bureaucracy, without ever being emancipated from their traditions of docility and the acceptance of direction from above. Aspects of a feudal mentality persisted within the nation after feudalism had been replaced by a modern capitalist order. Industry, commerce, and finance were concentrated in the hands of a few huge trusts, known collectively as the Zaibatsu, each controlled by a closely integrated family group and almost beyond the reach of public supervision. The Zaibatsu not only dominated the economic picture but also were affiliated with bureaucrats in the government and deeply influenced political parties.

*The illiberal character of
Japanese parties: the
Seiyukai*

The flimsy foundations of Japanese liberalism are revealed in the history and character of political parties during the 1920s and early 1930s, by which time two competing parties had risen to prominence. The Seiyukai was a descendant of the old Liberal party of Itagaki, but it exemplified a metamorphosis of liberalism into something almost its opposite. Itagaki's party, largely agrarian from the beginning, had passed under the domination of great landlords in place of the small tenants. To this conservative agrarian element was added the leading representative of big business, the house of Mitsui. Thus the Seiyukai constituted an alliance of landlords, monopoly capitalists, and bureaucrats, and it had connections also with the armed services. While the party favored constitutional methods, it was extremely conservative on domestic issues and rabidly expansionist on foreign policy, advocating forceful measures to improve Japan's economic position.

In 1927 an opposition party to the Seiyukai was formed, incorporating remnants of the old Progressive party of Count Okuma. This new party, the Minseito, was backed primarily by industrial rather than agrarian interests, and favored policies conducive to the health of the business community, including social-welfare measures to relieve working-class discontent. But while it was progressive in comparison with the Seiyukai, it could hardly be considered truly liberal in composition or principles. It was supported by one of the great Zaibatsu houses (the Mitsubishi) and was as intensely nationalistic as the Seiyukai, differing from the latter chiefly on the question of which methods would best advance the country's interests.

The Minseito

A hopeful interlude, of brief duration, began when a Minseito cabinet came into office in 1929 and attempted to reverse the "strong" policy of the previous ministry, which had thrown troops into Shantung province as the Chinese Nationalist forces advanced toward Peking. The impact of the world depression upon Japan's economy, however, jeopardized the position of the moderate Minseito cabinet, and the assassination of the premier by a fanatic not only weakened the cabinet but also gave ominous warning of the length to which intransigent nationalist groups would go in promoting their own cause. Then, in September 1931, the Japanese army stationed in Manchuria took matters into its own hands by attacking Chinese troops. By the following February, Manchuria had become the "independent" state of Manchukuo under Japanese auspices, and in 1933 Japan, branded publicly as an aggressor, defiantly withdrew from the League of Nations.

The failure of moderation; the Manchuria incident

Throughout the 1930s liberal elements in Japan never entirely abandoned their struggle to hold back the tide of militant nationalism. But when the issues became international, as in the struggle over Manchuria and, later, in the war against China, patriotic sentiments blunted the edge of popular opposition. The only groups strong enough to challenge the militarists were the financial and business interests, and these were easily seduced by the promise of profits in the offing. Most of the business leaders had come to regard expansion as essential to Japan's economy. They hoped it could be carried out peacefully and painlessly, but they had helped to build, and had profited from building, a war machine that would be extremely difficult to hold within bounds.

The omnipotence of nationalism

Of course, the primary center of aggressive truculence lay in the military services themselves, particularly the army. As previously pointed out, the Japanese army was composed largely of peasants, an unfortunate class, whose legitimate discontents were, under skillful direction, sublimated into an unreasoned and frenzied patriotism. After the Meiji period the army officers also were drawn chiefly from

The rise of fanatical militarism

small towns and rural communities, and they lacked the temperate and relatively broad-minded attitude that had distinguished the samurai leaders. Gradually a "young officer" group developed an ideology of its own, which began to permeate the rank and file. Idealists in the worst sense of the term, these soldier fanatics preached absolute loyalty to the emperor and affirmed that Japan, of divine origin and superior to other nations, had the right to extend its rule over other parts of the world. At the same time, reflecting their peasant affinities, they demanded agrarian reforms or even nationalization of the land and castigated both capitalists and politicians as selfish and corrupt. Their program, a medley of radical and reactionary principles, aimed to make Japan an invincible state, solidly unified under the imperial will, which they claimed to represent most faithfully. Although it has been likened to fascism, the "Imperial Way" proclaimed by the ultranationalists undoubtedly had more in common with the ancient Japanese concepts of the state as a patriarchal society and of the superiority of government by men to government by law.

The conquest of Manchuria as a prelude to war against China

The creation of the puppet state of Manchukuo in 1932 and its development under Japanese management did not yield the substantial benefits to Japan's economy that had been anticipated. To exploit the coal, iron, and oil resources of Manchuria required an extensive outlay of capital, and Japanese capital was not readily forthcoming, partly because of the fear that industry in Manchukuo would compete with Japan's and partly because of the rigid governmental controls imposed upon capital and industry in the puppet state. As plans matured for making Manchuria not simply a source of raw materials for Japan but a center of heavy industry for Asia, it became apparent that the assurance of access to a wide market area was imperative. Hence, Japanese expansionists attempted to convert China's northeastern provinces into an "autonomous" region, linked economically with Manchukuo. Finally they enlarged their objectives to encompass the creation of a "Greater East Asia Co-Prosperity Sphere." Instead of alleviating Japan's economy, this aggressive imperialistic policy saddled it with

Japanese Troops in the Walled City of Mukden, Manchukuo (Manchuria)

The Beginning of the Occupation in Japan. American troops entering Tokyo September 8, 1945. The devastating effects of the bombing raids are plainly evident.

additional burdens, entailing larger and large expenditures for armaments in support of a program that had no foreseeable limits and was bound to meet with resistance at every point.

The role of Japan in World War II, into which its conflict with China was merged, is discussed elsewhere in this volume. Japan's surrender in 1945 was the prelude to a new phase of history, in many ways different from anything experienced in the past. Never before had the Japanese nation been defeated in war and never before had the country been occupied by a foreign power. The occupation of a conquered country was also a new experience for the United States. At the very least it can be said that both the Japanese and the Americans conducted themselves in such a way as to produce a minimum of friction in relationships which were necessarily difficult.

The defeat of Japan in World War II

For six and a half years, authority in Japan was nominally held by the Far Eastern Commission in Washington and the advisory Allied Council for Japan in Tokyo. Actually it was held by General Douglas MacArthur as Supreme Commander for the Allied Powers (SCAP) under orders from Washington. From beginning to end the Japanese Occupation was an undertaking and a responsibility of the United States. Military rule was indirect, however, and was exercised through the regular Japanese government, which had not disintegrated with Japan's military defeat. The emperor accepted the surrender terms, called upon his subjects to cooperate with the occupying forces, and served as the connecting link between the old order and the new. In spite of the relative unimportance of the emperor politically in modern times, his role was of great value psychologically in

The American Occupation

providing a symbol of continuity when so much of the past seemed
to have been destroyed forever.

Japan's military defeat and subsequent occupation by the conqueror's troops marked the third time in the country's history that it
was subjected to strong doses of foreign influence. Unlike the earlier
occasions, the Japanese were not acting voluntarily. But although
forced to accept changes, they again succeeded to a remarkable degree
in adapting these to their own social and cultural traditions and in
using them to promote renewed growth and fresh achievements.

One of the first major tasks of the Occupation authorities was to
furnish Japan with a new constitution grounded in democratic principles. A draft prepared by a group of Japanese consultants was
replaced by an American document, which was approved by the
emperor and formally promulgated by him in the Diet in November
1946. It went into effect in May of the following year. Breaking
cleanly with tradition and with the Constitution of 1889, it declared
that sovereignty lay with the Japanese people and left the emperor
with only formal powers like those of the British monarch. The new
Constitution contained an elaborate Bill of Rights, in which to the
normal civil liberties were added such benefits as the right to work
and to bargain collectively, social equality, and equality of the sexes.
Universal adult suffrage was established, with a bicameral Diet, and
a cabinet responsible to the House of Representatives. The Constitution also incorporated the American principles of separation of church
and state and judicial review of acts of the legislature. Particularly
arresting was Article 9, which declared that "the Japanese people forever renounce war as a sovereign right of the nation" and that "land,
sea, and air forces, as well as other war potential, will never be maintained." Its highly utopian flavor made the new Constitution one of
the most remarkable documents of its kind ever issued. If its principles
could have been carried into active and complete realization, they
would have made Japan a more advanced democratic nation than the
United States.

While introducing political changes the Occupation authorities projected a far-reaching reform program. In conformity with the policy
of demilitarization, an extensive purge was conducted to remove from
office and from teaching positions all persons suspected of ultrana-
tionalist proclivities. A direct attack was launched against the Zaibatsu
groups with the passage of an Antimonopoly Law and the creation of
a Fair Trade Commission. Pursuant to the liberal economic provisions
of the new Constitution, labor organizations were encouraged.
Between 1945 and 1950 membership in labor unions increased from
5,000 to more than 6,000,000 and the government enacted a comprehensive labor welfare code. Perhaps most significant among the
reforms was that which dealt with the long-neglected problem of land
ownership. An agrarian law of 1946, providing for government pur-

chase of tracts from absentee landlords and for the sale of these tracts to tenant farmers at moderate prices, led to a sweeping transformation of agricultural land ownership.

The character of the Occupation and its accompanying reforms were clearly stamped with the complex personality of General MacArthur. Filled with a strong sense of mission that sometimes made him arrogant, he was nevertheless capable of sound judgment, and he strove vigorously and sincerely to promote what he believed to be Japan's long-range best interests. He successfully opposed demands to abolish the imperial office, realizing its value both as a symbolic link to the past and as a vehicle for legitimatizing institutional reforms. Honored as a military hero in America, MacArthur came to be looked upon almost as a demigod in Japan. His policies, however, were sometimes impractical and even contradictory. He insisted on the disestablishment of Shinto as a state religion to further the objective of complete religious freedom, yet he entertained hopes of converting the Japanese to Christianity. The purge directed against militarists and ultranationalists caught some liberals whose only fault seemed to be their adherence to ideals boldly announced in the new Constitution. Labor was prodded into organizing and collective bargaining, but strikes were restricted by the Occupation government. MacArthur took particular pride in his campaign to promote free enterprise by breaking up the huge Zaibatsu combinations. The ultimate results of this trust-busting program could hardly have been foreseen and were considerably different from what MacArthur intended. The efficient organizational structures that Mitsui and Mitsubishi had developed were, with their dissolution, replaced by a rigid bureaucracy created by the Occupation to enforce competition and control foreign trade. Clumsily and inflexibly managed, it temporarily disrupted the economy and hampered recovery. But the precedent of a centralized bureaucracy, remaining as a legacy of the Occupation,

Occupation policies

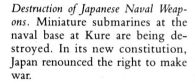

Destruction of Japanese Naval Weapons. Miniature submarines at the naval base at Kure are being destroyed. In its new constitution, Japan renounced the right to make war.

eventually proved useful in speeding Japan's economic growth. The Japanese government, which before the war had exercised relatively weak control over the private sector, at the end of the Occupation stepped into SCAP's role as chief economic planner and director. Although the great trusts were not formally reconstituted, Japan acquired a centrally guided rather than a laissez-faire economy. Beginning in 1948, the economic restraints imposed by SCAP were gradually relaxed. Occupation policy, reflecting the pressures of global power politics, shifted from reform to retrenchment and recovery. The program of decentralizing industry halted with the realization that if Japan's industrial strength were preserved it could be an asset to the West in the Cold War with the Communist powers.

The Peace of 1951 and end of the Occupation

A peace treaty between the United States and Japan was negotiated at San Francisco in September 1951, and ratified the following April. It was also signed by forty-eight other countries, not including the Soviet Union, however, which remained technically in a state of war with Japan until 1956. The peace settlement, although it ended the Occupation and restored formal independence to Japan, was very drastic territorially. Depriving the nation of all its empire, the treaty reduced Japan to the same area it had held at the time of Commodore Perry's visit in 1853, although its population was now three times as great. The peace treaty, supplemented by a security treaty, acknowledged Japan's right to arm for "self-defense" and authorized the stationing of foreign troops (meaning American) in Japan for the defense of the country.

Political trends in postwar Japan: The Liberal Democratic party

Encouraged by a democratic constitution, numerous political parties sprang into being, but the persisting tradition of loyalty to personalities, kinship groups, or local interests made it difficult to establish them on a nationwide basis with broad popular support. In 1955 two major organizations, successors respectively of prewar Seiyukai and Minseito, merged to form the Liberal Democratic party, which has held a predominant position ever since. In spite of its name the party is conservative, and its continual success reflects the conservative bias of the majority of voters. Deriving support from the business community, old-line bureaucrats, rural constituents—which are overrepresented in the Diet—and civil service officials, it has operated as a coalition of factions without a clear program or well-organized and active membership. In power for two and a half decades, the party became in effect the Japanese Establishment, nourishing the country's expanding economy and maintaining its ties with the United States. Revelation that officials had accepted bribes from Lockheed Corporation shook the party in 1974. The prime minister, Kakuei Tanaka, was forced to resign and later was tried and imprisoned. Bickering and rivalry among factions reached such a point in 1980 that an opposition coalition led by the Socialists won a vote of no confidence in the ministry. Parliament was dissolved for the second time within eight months, but in the election of June 1980 the Liberal Democratic party was returned to power with a comfortable majority. Unpopular government policies, scandals in high places, and even economic recessions have not sufficed to dislodge the LDP, largely because unprecedented material prosperity came about under a succession of conservative administrations.

The principal political opposition has come from the Socialists, who in 1955 won a third of the seats in the lower house of Parliament but were unable to repeat this performance. Groups challenging the dominant party have diverged widely in aims, and opposition parties have been plagued by factional disputes. A small Japanese Communist party, aligned neither with Moscow nor Peking, minimizes radical ideology and attempts to woo the electorate with such innocuous slogans as "Cover drainage ditches" and "Build more day nurseries." At the extreme right the Clean Government party, political arm of a militant Buddhist sect, has appealed primarily to middle- and lower-income groups.

The opposition

To what extent political democracy has taken root in Japan is a matter for debate. The Constitution, organs of government, judicial and electoral processes clearly meet democratic standards. The press is free and of high caliber. At the same time, Japanese political habits and psychology carry overtones of an earlier tradition. The tenacity of local loyalties and personality cults—a preference for government "by men" rather than "by law"—has prevented the rise of national parties with clearly defined policies, or even the development of a national political consciousness. Without presenting a distinctive platform on which to stand or fall the LDP has been able to keep the reins of office by balancing the claims of competing groups. Minorities and opposition parties, in spite of their poor showing at the polls, are not without political input. Their pressure is sometimes reflected in initiatives of the ruling party, which respects the Japanese fondness for reaching a consensus acceptable to all rather than a victory for one contestant.

Extent of democracy

The economic difficulties confronting Japan immediately after its surrender seemed practically insurmountable. Before the close of hostilities almost one-third of the homes in Japan's urban areas were destroyed by air attacks, and the direct economic loss caused by the war was staggering. Japan was shorn of its empire, industrial production had fallen 80 percent below the 1937 level, foreign trade stood at zero, and the country depended upon imports even for foodstuffs. Viewed against this dismal background, Japan's economic recovery and advance have been spectacular. By 1953 the index of production was 50 percent above the level of the mid-1930s, and it continued upward, with textiles, metal goods, and machinery leading the way. During the 1950s economic productivity doubled; in the next decade it overtook that of England, France, and West Germany to become

Japan's spectacular economic recovery and expansion

the third largest in the world. By the late 1970s Japan's gross national product was more than half that of the United States. A remarkable aspect of this economic expansion was that Japan both competed successfully in long-established industries and also pioneered in new fields. It became the world's largest shipbuilder, exported steel, light and heavy machinery, and gained a commanding position in such areas as chemicals, synthetics, optics, electronics, and computer technology. The Japanese outpaced most Western nations in the development of mass transit facilities, especially railways, famous in recent years for their "bullet trains." By the 1980 experiments were under way with magnetically levitated "floating trains," reportedly capable of speeds in excess of 300 miles an hour. Although the farm population declined to about 18 percent of the total, through the application of scientific methods Japan was able to increase agricultural output by 50 percent.

Explanation of Japan's rise to prosperity

Several factors explain Japan's seemingly miraculous rise from a condition of prostration to one of dizzying prosperity. First, in spite of devastating losses from the war, the Japanese retained their technical proficiency, labor force, and traditions of hard work. A determination to recover lost ground and to overtake and surpass the West became a national obsession, eliciting self-sacrifice and mitigating disputes between management and underpaid labor. Employees of large corporations served them with a loyalty like that of the old feudal samurai to his lord. Statistics reporting the growth of the GNP were scanned with the avidity devoted in more leisurely societies to the sports pages. Postwar Japan achieved an extremely high ratio of savings to earnings, in some years amounting to 30 percent. A second factor helping to stimulate recovery was American financial aid, not only during the Occupation but especially by the purchase of goods and services for the Korean conflict. A third factor was the initiative of the government in stimulating and guiding the growth of an essen-

The Mitsubishi Shipyards. A Greek tanker is under construction.

Electronics Industry of Japan. Mass-production lines of television sets at the Matsushita Electrical Industrial Company plant in Ibaragi. Better than 90 percent of Japanese families own television sets. The Japanese electronics industry has also become a major factor in the American market for such products.

tially private-enterprise economy. The government encouraged capital investment by incentive tax and loan policies, operated an Economic Planning Agency to compile data and predict market trends, and through a Ministry of International Trade and Industry took the lead in directing industrial development. The Japanese economic system, combining governmental guidance with private ownership and initiative, has been called the "most successful economic model in the world in recent years."[1] Probably the most important asset of all was—paradoxically—the defeat and elimination of Japan's military establishment, which had systematically drained the country's resources. During a crucial period Japan enjoyed the distinction of being the only great industrial nation operating on a peace economy instead of a war economy. This situation is unlikely to continue indefinitely. Japan's strength in conventional weapons is already greater than it was at the peak of World War II and the country has moved up to seventh rank in military spending. Still, the Defense Agency has never consumed more than 1 percent of the GNP or more than 8 percent of the national budget. In 1969 the government allotted over three times as much to social security, education, and the promotion of science as to defense.

[1] E. O. Reischauer, *The Japanese*, p. 194.

The problems of Japan's changing society

Japanese society has been profoundly affected by the tremendous expansion of the nation's economy. A continual rise in the standard of living—the highest in Asia and approaching that of Western Europe—is illustrated by successive changes reported in the traditional Japanese conception of the "three sacred treasures" desired by every household. The mirror, jewel, and sword of ancient times gave way to the electric refrigerator, washing machine, and television set. By 1970, 90 percent of the families possessed these items, and they aspired to a color TV, "room cooler," and motor car; or even to the luxury of central heating, an electric cooking range, and a vacation cottage. Rising inflation and a decline in the rate of industrial growth that accompanied the world recession of 1974–1976 forced a lowering of expectations and a reassessment of goals. Far from solving all of Japan's problems, prosperity augmented some of them. A staggering rate of population increase, which brought the total to 115 million by 1978, has apparently been successfully halted, as it has in China. But half the inhabitants are concentrated on 2 percent of the land, the bulk of them in an urban belt stretching from Tokyo to Osaka. Tokyo, with nearly 9 million people, became the largest city in the world—until it yielded this dubious honor to Shanghai. Tokyo is still one of the dirtiest, noisiest, and most congested of cities. With population density in urban areas three times as great as in the United States, Japan faces a major problem of air and water pollution. While industrial progress has created large fortunes, it has done little to raise wages in the small shops and home factories that still employ a majority of the working force. Although Japan's GNP is the third largest in the world, the nation ranks only sixteenth in per capita income. Social services have lagged behind the need for better roads, sewers, environmental protection, and housing. Most residents of Tokyo live in tiny two-room apartments. One precarious element in Japan's situation is its dependence on external markets. Japan is the world's largest importer of oil, coal, iron ore, lead, copper, zinc, lumber, wood, cotton, and many other raw materials. It must also import about half of its food, including almost all feed grains, although it has become self-sufficient in rice. The Japanese depend on foreign fuels for 85 percent of their energy supply, 60 percent of which is provided by Persian Gulf oil. The development of nuclear power to the point where, by 1976, Japan ranked fourth in nuclear-produced kilowatts of electricity, has encountered popular resistance because of the hazards involved in this technology. In exploiting solar energy Japan has forged ahead, equipping more than 2 million houses with solar water heaters, in comparison with some 30,000 in the United States.

Japanese society, like politics and the economy, is a blend of innovation and tradition. In income distribution and in providing opportunities for advancement it has become more equalitarian than most societies. The old feudal class structure has disappeared along with

Pollution in Industrial Japan. Kawasaki is a heavily industrialized city in the Tokyo-Yokohama Industrial Zone. The works of numerous heavy and chemical industry companies are located here.

titles of nobility, and pedigrees are no longer important. But to a considerable extent society is still hierarchical, with status dependent not upon birth but upon identification with a group, rank in an organization, or, especially, educational credentials. Japan is one of the most literate and most educated nations in the world, its people benefiting from superior instructional standards in the lower and middle schools. Higher education is expensive and deficient in breadth and flexibility, but a degree from a prestigious institution, especially Tokyo University, is normally a stepping stone to a leadership career in business or politics. The persistence of paternalistic and patriarchal traditions tends to inhibit the development of individuality, while at the same time offering the individual a degree of security lacking in less closely organized societies. For example, although labor is much more fully unionized than in the United States, strikes are rarer. Employees of large firms—comparatively well paid, assured of gradual advancement, often kept on the payroll when no longer needed, or trained for other jobs to keep pace with technological change—develop a sense of identity with and loyalty to the corporate entity. The preservation of social harmony is valued above the attainment of abstract justice, and litigation is infrequent. Japan has only one-fifteenth as many lawyers per capita as the United States. There are unfortunate exceptions to the laudable ideal of equality of opportunity and merit as a determinant of status. About 2 percent of the population, known as *burakumin* or "hamlet people" and possibly a carryover from feudal times, are treated as outcasts. Although physically indistinguishable from other

Innovation blended with tradition

*Japan's economic
ascendancy in Southeast
Asia*

Japanese and equal before the law, they are generally socially ostracized. Another exception to the homogeneity of Japanese society is the failure to assimilate a resident Korean minority of some 600,000.

The position of women in Japan, reflecting the persistence of an antiquated feudal mentality in spite of constitutional and legal changes, constitutes the most glaring failure in the implementation of the democratic ideal. Women have not been accepted in significant numbers in positions of leadership, and they are still exploited economically and in family relationships. In 1972, although 57 percent of all factory workers were women, their average wage was less than half that of male workers. Regarded as temporary employees and forced to retire at an early age, women are not permitted to share in the benefits extended to labor by management. While the claim of one critic that Japanese women "are virtually as fully oppressed as they have been since the victory of the warrior culture in the Kamakura period of the twelfth century" is an exaggeration, it is doubtless true that they "continue as unrecognized and undervalued servants of Japan's prosperity."[2]

Since World War II Japan's foreign policy has been conditioned by two main factors: a struggle for economic recovery and ascendancy, and a close relationship with the United States. Striving to dispel the hostility and distrust remaining as a legacy from its imperialist era, Japan made generous reparations settlements with the small states of Southeast Asia that its armies had overrun, and contributed substantially to various development programs. When the Asian Development Bank was inaugurated in 1966, a Japanese became the first president of this regional organization. Japan's foreign aid, although extensive, has been criticized for being geared more to its own economic needs than to those of the recipient countries. Most of it has been in the form of loans, under terms profitable to Japanese investors and traders. Japan's successful penetration of the market in Indonesia, Malaysia, Singapore, the Philippines, and Thailand aroused resentment throughout Southeast Asia. The image of the "ugly American" gave way to one inspired by Japanese businessmen, bankers, and technicians, disparagingly referred to as "honorary whites" or "Yellow Yankees." But it is doubtful that Japan, through economic superiority, will dominate Southeast Asia completely, partly because the Japanese are sensitive to accusations of neocolonialism and, more importantly, because the Southeast Asian market is not adequate to fulfill their needs. To reap full benefit from their specialized and advanced technology they must have access to high-income areas, such as Australia, western Europe, and North America. In 1965 Japan's share of the Asian market was only 17 percent. It will undoubtedly grow larger, especially as Chinese-Japanese trade

[2]Joan Mellen, *The Waves at Genji's Door: Japan through the Cinema*, p. 27.

increases. Meanwhile the Japanese are seeking other areas for investment and are already active in Latin America.

Japan found it more difficult to reach an understanding with the Soviet Union than with any other of her former enemies. An agreement signed by the two countries in October 1956 restored diplomatic relations and paved the way for Japan's entrance into the United Nations, but it was not a formal treaty of peace. There have been frequent disputes—over Japanese prisoners of war never accounted for by Russia, fishing rights, and Japanese claims in the Kuril Islands, all of which are held by Russia. Russian attempts, beginning in the early 1970s, to enlist Japan's help in developing Siberian reserves of oil and gas have not met with much success.

The American presence continued to be felt in Japan by virtue of the Security Treaty of 1951, which pledged the two countries to mutual consultation and allowed the United States to retain military bases in Japan. Successive Japanese administrations followed Washington's lead in international diplomacy so dutifully that some critics accused the foreign ministry of being "the Asian Department of the United States State Department." Popular resentment provoked riotous demonstrations against renewal of the Security Treaty in 1960 and again in 1970, and escalation of the war in Indochina further intensified anti-American feeling. Friction between Japan and the United States, never severe enough to invalidate the relationship, was alleviated by the return to Japanese sovereignty, in 1968 and 1972 respectively, of the Bonin and the Ryukyu Islands, which had been heavily fortified and used as bomber bases in the Korean and Vietnam wars. The terms of the transfer agreement called for the removal of nuclear weapons but left the United States the right to continue to use the bases.

Automobile Assembly Line, Toyota Motor Company. In 1980 the Japanese automobile industry became the largest in the world.

*Changes in the
relationship*

Significant changes in the semipartnership between the United States and Japan resulted from the latter's growing economic strength, which stimulated dissatisfaction with a condition of dependence. The balance of trade between the two countries shifted in Japan's favor, by 1976 yielding an annual surplus of $5 billion and continuing upward. Moreover, as the islanders gained pre-eminence in specialized and sophisticated technologies, the United States in its trade with them played a "colonial" role, providing grains, lumber, cotton, and other raw materials in exchange for steel, machinery, cameras, watches, electronic components for radio and television, and innumerable other manufactures ranging from pianos to barber chairs. American automobile sales in Japan matched only a small fraction of Japanese car sales in the United States. A continual trade deficit, bringing the prospect of falling profits and rising unemployment, worried United States manufacturers. The president of Zenith Radio Corporation warned that the American consumer-electronics industry faced a threat "every bit as real as the threat of extinction faced by the coyotes, the bald eagles, the seals, the alligators, and the rattlesnakes." While Japanese exports were aided by government subsidies, the main reasons for their success were the innovative initiative of management and the high productivity of Japanese labor.

The "Nixon shock"

President Nixon's announcement in the summer of 1971 of his intention to visit Peking the following year surprised and angered the Japanese. Washington had pressured them into close ties with the Nationalist regime in Taiwan and had stressed the necessity of joint action in dealing with mainland China, yet had not consulted with nor informed them in advance of the United States' dramatic reversal of policy. Beyond suffering a temporary loss of face, the Japanese now felt impelled to mend their own diplomatic fences. In September 1972 Prime Minister Tanaka made his pilgrimage to a summit meeting in Peking, offered an apology to the Chinese people for Japan's past misconduct, and—in advance of the United States—established full diplomatic relations between Japan and the People's Republic of China. The Chou-Tanaka joint statement issued in Peking was a masterpiece of diplomatic finesse and graceful ambiguity which laid a basis for "peace and friendship" without a formal peace treaty and with important issues left unresolved. Japan recognized that Taiwan "ought to" belong to China, withdrew its ambassador from Taipei, but replaced its embassy there with unofficial liaison offices which effectively served the same purposes. (The United States adopted a similar procedure half a dozen years later.)

*The "oil shock" and its
consequences*

Japan's foreign relations have inevitably been affected by the recurring crises of the 1970s. Closely following the "Nixon shock" was the "oil shock" of 1974, the quadrupling of oil prices by OPEC. It struck no nation more severely than Japan, totally dependent on outside sources for this essential commodity. The recession following the oil crisis slowed the economic growth rate, brought the threat of unemployment—negligible heretofore—and caused the Japanese to re-examine national priorities and to question whether the "miracle of Japan" was reality or illusion. A factor hampering economic recovery was, ironically, the strength of the yen in comparison with the dollar and other depreciating Western currencies. The yen's high valuation made goods produced in Japan expensive (although products were exported at lower than the domestic prices), and the Japanese found they were being undersold by such Asian competitors as South Korea, Taiwan, and Hong Kong. Many small firms were forced out of business; in 1977 more than 18,000 bankruptcies were reported in Japan. To alleviate the situation the government promised to spend more on public works and, to help reduce huge trade surpluses with the United States and western Europe, sought to expand the market for exports and investments in less developed areas. In February 1978 Japan signed a $20-billion eight-year trade agreement with China, followed six months later by a formal peace treaty with the People's Republic.

In seeking new economic opportunities the Japanese have also been mindful of political and strategic factors, realizing that a major conflict in the Far East would place them in grave jeopardy. The nation that for centuries remained in almost complete isolation is today one of the least isolated, dependent for its survival upon reciprocal relations with many other countries. The Japanese have stepped warily around the Peking-Moscow confrontation, and they sense the danger, uncomfortably close, of eruption in a bitterly divided Korea—especially since neither of the two divisions exhibits friendly feelings toward Japan. Paralleling an active economic role in Southeast Asia, Japan has attempted to strengthen diplomatic ties there. In 1977 Prime Minister Fukuda strongly endorsed ASEAN (Association of Southeast Asian Nations, comprising the Philippines, Indonesia, Singapore, Malaysia, and Thailand) and announced a program of $1 billion to support regional projects. Premier Zenko Suzuki, for his first trip abroad after taking office in the fall of 1980, chose a tour of ASEAN capitals rather then the customary courtesy visit to Washington, D.C. Russian attempts either to woo Japan into partnership or to keep the nation isolated have failed. While cultivating relations both with China and with non-Communist Asian countries, Japan has remained within the United States defense system. Even the opposition parties in Japan no longer denounce the Security Treaty of 1951. There is pressure from the United States and from elements within Japan to convert the Defense Agency into a force with offensive capability. In 1978 the Japanese foreign minister asserted that defensive *nuclear* weapons were not prohibited by Article 9 of the Constitution. However, a drive to rearm Japan or take it down the nuclear road would meet with resistance because of the strong antimilitarist sentiment of a majority of the Japanese people.

From isolation to interdependence

SELECTED READINGS (*See also Readings for Chapters 23 and 32*)

• *Items so designated are available in paperback editions.*

CHINA

• Barnett, A. Doak, *China and the Major Powers in East Asia,* Washington, D.C., 1977. A careful study of recent international relations.

Bianco, Lucien, *Origins of the Chinese Revolution, 1915–1949,* tr. Muriel Bell, Stanford, 1971. A brilliant interpretive summary.

Brugger, Bill, *Contemporary China,* New York, 1977. An impressive historical interpretation of the period 1942–1973.

• Ch'en, Jerome, *Mao and the Chinese Revolution,* New York, 1965.

• Clubb, O. E., *Twentieth-Century China,* 3d ed., New York, 1978. One of the best surveys of recent Chinese history.

Davies, J. P., Jr., *Dragon by the Tail: American, British, Japanese, and Russian Encounters with China and One Another,* New York, 1972. An American diplomat's jolting account of bungling and intrigue.

De Crespigny, R. R. C., *China This Century,* New York, 1975. A concise introduction.

Dulles, F. R., *American Policy toward Communist China—the Historical Record: 1949–1969,* New York, 1972.

Fisher, Lois, *A Peking Diary: A Personal Account of Modern China,* New York, 1979. Intimate glimpses of lives of the common people.

• Floyd, David, *Mao against Khrushchev: A Short History of the Sino-Soviet Conflict,* New York, 1964. A readable account.

Gittings, John, *The World and China, 1922–1972,* New York, 1974. Informative for Sino-Soviet relations.

• Griffith, W. E., *The Sino-Soviet Rift,* Cambridge, Mass., 1964. An analysis with pertinent documents.

• Hinton, H. C., *China's Turbulent Quest: An Analysis of China's Foreign Relations since 1949,* Bloomington, Ind., 1972. Accurate; coldly objective.

Hsiung, J. C., *Ideology and Practice: The Evolution of Chinese Communism,* New York, 1970. Valuable for an understanding of the Cultural Revolution.

• Isaacs, H. R., *The Tragedy of the Chinese Revolution,* Stanford, 1964.

• Larkin, B. D., *China and Africa, 1949–1970: The Foreign Policy of the People's Republic of China,* Berkeley, 1973.

• Milton, David, and Nancy Milton, *The Wind Will Not Subside: Years in Revolutionary China—1964–1969.* New York, 1976. Vivid account of the Cultural Revolution.

Selden, Mark, *The Yenan Way in Revolutionary China,* Cambridge, Mass., 1971. Scholarly treatment of the "Border Region," 1935–1947.

• Shabad, Theodore, *China's Changing Map: National and Regional Development, 1949–71,* rev. ed., New York, 1972. A valuable reference work.

Sharmon, Lyon, *Sun Yat-sen: His Life and Its Meaning,* New York, 1934. A critical biography.

• Snow, Edgar, *Red Star over China,* New York, 1938. A classic account of the Communists' early years of struggle.

- Terrill, Ross, *800,000,000: The Real China*, New York, 1972. A vivid and discriminating account by an Australian journalist-scholar.
- Topping, Seymour, *Journey between Two Chinas*, New York, 1972. An able narrative of the Communist Revolution.
- Tuchman, Barbara, *Stilwell and the American Experience in China, 1911–1945*, New York, 1972.
- Waller, D. J., *The Government and Politics of Communist China*, Garden City, N.Y., 1971. Concise and informative.
- Wang Gungwu, *China and the World since 1949; The Impact of Independence, Modernity, and Revolution*, New York, 1977. An able, brief survey.
   Wilbur, C. M., *Sun Yat-sen: Frustrated Patriot*, New York, 1976. Provides fresh insights.
   Wilson, Dick, *The Long March: The Epic of Chinese Communist Survival*, New York, 1971.
   ———, ed., *Mao Tse-tung in the Scales of History*, New York, 1977. Ten essays of high quality.
   Zupnick, Elliot, *China's Economic Development: The Interplay of Scarcity and Ideology*, Ann Arbor, 1976. A penetrating study.

JAPAN

   Allen, G. C., *Japan's Economic Expansion*, New York, 1965.
   Axelbank, Albert, *Black Star over Japan: Rising Forces of Militarism*, New York, 1972. An alarming prognosis.
- Benedict, Ruth, *The Chrysanthemum and the Sword*, New York, 1967. A classic analysis of prewar Japanese society.
   Blaker, Michael, *Japanese International Negotiating Style*, New York, 1977. A study of diplomacy between 1895 and Pearl Harbor.
   Brzezinski, Z. K., *The Fragile Blossom: Crisis and Change in Japan*, New York, 1972. An analysis of Japan's economic, political, and strategic position.
   Buck, Pearl, *The People of Japan*, New York, 1966. A personal account.
- Burks, A. W., *The Government of Japan*, 2d ed., New York, 1964.
   Butow, R. J. C., *Japan's Decision to Surrender*, Stanford, 1954.
   ———, *Tojo and the Coming of the War*, Princeton, 1961.
   Emmerson, J. K., *Arms, Yen and Power: The Japanese Dilemma*, New York, 1971. Balanced, informative, optimistic.
- Ishida Takeshi, *Japanese Society*, New York, 1971.
   Kawai Kazuo, *Japan's American Interlude*, Chicago, 1960.
- Maki, J. M., *Government and Politics in Japan: The Road to Democracy*, New York, 1962.
- Mellen, Joan, *The Waves at Genji's Door: Japan through the Cinema*, New York, 1976. Provides a feminist critique of Japanese character and society.
   Minear, R. H., *Victors' Justice: The Tokyo War Crimes Trial*, Princeton, 1972. Challenges the moral and legal validity of the trials.
   Morris, Ivan, *Nationalism and the Right Wing in Japan: A Study of Post-War Trends*, London, 1960. A clear and forceful study.
- Nakane Chie, *Japanese Society*, Berkeley, 1972. A social anthropologist's analysis.

Packard, G. R., *Protest in Tokyo: The Security Treaty Crisis of 1960,* Princeton, 1966.

• Reischauer, E. O., *The Japanese,* Cambridge, Mass., 1977. A highly informative survey by an eminent scholar.

———, *The United States and Japan,* 3d ed., New York, 1965.

Thayer, N. B., *How the Conservatives Rule Japan,* Princeton, 1969.

Tsuneishi, W. M., *Japanese Political Style: An Introduction to the Government and Politics of Modern Japan,* New York, 1966. An excellent brief study.

• Van Alstyne, Richard W., *The United States and East Asia,* New York, 1973.

Vogel, E. F., *Japan As Number One: Lessons for America,* Cambridge, Mass., 1979.

Yanaga Chitoshi, *Big Business in Japanese Politics,* New Haven, 1968.

SOURCE MATERIALS

• Brandt, C., B. F. Schwartz, and J. K. Fairbank, *A Documentary History of Chinese Communism,* London, 1952.

• Chai, Winberg, ed., *The Essential Works of Chinese Communism,* New York, 1969.

Chiang Kai-shek, *China's Destiny,* New York, 1947.

• de Bary, W. T., ed., *Sources of Chinese Tradition,* Chaps. XXVII, XXVIII, XXIX, New York, 1960.

• ———, ed., *Sources of Japanese Tradition,* Chaps. XXVI, XXVII, XXVIII, XXIX, New York, 1958.

Grew, Ambassador Joseph C., *Ten Years in Japan,* New York, 1944.

• Lin, N. T., tr., *In Quest: Poems of Chou En-lai,* Cambridge, Mass., 1979.

• Minear, R. H., ed., *Through Japanese Eyes,* 2 vols., New York, 1974. Selections from the period of the Pacific War to the 1970s.

• Schram, Stuart, ed., *Chairman Mao Talks to the People: Talks and Letters, 1956–1971,* New York, 1975.

• Starr, J. B., *Continuing the Revolution: The Political Thought of Mao,* Princeton, 1979.

Chapter 40

NEW POWER RELATIONSHIPS

Africa, all I ask from you is the courage to know: to look about you and
see what is happening in this old and tired world; to realize the extent and
depth of its rebirth and the promise which glows on your hills.

—W. E. B. Du Bois, *Autobiography*

Put any economist in the capital of an underdeveloped country and give
him a few assistants, and he will in no time produce a plan.

—Gunnar Myrdal, *Against the Stream*

W orld War II left the political world of Europe, Asia, and the
United States in a state of disorder. As victory approached,
wartime allies began to mistrust each other and to protect
themselves against those whom they now perceived as prospective
rivals. In addition, the war spawned nationalist revolts throughout the
world. Many of these struggles were attempts by colonies to gain independence. Although these wars were often no more than local, they
threatened to lead to major conflict and, because of the increasing proliferation of nuclear weapons, to general holocaust. This threat, if it
did not reduce tensions, may in fact have operated to prevent nations
from pursuing their interests to the point of no return.

Tensions in the postwar world

1. SOVIET-AMERICAN WORLD RIVALRY

As a result of the Second World War, world power relationships were
drastically altered. Germany, Italy, and Japan had been defeated so
overwhelmingly that they seemed for a time destined to play a subordinate role in world affairs. Officially, the list of great powers included five states—the Soviet Union, the United States, Great Britain,
France, and the Republic of China. These were the Big Five that, as
the war ended, seemed fated to rule the world. China was soon over-

Changing power relationships

whelmed by a communist revolution, however, while Britain and France became increasingly dependent upon the United States. As a consequence, the world of nations, during the ten years after 1945, took on a bipolar character, with the United States and the Soviet Union contesting for supremacy and striving to draw the remaining states into their orbits.

The United States after World War II

From the standpoint of economic power, the United States had far outdistanced the rest of the nations. Since 1939 Americans had doubled their national income and quadrupled their savings. Though they constituted only 7 percent of the world's population, they enjoyed over 30 percent of the world's estimated income. For the first time in its history the United States was in a position to be the arbiter of the destinies of at least half the earth. Japan was virtually its colony; the U.S. controlled both the Atlantic and Pacific Oceans, policed the Mediterranean, and shaped the development of international policy in western Europe. Until 1949, America had a monopoly of death-dealing atomic weapons. When the Soviet Union cracked this monopoly U.S. policy-makers remained convinced that their assumption of superior strength was still valid. All that was now necessary was to add new and more deadly weapons, thereby making sure that no rival could successfully challenge the United States.

Russia's strengths and weaknesses

Soviet Russia emerged from World War II as the second strongest power on earth. Though its navy was small, its land army and possibly its air force by 1948 were the largest in the world. Soviet population was climbing rapidly toward 200 million and this in spite of the loss of 7 million soldiers and about 8 million civilians during the war. In mineral wealth Russia's position compared favorably with that of the richest countries. After 1946 it claimed a large percentage of the world supply of petroleum. On the other hand, there can be no doubt that its industrial machine had been badly crippled by the war. No fewer than 1700 Russian cities and towns had been totally destroyed and about 40,000 miles of railway and 31,000 factories. Stalin declared in 1946 that it would probably require at least six years to repair the damage and rebuild the devastated areas.

Russia in eastern Europe

It seems reasonable to suppose that much of the hostility displayed by the USSR in its dealings with other nations during the years after 1945 was attributable in some measure to the losses sustained during the war. Resentful of the fact that they had been compelled to make such sacrifices, the Soviets became obsessed with security as a goal that must be attained regardless of the cost to their neighbors. Fearful that poverty and hardship might make their own people rebellious, Russia's rulers encouraged their people to think that their country was in imminent danger of attack by capitalist powers. Following the end of the war, the Russians were determined to maintain the influence their military advance had secured for them in eastern Europe. Building on the agreements reached at Yalta, the Soviet

Union remained as an occupying force throughout that area, working meanwhile to establish "people's republics" sympathetic to the Soviet regime. By 1948, governments which owed allegiance to Moscow were established in Poland, Hungary, Rumania, Bulgaria, and Czechoslovakia. Albania and Yugoslavia, liberated by their own anti-Nazi forces, were not directly linked to Russia as satellites, although the governments of those two countries were also communist. The nations of eastern Europe did not succumb without a struggle. Greece, which the Russians wished to include within their sphere of influence, was torn by civil war until 1949, when with Western aid its monarchy was restored. Perhaps the most direct challenge to the Yalta guarantee of free, democratic elections occured in Czechoslovakia, where in 1948 the Soviets crushed the coalition government of liberal leaders Eduard Beneš and Jan Masaryk.

The United States countered these aggressive moves with massive programs of economic and military aid to western Europe. In 1947, President Truman proclaimed the so-called Truman Doctrine, which provided assistance programs to prevent further communist infiltration into the governments of Greece and Turkey. The following year, the Marshall Plan, named for Secretary of State George Marshall who first proposed it, provided funds for the reconstruction of western European industry. The plan was notable in two respects: first, it represented an attempt by the United States to restore the strength of its most serious economic competitors, and of its former enemy Germany, under the notion that an economically independent Europe would be less likely to fall prey to Soviet domination. Second, it relied upon a willingness on the part of the western European nations to coordinate their economic efforts, substituting, at least to some degree, cooperation for competition.

The Marshall Plan

At the same time, the U.S. moved to shore up the military defenses of the West. In April 1949, a group of representatives of North Atlantic states together with Canada and the United States signed an agreement providing for the establishment of the North Atlantic Treaty Organization (NATO). Subsequently Greece, Turkey, and West Germany were added as members. The treaty declared that an armed attack against any one of the signatory parties would be regarded as an attack against all, and that they would combine their armed strength to whatever extent necessary to repel the aggressor. It was decided also that the joint military command, or NATO army established in 1950, should be increased from thirty to fifty divisions in 1953, and that West Germany should be rearmed and invited to contribute twelve of the divisions. It was thereby hoped that NATO would be ready for an emergency that might arise as a consequence of the expansionist policies of Soviet Russia.

NATO

The Russians reacted with understandable alarm to the apparent determination of the United States to strengthen western Europe eco-

Crises in Berlin. Left: The Berlin Airlift, 1948. For fifteen months the United States, Britain, and France airlifted over two million tons of supplies into West Berlin, around which the Russians had imposed a land blockade. Right: The Berlin Wall, 1961. Thirteen years after the blockade, the East German government constructed a wall between East and West Berlin to stop the flow of escapees to the West.

The Berlin Blockade

nomically and militarily. They were particularly concerned when U.S. money began to flow into those areas of western Germany occupied by British, French, and U.S. forces. In 1946, the joint administration of Germany by the four powers collapsed. Russia remained in control of its satellite, which eventually became the nominally independent German Democratic Republic (East Germany), while the Western powers continued to support the industrial recovery of that area under their control—in its turn to emerge as the Federal Republic of Germany (West Germany). A crisis arose in 1948 when, in retaliation for the reunification of the western zones of control under one authority, the Russians closed down road and rail access from the west to Berlin. Berlin, though within the territory of East Germany, was administered by all four powers. The Western powers countered with an airlift of food and other necessary supplies which prevented the collapse of the city into Soviet hands. After almost a year the Russians lifted the blockade. For many years to come, however, Berlin was to remain one of the hottest spots in the ongoing "Cold War," as it came to be called, between Russia and the West.

The Korean war

The most serious armed clash of the immediate postwar period was the Korean war of 1950–1953. At the end of World War II it had been agreed that Korea, under Japanese rule since 1910, was to become an independent and united country. The United States and the Soviet Union left occupying forces there until 1949, however, the Americans south of the thirty-eighth parallel, the Russians to the north of it. During this period of occupation, the Soviets refused to cooperate with the United Nations–sponsored plan to hold free elections for the entire country. Instead, they established in the north a people's republic similar to those they had erected in eastern Europe. In June 1950, troops from this republic crossed the thirty-eighth parallel and invaded the south. Taking advantage of a temporary Russian boycott of the United Nations, the United States was able to avoid a Soviet veto of its plan to counter this invasion by sending a contingent of troops to oppose it. The troops, though nominally under United Nations command, were largely American, directed and supplied by the United States. Initial military gains by this force were countered in November by the invasion into Korea of troops from the newly established People's Republic of China, sent into the peninsula after General Douglas las MacArthur had, without authorization, advanced to the Chinese border. A stalemate ensued, President Truman and his advisers being as unwilling to widen the conflict into China as they were to abandon their South Korean allies. After two years of military and diplomatic deadlock, a peace settlement was concluded, recognizing the existence of both North and South Korea.

The Korean conflict, unprecedented in its savagery, revealed the disastrous effects of letting superpower rivalry erupt into open conflict. By the second year of the war, half of South Korea's population had been driven from their homes. After military targets were exhausted without bringing the enemy to its knees, American bombing planes systematically destroyed mines, factories, power plants, and irrigation dams. Casualties of military personnel and civilians numbered 6 million; one third of South Korea's surviving population was left destitute. The war adversely affected relationships between the United States and the nations of the Far East. While Japan had welcomed American intervention as a sign of its determination to halt the spread of communism, other countries had looked on America's role with suspicion. The United States claimed to be acting in accordance with United Nations principles. Powers such as India, Burma, and Indonesia, however, saw the war as a neocolonialist intrusion by America on behalf of its client state, South Korea. China's determination to understand the war in this light contributed greatly to the deep hostility that characterized Sino-American relations during the next twenty years.

The tensions between the United States and Russia eased somewhat during the late 1950s and 1960s. America, it is true, continued to adhere to a policy of Soviet "containment," seeking as allies those most willing to oppose by military force, if necessary, the spread of international communism. And Russia was never afraid to risk Western military reaction when suppressing revolts within the countries of its satellite allies. Yet the period has not incorrectly been labeled one of

Effects of the Korean war

The "thaw"

Nikita Khrushchev

Continued tensions

"thaw." A change in direction was signaled by the death of Stalin in 1953 and the accession to power after a brief interregnum of Nikita Khrushchev (1894–1971) in 1955. Khrushchev created the impression that the Soviet Union was prepared to pursue a new diplomatic line: for example, he denounced Stalinist tyranny and continued the program of destalinization begun after Stalin's death. In addition, he and his colleagues announced their approval of the doctrine of "more than one road to socialism." In accordance with this new attitude, the Russians concluded peace with Austria and withdrew their occupying troops. In 1955 they agreed to a "conference at the summit" with the chiefs of government of Great Britain, France, the United States, and the USSR as the participants.

This change in policy was undoubtedly prompted in part by discontent within the country. The Russian people had no desire for another war, and were weary of the restrictions and rigidities imposed by the Stalin regime. They believed that the time had come for less emphasis on expanding the production of heavy industry and armaments and more on providing the amenities of life. This switch in emphasis would mean a lessening of the Soviet role as overlord of the socialist world. Khrushchev was disposed to sympathize with the demands of the Russian people. The new policy, however, soon ran into trouble. The first sign of change was the Soviet suppression of revolts in Poland and Hungary in 1956. The Poles escaped serious repressions when they promised to remain within the Soviet orbit in return for permission to make various modifications in their socialist system. The Hungarians, however, were repressed with bloody violence when they attempted not merely to change the economic system but to break all ties with the Soviet Union.

At the beginning of another "summit" conference in Paris in May 1960 with President Dwight D. Eisenhower (1890–1969), Premier Khrushchev erupted violently when he learned that the Russians had shot down an American high-altitude reconaissance plane far over Soviet territory, whose mission was to discover the location of bases and other military installations. Though at first Washington officials denied these flights, they later admitted them and sought to justify them as necessary for the military security of the United States. The summit conference terminated immediately, with nothing but a poisoned atmosphere to mark its effects, despite the subsequent suspension of these flights. Yet Khrushchev was not ready to completely abandon his policy of conciliation. Later in 1960 he enunciated his principle of "peaceful coexistence." Though he did not renounce the ultimate triumph of communism, insisting that "we will bury you," he refused to admit that this triumph must be accomplished by force of arms.

With respect to Germany, Soviet leaders remained unyielding. They nurtured the fear that Germany might launch a new war, aided and abetted by its capitalist allies. For this reason they staunchly op-

Revolt in Hungary. By 1956 discontent with Soviet domination manifested itself in several of the satellite states. Violent revolt broke out in Poland and Hungary. Left: The photograph indicates the extent of the violence in Budapest. Right: A group of Hungarian freedom fighters.

posed unification of the country and insisted upon recognizing East Germany as one of their satellites. In 1961 the East German government built a high wall separating the two sectors of Berlin, in order to cut off the escape of thousands of East Germans to West Berlin and thence to western Germany. Many did make their escape, but the wall remained as a symbol of Soviet determination to prevent the formation of a united Germany. Khrushchev eventually fell prey to political rivals and was deposed in 1964, reduced to the level of a "non-person." The reins of power passed into the hands of a joint dictatorship of Aleksei Kosygin as premier and Leonid Brezhnev as secretary of the Communist party. The government did not return to Stalinist policy, but some of the new trends moved noticeably in that direction. A cardinal example was the occupation of Czechoslovakia in 1968. The Soviet dictators accused the Czechs of flirtation with West Germany to such an extent as to threaten the Soviet system and weaken its ties over eastern Europe. In particular, they resented the economic and social privileges allowed by the Czech government to its own citizens. Accordingly, they sent in armored troops and puppet rulers to take over the country. They followed this action by issuance of the Brezhnev Doctrine, which asserted the right of Moscow to interfere in the affairs of any satellite that strayed from the path of Soviet leadership.

The Berlin Wall

During the 1970s, the Soviets showed, by their intervention in the affairs of newly emerging nations of the so-called Third World—Africa, Asia, and Latin America—that they remained vitally interested in extending their sphere of influence wherever they could. At the same time, they continued to adhere to a policy which allowed for a further easing of tensions, a policy pursued with some enthusiasm, as well, by American diplomats. Henry Kissinger, secretary of state under Presidents Richard Nixon and Gerald Ford in the 1970s, proclaimed détente with the Russians as his goal, and devoted much time to

Arms limitation

The Occupation of Czechoslovakia. In 1968 the liberalized regime of Alexander Dubček was suppressed by the Soviets. The violent response by the citizens was put down by military force.

negotiations aimed at defusing potentially explosive areas of conflict between the two nations. Both countries were particularly concerned to curb the spread of nuclear weapons and to limit, if possible, the apparently endless expansion of their own arsenals. The Strategic Arms Limitation Treaty (SALT) talks, in which the Russians and Americans engaged during the 1970s, were an indication of mutual willingness to recognize and tackle a problem of awesome dimensions, even if their initial attempts to solve that problem resulted in at least temporary stalemate.

The European Common Market

Meanwhile, developments in Europe assisted in altering the balance of power and hence the nature of the international rivalry between the United States and Russia. European economic recovery led in 1958 to the establishment of a Common Market, or tariff union. By the mid-1970s, most of the major western European nations, including Britain, France, and West Germany, were members. Although the market was by no means the equivalent of a United States of Europe, its formation and continuing operation declared the existence of a new and important power bloc which, while more generally sympathetic to U.S. than to Soviet aims, nevertheless was determined to speak with a voice of its own.

2. IMPERIAL DECLINE AND THE EMERGENCE OF THE THIRD WORLD

The Third World

Probably more significant in the long run than U.S.-Soviet rivalry in the postwar period has been the decline of the Western imperial powers and the concurrent emergence of the Third World. Many of these countries have established themselves in territories which were formerly part of European empires. Others—China and the various nations of the Middle East, for example—while nominally independent of the West before 1945, nevertheless existed under European hegemony and were forced to acquiesce to European demands. Such is the case no longer. Although most of these so-called emerging nations are poor, and although the people of the Third World are by no means a united bloc, they represent a new and increasingly independent factor in the world power equation.

Some of these countries are rich in natural resources. Nations in the Middle East, Venezuela in South America, and Nigeria in Africa, possess oil in quantities sufficient to make their every move of vital importance to the West. Other African nations, Zaire and Angola, for example, are immensely rich in many mineral resources. Population is both a liability and an asset in the Third World. The people of China, by their sheer numbers, constitute an implicit threat to the balance of power at all times. The people of India, again by their sheer numbers, and lack of food, represent a perpetual threat to the stability of their own country and hence to all Asia. Every area in the Third World is a potential "trouble spot." This is so not only because the problems of racism, poverty, hunger, and overpopulation make them particularly vulnerable to violent civil conflicts. It is so, as well, because the superpowers, the United States and Russia—and lesser powers, including European nations and China—engage each other through the medium of Third World adversaries, thus increasing the possibility of conflict by their willingness to encourage it. To protect themselves from direct confrontation with each other, these developed nations interfere in the civil wars of others, on opposite sides and with an intensity that frequently belies their declared interest in avoiding general world war.

Relations with the West

The most radical change affecting both the Third World and established power relationships was the Chinese Revolution, described in the preceding chapter. Of comparable importance was the emergence of independent states in the Indian subcontinent, revolutionary upheavals in the Middle East, and the rise of black Africa (discussed in Chapters 37 and 38, respectively). Great Britain, having surrendered India and Burma, was further constrained to give up most of the remaining portions of its empire. Over a period of years Britain liberated Ceylon, Malaysia, Mauritius, Fiji, Singapore, and Nauru, among others, together with the Caribbean colonies of Guyana, Trinidad and Tobago, Jamaica, and Antigua, and significant territories in sub-Saharan Africa as well. The years following World War II also witnessed the liquidation of Dutch and French colonial empires in Southeast Asia.

Liquidation of empires

Indonesia, known for more than two centuries as the Netherlands Indies, was the most valuable jewel of the Dutch imperial crown. Indeed, it was one of the richest countries in the world in natural resources. When Japan extended its aggressions to Southeast Asia in 1941, the empire of the Dutch was a prize conquest. But toward the

Indonesian independence

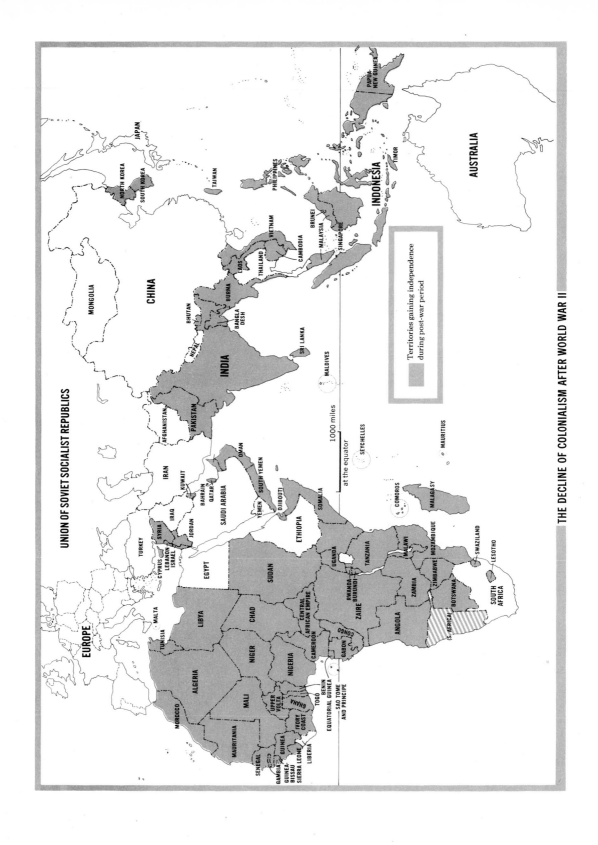

THE DECLINE OF COLONIALISM AFTER WORLD WAR II

Territories gaining independence during post-war period

end of the war, nationalists, under the leadership of Achmed Sukarno, a one-time architect and flamboyant politician, rebelled and proclaimed an independent republic. Although the Dutch attempted for four years to regain their sovereignty, the opposition of the indigenous population proved too strong. In 1949 the kingdom of the Netherlands recognized the independence of its former colony.

*Developments in
Indonesia*

Under the colorful but erratic President Sukarno, the Republic of Indonesia assumed an aggressive role in Asian politics, but his reckless policies brought both economic disaster and internal discord. With encouragement from China, and to some extent from Sukarno, communist influence increased, and the Indonesian Communist party for a few years was the third largest in the world. An abortive coup in September 1965, attributed to the Communists, led to the imposition of a military regime which stripped Sukarno of his power. The Indonesian Communist party was shattered but at the price of a reign of terror lasting several months and a bloodbath that took the lives of at least half a million people. General Suharto, who replaced Sukarno as president, projected an ambitious program of industrial development for Indonesia, while maintaining a rigid dictatorship, stifling dissent, and incarcerating thousands of political prisoners. The nation of 130 million, fifth largest in the world, is among the poorest, with a per capita income of about $130 a year. But the sprawling republic has the potential to become highly prosperous. It has attained a favorable balance of trade, owing to the strong demand for its exports—petroleum, timber, rubber, palm oil, tin, and coffee.

Ho Chi Minh

France after World War II faced almost simultaneous revolts in two of its richest colonies, Algeria and Indochina. Indochina had been a casualty of Japanese conquests, and after the defeat of Japan in 1945 France sought to recover its lost empire in the Far East. These efforts ended in failure, however. The French were immediately confronted by a rebellion of Vietnamese nationalists under the leadership of Ho Chi Minh (1890–1969). The rebels resorted to guerrilla warfare and inflicted such costly defeats upon the French that the latter decided to abandon the struggle. An agreement was signed at Geneva in 1954 providing for the division of Vietnam into two zones, pending elections to determine the future government of the entire country. Ho Chi Minh became president of North Vietnam and established his capital at Hanoi. His followers, who came to be called Viet Cong, were numerous in both halves of the country. Had elections been held as provided by the Geneva Agreement, Ho Chi Minh would probably have been elected president of all of Vietnam. But the government of South Vietnam, backed by the United States, refused to permit elections to be held.

The war in Vietnam

From this point on, involvement by the United States in the Vietnamese civil war steadily increased. President Kennedy was convinced that the Chinese Communist juggernaut would soon roll over all of Southeast Asia. The first victims would be Vietnam, Laos, Cambodia,

*Kennedy's intrusion into
Vietnam*

Malaysia, and Singapore. Then would come Thailand, Burma, and India. How far Kennedy would have gone in his crusade against communism had he escaped assassination in 1963 is impossible to say with certainty. Kennedy's successor, Lyndon B. Johnson (1908–1973), hoped that a relatively small force of perhaps 100,000 men would be sufficient to defeat the Viet Cong and drive them back into their own country. Little consideration was given to the fact that these forces were solidly entrenched in both states of Vietnam, and that they had been waging a bitter national struggle for upwards of eighteen years. They had succeeded in driving out the French in 1954 and were not likely to surrender to a new invader, as they conceived the Americans to be. The Viet Cong and the North Vietnam regulars, though less well-equipped, nevertheless fought the South Vietnamese and their American allies to a standstill on several occasions. During the Tet offensive of 1968 they came close to capturing Saigon, the South Vietnamese capital.

President Johnson escalates the war

Exasperated by failure to win an easy victory in South Vietnam, the American civilian and military chiefs determined upon aerial bombing. A series of incidents in 1964 provided the justification. Reports, of doubtful veracity, indicated that North Vietnamese ships had attacked American naval vessels in the Tonkin Gulf. President Johnson pronounced these incidents acts of war and immediately obtained from Congress authorization to use whatever measures necessary to repel communist aggression. Soon afterward American bombers unloaded their first cargoes upon towns and villages occupied by the North Vietnamese and the Viet Cong. Although evidence accumulated which cast doubt on the efficacy of these raids, they continued to be used. It has been estimated that the total American bomb tonnage dropped on Indochina (an area about the size of Texas) was more than three times as much as the United States dropped on enemy territory during all of World War II. In a single year (1974) the 250,000 tons of bombs dropped on tiny Cambodia exceeded the total expended on

War in Vietnam. Confronted with a new kind of warfare, the American military sought to adapt its methods to the Vietnamese situation.

Japan before Hiroshima. Still the deadly onslaught continued. The only answer of those responsible for strategy in Washington and Saigon seemed to be "Cover up the failure by escalating the war." As the struggle entered its fifth year, with no end in sight, disillusionment spread throughout the United States. Criticism of President Johnson was so harsh in 1968 that he was forced to abandon his plans to run for a second term.

Johnson's successor, Richard M. Nixon, was elected on the strength of promises to end the war. But this turned out to be a shadowy promise. While ground troops were being withdrawn from Vietnam, in May 1970, the United States invaded Cambodia and a few months later the kingdom of Laos. In April 1972, the North Vietnamese, with massive aid from Russia and China, launched a powerful counteroffensive with the apparent objective of conquering South Vietnam and driving all foreign armies out of the country. A number of South Vietnamese strongholds were captured and the offensive seemed more dangerous than the famous Tet offensive of 1968. Nixon countered with increased bombing of North Vietnam's factories and railroads and by mining its harbors, including savage raids while negotiations were under way in December 1972. A cease-fire, early in 1973, did no more than postpone the inevitable. Two years later, South Vietnam fell to the Viet Cong and the North Vietnamese. The massive intervention had proved a ghastly failure.

The Nixon policies

A focal point in a global power struggle, Indochina remained the most distressed area in all of Southeast Asia. The Vietnam War foreshadowed the possibility of the total annihilation of a country by the technology of modern warfare. In South Vietnam alone, besides those killed and wounded, at least 8 million people were turned into homeless refugees. Crops had been destroyed and farmlands ravaged. Exposure to the highly toxic defoliant, Agent Orange—sprayed on forests over a nine-year period—may have inflicted permanent genetic damage upon human survivors. One casualty of the Indochina conflict was the downfall of Prince Norodom Sihanouk's government in Cambodia, which in the midst of conflict had managed to remain neutral. Under pressure from both sides, Sihanouk succeeded in holding communist influence to a minimum, until he was ousted by a military coup in 1970 and replaced by Marshal Lon Nol. Although supported by the United States, Lon Nol was so corrupt and incompetent that he reduced his country to a shambles and soon lost three-fourths of it to the Communists.

Disastrous effects of the war in Indochina

The aftermath of the Indochina war bore little resemblance to what either United States planners or their revolutionary adversaries had intended. Expulsion of the foreign invaders led not to peace, but to desperate internal struggles and renewed warfare. In Cambodia the Communist Khmer Rouge, which had overthrown Lon Nol's regime, proclaimed the new state of Kampuchea in January 1976 and instituted a reign of terror that came close to a policy of genocide. The

Prince Norodom Sihanouk of Cambodia

paranoid leader Pol Pot, in his determination to create an agrarian society more radically equalitarian than that of China, liquidated bourgeoisie and intellectuals and forced entire city populations to move to the country. Khmer Rouge zealots abolished currency, private property, and private households, and were responsible for the death of some 2 million Cambodians. The Communist rulers of the Socialist Republic of Vietnam (SRV), whose forces had borne the brunt of the fighting, appeared more conciliatory than the fanatics of Kampuchea and placed a high priority on rebuilding Vietnam's economy. The task of reconstruction was staggering, with industry destroyed, per capita annual income only $150 and declining, and foreign aid not readily forthcoming.

Regional antagonisms and realignments

The conflicts in Indochina of the late 1970s and beyond, although aggravated by great power rivalry, stemmed basically from the resurgence of centuries-old ethnic and national rivalries that had been temporarily suppressed by the common effort against French and American imperialism. Both Thailand and Vietnam aspired to dominance in the area, forcing the smaller states of Laos and Cambodia to serve as pawns or buffers between them. A Communist regime installed in Laos in 1975 was held closely aligned with Vietnam, but antagonisms rankled between Vietnamese and Cambodians, and Pol Pot, with only a shaky hold over his own Kampuchea, staged military incursions into Vietnam. Relations between Vietnam and China had never been cordial, even while they were nominally allied. The Chinese viewed Vietnamese with the same disdain the Vietnamese felt toward Cambodians, and the Vietnamese remembered their long struggle to win independence from imperial China. When Peking terminated its aid program with Hanoi, the SRV was forced to look for support elsewhere. Hoping to balance aid from the socialist countries with contributions from the United States and its allies, the Hanoi government participated in a United States—North Vietnam Joint Economic Commission. Although Secretary of State Kissinger broke off these negotiations in July 1973, the Vietnamese did not abandon hope of winning American diplomatic recognition and financial assistance until 1978, when Washington's Indochina policy—reflecting National Security Adviser Brzezinski's determination to play the "China card"—shifted toward closer alignment with Peking. Rebuffed by the United States, the Vietnamese yielded to Russian pressure to sign a Treaty of Friendship and Cooperation with the Soviet Union in March 1978.

Pol Pot of Kampuchea

Vietnam's wars with Kampuchea and China

War between Vietnam and Kampuchea was preceded by Khmer Rouge raids into Vietnam and punitive strikes by Vietnamese troops deep into Cambodia. Unable to induce Pol Pot to accept a demilitarized zone, Hanoi opened a full-scale assault in December 1978 and toppled the Khmer Rouge government the following month. The war threatened to destroy what little was left of Cambodia. After the fall of Phnom Penh, the capital, fighting continued between the new

Vietnamese-backed regime and various guerrilla groups, including a sizable remnant of Pol Pot's Khmer Rouge. Thousands of sick, wounded, and starving refugees swarmed to the Thai border. International relief agencies, attempting to avert famine, were frustrated by the dictates of rival political authorities. The war put a heavy strain on Vietnam's stunted economy. Finally, Vietnam's Cambodian adventure provoked an attack by the People's Republic of China. In line with its socialization program, Hanoi had in 1978 decreed the nationalization of small businesses and banks, most of which in the vicinity of Saigon (Ho Chi Minh City) were owned by resident Chinese. Before the border was closed, 170,000 had returned to China. Although the SRV's treatment of "bourgeois tradesmen" was precisely that which the Chinese Communists had meted out to the bourgeoisie in their own country, the procedure intensified hostile feelings between the two socialist states. The Chinese felt it necessary to support Pol Pot—in spite of his unsavory reputation—because his was the only regime in Indochina aligned with Peking and because its destruction would remove a check on Vietnam's expansionist ambitions. The Chinese invasion of Vietnam, which began on February 17, 1979, and lasted only seventeen days, destroyed bridges, utilities, mining operations, and thousands of homes, without producing any discernible advantage for either side to offset the heavy losses. Peking claimed its intent was to "teach" Vietnam "a lesson." Actually, the brief but costly encounter failed to change the status quo in the peninsula. The Vietnamese continued to occupy the greater part of Cambodia and, utilizing emergency supplies donated by private relief agencies, began to revive the economy. Because Hanoi refused to withdraw its troops as long as China was helping the Khmer Rouge, the United States and its allies continued to support the Khmer Rouge's dubious claim to represent Kampuchea in the United Nations General Assembly. A majority of the Cambodians, while displaying

The Flight from Cambodia. Thousands of Cambodian refugees fled the fighting between the Pol Pot regime and the Vietnamese army. Here civilians, wearing traditional Khmer head scarves, are streaming across the border into Thailand. On this day alone (April 27, 1979) some 12,000 sought refuge in Thailand, where the facilities for caring for them were woefully inadequate.

little affection for the Vietnamese invaders, apparently preferred their continued occupation of the country to the return of the hated Pol Pot.

The nations of the Third World differ widely in degree of development and in potential, ranging from the fabulously wealthy Persian Gulf oil emirates to the semitribal peasant communities of Africa. The most impoverished areas are sometimes referred to as the "Fourth World." The overall disparity between the new or developing nations—constituting a majority of the world's population—and the minority of advanced industrial societies is startling. A recent report of the U.N. Food and Agricultural Organization disclosed that a billion people—one-fourth of the earth's inhabitants—live in "absolute poverty and destitution," and the situation is worsening. This presents a problem for the countries enjoying high levels of consumption as well as for those suffering deprivation. As ideologies fade and superpower rivalry reaches a stalemate, the most critical confrontation may prove to be between the industrially advanced "have" nations and the dispossessed—a confrontation sometimes phrased as "North" versus "South." Prosperous nations of the "North" are by no means indifferent to the Third World. They have supplied billions of dollars in "aid," but much of this has gone to feed military establishments or has been in the form of loans designed to benefit the donor's economy rather than the recipient's. Contrary to a widely shared notion, wealthy nations have on the whole been niggardly rather than generous. In 1975 the foreign aid contributed by western European nations averaged .36 percent of their GNP. The figure for the United States was .27 percent. The Soviet Union—professed friend and benefactor of the Third World—did worse, giving proportionately one-tenth as much as the United States. Underdeveloped nations could help improve their condition by forgoing excessive purchases of armaments. Unfortunately, they have followed the opposite course, yielding to the enticements of the arms-exporting states. Third World countries—some of which cannot feed or house their own people—doubled their expenditures on armaments between 1960 and 1975.

Many of the countries born of revolutions following World War II were at first inclined to throw in their lot with the Communist half of the postwar world. This was partly because their revolutions had been against Western capitalist governments and partly because they were anxious to achieve rapid economic growth and believed this could be done only through centralized planning and controls, which might require the curtailment of individual freedom of choice. Third World countries, however, soon showed that they were determined to remain independent and preferred not to attach themselves to either of the global power blocs, pursuing generally a policy of nonalignment.

The artificiality of the divisions between the several "worlds" is illustrated by the situation in Korea, where an imaginary line—the thirty-eighth parallel (plus real fortifications)—separates the two competing spheres of communism and capitalism. Both Koreas actually display characteristics common to the Third World. The Republic of Korea, with its capital at Seoul, and the Democratic People's Republic of Korea in the north, with Pyongyang as its capital, not only survived as separate political entities but showed remarkable recuperative ability. Both capitals were rebuilt and industrial complexes restored and expanded. In each case the price of economic progress has been submission to the dictates of a police state, as repressive in South Korea as in the northern Communist republic. Hostility between the two divisions of the peninsula has forced each to maintain an army of more than half a million troops and has repeatedly threatened to ignite another Far Eastern conflagration. However, even in 1979–1980, when South Korea was shaken by internal upheaval and the threat of civil war, there was no overt move on the part of North Korea to seize the opportunity provided by confusion in Seoul to attack its southern neighbor. It is doubtful that either of the two republics will resort to war unless prodded into it by one or both of the superpowers. On the contrary, there are occasional signs that, if left alone, they may eventually effect a peaceful reunification of the peninsula.

The United States, resolved to keep South Korea within its alliance system, supplied military and economic aid—amounting to nearly $200 billion—in spite of flagrant violation of human rights by the Seoul government. In the mid-1970s it was revealed that agents of the Korean C.I.A., operating extensively in the United States, had engaged in wholesale bribery of congressmen to ensure continued support. South Korea's president, General Park Chung Hee, after seven years of absolute rule, was assassinated in October 1979 by the head of the Korean C.I.A. The hope that Park's removal might open the door to democratic progress—or that Washington might use the occasion to apply pressure for reform—was not fulfilled. General Chun Doo-hwan, who seized power in a coup in December, proved himself an apt pupil of the slain dictator. Widespread demonstrations demanding a return to constitutional government reached a climax in May 1980, when 100,000 students marched on Seoul and other cities and popular uprisings spread throughout an entire province. Chun crushed the revolt with 10,000 armored troops, reinvoked martial law, and jailed all resisters. In August he made himself president and soon afterward appointed a rubber-stamp assembly to legalize the muzzling of every political leader disapproved by Chun. Most prominent among the many persons arrested and tried for the May uprising was Kim Dae-jung, battle-scarred veteran of a long campaign for democratic government. Although he had been in prison at the time of the riots, Kim was charged with sedition and sentenced to death. The sentence was commuted to life imprisonment after vehement protests from abroad and a threat from Japan to cut off economic aid. In February 1980 the newly inaugurated American president, Ronald

Progress in the two Koreas

Upheaval and continued dictatorship in South Korea

Chun Doo-hwan, President of South Korea

Reagan, gave Chun a warm reception in Washington, promised to retain U.S. troops at full strength in Korea, and declared, "We share your commitment to freedom."

Of the several attempts to promote solidarity among nations of the Third World—beginning with the Asian-African Conference of twenty-nine states held at Bandung, Indonesia, in 1955—the most promising to date is the Association of Southeast Asian Nations (ASEAN), established in 1967 by Indonesia, Singapore, Malaysia, Thailand, and the Philippines. Not a military alliance, the organization sought at the outset to win recognition of Southeast Asia as a "zone of peace, freedom, and neutrality." It aims to develop regional interdependence among a significant group of Third World states and has the potential to make their collective weight felt in international affairs. An ASEAN summit meeting in 1976 produced a Treaty of Amity and Concord, providing for mutual economic assistance and trade. ASEAN undertakes to strengthen ties among states scattered over a wide geographical area and differing in culture and in degree of economic development. Each has internal problems; the government of each is anti-Communist but repressive. Indonesia and Thailand are under military rule, while the Philippines and Singapore are civilian dictatorships. Thailand, nominally a monarchy, has experienced frequent coups. The ASEAN countries have high potential for economic development, and they have sustained impressive growth rates during the past two decades. Indonesia, though presently poor, ranks first in size, population, and natural resources. The island of Singapore, tiny by comparison, is a thriving port and financial center. Although the military regimes of Indonesia and Thailand have depended upon United States support and the Philippines are the site of important American bases, the ASEAN countries may be useful as a bridge between opposing camps. Vietnam's hostilities with Cambodia and China forced Hanoi to improve relations with staunchly anti-Communist Thailand and to revise its stance toward ASEAN, which it had previously denounced as an American "scheme of aggression and intervention." In 1978 the Vietnamese prime minister toured all the ASEAN capitals and pronounced ASEAN "a genuine regional organization for economic cooperation." Rebuffed by Thailand and Singapore, Vietnam's overtures were viewed more sympathetically by Malaysia and Indonesia, both of which had had experiences that made them distrustful of China. If ASEAN could succeed in forging a link between Communist-oriented Indochina and anti-Marxist Indonesia, it could prove to be an effective counterbalance to the superpowers of East and West.

3. THE LIMITS OF POWER

The period embraced by the two world wars brought not only nationalist revolutions but also fundamental changes in power relationships.

The postwar emergence of two "superpowers" marked the climax of an evolutionary process which seemed to leave the world at the mercy of two rival colossi, commanding tremendous material and human resources and, temporarily, a monopoly of nuclear weapons. This concentration of power, with its accompanying pressure upon weaker states, eventually reached the point of diminishing returns and began to frustrate the national objectives of the superpowers themselves. The reasons for this paradox are several. First, both Russia and the United States, in seeking military superiority, neglected the needs of their own societies. Fifty years after the Revolution of 1917 the Soviet Union had not succeeded in overtaking a single country—with the possible exception of Italy—in per capita income. In this category the U.S.S.R. ranked twentieth in a list of 130 countries. Agriculture was too inefficient to free the Soviets from the need to import foodstuffs, and they required foreign capital to implement plans for developing the oil and gas deposits of Siberia. At the same time the United States, boasting the world's largest GNP and displaying record-breaking affluence, was becoming a poor society in terms of the quality of life. In the mid-1970s the United States ranked thirteenth in the number of teachers per school-age population; seventeenth (just below Poland) in the ratio of physicians to population; seventeenth (tied with East Germany) in the infant mortality rate; and twentieth in life expectancy. An industrial slump triggered by the oil crisis of 1974 curtailed vital services, including police and fire protection, and threatened major American cities with bankruptcy. By 1980 a huge foreign trade deficit, runaway inflation, and rising unemployment underlined serious weaknesses in the economy and sapped public confidence in the government's ability to cope with them. The United States and the Soviet Union, superpowers militarily, were like two exceedingly dangerous but partially crippled giants.

A second factor limiting the usefulness of massive power was the difficulty of enforcing compliance from allies and client states. The Soviet Union, besides suffering a major blow when Communist China embarked on an independent course, has met with formidable resistance in its east European satellites. In 1980, Polish workers—over a period of months and at the risk of Soviet military intervention—defied both their own Communist rulers and the Kremlin. Through a series of strikes that almost paralyzed the economy, they forced the party bosses to grant major concessions, including recognition of an independent union (Solidarity), labor's access to the media, and, in February 1981, the dismissal of four provincial officials accused of corruption. In July 1981 the impact of Solidarity's demands on the Communist Party was dramatically manifested at an extraordinary congress of the Polish Communist Party where the 1,955 delegates (90% of whom were attending their first congress), utilizing the secret ballot for the first time, completely reshaped the Party's central committee and politburo. The United States, while retaining and

Limiting factors in the supremacy of the superpowers

The unreliability of alliances

Proliferation of armaments

*Confrontations and pull-
backs*

shoring up NATO, had only limited success in building alliance systems elsewhere, in spite of great expenditure of time and money.

A third negative factor was the proliferation of weapons among nations rich and poor and, ominously, a shattering of the dream of an elite "nuclear club." It became evident that sooner or later midget states, or even private gangs of terrorists, could procure atomic weapons for purposes of blackmailing or destroying an enemy. Finally, the "balance of terror" created by the superpowers was, in effect, a continuing crisis that made peace impossible. The nuclear giants, armed with the power to destroy the world, could not police it; they could not effectively restrain even their own dependents. They were impotent to prevent conflict from erupting or to extinguish it when it came, because armed intervention by a nuclear power carries the risk of triggering Doomsday. This fact has not escaped the notice of small states embroiled in regional feuding, especially when these states are equipped with conventional weapons conveniently supplied by one or both of the superpowers.

The limitations upon power as an instrument for achieving political solutions was illustrated during the Korean War of 1950–1953. The United States government refused to permit General MacArthur to invade China or to employ nuclear weapons, as he had requested, for fear that such moves might lead irrevocably to a world war. This

Defiance in Poland. Thousands of striking workers take part in religious services in the Lenin Shipyards in Gdansk on August 24, 1980. This was the scene of the first in a series of strikes that paralyzed an already troubled economic and political system and challenged Soviet domination of Polish governmental policy.

General Douglas MacArthur Returns from Korea. MacArthur, who had recently been relieved of his command for disobeying President Truman's orders, was given a hero's welcome in New York on April 20, 1951. This effusive approval of MacArthur's behavior reflected the frustration felt by many Americans at the inability of the United States government to bring the Korean conflict to a swift and victorious conclusion.

policy puzzled and angered many Americans, accustomed to the concepts of all-out war and unconditional surrender. Especially galling to them was the fact that President Harry Truman saw fit to fire General MacArthur, hero of the Pacific theater in World War II and now commander of the United Nations forces, because MacArthur refused to fight a limited war. In 1962, the United States and the Soviet Union were again forced to ask themselves how much they were willing to risk in order to protect their own strategic interests. During the early 1960s, President John F. Kennedy and his advisers grew increasingly concerned about the activities of Premier Fidel Castro of Cuba. In October 1962 Kennedy ordered a naval blockade of the island to prevent delivery of missiles and other war matériel the Russians had promised to supply. The Soviet government, alarmed by the threat of war, agreed to remove the bombers and missiles already on Cuban soil. The incident posed an extremely difficult question for the two superpowers. How could one nation convince another of its determination to brook no further interference with its plans, if its adversary could be fairly certain that because of the fear of nuclear war the threat was no more than a bluff?

Its unhappy adventure in Indochina provided the United States with the most searing demonstration of the futility of a policy based solely on force. Although the American commander, General William Westmoreland, claimed a victory in Vietnam, it would be hard to conceive a more decisive reversal than the United States had experienced. After fifteen years of struggle, a sickening toll of lives, and the expenditure of $150 billion, the result was the triumph of communism and the overthrow of every American-sponsored government in Indochina except Thailand, which had remained neutral. In retrospect it seems obvious that American objectives could have been better served at far less cost. Following the withdrawal of American trooops the states of Southeast Asia did not "fall like dominoes," but the Indochinese Communist regimes—temporarily forced into union against foreign intervention—fell upon one another in a regional power struggle. A senior U.S. diplomat who had been associated with the Vietnam commitment, observed aptly that the United States was better off than if it had won the war. The lessons of Indochina, not yet fully assimilated, are probably not yet finished. Before attacking Cambodia in the fall of 1978, the Vietnamese Communists allied themselves by treaty with the Soviet Union, hoping thereby to discourage China from interfering. The alliance did not keep China from invading Vietnam, but, by the same token, neither did China's alliance with Kampuchea deter the Vietnamese from attacking that pitiable country.

The U.S.S.R., as if to prove that it had learned nothing from the experience of the French and the Americans in Vietnam, decided to compel obedience from Afghanistan, a Middle Eastern country bordering on Russia, where a pro-Soviet regime had been installed in April 1978. Weary of the stubborn resistance offered by the Muslim population of Afghanistan, the Soviets attacked in strength in December 1979 and installed a compliant puppet as prime minister in Kabul. While Russian troops policed the cities, Afghan tribesmen inflamed the countryside with guerrilla attacks from their mountain strongholds, foreshadowing a long and ruinous civil war.

Recent decades have recorded the weakening or dissolution of alliance systems originally designed to bolster the shaky bipolar balance of power or to give one side an advantage over the other. Nations of the Third World, weak and dependent as they are, have resisted interference in their domestic affairs as well as attempts to absorb them into power blocs. Communist China hoped in vain to manipulate Indonesia through that country's large Communist party. The U.S.S.R., frustrated in Egypt and Iraq, struggled laboriously to gain footholds in the new African states. While accepting a Soviet alliance, born of desperation, in 1978, the Vietnamese rejected Russia's request for naval bases in their territory. In the Western Hemisphere, the United States is no longer able to dictate to the Organization of American States. After pouring billions of dollars into the Shah's Iran to make it a Middle East bastion, Washington's influence collapsed to zero with the revolution of 1979, and it could only watch helplessly as American nationals, seized as hostages by militant revolutionaries, were imprisoned for fourteen months. For a couple of decades United States strategists hoped to retain leverage with an alliance they had organized for Southeast Asia in 1954. The Southeast Asia Defense Treaty (SEATO) was designed as a counterpart to NATO, in an overall program for containing communism. The organization was never popular nor effective. Only three of its eight members were Asian states (Thailand, Pakistan, and the Philippines); by 1967 France had virtually withdrawn from the alliance, and Pakistan left in 1972. In June 1977 what remained of SEATO was quietly laid to rest with a brief ceremony in Bangkok. The Southeast Asian states, disinclined to revive the Cold War, looked toward ASEAN as an association more suitable to promoting their common interests.

SELECTED READINGS

* *Items so designated are available in paperback editions.*
* Brzezinski, Z. K., *The Soviet Bloc: Unity and Conflict,* rev. ed., Cambridge, Mass., 1967.

  Cady, J. F., *Southeast Asia: Its Historical Development,* New York, 1964.

  Chaliand, Gérard, *Revolution in the Third World: Myths and Prospects,* New York, 1977. Gloomy but insightful.
* Degler, Carl N., *Affluence and Anxiety: The United States Since 1945,* Glenview, Ill., 1968.
* Dehio, Ludwig, *Germany and World Politics in the Twentieth Century,* London, 1959. A series of essays assessing Germany's twentieth-century drive for European hegemony.

  Ehrmann, Henry W., *Politics in France,* Boston, 1968. French politics since 1958.
* Falk, Richard, *A Study of Future Worlds,* New York, 1975.

  Fall, Bernard B., *The Two Vietnams: A Political and Military Analysis,* rev. ed., New York, 1967.
* Fanon, Frantz, *The Wretched of the Earth,* New York, 1968. The extraordinary and brilliant delineation of the oppression of Third World peoples.

  Fitzgerald, Frances, *Fire in the Lake: The Vietnamese and the Americans in Vietnam,* Boston, 1972. A detailed and moving account.

  Henderson, W. O., *The Genesis of the Common Market,* Chicago, 1963.

  Hoffman, Stanley, et al., *In Search of France,* Cambridge, Mass., 1963. Essays providing perceptive analyses of postwar French politics and society.

  Knapp, Wilfrid, *Unity and Nationalism in Europe Since 1945,* Elmsford, N.Y., 1969.

  Kolko, Gabriel, *The Politics of War: The World and United States Foreign Policy, 1943–45,* New York, 1969. Argues that the blame for the Cold War rests with the Western allies.

• Moore, Barrington, *The Social Origins of Dictatorship and Democracy: Lord and Peasant in the Making of the Modern World,* Boston, 1966.

Mozingo, David, *China's Policy toward Indonesia, 1949–1967,* Ithaca, 1976.

Myrdal, Gunnar, *Against the Stream: Critical Essays on Economics,* New York, 1972. Offers pertinent comments on problems of the Third World.

———, *The Challenge of World Poverty: A World Anti-Poverty Program in Outline,* New York, 1970.

Nogueira, Franco, *The Third World,* London, 1968.

Reischauer, Edwin O., *Beyond Vietnam: The United States and Asia,* New York, 1968.

Seabury, Paul, *The Rise and Decline of the Cold War,* New York, 1967.

Shawcross, William, *Sideshow: Kissinger, Nixon and the Destruction of Cambodia,* New York, 1979.

• Williams, Lea E., *Southeast Asia: A History,* New York, 1976. From the fifteenth century to the present.

• Worsley, Peter, *The Third World,* 2d ed., Chicago, 1970.

• Wylie, Laurence, *Village in the Vaucluse,* rev. ed., Cambridge, Mass., 1974. Analyzes the social structure of French rural life in 1950. An afterword reveals the changes wrought by the intrusion of modern life in the ensuing twenty years.

SOURCE MATERIALS

Adenauer, Konrad, *Memoirs, 1945–53,* Chicago, 1966. Adenauer served as chancellor of the Federal Republic of Germany from 1949 to 1963 and sought both American support and the reunification of dismembered Germany.

Barnes, Thomas G., and Gerald D. Feldman, comps., *Breakdown and Rebirth: 1914 to the Present,* Boston, 1972. An excellent documentary collection of contemporary history, primarily European.

• Caputo, Philip, *A Rumor of War,* New York, 1977. The best memoir of the American experience in the Vietnam war.

De Gaulle, Charles, *Memoirs of Hope: Renewal and Endeavor,* New York, 1971.

Kennan, George F., *Memoirs, 1925–1950,* New York, 1967. Kennan, a career diplomat, was America's leading expert on Russia and instrumental in the formation of the containment policy.

Chapter 41

PROBLEMS OF WORLD CIVILIZATION

This conjunction of an immense military establishment and a large arms industry is new in American experience. The total influence—economic, political, even spiritual—is felt in every city, every statehouse, every office of the federal government. . . . We must guard against the acquisition of unwarranted influence, whether sought or unsought, by the military-industrial complex. The potential for the disastrous rise of misplaced power exists and will persist.

—Dwight D. Eisenhower, "Farewell Address"

The writing of a final chapter in a text book of this sort is, for the authors, a difficult task. Not only are they called upon to attempt an instant analysis of their own society and time; they are expected as well to discern in present events patterns that will continue to be of some consequence five to ten years hence. In other words, they are called upon to pick historical winners, to decide not what *has* mattered, which is difficult enough, but what *will* matter. Historians, whose job it is to acknowledge the way in which human idiosyncrasies make prediction a tricky business, are particularly loath to single out this movement or that trend and to pronounce it "significant" in terms of the future. We shall therefore merely content ourselves with a discussion of some of the most serious problems confronting society in the 1970s, calling attention at the outset to the fact that these problems are rooted in many of the historical developments—industrialization, urbanization, and international competition, for example—that we have traced in the preceding chapters.

The present as history

I. THE GROWTH OF CENTRALIZED GOVERNMENT AND ITS CONSEQUENCES

Centralization and social welfare

The responsibilities central governments assumed, and the power they arrogated to themselves to discharge those responsibilities, increased significantly around the world after World War II. In almost all countries, successive administrations either intitiated or expanded social welfare programs, insuring that entire populations would receive protection from the depredations of unemployment, sickness, and old age. Building upon the examples set by Germany and Britain before World War I, Western nations instituted increasingly comprehensive national programs for health and social security. Socialist and Third World countries likewise moved, in some cases with remarkable speed, to alleviate the problems and disabilities of people who for generations had been denied the chance of a healthy and secure existence.

Reasons for the increase

This movement to expand social welfare systems resulted in an increased tendency on the part of governments to manage and control their citizenry. Programs of social insurance were designed to benefit and hence to regulate the lives of all classes of men and women, not just the destitute. New agencies, staffed by armies of newly recruited bureaucrats, imposed rules while they dispensed assistance to a clientele that grew to include the entire citizenry. Many of those responsible for the institution of these programs were motivated by a genuine desire to provide a decent life to all citizens, regardless of economic class. An equally powerful incentive, however, was the conviction of governments that without a strong and generally satisfied population a country was doomed to recurring unrest, that social insecurity would contribute to rapid national decline into domestic inefficiency and international ineffectiveness.

The role of international competition

Concern to improve or at any rate to stabilize a nation's international position, within a world in which power relationships were constantly shifting, contributed further to the growth of centralized government. New nations wanted to attain some new measure of international power. Older nations wanted to retain whatever measure had been theirs. In either case, governments recognized the importance of a stable economy and a strong military defense. Few countries, old or new, managed to attain those twin goals in the 1970s to the extent they deemed necessary. Inflation in particular proved an intractable obstacle to their achievement. Nevertheless as nations strained to assert themselves, their governments tightened their hold on the economy, working to do so with the forces of both management and labor, while investing enormous sums in the most sophisticated and up-to-date armaments of war. The result of these activities was a further growth of the power and control of government.

What have been the consequences of such growth? Some observers have argued that the general worldwide increase in the authority of central governments is a symptom of a decline in the importance of political and economic ideology. Whether a nation declares itself to be a capitalist democracy (as does the United States), a socialist commonwealth (as does the Soviet Union) or something in between (as do many of the nations of western Europe), all appear to some degree to have blunted ideological differences as they have attempted to rationalize—or nationalize—their industries, manage their economies, provide for the well-being of their citizens, and arm themselves against the possibilities of future war. Fewer socialists now advocate collective ownership of the means of production; they have become instead exponents of the welfare state. Defenders of capitalism still exist in theory but few would recognize it if they saw it in full swing. Capitalist economies are no longer free enterprise systems but "mixed" economies, involving government controls, managed currencies, and forced distribution of profits. Small-time capitalists are permitted to enjoy their gains only until they turn them over to the government to finance its wars, armaments, and social welfare programs.

Political reaction to centralization

To suggest that there has been some ideological blurring in the movement toward more generally accepted goals does not mean, however, that men and women do not continue to call themselves capitalists or socialists, or that those terms have lost their meaning. Nor should it imply that there is not continuing and heated debate about both ends and means. During the mid-1970s a reaction of some magnitude occurred in several Western countries against the notion that governments should manage the lives of their citizens to the extent they were. Social reform, critics said, has cost too much, and has not really achieved what it was supposed to. There is still poverty and misery. Admit that they will always exist, these people argued, and moderate your goals accordingly; in the process, put an end to big government. This viewpoint was occasionally translated into political victory. The socialist government of Sweden, in power for decades, was succeeded by a conservative one. Margaret Thatcher, arch-conservative leader of Britain's Tory party, became the first woman prime minister of that country in 1979, as well as the first woman head of state of a Western nation, on a platform which blamed her country's economic decline in the 1970s on the fact that the government had overextended itself. In the United States there was a relatively successful campaign by citizens to curb government activity by limiting taxation.

Critics of bureaucratic centralization

This debate has been carried on not only in the political arena but in the writings of thoughtful and angry critics of modern society. Two of the most powerful voices raised against the growth of worldwide governmental expansion and authoritarianism were those of Alexsandr Solzhenitsyn and Herbert Marcuse. Solzhenitsyn, an exiled Russian novelist, attacked the brutal methods employed by the Soviet Union in its rapid climb to world power. His *Gulag Archipelago,* published in 1973, is a fictionalized account of the fate of those whose

Margaret Thatcher

Alexsandr Solzhenitsyn

President Nixon Resigns. Here Nixon bids his last farewell to the White House in the wake of his resignation.

willingness to stand in the way of Soviet "progress" sentenced them to life in Siberian labor camps. Marcuse, an American, charged that authoritarianism was just as much a fact of life under capitalism as under communism. He argued that industrial capitalism had produced a "one-dimensional" society, in which the interests of individual citizens had been ruthlessly subordinated to those of the powerful corporate interests which were the true governors of the world.

Marcuse urged the adoption of revolutionary measures to accomplish the overthrow of authoritarian capitalist imperialism. Those unwilling to follow him to that extreme nevertheless concurred in his denunciation of the manner in which big government and big business together appeared to be draining power from individual citizens. Indeed, as devoted a capitalist as Dwight D. Eisenhower, general in the U.S. Army during the Second World War and president of the United States in the 1950s, warned in his farewell presidential address of the growing might of what he called "the military-industrial complex." In those countries calling themselves democracies, democracy seemed to many to have less and less meaning, as people appeared to enjoy little control over their government and hence over their lives. Concerns of this sort received apparent confirmation in the late 1960s and early 1970s, when the United States was at war in Vietnam. Evidence subsequently published showed that the democratically elected Congress was misled by President Lyndon Johnson and his advisors into believing that hostile North Vietnamese attacks on American ships had compelled U.S. intervention, whereas the attacks had instead been "manufactured" to allow the government to pursue its own aggressive policies. Concern about the arrogance of governmental power reached its peak in the United States during the Watergate investigations leading to the resignation of President Richard Nixon in 1974, when it was learned that Nixon had authorized domestic spying in the name of national security but without proper regard for the constitutional rights of American citizens. Following that dramatic episode came revelations about the role played in secret by the U.S. Central Intelligence Agency in subverting leftist Third World governments, along with the intervention of giant multinational corporations and the C.I.A. together in assisting to overthrow a democratically elected socialist government in Chile. Knowledge of these events brought home the extent to which centralized authority in supposedly democratic governments had removed itself from popular control and accountability.

2. COMMITMENT: THE GROWTH OF BLACK CONSCIOUSNESS

Partly in response to revelations of this sort, partly as a result of longstanding grievances and dissatisfactions, groups that had hitherto lived as subordinates in society, kept powerless and in large part silenced, raised their voices in the 1960s and 1970s, demanding not only to be heard but to have their demands met. At the very time when democracies were being charged with ignoring the wishes of their constituents, blacks, youth, and women, in particular, began to assert their right to equality.

The growth of insurgency among American blacks has to some extent paralleled the rise of black nations in Africa and the Caribbean. Through most of the years from the Civil War to 1900, black people were condemned, in the North as well as the South, to a subordinate role within a predominantly white culture. The emancipation of slaves, and the Thirteenth and Fourteenth Amendments to the Constitution brought little change in a quality of existence which was centuries-old and which was underwritten by the racist attitudes and practices of most whites. These attitudes and practices were realized in substandard education, lack of jobs, poor housing, inequality under the law, lynching of both black men and women, and other conditions of life with which black people were faced. Any changes in this reality might have been indefinitely postponed had it not been for the spread of black political consciousness and the rise of a number of black leaders, both male and female, during the course of the twentieth century. Black political consciousness and black leaders were not unknown before the turn of the century: Harriet Tubman, Sojourner Truth, Frederick Douglass, Nat Turner, and others, were eloquent and powerful spokespeople and activists. But with the twentieth century came a massive emigration of blacks from the South to the North. Although the North shared most of the attitudes of the South, there were more opportunities for blacks in the industrial cities than in the primarily agrarian South. Many thousands of black people emigrated to the North during the years of the First World War, when the lack of white labor created a need for their services; it should also be mentioned that over 400,000 blacks were made to serve in the war even though, in most parts of the United States, they were essentially disenfranchised citizens. During the postwar depression, however, black workers were the first to suffer and to lose their jobs. But the emigration brought a changed political consciousness for black people; more voted, for example.

U.S. blacks after the Civil War

In 1910 the National Association for the Advancement of Colored People was founded and contributed to this political progress and the growing awareness among black people that they were an oppressed group and that this should be changed. The work of the NAACP was supplemented in 1911 with the founding of the National League on Urban Conditions Among Negroes (later known as the National Urban League). The work of black leaders of this time—for example, Ida Wells-Barnett (1862–1931), A. Philip Randolph (1889–1979), W. E. B. Du Bois (1868–1963), Mary Mcleod Bethune (1875–1955)—who were visible and vocal opponents of lynching, promoters

W. E. B. Du Bois

of educational opportunities for blacks, and labor union organizers, kept this movement toward equality and against oppression a vital force in American history, which would culminate in the civil rights movement of the 1960s.

The year 1919 saw the rise to prominence of another important black leader, Marcus Garvey (1887–1940), a native of Jamaica. Garvey's political base was Harlem in New York City, a major black ghetto. Garvey emphasized the African origins of black Americans and taught his followers to refer to themselves as "black" rather than "Negro." He claimed his people were the descendents of the "greatest and proudest race who ever peopled the earth," and generated a movement of black emigration from America to Africa. Garvey encouraged and influenced an important black literary movement, the so-called Harlem Renaissance of the 1920s. Several of its leaders derived inspiration from him, notably Langston Hughes and Countee Cullen.

Garvey's philosophy also extended indirectly to the Black Muslim movement, through his influence on the father of its most vigorous proselytizer, Malcom X (1925–1965). Malcolm X was converted in prison by his brother to the religion of Islam. After his release he became a spokesman for Elijah Muhammad, founder of the movement. Most of his followers were people of the same background who had flocked to Garvey's standard—recent migrants from the South who now lived in poverty in the black ghettos of northern cities. Malcolm X attempted to overcome their feeling of helplessness by giving them a new religion to take the place of the white man's Christianity and by restoring black pride. This new religion was Islam, which Malcolm X described as the true faith of Africans. Though he and his followers were firm believers, they were not fanatics. They did not renounce worldliness as a life of sin. They urged blacks to pool their resources and establish black-owned businesses. This would lead to economic independence and a heightened sense of self. The Muslims taught their adherents to avoid aggression and to fight only when attacked. Their charismatic minister broke with the Black Muslims in 1964. In February 1965 he was assassinated as he started to speak at a rally in Harlem.

In the meantime black consciousness was being expressed through other forms. One was the Congress of Racial Equality (CORE), founded by James Farmer in 1942. His announced aim was to translate "love of God and man" into specific crusades against injustice. By 1960 CORE had combined its efforts with those of other political organizations seeking to end discrimination against blacks. It helped in promoting "freedom rides" for civil rights into the South and boycotts against racist shopkeepers. After 1955 Farmer often collaborated with Martin Luther King, Jr. (1929–1968), a young Baptist minister. Like Farmer, King also embraced the Gandhian philosophy of nonviolence. For more than ten years he was widely regarded—and

Martin Luther King, Jr.

feared—as the most effective defender of black rights. His career was brought to a tragic end by an assassin's bullet as he stood on the balcony of a motel in Memphis in 1968.

Important successors to King, Farmer, and in a sense the Black Muslims, were the Black Panthers. Their movement began during the civil rights confrontations of the 1950s and 1960s in Alabama and Mississippi. From there it rapidly spread northward and about 1968 established its headquarters in Oakland, California. Its leaders—such men as Huey Newton, Bobby Seale, and Eldridge Cleaver—adopted for their party the name of Black Panthers. They saw in the panther an animal slow to take the initiative of aggression but fierce in retaliation when attacked by its enemies. The Panthers differed from other black activists in a number of ways. First of all, they were frankly revolutionary and not nonviolent. They believed that only by seizing power could they redress society's wrongs against black people. Second, the Black Panthers, unlike some of their forerunners, did not advocate a return to Africa, but sought an end to racism in America. The Black Panthers also professed a kind of internationalism similar to that of other revolutionaries.

Black movements in the 1970s to some degree retreated from militant commitment. Even the Black Panthers declared their willingness to work within the existing system for reform. Civil rights laws enacted under the Johnson administration in the 1960s have brought U.S. blacks some measure of equality with regard to voting rights—and, to a much lesser degree, school desegregation. In other areas, such as housing and job opportunities, blacks continue to suffer disadvantage and discrimination, as a result of white racism, which underwrites the belief that blacks should be satisfied with the gains they have made, and the general recalcitrance of administrations following Lyndon Johnson's domestically innovative one. These problems are not confined to the United States. In Great Britain, for example, where there has been a large immigration of blacks from former colonies, extreme discrimination in jobs and housing menaces the chances for early or satisfactory integration. Because the momentum for reform has slowed, black leaders are less able than in the 1960s to chart their movement's direction. Meanwhile black people derive continued strength not only from the conviction that the battle for equality is both justified and still to be won, but from the example of African and Caribbean nations emerging into independent statehood.

3. COMMITMENT: YOUTH AND WOMEN

The years from 1964 through 1972 were marked by a protest and upheaval by the younger generation more rampant than the world had witnessed in many decades. They were committed, as were blacks, to

Vietnam Protest, 1971. Veterans of the U.S. Armed Forces march on the capitol to protest continued U.S. involvement in the war in Vietnam.

The youth rebellion

the assertion of their right to be heard. In the United States this rebellion was fueled by the war in Vietnam. Young men, drafted to fight in a war they despised, rebelled against the idea that it was their "duty" to serve. Together, young men and women proclaimed instead their duty to question anew the presuppositions that had led the U.S. into its unhappy military predicament. Science antagonized them because of its association with war-making. Knowledge that was not "relevant" to the world's problems was questioned with regard to its worth. Young leaders urged their peers to leave their college books and address the problems of the "real" world: overpopulation, industrial pollution, mistreatment of blacks and other minorities. It was this rebellion that exposed the inhumanity of the American adventure in Southeast Asia. Long before adult liberals spoke out against the bombing raids and body-counts of that war, students in colleges and universities stormed the institutions of the Establishment in angry protest. Although they did not stop the war, they helped to bring about President Johnson's retirement in 1968. Their *compères* in France, who rioted in May 1968, contributed to the defeat of President Charles de Gaulle.

Radicalism in the 1970s

Political radicalism no longer shapes the mind of the West's youth as it did in the late 1960s, a fact explained in large part by the end of hostilities in Vietnam. Radicalism's much-distorted reflection, however, appears in the activities of terrorist gangs such as that which in 1978 abducted and eventually killed the moderate Italian political leader Aldo Moro. Hoping their extremist tactics would help divide Italy and somehow produce a revolution, the gang's leaders discovered instead that they had conducted a sterile exercise in terror for its own sake.

Not all young rebels in the 1960s and 1970s committed themselves to a life of radical political activism. Some turned for spiritual or psychological comfort to fundamentalist religious movements. Some declared their disgust with the world by "dropping out," living in communities of their own design apart from society. Others devoted themselves to a counterculture reflected in the intensely personal music and lyrics of young popular musicians, in the custom of drug-taking, and in the freedom to live with each other without marriage. Social rebellion of this sort infected various countries to various degrees. It was primarily a movement of urban middle-class youths. Though in some cases their rejection of older values was the result of deeply held and enduring convictions, in many others their declaration of independence was short-lived, amounting to little more than the customary behavior of uncertain and impatient adolescents.

Youthful counterculture

Women, like blacks and young people, began to assert themselves during the 1960s and 1970s. As was the case with the youth rebellion, the women's movement began in the United States and was first directed from within the middle class. Some women in western European countries joined in the struggle for equal rights; by the mid-seventies the movement had spread worldwide, including the Third World nations, and was no longer limited to the middle class. Many of the early activists within the movement had been part of the youth rebellion during its most intense phase in the sixties. Their activism, in part, stemmed from a realization that even in a radical political atmosphere, women were relegated to second place. Women's position within society had changed radically since the nineteenth century. The assumption that the middle-class woman's place was in the home had been challenged by the ever-increasing demand for women workers and by the need experienced by more and more women to hold a job—either for financial reasons or because housework was for a growing

The women's movement

Students of the University of Paris During the Uprisings of 1968

Margaret Sanger, a Leader in the Movement to Awaken the World to the Necessity of Birth Control

Abortion as a central issue

number an unfulfilling occupation. The increased availability and social acceptance of birth-control devices meant that women were having fewer children, and that they could begin to exercise more control over the pattern of their lives.

Yet society seemed loath to acknowledge the implication of these changes: that women are equal to men. Women were paid less than men for similar work. Women with qualifications no different from men were turned down because of their gender when they applied for jobs. Women with excellent employment records were forced to rely on their husbands to establish credit. Political action helped alleviate some of these inequities in the late 1960s and the 1970s. The U.S. government instituted programs of "affirmative action" which mandated the hiring of qualified women as well as members of racial minority groups. The campaign for equality did not meet with universal approval, however. A particularly volatile subject was a woman's right to an abortion. Feminists argued that women must enjoy the freedom to plan for their future unencumbered by the responsibilities of motherhood if they choose, and that their bodies are theirs to govern. Their opponents, which included members of the so-called right-to-life movement, countered with the argument that abortion encouraged sexual irresponsibility; some declared that abortion is the equivalent of murder. By the end of the seventies the campaigners for women's equality, though still battling in the United States for passage of a constitutional Equal Rights Amendment, had a good many successes to their credit. Unlike the youth rebellion, which had run its course by that time, the women's movement, like that of black people, was based not on the disaffections of only one generation, but on a history of discrimination experienced by great numbers and recognized as unjust by a sizable proportion of majority opinion.

4. LITERATURE AND ART AS REFLECTIONS OF CONTEMPORARY PROBLEMS

Postwar authors

Not surprisingly, the work of many of the West's leading writers reflect the difficulties and commitments we have been surveying. During the immediate postwar years novelists concerned themselves with the horrors of war and of the totalitarian systems which had spawned the conflict of the 1940s. The Americans James Jones and Norman Mailer, in *From Here to Eternity* and *The Naked and the Dead,* portrayed the coarseness and cruelty of military life with ruthless realism. The German Günter Grass's first and probably most important novel, *The Tin Drum,* depicted the vicious and politically diseased life of Nazi Germany in the 1930s. In France, Jean-Paul Sartre, as a result of his own and his country's wartime experiences, recommitted himself in his novels, plays, and other writings to a life of active political involvement as a Marxist. Whereas he had previously defined hell in terms of individual hostilities, he now defined it in terms of class inequality. Unlike Sartre, his compatriot Albert Camus (1913–1960) was unable to construct a secular faith from his own perceptions of the world and its apparent absurdities. Though idealist enough to participate in the French resistance movement against the German occupation in World War II, and though proclaiming the virtues of rebellion, Camus remained tortured in novels such as *The Fall, The Plague,* and *The Rebel* by the problem of humanity's responsibility for its own miserable dilemma and by the limitations placed upon the ability of men and women to help each other.

The theme of individual alienation and helplessness, a reflection of the problems arising from the growth of state power, was one which writers addressed themselves to with increasing frequency in the 1960s and 1970s. The Russian Boris Pasternak, in his novel *Dr. Zhivago,* indicted the Soviet campaign to shape all its citizens to the same mold. Although both Pasternak and his compatriot Solzhenitsyn were awarded the Nobel Prize for literature, the former in 1958 and the latter in 1970, their works were condemned by the Soviet government and Solzhenitsyn was sent into exile. Western novelists dealt with the threat to individuality as well, building upon a prewar tradition most forcefully expressed in the writings of the Austrian Franz Kafka (1883–1924). Kafka's novels present a vision of humans in a hostile universe, hopelessly striving to come to terms with a remote and unknown power. It is not so much a dream as it is a nightmare composed of weird, fantastic details brought together in a terrifying pattern. His best-known work, *The Castle,* is at once a satire on bureaucracy and a philosophical representation of the isolation of the individual in the universe. The American novelist Saul Bellow (1915–   ) was concerned with many of these same themes, though Bellow spoke with a far gentler, if less compelling, voice than Kafka. He chose the modern city as the milieu for his fiction. His heroes in novels such as *The Adventures of Augie March, Henderson the Rain King,* and *Mr. Sammler's Planet* were all men trapped in a world turned upside down, condemned to seek personal understanding—indeed to maintain their sanity—in an environment at worst savage, at best absurd.

Women authors wrote not only of the general loneliness of the human condition, but of the particular plight of women trapped in a world not of their own making. The Frenchwoman Simone de Beauvoir (1908–   ) in *The Second Sex,* a germinal study of the female condition, denounced the male middle class for turning not only workers but also its own women into objects for its own ends. American writers like Adrienne Rich, Tillie Olsen, and the philosopher Mary Daly helped define the politics and culture of the women's movement.

The specific issues that drove men and women to committed action

Alienation and helplessness

Simone de Beauvoir

Women writers

James Baldwin

Black women authors

The absurd and fantastic

in the mid-1960s compelled writers to take sides as well. Günter Grass, in *Local Anaesthetic,* published in 1970, wrote of student unrest and political involvement. The movement for black equality encouraged a tradition in America that had burgeoned in the wake of the depression and World War II. One initiator of this tradition was Richard Wright (1908–1960), who grew up amid the rural poverty and violent racism of Mississippi. As a youth Wright drifted to Chicago and became a resident of and spokesman for the black ghetto. In his novel, *Native Son,* and his autobiography, *Black Boy,* he portrayed with scathing realism the oppression of working-class blacks. Despite the pretensions of the New Deal, he found that the burdens of that group had not been appreciably lightened. One of the most effective articulaters of black aspiration and disenchantment in the 1960s was James Baldwin, the son of a Harlem clergyman. Living under the dual stigmas of his blackness and his homosexuality, Baldwin remained a self-exile in Paris for ten years following the Second World War. He returned to the United States to warn, in his most powerful book, *The Fire Next Time,* that unless whites awoke soon to the extent and pervasiveness of their racism, American society would be consumed by its own animosities.

Not only black men, but black women also wrote of the oppression and struggle of their race. Zora Neale Hurston (c. 1901–1960) was a novelist, anthropologist, and folklorist. In both her novels and anthropological studies Hurston wrote eloquently of the history of black people, their language and traditions. Her major novel, *Their Eyes Were Watching God* (1937), is about the strength of one black woman and her belief in her own strength and in herself. The poet Audre Lorde and the novelist Toni Morrison are two black women writers who also deal in detail and with an assured sense of history with the experience of black people, particularly with the black female experience. One of the most sensitive of contemporary black women writers was Lorraine Hansberry (1930–1965). A poet and dramatist, Hansberry won distinction in her tragically brief lifetime for her play *A Raisin in the Sun,* specifically the story of one black family in Chicago but actually the story of many black families existing under racism. Her dramatic talent was displayed even more clearly in *To Be Young, Gifted, and Black,* produced four years after her death. Hansberry wrote with defiance and anger, and sometimes in bitterness, when the beauty she saw in life was dimmed by bigotry and extinguished by repression.

Some authors, although they agreed with indictments of contemporary civilization, believed the human condition too hopeless to warrant direct attack. These writers expressed their despair by escaping into the absurd and fantastic. In the plays of Samuel Beckett (1906–   ), an Irishman who wrote in French, and of the Englishman Harold Pinter (1930–   ), nothing happens. Characters speak in the banalities that have become the hallmark of modern times. Words which are meaningless when spoken by human beings nevertheless take on a logic of their own; yet they explain nothing. Other authors, less willing, perhaps, to attempt to make a statement out of nothingness, have invaded the realms of hallucination, science fiction, and fantasy. The novels of the Americans William Burroughs and Kurt Vonnegut convey their readers from interior fantasizing to outer space. Significantly one of the most popular books among the youth of the sixties and seventies was *The Lord of the Rings,* a pseudosaga set in the fantasy world of "Middle Earth," written before the Second World War by the Englishman J. R. R. Tolkien.

Film

Filmmakers, in the decades after the Second World War, made films which mirrored the problems and concerns of society, with a depth and artistic integrity seldom attempted or achieved previously. The Swede Ingmar Bergman, the Frenchmen Jean-Luc Godard and François Truffaut, the Italians Frederico Fellini and Michelangelo Antonioni, to name but a few of the most gifted directors, dealt in their films with the same themes that marked the literature of the period: loneliness, war, oppression, and corruption. One important factor facilitating the achievement of artistic quality was the general willingness on the part of censors—state or industry sponsored—to reflect public taste by permitting filmmakers great license in the handling of themes such as racism, violence, and sexuality. While there is no question that this relaxation led to exploitation, it cleared the way for extraordinarily powerful film statements, such as the American Arthur Penn's *Bonnie and Clyde* (1967) and the Italian Bernardo Bertolucci's *Last Tango in Paris* (1972), shocking declarations about humanity made possible by explicit depictions of violence and sex. Film, while gaining a general maturity it had heretofore lacked, did not desert its role as entertainment. The international popularity of the British rock-and-roll group, the Beatles, was translated, for example, into equally successful films, charming, slapstick escapism which nevertheless proclaimed the emancipation of youth from the confining formalities and conventions of their elders.

Fine arts

Unlike writers or filmmakers, the majority of postwar artists did not use their work as a vehicle to express either ideological commitment or a concern for the human situation. Following trends established by the impressionists and cubists, they spoke neither about the world or to the world, but instead to each other and to the extremely small coterie of initiates who understood their artistic language. Foremost among the postwar schools of art was abstract expressionism, whose chief exponents were the painters Jackson Pollack (1912–1956), William deKooning (1904–   ), and Franz Kline (1910–1962). Their interests lay in further experimentation with the relationships between color, texture, and surface, to the total exclusion of "meaning" or "message" in the traditional sense. Jasper

Mahoning by Franz Kline. A work representative of the abstract expressionists' desire to explore the varieties of light, texture, and surface.

See color plates following page 1088

Johns's painting of the American flag insisted that the viewer see it not as *a* painting—that is, something to be interpreted—but instead as painting, the treatment of canvas with paint. Robert Rauschenberg, in revolt against the abstract expressionists, exhibited blank white panels, insisting that by so doing he was pressing art to the ultimate question of a choice of medium. Painters fought the notion that their work in some way expressed disgust with an empty civilization. "My paintings are based on the fact that only what can be seen is there," declared the American Frank Stella, who painted stripes on irregularly shaped canvases. "Pop" art, a phenomenon of the late sixties which took as its subject everyday objects such as soup cans and comic-strip heroes, was likewise, according to its practitioners, not a protest against the banality of industrialism but another experiment in abstractions.

Rothko

Even the remote and yet extraordinarily compelling abstractions of Mark Rothko (1903–1970), glowing or somber rectangles of color imposed upon other rectangles, were said by the artist himself to represent "nothing but content—no associations, only sensation." Only with the coming, in the 1970s, of the so-called hyper-realists, artists such as the American Duane Hanson, who recreates his invariably depressing human subjects in plastic down to the last eyelash, can we perhaps say that some artists are making a statement not only about technique but about what they perceive as the vacuity of life.

5. THE CRISIS OF ECOLOGY AND POPULATION

Pessimism about the human condition derived not only from concern for the problems of the present that we have been considering. It stemmed as well from a fear about the future, the future of the earth's human beings, of the earth itself, and of what is termed its ecology. The word "ecology" is often used primarily to refer to human beings and their environment, but it is much broader than that. Ecologists think of humans as a link in a vast chain of life which extends all the way back through mammals, amphibians, invertebrates, and the simplest microorganisms, which may be either plants or animals. In popular usage ecology may be synonymous with pollution problems. Again this is an oversimplification. The causes and prevention of pollution make up important elements in the study of ecology, but they are not the whole subject. Equally important is the use of our environment in ways that will safeguard the heritage of fertile soil, pure air, fresh water, and forests for those who come after us.

Ecological violations consist not merely of poisoning the atmosphere and contaminating oceans, rivers, and lakes by dumping wastes into them, but of any assault upon them that makes them less valuable for human survival. The excessive construction of dams, for example, causes the silting of rivers and the accumulating of nitrates at a faster rate than the surrounding soil can absorb. The use of insecticides, especially those containing DDT, may result in upsetting the balance of nature. An example in the recent history of Malaysia illustrates such an occurrence. The Malaysian government resorted to extensive spraying of remote areas with DDT in the hope of stamping out malaria-carrying mosquitoes. The DDT killed the mosquitoes but also poisoned the flourishing cockroaches. The cockroaches in turn were eaten by the villages cats. The cats died of the DDT poison. The net result was a multiplication of rats formerly kept from a population explosion by their natural enemies, the cats. So badly disturbed was the balance of nature that a fresh supply of cats had to be airlifted from other regions. Other assaults upon the balance of nature have been even more serious. The Aswan High Dam of Egypt, undoubtedly valuable for increasing the water supply of that country, has at the same time cut down the flow of algal nutrients to the Mediterranean, with damaging effects on the fishing industry of various countries. From the ecological standpoint the rapid development of industry in modern times is almost an unmitigated disaster. For thousands of years the human race introduced into the environment no more waste substances than could easily be absorbed by the environment. But modern technology has introduced into nature a variety of wastes never abundant before. Among them are carbon monoxide, sulfur dioxide, and nitrogen oxides. And this is to say nothing of the discharge into nature of pesticides, the great host of synthetic products that are not biologically degradable, and the fruits of nuclear weapons testing.

The ecological problem is caused not simply by the dumping of harmful and nondegradable products. It is also the result of wastage of land as our most valuable natural resource. In many parts of the world

Industrial Pollution. This photo shows steel mills in Westfalenhuette, West Germany. While polluting gases and particular matter are released into the air, industrial wastes, both thermal and chemical, are released into nearby waters.

Diminishing land resources

rivers run brown because they are filled with earth washed from the fields bordering them. In some of the largest American cities two-thirds to three-quarters of the land area is paved with streets and parking lots. Meanwhile, the nation's crop land is shrinking at an alarming rate. Ecologists say that much of this land will probably have to be abandoned.

Ecology and the population explosion

A close link exists between the problems of ecology and the population explosion. Indeed, if population control had remained a reality, the problems of ecology might well have passed unnoticed for many years. For example, New York City on the eve of the Civil War had a total population of 700,000. The area was not essentially smaller than what it is now. Yet the inhabitants of the five boroughs constituting the city have multiplied ten times over. This increase has been accompanied by physical transformations that have facilitated crowded living by masses of people. Oil lamps were replaced by gaslight and then by electricity, horse-drawn wagons and carriages by trolley cars, automobiles, subways, and buses. While some of these inventions eliminated a few forms of pollution, the general effect was to multiply sources of contamination and abuse of the natural environment. The example of New York City can be duplicated in many other over-crowded areas, not only in America but especially in Asia. Calcutta now has a population of 7 million, compared with 3 million in 1961. Tokyo has grown from 9 million to over 11.5 million in little more than fifteen years.

As the population increases, human beings create more and more problems and the damage done by each person escalates rapidly. Conditions in Los Angeles illustrate the danger. Despite excellent laws, the city makes little progress in carrying them out. Increases in the number of smog-producers nullify every victory the smog-control experts succeed in gaining. The worst offenders in vitiating ecological progress are the big industrial powers. They combine exhaustion of natural resources with contamination of the environment by industrial poisons, and consume hundreds of times more natural products than do most of the inhabitants of the Third World. The oil shortages of the 1970s, produced by the uncertain political state of the Middle East, forced the West—and particularly the United States—to become aware of its wasteful ways. Whether those shortages will also compel the West to expend its resources less extravagantly remains to be seen.

*Effects of population
explosion*

Most nations of the contemporary world are in danger of being overwhelmed by a population explosion. Its major cause has been what the experts call the demographic revolution. By this is meant an overturning of the ancient balance between births and deaths, which formerly kept the population on a stationary or slowly rising level. This balance is a biological condition common to nearly all species. For thousands of years humankind was no exception. It is estimated, for example, that the total population of the earth at the beginning of the Christian era was about 250 million. More than sixteen centuries passed before another quarter-billion had been added to the total. Not until 1860 did the population of the globe approximate 1 billion. From then on the increase was vastly more rapid. The sixth half-billion, added about 1960, required scarcely more than ten years.

*The demographic
revolution*

What have been the causes of this radical imbalance known as the demographic revolution? Fundamentally, what has happened has been the achievement of a twentieth-century deathrate alongside a medieval

An Oil Spill off the Coast of California. Offshore oil drilling has been responsible for numerous spills. Here, from an altitude of 1,800 feet, spreading oil can be seen moving from the offshore rig to pollute the nearby shores.

Causes of the demographic revolution

birthrate. Infant mortality rates have markedly declined. Deaths of mothers in childbirth have also diminished. The great plagues, such as cholera, typhus, and tuberculosis, take a much smaller toll than they did in earlier centuries. Wars and famines still number their victims by the millions, yet such factors are insufficient to counteract an un-curbed rate of reproduction. Though the practice of contraception has been approved by the governments of such nations as India, China, and Japan, only in the last decade have the effects been worthy of notice. In some countries poverty, religion, and ignorance have made the widespread use of contraceptives difficult. Leaders in Third World countries charge that attempts by Western powers to encourage them to limit population growth, either by contraceptive devices or by sterilization, is a not-so-subtle form of genocide.

The uneven growth of world population

The demographic revolution has not affected all countries uniformly. Its incidence has been most conspicuous in the underdeveloped nations of Central and South America, Africa, and Asia. Whereas the population of the world as a whole will double, at present rates. of increase, in thirty-five years, that of Central and South America will multiply twofold in only twenty-six years. An outstanding example is that of Brazil. In 1900 its population was estimated to be 17 million. By 1975 this total had grown to 98 million, more than a fivefold increase. Mexico and Venezuela have two of the highest birthrates in the world. The population of Asia (excluding the USSR and Japan) grew from 813 million in 1900 to approximately 2 billion in 1975. By way of summary, at mid-century, the population of the underdeveloped portions of the globe was more than twice that of the developed portions. Their total land areas were about equal.

6. ACHIEVEMENTS AND LIMITATIONS OF SCIENCE AND TECHNOLOGY

Science and technology: cause and cure of the world's problems

The magnitude of the world's problems has encouraged doubt and pessimism among some of its most creative thinkers. Yet the majority of those charged with the responsibility of finding solutions to the problems—primarily politicians and civil servants—remain cautiously optimistic. For solutions they have continued to turn, paradoxically, to those agencies responsible, in many cases, for the creation of the problems: science and technology. Scientists and technicians invented and perfected the internal combustion engine and the chemical DDT. Now other scientists and technicians are seeking ways to combat their deleterious effects. Scientific research has been responsible for the medical advances which have helped to produce worldwide population increase. No one would argue, of course, that the research should not have taken place, or that the continuing battle against disease is not one of humanity's most worthwhile engagements. Most would agree, however, that science must move as quickly as possible to come up with a safe and simple method of controlling birth, as it continues to fight to prolong life.

The achievements of science in the field of health during the past half-century have been truly remarkable. Two discoveries of great importance have enabled scientists to understand more clearly the ways in which the human body receives and transmits disease. The discovery of viruses was the result of experimentation conducted chiefly by the American biochemist Wendell Stanley in the 1930s. Viruses are microscopic organisms which show signs of life—including the ability to reproduce—only when existing inside living cells. They are the cause of many human diseases, including measles, poliomyelitis (infantile paralysis), and rabies. Not until the nature of viruses was understood could scientists begin to develop means of treating and preventing the virus-produced illnesses in human beings. A second most important discovery that has increased our understanding of human life occurred in 1953, when the Englishman F. H. C. Crick and the American James D. Watson further unlocked the mysteries of genetic inheritance that had been explored by Gregor Mendel at the end of the nineteenth century. Crick and Watson successfully analyzed deoxyribonucleic acid, or DNA, the chemical molecular structure that occurs in the nuclei of gene cells. They discovered that DNA is composed of smaller molecules of four different kinds, linked together in spiral chains. The arrangement of these molecules in each cell forms a

The discovery of viruses; DNA

The Decoding of DNA. Left: F. H. C. Crick and James D. Watson discuss their efforts to analyze the molecular structure of DNA. Right: A model of the molecular structure of DNA. The dual spiral chains are called a double helix.

distinct chemical message which determines the character of the genes and therefore of the human organism of which they are a part. The knowledge gained through analysis of DNA has enabled scientists and doctors to understand the causes of hereditary disease and also, by altering a patient's body chemistry, to prevent it. Despite the great benefits that have resulted from this recent discovery, scientists and others have warned that an understanding of the workings of DNA could lead to dangerous tampering with the genetic processes, as, for example, in attempts to produce artificially a breed of more "perfect" human beings.

Medical advances: sulfa drugs, antibiotics, tranquilizers

Experimentation based upon a fuller understanding of the causes of disease has led to the discovery of new medicines to treat it. In 1935 a German named Gerhard Domagk discovered the first of the sulfa drugs, which he called sulfanilamide. Soon others were added to the list. Each was found to be marvelously effective in curing or checking such diseases as rheumatic fever, gonorrhea, scarlet fever, and meningitis. About 1930, the Englishman Sir Alexander Fleming described the first of the antibiotics, which came to be known as penicillin. Antibiotics are chemical agents produced by living organisms and possessing the power to check or kill bacteria. Many have their origin in molds, fungi, algae, and in simple organisms living in the soil. Penicillin was eventually found to be a drug that could produce spectacular results in the treatment of pneumonia, syphilis, peritonitis, tetanus, and numerous other maladies hitherto frequently fatal. Scientists used knowledge obtained through the analysis of DNA to strengthen the cultures used to develop penicillin. In the 1940s the second most famous of the antibiotics—streptomycin—was discovered by the American Dr. Selman W. Waksman. Streptomycin seems to hold its greatest promise in the treatment of tuberculosis, though it has been used for numerous other infections that do not yield to penicillin. Another category of so-called miracle drugs is tranquilizers. Introduced in 1955, they came to be used frequently in the treatment of mental disorders such as manic-depression and have achieved success in making violent patients more tractable. Although these drugs do not themselves effect cures, they help make patients more accessible to other forms of therapy and enable them in many instances to lead relatively normal lives outside institutions in which they would otherwise be incarcerated. That tranquilizers have been misused by men and women indiscriminately as a dangerously simple method of achieving a desired state of mind is no more than further confirmation of the fact that science continues to create new problems as it solves old ones.

Dr. Jonas Salk in His Laboratory

As important as the discovery of new drugs to treat disease has been the development of new means of preventing it. Sir Edward Jenner discovered the first successful vaccine, used to prevent smallpox, in 1796. But not until the 1950s were vaccines found that could protect from diseases such as mumps, measles, and cholera. One of the most exciting breakthroughs occurred with the development of an innoculation against poliomyelitis by the American Dr. Jonas Salk, in 1953. Still to be discovered are effective agents for the successful treatment of two of the world's most deadly killers, heart disease and cancer. The technique of transplanting a heart from a recently dead human being to a live but ailing heart patient, first perfected by the South African, Dr. Christiaan Barnard, has proved of limited usefulness. More effective have been operations substituting plastic valves for defective arteries leading to the heart, and the insertion of electrical devices—"pacemakers"—to steady or stimulate heartbeat. Testing has produced a definite link between cancer and cigarette smoking, as well as industrial and urban pollution—another example of the way in which technology generates difficulties as it resolves others. Doctors continue to experiment with cancer treatment by X-ray and chemical therapy. But despite the dedication of researchers and the expenditure of large sums to assist their work, a cure eludes them.

Vaccines, heart disease, and cancer

Few would today oppose continued campaigns by scientists intent upon eradicating disease. Governments have found it increasingly difficult, however, to justify the spending of vast sums of public money on programs designed to facilitate the exploration of outer space. From their inception, these "experiments" have resembled international competitions between the United States and the Soviet Union as much as they have scientific and technological investigations. On October 4, 1957, the government of the Soviet Union rocketed the first artificial satellite into space at a speed of about 18,000 miles an hour. Though it weighed nearly 200 pounds, it was propelled upward higher than 500 miles. This Russian achievement gave the English language a new word—Sputnik, the Russian for satellite or fellow traveler. A month later the Soviet scientists surpassed their first success by sending a new and much larger Sputnik to an altitude of approximately 1,000 miles. These Sputniks were the forerunners of others of greater significance. In April 1961, the Russians succeeded in sending the first man into orbit around the earth. Meanwhile, scientists and military specialists in the United States had been competing to match the Soviets' achievements. After a number of successes with animals and "uninhabited" capsules, and the suborbital journey of a manned capsule, they succeeded, on February 20, 1962, in launching the first American manned spaceship into orbit around the earth. The successful astronaut was Lieutenant-Colonel John H. Glenn, Jr., who circled the globe three times at a top speed of over 17,000 miles per hour. In 1966 a United States Navy officer left the cabin of his spacecraft and walked in space for forty-four minutes, hundreds of miles above the earth. His feat was surpassed in July 1969, when Neil Armstrong, a civilian astronaut, left his lunar landing module and became the first man on the moon's surface. All over the world these successful voyages and those that followed were hailed as events of capital importance. They did promise an extension of our knowledge of outer space and could doubtless prepare the way for exploration of the

Space exploration

The First Lunar Landing. Astronaut Edwin E. Aldrin, Jr., is photographed walking near the lunar module of Apollo 11. Astronaut Neil Armstrong, who took the picture, and part of the lunar module are reflected in Aldrin's face plate.

moon and eventually of distant planets. But by the mid-1970s, both the United States and the Soviet Union had drastically cut back their space programs in response to demands on their economies from other quarters. Plans for a space "shuttle" and laboratory, plus continuing experiments of a minor nature, kept the programs alive. But their value was being questioned, in view of the billions required to keep them operational.

Nuclear science: Einstein's discoveries

Undoubtedly it was in the area of nuclear science that the largest and most disturbing questions arose as to the capabilities, limitations, and implications of science and technology. Most of the eventual twentieth-century developments in this area were based upon the pioneering work of the physicist Albert Einstein (1879–1955). In 1905 Einstein began to challenge not merely the older conceptions of matter but practically the entire structure of traditional physics. The doctrine for which he is most noted is his principle of relativity. During the greater part of the nineteenth century, physicists had assumed that space and motion were absolute. Space was supposed to be filled with an intangible substance known as *ether,* which provided the medium for the undulations of light. But experiments performed by English and American physicists near the end of the century virtually exploded the ether hypothesis. Einstein then set to work to reconstruct the scheme of the universe in accordance with a different pattern. He maintained that space and motion, instead of being absolute, are relative to each other. Objects have not merely three dimensions but four. To the familiar length, breadth, and thickness, Einstein added a new dimension of *time* and represented all four as fused in a synthesis which he called the *space-time continuum*. In this way he sought to explain the idea that mass is dependent upon motion. Bodies traveling at high velocity have proportions of extension and mass different from what they would have at rest. Included also in the Einstein physics is the conception of a finite universe—that is, finite in space. The region of matter does not extend into infinity, but the universe has limits. While these are by no means definite boundaries, there is at least a region beyond which nothing exists. Space curves back upon itself so as to make of the universe a gigantic sphere within which are contained galaxies, solar systems, stars, and planets.

The Einstein theories had a major influence in precipitating other revolutionary developments in physics. By 1960 it had been discovered that the conception of the subatomic world as a miniature solar system was much too simple. The atom was found to contain not only positively charged protons and negatively charged electrons, but *positrons,* or positively charged electrons; *neutrons,* which carry no electric charges; and *mesons,* which may be either negative or positive. Mesons, it was discovered, exist not only within the atom (for about two millionths of a second) but are major components of the cosmic rays that are constantly bombarding the earth from somewhere in outer space.

Several of the developments in physics outlined above helped to make possible one of the most spectacular achievements in the history of science, the splitting of the atom to release the energy contained within it. Ever since it became known that the atom is composed primarily of electrical energy, physicists had dreamed of unlocking this source of tremendous power and making it available for man. As early as 1905 Einstein became convinced of the equivalence of mass and energy and worked out a formula for the conversion of one into the other, which he expressed as follows: $E = mc^2$. E represents the energy in ergs, m the mass in grams, and c the velocity of light in centimeters per second. In other words, the amount of energy locked within the atom is equal to the mass multiplied by the square of the velocity of light. But no practical application of this formula was possible until after the discovery of the neutron by the Englishman Sir James Chadwick in 1932. Since the neutron carries no charge of electricity, it is an ideal weapon for bombarding the atom. It is neither repulsed by the positively charged protons nor absorbed by the negatively charged electrons. Moreover, in the process of bombardment it produces more neutrons, which hit other atoms and cause them in turn to split and create neutrons. In this way the original reaction is repeated in an almost unending series.

In 1939 two German physicists, Otto Hahn and Fritz Strassman, succeeded in splitting atoms of uranium by bombarding them with neutrons. The initial reaction produced a chain of reactions, in much the same way that a fire burning at the edge of a piece of paper raises

Albert Einstein

Releasing the energy within the atom

The development of the atomic bomb

the temperature of adjoining portions of the paper high enough to cause them to ignite. Scientists in Germany, Great Britain, and the United States were spurred on by governments anxious to make use of these discoveries for military purposes during the Second World War. The first use made of the knowledge of atomic fission was in the preparation of an atomic bomb. The devastating weapon was the achievement of scientists working for the War Department of the United States. Some were physicists who had been exiled by Nazi or Fascist oppression. (Einstein himself, a native of Germany and a Jew, had left that country in the 1930s for the United States.)

The hydrogen bomb

Even more disturbing than the results of the bombs dropped on Japan at the end of World War II were the first tests of a hydrogen bomb by the United States Atomic Energy Commission in November 1952. The tests were conducted at Eniwetok Atoll in the South Pacific; an entire island disappeared after burning brightly for several hours. The hydrogen bomb, or H-bomb, is based upon fusion of hydrogen atoms, a process which requires the enormous heat generated by the splitting of uranium atoms to start the reaction. The fusion results in the creation of a new element, helium, which actually weighs less than the sum of the hydrogen atoms. The "free" energy left over provides the tremendous explosive power of the H-bomb. The force of hydrogen bombs is measured in *megatons,* each of which represents 1,000,000 tons of TNT. Thus a 5-megaton H-bomb would equal 250 times the power of the A-bombs dropped on Hiroshima and Nagasaki.

Clearly the scientists had, at the behest of their government, unleashed a weapon of devastating proportions upon the world. By the 1970s, not only the United States, but the Soviet Union, China, Brit-

An H-Bomb Mushrooms. The cloud spreads into a huge mushroom following a 1952 explosion of a hydrogen bomb in the Marshall Islands of the Pacific. The photo was taken 50 miles from the detonation site at about 12,000 feet. The cloud rose to 40,000 feet two minutes after the explosion. Ten minutes later the cloud stem had pushed about 25 miles. The mushroom portion went up to 10 miles and spread 100 miles.

Calder Hall. Built in 1956 in England, this was the world's first large-scale atomic power station. The two towers on the left are for cooling. Since this time such power plants have proliferated around the world. However, the near-catastrophic accident at the Three Mile Island Power Station close to Harrisburg, Pennsylvania, in March 1979 has spurred opponents to press even harder for a reexamination of the use of nuclear power.

ain, France, India, Israel, and other nations either possessed atomic weapons or were in the process of developing the technology to do so. Science was once and for all proved to be something other than "pure," that is, without practical and political implications. The application of its discoveries had become a burdensome fact of life for humanity the world over.

The proliferation of nuclear weapons

Governments experimented with schemes to harness nuclear energy for peaceful purposes. Some progress has been made in the development of atomic power as an alternative source of domestic and industrial fuel. But the dangers of radiation as a by-product suggest that this scheme may prove of limited value. During the late 1970s, when the West's supplies of oil were threatened, heated debate continued between advocates of further construction of atomic power plants and those who argued in favor of other energy forms—among them solar—as safer and cheaper alternatives. Meanwhile, technologists working for private industry made use of discoveries in atomic physics to pioneer the field of electronics. Electronics derives from that branch of physics which deals with the behavior and effects of electrons, or negative constituents within the atom. Electronic devices have multiplied in staggering profusion since World War II. Among them are devices to measure the trajectory of missiles, to give warnings of approaching missiles or aircraft, to make possible "blind" landings of airplanes, to store and release electrical signals, to amplify and regulate the transmission of light and sound images, and to provide the power for photoelectric cells that open doors and operate various automatic machines. The spacecraft industry, which has made possible the exploration of outer space, is closely dependent upon electronics.

The uses of atomic energy; electronics

The Age of Television. Left: The first working television pickup camera, 1929. Right: The Telstar communications satellite. Weighing only 170 pounds, and measuring 34 inches in diameter, it is powered by 3,600 solar cells. It circles the earth at a speed of 1,600 miles per hour, at a height of from 500 to 3,000 nautical miles.

Automation

The use of electronic devices for radio reception led to initial progress in automation. Automation should not be confused with mechanization, though it may be considered the logical extreme of that process. More correctly conceived, automation means a close integration of four elements: (1) a processing system; (2) a mechanical handling system; (3) sensing equipment; and (4) a control system. Though all of these elements are necessary, the last two are the most significant. Sensing equipment performs a function similar to that of the human senses. It observes and measures what is happening and sends the information thus gained to the control unit. It employs such devices as photoelectric cells, infra-red cells, high-frequency devices, and devices making use of X-rays, isotopes, and resonance. It operates without fatigue and much faster and more accurately than do the human senses. Moreover, its observations can be made in places unsafe for, or inaccessible to, human beings. A control system receives information from a sensing element, compares this information with that required by the "program,'" and then makes the necessary adjustments. This series of operations is continuous, so that a desired state is constantly maintained without any human intervention, except for that initially involved in "programming." This revolution has been greatly extended by the invention of lasers. A laser is a device for amplifying the focus and intensity of light. High-energy atoms are stimulated by light to amplify a beam of light. Lasers have demonstrated their value recently in medicine. They have been used effectively in arresting hemorrhaging in the retina in eye afflictions. Through automation, expensive and complicated machines are constantly taking the place of much human labor. Data processing machines and electronic computers are employed to control switching operations in railroad yards, to operate assembly lines, to operate machines that control other machines, and even to maintain blood pressure during critical operations in hospitals.

Electronic inventions have proved no more an unmixed blessing than have the other discoveries and developments of scientists and technicians. One obvious problem generated by devices that can do the work of humans is that they put humans out of work. Technological unemployment has become an important problem for the modern world. Though new industries absorbed many workers, others were bound to be displaced by automation. While the demand for skilled labor remained high, the so-called entry jobs performed by the unskilled were fast disappearing. They were being eliminated not by computers so much as by fork-lift trucks and motorized conveyors and sweepers. Mechanization of agriculture also eliminated thousands of jobs for unskilled and uneducated workers.

Technological Unemployement

Science and technology provide no panaceas for the problems of the world. If those problems are to be solved, men and women, not machines, will have to do the work. They will be better equipped to do so if they possess some sense of their own past. The lesson of history is not that it repeats itself. The lesson is, rather, that the present can be clearly perceived, and the future intelligently planned for, only when those responsible for the world's destiny understand the workings of human nature. And for knowledge of that extraordinarily complicated and fascinating mechanism, there is no better source than history.

SELECTED READINGS

• *Items so designated are available in paperback editions.*
• Banfield, Edward C., *The Unheavenly City: The Nature and Future of Our Urban Crisis,* rev. ed., Boston, 1974.
• Bell, Daniel, *The End of Ideology: On the Exhaustion of Political Ideas in the Fifties,* Glencoe, Ill., 1960.
  Beynon, Huw, *Working for Ford,* London, 1973. A recent analysis of England's industrial and labor problems. Stimulating and perceptive.
  Collins, Doreen, *The European Economic Community, 1958–72,* London, 1975. A thorough analysis of the Common Market, emphasizing the social policies that have emerged in Europe since 1958.
• Erlich, Paul, *The Population Bomb,* New York, 1968.
• Galbraith, John Kenneth, *The New Industrial State,* Boston, 1967. A penetrating analysis of the changes in capitalism wrought by advanced technology.
• Harrington, Michael, *The Other America: Poverty in the United States,* New York, 1962.
• Heilbroner, Robert, *The Future as History,* New York, 1960.

• ———, *An Inquiry into the Human Prospect*, New York, 1975, 1980.

Infeld, Leopold, *Albert Einstein: His Work and Its Influence on Our World*, New York, 1950. A general introduction.

Lerner, M., *The Age of Overkill*, New York, 1962.

• McKenzie, A. E. E., *The Major Achievements of Science*, New York, 1960.

• Marcuse, Herbert, *Counterrevolution and Revolt*, Boston, 1972.

• Popper, Karl, *The Open Society and Its Enemies*, rev. ed., London, 1962. A vigorous comparison of the totalitarian and democratic philosophies by a libertarian.

Rosenberg, Harold, *The Anxious Object: Art Today and Its Significance*, New York, 1964.

• Shonfield, Andrew, *Modern Capitalism: The Changing Balance of Public and Private Power*, New York, 1965.

• Toffler, Alan, *Future Shock*, New York, 1971. An extended essay on the consequences of rapid change in modern industrial society.

Von Laue, T. H., *The Global City: Freedom, Power and Necessity in the Age of World Revolutions*, Philadelphia, 1969.

SOURCE MATERIALS

Bowges, Hervé, comp., *The Student Revolts: The Activists Speak*, London, 1968. Interviews with participants of the student riots of May 1968 which shook France and almost toppled the government.

• Jackson, George, *Soledad Brother: The Prison Letters of George Jackson*, New York, 1970.

• Rich, Adrienne, *On Lies, Secrets, and Silence*, New York, 1979. Essays by a leading feminist thinker.

Snow, C. P., *The Two Cultures and a Second Look: An Expanded Version of the Two Cultures and the Scientific Revolution*, Cambridge, 1965. Argues that in the modern world the great divergence between science and the humanities has been a disastrous process.

• Solzhenitsyn, Alexsandr, *The Gulag Archipelago, 1918–1956*, New York, 1974–75. An account of prison camps during the Stalinist era by the exiled Russian novelist.

RULERS OF PRINCIPAL STATES SINCE 700 A.D.

The Carolingian Dynasty

Pepin, Mayor of the Palace, 714
Charles Martel, Mayor of the Palace, 715–741
Pepin I, Mayor of the Palace, 741; King, 751–768
Charlemagne, King, 768–814; Emperor, 800–814
Louis the Pious, Emperor, 814–840

MIDDLE KINGDOMS

Lothair, Emperor, 840–855
Louis (Italy), Emperor, 855–875
Charles (Provence), King, 855–863
Lothair II (Lorraine), King, 855–869

WEST FRANCIA

Charles the Bald, King, 840–877; Emperor, 875
Louis II, King, 877–879
Louis III, King, 879–882
Carloman, King, 879–884

EAST FRANCIA

Ludwig, King, 840–876
Carloman, King, 876–880
Ludwig, King, 876–882
Charles the Fat, Emperor, 876–887

Holy Roman Emperors

SAXON DYNASTY

Otto I, 962–973
Otto II, 973–983
Otto III, 983–1002
Henry II, 1002–1024

FRANCONIAN DYNASTY

Conrad II, 1024–1039
Henry III, 1039–1056
Henry IV, 1056–1106
Henry V, 1106–1125
Lothair II (of Saxony), King, 1125–1133; Emperor,
    1133–1137

HOHENSTAUFEN DYNASTY

Conrad III, 1138–1152
Frederick I (Barbarossa), 1152–1190
Henry VI, 1190–1197
Philip of Swabia, 1198–1208 ⎫ Rivals
Otto IV (Welf), 1198–1215 ⎭
Frederick II, 1220–1250
Conrad IV, 1250–1254

INTERREGNUM, 1254–1273

EMPERORS FROM VARIOUS DYNASTIES
Rudolf I (Hapsburg), 1273–1291

Adolf (Nassau), 1292–1298
Albert I (Hapsburg), 1298–1308
Henry VII (Luxemburg), 1308–1313
Ludwig IV (Wittelsbach), 1314–1347
Charles IV (Luxemburg), 1347–1378
Wenceslas (Luxemburg), 1378–1400
Rupert (Wittelsbach), 1400–1410
Sigismund (Luxemburg), 1410–1437

HAPSBURG DYNASTY

Albert II, 1438–1439
Frederick III, 1440–1493
Maximilian I, 1493–1519
Charles V, 1519–1556
Ferdinand I, 1556–1564
Maximilan II, 1564–1576
Rudolf II, 1576–1612
Matthias, 1612–1619
Ferdinand II, 1619–1637
Ferdinand III, 1637–1657
Leopold I, 1658–1705
Joseph I, 1705–1711
Charles VI, 1711–1740
Charles VII (not a Hapsburg), 1742–1745
Francis I, 1745–1765
Joseph II, 1765–1790
Leopold II, 1790–1792
Francis II, 1792–1806

Rulers of France from Hugh Capet

CAPETIAN KINGS

Hugh Capet, 987–996
Robert II, 996–1031
Henry I, 1031–1060
Philip I, 1060–1108
Louis VI, 1108–1137
Louis VII, 1137–1180
Philip II (Augustus), 1180–1223
Louis VIII, 1223–1226
Louis IX, 1226–1270
Philip III, 1270–1285
Philip IV, 1285–1314
Louis X, 1314–1316
Philip V, 1316–1322
Charles IV, 1322–1328

HOUSE OF VALOIS

Philip VI, 1328–1350
John, 1350–1364
Charles V, 1364–1380
Charles VI, 1380–1422
Charles VII, 1422–1461
Louis XI, 1461–1483
Charles VIII, 1483–1498
Louis XII, 1498–1515
Francis I, 1515–1547

Henry II, 1547–1559
Francis II, 1559–1560
Charles IX, 1560–1574
Henry III, 1574–1589

BOURBON DYNASTY

Henry IV, 1589–1610
Louis XIII, 1610–1643
Louis XIV, 1643–1715
Louis XV, 1715–1774
Louis XVI, 1774–1792

AFTER 1792

First Republic, 1792–1799
Napoleon Bonaparte, First Consul, 1799–1804
Napoleon I, Emperor, 1804–1814
Louis XVIII (Bourbon dynasty), 1814–1824
Charles X (Bourbon dynasty), 1824–1830
Louis Philippe, 1830–1848
Second Republic, 1848–1852
Napoleon III, Emperor, 1852–1870
Third Republic, 1870–1940
Pétain regime, 1940–1944
Provisional government, 1944–1946
Fourth Republic, 1946–1958
Fifth Republic, 1958–

Rulers of England

ANGLO-SAXON KINGS

Egbert, 802–839
Ethelwulf, 839–858
Ethelbald, 858–860
Ethelbert, 860–866
Ethelred, 866–871
Alfred the Great, 871–900
Edward the Elder, 900–924
Ethelstan, 924–940
Edmund I, 940–946
Edred, 946–955
Edwy, 955–959
Edgar, 959–975

Edward the Martyr, 975–978
Ethelred the Unready, 978–1016
Canute, 1016–1035 (Danish Nationality)
Harold I, 1035–1040
Hardicanute, 1040–1042
Edward the Confessor, 1042–1066
Harold II, 1066

ANGLO-NORMAN KINGS

William I (the Conqueror), 1066–1087
William II, 1087–1100
Henry I, 1100–1135
Stephen, 1135–1154

Angevin Kings

Henry II, 1154–1189
Richard I, 1189–1199
John, 1199–1216
Henry III, 1216–1272
Edward I, 1272–1307
Edward II, 1307–1327
Edward III, 1327–1377
Richard II, 1377–1399

House of Lancaster

Henry IV, 1399–1413
Henry V, 1413–1422
Henry VI, 1422–1461

House of York

Edward IV, 1461–1483
Edward V, 1483
Richard III, 1483–1485

Tudor Sovereigns

Henry VII, 1485–1509
Henry VIII, 1509–1547
Edward VI, 1547–1553
Mary, 1553–1558
Elizabeth I, 1558–1603

Stuart Kings

James I, 1603–1625
Charles I, 1625–1649

Commonwealth and Protectorate, 1649–1659

Later Stuart Monarchs

Charles II, 1660–1685
James II, 1685–1688
William III and Mary II, 1689–1694
William III alone, 1694–1702
Anne, 1702–1714

House of Hanover

George I, 1714–1727
George II, 1727–1760
George III, 1760–1820
George IV, 1820–1830
William IV, 1830–1837
Victoria, 1837–1901

House of Saxe-Coburg-Gotha

Edward VII, 1901–1910
George V, 1910–1917

House of Windsor

George V, 1917–1936
Edward VIII, 1936
George VI, 1936–1952
Elizabeth II, 1952–

Prominent Popes

Silvester I, 314–335
Leo I, 440–461
Gelasius I, 492–496
Gregory I, 590–604
Nicholas I, 858–867
Silvester II, 999–1003
Leo IX, 1049–1054
Nicholas II, 1058–1061
Gregory VII, 1073–1085
Urban II, 1088–1099
Paschal II, 1099–1118
Alexander III, 1159–1181

Innocent III, 1198–1216
Gregory IX, 1227–1241
Boniface VIII, 1294–1303
John XXII, 1316–1334
Nicholas V, 1447–1455
Pius II, 1458–1464
Alexander VI, 1492–1503
Julius II, 1503–1513
Leo X, 1513–1521
Adrian VI, 1522–1523
Clement VII, 1523–1534
Paul III, 1534–1549

Paul IV, 1555–1559
Gregory XIII, 1572–1585
Gregory XVI, 1831–1846
Pius IX, 1846–1878
Leo XIII, 1878–1903
Pius X, 1903–1914
Benedict XV, 1914–1922

Pius XI, 1922–1939
Pius XII, 1939–1958
John XXIII, 1958–1963
Paul VI, 1963–1978
John Paul I, 1978
John Paul II, 1978–

Rulers of Austria and Austria-Hungary

*Maximilian I (Archduke), 1493–1519
*Charles I (Charles V in the Holy Roman Empire), 1519–1556
*Ferdinand I, 1556–1564
*Maximilian II, 1564–1576
*Rudolph II, 1576–1612
*Matthias, 1612–1619
*Ferdinand II, 1619–1637
*Ferdinand III, 1637–1657
*Leopold I, 1658–1705
*Joseph I, 1705–1711
*Charles VI, 1711–1740
Maria Theresa, 1740–1780

*Joseph II, 1780–1790
*Leopold II, 1790–1792
*Francis II, 1792–1835 (Emperor of Austria as Francis I after 1804)
Ferdinand I, 1835–1848
Francis Joseph, 1848–1916 (after 1867 Emperor of Austria and King of Hungary)
Charles I, 1916–1918 (Emperor of Austria and King of Hungary)
Republic of Austria, 1918–1938 (dictatorship after 1934)
Republic restored, under Allied occupation, 1945–1956
Free Republic, 1956–

*Also bore title of Holy Roman Emperor.

Rulers of Prussia and Germany

*Frederick I, 1701–1713
*Frederick William I, 1713–1740
*Frederick II (the Great), 1740–1786
*Frederick William II, 1786–1797
*Frederick William III, 1797–1840
*Frederick William IV, 1840–1861
*William I, 1861–1888 (German Emperor after 1871)

Frederick III, 1888
William II, 1888–1918
Weimar Republic, 1918–1933
Third Reich (Nazi Dictatorship), 1933–1945
Allied occupation, 1945–1952
Division into Federal Republic of Germany in west and German Democratic Republic in east, 1949–

*Kings of Prussia.

Rulers of Russia

Ivan III, 1462–1505
Basil III, 1505–1533
Ivan IV, 1533–1584
Theodore I, 1584–1598
Boris Godunov, 1598–1605

Theodore II, 1605
Basil IV, 1606–1610
Michael, 1613–1645
Alexius, 1645–1676
Theodore III, 1676–1682

Ivan V and Peter I, 1682–1689
Peter I (the Great), 1689–1725
Catherine I, 1725–1727
Peter II, 1727–1730
Anna, 1730–1740
Ivan VI, 1740–1741
Elizabeth, 1741–1762
Peter III, 1762

Catherine II (the Great), 1762–1796
Paul, 1796–1801
Alexander I, 1801–1825
Nicholas I, 1825–1855
Alexander II, 1855–1881
Alexander III, 1881–1894
Nicholas II, 1894–1917
Soviet Republic, 1917–

Rulers of Italy

Victor Emmanuel II, 1861–1878
Humbert I, 1878–1900
Victor Emmanuel III, 1900–1946
Fascist Dictatorship, 1922–1943
   (maintained in northern Italy until 1945)

Humbert II, May 9–June 13, 1946
Republic, 1946–

Rulers of Spain

Ferdinand { and Isabella, 1479–1504
{ and Philip I, 1504–1506
{ and Charles I, 1506–1516
Charles I (Holy Roman Emperor Charles V),
  1516–1556
Philip II, 1556–1598
Philip III, 1598–1621
Philip IV, 1621–1665
Charles II, 1665–1700
Philip V, 1700–1746
Ferdinand VI, 1746–1759
Charles III, 1759–1788
Charles IV, 1788–1808

Ferdinand VII, 1808
Joseph Bonaparte, 1808–1813
Ferdinand VII (restored), 1814–1833
Isabella II, 1833–1868
Republic, 1868–1870
Amadeo, 1870–1873
Republic, 1873–1874
Alfonso XII, 1874–1885
Alfonso XIII, 1886–1931
Republic, 1931–1939
Fascist Dictatorship, 1939-1975
Juan Carlos I, 1975-

Principal Rulers of India

Chandragupta (Maurya Dynasty), c. 332–298 B.C.
Asoka (Maurya Dynasty), c. 273–232 B.C.
Vikramaditya (Gupta Dynasty), 375–413 A.D.
Harsha (Vardhana Dynasty), 606–648
Babur (Mogul Dynasty), 1526–1530
Akbar (Mogul Dynasty), 1556–1605
Jahangir (Mogul Dynasty), 1605–1627
Shah Jahan (Mogul Dynasty), 1627–1658

Aurangzeb (Mogul Dynasty), 1658–1707
Regime of British East India Company, 1757–1858
British raj, 1858–1947
Division into self-governing dominions of India
  and Pakistan, 1947
Republic of India, 1950–
Republic of Pakistan, 1956–
Republic of Bangladesh, 1971–

Dynasties of China

Hsia, c. 2205–1766 B.C. (?)
Shang (Yin), c. 1766 (?)–1100 B.C.
Chou, c. 1100–256 B.C.
Ch'in, 221–207 B.C.
Han (Former), 206 B.C.–8 A.D.
Interregnum (Wang Mang, usurper), 8–23 A.D.
Han (Later), 25–220
Wei, 220–265
Tsin (Chin), 265–420
Southern Dynasties: Sung (Liu Sung), Ch'i, Liang,
  Ch'eñ, 420–589

Northern Dynasties: Northern Wei, Western Wei,
  Eastern Wei, Northern Ch'i, Northern Chou,
  386–581
Sui, 589–618
T'ang, 618–907
Five Dynasties: Later Liang, Later T'ang,
  Later Tsin, Later Han, Later Chou, 907–960
Sung, 960–1279
Yüan (Mongol), 1279–1368
Ming, 1368–1644
Ch'ing (Manchu) Dynasty, 1644–1912

Periods of Chinese Rule

Chinese Republic, 1912–1949

Communist Regime, 1949–

Periods of Japanese Rule

Legendary Period, c. 660 B.C.–530 A.D.
Foundation Period, 530–709 A.D.
Taika (Great Reform) Period, 645–654
Nara Period, 710–793
Heian Period, 794–1192
Kamakura Period, 1192–1333
Namboku-cho ("Northern and Southern Dynasties")
  Period, 1336–1392

Muromachi (Ashikaga) Period, 1392–1568
Sengoku ("Country at War") Period, c. 1500–1600
Sengoku Period, c. 1500–1600
Edo (Tokugawa) Period, 1603–1867
Meiji Period (Mutsuhito), 1868–1912
Taisho Period (Yoshihito), 1912–1926
Showa Period (Hirohito), 1926–

Rulers of Principal African States

Ewuare the Great, Oba of Benin, 1440–1473
Muhammad Runfa, King of Kano, 1463–1499
Afonso I, King of Kongo, 1506–1543
Ibrahim Maje, King of Katsina, 1549–1567
Idris Alooma, Mai of Bornu, 1569–ca. 1619
Osei Tutu, King of Asante, ca. 1670–1717
Agaja, King of Dahomey, 1708–1740
Sayyid Said, ruler of Zanzibar and Muscat, 1804–1856
Shaka, King of the Zulu, 1818–1828
Moshesh, King of Basutoland, 1824–1868
Menelik, King of Shoa, 1865–1889; Emperor
  of Ethiopia, 1889–1913
Haile Selassie, Emperor of Ethiopia, 1930–1974
H. F. Verwoerd, Prime Minister of South Africa,
  1958–1966

Gamal Abdul Nasser, President of Egypt, 1956–1970
Leopold Sedar Senghor, President of Senegal, 1960–
Felix Houphouet-Boigny, President of the
  Ivory Coast, 1960–
Kwame Nkrumah, President of Ghana, 1960–1966
Julius K. Nyerere, President of Tanzania, 1962–
Jomo Kenyatta, President of Kenya, 1964–1978
Sese Seko Mobutu, President of Zaire, 1965–
Houari Boumedienne, head of Algeria, 1965–1978
Anwar el Sadat, President of Egypt, 1970–
Agostinho Neto, President of Angola, 1975–1979
Olusegun Obasanjo, head of Nigeria, 1975–1979
P. W. Botha, Prime Minister of South Africa, 1978–
Robert Mugabe, Prime Minister of
  Zimbabwe, 1980–

ILLUSTRATIONS IN COLOR

(Illustrations appear facing or following the pages indicated)

ILLUSTRATIONS IN THE TEXT

Index

Guide to Pronunciation

The sounds represented by the diacritical marks used in this Index are illustrated by the following common words:

āle   ēve   īce   ōld   ūse   bōot
ăt   ĕnd   ĭ11   ŏf   ŭs   fŏot
fătality ēvent   ōbey   ūnite
câre   fôrm   ûrn
ärm
ȧsk

Vowels that have no diacritical marks are to be pronounced "neutral," for example: Aegean = ē-je′an, Basel = bäz′el, Basil = bă′zil, common = kŏm′on, Alcaeus = ăl-sē′us. The combinations ou and oi are pronounced as in "out" and "oil."

Gothic style, 476–79, 511, 714
Goths, 261
Gottfried von Strassburg, 473, 474
Goulart, João, 1165–66
Gournia, town of, 100
Government of India Act of 1858, 1211
Government of India Act of 1919, 1216
Goya, Francisco, 894
Gracchi (gräk'ē) revolt, 241–42
Gracchi brothers, 241
Gracchus, 241
Granada, 435, 507
Gran Colombia, republic of, 1152
Grand Canal (China), 529
Grande Armée, 809
Grand National Consolidated Trades
    Union of Great Britain, 876, 877
Grapes of Wrath, The (Steinbeck), 1105,
    1113
Grass, Günter, 1366, 1368
gravity, law of, 598–99, 962
Great Bharata War, 122
Great Britain, 215, 265, 866, 927, 995,
    998, 1053, 1076, 1081, 1119, 1135,
    1157, 1204, 1249, 1260, 1261, 1266,
    1273, 1275, 1277, 1282, 1291,
    1312–13, 1321, 1333, 1334, 1336,
    1338, 1359, 1380–81
    see also British Empire; Common-
    wealth of Nations; England; names
    of cities
    alliances and rivalries (before 1914),
        1001–3
    colonialism, 728, 741
    Common Market, 1340
    competition with Germany (1870–
        1914), 938–40
    Congress of Vienna, 862–64
    consequences of industrialism (1800–
        1850), 834–35, 838–39, 840–42, 844,
        848, 852, 853, 858
    Crimean War, 907, 914
    democracy, 1099, 1100, 1101, 1102
    discrimination against blacks, 1363
    French Revolution and, 776, 782, 794,
        797, 806, 822
    imperialism, 943–44, 945, 946, 948,
        950, 960, 1012–14, 1019, 1020, 1027,
        1031, 1040, 1043, 1045, 1048–49,
        1207–24
    industrialism, 928, 929, 931, 936,
        938–41
    Industrial Revolution, 814–21, 822,
        823, 824, 829–30
    liberalism, 861, 867–70, 873–75, 876–
        78, 885–86, 889, 900
    moderation and militancy (1870–
        1914), 987–91
    Napoleonic wars, 806, 807, 808, 822,
        1149, 1152
    nationalism, 960
    Opium War, 1014
    Paris Peace Conference, 1068–71
    public education, 941
    Quintuple Alliance, 865–66, 868
    railway lines, 826, 827, 828, 829
    romanticism and nationalism, 891,
        893–94
    slave trade, 1040, 1041, 1042, 1148

socialism, 955, 958, 959
tariff policies, 941–42
trade deficit (1965), 1188
United Nations, 1131–32
Victorian period, 842
War of the Spanish Succession, 688–89
World War I, 1057–58, 1059, 1061,
    1062, 1067, 1090
World War II, 1123–24, 1127, 1333
    Zionism in, 1252
Great Depression of 1929, 1095, 1105,
    1314
    causes of, 1101
    results of, 1101
Great Dictator, The (motion picture), 1112
Greater East Asia Co-Prosperity Sphere,
    1316–17
Great Exhibition of the Works of Indus-
    try in All Nations (1851), 855
Great Lakes, 637, 675
Great Leap Forward program, 1298–99
Great Mother, *see* Earth Mother cult
Great Mutiny of 1857, 1210–11
Great Sphinx at Gizeh, 38–39
Great Trek, 1048
Great Wall of China, 149, 318, 323
Great Western, The (steamship), 840
Great Zimbabwe, 552
Greece, 18, 298, 360, 998, 1006, 1074,
    1075–76, 1123, 1247
    civil war, 1325
    independence of, 1243
    Marshall Plan aid to, 1335
    Turkish rule of, 867
    World War II, 1124
Greece (ancient), 1, 46, 67, 87, 93, 117,
    119, 132, 155, 157, 167, 171–228,
    229, 230, 253, 351, 440
    attitudes toward work, 204–5
    banks, business, and finance, 215–16
    break and continuity (between Hel-
        lenic and Hellenistic eras), 211–12
    city-states, 175–77, 212, 213, 232
    classes of population, 178–79, 203–4
    contempt for "barbarians," 209
    Enlightenment philosophers on, 703
    growth of cities, 216–17
    Hellenic civilization, 171–210
    Hellenistic civilization, 211–28
    Minoan and Mycenaean civilizations,
        96–104
    morality, 174
    Roman conquest of, 240
    social and economic equality, 204
    tyrants, 176–77, 185
Greek language, 65, 98, 106, 211, 226,
    245, 289, 296, 357, 359, 466, 564,
    568, 941
Greek Orthodox Church, 449
Greek Slave, The (Powers), 855
Greek tragedies, 196–97
Greenback party, 1000
Greenland, 401, 484
Gregorian chant, 387
Gregory I (the Great), Pope St., 293,
    387, 389, 395, 448
Gregory VII, Pope, 420
Gregory XI, Pope, 496
Gregory XIII, Pope, 243

Grey, Sir Edward, 1057
Grey, Lord, 869, 870
Griffin, W. B., 1199
Grimm brothers, 893
Grimm's Fairy Tales, 893
Gropius, Walter, 1111–12
Grosseteste (grŏs'tĕst), Bishop Robert,
    467
Grosz (grōs), George, 1108
Grotius (grō'shĭ-us), Hugo, 691
Group Areas Act (South Africa), 1269
Guadalajara (gwä'dhä-lä-hä'rä), 1155
Guadeloupe (gwäd'lōōp'), 689
Guanajuato (gwä'nä-hwä'tò), 1155
Guantánamo Bay, U.S. naval base at,
    1176
Guatemala, 17, 1141, 1143, 1175, 1182
Gueiler, Lydia, 1173–74
guerrilla warfare, 182, 1174, 1181, 1183,
    1236, 1239, 1253, 1282
Guesde, Jules, 959
Guiana, 689
Guicciardini (gwēt'chär-dē'nē), Fran-
    cesco, 570
guilds, 542, 570
Guinea, 636, 1275, 1280, 1282
Guise family, 630
Guizot (gē'zō'), François, 875–76, 879,
    885
Gulag Archipelago (Solzhenitsyn), 1359–60
Gulf of Mexico, 1165
Gulf of Tonkin, 321
Gulliver's Travels (Swift), 720
gunpowder, invention of, 513
Gunpowder Plot, 665–66
guns, invention of, 513–14
Gupta Dynasty (India), 304–5
Gurage people, 1050
Gustavus II Adolphus, king of Sweden,
    677, 686
Guyana, 1185, 1341
Guzmán, Antonio, 1175, 1180
Gwato, seaport of, 756
gypsies, 1098, 1126

haciendas, 1161
Hades, 206
Hadrian, Emperor, 249
Haeckel (hĕk'el), Ernst, 965
Hafiz, 382
Hahn, Otto, 1379–80
Haiti, 1175
    independence of, 1154
Halley, Edmund, 709
Halley's comet, 709
Halys (hăl'ĭs) River, 65, 105
Hamlet (Shakespeare), 563, 593
Hammurabi, King, 51, 62
Hampden, John, 667
Hampton Court, 715
Handbook of the Christian Knight, The (Eras-
    mus), 584
Handel, George Frederick, 721
Han Dynasty, 319–22, 323, 325, 327,
    328–29, 335
Hangchow, port of, 149, 527, 530, 534
Hankow (hän'kō'), 1023
Hannibal, 239
Hanover, 673

Morocco, 346, 384, 546, 548, 1003, 1004, 1006, 1281
Morrison, Toni, 1368
Morse, H. B., 1012
Moscow, 682, 683, 809, 1125
Moses, 76, 81, 82, 85
Moses (Michelangelo), 576
mosques, 373
Mossadegh (mô'sä-dĕk'), Muhammed, 1261
Mosul, 384
Mo Ti (or Mo-tzu), 161–62, 330
motion picture industry, 1112, 1113, 1369
Mountbatten, Lord, 1224
Mount Kenya, 1044
Mount Kilimanjaro, 1044
Mount Olympus, 173
Mount Sinai, 82
Mozambique, 347, 551, 761, 946, 1044, 1045, 1280
  independence, 1272
Mozart (mô'tsärt), Wolfgang Amadeus, 722–23, 724
Mr. Sammler's Planet (Bellow), 1367
Mugabe, Robert, 1282
Muhammad (the Prophet), 369–72, 373, 374, 375, 378, 736, 1245
  background of, 370–71
  Hegira of 622, 371
Muhammad, Elijah, 824
Muhammad Touré, Askia, 547–48
Muller, Herbert J., 3
Mun, Thomas, 635
Munich, 414, 1095, 1097
Municipal Ordinance of 1808 (Prussia), 898
Munster (mŏŏn'stûr), 618
Münzer, Thomas, 616–17
Murray, Gilbert, 1059
Muscat, 761, 1044
music:
  atonal, 1109–10, 1112
  Buddhist, 330
  break from the romantic tradition, 976
  following World War I, 1109–10
  High Middle Ages, 479
  homophonic, 479
  polyphonic, 479, 720–21
  Renaissance, 593–95
  seventeenth and eighteenth centuries, 720–24
Muslim League, 1215, 1217, 1218, 1222, 1223, 1234
Muslims, 317, 347, 352, 388, 391, 399, 459, 626, 628, 720
  see also Islam; Islamic civilization
  conquests in India, 520–26
  Crusades, 450–51
  moneylending business, 611
Mussolini, Benito, 1248
  Munich Conference (1938), 1121–22
  rise to power, 1090–93
Mustafa Kemal (mŏŏs-tä-fä' kĕ-mäl'), 1075
Mutsuhito (mŏŏ-tsŏŏ-hĕ'tŏ), Emperor, 1027
Mwenemutapa, 754, 761
Mycenae (mī-sē'nē), 97, 103, 171, 177

Myron, 202
Mysore, 526
mysticism, 73, 226, 247, 262, 327, 365, 499–500, 513, 568
  see also names of mystery cults
Mystic Nativity (Botticelli), 571

Nabopolassar (năb'ō-pō-lăs'ēr), King, 51
Nadir Shah, 735
Nagasaki (nä'ga-sä'kĕ), 752
  atomic bombing of, 1127, 1380
Naguib (nä'gĭb), Major General Muhammad, 1249
Naked and the Dead, The (Mailer), 1366
Nalanda (nà-lān'dà), Buddhist university at, 308–9, 524
Namibia, 1282
Nanak (nä'năk) (preacher), 732–33
Nancy, Battle of (1477), 505
Nanking, 1017, 1024, 1290–91, 1293
Nanking, Treaty of (1842), 1014
Nanshe (goddess), 55
Nantes (nănt), Edict of, 630, 675, 677
Napata, 45
Napier, Lord, 1013–14, 1210
Naples, 231–80, 414, 502, 578, 902
  see also Two Sicilies, kingdom of
Naples, University of, 464
Napoleon I, Emperor, 644, 802, 803–10, 822, 823, 863, 865, 876, 893, 897, 1149–51, 1152, 1154, 1159
  Catholic Church and, 805
  death of, 809
  Directory government, 802–3
  downfall of, 808–10
  in Egypt, 803
  Europe and, 803–7
  as first counsel, 803–5
  Grande Armée retreat, 809
  Paris shrine, 889–90
  reforms of, 804–7
Napoleon III, Emperor, 881–82, 883, 884, 956, 983, 984, 1159
  foreign policy, 884
  Italian War for Liberation, 911, 912
  plebiscite, 882, 909
  Sedan defeat, 909
Napoleonic Code, 299–300, 823
Napoleonic Wars, 808–9, 822, 823, 824, 867, 1048, 1053
  conservative reaction to (1815–1830), 862–67
  Latin America and, 1149–51, 1152, 1153
  Russian campaign, 809, 863
Nara, 341
Narayan, Jayaprakash, 1185, 1231
Nasser (nä'sēr), Gamal Abdel, 1249, 1250
Nathan the Wise (Lessing), 706
National Assembly (France), 789–92, 799
National Association for the Advancement of Colored People (NAACP), 1361
National Association for the Protection of Labour, 876
national consciousness, 604
National Convention (French Revolu-

tion), 799, 801–2
National Guard (French), 801
National Health System (Australia), 1202
nationalism, 631, 960, 1004–5, 1025, 1049, 1054, 1076, 1215, 1216–17, 1221, 1222–23, 1313, 1315
  cultural, 517
  economic, 647
  Italian fascism and, 1092
  liberalism and, 890, 901–5
  meaning of, 889
  Middle East, 1243, 1244, 1248, 1261, 1265
  nation-building (1800–1848), 897–901
  nation-building (1850–1870), 906–16
  nineteenth-century, 889–917
  Protestant Revolution and, 608–9
  revolutions of 1848, 901–5
  and romanticism, 890–97
National Labor Front, 1099
national monarchies, rise of, 419–36
National Reconstruction Government (Nicaragua), 1182
National Security Council, 1169
National Socialist German Workers' party,
  see Nazi party
National Urban League, 1361
Native Labour Act (South Africa), 1269
Native Land Act (South Africa), 1269
Native Son (Wright), 1368
Natural History (Buffon), 712–13
Natural History (Pliny the Elder), 255
naturalism, 509–12, 971, 973
natural law, 850
Nauru, 1341
Naval Arms Limitation Agreement, 1312
Navarre, 435
Navigation Acts (England), 647
Nazi party, 1111–12, 1120, 1124, 1126, 1366
  anti-Semitic policies, 1096, 1097
  architecture, 1112
  racism, 1098
  rise of, 1093–99, 1101
  theories of, 1098–99
  West German restitution for, 1254
Nazi-Soviet Pact (1939), 1122
Ndebele people, 1049
Neanderthal (nē-ăn'dēr-täl') man, 7, 8, 9, 13
Neander Valley, 7
Nebuchadnezzar (nĕb'ū-kăd-nĕz'ēr), King, 51–52, 62, 63, 79
Necker, Jacques, 780
necromancy, 81, 85
Nefertiti (nĕ'fēr-tē'tĕ), Queen, 33, 39
Nehru (nā'rōō), Jawaharlal, 1185, 1218, 1228, 1229–30, 1233
Nejd (nĕjd), 1258
Neo-Babylonians, *see* Chaldeans
neoclassicism, 893
Neo-Confucianism, 533, 742
Neolithic culture (New Stone Age), 12–16, 44, 98, 112, 140–41, 142, 230, 332, 340, 344
neo-Palladianism, 717
Neoplatonism, 262, 277, 380, 568, 571,